Reader's Digest

America's
Fascinating
Indian
Heritage

Reader's Digest

America's Fascinating Indian Heritage

The Reader's Digest Association, Inc.
Pleasantville, New York   Montreal

America's Fascinating Indian Heritage

Editor: James A. Maxwell
Art Editor: Richard J. Berenson
Research Editor and
Assistant to the Editor: Helen E. Fisher
Research Editor: Monica Borrowman
Art Associate: Evelyn S. Bauer
Picture Researcher: Margaret Mathews
Copy Editor: Rosemarie Conefrey
Art Assistant: Janet G. Iannacone
Project Secretary: Catherine A. McAleenan

Contributing Editor: Peter M. Chaitin
Contributing Research Editor: Patricia H. Murphy

Chief Consultant

Stanley A. Freed, Ph.D.
Curator, Department of Anthropology
The American Museum of Natural History

Special Consultants

Raymond S. Baby, D.Sc.
Curator of Archeology
Ohio Historical Center

Asen Balikci, Ph.D.
Professor of Anthropology
University of Montreal

Melvin L. Fowler, Ph.D.
Professor of Anthropology
University of Wisconsin,
Milwaukee

Robert F. Heizer, Ph.D.
Professor Emeritus of Anthropology
University of California, Berkeley

Bill Holm
Curator of Northwest Coast Indian
Art at Thomas Burke Memorial
Washington State Museum

Charles M. Hudson, Jr., Ph.D.
Professor of Anthropology
University of Georgia

Elden Johnson, M.A.
Professor of Anthropology
University of Minnesota,
Minneapolis

Laura F. Klein, Ph.D.
Assistant Professor of Anthropology
Seton Hall University

Alfonso Ortiz, Ph.D.
Professor of Anthropology
University of New Mexico

Edward S. Rogers, Ph.D.
Professor of Anthropology
McMaster University

Elisabeth Tooker, Ph.D.
Professor of Anthropology
Temple University

Deward E. Walker, Jr., Ph.D.
Professor of Anthropology
University of Colorado, Boulder

Joe Ben Wheat, Ph.D.
Curator of Anthropology
University of Colorado Museum

About This Book

The New World is a land without a truly native population. Except for the Indians, all of us are either immigrants or the descendants of the Europeans, Africans, Orientals, and others who came to the Americas after Columbus made his landfall at San Salvador in 1492. But even the dark-skinned men and women waiting onshore to greet the crews of the *Pinta*, the *Niña*, and the *Santa María* were of foreign lineage. Columbus, whose knowledge of global geography was understandably vague at the time, called them *Los Indios* because he thought he had landed in the Orient. But though the mariner misnamed these people, his error, as it turned out, was not quite as gross as it seems. Their forebears, at least, did come from Asia.

The First Immigrants

Some 30,000 to 50,000 years ago an ice age created a land bridge between Siberia and what is now Alaska, thus providing a means of passage for the first immigrants to the New World. Those who made the crossing were neither explorers nor settlers nor adventurers. They were simply hungry men and women following the game on which their livelihood depended.

Over the centuries their descendants spread out over the two continents, from Alaska to the tip of South America. As each pioneer group reached a new area, they came upon a wide variety of animals, many of which they had never seen before. But never once did they encounter another human being who had preceded them—a true native. The reason? There was a blank page in the natural history of the New World.

In Asia, Europe, and Africa the human species had, over millions of years, evolved from apelike creatures to Homo sapiens, modern man. But, oddly enough, this evolutionary process of mankind never took place in the Western Hemisphere. And so the first people to set foot here, those who followed, and their descendants, whom we call Indians, were all Homo sapiens, men and women like ourselves, with the same mental and physical capabilities we have.

Adapting to a New World

Certainly the Indians and the Eskimos—the last group to cross the land bridge—needed human reasoning and imagination to adapt and survive in this wondrous, variegated place. In North America alone, the land stretches from the Arctic Circle to subtropical Mexico. People had to learn to live in frozen tundra, in forests, on grassy plains, and in arid deserts, on high mountains and in deep canyons, along rugged coastlines and lakeshores and in fertile river valleys.

To maintain life in these various environments, the Indians had to invent new weapons and develop new techniques for hunting, to learn to farm, to forage for food, to fish collectively for the large catch needed, to utilize the natural medicines the earth provided. A host of different kinds of dwellings— from simple windbreaks to houses made of ice to huge apartment buildings— had to be devised for many climates and constructed from whatever materials were available in a given region. Water transportation was required, and the Indians proved capable of designing and constructing craft suitable for everything from traveling on placid rivers to killing whales in the ocean. There was clothing to be made from the cured skins of animals and even from the woven bark of trees. Tools, of course, were a prime requisite for such tasks, and the people showed enormous ingenuity in fashioning them from rock, wood, bone and, in time, copper.

Combining great artistry with utility, the Indians produced magnificent pottery, basketry, blankets, and other artifacts that are treasured by museums and collectors today. Trade also flourished. People in various sections of the country early recognized the advantage of exchanging their surplus raw materials and handicraft for goods either nonexistent or in short supply in their particular region.

A Multiplicity of Peoples

Although we tend to think of Indians as a single people, they were, in fact, as diverse as the various nationals of Europe. The Tlingits, for example, were as different from the Sioux as Greeks are from Danes. As the people spread over the North American continent, more than 200 languages and dialects developed, and any two were usually no more alike than, say, Russian and Spanish.

The environment obviously played a major role in determining primary means of sustenance. Some groups in areas where game was plentiful and varied became almost exclusively hunters. The rich resources of rivers, lakes, and the sea made fishing the logical choice of others. When good soil and ample water were available, many tribes became farmers and even developed elaborate irrigation systems. Still other bands, living in areas where animals were few, rainfall was sparse, and fish were nonexistent or minimal in number, became gatherers and foragers, and lived off the land. And there were even groups that gained a substantial part of their sustenance by acting as middlemen in the exchange of goods between other tribes.

Social and political structures were equally diverse. Many Indians felt intense tribal loyalty, but the concern of others did not extend beyond the family unit. There were areas where a hierarchy exercised near-absolute power, and regions where there was a total absence of centralized authority. Many groups observed complete equalitarianism. In others, all individuals were rigidly ranked by lineage and wealth, with no two persons on exactly the same level.

The Varying Roles of Women

The status of women spanned a complete spectrum. In some groups a female was little more than a childbearer and worker, completely dominated by her husband who could, at his discretion, even send her off to the bed of another man. In contrast, women of certain tribes held a monopoly on political power. For example, women not only appointed the men who served as representatives to the Iroquois council but could strip them of office if they failed to vote as instructed or displeased their female mentors in other ways. Women also enjoyed vast economic power in many Indian societies. The woman owned the dwelling and all its furnishings, the tools, the crops, the horses and sheep. The man's possessions were restricted to his clothing and weapons.

Sexual mores were no less varied. Among some Indian groups the chastity of young women was guarded as carefully as that of adolescent females in proper Victorian families. In other Indian societies premarital sex was casually accepted; in a few, girls were even encouraged to charge for their favors so that they could accumulate dowries for their marriages. Marriage itself was sometimes arranged by the elders, sometimes left to the inclinations of the young people involved. Here, the betrothed would go through an elaborate ceremony; there, the man and woman would simply begin living together.

The Man's Domain

Although the authority of the man differed enormously from group to group, he bore primary responsibility for the welfare of the family. But what was considered "man's work" and "woman's work" varied between tribes. With minor exceptions, however, he was always the hunter and the warrior—if the latter role existed in his particular group. Contrary to popular belief, not all tribes engaged in warfare. Some held firmly to a pacifist position and would not fight even to avenge a raid on one of their villages.

In any case, the Indians rarely engaged in large battles. Most armed combat was on a small scale, usually motivated by a desire for revenge. Among some groups the objective of fighting was less the killing of the enemy than the gaining of personal glory by the individual warrior. Touching an enemy leader in the heat of battle, for example, was more important than bringing him down with an arrow. (This approach to warfare as a kind of game was to cost the Indians dearly in many encounters with the whites, whose uncomplicated goal was simply to slaughter as many of the opposition forces as possible.) Treatment of captives ranged from unspeakable torture to adoption by the victors.

The Supernatural World

There were many gods in the Indians' pantheon, and many different beliefs about the origin of man and this earth, about spiritual realms, and about afterlife. Some of the spirits were benign, some were evil, but all had to be placated. One tribe would have elaborate ceremonials to enlist the aid or avoid the wrath of supernatural beings; another would have few, if any, rites but would live by a set of rules calculated to appease the unseen powers.

But almost uniformly held throughout Indian cultures was the tenet that all living things—plants as well as animals—had souls and were to be shown proper respect and consideration. Thus the Indians existed in rare harmony with their environment.

The Europeans brought a wholly different attitude to the New World. To them land was property to be acquired and utilized in any way the owner saw fit. And when one generation died, title passed on to the next. To the Indians such a concept was incomprehensible; one could no more own the earth and its bounties than hold a monopoly on sunshine and rain. The Indians, of course, had no academic theories about the ecology, but they did have a basic understanding of the interdependence of all living things. The importance of their protective attitude is still only dimly understood by the modern world.

Invitation to Exploration

In this book we bring the multifaceted universe of the North American Indians and Eskimos into focus and present a realistic picture of how these remarkable people lived and died. (At certain places in the book we have dramatized the lives of various Indian and Eskimo groups to give immediacy to their experiences. Although a fictional form is used, the narrations are based on reality. Such sections are set in *italicized type* to separate them from the main body of the text. This device is also used for lengthy Indian legends and similar matter.)

The coming of the Europeans, of course, completely changed the Indians' existence, and this, too, is part of our story. An account of how they are faring in contemporary times ends this volume. We hope that when the reader finishes this work he will have the feeling that he has been on an exciting and informative trip of exploration.

—The Editors

ARCTIC

SUBARCTIC

NORTHWEST
COAST

PLATEAU

GREAT PLAINS

NORTHEAST
AND
GREAT LAKES

CALIFORNIA

GREAT
BASIN

SOUTHWEST

SOUTHEAST

Contents

THE FIRST INDIANS
Finding a New World

Along Alaska's river valleys, such as this one in the Brooks Range, America's earliest immigrants inched their way south tens of thousands of years ago. By 9000 B.C. some were in the Southwest hunting bison with Sandia points (inset) lashed to spears.

Asian hunters, the forebears of American Indians and the first humans to set foot in the New World, came when an ice age created a land bridge between the Orient and North America.

T here was a time when our people covered the whole land as the waves of the wind-ruffled sea cover its shell-paved floor. But that time has long since passed away with the greatness of tribes now forgotten. I will not mourn over our untimely decay, nor reproach my paleface brothers with hastening it."
—*Chief Seathe of Duwamish tribe, 1855*

Eons before the coming of the European in the 15th century, men and women from Asia came to the continent of North America. We do not know their names. We do not know with absolute certainty when they came. But, nonetheless, they were the true American pioneers. Over many millennia they spread to every part of the continent and to South America as well. They came to live on plains and in deserts and forests. As they adapted to the demands of these various environments, they developed many diverse cultures. Yet, over the centuries, they and later migrants evolved into a distinct people whom Columbus erroneously labeled *Los Indios*, thinking he had landed in the East Indies. Today, as a result, they are known universally as the American Indians.

It may have been 50,000 years ago or more that mankind began its epic journey into the New World. No written chronicles exist, of course. But generations of archeologists, anthropologists, and geologists—in their quest for the American past—have sifted the evidence, pondered it, and tried to put the many pieces together. Their scientific labors make it possible for us to recreate this momentous adventure of man with a reasonable measure of certainty.

It was late in the history of human evolution when man first set foot in the New World. For thousands of centuries ape-men and primitive forms of humanity wandered across Africa, Europe, and Asia, but these forerunners of modern man never appeared in the Americas. The first migrants to the New World were men of the "modern" type—Homo sapiens. Almost certainly, their forebears had lived for numberless generations in the Siberian tundra, hunting whatever animals they could find and kill with their primitive weapons.

There were perhaps two dozen in the band of fur-clad hunters. They camped in the Siberian tundra in a small cluster of tents fashioned of caribou fur and wood. Inside the tents the ground had been dug out a foot or so below the surface to help protect the hunters from the bitterly cold Arctic wind. Soon it would be time to break camp and move on. The herds of caribous, bison, and horses, whose carcasses gave the hunters food and clothing and the materials for shelter, were migrating once again. The hunters must gather up their weapons, fold their tents, and follow the animals—or perish.

At the time, the world was still in the grip of the last of the great ice ages. Four times in the last million years glaciers moved slowly from the poles into the temperate zones, burying thousands of square miles under thick layers of ice and turning the northern regions into desolate places numbed by freezing Arctic winds. In the last age, as in the previous ones, the advancing glaciers absorbed a vast quantity of seawater and locked it into the ice. This caused a drastic lowering of the level of the oceans. The immense weight of the glaciers also depressed the continental landmasses, causing a corresponding rise in the level of the seafloor.

Creating a Natural Bridge

These epochal changes on the surface and in the crust of the earth were to have profound implications for North America and the migration of mankind from the Old World to the New. Bering Strait, the body of water separating Siberia from Alaska in modern times, is only 56 miles wide and 180 feet deep. Geologists have determined that the sea levels fell by 400 to

450 feet in the most recent ice age. This means that the region now covered by the waters of the Bering Strait then lay high and dry. This land bridge between Asia and America, called Beringia by some modern scholars, was later to become submerged again as the glacier withdrew. But off and on, over the centuries, it served as the highway from the Old to the New World.

Beringia was a forbidding place: a broad, water-logged plain broken occasionally by low, rolling hills. The winters were long, dark, and cruelly cold. But the migrant hunters pushed on. In some places, where the land was dry and grassy, game abounded and hunting was good. Over the centuries the hunters of Beringia pursued their quarry, moving eastward as the herds of caribous, horses, and mammoths moved before them—ever away from the ancestral homeland in Siberia. At one point, probably more than 40,000 years ago, the first band of migrants set foot in what is now Alaska. Mankind had come to the New World.

It must have been a daunting experience, for a great sheet of ice lay across southern Alaska and stretched across Canada, virtually from the Pacific to the Atlantic. A few ice-free corridors to the south did exist, but these pathways were narrow, the climate was punishing, and the route ahead was uncharted. In many periods it must have been all but impossible for the primitive wanderers to make much headway in the continent of North America. And many must have perished along the way.

At certain times, however, warmer interludes made the cold less dreadful, and then the corridors between the gigantic fields of ice became wider and more accessible. One such route led around the unglaciated foot-hills of what is now called Brooks Range, down the

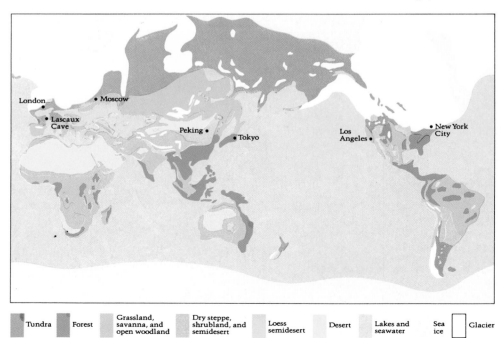

The world as it was 18,000 years ago (right) looked much different than it does today. Glaciers penetrated deep into the Northern Hemisphere and locked up so much of the world's ocean water that the overall sea level was some 400 feet lower than in our times. The sites of today's coastal cities, such as New York, were well inland, and the lowered sea level exposed a 1,000-mile-wide land bridge—Beringia—connecting Alaska and Siberia. It was across Beringia—which vanished and reappeared with the ebb and flow of the glaciers—that the first immigrants to America came. Their goal was neither to explore nor to settle, but merely to pursue the migrating animal herds—such as caribou—for food.

London • Moscow
• Lascaux Cave
Peking •
• Tokyo
Los Angeles •
• New York City

Tundra | Forest | Grassland, savanna, and open woodland | Dry steppe, shrubland, and semidesert | Loess semidesert | Desert | Lakes and seawater | Sea ice | Glacier

Stone Age Man: His Testimony Found in Caves

Whether in Europe, Asia, or America, the world of Stone Age man, some 15,000 years ago, shared a basic unity dictated by a common means of sustenance: the hunting of such large mammals as bison, reindeer, caribous, mammoths, and mastodons. Such differences in living patterns that did exist were relatively minor. Probably the hunter roaming the tundra of Alaska's ice-free corridor would have felt quite at home had he been suddenly and magically transported to so distant a region as the tundra of southern France. Here too he would have pursued the great herd animals, and when they were not available, he would have hunted smaller creatures, such as deer, rabbits, boars, and various kinds of fowl. He would have supplemented his meat diet with the gleanings of the tundra's wild vegetation. He would have erected warm-weather shelters of skins stretched over poles, and in the winter sought comfort and security deep in one of the many mountain caves.

It is within such caves, particularly in southwestern France, that modern man has discovered numerous wall and ceiling paintings dating back thousands of years. These tell much about the life of man in that region 13 millennia before Christ and, perhaps, as much about man throughout the far-reaching tundra. Archeologists believe that such paintings—of bison, reindeer, and other creatures—were a form of magic. The members of the hunting bands may have believed that by depicting these animals within human habitations the herds could be influenced to appear so that they might be hunted. Similarly, the Stone Age peoples of southern Europe embellished the walls and ceilings of their caves with pictures of feared predators—bears or lions—perhaps as a means of transferring the strength and courage of these animals to themselves. Often such illustrations were painted on a cave's convex surfaces, apparently to create the illusion of bas-relief, lending realism to the artwork.

Some of the cave paintings in southern France have been found in chambers with entrances so small that a full-grown man has great difficulty wriggling through them. Such chambers are thought to have been sacred places, and the figures

*A **spear-pierced bison** (top left), a human figure—perhaps a priest—in skins and antlers (top right), and a woolly mammoth (above) were discovered in three different caves in southern France. Such illustrations may have been painted to prophesy, and thus ensure, a successful hunt.*

painted there are often of wounded animals. These creations too may have been a form of magical prophesy. The artist may have believed that by depicting a desired condition he could bring it about.

Cave painting was not early man's only art form. In Europe, as in America, he carved decorations for his spear-throwers and made beads from bone and antler. And when he died, he was buried with suitable ceremony, his body surrounded by prized possessions so that he might be well supplied for the afterlife. Although man's knowledge of his remote ancestors of 15,000 years ago is far from complete, this much is certain: the hunting bands of that time had already adjusted to their environments and had evolved a technology suitable for their needs. Art and religion flourished, and mankind was moving steadily toward ever more complex cultures.

Corridors That Opened and Closed

The earliest immigrants to North America found a world bounded by glaciers that covered most of Alaska, leaving only some river valleys free of the ice floe. In their pursuit of game, these early hunters tended to roam southward into the heartland of the continent, but the periodic advance of the glaciers often cut off their routes south and the people would be imprisoned within the fastnesses of Alaska's Brooks Range (top left) for many centuries at a time. Then the glaciers would recede for a time, leaving ice-free corridors open through which hunting bands could freely move.

Though a glacier advances at an invisibly slow rate, it is a formidable juggernaut as it inches, year by year, toward the sea. Once it is launched by an accumulation of snowfalls that may reach a depth of 50 feet, the compacted mass moves downhill from its birthplace on the peaks of mountains. As it does so, it builds up more bulk, not only in the form of snow and ice but also in crushed boulders and millions of tons of soil that the glacier envelops. The lip, or snout, of a contemporary glacier (center), for example, is approaching a small stand of trees that it will eventually uproot and perhaps deposit hundreds of miles away.

A glacier is said to retreat when major changes in the climate bring about a melt, the water thus released causing both the sea to rise and vast new lakes to be created in the great depressions that the ice floe had gouged out of the earth during the advance of the glacier. As a glacier retreats, it also leaves behind the accumulated debris it had carried, a topsoil called moraine.

The first Americans who hunted in the glacier-free river valleys of Alaska lived on a terrain characterized by permafrost. Only the surface of the earth melted during the short warm season, and the land became a region of bogs and marshes much like the Alaska terrain shown in the photograph at bottom right.

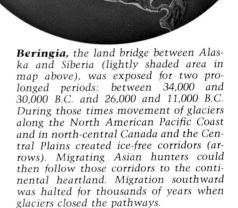

Beringia, the land bridge between Alaska and Siberia (lightly shaded area in map above), was exposed for two prolonged periods: between 34,000 and 30,000 B.C. and 26,000 and 11,000 B.C. During those times movement of glaciers along the North American Pacific Coast and in north-central Canada and the Central Plains created ice-free corridors (arrows). Migrating Asian hunters could then follow those corridors to the continental heartland. Migration southward was halted for thousands of years when glaciers closed the pathways.

valley of the Mackenzie River, and into the broad plains east of the Rockies. Another followed the Yukon Valley southward.

The bands of nomads had just emerged from the narrow land path between the great walls of ice. Ahead of them lay a wondrous sight, a beautiful expanse of country stretching apparently without end before them to the south and the west and the east. The vegetation was thick and various, and the plains seemed to swarm with animals. As the wanderers trekked southward, they marveled at the abundant fish, the gigantic beasts, and the mysterious blossoms. As the weather warmed, they began to discard some of their heavy fur clothing. In this new world memories of the chill Arctic mists were soon to be left behind. The pioneers chattered among themselves. The heartland of North America for the first time had heard the sound of a human voice.

By all scientific evidence the first Americans entered a land quite different from the America of today. The climate in those glacial times was cooler and rainier. Lakes and swamps existed where no water exists today. Present-day Nevada was covered by the huge body of water now called Lake Bonneville by the geologists. Even today's Death Valley included large bodies of fresh water. As the glacier continued its gradual retreat to the north, its place was taken by natural growth—by forests of spruce, pine, and birch, or by rich, grassy plains.

America's oldest artifact, *this 27,000-year-old caribou-bone scraper, its edges still intact, was found in the Yukon. A sketch of the whole-bone is at right.*

Glyptodon (huge armadillos), tapirs, and giant ground sloths abounded. Among these many herbivores stalked the predators: the ferocious dire wolf, the terrifying-looking saber-toothed cat, and the immense short-legged bear, bigger than today's grizzlies or Kodiaks.

Now man, the greatest predator of all, had arrived in the untouched, primeval land. But the very earliest Americans did little to deplete the vast game supplies they encountered. These people had only the crudest chopping tools of stone, and their weapons were wholly primitive. Almost certainly, they hunted with sharpened sticks or with spears fitted with points of bone or horn. Such weapons could not have been especially effective in hunting the huge animals that surrounded the first Americans, and they undoubtedly enjoyed their greatest success when the prey was crippled or aged. The chief sustenance of these people, however, probably came from nuts, berries, and small game.

Cut off from a retreat to their Asian homeland by the whims of the land bridge and the ice barriers, the pioneers moved ever more deeply into their new continent. And in the American land of plenty they not only survived but flourished. As generation followed generation, they spread from the Central Plains to present-day California and to the forests of the Atlantic Coast. They trekked through Mexico and the Central American jungles and reached the southernmost tip of South America. Above all, they learned to adapt to the many new environments the New World held in store for them.

The Fertile Earth

If their ancestral homelands to the north were largely barren of life-sustaining vegetation, the early Americans found a dazzling variety of edible plants in the heartland of the American continent. Although game was scarce in any given area from time to time, the good earth offered turnips and ground nuts and arrowroot. Wild berries as well as plums and persimmons could be found in many places. Hazel, hickory, and pecan trees hung with clusters of nuts.

In the plains the migrants came upon huge beasts grazing undisturbed in enormous herds. There were mammoths standing 14 feet high at the shoulders, and the slightly smaller mastodons; both had the same common ancestors as today's elephants. Horses, supersized bison, and even camels lived alongside deer, elk, and beavers the size of grizzly bears. Strange creatures like

Arrival of the Europeans

By the time the Europeans arrived, the descendants of the prehistoric pioneers and later migrants had formed a wide variety of tribes. Clearly, they were all related. But some of them were simple nomads, roaming the dry plateaus and deserts of the West, while others were forest-dwellers who sustained themselves as hunters and fishermen. In the Southwest lived the farming people of the Pueblo country, inhabiting substantial cities of stone or adobe. Along the Mississippi were the villages of the Mound People, who built giant earthworks atop which they worshiped their gods. By this time the Indians spoke many different languages, some as different from each other as Swahili from English. There were great variations in customs and traditions from place to place and tribe to tribe.

The Europeans were greatly puzzled over these

brown-skinned, befeathered people. In 1512 Pope Julius II proclaimed that the Indians were children of Adam and Eve—hence, human beings. More fanciful Europeans theorized that these strange people, unlike any other they had seen in Europe, Africa, or Asia, might have been refugees from some Old World catastrophe, such as the fall of Carthage, the sinking of Atlantis, or the scattering of the Children of Israel. Scholars professed to find linguistic similarities between the red man's tongues and those of the ancient Hittites, the Phoenicians, and the Welsh.

Most puzzling of all to the early Europeans, How came these people to the New World? The Indians were not great mariners, and it was difficult to imagine their sailing across the turbulent Atlantic or navigating the newly discovered, apparently boundless Pacific. As early as 1590 the Spanish priest José de Acosta reasoned that the Indians must have arrived by land. Acosta further surmised that somewhere on the unexplored western coast of America there was a place joined to eastern

Antler-shaped reindeer moss (grayish-white), dwarf willow (reddish leaves, upper left), lingonberries (red fruits), and lichens soak up the long day's sun of Alaska's short growing season in Mount McKinley National Park. Both the early human inhabitants of Alaska and some of the animals on the opposite page fed on such plants as they roamed the tundra in search of food. But in the Arctic these eatables were available for only a few months each year.

Asia, or at least "not altogether severed and disjoined."

Others carried these speculations further. In 1614 the English philologist Edward Brerewood concluded that the American Indians must be related to the Tartars, by which he meant the inhabitants of Mongolia and Siberia. But not until the years between 1728 and 1741 did Vitus Bering—a Danish sea captain in the service of the Russian czar—explore the tip of eastern Asia and prove that it was separated from North America by the narrowest of channels. Bering Strait was bleak and windswept and littered with dangerous ice floes, but Bering found Eskimos crossing it in their kayaks and traveling over the bridge of ice that formed in the coldest depths of winter. By the early 19th century most thoughtful people—including amateur archeologist Thomas Jefferson—were fully convinced that the Indians had indeed come to the New World from Asia via the Bering Strait area. Today few, if any, scientific authorities would care to dispute that hypothesis.

Much greater controversy surrounds the question, When did the Asians arrive in the New World? Geologists have argued that the early migrations probably were sporadic. When the warmer climate favored the opening of the corridors through the ice sheet, the sea would rise and envelop the land bridge. And often, when the land bridge was open, the way southward to the American heartland was closed off by the glacier. Geologists believe that conditions would have permitted Old-to-New-World migration starting 50,000 or 60,000 years ago. After that the climate worsened, so that those who did cross on the land bridge would have found survival on the American side virtually impossible. But in later times, when both the land bridge and the corridors were open, new bursts of immigration may have occurred. The geologists believe that proper combinations of conditions existed about 25,000 years ago and also from 11,000 to 13,000 years ago. After that the ice began to retreat, sea levels rose, and the Beringia land bridge was swallowed by the ocean waters that cover it today.

Establishing an Arrival Time

Despite the views of the geologists, most scientists in the first two decades of this century held with anthropologist Ales Hrdlicka of the Smithsonian Institution's Bureau of American Ethnology that the first arrivals in America could not have been more than three or four thousand years ago. In their view the migration would have been by boat. But important archeological finds during the 1920's and 1930's proved conclusively that America was relatively well populated during the waning centuries of the last ice age—between 15,000 and 25,000 years ago. More recent findings and the discovery of Carbon-14 (C-14) testing have enabled scientists to push their quest for the earliest Americans ever deeper and deeper into the past.

Developed in the 1940's, the Carbon-14 test has pro-

Woolly mammoth

American mastodon

Giant sloth

Camel

Dire wolf

Short-faced bear

Giant bison

Horse

Giant beaver

Armadillo

Peccary

Tapir

Saber-toothed cat

American lion

Ancestors of modern-day animals roamed the forests and plains of North America some 15,000 years ago, the herbivores foraging for leaves and branches, roots, and tubers while the carnivores lived off the flesh of their fellow beasts. Some of these animals originally migrated from Asia over the Bering land bridge. Others, such as the primitive armadillo and the giant ground sloth, moved north from South America. The sloth (upper right) used its muscular tail to steady its enormous bulk as it searched for tender shoots on the upper branches of junipers and pines. Other herbivores included the woolly mammoth—a three-ton, curved-tusked behemoth—and the only slightly smaller mastodon, as well as the giant bison, the horse and camel, the peccary (drinking at the water hole), and the curved-snouted tapir. The rivers of the continent abounded with fish, eagerly sought by the giant beaver (on log) that weighed some 300 pounds. Among the predators were the short-faced bear—one-third larger than the modern black bear—the dire wolf, the sabertoothed cat, the American lion, and that most fearsome hunter of all: man.

The World of the North American Paleo-Indians

Onion Portage, Alaska: Paleo-Indians hunted caribou here as long ago as 8000 B.C.

Old Crow Flats, Yukon Terr. 27,000-year-old caribou-bone tool, oldest American artifact yet found

MacHaffie, Mont.: Giant bison slain here, 8000 B.C.

Marmes, Wash.: Pieces of human skulls, 9,000 years old, found

Lindenmeier, Colo.: Giant bison and mammoth hunting site, 8000 B.C.

Olsen-Chubbuck, Colo.: Remains of giant bison, 10,000 years old, indicating successful hunting drive

Laguna Beach, Calif.: Human skull found. Tentatively dated at 15,000 B.C. Possibly oldest human remains yet discovered in Americas

Folsom, N. Mex.: Remains of extinct animals with human artifacts reveal this as one of the oldest North American campsites

Naco and Lehner, Ariz.: Bones of mammoths and spearpoints show this to be hunting ground 11,500 years old

Clovis, N. Mex.: Mammoth hunters made kills here, 9000 B.C.

Scharbauer, Tex.: Skull of woman who died c. 8000 B.C. found

Hudson-Meng, Nebr.: Bison bones with spearpoints reveal that some 400 bison killed here 10,000 years ago

Meadowcroft Rockshelter, Pa.: Layers of debris dating from 14,000 B.C. to historic times show this to be site of longest human habitation in Americas

Bull Brook, Mass.: More than 1,000 artifacts—drills, knife edges, projectile points—date back to 7000 B.C.

Debert, Nova Scotia: 4,000 flint tools and hunting points, 10,600 years old

Plenge, N.J.: One of the most varied collections of Paleo-Indian artifacts found here

Shoop, Pa.: Artifacts from non-native stone indicate intergroup trade, perhaps as early as 9000 B.C.

Flint Run, Va.: Numerous hunting, quarry, and camp sites dating from 9000 B.C.

Williamson, Va.: Quarry site where Paleo-Indians mined chert (a variety of quartz) for toolmaking

Plainview, Tex.: Earliest discovered site—9000 B.C.—of major bison cliff drive

Levi, Tex.: Rock shelter in forest where hundreds of flint tools were found

Tepexpán, Mexico: Human skull, possibly 10,000 years old, discovered

At a quarry site in New Mexico 11,000 years ago, two men from a hunting band create weapons and tools in anticipation of expeditions to kill mammoths, deer, and antelopes. As a woman tends to the children, the man in the foreground uses a bone to flake the edges of a stone and make a Clovis point (inset) for a spear tip. Meanwhile, another hunter is forming knives and skin scrapers from rocks.

After a successful hunt in New Mexico about 10,000 years ago, a band of huntsmen carry off huge chunks of meat from the carcass of a giant bison. They felled the massive animal with spears tipped with hollowed out Folsom points, like the one above, aiming their weapons at the bison's ribcage. If only a few animals were killed, nothing was wasted. The hide was scraped clean and tanned, the surplus meat dried for future use. But if the kill was large, much meat would be left to scavengers.

A herd of bison, terrified by shouting hunters waving skins, stampedes to its doom over a cliff during a hunt in about 8000 B.C. After the beasts had fallen to the bottom, the hunters used large stones to stun any animals that survived. These bison were then finished off with spears tipped with Plano points, such as the one above. (This tactic of mass slaughter of animals was employed by Indians as late as the 19th century.) By the Plano Era the giant bison had disappeared, and hunters pursued smaller varieties.

vided archeologists with a far more precise way of dating their finds than existed in the past. C-14 is a radioactive element that every living thing absorbs at a steady rate throughout its life. At death, the intake of C-14 ceases and the accumulated supply in the body begins to break down into nonradioactive carbon. By measuring the degree to which this breakdown has progressed, scientists can determine how long ago the death of the organism took place. The age of wood, bone, hair, and antler, for example, can be measured with a fair degree of precision up to the age of 50,000 years. However, such things as pottery, stone tools, and other inorganic artifacts cannot be tested in this way.

South American Findings

Modern scientists now believe that human beings dwelled in the New World 40,000 to 50,000 years ago, perhaps even earlier. Some of their evidence has come from South America. In Patagonia, at the extreme southern tip of Chile, signs of human habitation have been found that have been dated by C-14 tests to at least 12,000 years ago. The question arises, How many millennia had it taken those people to cover the 11,000 miles from Bering Strait to the Strait of Magellan?

Far to the north, signs of human habitation have been found in Peru (dating to 16,000 years ago), Venezuela (18,000 years ago), and Mexico (23,000 years ago). If mankind

This sculptured head of a Tepexpán man is based on an 11,000-year-old skull found near Mexico City. The work suggests the probable facial characteristics.

reached Mexico 23,000 years ago, the scientists reasoned, they must have left earlier traces farther to the north. That assumption proved to be a sound one. Man-made artifacts, dating back 25,000 and 29,000 years, have been found along the Old Crow River, in the Yukon Territory of Canada. Charcoal from what may have been ancient cooking hearths discovered in northeast Texas have yielded C-14 dates going back approximately 38,000 years.

One of the most intriguing of the early archeological sites is Santa Rosa Island, 45 miles off the coast of southern California. Fossils of an unusual dwarf mammoth, native only to the island, have been found there. This Santa Rosa mammoth, as the archeologists have dubbed it, stood just six feet high. It was, in effect, an elephant no bigger than a barnyard bull—and evidently it was an easy mark for hunters of the time.

The women and children of the island people were in a festive mood. Two days before, the men had killed six dwarf mammoths down by the beach, smashing in their skulls with their stone clubs. They had butchered the animals with blades of stone. Ribs, vertebrae, and

tails were removed. Then pieces of the meat were carried to the hearth site, a pit in the earth about two feet deep and eight feet across. Wood was heaped in the pit and ingnited. The meat, wrapped in the biggest leaves the women could find, was placed atop the smoldering wood. After more burning wood was added, a layer of soil was heaped over the cooking pit. Now the meat had cooked for a day and a half, and tonight there would be a joyful feast for everyone in camp.

No human bones were found on Santa Rosa, but charcoal samples from a cooking pit have been subjected to C-14 testing. In March 1977 the results were announced by Dr. Rainer Berger of the University of California at Los Angeles. The test indicated an age of greater than 40,000 years. "It clinches the argument," commented Dr. Berger, "that human presence and evolution [in North America] go back much further than we thought."

Dr. Berger and other scientists are cautious about calling the Santa Rosa mammoth-roasters ancestors of the Indians. The earliest Americans may have been precursors, and not necessarily direct ancestors, of today's Indians. If this is the case, the North American Indians of today are the descendants of the later migrants who departed from their Asian homeland.

New Hunting Skills

After the first generations of migrants the early Americans began to develop the skills needed to hunt large animals more effectively. Archeologists refer to that period of big-game hunting (roughly 50,000/10,000 to 5000 B.C.) as the lithic, or Paleo-Indian, period. ("Lithic" is from the Greek word for "stone"; "Paleo" from the Greek for "ancient.") This was succeeded by the Foraging, or Archaic, period (5000 to 1000 B.C.), during which the Indians hunted small game as well as the dwindling supply of big-game animals, foraged for vegetables and grain, and developed a wide assortment of tools. Finally, in the so-called Formative period (1000 B.C. to A.D. 1000), there were far more dramatic changes. The American Indians developed pottery, stable village life, trade, and the beginnings of agriculture.

These periods, of course, are not to be regarded as rigid chunks of prehistory. In most parts of North America the three periods blurred and overlapped as various tribes adapted to changing conditions or new environments. In some areas many ancient ways continued with little change. In others, the Indians sought out new methods of survival.

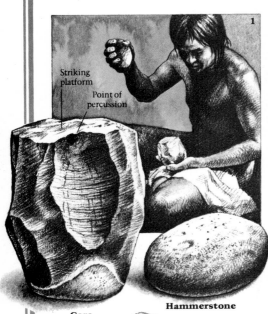

Striking platform

Point of percussion

Core

Hammerstone

Flake

Bulbar scar

Bulb

Splits

Ripple marks

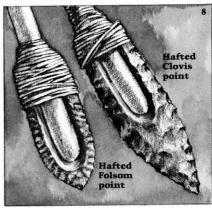

Hafted Clovis point

Hafted Folsom point

The Delicate Art of Stone Age Flaking

Gripping an egg-shaped stone he uses as a hammer, a Folsom toolmaker (fig. 1) prepares to knock a flake from a large piece of flint, the first step in making a spearpoint. The flake (fig. 2) bears little resemblance to the projectile point it will become. Head-on views of the flake are shown at the bottom of figures 2, 3, 5, and 7 to illustrate the progression of fluting characteristics of the Folsom point.

Additional flaking creates the generalized form of the point (fig. 3) and a ridge in the middle of both faces. The base is then notched (fig. 4) by hammering with the tip of some sharp instrument—perhaps an antler point—against that surface. This creates a striking point in the center of the base. By sharply hitting that striking point (fig. 5) with the antler,

the ridge on one face of the projectile head is flaked away, leaving a channeled (fluted) surface. The obverse face of the projectile point is now worked, with the antler tip first being used to make new notches in the base (fig. 6) and then to hit the center striking point to flake off a channel (fig. 7) on that side of the point.

The point is now finished and is ready to be lashed securely with sinew to the fork-tipped shaft of wood (left, fig. 8). A similar spear tip was the earlier Clovis point (right, fig. 8), but it was usually channeled on only one face. The method used to attach points to shafts, as shown in figure 8, is conjecture, but the characteristics of the points indicate this was probably the technique employed.

The Slaughter of the Mammoths

Perhaps a thousand generations have lived and died since the first migrants came to the Western Plains of North America. The glacier has withdrawn into the Arctic. And by now the forebears of the American Indians—the Paleo-Indians—have developed into formidable hunters. Responding to the presence of huge herds of gigantic animals on the continent, they have crafted weapons and evolved techniques capable of killing the biggest prey. By now man truly has become the most deadly predator in the New World.

Evidence of this Paleo-Indian period has accumulated steadily in recent decades. Many layers beneath the

surface inside Sandia Cave, near Albuquerque, New Mexico, weapon points have been found among the bones of extinct animals. Sandia points have been found at other sites in New Mexico, and studies indicate that the people who used them lived some 12,000 years ago. Because archeologists have no way of knowing with certainty whether these stone implements were mounted on lances, darts, or spears, they prefer to speak of them as "points" (short for "projectile points").

The Sandia people apparently did not spread widely, and their impact on the animal life of North America was minimal. But suddenly, about 12,000 years ago, a culture of big-game hunters appeared on the scene and had a dramatic effect on much of the continent. These were the Clovis people, named for a find made at Clovis, New Mexico, in 1932. Along the shorelines of ancient, long-vanished lakes, where mammoths, bison, and horses once grazed in a lush grassland, archeologists found the charred bones of all these animals and traces of the weapons that killed them.

New Hunting Weapons

Seemingly delicate, the so-called Clovis points were, in fact, lethal weapons in the hunt for the big game. Typically, they were about four or five inches long, shaped like the killing portion of a bayonet. They were carefully thinned down by chipping the stones until their edges were sharp and penetrating. These points were presumably lashed to wooden shafts with animal thong. They may have been used for jabbing, as with a lance, or throwing, as with a spear—quite possibly both.

Killing the great beasts could not have been an easy matter, even with those sharp-pointed spears and lances. The bow and arrow had not yet been invented, so that the early Clovis tribes had only the strength of their own bodies to launch their stone-pointed shafts. There is evidence that the Clovis man developed additional techniques for killing the mammoth—his favorite prey—as well as many other animals. Sometimes the hunters lighted grass fires and stampeded the beasts

over cliffs or into a ravine. On other occasions the men found ways to separate the younger, less dangerous mammoths from the herd and to slaughter them with their spears and lances.

Who were the Clovis people, the fiercest hunters yet to appear in America? We do not know with total certainty where they came from or how they evolved their superior technology for the hunt. It is possible that inventive minds among the existing tribes of North America created the superior stone point and thereby made big-game hunting far more productive. Or it is equally possible that an entirely new band of hunters came across the Bering land bridge, armed with a point-making technology that originated in Siberia.

If their origins are uncertain, the efficacy of the Clovis people as hunters is not open to doubt. With an astonishing swiftness they spread across thousands of square miles of North America. Traces of the Clovis hunts have been found from Alaska to Mexico and from California to Nova Scotia.

The hunters lay in wait in the hills above the pond, a drinking hole for a herd of mammoths that grazed in the nearby grasslands. The Indians knew what the prey would do next. After some hours a dozen of the huge, shaggy animals came lumbering down to the water's edge. Once the hunters spied them, the men gathered up their spears and pointed sticks and crept stealthily

On the hunt, *a Paleo-Indian armed with a spear and a device called an atlatl—from the Aztec word meaning "spear-thrower"—approaches two caribous. Before the animals can take flight and run off, the Indian will have sent his spear hurtling through the air with great force, and if his aim is true, he will bring down one of the caribous.*

No one knows when or where the atlatl was invented, but it was widely in use both in southwestern Europe and southwestern North America by 8000 B.C. Its effect was to revolutionize hunting techniques by allowing a man to hurl a spear with lethal force while remaining at a considerable distance from his quarry. Basically, the atlatl is nothing more than a two- or three-foot-long piece of wood with a small base carved in its butt end. The spear rests on the upper face of the atlatl and is held in place by the base and the hunter's hand. To throw the spear, the hunter merely lifted the atlatl over his shoulder and, with a whiplike motion, sent the weapon hurtling toward its target.

through the tall grass toward the unsuspecting brutes.

The leader of the hunters gave a signal, and the other spearmen, shouting and brandishing their weapons, closed in on the animals. Some of the frightened mammoths bolted and escaped in the brush. The others retreated into the shallow water. As the animals thrashed around in the pond, the men hurled their razor-sharp weapons into the mammoths' sides. Trumpeting in rage and pain, the huge beasts brought their eight-foot tusks into play. One mammoth impaled a hunter, then tossed him aside like a broken doll; another mammoth stomped a tormentor into the slime. But the hunters were relentless, hurling and jabbing their pointed weapons. Some of the mammoths began to lose blood and strength. As they weakened, the hunters thrust their sharply pointed spears into their lungs and hearts. Before long the wild cries ceased. The day's hunt was over.

The Extinction of Species

The improved weapons and hunting techniques introduced by the Clovis people and the progress in both areas made by those who followed them undoubtedly had some effect on the animal population of North America. But whether that effect was major or inconsequential is impossible to determine.

We do know, however, that during the Pleistocene epoch, which lasted nearly 3 million years, more than 60 species of large mammals—including the horse, the camel, the mammoth, and the saber-toothed cat—disappeared from the continent. More than half of those species died out during the 2,000-year period contemporary with the Clovis people. Another interesting phenomenon was taking place more or less concurrently. The size of some giant animals began diminishing about the middle of the Pleistocene era. The huge bison, for example, disappeared, but the smaller subspecies—the kind still to be found in the modern world—survived.

Many scientists are convinced that the extinction of some species and diminution of others was brought about by drastic climate changes during the Pleistocene epoch. As meadows became deserts, lakes disappeared, and chilly woodlands became temperate forests, perhaps the mastodon and other large mammals were unable to adapt. Other scientists have speculated that a plague of some sort, brought out of Asia by new waves of hunters, may have caused the elimination of many species.

But regardless of cause, as the big game began to dwindle, life must have become more difficult for the Clovis people. Being hunters, they roamed the countryside most of the time, in family-sized bands, following the game. In areas where animals were plentiful, perhaps several families would come together and form a temporary camp in some secluded part of the brush or prairie. At times, probably, they lived on small animals

or nuts. Many must have died, unable to adapt their Clovis hunting skills to new conditions.

The Coming of the Folsom People

About 10,000 years ago new immigrants arrived in the American Plains. The archeologists have labeled them the Folsom people because of a dramatic finding at Folsom, New Mexico, in 1925. Searching for a lost cow, a cowhand named George McJuhkin discovered some unusually large bones and some curious stone weapon points not at all like the arrowheads he had seen around the area. Archeologists soon determined that the bones were those of *Bison antiquus*, a giant, long-horned bison that inhabited the American Southwest until 8,000 or 10,000 years ago. The points, referred to as Folsom points, are long, elegantly worked flint weapons with flutings, or grooves, incised into the faces.

A New Tool for Killing

Also during this period a revolutionary invention appeared—a throwing device known today by the Aztec word atlatl. It was a deceptively simple mechanism, a wooden handle with a hooked tip. Used properly, it enabled a hunter to increase greatly the force and speed with which a spear could be thrown. In effect, the atlatl lengthened the hunter's throwing arm. The atlatl also permitted him to hunt game from a distance and not have to creep up to close quarters and take added risks to make his kill.

The Folsom people, like their predecessors, left slender clues to their way of life. They did have stone knives and hide scrapers, bone needles and awls—tools a hunting people would use in dressing meat and preparing skins for tents or clothing. A few small bone beads and pendants, bearing traces of red pigment, have been found at Folsom sites and indicate at least a rudimentary taste for ornament.

There is evidence that the Folsom people did not spread much beyond the Southern Plains, and they seem to have been supplanted rather quickly by a group that used unfluted weapon points—the so-called Plano hunters. Their chief prey was the huge bison, an ancestor of the modern buffalo.

The Plano people must have taken a heavy toll on the great bison herds of their time, for they had mastered the technique of stampeding large herds to their deaths. One Plano kill site, discovered near Kit Carson, Colorado, contained abundant evidence that Plano hunters had driven a herd of bison into an eight-feet-deep arroyo and slaughtered almost 200 of them.

It was early summer, and a large herd of bison—including many calves—grazed in the open field. Suddenly, the hunters appeared on three sides. On the fourth side was a deep gully. At a prearranged signal the hunters attacked, hurling their spears and uttering blood-chilling shrieks. In a moment the animals were

The Mystery of the Disappearing Mammals

Of all the unanswered questions about prehistoric North America, one of the most intriguing concerns the disappearance from the continent of scores of species of large mammals. Why, for example, did the mastodon, the mammoth, the camel, the horse, the giant sloth, the long-horned bison—to name just a few—become extinct? To date, no one has been able to answer that question with any degree of certainty, but there are clues to the mysterious event.

The onset of the disappearance seems to have coincided with the end of the last ice age, some 12,000 years ago, a period geologists call the Late Pleistocene. Some 6,000 years later, fully two-thirds of the species of North American mammals that weighed more than 100 pounds at maturity had become extinct. Some scientists blame changes in climate and topography. The climate in the Plains and the Woodlands had become generally warmer, the level of moisture was down, and

lakes and rivers disappeared. Clearly, such changes in environment must have put great stress upon the large mammals, most of which were herding creatures that migrated in large groups. But, by the same token, their migrating instincts might well have saved them from extinction, for nothing prevented them from searching out new territories where the weather and topography were more accommodating to the animals' needs. And, it is sometimes suggested, changes in temperature may have upset the breeding cycles of the mammals. Yet many of the same species that disappeared in the Late Pleistocene had survived earlier retreats of the ice.

During the Late Pleistocene, however, there was a new factor that had not existed in previous interglacial ages, and that was man, the superpredator. Though early emigrants from Asia had lived in North America long before the last ice age ended, the human population was relatively small. But when the

ice retreated to the Far North, innumerable bands of huntsmen trooped down the Alaska valleys and killed animals on the fertile, game-rich plains and forests of the North American heartland. These were men who had long since perfected their skills as hunters. They were armed with spears tipped with razor-sharp points. They were capable of organizing into large, disciplined bands, to set the grasslands aflame and drive large herds of lumbering beasts into surrounds or over the edges of cliffs. Such tactics are now called the Pleistocene Overkill. Given the likelihood that the herds were already somewhat diminished by the stresses of environmental change, it is possible that man, through his prodigal hunting techniques, applied the coup de grace to scores of species. And with the extinction of numerous herding species, many of the predators that fed upon them—the dire wolf, the saber-toothed cat, the American lion—were also doomed.

Waving torches and shouting, *hunters stampede a herd of long-horned bison into an arroyo where those not killed by the fall could be easily dispatched with spears. An excavated trench at right shows the results of such a hunt some 8,500 years ago, for here are the bones of 200 bison, obviously slaughtered in a single hunt.*

in a panic. Some tried to dash past the advancing hunters and were speared. The main portion of the herd stampeded away in the only open direction—toward the gully. In their fear the bison plunged straight into it. The first ones suffocated as the other animals crashed in on top of them. The gully was soon filled with writhing, bleating bison, and the hunters closed in for the final kill. Spear after spear went biting into the flanks of the tormented beasts. So many were killed that day that the hunters did not even bother to drag all the slain animals out of the death trap for butchering and storing. There were always plenty of scavengers around to consume the vast surplus of flesh.

***The stone mano and metate** were a primitive mortar and pestle for grinding seeds into meal. The wide use of these tools by 6000 B.C. indicates extensive reliance on plants as food.*

The Plano hunters, like the Clovis and Folsom peoples before them, butchered the animals with razor-sharp knives fashioned out of flint or obsidian. The butchering was done at the site of the killing, and then the meat was carried away to a nearby camp. The techniques used for such large-scale killing required bands of perhaps 150 people. This would imply that some sort of rudimentary social organization with a sense of discipline had been developed and that the concept of leadership had taken hold.

There was no sign at all of any agriculture being practiced during this era. The Paleo-Indians relied chiefly on meat and wild fruits and vegetables for their subsistence. Basically, they were hunters, and when the game began to dwindle and disappear, their day was over. No evidence exists that these fierce hunters of the American Plains ever became farmers and artisans and converted to a more sedentary life.

Foraging for Sustenance

As the huge animals—called megafauna by students of the Pleistocene epoch—disappeared from most of the American continent, the people who survived were those able to evolve techniques and a wider variety of tools for hunting smaller animals. Life no longer centered around the hunt for the mammoth, the ancient bison, or the giant ground sloth. Now prehistoric man turned to foraging for plants, for such smaller game as deer and antelope, and for fish and fowl. In some areas, along the seacoasts, he gathered shellfish, speared the seal, and even summoned up sufficient skill and courage to venture into the ocean to hunt the mighty whale.

Such fundamental changes in the approach to survival led, inevitably, to a period of immense cultural ferment. This period, called the Foraging, or Archaic, by the archeologists, saw people learn to make handsome and useful chopping and scraping tools of polished stone and to fashion elegant barbed or notched points for hunting the smaller game. Many Indians still moved with the seasons in order to follow the game, but semipermanent settlements began to develop and, with that, more complicated social patterns were created. Gradually, Indians in parts of America learned the rudiments of agriculture and began to domesticate livestock. Trade among various communities began to appear. The art of pottery-making was discovered and introduced into the Southwest. And, as we can tell from a growing number of artifacts of a ritualistic nature, deeper and more complex religious concepts began to spread among the prehistoric Americans.

But, to some extent, we are getting ahead of our story.

Decoy ducks, remarkably lifelike, were found in a cave in northwest Utah. Made by desert foragers some 3,000 years ago, the decoys were used to attract migrating ducks to nearby marshes. The decoys were made of reeds, as is the one at far right, and were sewn together with fiber thread. The bodies were then covered with paint (decoy at left) or a feathered skin. The actual means employed to take live ducks is a matter of conjecture. One possible method was for a hunter to submerge himself with the decoy tied to his head. While breathing through a reed he watched for a duck to land nearby, then reached up to grab it. Another method might have been to hide in the rushes and then hurl darts at the ducks.

Overlapping Cultures

As mentioned earlier, the various prehistoric eras blurred and overlapped, beginning and ending at different times in different places. Archeologists roughly date the height of the Archaic period as lasting from 5000 to 1000 B.C.—the years when it had spread to all parts of the continent. But even during the earlier era, cultures other than the Clovis or Folsom or Plano huntsmen had existed in some parts of the continent. And some of these cultures—possibly even older ones than the hunters—had begun to develop the traits of the foraging tradition. The big-game hunters were to perish along with their prey, but these other, more adaptable cultures managed to endure. From them, it seems likely, stemmed the rich and varied Indian tribes that were to inhabit America thousands of years later when the European explorers arrived on the continent.

One such precursor of the Archaic Americans, a group that lived in the Pacific Northwest, is known to modern archeologists as the Old Cordilleran Culture. Contemporaries of the Folsom and Clovis hunters, they were established in the Columbia River valley by 9000 B.C., and perhaps earlier. (The question of the antiquity of the Old Cordilleran Culture is still the subject of sharp debate among archeologists. The basic point of contention is whether it predated the hunting tradition of the Plains or was contemporary with it.) The Cordillerans were hunters, too, but they were not nearly as single-minded as the big-game hunters. The Cordillerans hunted the camel and the ground sloth, but primarily they lived on small mammals and fish. Far less specialized than the big-game hunters, the Old Cordillerans also developed the tools and techniques for the collection and preparation of edible plants. They appear to have been far more settled than the big-game hunters and occupied the same terrain for hundreds or even thousands of years.

To this day the archeological record of the area from 5000 to 1000 B.C. remains obscure. One commonly held hypothesis presumes that the Old Cordilleran Culture is considered to be the matrix from which the rich Northwest Coast Indian culture eventually was to evolve about 1000 B.C.

People of the Desert

Another ancient civilization that foreshadowed and merged into Archaic times was the so-called Desert

This sandstone rock, incised by a desert craftsman at least 600 years ago, may have had a function in ceremonies to ensure a good hunt or in healing rituals.

Culture. This appeared in the arid Great Basin region, which takes in present-day eastern California, Nevada, much of Utah, and parts of Oregon, Idaho, and Wyoming. Its best-known site is Danger Cave, on the edge of Great Salt Lake in western Utah, where Carbon-14 tests have shown human occupation as early as 11,500 years ago.

Before the archeologists came, the cave was known to the people of the region as Hands and Knees Cave—because it was necessary to crawl through a low tunnel to reach the main chamber. But the site is now firmly established in the annals of American archeology as Danger Cave, the name given it by E. R. Smith after a huge rock fall halted his excavations in 1941.

Not until the 1950's, when Jesse D. Jennings directed a team of excavators at the site, did Danger Cave reveal its most startling secrets. No bones of extinct ice age animals were unearthed, as they were at Etna Cave, a Desert Culture site near Las Vegas, but Danger Cave did yield the remains of mountain sheep, deer, and antelopes. Radiocarbon testing placed the age of the sheep dung and wooden objects at more than 11,000 years. Some objects in the newer layers ranged from 9,000 to 3,000 years in age—proof that Danger Cave had been occupied, though perhaps not continually, over many thousands of years.

In the lowest levels of the cave, diggers have found small points, apparently used as the tips of throwing-stick darts in the hunting of relatively small animals, such as deer and antelopes. But the next youngest level, dating to roughly 8000 B.C., yielded far more astonishing things: baskets woven from plant fiber and millstones that had been used to grind seeds. That long ago, apparently, the Desert folk had practiced the craft of basketry. It may very well be that they were the first people in the world to do so.

Treasures of Danger Cave

On various layers the cave yielded thousands of artifacts, including stone chopping tools and objects made of wood, bone, shell, fiber, or hide. Clothing clearly was at a minimum among the early inhabitants of Danger Cave, but as years passed—the evidence at the cave site shows—the Indians developed skill in the working of skins. The remains of one patched moccasin and three moccasin scraps have been unearthed at the site. The primitive shoes, made of antelope hide and stitched with sinew, were found encrusted in a slimy mud much like the earth found today in the nearby salt flats.

Evidence from the cave also shows that they gathered nuts, bulbs, and acorns, ground them into flour, and cooked them. This remarkable development is regarded by archeologists as one of the first steps in the eventual transition of prehistoric North American man from a hunting to a farming way of life.

Inside the cave the women of the band had spent much of the long winter making baskets. The older women patiently showed the girls how to take the willow splints they had collected and weave them into baskets of various shapes. Now, in early spring, the baskets were ready. Some would be used to carry the nuts, acorns, and berries the women would collect that day. The berries would be mashed into a flavorsome paste. The nuts and acorns would be ground into a flour on the millstone. Then the women would mix the flour with water and pour the thick dough into a flat cooking basket. They would then place the basket on stones heated by the fire, shaking the basket frequently to prevent it from scorching. When the cooking was over, they would have a fine, tasty mush to go along with whatever meat the men brought home that day.

The Ingenious Cochise

Perhaps the most inventive of the Desert Culture people—the Cochise—lived in southeastern Arizona. The climate there was cool and moist when these people arrived, and the region was blessed with plentiful wildlife. That was, perhaps, 10,000 years ago. But it soon was to grow hot and arid—another climatic consequence of the withdrawal of the glacier. As this change occurred, the few remaining bison in the area quickly disappeared. To survive, the people became foragers and food-gatherers. We know this group as the Cochise because the first evidence of its existence was uncovered in 1926 near the town of Cochise, Arizona. Carbon-14 testing dates the Cochise Culture to at least as early as 9,000 years ago.

Like the people of Danger Cave, the earliest Cochise had millstones to grind their seeds and nuts. At this stage they were not farmers. A few millennia later, however, it is possible that they had grasped the concept of actually *cultivating* a crop for food. In Bat Cave, New Mexico, archeologists uncovered a layer of debris that contained not only Cochise-style weapon points but a number of corncobs. They were not from wild corn but from a cultivated primitive species measuring no more than an inch in length. (See the following chapter for the story of how agriculture was to develop and spread in North America.)

Tens of centuries later the Cochise almost certainly evolved into the first true farmers north of Mexico. From the people to the south in Mexico they learned to grow a number of crops—including a primitive strain of maize as well as squash and beans.

Desert foragers of 5,000 years ago make camp in the shelter of an outcropping of rocks. The long summer day's foraging has ended, and the members of the band are preparing for the evening meal and readying their equipment for the next day's hunt. For these inhabitants of the southwestern desert there is scant time for relaxation, and the eventide scene is one of intense activity. Near the base of the hill an elderly man works a fire stick to light tinder for the cooking fire. Nearby, another man displays a reed decoy he will use to attract ducks to the pond in the distant background. Meanwhile, a huntsman inspects a net to be used to trap rabbits during a mass drive, for with fall approaching, small game—deer and antelopes, as well as rabbits—will become increasingly available. The skins of these animals will be used for clothing and blankets, and their meat will provide a welcome relief from the standard diet of wild vegetables, nuts, and berries. Already some game has been taken, and a young woman—her baby at her side—kneels over a pelt she will transform into a pair of moccasins. Behind her, two of the band enter the camp bearing wood and water while a pair of hunters (upper left) skin a deer. Some of the venison will be dried on the rack (center background) for future consumption. Near the rack a woman prepares seeds for grinding by tossing them with hot coals in a winnowing basket. When the parched shells have blown away, the woman seated beside her will grind the seeds into flour.

27

The Cochise people also learned to dig shallow pits for their houses and roof them over with twigs and small branches. They came to weave baskets out of the tough fibers of such desert plants as the yucca and the agave. The Cochise also came to make their own crude pottery figurines—again under the influence of the tribes from the south.

From studies of this period it is clear that the Cochise people were developing swiftly—paving the way for the Southwest Indian cultures that would succeed them in the modern era.

In other parts of the vast continent other Archaic peoples were also undergoing profound changes in their ways of life. At first only the Cochise practiced agriculture. But as the centuries passed, nearly all the Indians of North America learned the rudiments of farming. But perhaps the most astonishing thing that took place in Archaic times was the development of metalworking in the upper Great Lakes area, chiefly in the region of modern Wisconsin.

For decades archeologists had examined the well-made Wisconsin artifacts of copper—including chisels, spear points, axes, and knives—and pronounced them extraordinary, since they must have been made in the seventh or sixth century B.C. But in recent years Carbon-14 testing has yielded astonishing results: the Old Copper Culture of the Great Lakes area actually flourished between six and seven *thousand* years ago! These Archaic Americans may have been the first metalworkers in the world. Certainly they were the first in the Americas.

How such a stunning occurrence in mankind's adventure in the New World came to happen is a matter of some conjecture. The people are thought to have migrated into the northern Great Lakes area from the north or northeast. And on the southern shores of Lake

Returning from a day's foraging, *several women approach their village in a valley near the banks of the Illinois River. The time is some 5,500 years ago. Fires are burning in limestone pits where turkeys, venison, and geese killed in the forests, and fish and mussels taken from the river, will be roasted. The houses have thatched roofs and mud-and-wattle sides. Axes, much like the stone-headed model above, were used to chop sturdy marsh grasses that helped form the house walls.*

Superior and on Isle Royale they found the strange metallic substance in surface nuggets and exposed glacial deposits. At first they worked the copper as they had previously worked stone, by pecking and flaking it to make tools and projectile points. After a time, however, the flexibility of the metal became apparent to these Archaic people, and they learned that they could shape the copper by pounding it.

Perhaps a dozen men dressed in skins stood facing the stone wall of a cliff, hacking away at it with stone hammers and axes. As the chunks of rock fell loose, the men sorted out the pieces that held large nuggets of pure copper. The copper-bearing rocks were placed in a roaring fire and brought to a high heat, then plunged into cold water. The change of temperature cracked the rocks and freed the copper nuggets, and then the men, using stone hammers, chipped off the bits of rock still clinging to the copper. Once the men had accumulated enough of the soft metal, they set to work and hammered it into the shapes they wanted. Finally, they heated the metal objects slightly—a process that gave the copper strength enough to chop wood or slash and puncture the animals on the nearby Plains.

Skillful Coppersmiths

The tools, ornaments, and utensils these prehistoric Americans fashioned out of copper were skillfully—sometimes beautifully—made. And the variety was truly astonishing: axes, picks, gouges, wedges, awls, fishhooks, knives, drills, projectile points, breastplates, rings, earrings, pendants, beads, and coverings for wooden effigies. The metalworkers sometimes hammered the copper into sheets and drew the outlines of decorations on the metal. Then they indented the copper along the drawn lines with a sharp tool and produced the desired article by bending or breaking the metal. The objects made by the first metalworkers must have been in demand among the other tribes, because examples of their work have been found from the Great Plains to present-day Florida and New York.

The Wisconsin metalworking was a remarkable but isolated and temporary cultural phenomenon. By 3,500 years ago, in fact, it had disappeared. The increasing mildness of the weather had caused the caribou, lynx, beaver, and other game animals to migrate northward into Canada. The people of the Old Copper Culture followed them, eventually moving beyond their source of copper supply. The craft was long in returning. Not until the upsurge of

Copper artifacts—blades, dart heads, awls, and bracelets—were hammered from nuggets as early as 1500 B.C. by Great Lakes Indians. Such items, made from copper found along the shores of the lakes, eventually became trade goods and have been discovered as far away as the Atlantic and Gulf Coasts.

the Hopewell Culture about 2,500 years ago did copperworking revive on a widespread basis.

The Archaic tradition was also found in the forest land that then stretched from the Plains to the Atlantic coastal regions. Here the really big game of the West never had flourished. During the Archaic period hunters killed squirrel, possum, deer, and turkey, and the people—like their western relatives—often made do on wild nuts and berries. For their life in the forest they developed many specialized tools. They had mortars and pestles for crushing seeds, berries, and nuts. They had axes, drills, and gouges for work on the plentiful supply of wood. Evidence from sites in Tennessee and Kentucky is that these Archaic people also had developed fishhooks, harpoons, and nets for fishing.

It is now clear that these eastern Archaic peoples had begun to develop large, settled populations with complex cultural concepts. At the rich Archaic site at modern Indian Knoll, Kentucky, on the banks of an old channel off the Green River, more than 1,000 human skeletons

This multistrand necklace of shells was probably worn by an Archaic Indian woman thousands of years ago. Shells were also used in rings, pendants, and pins, and to decorate deerhide clothing.

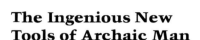

The Ingenious New Tools of Archaic Man

By 6000 B.C. the giant game of the Paleo period had become rare, and the peoples of North America were finding it necessary to adapt to a different way of subsistence centered on small-game hunting, gathering, and fishing. To exploit the changed environment Archaic man devised new implements—such as the bone harpoon (above), probably used for sea mammals—and improved techniques for fashioning the artifacts he needed. Many implements were now made by the peck-and-grind method. The craftsman first chose a hard stone with a shape similar to the implement he desired. Then he pecked slivers from the surface with a hammerstone until the implement was close to the necessary form. Final shaping and sharpening was done by grinding the implement against a sandstone block. Then the tool or weapon was polished with sand and a piece of leather. The plummet stones (top right), used for weighting fishing nets, and the ax heads (right) were all made by the peck-and-grind method. Craftsmen probably used a hammerstone much like the round rock in the picture at right.

dating back roughly 5,000 years have been unearthed. They were people who buried their dead according to well-established customs. Most of the bodies were smeared with a red pigment. Grave ornaments and burial offerings were found with many of the skeletons.

Approximately 55,000 artifacts, including a large variety of tools and utensils, were also found at Indian Knoll. In addition to the more practical articles, beads, pendants, rings, and rattles—made by inserting pebbles into box tortoise shells—were unearthed. One of the more extraordinary discoveries, however, was that the ancient inhabitants of Indian Knoll made gorgets and pins from conch, and used other marine shells to ornament their clothes. These marine shells did not exist near Indian Knoll and must have been imported from coastal people. Likewise, two thin sheets of copper and a copper pendant found at the site almost certainly were acquired from people of a different region. The implication was clear: a trade system already had begun in the area, one which linked various groups and not only served as a transmission belt for commerce but probably for cultural exchange as well.

Another extremely significant find at Indian Knoll

was the prepared clay floors that were scattered throughout the site. These must have been living areas. Fire-reddened marks on the floors evidently were left by primitive hearths, and around these fireplace areas were found the charred hulls of walnuts, acorns, and hickory nuts. There was also evidence that the inhabitants set vertical posts into the clay floors around the hearth areas to serve as rude windbreaks. The Indian Knoll discoveries, and the evidence from sites in Alabama and Florida, clearly demonstrate that large numbers of Archaic people lived in permanent settlements over a number of centuries.

Far to the north—in New England and the Maritime Provinces of Canada—the Archaic life-style had taken hold by 3000 B.C., and perhaps earlier. Indian cemeteries have been found throughout the area, and these gravesites show that the people there had also developed carefully prescribed burial practices. Of particular interest are the Red Paint People, a name given them by 18th-century farmers because these ancient Indians lined their burial pits with bright red hematite.

The most interesting Red Paint burial ground discovered so far is at Port au Choix, in northern Newfound-

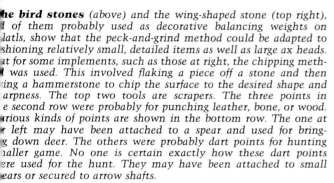

The bird stones (above) and the wing-shaped stone (top right), all of them probably used as decorative balancing weights on atlatls, show that the peck-and-grind method could be adapted to fashioning relatively small, detailed items as well as large ax heads. But for some implements, such as those at right, the chipping method was used. This involved flaking a piece off a stone and then using a hammerstone to chip the surface to the desired shape and sharpness. The top two tools are scrapers. The three points in the second row were probably for punching leather, bone, or wood. Various kinds of points are shown in the bottom row. The one at far left may have been attached to a spear and used for bringing down deer. The others were probably dart points for hunting smaller game. No one is certain exactly how these dart points were used for the hunt. They may have been attached to small spears or secured to arrow shafts.

land—the northernmost penetration of the people who practiced the Red Paint rites. Here, on an old abandoned beach a few yards above the present shore of the Gulf of St. Lawrence, the skeletons of 100 persons, buried 4,000 years ago, have survived in excellent condition. Judging by the remains, they were a robust group of people, quite similar in appearance to the Indians of New England during historic times.

The dead apparently were buried with the tools they valued most highly and might want to have in the next world. The graves contain axes, adzes, and gouges—heavy woodworking tools the Indians probably used to make dugout canoes. These fishermen and hunters also possessed firemaking kits of flintstone and pyrite, as well as a wide variety of tools and weapons of bone, stone, and antler. As findings at the Port au Choix site indicate, the people also crafted bone and antler into combs, pins, and effigies.

By 1500 B.C. the Red Paint People were already in decline, and by 500 B.C.—for reasons that are not entirely clear—the old cult had largely faded. Archeologists believe that these Red Paint People were almost certainly among the ancestors of the Algonquian Indi-

ans who roamed the forests of the Northeast when the Europeans came to the New World.

Beyond a doubt, one of the most extraordinary achievements of Archaic man is what is now known as the Boylston Street Weir in present-day Boston. The huge fish trap, built about 2000 B.C., was constructed of vertical sticks four to six feet long. Each stick was sharpened on one end with a stone ax and then driven into the blue-clay bed in the nearby water. There were 65,000 such stakes in the weir, and the spaces between them were closed up by bundles of brush. Such an elaborate construction must have taken many men to build and indicates a large and settled population in the Boston area well over 3,000 years ago.

All along the riverside the tribesmen gathered with their tools of stone and slate. On the shore lay a pile of wood they had hewn from fallen trees some days ago and left in the sun to dry. Now the men—perhaps a hundred in all—set to work. Some of them sharpened their axes and slate knives on hard whetstones and shaped the wood into strong, pointed staves. Others waded into the river, carrying sticks and heavy stones

31

Archeology in Action at the Koster Site

Every summer since 1969 a once peaceful field in Illinois has been the site of feverish activity. Bulldozers turn the upper layers of dirt; bronzed youngsters, armed with pickaxes and shovels, dig deeper into the earth; other workers, standing over sifting trays, carefully examine the dirt the shovelers provide. At this dig, called the Koster Site, professionals and students in such diverse fields as archeology, botany, geology, and osteology (the study of bones) are carrying on the most extensive archeological excavation in North America. Under the direction of anthropologist Stuart Struever of Northwestern University, experts have already uncovered 15 prehistoric settlements, stacked one upon the other like thick pancakes. "The mantle of soil," says Dr. Struever, "washed down from the bluffs nearby, preserved intact . . . the remains of stone tools and hunting gear . . . bones, nuts, seeds and other food remnants. We have excavated 34 feet below the present surface and have found evidence that men lived at this site more than 9,000 years ago."

By bringing together specialists from many fields, Dr. Struever expects that we will learn "more about prehistoric man than just identify the tools he used. . . . By studying culture, environment and human biology as interdependent systems," he says, "we . . . will eventually be able to explain changes that have occurred in the systems throughout the . . . prehistoric record."

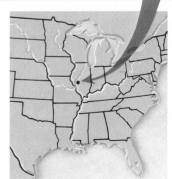

Within the Koster Site dig students and professionals (above) work at many different levels, sifting and digging out the remains of successive settlements; the lower the level, the older the community. Meanwhile, two geologists (left) stand on a makeshift scaffold as they chart a "profile wall." Their gridwork of cord marks off layers of soil that were stained by the ruins of many communities. The Koster Site (map at right), named for the owner of the farm on which the excavation is taking place, is located near the junction of the Illinois and Mississippi Rivers. They probably served as major sources of food—substantial amounts of fish remains were found during the digging—and as important trade routes to distant tribes.

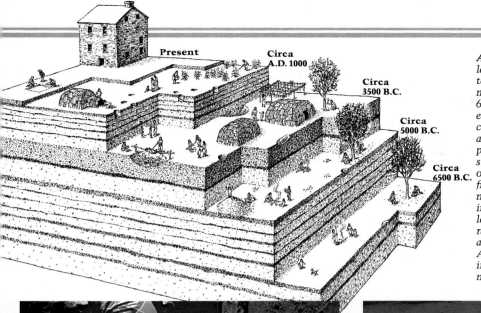

An artist's cutaway shows 4 of the 15 levels, or horizons, excavated at the Koster Site. One of the important findings made during the dig was that as early as 6500 B.C. the dog was domesticated, an event previously thought to have occurred only with the onset of agriculture, about 1000 B.C. By 5000 B.C. there were postholes, indicating the building of substantial dwellings. The large refuse pile on this level contained the bones of many fish, suggesting a semipermanent community in which groups cooperated in fishing the nearby streams. The 3500 B.C. level, with its large dwellings, fish drying racks, and limestone roasting pits, reveals an increasingly complex village life. By A.D. 1000 the inhabitants had evolved into an agricultural people with corn as a major source of food.

Student archeologists, using such small tools as dental picks and paintbrushes, gently clean away packed dirt from the ribcage of a skeleton dating back some 4,500 years. The fragments of bones will then be sent to a laboratory for analysis. The skeleton is one of 19 found in a burial pit, all of them in a flexed position (above right), indicating ceremonial interment. From such finds scientists learn much about how ancient peoples looked and the ills to which they were prey.

Using a triangular measuring device, a student at Koster records the position of an object when it was discovered. Such record-keeping is essential. Materials whose age cannot be gauged by such means as carbon analysis may be dated by their proximity to items susceptible to scientific dating techniques.

Shells and animal bones taken from the Koster Site rest in partitioned boxes. Each section will be marked to record the area where its contents were found.

to use as hammers. Near the center was a spot where the water current had loosened hundreds of sticks and carried them away, creating a number of large holes in the fish trap.

All day long the men drove the stakes into the soft riverbed. At dusk, finally, they had replaced all the missing sticks. The weir was almost mended. Tomorrow they would gather piles of muddy brush from the nearby forest and work it around the sticks in such a way as to close the spaces between them. When that was done, the weir, built generations ago by their forefathers, would be repaired once again. In a week or two schools of fish would swim into the trap. As they thrashed about in the water near the wooden barrier, the men would again wade into the river, this time carrying their slate-tipped spears, and kill the fish by the thousands.

By the first millennium before Christ the Foraging period was drawing to a close. By any measure, it had witnessed tremendous change. Animal life had altered radically, and so had the climate. As a consequence, the techniques of gaining food and shelter were radically revised and new social patterns began to evolve. For mankind in the New World, they had been eventful times; those to come would offer even more revolutionary change.

The Mound Builders

By 1000 B.C. the peoples of North America were many and diverse. The Eskimos, last of the Asians to cross over into the New World, had spread across the Arctic from Alaska to Labrador. In Subarctic Canada the ancestors of today's Canadian Indians had established a firm presence. In the Pacific Northwest, the lush coastal strip stretching from California to Alaska, the descendants of the Old Cordillerans and waves of more recent arrivals from Asia had created a relatively comfortable way of life based on foraging off the natural bounty of the area. All across what are now the United States and Canada, various groups hunted the smaller game, gathered plant food, and slowly improved their weaponry, tools, and skills.

It was a time of great, if gradual, innovation. To the south the Mexican cultures had already developed horticulture and pottery; they built houses, villages, and temples. Influenced by their southern neighbors and

This Adena effigy pipe, found in an Ohio mound, was made of red and yellow clay and is about 2,000 years old. The figure may be of a dwarf.

possibly by fresh ideas brought out of Asia and elsewhere, the peoples of North America were also undergoing a slow, but inexorable, change.

The basic foraging techniques of the Archaic period remained intact in most places. What set this so-called Formative period apart was the gradual spread of pottery, of pipes and tobacco, of ceremonial burial, of settled village life and, eventually, of agriculture.

The transition is best understood in the eastern half of the present United States, the vast Woodlands area stretching from the Plains to the Atlantic Coast. There the new influences were felt long before they reached the West. By 1500 B.C. pottery-making was known in many eastern areas. Some archeologists contend that pottery came to the Woodlands area from northeast Asia. Others argue that pottery-making techniques may very well have arrived from Scandinavia via the Faeroe Islands, Iceland, and Greenland. Still other archeologists detect a Mexican inspiration. Whatever the origin, pottery-making had become a widespread phenomenon in the Woodlands by 1000 B.C.

By far the most extraordinary development of this era, however, was the appearance of the so-called Adena-Hopewell Culture in the Woodlands area. Some scholars deal with the Adena people and the Hopewell people as one culture. Both left behind monuments in the form of vast earthworks—high, narrow ridges of earth, often enclosing large fields. In both cases burial mounds, some conical, some domed, are found inside many of the earthworks. Other archeologists prefer to deal with the Adena and the Hopewell as two separate groups, despite their similarities. For reasons of clarity, we will adopt this course.

The pioneer Mound Builders were the Adena, a people who lived chiefly in the Ohio Valley. Their name derives from the Ohio estate where their distinctive remains were first uncovered. Carbon-14 tests show that their culture took form around 3,000 years ago and endured for some 15 centuries. These people lived in circular houses with walls composed of wooden posts lashed together by flexible plant material, and roofs of matting or thatch. They clustered in small villages and hunted deer, elk, and raccoon. The Adenas also ate snails and freshwater mussels and such wild plants as raspberry, chestnut, pawpaw, and walnut. There is

The Great Serpent Mound uncoils gracefully in a woodland near Cincinnati, Ohio. A masterpiece of engineering, the 1,000-year-old Adena mound is a quarter-mile long, 30 feet wide, and 5 feet high. Other Adena effigy mounds are shaped like birds, bears, and alligators. Though these were not burial mounds, they may have been associated with interment rituals.

some evidence that late Adenas were able to cultivate pumpkins, squash, and sunflowers as well.

Honoring the Dead

The Adena, like many primitive people, placed great emphasis on honoring their dead. In their earlier stages they built low earthen mounds over burial pits. But as the centuries unfolded, they began to erect gigantic funeral mounds that must have required many workers and a good deal of social organization and leadership.

The men, some three dozen of them, had worked for many hours. An important member of the village had died the night before, and in the morning the men had placed him in a burial pit and smeared his body with red ocher. Then they carefully placed copper bracelets and rings, clay pipes, and headdresses crowned by the antlers of an elk into the pit with the dead man. Then each man went into the nearby fields, scooped up earth, walked back to the burial pit, and piled the dirt on top of the body. After some time, and many small loads of earth, a leader pronounced the mound to be finished. Strangely, it was not an unattractive sight. The ground had been brought from various places, and the burial mound thereby had taken on a pleasant, mottled look from the different earth colors that made it.

This deeply incised Adena tablet may have been used to stamp out a batiklike pattern on skins, or perhaps it was a whetstone used to sharpen awls and knives.

Some of the mounds were many-layered and contained numerous dead. This, and the richness and abundance of the artifacts placed in the graves, seems clear evidence that the Adena were a settled people with a complex sense of ritual. Certainly, only a well-organized, ritualistic group could have created the spectacular Great Serpent Mound in Ohio, one of the most impressive of the Adenas' accomplishments. This low, rounded embankment is shaped like a gigantic snake in the act of uncoiling, and it extends more than 1,200 feet from its tail to the tip of its upper jaw. A conical burial mound was built 400 feet away. What meaning did this spectacular earthwork have for the inhabitants of prehistoric Ohio? Archeologists pose the question, but so far none has advanced a satisfactory answer.

The Adena people themselves are a nagging mystery. They were tall, powerfully built people with massive skeletons, prominent foreheads bordered by sizable browridges, and large round skulls. The appearance of these round heads is extraordinary, for the typical Archaic Indians were long-headed, with high-vaulted, narrow skulls and slender bodies. It seems very much as though the Adena—a band of strikingly different people of great presence and majesty, with many women over six feet tall and men approaching heights of seven feet—had forced their way into the Ohio

The extent of cultural influences of the Adena (red) and Hopewell (yellow) civilizations is shown above. The centers of these overlapping cultures were in the present Ohio Valley, but the Hopewell (about 400 B.C. to A.D. 500) affected a far larger area than did the Adena (about 1000 B.C. to A.D. 400.)

Valley from somewhere else about 3,000 years ago.

But from where? Many archeologists believe they were emigrants from Mexico, where some customs similar to those of the Adenas were practiced. Others think they came from the Great Lakes region or some unknown point farther to the northeast. To this date the question remains unresolved.

Equally mysterious are the origins of the Hopewell people, who—some 2,400 years ago—drove a wedge into Adena territory. At first the Hopewells—named for the owner of an Ohio farm where many of their treasures were unearthed—occupied the Scioto Valley of south-central Ohio. We do not know whether the two groups actually battled it out with spears and knives, but we do know that, after the initial collision, the Adena Culture began to wane and the Hopewell people's realm grew steadily greater. It is quite possible that intermarriage took place between the two groups, and perhaps some of the Adena traits and customs were acquired by the newcomers. The result, at any rate, was the development of a vast and powerful Hopewell sphere of influence and the eventual departure of the Adenas to such places as modern Alabama, the Chesapeake Bay area, and New York.

For a thousand years the Hopewells dominated the Midwest from their Ohio center. And beyond a doubt they were a remarkable group of people. They excelled all other prehistoric Indians as craftsmen and artists. The Hopewells made decorated pottery, finely woven mats, and exquisitely carved bone, wood, and metal figures. They were also the finest metalworkers of their time, crafting tools and ornaments out of copper and, occasionally, silver and gold.

The Hopewell people, inheritors of a bounteous land, also made objects that must have seemed luxurious to tribes in other parts of the continent. The Hopewells clothed themselves in fine furs and robes, well-tanned skins, and woven cloth. They also decorated themselves with ornaments of copper, mica, shell, and bone. Men and women alike wore ear decorations and necklaces of animal's teeth and pearls.

Social life among the Hopewells was highly developed. Clues pieced together by scholars show a society of well-organized people led by an elite upper class. Some students of the Hopewells believe they also developed institutions akin to guilds or craft unions for carvers, woodworkers, and traders. The Hopewells were bound together in what was something like a loose con-

This stone figurine of a bearskin-clad shaman was found in the Hopewell earthwork enclosure in what is now Newark, Ohio. At the height of its splendor, this vast complex—evidently constructed to house the dead—contained numerous burial mounds, a great effigy of an eagle, and a two-and-a-half mile long corridor to the banks of the Licking River. Within the complex, which covered more than four square miles, were avenues, circles, and plazas. Much of what was once this center of Hopewell grandeur now lies within a golf course and an agricultural fair grounds.

federation of tribes. At its zenith it extended from the Atlantic to the plains of Kansas, and from northern Wisconsin to the Gulf of Mexico. But not all of these related groups followed exactly the same cultural paths. On the contrary, the local traditions and environment in each area modified the Hopewell Culture and gave it a particular flavor and direction.

These people, clearly, were not mere food gatherers, farmers, and hunters. They were all those things, but they were also the most talented tradesmen of the prehistoric world. And unlike the informal commerce practiced by the Archaic tribes, the Hopewells developed systematic trade ties that linked them with tribes in widely scattered parts of the continent.

A humdrum day in the village soon became one of great excitement. A band of strangers had come to the village with many wonderful things to trade. They had been on the trail for many weeks, visiting other peoples over the horizon, trading one object for another. Now they spread out many strangely colored feathers, hundreds of shells of the most striking hues, copper knives, and the tusks of sea creatures from the Far North. It was a friendly occasion. In turn, the villagers brought out things that they had made, especially the ornamental clay pipes for which they were praised by other groups. Over the next few hours goods were haggled over and exchanged. The strangers shared a pipe or two of tobacco with the villagers and slipped back into the forest. Their dugout canoes, which were tied up on the riverbank a mile or so away, would quickly carry them to another village and, they hoped, another peaceable exchange of goods.

A Center of Commerce

The central geographic position of the Scioto Valley was well suited for commercial enterprise. Northward lay the Sandusky and Maumee Rivers, giving access to the Great Lakes and to the copper-mining tribes of Lake

Hopewell traders load up their dugout canoes and prepare to leave their village on the banks of Scioto River in present-day Ohio for a distant trading center hundreds of miles away. There they will exchange their cargo of Ohio pipestone, flint, and freshwater pearls for such items as copper, grizzly bear teeth, and mica. The traders also carry such finished items as copper ear ornaments and ceremonial blades. As the men prepare for the journey, a small child bids his father good-bye, and women perform a variety of household tasks. Meanwhile, two men labor in a garden plot (far left). Beyond the small field is a burial mound where the body of a revered leader lies in a logged tomb lavishly provisioned with copper ornaments, knives, pearls, and silhouettes from sheets of mica. One object of trade was to obtain materials for tombs, but another was to provide luxury goods for the living.

Superior. East of Lake Erie lay Lake Ontario, which in turn provided routes into the St. Lawrence, Mohawk, and Hudson Valleys. To the south the Ohio River and its tributaries led into the Appalachians, where the inhabitants made objects from the mica found there in abundance. To the southwest the Ohio River coursed into the Mississippi, along which tribes from the south brought shells, sharkskin, and alligator teeth from the Gulf of Mexico. Westward, up the Missouri, lived people who provided grizzly bear teeth for beads and obsidian for spear tips.

The rivers of the area gave the Hopewells the highways along which they could expand their commercial and cultural ties with other Indian groups. In the area around the present-day city of Chillicothe, Ohio, they would load their canoes with trade goods—mica, flint, carved pipes and, perhaps, tobacco—and push off into the river bound for far-off trading centers. The canoes, made of oak logs hollowed out with fire and stone gouges, carried as many as six paddlers and a leader, who in some cases was also the chief of the settlement. Scholars surmise, from the practice of later Indians, that the primitive traders painted their faces in ornate patterns that divulged the rank of each man and the fact that he was on a peaceful mission.

Transcending Language Barriers

The trading center was, in a sense, a primitive country fair. Numerous tribes were represented, and many of the Indians did not understand more than a word or two of the other languages being spoken. But in the give and take of trade they managed to make themselves understood. It was a place of peace. Long-standing feuds were forgotten for a few days, and the traders conducted their business in spirit of goodwill and mutual self-interest. After the pipes and tobacco were traded for the shells and the furs, the Indian traders retired to their various camps for the night. In the camps jokes and insults were exchanged, good-natured scuffles arose, and the Indians huddled around the campfires to feast on roast meat and fowl. They gambled, they spun tales of tribal history, and they played the cup-and-pin game, trying to flip a bone pin into a conical cup made of bone.

The Hopewells were formidable builders as well as skilled traders. Among other things, they constructed enormous geometrical earthworks, huge embankments, broad avenues and, above all, thousands of burial mounds. Much of this is gone today, but enough survived into the 19th century to awe the early white settlers and inspire fantasies about lost races. Perhaps the most impressive Hopewell work was the great enclosure at Newark, Ohio, which once covered four square miles. "In entering the ancient avenue for the first time," wrote the archeologist Ephraim Squier more than a century ago, "the visitor does not fail to experience a sensation of awe, such as he might feel in pass-

A Treasure in Art From Hopewell Tombs

In their desire to honor their dead with magnificent grave offerings, the Hopewells of the Scioto Valley established vast trade network that covered about two-thirds of the present continental United States. From these distant regions they secured many of the raw materials they needed to make such objects as shown here. The trade routes, for example, reached west to the Rockies, where Indians in the Yellowstone region had access to great supplies of obsidian. Local traders probably carried this item eastward, and the Hopewells might have secured it at villages along the Mississippi. From Florida, either directly or through intermediaries, came barracuda jaws, alligator and shark teeth, and conch shells—raw materials for beads and necklaces. Mica, from which the Scioto people carved delicate silhouettes, came from North Carolina and Arkansas, while copper nuggets—to be hammered into ear ornaments, knives, rings, headdresses, axes, and numerous other items—originated near the shores of the Great Lakes.

Not all of the raw materials the Scioto people used in their artworks came from distant regions. From the Scioto River itself, laborers gathered thousands of freshwater pearls to decorate burial clothing or to drape around the necks of the deceased. Though most of the objects the villagers made were doubtless worn or carried by the living, the most beautiful creations were consigned to the graves, there to rest undisturbed until uncovered in recent decades to lend insight into a culture long gone.

A stylized spoon-billed duck, *a favorite Hopewell motif, adorns this ceramic vessel found in a burial mound. The incised background was probably made in the soft clay with a blunt stylus, and the vessel was fire-dried. Hopewell potters were among the most versatile of their times, turning out clay figurines and pipes, as well as pottery of various shapes.*

pipestone toad, one of many sculpted [vot]ive offerings, survived a burial ceremony [in]tact. Often Hopewells smashed [th]ese figurines, perhaps to lib[er]ate their spirits for the [aft]erlife.

A stone falcon forms the bowl of this platform pipe. Birds of prey may have been venerated for their role in burial rites. Apparently, some bodies were left exposed before burial so the birds could strip them of flesh.

Mica silhouettes, such as this bird's claw, were often placed in tombs. Shimmering and easily worked, mica was a much-valued trade item.

An obsidian ceremonial blade (left) in a reconstructed handle still looks lethal more than a millennium after it was fashioned. Because there was no obsidian in the region, the glossy volcanic rock was almost certainly imported from the Rocky Mountains or Black Hills region and then worked into the desired form by Hopewell craftsmen.

An eagle in flight, cut from a sheet of copper, may have graced the corner of a ceremonial lodge or, perhaps, was attached to the tip of an important Hopewell's staff as an emblem of status. Like earlier copper-working Indians, the Hopewells never learned to smelt the metal from ore but used almost pure copper nuggets imported from the north. Copper sheets were made by alternately heating and hammering a nugget over a hot fire. When the sheet had been hammered into its desired thinness, a coppersmith, using razor-sharp flint tools, cut out a variety of ornaments, such as headdresses, breastplates, ear spools, beads, and other objects to be worn by the living or placed in tombs to accompany the dead into the next life.

During an elaborate burial ritual *for a child, a Hopewell shaman (top) wears a hoodlike headdress made from pieces of hide joined to the front of a human skull. He is placing a clay effigy of the child beneath a shell-decorated shroud that covers the dead baby. Stripes of paint on the shaman's arms, three strands of pearls around his neck, copper ear spools, and a breastplate complete his ceremonial regalia. Because death was a major preoccupation of the Hopewells, human skulls were one of that people's most treasured cult symbols. The drawing was based on a reconstructed mask (above) and other evidence, portions of which were found in Ohio in 1951.*

ing the portals of an Egyptian temple." Today the great Newark enclosure is a public park, and part of it has been converted into a golf course. Even so, it continues to evoke wonder in the imaginative beholder.

But the burial mounds tell us the most about the Hopewell people. The contents of these innumerable tombs reveal much: the skill of the Hopewell artisans, the material wealth of the Ohio Mound Builders, and their taste for exotic raw materials. The tombs also reveal the people's fascination with death and an obsessive desire to send departed ones into the next world laden with treasure. A single grave in the Turner mound group of Hamilton County, Ohio, yielded 12,000 pearls, 35,000 pearl beads, 20,000 shell beads, and nuggets of copper, meteoric iron, and silver, as well as sheets of hammered gold, copper, and iron beads. From a mound at the Mound City group near Chillicothe came hundreds of pipes, copper figures of birds, turtles, and humans, a mask made from fragments of a human skull, and a copper-covered wooden effigy of the death cup mushroom. In the Seip Mound in Ross County, excavators uncovered a copper ax weighing 28 pounds, a set of copper breastplates, more thousands of pearls, and a skull adorned with an artificial copper nose.

Riches for the Dead

There is an attractive vigor about all this fondness for excess and flamboyance. To envelop a corpse from head to feet in pearls, to weight it down in pounds of copper, to surround it with masterpieces of sculpture and pottery, and then to bury everything under tons of earth shows a kind of cultural energy for which there is no previous parallel in prehistoric North America.

This fertile society took form about 2,500 years ago, reached its great peak about the dawn of the Christian era, and disappeared about 1,500 years ago. We do not know what caused its downfall. One authority, James B. Griffin, suggests that the Hopewells may simply have reached a cultural peak beyond which they found it impossible to go—and as a consequence suffered "culture fatigue." Griffin also has raised the possibility that climate changes caused repeated crop failures that undermined the Hopewell economy. Others have postulated famines, plagues, civil war, and the invasion of Hopewell territory by savage tribes.

Scholars freely admit they do not know what happened to the Hopewells. All that is certain at this stage is that when white settlers arrived in Ohio in the 18th century they found no trace of the Hopewell people. Instead, they discovered the most humble of local Indians living amid the ruins of the ancient Mound Builders. With the Hopewell people, 40 or 50 or even 60 thousand years of prehistoric man's adventure in the New World came to an impressive and mysterious close. It was a mighty ending. It was also an auspicious prelude to the Indian cultures that were soon to cover the North American continent.

A Louisiana burial mound in the process of being excavated in the mid-1800's is shown in this schematized cross-section commissioned by Dr. Montroville Dickeson, who supervised the work. This scene, part of a panorama, shows the various levels of the tomb with its skeletons and artifacts. Dickeson toured the nation with the painting, charging 25 cents to viewers.

Unraveling the Mystery of the Mound Builders

As American settlers in search of free land poured through the Appalachian's Cumberland Gap in the late 18th century and settled in what came to be called the Midwest, they were mystified by the many high mounds they came upon. These mounds—some 10,000 of them in the Ohio Valley alone—were obviously man-made. But why were they built, and who were the builders? It seemed highly unlikely that the semisedentary Indians, living in small villages, with whom the pioneers came in contact were capable of constructing such prodigies of engineering. One settler calculated that the great mound near Miamisburg, Ohio, was 68 feet high, 852 feet in circumference at the base, and contained 311,353 cubic feet of soil. Thousands of men from a highly organized society would have been required to achieve work of such proportions. Discipline, motivation, and considerable technical skill would also have been needed, and so far as the whites could tell, the local Indians had none of these attributes.

As a few artifacts—pottery vessels, small effigy sculptures, and the like—began to be excavated, a myth took shape that was to capture the imaginations of those Americans who felt they had come upon an exciting new chapter of ancient history. This legend envisioned a superior race, dubbed the Mound Builders, who had lived in North America in some remote era. They were civilized, unified, and highly sophisticated, a peace-loving people eventually wiped out by hordes of redskinned intruders. These Mound Builders were, perhaps, Vikings, or descendants of the Ten Lost Tribes of Israel, or even emigrants from the mythical lost island of Atlantis.

This vision of a separate race of Mound Builders remained in currency until the end of the 19th century. It was nourished by the speculations of scholars and embellished by the writings of novelists and poets. In 1832 William Cullen Bryant, reflecting on the earthworks, was moved to write:

The red man came— / The roaming hunter tribes, warlike and fierce/ And the Mound Builders vanished from the earth. . . ./ All is gone,/ All—save the piles of earth that hold their bones. . . .

In a best-selling novel, published in 1839, writer Cornelius Mathews galvanized the collective fantasy with a story about a mammoth that ravaged the cities of the Mound Builders. And, in the years before he was elected president of the United States, William Henry Harrison wrote fantastic yarns about the conquests and conflicts of the vanished people.

Not everyone lent credence to such fantastic speculations. Thomas Jefferson, for one, had used remarkably modern archeological techniques to excavate one mound, and in 1785 he admonished his countrymen to draw no conclusions in the absence of solid evidence. Several decades later the Grave Creek Mound in West Virginia was opened, unearthing a plethora of artifacts and artworks. After examining this evidence, anthropologist Henry Rowe Schoolcraft, in 1851, asserted that the mound could have been the work of people no more advanced than the ancestors of contemporary Indians. At the time few believed Schoolcraft.

Still, evidence was accumulating to support Schoolcraft's position. In 1894 the Smithsonian Institution, after compiling data on mounds in every part of the country, issued a report that finally put to rest the myth of non-Indian Mound Builders. Americans were at last forced to recognize that the American Indians were the inheritors of a cultural tradition of great complexity.

LOST INDIAN CIVILIZATIONS
Kingdoms of the Sun

The White House ruin, nestled near the cliffs of Arizona's Canyon de Chelly, was built by the Anasazis a millennium ago as shelter for hundreds of families. The black and white jar (inset) comes from another Anasazi ruin, this one at Mesa Verde in southern Colorad

Fascinating archeological discoveries provide conclusive proof of great and sophisticated Indian civilizations that existed long before Europeans ever came to the New World.

On a cold, snowy morning in December 1888, two ranchers named Richard Wetherill and Charlie Mason rode along Colorado's Mesa Verde looking for several missing steers. Suddenly Wetherill reined his horse, and for a moment he stared speechless at a remarkable sight across a canyon. "Charlie," he said, "look at that!"

What had stunned Wetherill was an arching entrance to a large cave in the canyonside, a cave that enclosed a strange and silent city, its multistoried stone buildings empty of all life. Wetherill's discovery—and others of a similar nature that would soon follow—would drastically alter the general view of the early North American Indian. Far from being a simple savage, he was the inheritor of a long and culturally rich tradition.

Richard Wetherill called his discovery Cliff Palace, an apt name that was seconded by one of its earliest visitors from the scientific community, a young Swedish anthropologist named Baron Gustav Nordenskiold. "Strange and indescribable," he wrote, "is the impression . . . of Cliff Palace . . . with its round towers and high walls rising out of the heaps of stones deep in the mysterious twilight of the cavern, and defying, in their sheltered site the ravages of time, it resembles . . . an enchanted castle."

As anthropologists and archeologists dug deeper into the mystery of Cliff Palace, two questions of supreme importance inevitably arose: on what did such a large population of Indians depend for their sustenance, and who were the progenitors of such obviously sophisticated civilizations? Archeological finds of projectile points, potsherds, jewelry, and other artifacts pointed to the probable answer to the second question. Cliff Palace and other southwestern urban centers apparently evolved from societies that had been located in the region for thousands of years. As for the first question, it quickly became apparent that these societies of apartment dwellers depended, in large measure, on the cultivation of corn for their support. In this century archeologists digging in a place called Bat Cave in New Mexico discovered ears of corn more than 5,500 years old: tiny ears, no more than an inch long, that were probably the first type of cultivated corn to be grown in North America.

But corn long presented a mystery of its own. Cultivated varieties—even the type found under thousands of years of debris in Bat Cave—are incapable of self-seeding. Wild corn has a relatively thin husk that opens on maturity, permitting the kernels to fall to the ground and germinate. Cultivated corn develops a heavy husk that does not open naturally; man must strip it away, remove the seeds from the cob, and sow them. The corn found in Bat Cave must have had a wild ancestor, capable of reproducing itself. But for decades this missing ancestor could not be found.

Major excavations in the Southwest and in Mexico turned up only smaller and smaller varieties, the oldest and smallest types apparently close to wild but still incapable of self-seeding. Then, in the early 1960's, Richard S. MacNeish, an American archeologist working in a Tehuacán Valley cave southeast of Mexico City discovered the long-sought ears of wild corn, plants that dated back to between 5200 and 3400 B.C. Above the layer of debris in which the tiny ears of wild corn were found were progressively larger ears of cultivated corn. Here then was a chronology from which the trained eye could deduce the path of civilization.

The effects of corn cultivation were enormous. The plant would eventually provide a stable food supply and even a surplus for trade. Over scores of generations the scattered hunters and foragers of the Tehuacán Valley began to rely less on game and wild plants and more on corn agriculture for their daily sustenance. The pattern of living changed, too. Farming meant that permanent villages could replace temporary campsites. And as the food supply increased, so too did the population—by 1,000 percent in the Tehuacán Valley between 3400 and 2300 B.C. Villages grew larger and, inevitably, the structure of society grew more complex.

By 1500 B.C. knowledge of corn cultivation—as well as that of squash, beans, and chili—had spread throughout the fertile valleys and coastlands of Mesoamerica, to transform tiny hunting and gathering bands into semi-settled farmers living along the banks of rivers and streams in true villages of rude huts made from sticks and wattles. Day in and day out the farmers trudged to their fields and, with primitive planting sticks and im-

Teosinte, *a wild grass, is one of the ancestors of the cultivated corn that made possible the growth of cities and cultures in ancient Mexico. The teosinte pollen, carried by the wind to other cornlike grasses, produced a hybrid whose cultivation helped ensure a stable food supply.*

plements of stone, sowed and harvested their crops. Hunting and gathering still played an important part in the lives of the villagers, but more and more, as the centuries passed, the people came to rely on farming, particularly of corn, for their day-to-day livelihoods.

To ensure bountiful crops, new gods came into prominence, deities that controlled the rainfall, the seasonal floods, the growth of crops, the fertility of man and beast. Now that there was a stable source of food—when the gods were kind—village life began to become more diverse. Both sexes ornamented their bodies with necklaces made from nuts and seeds, and women wore turbans of woven fiber cloth to enhance their beauty as well as to keep their hair out of their eyes. Although every adult in these villages could perform all the tasks required to sustain life and create the minimal comforts that their technology permitted, a specialization of labor was slowly coming into being as the range of skills increased. Long before 1500 B.C. Mesoamerican villagers were weaving strings of fiber into nets for fishing, and palm leaves were woven into mats. Basketry, too, was far advanced, and the potters' skills were growing rapidly. Even knowledge of cotton—its cultivation and its transformation from fiber to cloth—had become widespread.

For the most part, however, life revolved round the *milpa*—the "cornfield." From the harvest, women ground the kernels of maize on flat stones, called metates, with a mano of stone. They served their families a corn gruel that would come to be called *pinole*, or spread corn batter over a hot stone to make tortillas—two dishes that remain very much in evidence in the Mexico of today.

The Olmecs

While such changes were taking place over the centuries in much of Mesoamerica, a new, seminal civilization of the Western Hemisphere was being born. The time was about 1250 B.C. The place was a region about 350 miles due east of the Tehuacán Valley, near the Mexican Gulf Coast, northwest of the Yucatan Peninsula. The inhabitants of this region, now long-since vanished, are known as the Olmecs. For centuries, indeed well into our own times, their very existence was hidden by the ravages of time and jungle growth.

Although several Olmec communities grew up more or less simultaneously, the first great flowering of Olmec culture occurred at a place now called San Lorenzo, situated on a mesa that fronts the Coatzacoalcos River. When the remains of this civilization were uncovered, modern man marveled at its advanced state. And he wondered, too, about the strange, 18-ton busts the San Lorenzans carved from basalt. Simply transporting the stone must have been a tremendous task; the nearest basalt quarry lies scores of miles away through deep jungle. To obtain the stone, to load it on rafts and float it down river, to lift it up to the mesa plateau, obviously required a system of organization far beyond the capabilities of earlier societies in the region.

The massive busts that may have been depictions of contemporary leaders in helmetlike headdresses were only one form of Olmec art. There were, as well, clay figurines, expertly shaped in the attitudes of players of ball games, and lovely white-rimmed pottery vessels that proclaimed the skill of Olmec ceramicists.

But the Olmecs of San Lorenzo as well as those who lived in the nearby and roughly contemporary site of La Venta were far more than innovators of artistic and handicraft skills. Situated at the center of a great trade network, the Olmecs both adapted cultural advances from their trading partners and generated many of their own that they spread throughout the area. By the rivers of San Lorenzo and La Venta were found such architectural, intellectual, and artistic accomplishments as great temple pyramids, a calendar, a concept of numbering, and sculptures of the plumed serpent—an enduring motif that found expression throughout the Mesoamerican world.

San Lorenzo's Golden Age

The years 1150–900 B.C. probably encompassed the golden age of the Olmecs' San Lorenzo. On the mesa top a small religious center arose. About 2,500 people lived there—priests, bureaucrats, craftsmen, and merchants—supported by the farmers in the valley below. The incredibly rich soil in San Lorenzo's hinterland probably accounted for the community's growth and prosperity.

Like most of the succeeding civilizations of Mesoamerica, that of the Olmecs was a theocracy, for it was the priesthood that had a direct association with the gods that controlled the seasons and the weather. Only the priests could influence the deities to act on man's behalf, and only the priests could interpret the calendar and tell the peasants when to burn their fields, when to plow, when to seed, and when to harvest. In exchange for this vital information, the peasants labored on behalf of the priests, sharing a portion of their crops with them, building the great temple pyramids, and hauling the immense basalt boulders to the ceremonial sites—acts of labor that both sustained and glorified their theological masters.

It was this domination by the priests that may have caused the downfall of San Lorenzo, for sometime

A basalt head, *nearly nine feet high, dwarfs its discoverer, Dr. Matthew Stirling, who found hundreds of remains of the great Olmec civilization of southern Mexico. The head is one of five, all probably portrayals of priest-rulers. The Olmecs built great temple pyramids, devised a calendar and numbering system, and produced exquisite pottery and jadework. Their culture emerged about 1000 B.C. and vanished about A.D. 300.*

about 900 B.C. there was a revolution that ended with the abandonment of the site. Perhaps it was that the exactions of the priests had grown too great to bear, and this may have coincided with a series of crop failures that led the people to doubt their masters' powers. In any case, amid the ruins of the city there are signs of rebellion, the toppling of the great statues, their mutilation, and their burial. In a short time the mesa reverted to jungle. But the demise of this remarkable city-state did not mean the end of Olmec culture. While San Lorenzo was feeling the fury of its destroyers, another Olmec center was waxing strong at La Venta, an island rising amid the swamplands of the Gulf Coast.

From 800 to 400 B.C. the ceremonial city of La Venta dominated the Gulf Coast and, perhaps, a far-flung hinterland as well. As in San Lorenzo, a small population of priests and officials lived in splendor, supported by thousands of farmers and craftsmen. One can easily imagine the awe the farmers of the Gulf region felt as they entered the sacred precincts of the city, stared at the huge basalt head, and gathered before the high temple mounds to witness the elaborate rites thanking the gods for a bountiful harvest.

Yet, if this much can be imagined, much else remains elusive. For example, the significance of La Venta's pavements of greenish serpentine stone overlaid with mosaics remains a mystery. No sooner was one layer finished than it was apparently covered with dirt

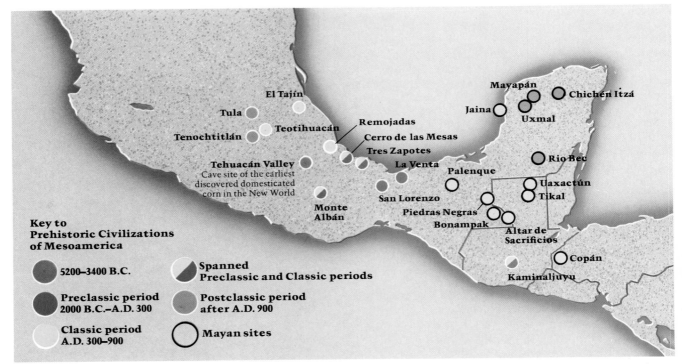

Key to
Prehistoric Civilizations
of Mesoamerica

● 5200–3400 B.C.

◐ Spanned
Preclassic and Classic periods

● Preclassic period
2000 B.C.–A.D. 300

● Postclassic period
after A.D. 900

○ Classic period
A.D. 300–900

○ Mayan sites

El Tajín
Tula
Teotihuacán
Tenochtitlán
Remojadas
Cerro de las Mesas
Tres Zapotes
La Venta
Tehuacán Valley
Cave site of the earliest
discovered domesticated
corn in the New World
Monte
Albán
San Lorenzo
Piedras Negras
Bonampak
Altar de
Sacrificios
Palenque
Uaxactún
Tikal
Río Bec
Mayapán
Jaina
Uxmal
Chichén Itzá
Copán
Kaminaljuyu

Three major civilizations of ancient Mesoamerica flourished in southern Mexico. First was the Olmec (c. 1000–300 B.C.) of La Venta and Monte Albán. It was succeeded by the Mayan (c. A.D. 300–1200), whose impressive ceremonial sites dotted the region. Greatly influenced by the Mayan culture were the people of Teotihuacán, the first true city.

and another layer placed on top, itself to be buried. Were these carefully and elaborately constructed pavements offerings to the gods? And then, as always, there is the question of how La Venta's massive stone heads were transported, for the boulders apparently came from a quarry 70 miles away. Until the Spaniards arrived in the 16th century A.D., there were neither wheeled vehicles nor pack animals. Only the labor of scores of thousands of human beings could account for such astonishing feats of transportation.

Equally impressive were the Olmecs' concave mirrors of magnetite that could kindle fires and reflect an image on a flat surface. Aids to priestly magic? And what significance had the innumerable statuettes of jade, stone, and terra-cotta, each bearing the face of a plump baby, some fanged, some snarling, some bawling, but all with jaguarlike characteristics? Apparently the jaguar, in spirit or in body, was the rain god of the Olmecs. One sculpted monument shows a woman coupling with a jaguar, and the cat-faced babies might well have been their offspring, half-human, half-divine spirits of the rain.

The fall of La Venta—and again there are signs of rebellion or invasion—marked the end of the Olmecs' dominance. But they left behind a cultural tradition that would be adapted by others. The arts and crafts that the Olmecs pioneered would not die, though they would be transformed. And their deities, the jaguar rain god and the great plumed serpent would reappear in later cultures, the serpent under the names of Kukulcán and Quetzalcoatl, the god-hero that brought learning and the arts to the people. Among those who would adopt these deities were two groups that brought Mesoamerica into its classic age: the Teotihuacán and the Mayan civilizations.

The Time of the Mayas

The achievements of Mayan civilization remain awe-inspiring. Their great age lasted from A.D. 250 to 900, and nowhere was it better exemplified than in their glittering ceremonial city of Tikal, at the base of the Yucatan Peninsula. The city's huge area was crowded with temple pyramids and splendid palaces. Among Tikal's 3,000 structures were six pyramids—skyscrapers of their kind—seven temple palaces, and several man-made reservoirs. Mayan architecture, even in its present decayed state, retains its massive dignity. Its art reflected a people's personality—a love of decoration and extravagance. The deep bas-reliefs on cylindrical stone monuments, for example, always show a single deity adorned with hieroglyphics and ornaments. Highly skilled workmanship and exuberant inventiveness are also reflected in the pottery and in the ceramic figurines of haughty nobles, beautiful women, playful monkeys, and flying parrots.

The art tells us, as well, much about the appearance

of the Mayas and the pattern of their daily lives. From their statues and carvings—found at such centers as Tikal, Palenque, Bonampak, Copán, Uxmal, and Chichén Itzá—we know that they had, or at least admired, aquiline noses, straight black hair, high cheekbones, and oriental eyes. Babies had their heads strapped between two boards so that their skulls would become elongated in keeping with the Mayan concept of physical beauty. Crossed eyes were also apparently admired, and babies sometimes wore beads that hung between their eyes so that they would develop the desired characteristic. We learn about the aristocrats and priests, carried from place to place on litters, their limbs covered with ornaments of jade, their bodies richly painted and tattooed, their teeth inlaid with semiprecious stones, and their heads covered with bonnets of quetzal plumes.

The priests stood at the apex of Mayan society, for they were the keepers of all learning, the stargazers, the formulators of the calendar that recorded the events of the past and predicted the course of the future. They were the counters of days, months, and years and were able to calculate in terms of vast stretches of time, literally covering thousands of years.

Measuring Time

No society in the history of mankind was more concerned with time and its division into measurable units. The Mayan priests evolved seven distinct calendars based on astronomical sightings, each time division within each calendar linked to a particular deity. Though the calendars all had different numbers of days and months per cycle, they were designed to mesh like the gears of an automobile. For the priests of Mayan society the primary task was to determine the precise moments when two, or three, or four, of these calendars would coincide, causing a meeting of the powers of associated gods. Would this conjunction or that conjunction of the deities bode good or ill for the people? Only the priests could know, and therein lay their power.

One of the most awesome times, for example, was the concurrent ending of a 365-day cycle and one of 260 days, a happening that occurred once in 52 years. It was primarily to keep track of the mass of mathematical calculations involved in time-keeping that the priests developed a system of hieroglyphics and numerical notations. The latter, which included the concept of zero, was based on time units calculated in multiples of 20.

Just below the priests in power and wealth were the hereditary oligarchs, the *Almehen*, or "Sun Children," and together with the clergy they ruled Mayan society. Priests and nobles alike lived in luxury, either on great estates or in the palaces of the ceremonial cities. For the nobility, life was filled with celebration. Banquets were common, and there was much feasting on roast fowl, washed down with chocolate-flavored beverages and a wine made from honey. Like the priests, the Mayan artistocracy had its own duties to perform. They were the managers, deciding such questions as who should work on public edifices and which crafts should be encouraged. They administered the collection of taxes, the dispensing of justice, the maintenance of roads and public monuments, and the education of the next generation of managers. To support the sumptuous lifestyle of the priests and nobles, the Mayas opened up far-ranging trade routes, their surpluses of honey, cotton cloth, cocoa, and quetzal feathers being exchanged for salt, jade, chert, shells, and obsidian.

Below the priests and aristocrats were the artisans—the stonecutters, carvers, painters, and jewelry-makers who designed everything from pyramids to tiny jade baubles. But the mainstays of Mayan culture were the farmers, whose corn made everything else possible. For the farmers, the lives of the priests and nobles were a world apart. But like their Olmec predecessors, these workers labored to support their superiors.

Though the Mayas were a relatively peaceful people and apparently had no professional military caste, warfare was not unknown, and in their treatment of prisoners the Mayas were no more humane than members of the warlike cultures that would later dominate Mesoamerica. Even today, centuries after the events depicted, viewers of the murals at the Mayan city of Bonampak cannot help but be affected by these exquisitely detailed representations of unlucky captives being stripped naked and tortured by their Mayan masters. One prisoner expires at the feet of his conquerors; others plead for mercy before an arrogant Mayan lord dressed in a jaguar skin. Nearby, a white-robed woman fans herself, watching the painful scene with indifference. It is probable that the captives were to be killed.

The Unseen World

Mayan religion grew into an elaborate tradition in which the worship of nature's forces was blended with a highly intellectualized concept of deified heavenly bodies and the Four Directions of the Universe, each one represented by its own god and color. And time itself was a godlike quality in Mayan belief. In the Mayan mind the earth was thought to be a great flat disk resting on the back of a mammoth crocodile that lived in a giant lake covered with water lilies. Above the earth was the sky, its four corners held in place by the gods, and surrounding the earth were no fewer than 13 heavens and 9 hells. It may well have been the Mayas who originated the legend—which spread all the way into what is now the United States—that the present world was superimposed on several previous ones.

As among many Indian groups, the need to propitiate the gods was central to Mayan religion. Great and ornate ceremonies before the temple pyramids were necessary to ensure the beneficence of the deities that would bring bountiful crops, successful hunts, profit-

Tikal: A Resplendent Center of Mayan Religious and Artistic Life

The Mayan civilization, which came into full flower about A.D. 300 and lasted for more than nine centuries, found its most impressive expression in the great ceremonial centers where religious rituals were celebrated and where the priests and nobles lived. The largest of these centers, Tikal, was built over several centuries, and many of its buildings were erected on the ruins of earlier structures.

When Tikal was completed about A.D. 750, it covered an area one mile square, within which were great plazas, wide causeways, sprawling single-story palaces perched on acropolislike heights and—most spectacular of all—six massive temple pyramids, the tallest of which towered over 200 feet. Each pyra-

mid was a pile of rocks faced with limestone.

A single steep flight of stairs on one side led to a truncated top on which stood a masonry temple with a lofty roof comb. Here the priests celebrated their rituals, probably in secret, for the temple rooms were too small to admit an audience.

The ceremonial centers were also focuses of art. Painted stucco reliefs decorated temple facades and roof combs; portraits in relief adorned lintels; murals covered the walls of some structures; rows of upright stone slabs in the plazas were ornamented with carved figures and inscriptions. The base of some temples served as burial grounds for the nobles and the priests.

Relief carving was a highly developed art form among the Mayas, who used it to decorate such materials as wood, stone, stucco, and jade. The photograph above shows carving on sapote wood: it is the upper portion of two beams that formed part of the lintel crowning the doorway at Tikal's so-called Temple IV. All of the temples at Tikal, which were built about A.D. 700, had carved sapote wood lintels above their doors as well as carved stucco reliefs on their facades. At right is a carved jade, ornamental breastplate, dating from the same period as the Tikal temples, but found at Nebaj, Guatemala, another Mayan site.

able trade, and other blessings. Perhaps there was even human sacrifice at the altars of the gods. We are not certain that this was so, but certainly succeeding civilizations in Mexico made such offerings an important part of their religion.

A classic question concerning the civilizations of Mesoamerica is why they lost their vigor. If archeologists are uncertain about the fate of the Olmecs, they are equally baffled by the waning of Mayan culture. As with the Olmecs, the Mayas may have experienced a major disaster because the peasants exhausted the land or because they rebelled against their masters. But sometime about A.D. 900 the great

Mayan ceremonial centers appear to have been suddenly abandoned, though smaller centers continued to exist. But in the main, in the course of a year, or a decade, or a half century, the sumptuous world the Mayas had built became little more than a relic.

The Glory of Teotihuacán

Mayan society was not the only complex cultural system in Mesoamerica during the first millennium of the Christian era. Several others vied with the Mayan in magnificence. The most remarkable of these existed in the city of Teotihuacán. (The massive, excavated ruins of this community are on public display 25 miles

The Temple of the Great Jaguar looms nearly 200 feet above the Great Plaza at the Mayan ceremonial center of Tikal. The plaza covers two acres, and at its far end stands another equally imposing temple pyramid, behind which stretches a wide causeway that leads to two more of these monumental structures. The complex of buildings at far right above is the Central Acropolis, one of three similar complexes at Tikal. Each is built high off the ground and has several levels on which stand a number of single-story palaces—many erected around interior courtyards—that may have been residences for nobles and priests. Behind this acropolis is the fifth of Tikal's temple pyramids, from which extends another causeway that leads to the sixth, the Temple of the Inscriptions. The inset shows a Mayan jade mask carved about A.D. 700.

northeast of Mexico City.) Teotihuacán differed from the Mayan centers in that it was not primarily a ceremonial site with a small permanent population of priests and nobles. As extensive excavations reveal, it was a city in the modern sense. At its height, Teotihuacán had a population of no fewer than 125,000 and, during religious festivals, could accommodate an equal number of visitors.

Teotihuacán had its beginnings about 150 B.C. and was finally abandoned 10 centuries later. It was a metropolis of broad boulevards, towering pyramids, ornamented temples, great apartment complexes, thousands of workshops, massive marketplaces, and a system of waterways that simplified the transportation of goods and provided irrigation water for nearby fields. Clearly, such a well-planned city could not have grown haphazardly. As population increased, urban planners and the authorities cleared away whatever lay in the path of their designs for a well-ordered town.

Eventually, Teotihuacán came to be laid out on a grid pattern, its main axis, the Avenue of the Dead, some two miles long and 60 feet wide. Along this ceremonial boulevard, temple after temple arose. Among the most magnificent was the Temple of Quetzalcoatl, with the great stone head of the plumed serpent god jutting out from its base. *(continued on page 52)*

Jaina figurines, recovered from Mayan graves and still bearing traces of the brilliant colors with which they were painted more than a thousand years ago, bring the people they depict vividly to life. Several of the figures are only four inches tall, and none is more than eight inches, yet all were modeled with a skilled attention to detail that makes each a portrait of a specific and unique person. At left is a dancing priest, his belt buckled with the huge mask of a god. Above him is a fierce-looking warrior, helmeted and carrying his shield, and a woman of high rank who is garbed in finery and has her hair in an elaborate, jewel-encrusted arrangement. The seated figure, wearing a tall headdress and bedecked with ornaments, is a cacique, or chief. To his right, with sling and shield in hand, is a young warrior, his face tattooed on cheeks and forehead.

Realistic Figurines Reflecting the Mayan World

Jaina, a mile-square island in the Gulf of Mexico, separated by only a narrow channel from the town of Campeche on the Yucatan mainland, is the site of some of the most charming and intriguing finds that have been made in Mayan archeology. These are small, painted terra-cotta figurines, quite realistic in style, that offer keen insights into Mayan daily life during the seventh century A.D. Although some temple ruins have been found, the island appears to have served primarily as a burial ground. Archeologists estimate that it holds more than 20,000 graves, and it is from the 400 or so that have been excavated that the figurines have been taken. The Mayas placed their children's bodies in large pottery containers covered with three-legged ceramic bowls, but they buried their adult dead directly in the ground, to-gether with one or more figurines on their chests or arms.

Other objects were also placed on the bodies or near them: stone and shell ornaments and necklaces and various kinds of pottery vessels. But the figurines showing men and women from every walk of life—warriors, ballplayers, priests, weavers, and women grinding corn—are by far the most fascinating. Most of the figurines are hollow and were made in molds, and some of them—either filled with clay pellets or perforated—could be used as rattles or whistles. Others are partially mold-made, with standard heads and individually modeled bodies and headdresses.

A smaller number—the most detailed, the most individual in style, and the most delicately modeled—are solid and were made entirely by hand.

A young Mayan couple, in an affectionate pose, wear tall hats, collars, and beads. Unlike the mold-made figurines, which are hollow, these handmade figures are of solid clay.

Using a mano and metate, a woman grinds corn for tortillas. As she works with an infant strapped to her back, an older child looks on. In its depiction of ordinary people doing ordinary work, this Jaina figurine is somewhat unusual. Most of the statuettes—particularly those modeled by hand and of solid clay, as is this one—are concerned with the lives of men and women of exalted rank, like the warriors, priest, noblewoman, and chief on the opposite page.

A weaver works at her loom, which is tied to a tree trunk. Weaving was important among the Mayas, and several figurines of weavers have been found. All wear wraparound skirts, ponchos, and beads, and have their hair severely coiffed.

This seated ballplayer, carrying his equipment with him, is wearing a flowing jaguar robe and has three skulls attached to the necklace of huge beads that he wears. Although ball games were an important activity among the Mayas, only a few figurines of players have been found among the hundreds dug up on Jaina by archeologists and by unauthorized persons who have been plundering the Jaina graves for years.

At one end of the avenue is the Pyramid of the Moon, large and imposing but dwarfed by the Pyramid of the Sun that stands a third of the way down the boulevard; the terraced sides of this pyramid rise some 200 feet from its 12-acre base.

Stretching out to the east and west from the Avenue of the Dead are more modest streets lined with apartment row houses, their street-side facades dull, drab, and lifeless. But the insides of these buildings, occupied by members of the wealthy and middle classes, were far more cheerful. The rooms were large and airy, and opened on wide interior courtyards where the residents could enjoy the morning sun and the evening breeze. The apartment houses were even equipped with storm sewers that conveyed rainwater to cisterns. On the outskirts of the city were the dwellings of the poor. These structures were much more modest but, nonetheless, equipped with at least some of the amenities of urban life.

Apparently, many of the apartment houses were arranged along occupational lines. Excavations have revealed that the city's tanners lived in one area, the pottery workers in another, the carvers of jade in yet a third, and the all-important obsidian craftsmen in still another. Near the dwellings were hundreds of workshops, small and large, where the workers carried on their crafts. Were the occupations closed guilds governed by the city's priests and administrators who decided who might work in each craft, how much their wares would sell for, and even where the workers might live? Some archeologists believe this was the case. It is clear, in any case, that for a city like Teotihuacán to have grown and thrived, and to have spread its influence far beyond the Valley of Mexico, a system of highly centralized government was necessary. Merely feeding the population must have been a problem of huge proportions. Fortunately, there was rich soil in surrounding areas for the growing of basic foods—corn, beans, and other crops. It also seems likely that the rulers of the city instituted a policy of strict game conservation; hunters of deer and rabbits were probably licensed and limited in the number of animals to be killed.

Manufacturing and trade, however, were the lifeblood of the city's existence; such Teotihuacán finished goods as tools, utensils, carvings made of obsidian, jewelry, pottery, cloth, and other products were exchanged for cocoa, raw cotton, and semiprecious stones and minerals.

This early calendar stone, 12 feet in diameter, has the Sun God at its center. The symbols represent earth, air, fire, and water, as well as the 20 days of each month. A year was made up of 18 months and five "bad luck" days.

To achieve favorable trade relations with foreign groups, near and distant, the priest-rulers of the city engaged in a kind of economic and cultural imperialism that extended Teotihuacán's influence hundreds of miles beyond its borders. As far away as Guatemala there is strong evidence of Teotihuacán's dominance, particularly at a place called Kaminaljuyu, near the site of Guatemala City. About A.D. 500 a delegation of Teotihuacáns, perhaps a few hundred in number, came to Kaminaljuyu to oversee the reorganization of that town along Teotihuacán lines. Although the northerners seemed to have had little interest in altering the living patterns of Kaminaljuyu's commoners, they instituted great changes among the ruling caste. With the Teotihuacáns probably acting as architects and advisers, an acropolis was built in Kaminaljuyu, its temples and pyramids smaller copies of those in the city far to the north. It is probable that the Teotihuacáns also helped the native rulers establish a strong, centralized government. After the work was completed, some of the visitors may have remained in Kaminaljuyu to represent Teotihuacán's interests.

What were these interests, and why go to such trouble to dominate a small settlement with perhaps 4,000 people? The answer is that Kaminaljuyu was strategically situated along the main route to the south where Teotihuacán's supplies of cocoa and jade originated. Even more important, Kaminaljuyu controlled one of America's richest sources of obsidian. In a world without iron, this glasslike rock was essential for the fashioning of projectile points, sharp-edged tools, and a variety of luxury items. During the sixth century A.D. there were about 350 obsidian workshops in Teotihuacán, employing thousands of people. Finished goods of obsidian were the city's main export, and upon this trade depended Teotihuacán's prosperity.

And the Teotihuacáns were certainly prosperous during their days of dominance. One can imagine the bustle around the city on feast days, when pilgrims and traders came from hundreds of miles around to throng the streets, gaze in awe at the stately processions of priests and aristocrats, and attend the rituals at the temples and pyramids.

The time for the ceremonies is not yet, and throughout the main market men and women engage in hundreds of sharp bargaining sessions, the sounds of scores of dialects filling the air. A potter, her wares balanced atop her head, tries to push her way past a noblewom-

The Pyramid of the Moon
rises 150 feet above the Avenue of the Dead, the principal boulevard of ancient Teotihuacán. Like its neighbors on the broad avenue—the even taller Pyramid of the Sun and the Temple of Quetzalcoatl—the Moon was a religious and ceremonial center not only for the city's population but for the people of the surrounding countryside. Excavations at Teotihuacán, which was a flourishing community from about A.D. 300 to about 600, show that it was a true city and not just a religious site. It had apartmentlike dwellings, workshops, marketplaces, and canals. The population exceeded 100,000.

an in a crowded alleyway. Both are headed for the market, and when the potter realizes whom she has bumped, she quickly backs away to make room for her superior. The market is also the destination of a sumptuously dressed gentleman borne on a litter. His retainers surround him and brandish thong whips over their heads as they force a path for their master.

Eventually, everyone in the crowd manages to push and shove his or her way into the market square. There everything is apparent confusion, but beneath the babble a kind of order prevails. At lines of neat stalls merchants hawk their wares, and buyers and sellers alike keep a wary eye open for city officials whose job it is to watch the bargaining and make sure that each seller gets the standard price, each buyer a proper measure. At one group of stalls, workers are fashioning ornaments of gold, jewels, and semiprecious stones, while well-dressed ladies bargain for the baubles to be paid for with cocoa beans. Suddenly a jade merchant lets out a bellow of rage, and two bureaucrats come running to his stall to investigate the commotion. To the merchant's dismay, he has discovered that a customer has paid for a figurine with counterfeit cocoa beans made of clay. Unfortunately, the buyer is now nowhere to be seen.

Across the square a tobacconist plies his trade, selling reed-wrapped aromatic cigars and contentedly puffing on one of his own wares. Next to him stands a tax collector waiting to take the state's share of each transaction. Perhaps on this day his exactions will be smaller than usual, for he has just been bribed with 12 cigars and is already smoking one of them. Elsewhere a woman buys a child's doll, and nearby groups of weavers and clothiers have spread out their wares—cotton robes, sisal cloth, feather mantles, mats, ropes, nets, and sandals. Here happy girls try on gaily embroidered hupiles, while men from near and far inspect the tanned hides of deer, otters, badgers, and jaguars.

About noontime an epidemic of hunger seems to affect shoppers and merchants alike. One by one the stalls are shut down for half an hour or so while the milling crowd surges to one corner of the square where food is sold. Here are sellers of beans, squash, turkeys, and pots of honey. At one stall the sound of bargaining is overlaid with yelps, barks, and whines, for at this place plump, juicy puppies are on sale.

Thus it was at Teotihuacán at the height of its power and glory. But it, too, would yield to the ravages of time, worn-out land and, perhaps, even rebellion. It was sometime about A.D. 750 that the rapid decline set in. Again we do not know exactly why. One possibility is that the rulers overextended themselves, and their demands for labor to build monuments and carry trade goods to the far corners of Mesoamerica just became too much for the surrounding population. And at some point there was a fire that destroyed many of the great ceremonial buildings at the city's core. A rebellious populace may have set the blaze, invaders from abroad may have been responsible, or the fire could have been an accident. But with Teotihuacán already sliding toward oblivion, this may have been the final blow.

By A.D. 800 Teotihuacán's population had declined to about 30,000, and the carefully constructed bureaucratic regime was no more. New cultures, new empires—led first by the Toltecs and then by the Aztecs—would arise. They would build on the Teotihuacán experience and would also adapt the Mayan and Olmec heritage to their own uses. Finally, in the 16th century, Spanish invaders would come and lay waste to the native cultures. But long before then, something of the Mesoamerican tradition had filtered to the distant north, into the wilds of the North American Southwest and as far east as the Mississippi Valley and beyond. There, in attenuated form, many of the customs, rituals, handicrafts, and living patterns of preconquest Mexico found a new birth and vitality.

Peoples of the Southwest

The American Southwest had been called the most beautiful and sublime of lands but also the wildest and toughest. In one corner of this vast region of soaring mountains, bone-dry deserts, mesas, plateaus, and high valleys girdled by arching peaks is the Gila River country of Arizona. Today little grows in this desert, save for saltbrush and mesquite. But a thousand years ago a traveler wandering through would have been astonished to find the desert suddenly yielding to a sea of green corn stretching as far as the eye could see. And amid the ripening plants, growing to a height of three or four feet, the visitor would encounter a sturdy people laboring in their fields, their brown bodies glistening in the sun as they dug irrigation canals and constructed earthen dams—complete with floodgates of woven mats to control the flow of water that would bring life to the parched land. Should the visitor continue his journey as much as 30 miles from the spot where desert and man-made oasis met, he would find himself beside the Gila itself, where yet other workers were cutting diversion channels to connect with the irrigation canals.

For our sojourner in time there would be yet more wonders. A careful examination of the canals reveals that these natives of the Southwest know about evaporation and have dug their canals deep and narrow to reduce the water surface exposed to the sun. A few of the canals have been emptied, showing once again the hand of cognitive man. The walls of the long ditches are lined with clay to prevent water absorption by the surrounding ground. Soon maintenance crews will appear to patch the walls with fresh clay and carry off accumulated silt from the bottom.

The people who created this complex irrigation system with nothing but the simplest tools of wood and stone were the Hohokam, the "Vanished Ones," as their modern-day descendants—the Pimas and Papagos—call them. The Hohokams themselves were probably the descendants of an earlier people, the Cochise, primitive planters and food gatherers who may have settled in the Southwest as long ago as 13,000 B.C. to evolve slowly over the millennia from gatherers and hunters to agriculturists.

Yet the Hohokams seem to have borrowed so much from the great civilizations of Mesoamerica—corn, cotton, irrigation farming, pottery styles, copper bells, mosaic plaque mirrors, stone carving, temple platforms, and ball courts—that some archeologists believe that they were really descended from Mexican immigrants. The ball courts, in particular, have long fascinated archeologists, for in size and shape they are similar to many that were constructed in Mesoamerica during the age of the Mayan empire. In a place called Snaketown is the largest of these Hohokam courts yet exca-

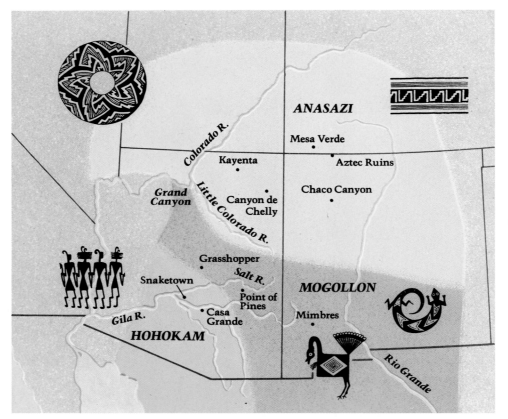

The ancient Southwest was the home of three cultures—the Hohokam, Mogollon, and Anasazi—each with its distinctive living patterns. The Hohokams, who lived in the Gila River region of present-day Arizona, were expert irrigation farmers who made the desert bloom. Their culture flourished for nearly 2,000 years, until about A.D. 1500, when—possibly because of drought—they abandoned their settlements. The Mogollons made their home in the high mountains of that name in present New Mexico. The Mogollons were primarily hunters and gatherers, and about A.D. 1300 their 1,500-year-old culture was absorbed by the more sophisticated Anasazi civilization, which dominated the Four Corners where Arizona, Colorado, New Mexico, and Utah now meet. By the first century A.D. the Anasazis had become successful farmers, and during the next 1,000 years their settlements prospered, reaching their zenith in the great communities of linked dwellings known as pueblos, some of which housed more than 1,000 people.

vated. It is an oval depression, and what appears to have been the playing surface is 132 feet long and about 33 yards wide at its broadest point. About half of this length is flanked by two earthen embankments, each some three feet high. Exactly what sort of game was played on the field is unknown, but it seems likely that a ball or balls were involved. These may not have been the stuffed skin type of balls relatively common among Indians, for archeologists have discovered within the Hohokam area balls made out of raw rubber.

Some archeologists believe that the Hohokams might have been colonists from the south, independent of political control from their homeland but still holding fast to many of the ancient ways.

Lovers of Peace

Perhaps that is what happened. But in one vital respect the Hohokam differed from most Mexican civilizations: they were a people who prized peace. In all their centuries-long history no evidence of war or violence has been found. The main Hohokam settlement was Skoaquick, or Snaketown, a stable, thriving community that, in time, covered about 300 acres and was continuously inhabited from about 400 B.C. until A.D. 1000. During this period Snaketown went through numerous stages of cultural development. At its time of greatest prosperity it consisted of about 100 houses—oblong rectangles with foundations sunk into shallow pits but otherwise built aboveground.

On most days Snaketown was half empty, for many of the residents were out in the fields tending to their crops and irrigation ditches while others were hunting. Although the Hohokams were primarily sustained by corn, they did seek out such game as was available in their desert environment. The jackrabbit and the cottontail—and to a lesser extent the mule deer—were important supplements to the diet of these people. Excavations have revealed that bison were also killed,

though probably only on rare occasions, for these animals seem not to have roamed often within the vicinity of Snaketown. There are indications that the carcasses of the bison were not used for food, but that the skins and heads played a role in Hohokam ceremonies.

Even on the days when most of Snaketown's residents were away from their homes, pursuing their chores, the settlement was a beehive of activity. Throughout its precincts women were hard at work grinding corn on the metates, making wine from the saguaro cactus fruit, and pursuing the handicrafts that resulted in clothing, implements, decorative jewelry, and trade goods. Of these, pottery-making was most important. The potters built up their vessels with layers of clay coils. When the coil work was completed, the vessel was placed—bottom up—over a small, mushroom-shaped clay anvil. As the potter turned the anvil with one hand, he used a wooden paddle in the other to shape the vessel into its final form. Then it was fired in an earth pit heated with a blaze of dry twigs. Finally, the red-on-buff pottery was decorated. The most common designs were either geometric forms, or people, animals, and birds so freely drawn as to impart an almost impressionistic quality to the eye of the modern-day viewer.

Pottery-making may have been women's work, but other handicrafts were probably the preserves of men, who wrought slender, delicately barbed arrowheads, stone dippers, and axes of diorite. But certainly the most unusual of all Hohokam artworks were their etched shells. The shells themselves were obtained through a trade network that extended westward to the Pacific and eastward to the Gulf Coast. Hundreds of years before Europeans discovered a similar process, the Hohokams were using a weak acid to create designs in relief on these shells. Hohokam craftsmen also carved handsome stone bowls and incense burners in the shapes of humans, lizards, and toads. Unfortunate-

The Remains of a Vanished Hohokam Culture

The traces left by the civilization of the Hohokams—the Vanished Ones, as their contemporary descendants call them—are both fascinating and tantalizing. The major Hohokam settlement, Snaketown, was occupied continuously for nearly 1,500 years—from about 400 B.C. to A.D. 1000—thus enabling archeologists to trace the civilization over a long period of time. But although important parts of that culture have been recovered—irrigation canals that turned the desert into fertile cornfields, copper bells, mosaic plaque mirrors, and huge sunken ball courts, for example—equally important elements have been lost.

The Hohokams cremated their dead, and with them their ceremonial and personal belongings of all sorts. In the process, they denied archeology some of its most important clues. Without them, for example, we will probably never know the true nature of the Hohokams' relationship with the culture of Mesoamerica. That there was some relationship seems highly probable; the things that have been recovered were as much a part of the great Mesoamerican civilizations as of the less sophisticated Hohokam culture. But though much in the Hohokam culture seems imitative or derivative, articles that show originality and uniqueness were equally important in Hohokam life. Among these are the red-on-buff pottery, stone palettes, and etched seashells shown in the photographs on this page.

A Hohokam deity cavorts along the inner surface of this red-on-buff pottery bowl made some time between A.D. 900 and 1100 when Hohokam culture was at its height. This color combination, which made its first appearance sometime about A.D. 400, became so widely used by Hohokam potters that early archeologists employed the term "the red-on-buff culture" to describe the people. In the early years the painted designs were quite simple—little more than linear patterns, straight or curved. But as time went on the designs increased in complexity and individuality to include representations of animals, masked dancers, and deities. The deity repeated several times here is Kokopelli, the humpbacked flute player who is thought to have been a fertility god among the Hohokams.

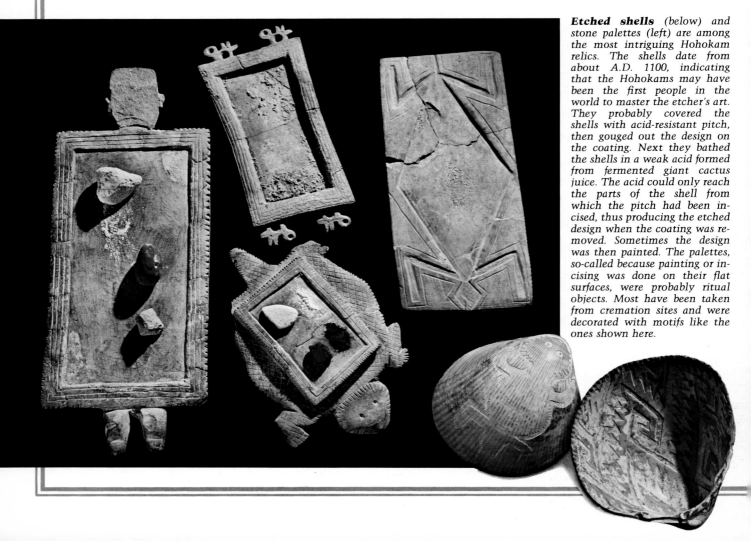

Etched shells (below) and stone palettes (left) are among the most intriguing Hohokam relics. The shells date from about A.D. 1100, indicating that the Hohokams may have been the first people in the world to master the etcher's art. They probably covered the shells with acid-resistant pitch, then gouged out the design on the coating. Next they bathed the shells in a weak acid formed from fermented giant cactus juice. The acid could only reach the parts of the shell from which the pitch had been incised, thus producing the etched design when the coating was removed. Sometimes the design was then painted. The palettes, so-called because painting or incising was done on their flat surfaces, were probably ritual objects. Most have been taken from cremation sites and were decorated with motifs like the ones shown here.

*A **Mogollon pit house*** *was built partly underground, its mud-plastered roof supported by a framework of saplings. This semi-subterranean construction was well adapted to the climate of the southwestern mountain valleys where Mogollon culture arose, the dwelling providing excellent insulation against the* *extremes of temperature that could range from 100° F during the day to near-freezing at night. There were seldom more than 30 such houses in a village, for even at the height of their culture, about A.D. 1000, Mogollon agriculture was not sufficiently developed to permit large settlements.*

ly for archeologists, the Hohokams deliberately smashed all of their great stone effigies, which may have been one of the highest expressions of their art. Perhaps they believed that they had to "kill" these funereal offerings if they were to be of use to the spirits of the dead. The practice of smashing the offerings was probably related to other Hohokam customs, which included cremating their dead. Thus they destroyed not only the bodies but also clothing and other flammable grave offerings, depriving archeologists of much basic research material.

The civilization of the Hohokams was somewhat broadened in the 14th century A.D. when the Salado people, probably from the Little Colorado Basin of present-day Arizona, moved in with them. The Salados evidently came as guests and not as invaders. They lived peacefully among their hosts, maintaining their own traditions and building their own walled villages and three- or four-story apartment dwellings hard by the simple hamlets of the Hohokams. Together these two distinct peoples worked on the irrigation canals and farmed the land in peace and harmony.

Yet the peaceful and relatively bountiful society of the Hohokams was not to last. Sometime about A.D. 1500 Snaketown and other centers were abandoned. Though we do not know why this happened, a reasonable guess is that a prolonged period of drought forced the Hohokams to abandon their large villages and scatter throughout the area in small groups to pursue agriculture as best they could. In time they would imperceptibly fade into the Papago and Pima peoples, who were also irrigation farmers.

The Mogollon: People of the Pit Houses

Near the Hohokam homeland and generally contemporary with its civilization was another Southwestern culture, that of the Mogollons, so named for the mountains many of them inhabited along the southern reaches of the New Mexico-Arizona border. Mogollon civilization flourished between 300 B.C. and A.D.

1250–1300, but unlike the Hohokams, who shaped the desert to their needs, most Mogollons sought the mountains for their homes. Here, in high mountain valleys, they evolved a civilization partly based on farming but also dependent on gathering nuts and wild grasses and on hunting.

In most respects Mogollon life was considerably less sophisticated than that of the Hohokams, partly because the semi-isolated villages of the Mogollons were far from the major trade routes, making the people less susceptible to outside influences than their neighbors. But in one respect, at least, the Mogollons excelled. They developed the pit house, a dwelling that was mostly underground with a roof of reed-covered saplings daubed with a mud plaster. No home could be better suited to the great temperature variations of the Southwest. The natural insulation provided by the underground earth walls served admirably to protect residents from both the heat of day—when temperatures might rise to 100° F—and the near-freezing chill of night.

For centuries life for the Mogollons was secure. The villages grew slowly, each reaching a maximum size of 30 or so pit houses about A.D. 1000. As these hamlets were usually situated near streams, water was generally available for the growing of corn, squash, beans, and tobacco. With a village population probably not exceeding 200, and water readily available, an ample food supply was rarely a problem. There was time, therefore, for a variety of activities centered about the community.

Imagine a Mogollon village scene in the year A.D. 800. People are busy in the sunny dirt plaza around which the pit houses are grouped. Near one of the houses a man, clad in a breechclout, his body richly painted and adorned with bracelets of shell and necklaces of hackberry seeds, sits on his haunches twirling a drill that produces enough heat to start a fire for the deep pit nearby. That morning young men from the village killed a buck deer, and its carcass has already

The Sophisticated Art of Mimbres Potters

The Mimbres—a Mogollon people named for the river in southern New Mexico near which they lived—created some of the most elegant and imaginative pottery bowls ever made in North America. The Mogollons were among the first people of the Southwest to fashion pottery, but it was not until about A.D. 700—probably as a result of dealings with their Hohokam neighbors to the west—that they began to decorate their ware with painted designs. Some 200 years later—possibly because of Anasazi influence—they began to make the black-on-white ware for which they are remembered. Over the next 300 years, while the Mogollon culture as a whole was beginning to decline, Mimbres potters, despite the extreme simplicity of their materials and techniques, raised their art to extraordinary levels of sophistication and originality. The potters formed their bowls by coiling—rolling a large chunk of clay into a long, thin strip and then, starting at the center of the base, building up the bowl by braiding strip upon strip to create the desired shape. Next they smoothed it, inside and

This painted bowl shows a man and woman under a blanket, a symbol of marriage in Mesoamerica. It may have had the same meaning for the Mimbres.

out, with a scraper and burnished it with a smooth stone. After the pot had dried, they covered it with a white slip and, after the slip had dried, burnished it again. Now it was ready for painting with an extract of a dried plant—probably mustard—applied with a brush made of yucca leaves shredded at one end to form bristles. With this primitive equipment a Mimbres potter, most likely a woman, could paint lines so thin, firm, and even that 15 of them—all parallel—could fit inside a border less than three-quarters of an inch wide. As decoration, the Mimbres used both naturalistic and geometric designs, often combining the two on the same object. The geometric patterns were usually quite elaborate: the bold and the delicate, the simple and the ornate appearing together. The naturalistic designs, although highly stylized and fanciful, are always easy to recognize. Moreover, there seems to have been nothing in the living world around them that these artists did not paint: flowers, humans, fish, turkeys, bears, insects, mountain lions, lizards, rams. Nor were the paintings created from set patterns. It is virtually impossible to find two Mimbres bowls of identical decoration.

Black-on-white pottery (above) played an important role in the cermonial and religious life of the Mimbres people. They buried their dead under the floors of their dwellings and covered the head of each corpse with a bowl. Pottery vessels used for this purpose were themselves ceremonially "killed" by punching a hole through the bottom of each one, as shown here.

Mogollon jewelry reflects trading. The turquoise chips (right)—possibly from earrings—are native stone, but the copper bells were probably from Mexico, and the shells used for the necklace and the circular bands came from the Hohokams.

been skinned and its entrails removed. By late afternoon the buck will be hung over the pit to roast, and in the evening the entire village will share in a feast. The man with the drill has started the fire, and he anticipates the evening meal with particular pleasure. Only a day ago the villagers, their crops not yet ready for harvest, had only roasted locusts to eat.

Across the square from the fire maker, three young women cheerfully converse about the feast to come and make their own preparations. They are bent over grinding stones that crush seeds and wild nuts into a paste. Later the women will shape the paste into patties and cook them on hot stone slabs. As they talk, one expresses the hope that the men will kill a rabbit or two, or perhaps a turkey, that will add variety to the venison dinner. Should the men be successful, these smaller animals will be boiled, either in pitch-lined baskets or clay pots.

Not everybody in the village is directly concerned with preparing food. Darting in and out between the roofs of the pit houses are half a dozen small naked children who shout and laugh as they chase about in their game of tag. As one of the children dashes across the plaza, his foot grazes a large basket to spill its contents of several hundred pieces of turquoise, mined from a nearby mountain. Two men, one old and the other young, working on the turquoise chips, look up from their labors and shout admonitions at the fleeing youngster. Then the men begin gathering up the chips. In the months to come these men will spend literally hundreds of hours laboriously grinding the chips against a sandstone slab to a uniform thickness. But this is only the first of several steps in the turquoise-

worker's art. Each chip will also be scored and broken into a square shape, then drilled through the center with either a sharp stone point or a cactus spine. Finally, after months of labor by the two men, the beads will be strung into a necklace and once more ground against the sandstone to a uniform roundness. Only then will the necklace be ready for wearing or trade—a shimmering ornament of green to adorn the neck of a wealthy person.

Among the most skilled of Mogollon artisans were the potters who lived along the Mimbres River of present-day southeastern New Mexico. With a sureness of touch and bold inventiveness, they evolved a style of pottery painting that is famous not only for its depiction of ceremonies and daily life but for its gentle sense of humor as well. Indeed, the bowls with their graphic illustrations are almost a form of writing. By arranging these vessels in chronological order, the biography of a typical Mimbres-Mogollon family might be "read," even though it is unlikely that the potters had any one family in mind when they made and decorated the bowls.

On one bowl, for example, we see a young girl, her hair done up in the whorls that connote her unmarried state. She is wearing a fringed skirt, a blanket around her shoulders, and sandals. On the next bowl a young man appears in the girl's life. His body is protected by quilted armor and thick leggings, and his quiver is filled with arrows. Turn the bowl, and the warrior is killing a bear, impaling it with his arrows. With the help of friends he drags the bear back to the village.

Other bowls, other times of life. Now the girl is a woman and wed to her warrior. Together they lie on a square blanket, an image symbolic of marriage among Mexican societies and probably among the Mimbres as well. Soon the woman becomes pregnant; then she

A wooden bird and two wooden sunflowers have retained their delicate beauty two millennia after Anasazi craftsmen carved them. They owe their remarkable state of preservation to the relatively low humidity in Sunflower Cave in Arizona, where archeologists uncovered them.

Skillful weaving was a hallmark of early Anasazi culture—a period known as the Basket Maker phase because baskets were used not only as containers but also cooking vessels. (Anasazi pottery was still extremely crude at the time.) Baskets were woven in an extraordinarily wide variety of designs and sizes. Weaving was also employed to make numerous other articles. The objects at right were all found in the southern section of modern Utah and date back to A.D. 400–500. They are woven of yucca and are still in remarkably good condition. Yucca and apocynum—a relative of milkweed—were the most widely used fibers. The long band at left, with its red and black decorations, was probably used as a carrying strap, and the basket next to it was for sifting seeds. The striped sack at upper right, which is ripped down one side, was woven without seams. At the bottom are two sandals. The one at left is made of yucca fibers; the other, of unsplit yucca blades.

gives birth to a son. She welcomes a medicine man to her abode, and he plays with the newborn, shakes his ceremonial rattle, and sprinkles sacred cornmeal over the infant. The woman's husband must now provide for a family, and in a series of scenes he is shown bringing home a pot of honey, angry bees pursuing him; killing an antelope; and tending his corn crops. On another bowl the scene shifts to the child as he learns to hunt at his father's side and talks gravely with his mother as she cooks a rabbit the youngster has trapped. On the last bowl the father is shown as old and fat, and he can walk only with the help of a stick. In the final scene he is swallowed up by a huge fish, a painting possibly symbolizing his sudden death in a flash flood.

But Mogollon culture was not to last in an unadulterated state. Influences from the north were eventually felt, and by the end of the 11th century many of the customs and patterns that had distinguished the Mogollons from their neighbors began to become blurred.

By A.D. 1100, for example, the Mimbres-Mogollons had abandoned the pit house as a dwelling. (It remained, however, in use as a place of ritual and worship, a structure

This flint-bladed knife dates from the Basket Maker period. Its resemblance to a modern jackknife is deceptive; the blade is fixed to the wood handle at an angle.

known as a kiva that is to this day an important element in the lives of the Pueblo Indians.) Instead, the pueblo became the standard family shelter. Among the Mimbres, this was a single-story adobe structure, containing as many as 50 rooms. Scores of families lived in each pueblo. But in room placement and design the pueblo reflected the architecture of the Mogollons' traditional pit house, even though the new abode was built mostly aboveground.

The disappearance of the Mogollon as a distinct cultural entity was probably slow and, at the time, almost imperceptible. It occurred, possibly over many decades, sometime between the years A.D. 1200 and 1400. Many of the Mogollons migrated north into the desert and mesa country to merge their own culture with that of the natives and were apparently absorbed into the well advanced Anasazi society. The Zunis of historic and contemporary times may be the descendants of the Mogollons.

Anasazi: People of the Cliffs

In the Navajo language the word Anasazi means "Old Ones" and connotes a people long gone but well remembered through legend, myth, and the remains of the complex and sophisticated culture they left behind. It was the Anasazis who created the third and best known of the Southwest's great ancient civilizations. The Anasazi heartland was the Four Corners, a region where present-day Colorado, Utah, New Mexico, and Arizona meet. It is a land of natural wonders and spectacular prehistoric sites. Here is an archeologist's paradise, for the dry mountain air has not only preserved human remains but also textiles, furs, and even feathers. The most fragile baskets dating back a thousand years are found perfectly intact, their colors as bright as the day they were made. Here, too, are the ruins of the great Anasazi population centers, some of them ruins only in the sense that they have been long abandoned but otherwise remarkably untouched by the passage of time.

Basket Makers, Anasazis, and many of today's pueblo dwellers are the same people at successive stages of development. The ancestors of the early Basket Makers had probably been living in the region of the Four Corners for thousands of years before the Christian era, but in the first century A.D., when they started to cultivate corn, their society began evolving distinct cultural patterns that set them somewhat apart from neighboring groups.

Some settled down in mountain caves large enough to house scores of families, while others took shelter in shallow, sunlit hollows at the base of towering red or yellow sandstone cliffs.

The Basket Makers fully deserve the name that archeologists have given them, for rarely, if ever, has any people been more adept at basketry. They made beautiful baskets of every kind: huge, handsomely decorated burden baskets carried on the back with the help of a strap slung across the forehead; flat basket-trays; sifting and winnowing baskets; pitch-lined baskets for holding water; tiny baskets for trinkets; and baskets shaped to fit the shoulders like modern-day backpacks. Weaving was also employed for other artifacts. One Basket Maker specialty was extraordinarily long nets for trapping small animals. One of these is some 240 feet long and 4 feet high. It was made to be stretched across a gully while hunters beat the bushes for rabbits, chasing them into the net that was painted black in the middle to mislead the quarry into mistaking it for a hole through which to escape.

For the ancestors of the Basket Makers the land and weather played the major role in their evolution from a hunting and gathering society to one principally dependent on farming. Their homeland on high plateaus received a goodly amount of rainfall each year, and seepage from numerous springs and brooks provided

Rings That Reveal the Past

Dendrochronology—the science of dating wood—has revealed much about the prehistory of the Southwest. It has told us, for example, that the oldest wood used in Pueblo Bonito was cut down in A.D. 919; the newest wood, from trees felled in A.D. 1130. This archeological tool was developed almost by accident by astronomer Dr. Andrew Douglass during research into a problem related to climate in the past. As part of his study Dr. Douglass examined the horizontal rings within the trunks of certain trees. He found that the rings show the annual growth of a tree and thus its age. And because the rings are of varying widths—those formed in dry years are narrow; those in wet years, wide—they reveal also the cycle of rainfall over long periods. Since trees of the same kind in the same region and during the same period exhibit virtually identical rings, examination of the bands on several trees enabled him to trace the climate over scores of centuries: the inner rings of a newly felled tree would match the outer rings of one that was felled when the first was a sapling. By carrying this principle back in time—matching rings as shown in the diagram at right—it is possible to tell when a particular tree was cut down. As Dr. Douglass matched rings from a number of pueblos, he was able to construct a master chart of the rainfall pattern back to 53 B.C. At the same time he could date the logs used in building the pueblos. The chart has one limitation: it cannot reveal when lumber was put to use.

Beam from pueblo built in 1300

Beam from house built in 1600

Tree felled in present day

1000   1300   1600   1970

The Lost Pueblos of the Anasazis

Starting about A.D. 750, the Anasazis began to make a dramatic change in their type of dwelling. Before, they had lived in pit houses, partly sunk beneath the desert surface and surmounted by thatch roofs. Now they began to use adobe and stone to build aboveground structures and to connect several of these to form a pueblo. As time went on, more and more houses were joined until, by about A.D. 1100, the pueblos had evolved into villages, each one a huge structure not unlike an apartment house, with several stories, hundreds of rooms, and often more than a thousand residents. Still, traces of the simpler past remained. As with the pit houses, entry into the pueblos was through ceiling openings. And the pit house itself was retained for underground chambers of worship—the kivas. In the last years of the 13th century the age of the great pueblos ended. Drought made it impossible for the hinterland to support large population centers, and the Anasazis scattered. Some traveled south where their descendants live today in pueblos that echo, but do not equal, the monumental structures of their ancestors.

An interior view in Pueblo Bonito *shows the series of doorways that connected one dwelling unit to the next. The walls are of stone set in mud mortar; the ceiling, supported by wooden beams, is made of sticks, grass, and several inches of mud.*

Pueblo Bonito, *the great Anasazi village in Chaco Canyon, New Mexico, lies in ruins today, as shown above. Construction began about A.D. 900, and for nearly 400 years Pueblo Bonito was a thriving community. At its peak, it was home for about 1,200 people. The residents lived in a huge, semicircular masonry structure covering more than three acres and built around a great central plaza. The artist's reconstruction at left shows how Pueblo Bonito probably looked during those years: 800 rooms built on a series of graduated terraces that served as streets, the entire complex rising to a height of four or five stories around its curved outer rim and enclosed along the front by a long wall.*

additional water, thus obviating the need for extensive irrigation. For the Basket Makers and their Anasazi descendants, agriculture, particularly the cultivation of corn, gave birth to permanent villages, and by A.D. 500 the Basket Makers had evolved into the Anasazi stage.

One sign of change was that pottery bowls as well as baskets were now in use. At first Anasazi pottery was not particularly notable. The basic designs were few in number, the fabrication crude with surfaces smoothed by hand and left uncoated. Most of the early decorations, usually done with black paint on the vessels' gray surfaces, were adaptations of forms used on baskets or of pictographs the people had long painted on cliff walls. With

A cylindrical wickerwork vessel, inlaid with shell beads and chips of turquoise, is just one of the many beautiful objects excavated at Pueblo Bonito.

time and experience, however, the Anasazis became expert potters and developed decorative motifs of great charm.

At about the same time that pottery was being introduced among the late Basket Makers or early Anasazis, changes were occuring in the kinds of dwellings these people inhabited. Their old house-styles—built either entirely aboveground or sunk into shallow pits—were giving way to true pit houses with many features adopted from the Mogollons. Each village consisted of some 20 to 30 pit houses, either set out in the open or built into the mouths of caves. The pit house was both a place of residence and the site of religious ceremonies. Eventually, the pit house as a dwelling would disappear, but in the pueblos of the Anasazis it was retained as a ceremonial center and a kind of men's clubhouse.

A new form of dwelling evolved during the years A.D. 750-900. Small and large houses of adobe and stone were built in the form of a crescent fronting on a large open plaza. These were multifamily dwellings, some of them containing as many as 300 rooms. Though many of these "apartment houses" had doors that opened onto the plazas, the primary means of entrance was through roof openings via ladders.

During the next two centuries construction techniques improved greatly, but the basic dwelling style remained much the same, though increasingly during this period each village came to have one kiva that was more important than the others and was recognized as the primary ceremonial center. Finally, in what has been called the Golden Age of the Anasazis (A.D. 1100-1300), the villages took their ultimate form: huge apartment compounds in the shape of crescents, made partly of stone and partly of adobe. The walls were covered with plaster and often painted, and wherever possible the building site was on a narrow ledge or set

into the high and broad mouth of a shallow cave or a canyon wall. The outer facades of these "cliff palaces" were solid, perhaps for protection against invaders, but the facade facing the plaza had windows and doors, though the roof hatch was still widely used as a means of entry.

Such a place was Pueblo Bonito, the "Beautiful City," probably the most magnificent of all of the Great Houses. It was begun about A.D. 900 and lies in the Chaco Canyon of northwestern New Mexico. When completed, Pueblo Bonito was a focal point of Anasazi culture. A gigantic single-structure housing project, Pueblo Bonito's back wall presented an almost unbroken vertical slab of masonry, offering, at least along its lower portions, neither windows nor doors nor even footholds through which would-be invaders might gain entry. Its inner side, however, presented a far different picture: a beautiful, terraced crescent containing a multitude of windows and roof entryways that fronted on a great plaza. All told, Pueblo Bonito contained 800 rooms and could accommodate 1,200 people. In the central plaza, around which Pueblo Bonito arched, were several kivas—enormous subterranean chambers, each of which

A kiva wall at Salmon Ruin, north of Pueblo Bonito, is the backdrop for this collection of domestic items used by the Anasazis. On the mano and metate at right are ears of corn, 600 to 800 years old; the pottery dates from the same era.

could accommodate hundreds of people for the sacred rites performed there.

In its heyday Pueblo Bonito was a vibrant and exciting place. In our minds we can see the fast pace of its city life. Along its plaza there is a constant procession: girls carrying water-filled ollas on their heads; groups of farmers returning from their fields, many of which are miles away; traders from distant regions haggling with the locals for their wares; and medicine men carrying feathers and gourd rattles on their way to their kivas to prepare for one of the many ceremonies that take place each season. Here a pack of dogs sets up a mournful howl, there several turkeys strut their ways along the ground. A young man, fresh from the hunt, enters the plaza, the carcass of a deer slung over his shoulder. Gently he lowers the animal to the ground, then disappears into a kiva for a few minutes. When he returns to his quarry he carries a blanket of turkey feathers to place over it and a pillow of piñon boughs to put beneath its head. Around the body the hunter places prayer sticks and then stands before the carcass to pray aloud, asking the animal's spirit for forgiveness and thanking it for yielding its life so that he might feed his family.

Suddenly, a group of important looking men, dressed in gorgeously feathered robes, strides into the central plaza of Pueblo Bonito, behind them a long file of bear-

The black-on-white Anasazi pottery *shown here was made during the classic Pueblo Period that began about A.D. 1100 and ended three centuries later. The vessels were painted with a dye obtained by boiling shoots of woodland aster.*

The Ruins of Mesa Verde Tell of a Vanished Civilization

Some of the most extraordinary archeological finds in Southwest have been made at Mesa Verde. It is a 20-mile-l stretch of tableland that looms 1,000 to 2,000 feet above Colorado countryside and is cut into numerous finger-sha plateaus by rugged canyons.

Here many Anasazis made their homes for more than years, until the end of the 13th century A.D. when their g pueblos were abandoned. The discovery of Mesa Verde rich lode for archeologists came in 1888 when two ranc happened upon the ruins of one of the great pueblos, called Cliff Palace. From that moment Mesa Verde and cliff dwellings exerted an irresistible pull on both popular scientific imaginations.

In 1891 the first archeological excavations were be and 15 years later the federal government placed Mesa V and its ruins under the protection of the Department of Interior. The protection was badly needed. The site had come a magnet for amateur collectors who had taken l quantities of relics and artifacts before they could be stu by experts. Undoubtedly, much valuable evidence was l

Within the ruins of Mesa Verde is the story of centu of developing culture, from the days when the Anasazis li in pit houses gathered in small villages—most of which scattered atop the mesa—to the height of Anasazi civiliza when the people constructed massive apartment dwelling the mouths of caves and on cliffsides.

In their period of greatest prosperity, just before the a donment, the pueblos of Mesa Verde may have been hom some 7,000 men, women, and children. Cliff Palace, wit 200 rooms, was the largest Mesa Verde pueblo, but there others nearly as large, including Long House, with 150 roc and Spruce Tree House, with 120. In addition, there scores of other smaller pueblos.

The Anasazis did not, however, always live in puel Until about the middle of the eighth century pit houses the people's dwellings. Then the Anasazis began construc aboveground—mud-covered, pole-and-thatch houses were connected to one another in long, curving rows. A 250 years later came the pueblos—houses built of stone mortar, some of them with more than 50 rooms and stand several stories high. But subterranean buildings did not di pear entirely; now they became ceremonial chambers ca kivas.

But toward the end of the 12th century the peopl Mesa Verde radically changed their living pattern. T abandoned most of the mesa top pueblos and built new sive pueblos inside the entrances to the huge caves that e ed in the precipitous canyon walls. We can only guess at reasons for the change. The cliff houses must have beer less convenient than the pueblos on the mesa tops. Sin getting to the tableland where the people grew corn, be and squash, for example, must have been hazardous and ing. The most likely guess is that the building of the g apartmentlike dwellings in the cave mouths was a defen measure against raiders. These structures offered far n natural protection than the exposed pueblos. The presenc watchtowers supports this theory. But however well prote the cliff dwellings were, the Anasazis remained within tl for only about 100 years. By the end of the 13th cen populations had probably grown too large for the region' sources, and killing droughts left the fields barren, forcing Anasazis to leave Mesa Verde.

An artist's reconstruction of Cliff Palace shows how this largest of the Mesa Verde pueblos probably looked on a typical day in the late 13th century—the last years of its occupancy. Along the floor of the lowest terrace are several openings leading to ceremonial chambers, for Cliff Palace had 23 kivas in addition to its 200 rooms. And everywhere are ladders—for entering and leaving the kivas; for moving from one terrace level to another; for reaching roofs, on which women spread their corn to dry before removing it to the storage rooms for wintertime use. Here at Cliff Palace, as at other Mesa Verde cliff dwellings, the storage rooms were built toward the backs of the caves and the family rooms toward the front, with the kivas the farthest forward. Not all portions of the cliff dwellings had ceilings: where the top of the cave was low enough, it served as the roof for the highest story. As can be seen in this painting, there were always more women and children than men at the pueblo during the day. Most of the men were off farming the fields or out hunting. A returning hunter, a rabbit slung from his shoulder, can be seen climbing the ladder at the bottom of the painting. While the men were gone, the women tended the children, ground corn, cooked, made pottery, replastered failing walls, and took time out to gossip on the roofs and terraces. Underfoot, there were always dogs and turkeys, these being the only domestic animals the people had.

ers carrying huge baskets and pottery vessels. They are yet another group of traders, and to greet them hundreds of Anasazis stream out of their rooms.

The traders bring what Pueblo Bonito wants: salt from the Zuni lakes, turquoise from the Galisteo Basin, delicate seashells from distant shores, glinting metal objects from Mexico, and a gaudily feathered macaw screeching a few words in an unintelligible tongue. All is quickly traded for Anasazi pottery, turquoise jewelry, and cornmeal. The priest, upon sighting the macaw, hurries down from his vantage point on the kiva roof and quickly exchanges several of his finest pipes for the bird. Though the holy man already has 13 macaws, he is an insatiable collector, for these birds are a necessary part of the kiva rituals.

A Shortage of Wood

Like cities everywhere and in every time, Pueblo Bonito was not without its problems. Many natural resources necessary for the life of the city were in short supply. Massive wood beams for house posts, for example, had to be hauled from scores of miles away along a network of rude paths. This activity alone probably required the efforts of a high percentage of the city's adult male population, creating periodic shortages of farmers, hunters, and gatherers. And wood for cooking fuel—piñon and juniper—which did grow in Pueblo Bonito's immediate hinterland, was probably not plentiful, particularly in terms of the city's burgeoning population. As the city grew and the surrounding area was denuded of its trees, it may have become necessary to send out foraging parties into distant regions merely to gather firewood.

The great kiva at Aztec Ruin, once an Anasazi pueblo, was used for sacred rites. Above is a reconstruction of its circular chamber with its central firepit, two rectangular pits—perhaps used for sweatbaths—and columns supporting a 90-ton roof.

There are also indications that during the 13th century the Anasazi settlements became embroiled in warfare. Possibly neighboring cities battled one another for the rights to a stand of trees. And it appears that during this period fierce warriors from the north—Apaches and Utes—invaded the region and created havoc.

But most threatening and devastating of all during this time was the problem of water. From A.D. 1276 to 1299 almost no rain fell. The Chaco River ran dry. One authority has speculated that even where rivers retained some of their moisture, the beds had by then cut so deep that the Anasazis' irrigation ditches were now well above the rivers' waterlines, making it impossible to irrigate the fields. Why not dig the ditches deeper? One can only guess. Perhaps by then the combination of warfare, wood shortages, and drought had so sapped the people's energies that they were no longer capable of sustained effort.

In any case, it is likely that the Anasazis turned to their gods and made prayer sticks to appease them and turn away their wrath. But the gods did not relent. Warfare continued. The drought grew even worse. Little by little the people of Pueblo Bonito began to leave their magnificent but doomed city to seek a better life elsewhere. So, too, did the peoples of dozens of other Chaco Canyon communities, and by A.D. 1300 almost all of the great settlements in the region lay deserted.

Nor was it only the cities of Chaco Canyon that were destroyed by the drought. In present-day Colorado the magnificent Anasazi settlement of Mesa Verde was also abandoned. And some 68 miles north of Pueblo Bonito another group of Anasazis had built their own great city, now called Aztec Ruin. At the height of its glory Aztec Ruin sheltered about 2,000 people who lived in hundreds of connected rooms grouped around a great central plaza with a kiva even bigger than any at Pueblo Bonito.

But scarcely was Aztec Ruin completed than it, too, was abandoned, its windows and hatchways sealed and all possession left in place, as if the inhabitants intended to return to reclaim their homes. But they never did come back. Instead, the Anasazis evacuated the most northern of their settlements and concentrated themselves along the Little Colorado River and Rio Grande where they established new pueblos. That is where they were located when the Spaniards pushed north from Mexico in the 16th century, and there they remain today. They are known as the Hopis, Tewas, Keres, and Tanos. As for huge Aztec Ruin, it was left to the elements for more than half a millennium. Then, in the late 19th century, white ranchers moved into the region and discovered the great ruin. For them it was an interesting site, but more important, it served as a quarry from which they took building stones for their own houses. To this day masonry from the once bustling city provides comfortable shelter for the grandchildren of these white pioneers.

The entrance to the painted kiva was by a ladder extending to a square hole in the wood-beam-supported roof. Behind the ladder stands the chamber's altar, made of layers of plaster over a framework of reeds. The reeds were woven in and out of four wooden posts embedded in the dirt of the kiva's floor.

The Painted Kiva at Kuaua: Sacred Art of the Pueblo Past

In 1934 archeologists began excavating the ruins of Kuaua, a New Mexico pueblo established in the 14th century when drought had driven the Anasazis from their homes farther north and the Mogollons had begun leaving their homes in the southern mountains. It soon became clear that Kuaua had been a meeting ground for the two cultures and there, for a century, the two peoples lived together in peace, each maintaining its own rituals. Two kinds of kivas were excavated at Kuaua, the round chambers of the Anasazis and the square ones of the Mogollons. One of the latter proved to be a spectacular find. On three of its walls was a mural, a rare decoration in a kiva. Even more unusual was the discovery that the walls had been replastered more than 80 times and that 17 of the plaster layers contained the remains of other paintings, all with religious themes that were immediately recognizable to modern Pueblo Indians. The themes varied from layer to layer, showing the development of an increasingly complex ceremonial life. The painting fragments that were recovered were carefully removed and are on display at the Museum of New Mexico in Santa Fe. Shown here is a reconstruction of the kiva itself, its walls painted with a replica of the best-preserved mural that was found.

The Kuaua kiva mural reflects the ever-present need for rain. Everything seen here has an association with the weather, crops, and good fortune. The masked human figure is Kupishtaya, the chief of the lightning makers. The great black and white bird to his right is an eagle, which was believed to have the power to ward off evil. Issuing from the eagle's mouth are symbols of fertility: a jagged bolt of lightning, an arched rainbow, and a great number of seeds—the yellow dots.

The Temple Mound Builders

Hard by the Mississippi River, on the outskirts of the present Illinois town of East St. Louis, is a typical example of American suburban sprawl. To the casual passerby there is nothing remarkable about this area of supermarkets, shopping plazas, automobile showrooms, and office buildings lined up along broad highways. If asked to find something a bit out of the ordinary, a keen-eyed observer might mention the presence of hills that contrast with the generally flat landscape but, having so remarked, he would be unlikely to think any more about it. To the practiced archeological eye, however, these hills are indeed remarkable, for they were not created by an ice age nor by some great prehistoric explosion of nature, nor do they represent the efforts of modern-day bulldozers. Instead, they are remnants of a civilization long gone and a city called Cahokia. To the archeologist each one of these hills is a testament to the labors of thousands of Indians who toiled for generations to construct massive pyramids as upland sites for the residences of their leaders and for great temples dedicated to their gods.

In fact, upon this site where shoppers and business people now go about their workaday concerns, proud priests and haughty aristocrats were once borne on litters by platoons of common people. Six or seven hundred years ago priests, clad in ornate headdresses and adorned with jewelry of hammered copper and freshwater pearls, stood on the flattened tops of some of these pyramids and summoned the thousands of faith-

A duck-shaped bowl, carved from diorite, is one of the best-preserved artifacts of the Temple Mound people yet discovered. It dates from about A.D. 1300 and was found in Moundville, Alabama, where hundreds of relics have been unearthed.

ful to the great plaza below. There simple farmers, huntsmen, and artisans watched the mysterious rituals of the ancestor cult with its elaborate ceremonials dedicated to the interring of the remains of departed aristocrats and priests.

Yet in one respect, at least, the world of the Mississippi Valley is little different today than it was in the time of these Temple Mound Builders. Then, as now, a man standing atop one of the mounds in midsummer would see field upon field of ripening corn stretching out into the distance.

It was corn planted in the rich alluvial soil along the Mississippi and its tributaries that made possible the creation and prosperity of a civilization that spread westward as far as present-day Oklahoma, southeastward into Alabama, Georgia, and the Gulf Coast, and northward into Wisconsin. For Cahokia in particular, and the other centers of Mississippian culture in general, their locations along broad river courses made possible the widespread and far-reaching trade that added to the wealth of the towns and facilitated cultural exchange. This civilization, characterized by the construction of villages and cities dominated by temple and residential mounds, took in scores of tribes, most of whom probably spoke some dialect of the Muskogean tongue.

The classic features of this Mississippian society, as archeologists call it, began to make themselves manifest as early as A.D. 700. This was two centuries or so after the decline of the Hopewells, who were also mound builders (see previous chapter) but differed greatly in most respects from the Mississippians who succeeded them. One basic difference, of course, was the role of agriculture, particularly the cultivation of corn. In the days of the Hopewells corn was not unknown, but the varieties then grown were less hardy and smaller than the hybrids that the Mississippians grew. In fact, corn among the Hopewells may have been little more than a

The Mound Builders' culture covered a large portion of today's southeastern United States and extended west to Oklahoma and north into Wisconsin. The map shows the location of seven major ceremonial centers, each covering a huge area dotted with clusters of truncated pyramids, some of them rising to a height of 100 feet.

ceremonial food, used only during religious feasts. Among the Mississippians, however, it was a major part of the diet, grown so intensively and with such success that harvests were able to support an ever-increasing population of city and village dwellers.

The corn hybrids that the Mississippians cultivated bore a striking resemblance to the varieties grown with similar success in Mexico. Some—but by no means all—anthropologists believe that there were other similarities between the world of the Mississippi Valley and that of cultures thousands of miles to the south. Designs appearing on Mississippian pottery are like many found in Mexico. Among the Mississippians, for example, the feathered serpent appears as a decorative motif on pottery vessels and in stone carvings. In Mesoamerican cultures the feathered serpent is the great god Quetzalcoatl. Similarly, the great mounds of the Mississippians, with their truncated, flat tops and the vast open plazas below, the class structure of town life, and the worship of the sun god all suggest the pervasive influence of Mesoamerica.

If the cultures of Mexico did influence the world of the Mississippians, trade, rather than warfare or emigration from the south, probably accounted for the infiltration of Mesoamerican forms and customs to the north and east. Perhaps seagoing traders from the Yucatan made the North American Gulf Coast a regular stopping place in the journeys. From there, many cultural traits of their homeland may have been diffused into the great river's valleys to permeate and transform many native cultures.

As Mississippian culture spread throughout the Southeast and Midwest in the centuries after A.D. 700, a typical kind of society began to emerge, focused about either a single center or a group of villages that would dominate a hinterland stretching for scores of miles in every direction. One of these sites, near the present-day, appropriately named town of Moundville, Alabama, contained 19 mounds that ranged in height from 3 to 23 feet and were arranged in a circle to create a great plaza. Outside the circle there were two other mounds, one 22 feet, the other 57 feet high. Some of the mounds were for burials, others for temples and the residences of notables. Excavations of these mounds, particularly the burial sites, have revealed a treasure of art, much of it defying contemporary interpretation. What, for example, does one make of a figure combining the characteristics of a heron, a woodpecker, and a serpent? What is the significance of a face devoid of all

This Mississippian mask, *combining the features of man and deer, was probably used in religious rites. The eyes and mouth are shell inlays.*

features save for eyes—which are weeping? There is, in fact, a sense of brooding and even despair in much of the art uncovered at the Moundville site.

There are strong indications that throughout the Mississippian culture an obsession with death—often related to human sacrifice—was pervasive. At one Cahokia burial mound, for example, the remains of four men, their heads and hands cut off, were found. In a pit beside them were the corpses of 50 young women. Evidently, all of them had been sacrificed simultaneously, perhaps in a ritual related to the burial of a notable.

If such conjectures are valid, the rich and powerful must have gone to their graves accompanied by their retinues, who would continue to see to their comforts for all eternity. And, presumably, the aristocracy in afterlife would continue to perform the same functions that they discharged on earth. One expert speculates that the rulers "gave orders for all able-bodied men and women to work in the public (or chief's) fields, and criers walked through the towns and villages to call out the man and woman power. The produce from these fields did not become the personal property of the chief, but was stored in a public granary. While the chief's immediate family subsisted on the results of this community enterprise . . . they were also obligated to feed . . . needy local families from public stores. Food for public ceremonies also came from the same store-

A stone pipe *found in Muskogee County, Oklahoma, is carved in the shape of a man preparing to play chunkey, a game popular throughout the area of the Temple Mound Builders. In chunkey, one man rolled a rimmed stone disk like the one the figurine is holding; then he and a teammate ran after it down a court as long as 100 feet and threw wooden poles as close as possible to the spot where they expected the disk to fall over. Every Mississippian town had its chunkey court and a supply of stone disks, all carefully crafted and highly polished. Chunkey remained popular into the historic era; early European travelers left accounts of games that lasted all day.*

The Good Life of Rich Mississippians

Of all the vanished Indians cultures north of Mesoamerica, none was more prosperous or sophisticated than that of the Mississippians—the Temple Mound Builders of the Southeast. Their huge ceremonial sites were not only religious centers for the tens of thousands of ordinary people—hunters and farmers—who lived in the outlying villages but trading centers for both local merchants and travelers from hundreds of miles away. The principal beneficiaries of the wealth this trade produced were the aristocrats and priests. The great mounds of the ceremonial complexes were labori-ously constructed to serve as their homes, tombs, and temples. Archeological findings have provided ample evidence that these leaders lived at a level of comfort and luxury that befitted their exalted stations. They had splendid houses and retinues of servants who waited on them, bore them through the streets on litters, and may even have followed them to the grave to serve their masters in the next world. Some of the tombs contain large numbers of decapitated remains—probably servants sacrificed at their leaders' deaths. Even in appearance, the nobles and priests were set apart from commoners. The aristocrats painted their faces and wore elaborately coiffed hair topped with ornate headdresses. They adorned themselves with earrings, necklaces, arm and leg bands of copper, pearls, and shells, and bedecked themselves in gaudy feathered capes.

"The Princess" and "Big Boy"—as the skeleton and the stone ceremonial pipe (left) are popularly known—illustrate the Mound Builders fondness for adornment. The Princess is encircled at shoulders, waist, and legs with almost 2,000 shell beads in long loops. Big Boy wears earrings, necklaces, and a headdress, and has a carved feather mantle on its back.

The Mississippians' use of shells for je ry, such as a necklace, and for a surface t decorated is shown at right. The incised de on the foot-long conch shell depicts Eagle a mythical figure that has often been foun artifacts uncovered in a number of excavat of Mississippian sites.

houses. The role of chief, then, was that of custodian of a public reserve of food."

It was at Cahokia that Mississippian culture reached its apex sometime about A.D. 1200. Nowhere else in the far-reaching Mississippi Valley was art so sophisticated, ceremonies so resplendent, religious fervor so great, trade so profitable, or industry so diverse as in Cahokia. Here were earthen pyramids higher and broader than any others north of the Rio Grande. Here resided some 75,000 persons within Cahokia and in the scores of smaller settlements nearby, as well as in a rural hinterland that stretched for hundreds of miles. The priests and aristocrats of Cahokia lived atop the pyramids or on the terraces beneath their summits—the higher one's house, the more lofty one's status. The main pyramid was Monk's Mound, so named because French Trappists once raised vegetables on its terraces. The pyramid was truly a colossus of its kind, rising to a height of 100 feet, its base 1,000 feet long and 700 feet wide. In the New World only Teotihuacán's Temple of the Sun and Cholula's Great Pyramid exceeded it in size.

Archeological studies have revealed that Monk's Mound was built in 14 stages, the initial structure having been begun in A.D. 900, and the final layers having been added sometime about A.D. 1150. On the flat summit of Monk's Mound there once stood a great building that spread over an area that could have contained three modern tennis courts. Probably this post-and-wattle structure surmounted by a thatch roof was a temple, but it may also have been the residence of Cahokia's priest-ruler.

Fronting on the Great Pyramid and surrounded by smaller mounds was an immense plaza that may have served a dual function as the city's chief marketplace and, on ceremonial occasions, the gathering spot for city residents. Thanks to the investigative work of archeologists we are able to reconstruct with some degree

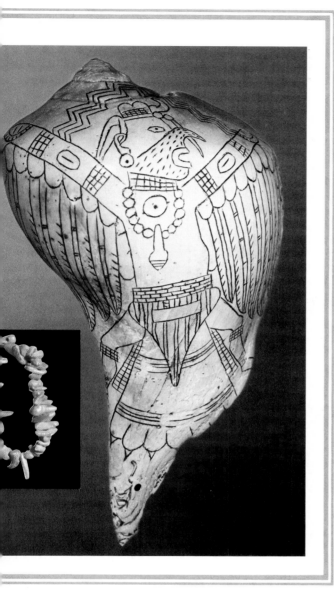

of accuracy what life in Cahokia might have been like at the height of its influence. The time is a few hundred years before the arrival of the white man.

A long line of men bearing blocks of salt approaches the log palisade that surrounds the center of Cahokia. The men are from a nearby area, and the salt, which they obtain by evaporating salt springwater, is one of the city's chief exports. Within the marketplace merchants eagerly await the bearers. But the merchants must be patient, for no one enters the inner city until he has been properly identified by soldiers standing on platforms atop the wall. Only when the soldiers are certain that the visitors are whom they appear to be and not invaders seeking entry is the caravan allowed to pass into the main gate's L-shaped vestibule (a device to slow down a mass attack of raiders) and thence into the city proper.

Meanwhile, a second caravan has halted behind the

first, this one with 40 men laden down with chert from a distant quarry. When they finally receive permission to enter, their burden will be distributed among craftsmen who will fashion this flintlike stone into various implements. Those carrying the salt and chert are but a few among Cahokia's common people, who form the work force that sustains the priests and aristocrats.

Passing single file through the narrow entrance to the inner city, the chert bearers almost collide with an outgoing caravan of foreign traders—travelers from the mountainous areas to the west who have bartered their cargo of grizzly bear teeth for salt, copper ornaments, and pearl necklaces. No sooner have the traders passed by than the laborers encounter two haughty nobles, one of them adorned with a profusion of feathers and copper brooches, the other weighed down by a fantastic antlered headdress. The humble folk quickly give way. Only when the nobles are out of sight do the bearers reform their line and shuffle wearily down the avenues past arrowhead makers, leatherworkers, potters, weavers, and other craftsmen creating goods for trade with local aristocrats and for the export market. The artisans are highly valued members of society and are a cut above farmers and common workers in Cahokia's class structure.

Finally, the chert bearers reach the great plaza that fronts on the 100-foot-high pyramid. There they lay down their burden while their leader engages in lively bargaining with local craftsmen who buy the chert for several strings of freshwater pearls and five baskets of berries. But nearby a noisy argument begins. A half dozen farmers and their wives have hauled many baskets of corn into town, and now they stand before a hoe maker arguing over the rate of exchange. The farmers want eight sharp-edged shell hoes for their produce, but this year the harvest has been so ample that corn commands but a small price. The artisan offers four hoes, and the farmers gesticulate wildly and spew out their fury. In the end they will accept the offer and return to their fields while muttering curses. At yet another part of the plaza a craftsman deals with an aristocrat interested in purchasing a bracelet of pearls. The two argue over the price for several minutes but fail to strike a bargain, and the nobleman finally walks off in a huff to search out a jeweler whose charges are more reasonable.

All of the activity in the plaza does not go on unobserved, for atop the Great Pyramid stands Cahokia's priest-king, who occasionally peers down on the scene below. But it is not the bartering in the plaza that concerns this mightiest of rulers. Rather, it is the doings within a circle of evenly spaced upright logs just outside the city walls that commands his attention. Within the circle are several lesser priests, one of them sitting on a post set exactly at the center of the ring. The seated priest peers at the (continued on page 74)

The funeral of White Woman, mother of the Great Sun, will also see the death of a number of Natchez men and women who are pledged to accompany her into the world beyond. Her husband—a commoner, as dictated by law—has already been garroted by his firstborn son and lies beside her on the bier. The victims, with their executioners behind them, can be seen on the various platforms in the plaza. Those who are to die will first be administered a drug to render them unconscious and will then be strangled.

At the top of the main mound stands White Woman's firstborn son, the all-powerful ruler of the Natchez, and her firstborn daughter, who will become the next White Woman. Leading the procession up the steps is the high priest well versed in

rituals for the dead. White Woman's house, atop a distant mound, is being burned according to custom.

According to Natchez belief, White Woman was the direct descendant of the original Great Sun, who brought religion and stable government to the Natchez people, and through her the sacred lineage was maintained. White Woman had lived a luxurious life. She had worn magnificent feather cloaks and precious pearls, eaten the finest food from special dishes, and had been borne everywhere on a litter. Only she had been permitted to accompany the Great Sun and the high priests into the temple each morning, where she had communed with the Great Spirit. Later she had relayed the messages from the supernatural world to the villagers waiting for her at the bottom of the temple steps.

The Symbols of the Buzzard Cult

According to the archeological evidence, a new religious cult began to flourish in many major Mississippian centers about A.D. 1200. The origins of the cult are unknown, but some of the symbols and motifs (right) associated with it resemble those common in Mesoamerica. Others appear to be derived from the earlier Hopewell culture, and still others may well have been indigenous. The symbolic meanings of these motifs and the details of the cult beliefs and rituals are not clearly understood.

But the sheer number of articles uncovered and the extraordinary care and skill that went into making them suggest that what is known as the Buzzard, or Southern, Cult played a major role in the life of the people. The preponderance of certain kinds of objects and symbols indicates that the cult was largely concerned with death.

The objects include gorgets (armor for the throat), ceremonial stone axes, shell pendants, masks, pottery, and copper plates—all of which are engraved or embossed with one or more of the motifs at right. Some of these symbols have several forms: the Cross, for example, is sometimes transformed into a swastika, or it may form the central element in a Sun Circle (second from top). And the Sun Circle itself may be seen with rays or with a scalloped edge. The Bi-Lobed Arrow appears frequently on hair ornaments and in the hair knot of Eagle Man—a mythic figure depicted on many Mississippian artifacts. Similarly, the Forked Eye is often associated with Eagle Man as well as with Bird Serpent, another mythic creature. Though there are variations of the Forked Eye symbol, all include an eyelike shape within a form resembling a stylized bird's head. An eye also appears on two other motifs: the abstract Open Eye and the Hand and Eye. Of all the symbols, the bottom two are most clearly associated with death: the first is a stylized skull; the other, a bone.

Cross

Sun circle

Bilobed arrow

Forked eye

Open eye

Hand and eye

Death motif

Death motif

sun and then at the shadows cast by the logs. Over and over again his eyes move from the sky to the ground, and from time to time he whispers a word to one of his associates. The priests are making solar calculations. They are the keepers of time, and from this "woodhenge"—which Europeans would find remarkably similar to ancient Britain's Stonehenge—they calculate propitious moments for such activities as planting, harvesting, and the commencement of religious festivals. On this day the priests are seeking solar signs that the time is ripe to begin a ritual celebrating the autumnal equinox.

Rites and Ceremonies

What were the rites and ceremonies important to the Mississippians? And what was the nature of their beliefs, and how did these fit into the society they had established? No one can say for certain how these questions might be answered in terms of Cahokia. The Cahokians never devised a form of writing, and by the time Europeans appeared on the scene, the city had disappeared as a center of Mississippian culture.

Cahokia may have been a victim of its own success, the town's burgeoning population and growing bureaucracy requiring more sustenance than the surrounding countryside could provide. Or conceivably there might have been a rebellion among the farmers, though there is no evidence of that. Indeed, most of the centers of Mississippian life had vanished from the river valley by the time the first European explorers began traversing the North American heartland. One theory is that European diseases preceded the foreigners themselves, causing great epidemics of smallpox and measles that all but wiped out the populations of the Mississippian cities. But as late as the early 18th century one culture that exhibited numerous Mississippian traits survived: the Natchez who lived near the site of the modern-day Mississippi city that bears their name.

In the 17th century French explorers penetrated into Natchez country, and they were soon followed by administrators, missionaries, and traders who lived among these Indians. Some of the Frenchmen kept journals and diaries of their experiences. It is through their eyes that we can gain some knowledge of the final flowering of a neo-Mississippian culture.

Natchez society in the early years of the 18th century may have been atypical of the Mississippians as a whole. By then the Mississippian culture had greatly decayed, and what the French saw may have been almost a parody of earlier glories. Like the Cahokians of centuries gone by, the Natchez were ruled by a living deity, the Great Sun, who lived atop a pyramidal mound in the tribe's primary village. His residence was on the highest mound and was far more imposing than the houses of the lesser people. When a Great Sun died, his house was burned to the ground, the mound on which it stood was then made bigger, and a new

Art to Celebrate Death

The preoccupation with death that marked the Buzzard, or Southern, Cult is evident in many of the artifacts found at Mississippian sites. Not only do they carry the cult symbols shown on the opposite page, but the objects themselves speak of violence and death, either in the manner in which they were used or in the themes they portray. Human sacrifice, usually through beheading, or warfare are associated with each of the objects shown here.

The mace (upper right corner) could have been used either as a weapon of war or as a club to kill victims in ritual sacrifice. Similarly, the figure on the gorget (right) holds a war club in one hand and a trophy head in the other. The head pot (below) bears the visage of a trophy head, and the platform-based pipe (bottom right) depicts a human sacrifice, the executioner standing over his victim.

Craftsmen of the Temple Mound Builders culture were expert in many decorative techniques and in the use of a wide variety of materials. The gorget directly above is fashioned of shell. The mace (upper right) was chipped out of stone. The face on the clay pot is painted with vegetable dyes. Clay was also used to make the ritual pipe (right) with its sacrificial theme. Both the gorget and the head pot carry symbols of the Buzzard Cult: a Forked Eye and Bi-Lobed Arrow on the former, a Cross on the latter.

residence for his successor was built on the same site.

Across an open plaza from the Great Sun's residence mound was the temple mound, rising perhaps 20 feet with steps on its eastern slope to make access easy. Atop the mound was the temple itself, a structure built of cypress logs and enclosing an area somewhat under 30 feet square and 10 feet high. The temple was divided into two rooms. In one an eternal fire—gift of the sun itself—was kept burning. Nearby were the remains of the current Great Sun's immediate predecessor reposing in a cane coffin. The second and somewhat smaller chamber may have been the repository for a stone statue of the original Great Sun, who was said to have

mysteriously appeared among the Natchez during a time when that people lived in chaos. This messenger from the Great Spirit established himself as ruler and laid down the structure of society, the laws and customs by which the people were to live forever after. When his work was done and old age had enfeebled him, this Great Sun metamorphosed himself into the statue to be venerated by coming generations.

The Great Sun was the absolute ruler of the Natchez, but he was aided by his mother, White Woman, his brothers called Suns and his sisters and other female relatives, Women Suns. From the ranks of the Suns came the war chief and the head priest. The Great Sun with his retinue of Suns and Women Suns formed the highest class of Natchez society. Beneath them were the nobles, the honored men, and finally, the commoners whom the higher orders referred to as stinkards. The stinkards, of course, were the workers who performed the farming, hunting, and mound building that their betters demanded.

Among the Natchez, nobles and commoners alike, households were made up of extended families, the oldest male—perhaps himself a great grandfather—enjoying the title of father to all of the children. But it was to their real father that every child felt responsible for his or her acts and, for as long as he lived, a man could exercise almost absolute control over the actions of his offspring. When children were very young, little differentiation was made between males and females, but as they grew toward puberty they began to learn the different skills they would be expected to practice as men and women. Girls were taught to plant crops, cook meals, and make clothing while boys concentrated their efforts on the arts of war and hunting, though they too would be expected to help with the cultivation of crops.

After puberty there were few inhibitions on sexual activities, though young girls were encouraged to charge for their favors so that they might accumulate possessions as a kind of dowry when the time came to wed. Indeed, the worth of a bride seems to have been calculated, at least in some measure, by the quantity and quality of goods she had accumulated as rewards for her amorous activities. When a man married a woman with a rich dowry, he enhanced his own status.

Corn cultivation was the major economic function of Natchez commoners. They cleared the fields of wild cane growths and planted two types of corn, from which they prepared no fewer than 42 dishes. Beans, pumpkins, and tobacco—the Natchez were inveterate

Mississippian pottery vessels *often took elaborate shapes, like those shown here. Of highly polished blackware, they are decorated with scrollwork incised with a fingernail.*

smokers—were also important crops. Fishing and hunting were less vital to the economy, though Natchez warriors pursued bears, buffalo, and deer. Sometimes deer were hunted primarily for sport. On such occasions a group of Natchez, sometimes as many as 100 men, would beat through the forest in search of their prey. When a deer was found, it was not killed on the spot. Rather it was surrounded and kept in a state of panicky running—as it tried to escape from the closing circle of men—until it dropped to the ground in exhaustion. The animal was then taken alive to some notable, often the Great Sun, who ceremonially slaughtered it and divided the meat up among the hunters.

Aside from working there was one other role that the commoners performed. From their ranks came the mates—both male and female—of every noble in the land. No aristocrat, be he a mere honored person or the Great Sun himself, was immune from the requirement that he choose his mates from the lowest order of society. Though a commoner spouse did not rise to the rank of the husband or wife, the children of these unions in all but one instance remained in the ranks of the nobility.

Yet here, too, there were complications. The offspring of a male Sun and a female commoner lived as a noble but was reduced one rank from the father's lofty estate. But rank held firm along the female line. The children of a female Sun (the sister of a Great Sun) and male commoner remained a Sun. No office or rank was immune from the dictates of female lineage. When a Great Sun died, his successor came neither from his own male children nor his brothers' but rather from among the sons of his closest female relation—usually a sister.

Once installed as the Great Sun, this god-man became absolute master of the domain. One French observer recalled that when the Great Sun "gives the leavings [of his meal] to his brothers or any of his relatives, he pushes the dishes to them with his feet. . . . The submissiveness of the savages to their chief, who commands them with the most despotic power, is extreme. . . . If he demands the life of any one of them he comes himself to present his head."

According to another French commentator, the priest Maturin Le Petit, the Great Sun was considered the actual brother of the celestial body. "The great chief of this nation," wrote the missionary, "who knows nothing on earth more dignified than himself, takes the title of brother of the Sun, and the credulity of the people maintains him in the despotic authority which he claims. . . . Every morning the great chief honors by his presence the rising of his elder brother, and salutes him with many howlings as soon as he appears above the horizon. . . . Afterwards, raising his hands above his head and turning from east to west, he shows him [the sun] the direction which he must take in his course."

The French found such concepts fascinating, perhaps in part because their own recently deceased king, Louis XIV, had styled himself the Sun King and had often dressed in eye-dazzling raiments suggestive of that heavenly body. And it was Louis who spent a lifetime scheming to reduce the power of the French nobility and establish himself as his nation's absolute master. Yet within his limited realm, the Natchez Great Sun far outshone his would-be French counterpart. Courtiers and servants at the French court did not commit suicide, for example, upon learning of their monarch's death. For the Great Sun of the Natchez, however, it was traditional that those closest to him would accompany him into the next world. Indeed, any aristocrat among the Natchez knew that when he died he would lead a phalanx of followers into the realm of the dead. As Maturin wrote, the Natchez believed that the righteous among them would find in the next life "all kinds of exquisite viands . . . and that their delightful and tranquil days will flow on in the midst of festivals, dances and women." Presumably, such visions helped overcome the natural reluctance of the living to join the dead.

Typical, perhaps, were the rites that surrounded the death in 1725 of Tattooed Serpent, war chief of the Natchez and brother of the Great Sun. Much beloved by all, Tattooed Serpent's death caused widespread grief, and even the Great Sun himself was said to have considered suicide. Though the Great Sun was dissuaded, Tattooed Serpent's funeral procession included his two wives, his pipe bearer, chancellor, doctor, and a host of other retainers. In keeping with tradition, all of these offered their own lives so that they might continue to serve their master in the world beyond. The self-condemned were drugged, their heads were covered with skin bags, and then they were publicly strangled.

But it was not only Tattooed Serpent's immediate entourage who accompanied him in death. Others, whose relationship with him had been more casual, offered themselves up too. Thus one noble woman, whom the French called La Glorieuse, in tribute both to her beauty and her generosity with her favors, insisted on dying, much to the dismay of her white lovers. And during the funeral procession one commoner couple threw the body of their child, whom they had just killed, beneath the feet of the pallbearers. Among the Natchez, such acts were deemed to have particular merit, and this was one of the few ways that commoners could rise to the ranks of honored persons.

As would happen so often in the history of Indian-white affairs, the friendship that had characterized the early relations between the French and the Natchez soon turned sour. In 1729 the French governor ordered the Natchez to evacuate their main village so that he might build himself a plantation on its site. Quite naturally, the Natchez resisted, at first verbally and finally with action. In a surprise attack in the autumn of that year the Natchez fell upon the French and massacred some 200 of them. Among the victims was the governor, who was beaten to death.

The French, from their newly built redoubt at New Orleans, soon struck back, sending troops into Natchez territory and, with the help of Choctaw allies, crushed their enemies. Eventually, a large group of the Natchez, including the Great Sun, surrendered. Some were burned at the stake as a warning to other Indians, but most were shipped off in slavery to labor on the plantations of Santo Domingo in the Caribbean. With the destruction of the Natchez the final chapter in the history of the Mississippian culture came to a close.

North America in 1500

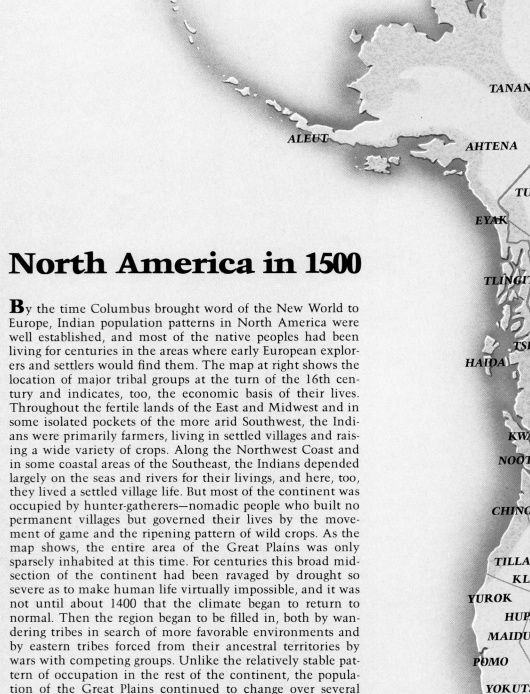

By the time Columbus brought word of the New World to Europe, Indian population patterns in North America were well established, and most of the native peoples had been living for centuries in the areas where early European explorers and settlers would find them. The map at right shows the location of major tribal groups at the turn of the 16th century and indicates, too, the economic basis of their lives. Throughout the fertile lands of the East and Midwest and in some isolated pockets of the more arid Southwest, the Indians were primarily farmers, living in settled villages and raising a wide variety of crops. Along the Northwest Coast and in some coastal areas of the Southeast, the Indians depended largely on the seas and rivers for their livings, and here, too, they lived a settled village life. But most of the continent was occupied by hunter-gatherers—nomadic people who built no permanent villages but governed their lives by the movement of game and the ripening pattern of wild crops. As the map shows, the entire area of the Great Plains was only sparsely inhabited at this time. For centuries this broad midsection of the continent had been ravaged by drought so severe as to make human life virtually impossible, and it was not until about 1400 that the climate began to return to normal. Then the region began to be filled in, both by wandering tribes in search of more favorable environments and by eastern tribes forced from their ancestral territories by wars with competing groups. Unlike the relatively stable pattern of occupation in the rest of the continent, the population of the Great Plains continued to change over several centuries, even after the Europeans had arrived and established themselves as permanent residents of North America.

MO

WKNIFE

PEWYAN

ESKIMO

NASKAPI

BEOTHUK

CREE

MONTAGNAIS

GROS VENTRE
CROW
OJIBWA
MIOMAC

HIDATSA
ABNAKI

ASSINIBOIN

DAKOTA MENOMINEE   ALGONQUIN
WINNEBAGO   HURON   IROQUOIS PENOBSCOT

MANDAN
FOX   POTAWATOMI

ARIKARA   OTO   ERIE   DELAWARE
IOWA

PAWNEE   CHEYENNE
SUSQUEHANNOCK

KANSA   MIAMI
OMAHA   POWHATAN

WITCHITA   MISSOURI   SHAWNEE

HE
OSAGE   CHEROKEE   TUSCARORA

CHICKASAW

CADDO   CREEK

CHOCTAW

NATCHEZ

TIMUCUA

CALUSA

KEY TO SUBSISTENCE AREAS

*Colors indicate the primary
means of sustenance.*

**HUNTING AND
GATHERING**

AGRICULTURE

FISHING

The Five Civilized Tribes

The Tennessee River *flows toward the west and carries loamy deposits that enrich the surrounding soil. In this fertile environment lived the peoples of the Southeast, among them the Cherokees whose craftsmen carved this elegant pipe (inset) found in a burial groun*

Knowledgeable in the use of medicines, skilled builders, craftsmen, and farmers, the Southeastern Indians created a great civilization that was to perish on the Trail of Tears.

The first explorers to penetrate the Southeast of what is now the United States encountered one of the most advanced Indian societies north of Mexico. The Southeastern Indians were accomplished and prolific builders. Their artisanship was well developed. Skilled agriculturists and fishermen as well as hunters, they lived according to a complex set of beliefs that encompassed both the natural and supernatural worlds. They were well versed in the use of herbs as medicines, many of which have modern counterparts. Their thinking about the conservation of natural resources was knowledgeable; indeed, their concepts foreshadowed much of what we now call environmental and ecological concerns and attitudes. And though they probably comprised between 150 and 200 separate groups or tribes and were often at war, combat was usually limited to small-scale raids in which casualties were few.

We can draw these conclusions about the Southeastern Indians with considerable assurance even though their society began to disintegrate almost immediately upon contact with the white intruders. From a scholarly point of view, to be sure, much vital information is lacking or incomplete. But fortunately, the oral traditions of these Indians survived for several hundreds of years, long enough for ethnologists—students of cultural structures and traditions—to get them down on paper. These oral traditions took the form of fables and legends about man and beast, deities, and witches and other forces of evil. Because these tales so persuasively present their view of themselves and their society, they will be quoted here frequently to supplement the scanty information yielded by archeological studies and the reports of the explorers and settlers who came into early contact with these peoples.

The Southeastern Indians inhabited a large area, diverse in topography, rich in flora and fauna, varied but generally healthful in climate. Their homelands were bounded on the east by the Atlantic Ocean, on the south by the Gulf of Mexico, on the west by the arid land beyond the Trinity River in what is now southeastern Texas, and on the north by the colder regions of the upper Mississippi and Ohio Valleys. In terms of political divisions of the United States, they lived in Georgia, Florida, South Carolina, western North Carolina, Alabama, Mississippi, Louisiana, southern and eastern Arkansas, Tennessee, a strip of eastern Texas, and those areas of Missouri, Illinois, and Kentucky that border the Mississippi River.

In terms of numbers it is exceedingly difficult to do more than make a conjecture based on incomplete and, on the whole, carelessly collected and reported information. But it is probably safe to assume that at the time of contact with Europeans there were as many as 1 million but fewer than 2 million Indians living in the region.

In addition to being divided into a large number of groups, they spoke a wide variety of languages. Some of these were similar in vocabulary and construction, and their speakers were comprehensible to each other. Others, however, were wholly dissimilar, as different, say, as Russian and German.

Arrayed against these evidences of division and diversity, however, is a whole assortment of beliefs common to all of them—about themselves and their world, about good and evil, about proper conduct, about the relationship of humanity to the supernatural, to the animals of the natural world, and much more. Furthermore, when one tribe was seriously reduced in

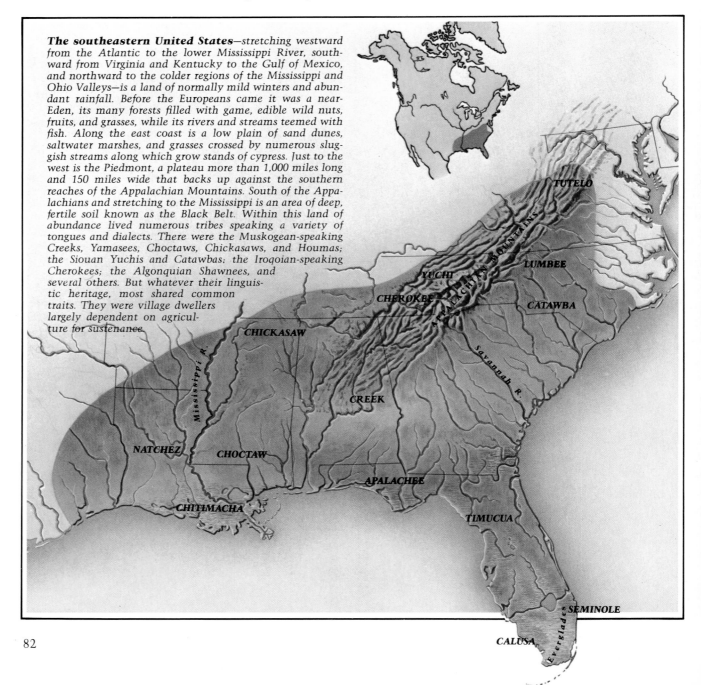

The southeastern United States—stretching westward from the Atlantic to the lower Mississippi River, southward from Virginia and Kentucky to the Gulf of Mexico, and northward to the colder regions of the Mississippi and Ohio Valleys—is a land of normally mild winters and abundant rainfall. Before the Europeans came it was a near-Eden, its many forests filled with game, edible wild nuts, fruits, and grasses, while its rivers and streams teemed with fish. Along the east coast is a low plain of sand dunes, saltwater marshes, and grasses crossed by numerous sluggish streams along which grow stands of cypress. Just to the west is the Piedmont, a plateau more than 1,000 miles long and 150 miles wide that backs up against the southern reaches of the Appalachian Mountains. South of the Appalachians and stretching to the Mississippi is an area of deep, fertile soil known as the Black Belt. Within this land of abundance lived numerous tribes speaking a variety of tongues and dialects. There were the Muskogean-speaking Creeks, Yamasees, Choctaws, Chickasaws, and Houmas; the Siouan Yuchis and Catawbas; the Iroqoian-speaking Cherokees; the Algonquian Shawnees, and several others. But whatever their linguistic heritage, most shared common traits. They were village dwellers largely dependent on agriculture for sustenance.

number by disease or other catastrophe, the survivors could easily move in with another people and quickly coalesce with them. All the Southeastern Indians also had in common a clan system, and everywhere the matrilineal family prevailed, that is, blood relationships were determined by descent from the mother, not the father. In marriage they all followed the practice of exogamy, which forbids a union between a man and woman of the same clan.

The universal symbol of war throughout the Southeast was the military club, and red was the color worn by warriors and associated with battle. Finally, the early Spanish marauders who traveled extensively throughout the whole area found the inhabitants more alike than unlike in social behavior. Hernando de Soto, for example, who ventured north and westward from Florida, did not encounter a different kind of people until he came to the Caddoan-speaking Tulas in western Arkansas.

Three Worlds

The Southeastern Indians believed that the universe in which they lived was made up of three separate, but related, worlds: the Upper World, the Lower World, and This World. In the last lived mankind, most animals, and all plants.

This World, a round island resting on the surface of waters, was suspended from the sky by four cords attached to the island at the four cardinal points of the compass. Lines drawn to connect the opposite points of the compass, from north to south and from east to west, intersected This World into four wedge-shaped segments. Thus a symbolic representation of the human world was a cross within a circle, the cross representing the intersecting lines and the circle the shape of This World.

Each segment of This World was identified by its own color. According to Cherokee doctrine, east was associated with the color red because it was the direction of the sun, the greatest deity of all. Red was also the color of sacred fire, believed to be directly connected with the sun, with blood and, therefore, with life. Finally, red was the color of success. The west was the moon segment; it provided no warmth and was not life-giving as the sun was. So its color was black, which also stood for the region of the souls of the dead and for death itself. North was the direction of cold, and so its color was blue (sometimes purple), and it represented trouble and defeat. South was the direction of warmth; its color, white, was associated with peace and happiness.

The Creeks held a similar conception of the four segments of the world, though they differed somewhat from the Cherokees in the attributes and colors assigned to the directions.

In any case, the Southeastern Indians' universe was one in which opposites were constantly at war with each other, red against black, blue against white. This World hovered somewhere between the perfect order and predictability of the Upper World and the total disorder and instability of the Lower World. Mankind's goal was to find some kind of halfway path, or balance, between those other two worlds.

The Upper World, in addition to order and stability, was characterized by other attributes the Indians valued highly: it had continuity and structure, known boundaries, and perhaps most important, it was pure, unpolluted. The Lower World was the source of pollution and madness, but it was also the fountainhead of fertility and invention; it stood for changeability rather than stability.

In the beginning only those two worlds existed. After This World came into being, many superhumans and animals from the Upper World came to live in it with mankind. But, in time, those from the Upper World found This World more and more uncomfortable, presumably because its order and stability were less than perfect. So they returned to the Upper World, leaving This World to be inhabited by man, by some of his natural enemies, the animals, and his natural friends, the plants.

If some order was to be achieved, it was necessary to classify animals. Three categories were established: (1) four-footed animals, of which the deer was considered the purest representative; (2) birds, whose ability to fly caused them to be associated with the Upper World toward which their wings could transport them; the eagle was a particularly respected bird; (3) in the last group vermin, snakes, lizards, and fish were lumped together as being part of the Lower World. The rattlesnake was the chief representative of this category.

However, certain animals were perceived as belonging to more than one group. Among these were the bat, which has four feet (like the deer) but could fly (like the eagle); the same could be said for the flying squirrel; the frog had four feet but swam like a fish, as did the turtle. Bears could walk on all fours, like ordinary animals, but also on two, like a man. (Indeed, according to one Indian legend, bears were once men, but being too lazy to endure the rigors of human life, allowed themselves to be transformed into animals.) The owl and the cougar were nocturnal and could see in the dark; hence they too did not fit into precisely one category. Some plants and trees also were hard to categorize. The Venus's-flytrap and the pitcher plant "ate" insects. Evergreen trees did not shed their leaves as did "normal" trees. Snakes refused to stay in one category: they swam, they climbed trees and hung in them, they moved along the ground. So all of these, from the bat to the evergreens, could not be fitted neatly into a single category. They overlapped and were therefore difficult to classify. At best, they were considered with awe; at worst, with deathly fear.

Most unclassifiable of (continued on page 88)

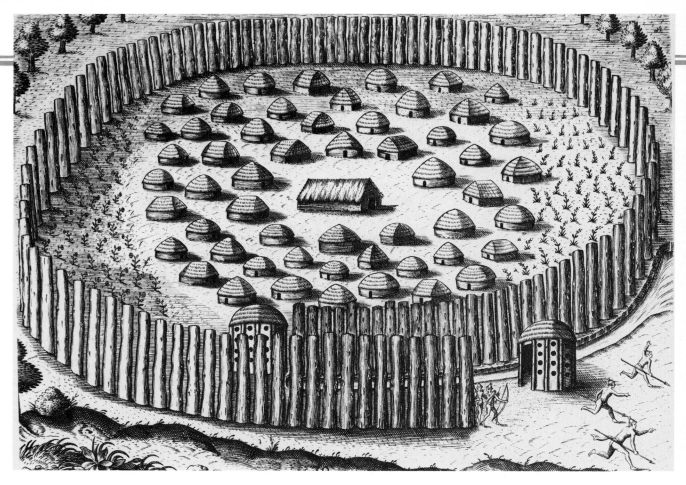

A European View of Life Among the Timucuas

Among the first Europeans to visit the Southeast was a keen-eyed Frenchman named Jacques le Moyne, who arrived in Florida's northern lake region with an expedition of his countrymen in 1564. The French hoped to establish sovereignty over the area, and Le Moyne's charge was to map the coast and "portray the dwelling of the natives and anything else in the land worthy of observation." The Frenchman fulfilled both assignments admirably. He made scores of paintings and drawings depicting the life of the Timucua Indians. These pictures were later converted into engravings by the Flemish artisan Théodore de Bry and published, together with Le Moyne's commentaries, in 1591. A number of Le Moyne's illustrations are shown on these pages, and all quotes are from his commentaries.

At the time of Le Moyne's visit the Timucuas—a confederation of several tribes—controlled large reaches of northern Florida. They were a tall, handsome people who built palisaded villages (above), harvested two crops of corn a year, fished and hunted, and made war both for glory and to protect their traditional hunting grounds. But their pattern of life was soon to perish. A year after Le Moyne's arrival, the Spanish attacked and drove off the French. The Timucuas were soon converted to Christianity, but the diseases carried by the Europeans greatly reduced the Indians' number. In the 17th and 18th centuries English colonists to the north encouraged tribes under their control to launch raids into Spanish Florida, and often the targets were the remnants of the Timucuas. By the time Florida was annexed by the United States in 1819, few traces of the Timucua people remained. Much of what we know of them comes from these engravings.

While on an evening stroll, *the great Timucua chief Saturiwa is accompanied by his wife and three other women. At his side are "two young men . . . carrying fans to make a breeze for him: while a third . . . goes behind and holds up the [chief's] deer's hide, so that it shall not drag on the ground." Le Moyne referred to Saturiwa as king, but actually he was the primary chief, ruler of 30 subchiefs and their villages. A typical Timucua village is shown at top. Everything was arranged for defensive purposes, with the chief's house—the only rectangular structure—surrounded by those of his villagers. The log palisade was about twice the height of a man, and its overlapping entryway was so narrow that no more than two men could pass through it abreast. A gatehouse stands at each end of the entryway, and there guards were posted. According to Le Moyne, the sentinels could detect the approach of enemies by smell.*

A village council meets, and a notable (standing with arms extended) invokes a blessing on the chief (seated at center of semicircle) while Frenchmen look on. As discussions continue, several women are preparing enormous amounts of strong herb tea, some of which a cupbearer carries in a large conch shell. Each councillor will partake of the tea many times during the meeting. The Timucuas, wrote Le Moyne, "esteem this drink so highly, that no one is allowed to drink it in council unless he has proved himself to be a brave warrior. Moreover, this drink has the quality of at once throwing into a sweat whoever drinks it. On this account, those who cannot keep it down, but whose stomachs reject it, are not entrusted with any difficult commission or any military responsibility." By sharing this heady brew the men reinforced tribal bonds, and outsiders earned their hosts' respect by participating in the drinking ceremony. "In military expeditions, the only supplies . . . consist of gourd bottles . . . full of this drink. It strengthens and nourishes the body, and yet does not fly to the head."

A bridal procession bears a chief's wife-to-be to the ceremonial site. "When the king is ready to take a wife," wrote Le Moyne, "he gives orders that from among the daughters of the principal men the tallest and most beautiful shall be chosen. The newly selected queen is brought to him on a litter covered with the skin of some rare animal and fitted with a canopy of boughs to shade her head." As the procession moves forward, its coming is heralded by two trumpeters blowing on horns of bark. Beside the litter walk two men, "each carrying on a staff a round screen, elegantly made to protect the queen from the sun's rays." Behind the litter bearers are "The most beautiful girls that can be found, clad in skirts made of pendant Spanish moss, their necks and arms decorated with necklaces and bracelets of pearls, each carrying a basket of choice fruits. At the end of the procession are the bodyguards."

At the wedding reception the chief and his consort are seated on a high platform, flanked by tribal notables. During these festivities "The queen is congratulated by [the chief] on her accession, and told why he chose her for his . . . wife. She, with a certain modest majesty . . . answers with as good a grace as she can." Then the village maidens dance. They "form a circle without joining hands, and with a costume differing from the usual one, for their hair is tied at the back of the neck, and then left to flow over the shoulders and back; and they wear a broad girdle . . . having in front something like a purse, which hangs down to cover their nudity." While chanting "the praises of the king and queen . . . they all raise and lower their hands together." Much impressed by the elaborate ceremony, Le Moyne commented, "It is wonderful that men so savage should be capable of such tasteful inventions."

Life Among the Timucuas (continued)

Preparing to make war, Chief Saturiwa gathers his warriors around him for propitiatory rites. "Taking a wooden platter of water, he turned toward the sun, and worshipped it.... Then he flung the water ... up into the air; and, as it fell down upon his men, he added, 'As I have done with this water, so I pray that you may do with the blood of your enemies.'" As part of their agreement with Saturiwa, the French had promised him firearms, but the white men refused to deliver them and instead offered to be peacemakers, an offer the chief refused.

Marching off to another war, Outina, who was also a major Timucua chief (front left), leads a large force that includes a number of French soldiers armed with guns called arquebuses. Many of the Indians carry heavy clubs to be used in close combat, and their fingernails are filed to sharp points to facilitate the gouging of the enemies' foreheads in order to blind them with the flow of blood. According to Le Moyne, the French were eager for Outina's friendship because they believed he controlled routes into the mountains that would lead to silver and gold.

Timucua archers, their arrows bearing clumps of flaming moss, stage a raid on a palisaded enemy village. Such raids were often conducted for their nuisance value. The attackers frequently fled after launching their arrows, which set fire to the easily rebuilt palm frond roofs. Some archers wear bark to protect their forearms from bowstrings.

Surrounded by grisly trophies, Timucua warriors and villagers celebrate a victory over a foe. They have brought the severed "legs, arms and scalps which they have taken from the enemy" to the meeting ground and display them on poles. Two of the celebrants shake rattles, a third pounds time on a stone, and a dancing shaman curses the enemy.

Spring planting engages the efforts of several Timucua villagers, the men turning the soil while the women sow. This picture is one of Le Moyne's least accurate depictions. While he correctly reported that the tribesmen used "a kind of hoe made from fish bone fitted with wooden handles," he shows the men with European-style mattocks. The method of sowing is also poorly portrayed. Instead of scattering seeds as shown, one woman made a hole in the soil with a digging stick and a second followed to drop the seeds into the depression. Although the Timucuas harvested two crops of corn, pumpkins, beans, and squash each year, hunting and gathering remained important activities.

Storing up foodstuffs against lean times, Timucuas paddle a dugout canoe filled with edibles to a storage house. "There are in that region," wrote Le Moyne, "a great many islands producing an abundance of various kinds of fruits, which they [the Timucuas] gather twice a year, and carry home in canoes and store up in roomy low granaries built of stone and earth and roofed thickly with palm branches. . . ." From these common stores the Indians were permitted to draw food for their families when their own supplies were exhausted. All villagers were expected to contribute to the granaries, reserving a portion of what they grew and gathered for the common hoard. Therefore, all had equally free access to the supplies when the need arose. Le Moyne was most favorably impressed by this system, and particularly by the fact that no one seemed to demand more than his fair share. "Indeed, it would be good," the Frenchman commented, "if among Christians there was as little greed to torment men's minds and hearts." The typical granary was "usually erected near a mountain or in the shade of a river bank, so as to be sheltered from the direct rays of the sun." Locating a storage house beside a river had the added advantage of making it easily accessible by canoe, the means of transport.

Timucua men smoke meat for winter storage over an open fire. "They set up in the earth four stout forked stakes," wrote Le Moyne, "and on these they lay others, so as to form a sort of grating. On this they lay their game, and then build a fire underneath, so as to harden them in the smoke. In this process they use a great deal of care to have the drying perfectly performed, to prevent the meat from spoiling." Among the game preserved were fish, deer, brown bears, wild cats, turkeys, lizards, and alligators. Although the carcasses for smoking were gutted, the Timucuas left the heads and the scales or skin intact. The Timucuas had dogs as their sole domesticated animals but, unlike some other tribes, apparently did not use the animals for food. Lakes, streams, and the waters of the Gulf of Mexico were important to the Timucuas as a source of both fish and shellfish. The Indians speared turbots, mullets, flounders, and trout from the prows of their dugout canoes, or wove labyrinthlike weirs from reeds that they sank in streams to trap the fish. They dug for clams, caught crayfish and crabs, and took oysters from the many inlets along the coast. Despite this abundance and their care in storing up food against shortages, the Timucuas' needs sometimes outran their supplies, particularly during a winter that lasted far longer than usual.

On an alligator hunt several Timucuas jam a 10-foot pole down the throat of one of the dangerous beasts while a second group of huntsmen (background), having flipped their prey on its back, dispatch it with clubs and arrows. According to Le Moyne, these Indians kept constant watch for alligators, posting men in little huts by the rivers from which the reptiles emerged when they were "driven to the shore by hunger." The alligators gave "themselves away by their loud bellowing, which can be heard at a great distance." Though the Timucuas hunted alligators, they also feared them, and the watchmen were posted as much to warn the populace of the beasts' approach as to alert the hunters. An alligator in search of food "usually crawls along with open mouth, ready to attack." Thus it was relatively simple to render the animal less dangerous with a pole.

all was the monster known as Uktena, the incarnation of evil. It combined attributes of the snake, the deer, and the bird. Depictions on pottery of dancers in Uktena costumes show them with forked tongues, serpent's bodies, and bird's wings. Merely sighting an Uktena was believed to bring serious misfortune; smelling its breath brought death. It could be repelled only by sacred fire.

A Cherokee account of the Uktena, as recorded from an Indian who knew it from oral tradition, goes as follows:

"The Uktena is a great snake, as large around as a tree trunk, with horns on its head, and a bright, blazing crest like a diamond upon its forehead, and scales glittering like sparks of fire. It has rings or spots of color along its whole length. . . . The blazing diamond is called Ulunsuti [transparent], and he who can win it may become the greatest wonder worker of the tribe, but it is worth a man's life to attempt it, for whoever is seen by the Uktena is so dazed by the bright light that he runs toward the snake instead of trying to escape. Even to see the Uktena asleep is death, not to the hunter himself, but to his family.

"Of all the daring warriors who have started out in search of the Ulunsuti only [a great magician or conjuror] ever came back successful. The East Cherokee still keep the one which he brought. It is like a large transparent crystal, nearly the shape of a cartridge bullet, with a blood-red streak running through the center from top to bottom. . . . Twice a year it must have the blood of a deer or some other large animal. . . . No white man must ever see it.

"Whoever owns the Ulunsuti is sure of success in hunting, love, rain-making, and every other business, but its great use is in life prophecy. When it is consulted for this purpose the future is seen mirrored in the clear crystal as a tree is reflected in the quiet stream below, and the conjuror knows whether the sick man will recover, whether the warrior will return from battle, or whether the youth will live to be old."

While the Ulunsuti, the Uktena crystal, was not to be had by any ordinary healer or conjuror, the Southeastern Indians did believe in divining crystals, which were always among the objects carried along by a war party in its collective medicine bundle.

Above their home in This World, the Indians believed, was the vault of the sky, which they envisioned as an inverted rock bowl. Twice each day, at dawn and twilight, the bowl rose and fell to allow the sun and the moon to pass underneath and shine on This World.

The greatest deity, the sun, had a representative on This Earth. This was sacred fire, representing the highest degree of purity. The Cherokees, who believed that the sun was female, thought of sacred fire as an old woman, and they fed it a portion of each meal. To

The Mystery of Key Marco

When, in 1884, archeologist Frank Hamilton Cushing arriv[ed] at Key Marco, an island lying off Florida's western co[ast] about 15 miles south of Naples, he found it one [of] the world's less attractive places. But for Hamilt[on] and posterity, the trip proved well worth t[he] effort, for upon the deserted islet he found t[he] remains of a sophisticated culture that h[ad] exploited the surrounding sea and its bounty [to] the fullest. Here were man-made seawalls a[nd] drainage basins and a plethora of tools ma[de] from shells. There were long timber jett[ies] stretching out into sea, the timbers fa[sh]ioned with saws made from the flat-tooth[ed] lower jaws of kingfish. Most fascinati[ng] of all were the more than 100 exquis[ite] wooden sculptures, the carvings ma[de] with the sharp edges of sharks' tee[th.] No one knows what tribe once inh[ab]ited Key Marco, though it seems li[ke]ly that they were Calusa, re[la]tives of the southern Muskoge[an] people. Today, with the arch[eo]logical exploration of Key Mar[co] far from complete, the islet (n[ow] known as Marco Island) is be[ing] transformed into a resort co[m]plex, which may forever bu[ry] the mystery of its pa[st.]

A wooden ceremonial mask is one o[f a] dozen such objects found on Key Marco. [It] is eight inches high and has holes in [its] sides through which thongs were strung [for] tying the mask on the wearer's hea[d.] Though the paint from these masks h[as] faded, some retain their conch shell ey[es.] When used in rites, feathers were proba[bly] inserted in tops of the masks.

profane a sacred fire by spitting in it or by dousing it with water was to court swift retribution, usually by being afflicted with a disease.

Some Southeastern peoples built their sacred fire in the form of a cross, with the blaze lighted where the two lines crossed. Others built or laid out the fire in the form of a circle or a spiral so that the flames traveled in a circular pattern. In both methods the universal symbols of a cross or a circle were represented.

The sacred fire, usually set in the principal building of each community, was kept going throughout the year. From it all the household cooking and heating fires were ignited. When it was ceremoniously extinguished during the greatest annual event of the Southeastern Indian calendar, it was in a ritual that marked both the culmination of the old year and the inception of the new.

An important tenet of the Indians' belief, in accordance with their goal of achieving balance between the

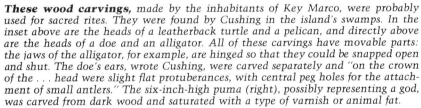

These wood carvings, *made by the inhabitants of Key Marco, were probably used for sacred rites. They were found by Cushing in the island's swamps. In the inset above are the heads of a leatherback turtle and a pelican, and directly above are the heads of a doe and an alligator. All of these carvings have movable parts: the jaws of the alligator, for example, are hinged so that they could be snapped open and shut. The doe's ears, wrote Cushing, were carved separately and "on the crown of the . . . head were slight flat protuberances, with central peg holes for the attachment of small antlers." The six-inch-high puma (right), possibly representing a god, was carved from dark wood and saturated with a type of varnish or animal fat.*

forces of Upper and Lower Worlds, was to use good to counter evil wherever possible. This was the basis for their extensive use of herbs and other plants in treating disease.

A Cherokee tale, recorded by an ethnologist, explains that the need for medicine began because man profoundly offended the animals by killing them for food and by proliferating his own kind to the point where the beasts began to feel crowded. In a series of separate councils the bears, deer, fishes, reptiles, birds, and insects plotted their revenge on man. Among other punishments devised was a great variety of diseases that the animals would visit on their human enemy. Fortunately, he had allies as well as foes.

"When the Plants, who were friendly to Man, heard what had been done by the animals, they determined to defeat the latters' evil designs. Each Tree, Shrub, and Herb, down even to the Grasses and Mosses, *agreed to furnish a cure for some one of the diseases named, and each said: 'I shall appear to help Man when he calls upon me in his need.' Thus came medicine; and the plants, every one of which has its use if we only knew it, furnish the remedy to counteract the evil wrought by the revengeful animals. Even weeds were made for some good purpose, which we must find out for ourselves. When the doctor does not know what medicine to use for a sick man the spirit of the plant tells him."*

The Southeastern Indians did indeed find out for themselves the properties of many drugs found in nature. Among those that we can be certain about were salicylic acid and caffeine, although there are others, such as morphine, reserpine, and digitalis, that the Indians may have used. Both salicylic acid and caffeine are in widespread use in the world today for a number of specific ailments. Salicylic acid is the essential ingredient of the pain-relieving aspirin, probably the medication most utilized throughout the world today. Caffeine, employed as a stimulant, is a colorless, crystalline substance found in coffee, tea, the kola nut and, in much smaller quantities, in cocoa. Along with its effect on the nervous system, caffeine also serves as a diuretic, causing greater production of urine.

These herbal drugs are merely the ones we know the region's Indians used. It is likely that the Southeastern tribes obtained scores of other effective medicines from a wide variety of plants. Some pharmacologists believe that the Indians' knowledge of herbal curatives and palliatives equaled, and perhaps even surpassed in some respects, modern man's expertise with natural drugs.

The legend concerning the development of herbal medicines reveals something basic about the Southeastern Indians and their relationship to their environment. They understood the resources of the world were finite, that man could not wantonly take all he wanted. Even those animals the Indians considered enemies were respected and killed only when the need for food and skins arose.

For the most part the tribes of the Southeast stood somewhere in between those of the West and Midwest and the nation-states of Mesoamerica in their government structure. On the one hand, the chiefs had more power to command obedience than did their counterparts on the plains or prairies; but in practice, the Southeastern chiefs and other notables led by example and persuasion rather than by force. Each chiefdom had a hierarchy in which a man's place was determined by his achievements in war or in such other pursuits as religion or healing. By custom, the words of leaders carried more weight in the councils than did those of ordinary warriors. And the titular head of each village was chosen by the leaders of the community, but this head chief's power was greatly circumscribed by tradition and he served mostly as a ceremonial leader.

There were some exceptions. Among the Natchez (see previous chapter), who had been influenced by

Chunkey yard

Granary and storehouse

Summer and guest house

Square ground

Household garden

Warehouse

Kitchen and winter lodge

the Mississippian culture, the hereditary chief, known as the Great Sun, had nearly absolute power over his subjects. But among most tribes of the region a man who distinguished himself as a warrior almost automatically attained a leadership role within the community council.

The community councils met to discuss issues of all kinds that were of common concern—tilling the fields owned by the community, making repairs on public buildings, or constructing a barricade around the village. Anyone could speak and would be listened to with respect. The aim was to reach agreement on any course of action. If unanimous agreement was impossible to achieve, then those who were opposed, if they saw they were a minority, would thereafter remain silent. No force was used, no one was punished for refusal to go along with the prevailing opinion.

People within a chiefdom were organized by clans named for animals. How clans came into being is set forth in a Creek legend:

An 18th-century Creek village, shown in an artist's reconstruction, reflects the highly organized nature of tribal life. Houses were arranged in clusters, each cluster including airy summer shelters and well-insulated winter lodges. The focal point of the village was the game field (upper left), often used for a rod-throwing contest called chunkey. The 40-foot pole at its center was sometimes topped with an object used as a target for archery and spear-throwing. The two poles at its rear were usually decorated with scalps or skulls, trophies of military triumphs. Next to the field is the square ground, a quadrangle of openwork structures where tribal elders met beneath the shade of the thatched roofs during the warm months. The round town house, 25 feet high at its center, was the winter council house. It also provided shelter for the aged and homeless and was the place where villagers gathered for ceremonies, dances, and socializing.

"When the Creek Indians came to know anything of themselves, it was to find that they had been for a long series of generations completely buried and covered . . . in a dense fog impenetrable to their powers of vision. Being unable to see, they were dependent on their other senses, especially that of touch, in their efforts to obtain subsistence.

"In their quest for food, the people very naturally became separated, straying away from each other in groups, and each group was aware of the existence and locality of its neighbors only by calling to them through the obscuring fog, each adopting the precaution not to stray out of calling distance of some other of the scattered groups.

"After a great while there arose a wind from the east that gradually drove the fog from the land. The group of people who first saw clearly the land and the various objects of nature, now rendered visible by the dissipating fog, were given the name of the Wind clan. It is related that, among the many things they were now able to see, the first animate objects observed by the people of the Wind clan were a skunk and a rabbit which appear to have accompanied them during their existence in the obscuring fog. While the people did not adopt either of these as their [clan symbol], they did declare them their nearest and dearest friends. So well is this understood . . . that it is universally understood to be the duty of the sons of the Wind clansmen always to extend to these animals protection and defense from physical injury and ridicule. . . .

"As the fog continued to recede and disappear before the driving east wind, other groups of people came to light; and, as each looked about, it adopted as the [symbol] of the clan by which it would thereafter be known, the first live animal which had emerged from the fog along with it."

Belonging to a clan was a matter of kinship, of blood ties. The members of a clan were all related to one another matrilineally—that is, they were all descendants from a common ancestress through the female line. (There were exceptions: under some circumstances an unattached person could be adopted into a clan, but this was rare.)

In keeping with the matrilineal nature of clan membership, the son of a married couple was considered the mother's progeny and only casually related to the father. In large measure the paternal role was taken over by the mother's brother, usually the oldest if she had more than one. It was he who taught a boy the communal games, hunting, fishing, the art of war, and other needed skills. The boy's father performed these duties for the male children of his sister.

Clan loyalty dominated the tribesman's life. Certain matters that in most other societies were the concerns of the larger community tended to be settled on the clan level by Southeastern Indians. The all-important matter of revenge was one example. The Southeastern Indians believed unswervingly in the principle of exacting revenge for any offense, from murder to the slightest hurt. If a boy were accidentally scratched in a friendly tussle with a friend, he would take the earliest opportunity to retaliate in kind, and that ended the matter. If someone was murdered, his clan had the duty to avenge the wrongdoing. The murderer was himself killed by a blood relative, that is, by someone related to the victim through the female side. If the murderer could not, for any reason, be executed, a member of his clan would be killed in his place. Sometimes a clansman would volunteer to die in place of the slayer. Even if years of scheming and planning and arduous travel were necessary, a murder was revenged if it were humanly possible to do so. In fact, many of the wars between chiefdoms were really clan wars, undertaken in retaliation.

Launching a War

However, the decision to make war was not taken casually or impetuously. There was a formal procedure of discussion and debate. First the members of the men's council of a chiefdom—made up of notables revered for their wisdom—conferred with the chief and debated the actions to be taken. When they decided that hostilities were unavoidable, the proceedings were turned over to the Great Warrior who, together with veterans of earlier wars, would begin to exhort the young men and whip up their ardor for combat. A war club, painted red, was displayed and a red flag was flown. Among the Natchez the flag was hung from a pole, also painted red, that was about seven feet long and was implanted in the ground in such a way that it leaned in the direction of the enemy whom they intended to attack. There were more speeches by the war leader and his aides. One such address was taken down in the early 19th century by a U.S. government ethnologist:

"My comrades. . . Oh, that I were young enough and strong enough to accompany you to this war and to do against our enemies now as I did against a nation from which I have taken three scalps, against another nation from which I have taken five, and four from such another. And how many blows of the war club have I made against our enemies in order not to be taken? . . .

"So, my comrades, leave with great courage, always have strong hearts, walk on the toes, keep the eyes open, never shut your ears, have no fear of the cold, do not hesitate to throw yourselves into the water in order to escape if it is necessary, and in that case conceal your retreat well. Especially never fear the arrows of the enemy and let it be seen that you are men and true warriors. Finally, if you find the occasion for it, use all your arrows on the enemies and afterward strike, kill, until your war clubs are drunk with the blood of the enemies."

After the speeches the women sang war songs with high-pitched howls that apparently roused those who had volunteered to fight—no one was ordered into combat—and heightened their desire to give a good account of themselves.

When an adequate force had been raised, the volunteers gathered at the dwelling of the war leader. There they spent three days fasting, an ordeal broken only by drinks of herbal potions, including snakeroot, a powerful emetic. Vomiting was thought to purify the body and spirit and make a man fit for combat. During this period the men were forbidden to have contact with women. This rule and others were sternly enforced by veterans among the volunteers. Even a minor infraction, it was thought, could bring great danger to the entire party.

As the volunteers fasted, the older men among them recounted tales from earlier wars, stressing their own heroic roles in battle. All sang and took part in war dances. Among the Natchez, and perhaps other tribes as well, the period of fasting ended with a ceremonial feast. All the warriors ate venison—so that they might attain the swiftness of deer—and dog meat, a dish symbolic of their steadfastness in battle and loyalty to their leader.

Only after these preliminaries were concluded and the warriors had painted themselves red and black were they ready to take to the trail. They did not depart quietly, but left the encampment with war chants and shouts upon their lips. Heading the column was their leader. He carried a medicine bundle containing sacred objects, including horns and bones thought to be relics of the mythical Uktena and Water Cougar, talismans to make the warriors immune to the enemy's spears and arrows. Behind the leader came the warriors—usually from 20 to 40 in number—striding in single file, three or four feet apart. From the moment they took to the trail, each man kept a watchful eye for ill omens—such as an oddly shaped tree trunk or a peculiar looking animal—and if any were spotted, the war party would return to camp at once.

But if no bad omens were encountered and the march continued, the joyful shouts ended and a deathly silence settled over the group as it approached enemy territory. Clad only in breechclouts and moccasins, the warriors moved quietly, stealthily through the woods, one man stepping into the footprints of the man in front so as to leave no evidence in the soil that a party of men had passed by. Such caution became even more intense as they moved deeper and deeper into the foe's domain. If a man so much as broke a twig, he carried it with him until battle was joined, lest an enemy find the bit of wood and have his suspicions aroused.

Typically, a party planning an attack armed itself with a variety of weapons: pikes, lances, darts, slings, clubs, and bows and arrows. The bows were particularly fearsome weapons. They were strung so tightly that

Covered by deerskins (left), bows at the ready, Timucuas approach to within easy range of three bucks, as shown in this engraving based on the paintings of 16th-century Frenchman Jacques le Moyne. "They manage," wrote Le Moyne, "to put on the skins of the largest [deer] . . . so they can see through the eyes as through a mask. Thus accoutered they can approach close . . . without frightening [the deer]." The mask above was worn as a disguise during turkey hunts.

The Ingenious Hunting Tactics of Southeastern Indians

Of all the animals that inhabited the game-rich forests of the Southeast, deer were the most highly prized among the Indians. Not only were the animals a major element in the diet, but their skins were the primary material for clothing. The Indians devised several effective tactics for the hunt. Sometimes they worked individually or in small groups, disguising themselves in whole deerskins so that they might approach to within easy arrow shot of the prey. They were also masters at imitating deer calls to bring an animal closer. In large-scale drives the Indians sometimes set fire to a forest to flush the deer into the open and into a surround. Bears were also hunted, though more for their fat than their flesh, and birds, particularly turkeys, were prime targets. Before the hunt Indians prayed to the spirits of their quarry, a rite to ensure the rebirth of the animals they killed, thus guaranteeing an abundance of game.

Blowgun at his lips, a modern Cherokee demonstrates this ancient hunting device made of hollowed-out cane. A dart, such as the one in his hand, can kill a small animal at 60 feet.

the early Spanish explorers found they could not pull the strings back even to their faces. An Indian warrior, however, was usually able to pull the strings back to his ear and send an arrow zinging through the air over great distances and with deadly accuracy. This prowess came from years of training. A boy was given a bow before the age of four and spent much of his childhood hunting small game, such as lizards and mice, to perfect his aim and strengthen his arms.

Surprise was the primary tactic the Indians employed in warfare. If a band of warriors was discovered before they could attack, they retreated without striking a blow or launching an arrow. Sometimes, however,

chance forced a confrontation. Then the opposing parties would exchange insults and threats of mayhem to come. Despite such verbal abuse, both sides tended to back away from combat, if this could be done with honor. Occasionally, however, there were miscalculations. The insults became so excessive that one war leader or the other suddenly blew his bone whistle, and the battle was joined.

If an attack could be made without prior detection, the war party split into small groups so that they could descend upon the enemy from different directions, surround the foe, and cut off their avenues of retreat. The attackers maintained communication with one another by imitating bird and animal cries, a skill at which most Indians were highly proficient. On signal, the attack began. First, a rain of arrows descended upon the unsuspecting foe; then the howling, screeching warriors appeared brandishing clubs and lances. In a matter of minutes the battle might be over, the victors taking the scalps of the fallen losers or occasionally cutting off an enemy's head to be displayed in the home village as a trophy of war. If a raiding party managed to destroy their foe, killing all, save for captives, the victors would often leave behind some kind of mark that proclaimed the identity of the warriors who had done the deed.

The return trip of a successful war party usually began in silence, but once out of enemy territory the warriors raised a chorus of victory shouts that could be heard in their home village long before the men themselves appeared. Once home, the war party returned to the war leader's dwelling, and because shedding human blood was an act of pollution, the warriors again fasted there for three days. But this time the ordeal was lightened by the songs chanted by admiring women who squatted through the nights outside the men's retreat.

Finally, there was the question of the captives' fates. Among the Southeastern peoples there seemed to be no set rule. A captive might be adopted into a clan and treated as if he had the status of a kinsman. Or he might be made a slave, maimed in some way to prevent his escape, and forced to labor for his captors.

Still another destiny, death by torture, was the common fate for an enemy feared because of his reputation as a great warrior. Among other torments, he would be scalped while still alive, and he was expected to show his bravery in the face of such agony by singing his death song until pain and weakness had rendered him unconscious.

The Indians as Builders

Because of the frequency of raids, many of the larger settlements, especially in the region's northeast section, were enclosed by palisades as high as 16 feet. The walls were made of stout logs set vertically in the ground and faced with smaller logs that were plastered with a mixture of mud and grass. The effect was that of stucco. There were watchtowers at regular intervals along the palisades, and holes in the walls provided defensive positions for archers.

But whether fortified or not, villages were generally laid out around a central plaza. Two public structures stood there. One was fully enclosed and provided quarters for the winter meetings of the council of men. Across the plaza was a small compound of open sheds—usually three or four in number—that served as the summer council houses. Three poles also stood in the plaza: the tallest was for the poleball game, an important communal activity; the other two were war poles where scalps were displayed and prisoners of war tied while their fates were being determined.

All winter buildings, public and private, were constructed in the same manner. Walls were begun with a series of narrow posts set into the ground. Split saplings were interwoven with the posts and then plastered with clay and dried grass. The roof, supported by the walls, rafters, and interior posts, was also made of interwoven split saplings, but it was covered with cypress bark.

The typical winter dwelling provided good protection against the weather. Doors were low and narrow,

Two human scarecrows stand on high platforms overlooking a cornfield. The woman in the foreground bangs a metal bowl while her associate (background) waves a piece of cloth in an effort to frighten away a flight of birds intent of feeding on the ripening crop. Among the Southeastern Indians several methods were used to protect their gardens from loss, particularly to crows and blackbirds. At night the Indians built bonfires around their fields, and sometimes they erected birdhouses for purple martins, which attack blackbirds and crows.

In the Southeast, a favorable climate usually permitted the harvesting of two corn crops each year, and often the Indians planted squash and beans between the cornstalks.

Twilled plaiting— a form of basketwork producing diagonal, zigzag, and circular patterns—was a speciality of Southeastern tribes. The two Choctaw baskets (left and right) and the one by the Chitimachas at center are typical examples. Dried cane, which is either yellow or green, was the raw material for such baskets and provided two of the four colors generally found in them. The two other colors were prepared from vegetable dyes. Black came from black walnuts; red, from a combination of Texas oak bark and black gum.

To achieve the diagonal effect, a split cane weft (horizontal) strand was passed over and under two or more warp (vertical) strands. On the next level the process was repeated, except that the weft advanced, passing under one of the warp strands it had skipped on the level below. This can be seen in the sketch at top, near right. Often receptacles were woven on a true diagonal by orienting the strands on the oblique, as shown at far right above.

and the only ventilation came from a smoke hole in the roof. A fire for cooking and heat was always burning, making each dwelling both smoky and hot. Consequently, the Indians wore little clothing indoors, and dressed lightly outdoors as well, having been trained from childhood to endure both rain and chill.

Furniture within the dwellings was generally limited to platforms used both for sitting and for sleeping. These were made of split white oak saplings and cane, and were covered with mats of cane and skins. They were set on posts that raised them two or three feet off the ground. In the southern reaches of the region, where the winters were mild, the Indians lived in much lighter structures with one or more open sides. Such dwellings, sheltering several different families from a single clan, were also used by more northerly groups during the warm weather months.

Arranging a Marriage

Marriages were arranged by the older women, but the young couples concerned made the ultimate decisions. When a boy was attracted to a girl—who had, of course, to be of a different clan—he did not speak to her directly. Instead, he turned to a maternal aunt for help, and she would approach the girl's maternal aunt to determine if the outlook was favorable and a marriage might be arranged. A series of discussions followed between the female members of both clans. Neither the boy's nor the girl's father was consulted on his views, but as a matter of courtesy the two men were usually kept informed on the progress of negotiations.

If the boy's suit won the approval of both sides, the next step would be to obtain the girl's consent. Her maternal aunt would formally apprise her of the situation, even though the youngster had probably already discovered what was afoot. The girl now signified her acceptance or rejection with a little ceremony. On a prearranged morning she set a bowl of hominy outside her dwelling. The boy then came by and requested permission to eat the gruel. If the girl forbade him to do so, it meant that she did not give her consent to the marriage. This was a means of letting her say no without directly rejecting her suitor, thus sparing his feelings. If, on the other hand, she permitted the young man to eat the hominy, her answer was yes. Now the members of the boy's clan prepared gifts for the bride-to-be, and the two were free to have sexual relations even though they were not yet wed.

Before the couple began living together, the boy was required to prove his manhood, first by building a dwelling for himself and his bride, and then by killing an animal for food—preferably a deer or a bear. He butchered the animal and presented some of the meat to her. She, in turn, gave him an ear of corn or some food that she had cooked, by way of proving her womanly accomplishments. This exchange of gifts was in fact the wedding ceremony, but only for a trial marriage. The couple began living at the house the youth had erected, but either was absolutely free to depart. If they were still together after a ceremony marking the end of the year, the marriage was generally considered a firm union. If not, their ties to each other were automatically dissolved. In either case, the house now belonged to the woman.

Monogamy, though often practiced, was not considered a moral imperative for men. A man could take a second and even a third wife if he so desired and could afford them. But he had to obtain his first wife's consent. A woman taken as a second or third wife had to be courted in the same manner that the first wife had been. Often there was no difficulty at all with the first wife when a man announced he wished to take another, particularly if the intended was the sister of the first wife, as often was the case. The first wife would attain the status of primary spouse, and she would have a helper for domestic and agricultural chores. But if the second wife was unrelated to the first, the new spouse had the right to a dwelling of her own.

In general among the peoples of the Southeast, women were not permitted as much license as men. In many tribes, however, it was customary for an unmarried young girl to have such affairs as she thought desirable. But once wed, a woman was expected to remain faithful, and she was sometimes punished for an act of adultery by having her ears cut off. Her marriage was

usually dissolved under such circumstances. Even so, the offending woman retained ownership of the dwelling in which she lived. And when a woman found herself a widow, she was, in some tribes, expected to observe a four-year period of mourning before remarrying. But this period might be considerably shortened if the woman married a man from the same lineage as her dead husband or if that lineage formally released her from the bonds of widowhood.

Like most North American Indians, those of the Southeast looked upon menstruating women with awe tinged by fear. During her periods a woman could not remain in her own dwelling but was required to live in one of a number of small huts set aside for this purpose. No one was supposed to touch her, and food was left for her in special containers. Nor was she allowed to position herself upwind from any man during this time nor bathe upstream from a male. When her period had passed, she was required to take a ritual bath and then put on clean garments before rejoining the community.

It was also in a menstrual hut that a woman gave birth. Well before that time—in fact as soon as she

Two Timuacas, their bodies elaborately tattooed and dressed in characteristic garbs, were drawn by 16th-century Englishman John White. The woman's dress is made of Spanish moss; during the chill of winter she probably donned a cloak of feathers or skins for additional warmth. She holds symbols of her duties—an ear of corn in one hand and a pottery bowl, probably containing cornmeal, in the other. The women did most of the gardening, prepared the food, and molded clay into vessels. Her body is covered from head to ankles with tattoos, the designs representing her status in the tribe and, by implication, the position of her husband. The warrior is also tattooed to denote his ranking. Tattooing was accomplished by pricking the skin with needles dipped in cinnabar or lampblack. (A warrior who decorated his body with a design to which he was not entitled by rank or accomplishment was forced to remove it—a very painful process.)

The man wears a ceremonial headdress, perhaps fashioned from animal skins, a precursor of the cloth turban later worn by the Seminoles. A metal gorget, another indication of rank, hangs from his neck, and cymbals encircle his upper arms and knees.

learned she was pregnant—she was expected to perform certain rituals to ensure the birth of a healthy child. Among the Cherokees, for example, she and her husband would visit a holy man at frequent intervals. There the woman drank an herbal potion intended to ensure an easy delivery. The drink included slippery elm bark, to make the woman's womb smooth, thus facilitating the baby's passage, and spotted touch-me-not stems, whose purpose was to frighten the fetus and cause it to "jump down" at the appropriate time. Two other ingredients were added to guarantee health and a long life to the child: roots of common speedwell and cones of the prickly pine tree. Certain foods were forbidden to pregnant Cherokee women. Squirrel meat was barred because that animal, when startled, goes up a tree, and the baby, under the influence of squirrel, might go up rather than down. Speckled trout was also banned because the fish was thought to produce birthmarks. No salt could be used because it makes meat swell and the fetus might grow too large to descend through the birth canal. Finally, rabbit meat was forbidden, for rabbits were thought to have abnormally large eyes. An expectant mother was also advised not to linger in doorways, lest the baby, following her example in dilatoriness, take his time in jumping down. The expectant mother was further warned against wearing neckerchiefs, lest the umbilical cord be wrapped around the child's neck.

When labor began, the mother was attended by one or more midwives. The newborn child was taken at once to a creek or river, where the baby was dipped in the stream or sprinkled with water. In winter the infant was rolled in the snow. Then he was rubbed all over with bear's grease and bound tightly to a cradleboard where he would spend the first year of life. Among most Southeastern Indians, the baby's forehead as well as his body was tied to the board. This was done in order to flatten the back of his skull. Some Indians believed this enhanced the child's appearance; others thought it improved his eyesight.

A child's training for his or her role in life began early. Under the tutelage of her mother or maternal aunts, a girl lent a hand in housework, gardening, pottery-making, basketry, and fire-tending. And, as maternal uncles looked on, a boy began honing his skills as hunter and warrior, for until a boy earned a war title, he remained a child in status, fit only for menial tasks. But once he had participated in battle and demonstrated his courage by killing, or at least harming, an enemy, he was accepted as a man among men and could take his place with the council. Symbolic of that new status was a new name—often that of an animal, such as Alligator or Bear, whose characteristics the youngster was thought to have. In addition, he was granted a war title that recalled his martial feats, such as One Who Killed an Enemy.

Among the Chickasaws, the day on which names

This eagle-feather cloak was made by Cherokee craftsmen in 1950, but it reproduces a style that dates back to precontact times. So elegant a garment probably would have been donned by a village headman for important ceremonial occasions rather than worn for everyday use.

and titles were awarded was considered a most important ceremonial occasion. The honored warriors wore red moccasins and white feather collars, anointed their bodies with bear's oil, and painted their faces various colors. Among the Natchez, the honored young warriors were borne on litters to the ceremonial site, the procession being led by two music makers: a drummer and a man shaking a rattle. Other warriors danced about and shouted war cries. At the ceremony itself, the novices dipped their hands into a specially brewed war medicine that they then smeared on their faces.

The next day the new warriors spent half an hour in a sweathouse, then plunged into a river. A celebratory feast was served, followed by dancing. For three days the ceremonies continued, during which time the young warriors were denied sleep. Finally, they climbed onto their litters once more and were borne back to their own dwellings. These ordeals were to demonstrate that the warriors were prepared to endure heat and cold and undergo sleepless nights when called upon for duty.

Warlike Games

War was such an obsession among Southeastern Indians that even some of their games mimicked the rigors of combat and, in some instances, were nearly as bloody as battle itself. Among the most popular of these pastimes was the stickball game the Southeastern tribesmen aptly called the little brother of war. It was a team contest that, in modified form, we know as lacrosse. This game, which had variants throughout North America, was played in a particularly savage fashion in the Southeast. Each participant had two sticks, each between two and a half and three feet in length, with one end bent to make a loop. A shallow pocket of animal skin was attached to the loop. The ball was animal hair encased in skin. The number of players to a side varied from region to region, but the object was always to hurl the ball between goalposts set up at either end of a field. The action was pure mayhem, as the players swung their sticks wildly, ran, pushed, and shoved to gain possession of the ball as it flew through the air. Players might be bashed on the head with the sticks or trampled underfoot if they stumbled and fell. Permanent maiming or even death was not an uncommon result of playing this version of lacrosse.

Not all games, however, were so savage. A milder ball game, played by both men and women around a post in the village plaza, was engaged in purely for the fun of it. The object was to hit the pole with a ball. The men were handicapped by being allowed to handle the ball only with sticks—much like those used in the little brother of war—while the women could use their hands. After the game there would be a feast, followed by dancing.

Among the many dances performed by both men and women was one called the friendship dance. It began with two men providing music with a drum and a gourd rattle. Then two other men would dance around the fire, side by side, a slow shuffle. After a single circle they picked two women to join them, and there was another shuffle about the fire. Then the two women picked two more men, and so on until the entire village was dancing except for the musicians who continued to beat out the rhythm. Finally, the song changed and two circles were formed, one of men, the other of women. These moved around the fire four times, the women dancing in one direction, the men in the other.

Other dances imitated animals. In the bear dance, the Indians moved awkwardly and pawed the air; in the mosquito dance, the women pricked the men with thorns as the latter circled the fire.

Although both men and women danced and played the poleball game together, there was a clear distinction by sex in most activities, and especially in work. It was the men's responsibility to provide meat and clear the fields for farming, the women's to plant, tend the gardens, and reap the harvest. In new fields the men killed the trees by girdling them and then letting them rot. In fields previously used they hoed up the weeds that had grown since the last harvest, dried them in the sun, and burned them. Corn was planted in rows of little mounds. When the corn sprouted, beans were planted on the same mounds and the two crops grew together, the cornstalks providing support for the climbing bean

The Southeastern Indians' Lacrosse: The Ultimate Contact Sport

Of the several games played by the Choctaw and other Southeastern tribes, none roused their enthusiasm more than *ist boli* (sometimes called *tolik*), a contest we know today, highly modified form, as lacrosse. Major games, played tween residents of villages of neighboring tribes, genera great excitement through a wide area, and often more tha thousand spectators would show up at the scene of the tion. Careful preparation for the game was necessary. A s ably level field, about 230 feet long, had to be selected a cleared, and 20-foot-high goalposts of branches erected each end. Formal invitations had to be sent out to the oppo tion. These took the form of painted and beribboned stic carried by messengers. By touching one of the sticks, a pla signified his acceptance of the challenge. During the two three days preceding the game, spectators arrived at the pl ing field, each loaded down with possessions—furs, skins, a trinkets—to wager on the game's outcome. Pregame cerem nies reached a climax on the night before the contest. Me bers of each team—75 to 100 men—painted their bodi drank sacred medicine, danced, and sang. Medicine m from opposing sides vied with each other in pronounc incantations, each believing that his magic would strength his own team and weaken the other.

The next morning, according to one white witness, t rival squads approached each other from opposite directio "making the heretofore silent forest ring with their defia shouts of 'hump-he!' as intimations of the great feats strength and endurance, fleetness, and activity they wo display before . . . their admiring friends." An old man thr the skin-covered ball into play, and the game was on, hours-long, bloody struggle, a game that was, in fact, m like war than sport.

The Ball Play Dance (left), here depicted by 19th-century artist George Catlin, was one of the colorful pregame activities. Two columns of women—squatting medicine men between them—are shuffling and chanting while stick-wielding players dance around the goalposts. The women, wrote Catlin, asked for the aid of the Great Spirit "in deciding the game to their advantage." This dance was repeated a dozen times during the night before the contest and was believed to whip the players into a combative frenzy. In the right foreground of the painting is a large pile of goods that has been bet.

ailing furiously with their webbed sticks, like ose at right, scores upon scores of players seek control the ball that they try to fling at the opposition's goalpost. Each yer was permitted to carry two of the sticks, as the Catlin ntings at left and above show. In gaining and maintaining control the ball just about any violence—stomping, tackling, hitting, kicking, mpling—was permitted. During the course of this mayhem many of the players e hurt, some seriously. Deep gashes, broken bones, torn ligaments, and even death were considered part of the play. "In these desperate struggles for the ball," wrote Catlin, ". . . hundreds e running together and leaping, actually over each other's heads . . . tripping and throwing, and foiling ch other in every possible manner. . . ." When a point was scored, the successful players mocked and raged their opponents with insults. Gobbling like turkeys was one way of taunting. The game ended en a team scored a predetermined number of points, often 12.

The Many Uses of the Miraculous Tobacco Plant

Of all the plants in nature's domain, none held more significance to the Indians of the Southeast than tobacco. When used in accordance with time-honored tradition, tobacco was thought to have awesome supernatural powers to heal or to hurt, to bring good fortune or ill, to supress hunger, induce hallucinations, ward off evil spirits, bring forth beneficent ones, and ensure long-lasting affection between a husband and wife.

In most instances tobacco was grown in small clearings in the woods. The soil was ritually prepared by burning over the brush with a fire made from branches that had been struck by lightning. The young shoots were, of course, carefully tended, and the leaves were picked when ripe. But at that point the tobacco was not deemed to have any particular power. That came only when the leaves were infused with the force of the supernatural through rigidly prescribed rituals, a process known as remaking. If, for example, a particular bundle of tobacco leaves was to be employed to call forth evil spirits, thus bringing harm to one's enemies, a medicine man would hold the leaves up to the rising sun and murmur the appropriate incantation. While doing this, he would knead the leaves into a wad, with the tobacco rolled in a counterclockwise direction. Finally, he might spit into the sticky mass. A similar ceremony took place when the tobacco was to be used to conjure up the forces of good. This time, however, the medicine man took the leaves to the edge of a stream at dusk or midnight and then rolled the tobacco clockwise.

According to anthropologist Charles Hudson, remade tobacco might be used as follows: "It could be smoked near the person who was the target of the conjury, so that the smoke would actually touch him; it could be blown in the direction in which he was likely to be located; it could be smoked so that [it] would pervade and affect everyone in a general area; and bits of tobacco leaf could be left where the person to be affected would come in contact with them."

There were other ways, as well, to employ this miraculous plant. A Cherokee who wished to rekindle or ensure his wife's love approached her when she was asleep and rubbed a

A pipe-smoking Timucua is offered tobacco leaves by a female healer in this Le Moyne drawing. The smoker, according to Le Moyne, was perhaps suffering from "humors." Tobacco was often used to induce vomiting, thus purifying the body.

mixture of tobacco and saliva over her body while he pronounced the necessary incantation. And as a healer of bodily ills, tobacco was thought to be of particular merit. Among the Creeks, a man afflicted with "the dog disease" (stomach cramps) called on a medicine man, who rubbed the patient's body with a mixture of water and tobacco, a concoction that the afflicted person also drank. Another Indian nostrum included a mixture of red sumac, which had been boiled in water, and tobacco. "This preparation," wrote one early observer of Southeastern life, ". . . the Indians constantly smoke and consider a sovereign Remedy in all cephalic [head] and pectoral [chest] complaints."

In the Southeast tobacco was also used to achieve an altered state of consciousness, and like Indians in much of North America, the peoples of the region smoked the plant during discussions in tribal or village councils and offered it to guests as a gesture of hospitality.

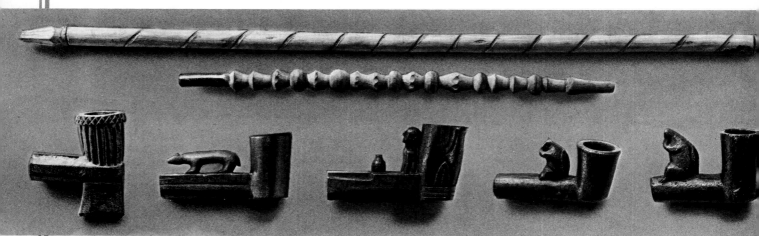

Beautifully designed stone pipes, normally decorated with human or animal figures, are evidence of the craftsmanship of Cherokee artisans. Although the pipes were sometimes made of pottery, stone, ground to a smooth finish, was the usual material. When the bowls were attached to softwood stems (top), most pipes measured about two feet in length. Made with painstaking care, a single pipe often took several weeks—sometimes even months—to complete.

vines. Squash, pumpkins, gourds, and sunflowers were also grown.

But corn was the principal crop, and the women planted two varieties: a fast-maturing strain that ripened in two months and was eaten during the summer; and a slower-growing variety that yielded larger ears but did not ripen until fall, when it was harvested and dried for winter storage. The dried corn was made into a gruel or into a bread dough that was baked on a stone in the fire, wrapped in cornhusks and boiled, or fried in bear's grease to make a kind of flat cake.

Though the women spent much of their time tending the crops and preparing meals, they were also responsible for making pottery, weaving baskets and mats, tanning animal skins, and making skirts for themselves and breechclouts, leggings, and cloaks for their men.

Among the Southeastern Indians, the year's most sacred holiday was the Busk, which coincided with the ripening of the fall corn and marked the end of the old year, the beginning of the new. Details of the celebration varied from group to group. Typically, however, on the first day of the Busk the men and women were separated. The women thoroughly cleaned and neatened their wigwams in honor of the occasion. The men swept the council house, replastered its walls, and laid fresh mats on the platforms. Then the sacred fires in the council house and the cooking fires in the wigwams were extinguished.

The second day of the Busk was marked by a fast. A day of feasting followed. The most important day was the fourth. At dawn the men went to a river to bathe, and then a shaman prepared to relight the sacred fire in the council house. He added four ears of new corn to the fire logs before kindling them with a flame sparked by a ceremonial fire drill. He fanned the flame to a blaze with the wing feathers of a white swan.

And thus the new year officially began. As part of the ceremonial all crimes, except murder, were formally forgiven. Then coals from the sacred fire were distributed to the women, who used them to relight their

Booger masks *were used by Cherokees to ward off the Europeans' evil influence and diseases. The mask above represents the black slave of a white man. While wearing such effigies during the Booger Dance, the Cherokees acted out the sad history of the postcontact period. In this way they sought protection of the spirits against continued white depredations. Not all masks in the dance represented foreigners. Animal effigies, such as the buffalo mask below, symbolized the Indians as hunters.*

own wigwam fires. The fast was then broken with one feast for the men and another for the women and children. Finally, the women and children were summoned to a gathering of the men in the plaza to listen as the village chief admonished every one to abide by the ancient traditions and beliefs. Busk ended as all took a ceremonial bath in a river.

Arrival of the Spaniards

For the Southeastern Indian the death knell for their way of life sounded on that day in 1513 when the Spanish explorer Juan Ponce de León made landfall off Florida. He was but the first of many European explorers, conquerors and, finally, colonists to arrive. Though the goals of the different European groups who penetrated the Southeast varied, the ultimate effect on the Indians was the same: catastrophe. The Spaniards pillaged, burned, killed, and enslaved as they marched inland from the Florida coast, but far worse than their direct actions were the ailments they brought with them from Europe: smallpox, measles, typhus, tuberculosis, chicken pox, influenza, and cholera. These diseases would kill the Indians by the thousands, wiping out whole villages, decimating whole tribes.

Even so, the Southeastern Indian culture might have survived had not the natives become enmeshed, first in the colonization of the area by Spain, France, and Britain, then in the struggle for colonial empire known as the French and Indian War, and finally in the rapacity of citizens of the new United States for virgin soil on which to plant their crops.

The Spanish conquistadors initiated this process of tribal disintegration. The most famous of these first invaders was Hernando de Soto, who came to Florida in 1539 with a royal commission ordering him to "conquer, pacify and people" the land. By the time he died in the field in 1542, he had achieved none of these goals. A veteran of conquests elsewhere in Latin America, he was interested only in locating and seizing loot, preferably gold, for which all Spanish explorers lusted. His expedition made a long, circular *(continued on page 104)*

A Time of Renewal: The Green Corn Rite

Among the many rituals of the Southeastern Indians that marked the passage of the months and seasons, the most important was the Green Corn Ceremony, celebrated near summer's end to coincide with the ripening of the late corn crop. Also called the Busk, the multiday ritual innaugurated a new year and was the occasion for giving thanks for a successful harvest.

Only a relative handful of men and women from each village were permitted to take part in the central ceremonies associated with the Busk. These participants included village chiefs and medicine men, male and female elders of recognized merit, and some young warriors who had particularly distinguished themselves.

With the beginning of the Busk, all village women scoured their houses and cooking utensils and put out their hearth fires. The men repaired communal buildings. All male-female contact was forbidden nor could anyone partake of the newly ripened corn. With the completion of domestic and village chores, participants gathered at the square used for such rituals, as seen at right. There they fasted for more than a day to purify themselves. After the fasting there was a meal, and then it was time for the most important ceremony, the lighting of the sacred fire, followed by a dance around its flames. With suitable ceremony and incantations, the high priest lighted the fire. Then the dance began. In the Creek version shown, six old women and six elderly male priests circle the flames to the beat of a drum. All carry branches of various trees, and the women wear conch shell rattles on their legs. Dancers and spectators alike are dressed in white, the color of the Busk. The spectators watch from three open-sided shelters, the highest-ranking men surrounding the village chief (center), who wears a duckskin headdress surmounted by a blaze of white feathers. The tribal elders sit in their own shelter (lower left), and opposite them are the honored warriors, whose faces and torsos are painted red. With the completion of the Green Corn Dance, other villagers joined the rites. Coals from the ceremonial fire were used to relight the hearth fires, and upon these the village women now cooked a great feast. Finally, everyone in the village took a communal bath in a nearby stream, once more to purify themselves for the new year.

journey north and westward into the interior. Frequently, De Soto was met with friendship. The Indians brought gifts to the intruders, often in the form of food that the Spaniards badly needed. On one occasion De Soto's party was greeted by a woman who presented the explorer with a strand of pearls she had worn about her neck. In return for such gifts the Spaniards enslaved their hosts, forcing them to become bearers, and plundered their villages. Soon all hopes of peaceful relations vanished. But there was no unity among the natives. The interlopers proved adept at setting one tribe against another and sponsoring a series of local wars that further reduced the Indians' ability to resist. Yet even with this division and the Spaniards' advantage of having horses, the Southeastern Indians exacted a heavy toll from the Spaniards in dead and wounded.

De Soto made no permanent settlements, but the Spaniards who came after him did. So did the French and British. By the beginning of the 18th century Spain was firmly in control of Florida. To the north from their base in Charleston, South Carolina, the British were rapidly expanding colonization along the Atlantic Coast. In the west the French were establishing outposts along the lower Mississippi. The aim of all three colonial powers was to gain control of the entire Southeastern region, but they went about it in different ways.

The Spaniards, for example, brought with them the cross as well as the sword. They established missions to convert the Indians to Christianity, schools to educate their children, and an agricultural system that required Indian labor. However, the Southeastern Indians were disinclined to work in the fields for the whites. Often troops stationed near missions had to be brought in to enforce discipline, and frequently mission Indians rebelled and killed the monks who manned the religious

outposts. But St. Augustine, founded in 1565, survived as a Spanish town as did numerous missions established by the Franciscan order.

The British characteristically relied on trade to gain control of their region. They bought deerskins as well as Indian slaves by exchanging tools and cloth with the natives, later adding rum and firearms to this bartering mix. The British traders penetrated deep into Indian territory, often taking up more or less permanent living quarters in native communities. Many of the British traders were renegades and outlaws, and nearly all of them were unscrupulous. They gained an economic stronghold on the Indians by offering goods on credit against the deerskins they would bring in during the coming winter hunt. Many of the natives soon found themselves burdened by towering debts in an economic system that was totally foreign to them.

The French by and large followed the British pattern, but they were limited in their capability to do so by a shortage of manpower. Unlike the British, who either went to the colonies freely or were sent there as indentured servants or as convicts banished from their native land, Frenchmen resisted emigration. Louisiana—as the French named the vast Mississippi Valley that had been explored by Joliet, Marquette, and La Salle—had a serious shortage of settlers. The French traded with the Indians to the extent that they could manage, however, bartering manufactured items for skins and human beings.

The result was that many Southeastern Indian communities found themselves hunting deer only for their pelts and raiding neighboring communities only to procure slaves to sell to Europeans for axes, knives, kettles, blankets, cloth, rum, and molasses.

Once a native raiding party had taken captives, the

Sequoyah (c. 1773–1843), shown at left with his syllabary of the Cherokee tongue, was the only man in history known to have single-handedly created a written language. The son of a Cherokee mother and an English father, Sequoyah believed that literacy was the source of the white man's power. Although he had no formal education, Sequoyah succeeded, by the early 19th century, in devising 86 symbols for the syllables of his tribal language. By the 1820's hundreds of Cherokees had learned the syllabary. In 1824 portions of the Bible appeared in the Cherokee language, and four years later the Cherokee Phoenix, a bilingual newspaper (above), was published. By then literacy had become a part of tribal life, as the amusing carved stone pipe at right shows.

Along the Trail of Tears *a column of dispirited Cherokees, guarded by bluecoated U.S. soldiers, moves westward in the 1830's. Forced from their mountain homes by the federal government, the Cherokee, like other major tribes in the Southeast, were forced to migrate to a sparsely populated region in the Indian Territory (now Oklahoma). For years the Cherokees fought this policy of Indian removal through the federal courts, but in the end the judiciary refused to recognize the Indians' rights to their ancestral lands. Though there was much suffering along the trail west, survivors managed to build a good life in their new homes.*

prisoners were sold to slave traders who took them to Charleston where they were sold again, either to local colonists or to merchants representing New Englanders or West Indian planters. Most Indian slaves wound up far from home because local planters discovered that the captives could easily escape into the backwoods where they would find shelter among their own people.

For the English the slave trade in Indians served several purposes. Not only did it provide field hands for farms and plantations near and far, but it helped clear whole regions of indigenous populations, thus making room for colonists. In addition, the intertribal wars engendered by the slave trade served the political interests of Britain. Southeastern tribes with strong trading ties with the British regularly swooped down on Indians living under Spanish sovereignty in Florida. By 1710 the whole northern half of the Florida peninsula was virtually deserted, save for a few communities of refugees huddled around the Spanish fort at St. Augustine. Into this empty land, over the years that followed, came numerous bands of Creeks whose own relations with the British had turned sour. They were joined by refugees from other tribes, by runaway slaves—both blacks and Indians—and still more bands of Creeks. Eventually, this mixture of peoples coalesced into a new Southeastern grouping known as the Seminole, from *semanoli,* derived from the Spanish word for "wild," or "runaway."

From time to time, when the exactions of the European traders became too great, the tribes would rise up in rebellion. Whites would be slaughtered, and those who escaped the Indians' wrath would flee to some safe haven. The whites would then send punitive expeditions against the Indians, and eventually new peace treaties would be signed. These sometimes "guaranteed" the Indians' rights to certain lands, but such pacts generally remained in force only as long as those territories were unwanted by the Europeans. Then settlers moved in, and the whole dolorous round of war-

fare and slaughter and reprisals would commence again.

After the French and Indian War ended French power on the North American continent, the British government, in 1763, declared white settlement beyond the ridge of the Appalachian Mountains to be illegal. Yet from the very first the colonists ignored this line, and whites continued to filter into the western reaches of Georgia and the Carolinas. And, by the end of the century, the hapless Indians had a new force with which to deal, the now independent United States of America. There was a new technology as well, generated by a machine called the cotton gin.

Until the end of the 18th century cotton had been a relatively minor crop along the Southeast Coast. Though the land and the climate were suitable for cultivation of the short staple variety, the problem of extracting the seeds from the blossom was so great that few planters cared to expend their slave labor on so expensive a project. All this changed when Eli Whitney invented his famous gin, which extracted the seeds through a simple mechanical process. Suddenly American cotton was in great demand, and the planters devoted an ever-increasing portion of their acreage to its cultivation. Unfortunately, the overplanting of cotton devastated the soil, and after several crops the land was worn out. Virgin soil was needed, and the planters began to look west. To obtain new lands, the Indians had to be displaced, and the pressure on them to sign away vast stretches of tribal domains, in exchange for cancellation of debts to white traders, grew ever more intense.

After the American Revolution the newly established states of Georgia, South Carolina, Alabama, and Mississippi took the lead in forcing the Southeastern Indians into exile. By then the white populations of these states already greatly outnumbered the Indians, who now were living in relatively small enclaves. Yet even these domains were to be denied the Indians. The state governments, under pressure from their citizens, demanded the removal of *(continued on page 108)*

A traditional shirt for an elderly Seminole man (above) is knee-length and appliquéd. Young men wore even longer shirts, which they hitched up when wading. Today Seminole men often wear black trousers and much shorter shirts.

A Seminole village (above), in the swar near Fort Lauderdale, Florida, consists o, grouping of open-sided, thatched-roofed dw ings called chickees, which are well adaptea the hot, wet climate. The chickee, usually ab 9 feet wide by 16 feet long, is constructed palmetto trees, the wood forming the pole fra and floor, the palm branches used for the re As can be seen in the picture at left, the floor platform raised a few feet off the ground to p tect the family within from the soggy earth c ated by torrential rains that drench the swam Beneath the roof there is an atticlike space storage, and poles pounded into the ground c side the chickee serve as convenient places which to hang household utensils.

Generally, a chickee is a single-family dw ing, but families themselves are often not v stable. Marriage is sometimes a rather casual lationship among the Seminoles of Florida, a divorce is traditionally a simple process: the h band merely leaves the chickee. Children are pected to help with chores at a very early a Even a four year old helps stir the soup, kne dough, and collects wood for the family fire.

Osceola (above), Georgia-born leader of the Seminoles in their struggle to remain in the Florida homeland, was being held by the federal government when George Catlin made this portrait shortly before the warrior's death in 1838. After the United States ordered the Seminoles to the west in 1832, Osceola quickly assumed leadership of Indian rebels who refused to comply. In an 1835 parlay with federal officials he made his stand clear by slashing the proposed removal treaty with a knife. His action triggered a general uprising that lasted until 1842. For the first two years of this guerrilla war, Osceola led some 5,000 warriors on raids from their redoubts in the Everglades. But in 1837 the chief fell victim to trickery. He had been assured a safe-conduct by the government for purposes of negotiations but was seized when he appeared. When Catlin portrayed him at Fort Moultrie, South Carolina, the artist wrote that Osceola was "ready to die . . . cursing the white man . . . to the end of his breath."

The Seminole: The Tribe That Defied the U.S. Government

Their ancestors were mostly Creeks, with scatterings from other Southeastern tribes. But in the 18th century they fled from British-dominated Georgia and Alabama and settled in Spanish-controlled Florida. There they came to be known as the Seminoles, more a loose grouping of peoples sharing a common culture than an actual tribe. For a time the Seminoles found peace and a degree of well-being under easygoing Spanish rule. But in 1817 U.S. Gen. Andrew Jackson led an expedition into northern Florida. His mission was obstensibly to round up runaway slaves who had found refuge among the Seminoles, but in the course of this action his troops engaged in an orgy of burning, looting, and slaughter. This was a mere portent of things to come. Two years later the United States purchased Florida from Spain, and the territory became a hunting ground for armed posses of slave-catchers who made little distinction between runaway blacks and their Seminole hosts. To escape these raids, the Seminoles fled to the edges of the Florida swamps, only to find scant sanctuary there.

In 1829 Jackson became president of the United States and soon moved to deport all Indians east of the Mississippi to the Plains. Unwilling to join their brother tribes on the long trek west, most of the Seminoles moved deeper into swamps, and from 1835 to 1842 they engaged in a bloody guerrilla war against U.S. troops sent to round them up. Only after 1,580 American soldiers and countless Indians had died was most of the tribe subdued and sent on the long, dolorous journey to the Indian Territory far to the west. Yet even then a remnant of the tribe remained in the vastnesses of Florida's Everglades to foray out against federal troops dispatched to imprison them. Eventually, the government wearied of the effort and withdrew its troops, leaving the Seminoles who remained in the Everglades at peace.

Today approximately 1,350 Seminoles remain in Florida on or around four reservations within the Everglades. Until recently, they lived in virtual isolation from the surrounding world, hunting and farming in much the way their ancestors had. Though far less isolated today, the Seminoles prize the distinct identity that they have fought to retain.

Representatives of 16 tribes and U.S. government officials meet at Tahlequah in the Indian Territory in 1843, shortly after the removal of the Five Civilized Tribes from their homelands in the Southeast to their new reserves in the trans-Mississippi region. The purpose of the conclave was to establish laws for the territory and create amicable relations among the many tribes that now lived there. Among those attending was John Ross, the Cherokee leader who had led the court fight against removal.

the tribesmen to regions far to the west. One rationale for their demands was that the tribes were uncivilized and therefore unworthy of maintaining their hold on land desired by white Christian farmers. Ironically, the Indians had, by then, adopted "civilization" and all its works. The remaining major tribes of the Southeast—the Choctaw, Chickasaw, Seminole, Creek, and Cherokee—were known as the Five Civilized Tribes, and many of the natives had adopted both European agricultural methods and Christianity.

Many Americans, apprised of this assimilation by publicists from the tribes themselves and by missionaries who had long lived among them, championed the cause of the Five Civilized Tribes. But the real power to dispose of the Indians' lands remained with the state governments, and they were adamant for removal. These governments, in the early 19th century, passed laws that "legalized" the eradication of the Indian communities and opened their lands to settlers. Such legislation even denied the Indians any right of appeal by depriving them of standing in court.

It was this denial of the Indians' most fundamental rights that led to a celebrated confrontation between two branches of the federal government in the persons of the venerable chief justice of the United States, John Marshall, and the president, Andrew Jackson. A Georgia law depriving the Indians of their rights was argued up to the Supreme Court, where it was ruled unconsti-

tutional. Jackson, who was determined to rid the eastern part of the nation of its Indian population, was reputed to have said of the decision: "John Marshall has rendered his decision; now let him enforce it."

Without the power of the federal executive behind him, Marshall's decision in favor of Indian rights was, in effect, null and void. And in 1830 Jackson signed into law a bill requiring all Indians living east of the Mississippi to leave their homes and be relocated far to the west in what was called Indian Territory. Now the federal government moved swiftly and brutally to enforce the new legislation. The first to feel the impact were the Choctaws of Mississippi. Bribed by agents of the government, a minority of Choctaw leaders in 1830 signed the Treaty of Dancing Rabbit Creek. All of the Choctaw land in Mississippi was ceded in exchange for territories in Arkansas and Oklahoma.

For the vast majority of Choctaws—about 20,000 of them—the situation was bleak. The land on which their homes stood was no longer legally theirs. The state government was foursquare against them and would do nothing to protect them from marauding whites. Yet the Indians knew that the journey west would be long and hard. If they or their relatives survived its rigors, they would arrive at their destination with nothing—no houses, no plows, no mules, no food. Would the federal government that had shown itself to be worse than indifferent to their fate now keep its promise to help them start a new life in a new land?

Whatever they thought of their prospects, most Choctaws realized that they had no choice but to go and hope for the best. In successive marches from 1830 to 1833, thousands of Choctaws set out on foot, under the watchful eyes of soldiers. To avoid the hot weather, they left in autumn, usually in October, but did not arrive at their destination until February or March. These long, cold marches, difficult at best, were made worse by shortages of wagons, horses, blankets, and food. Along the way the Indians were preyed upon by horse thieves, whose rapacity was matched by roadside merchants who charged extortionate prices for vital supplies. Woefully inadequate funds were quickly exhausted, and along the way people began to die. By the time Oklahoma was reached, more than a quarter of the migrants had succumbed to hunger, disease, or exhaustion.

The journey was equally horrible for the other Southeastern tribes when their turn came. Between 1834 and 1838 most of the Creeks, Cherokees, and Chickasaws suffered removal, as did many of the Seminoles. Still, many of those who survived the long trek west would eventually prosper. Although the tribes in their new Oklahoma territories never recovered the vitality of the old days, they did reassert their former way of life, albeit in somewhat diminshed form. They established farms, built schools and churches, revived their political institutions, and the Cherokees resumed publication of their newspaper.

Nor were the old Indian ways completely gone from the ancient homelands in the Southeast. Thousands of Choctaws, for example, managed to evade federal authorities and escape removal by scattering in small bands throughout the backwoods of Mississippi and Louisiana, there to live for decades on the periphery of non-Indian society. But to a greater degree than their brothers in Oklahoma, the eastern Choctaws kept their language, medicines, ball games, and old beliefs. Early in the 20th century the federal government finally abandoned efforts to expel those who remained. The Bureau of Indian Affairs established an agency among them in central Mississippi and purchased land there for a reservation.

The story of the eastern Seminoles is rather different. Though many were forced to go west, others forged themselves into a guerrilla army and waged bloody warfare against federal troops to retain their foothold in the East. One war lasted for seven years, from 1835 to 1842; a second war, in the 1850's, was much shorter.

In the course of the seven-year conflict, the Seminoles were forced from the prairies of central Florida into the inhospitable Everglades and the Big Cypress Swamp at the tip of the peninsula. The federal government pursued them there, wasting the lives of many U.S. soldiers in an effort to dislodge the Indians and force them to go west. For almost 30 years after the fighting stopped in 1856, the remnants of the eastern Seminole peoples lived in isolation.

About 1880 white observers began to travel among the Seminoles of Florida and describe their way of life. Parts of their Creek heritage remained intact, but in their new environment they had developed a culture that was unique. They lived in scattered compounds or camps that dotted the great swamp like little islands. Their open-walled houses, called chickees, were basically thatched roofs raised over wooden platforms. They tended gardens of corn, rice, sweet potatoes, bananas, and sugar cane. Though they kept livestock, especially hogs, they also hunted for meat.

By the 1890's white settlers began moving into southern Florida, pressing the Seminoles farther and farther back into the swampy interior. There they remained, relatively isolated, through the first half of this century. Today there are some 1,350 Seminoles in southern Florida, living on or around four reservations. Though they are no longer isolated and the young are increasingly adopting modern ways, all retain loyalty to their clans and many prefer the chickee to modern houses. On some of the reservations the Busk is still held, and during the course of that festival a boy can enter manhood in a manner prescribed by the ancient Creek ceremonies that have been handed down from generation to generation.

There are, as well, the remnants of the Cherokee nation in the Southeast. Like the Seminoles, a minority of Cherokees remained in the region by fleeing to land that was inaccessible to the outside world and generally considered worthless. Before removal, they had occupied the rolling Appalachian foothills in parts of Georgia, Alabama, Tennessee, and North Carolina, and their domains extended into the high mountains where scattered groups lived, including a community that had withdrawn from the tribe and obtained U.S. citizenship. When the order for removal came, these Cherokee citizens were exempt, and they were soon joined by hundreds of refugees who had evaded the government's roundup. At first the refugees were hounded and harassed by the authorities, but in time they were left alone. Before the 19th century ended, the eastern Cherokees were all living legally on reservation lands purchased for them in the mountains of North Carolina. They entered the 20th century as subsistence farmers and seemed much like their white neighbors. But they were not the same. They kept their language and dances and stories of their Cherokee forefathers. They continued to use Sequoyah's syllabary, and their medicine men wrote down the ancient formulas for herbal cures. While the Cherokee language is today spoken only by a minority of the tribesmen, it is in no danger of dying out. It is being taught in local public schools, along with other courses designed to preserve the ancient Cherokee heritage.

THE NORTHEAST AND GREAT LAKES
Woodland Warriors

The forested Adirondack Mountains, with their hundreds of sylvan lakes, was part of the Iroquois' home country. A favorite weapon of the Iroquois, in their wars with the Algonquians, was a heavy club of carved hardwood (inset).

From these tribes came great hunters, fishermen, farmers, and fighters, as well as creators of the most powerful and sophisticated Indian nation north of Mexico.

By A.D. 1492 the tree was almost everywhere in northeast America. Broad-leaved trees thrust their roots deep into the rich soil of valleys and grew so tall and thick that the noonday sun barely filtered through their interlocking branches. A man walking through the glades during the leafy season moved in a weird green glow, his moccasins cushioned by the soft earth. Higher up, on hillsides and mountain slopes, coniferous trees crowded even more closely together—millions of dark, spiky cones, all determinedly vertical. Higher still, wind-warped trees clung precariously to rocky peaks, sucking life from the thin pebbly soil.

Except for the lakes and rivers, the primeval forest of northeastern America extended in one vast sweep from swampy south to snowy north, from the cliffs and sandbars of the east to the edges of the prairie in the west. In aboriginal times this leafy universe was the home of the Eastern Woodlanders—half a million men, women, and children to whom the tree gave protection and sustenance. Nuts and fruit dropped from its branches to help satisfy man's hunger. Wildfowl roosted in the tree, rabbits and woodchucks burrowed between its roots. Beaver felled the tree to build dams, and the dams created pools that were soon full of fish.

Shaped into the shafts of spears and arrows, or pounded and woven into nets, the tree enabled a man to become hunter and fisherman. The tree's bark, when peeled, dried, and flattened, became the walls of a house. That same bark, when scraped smooth, curved, and stitched, became a container, a tray, or a canoe. Lopped of its branches and divided by fire into suitable lengths, the tree became a wall of stakes to fortify villages. When bent into frameworks, it became a litter, or a bow, or a snowshoe. Fashioned into an 18-inch board, fitted with supporting straps, and suspended from a convenient hook, the tree became a baby-frame—a kind of cradle—a safe, comfortable place to hold an infant while the mother was at her chores.

The Woodlands began to show unmistakable signs of human presence in the second millennium A.D. Many patches of open country had been hacked from the wilderness. There were green squares of corn and tobacco, as well as patches of ground farmed into sterility and then abandoned. Fishing camps dotted the riverbanks, and hunting paths were gradually hardening into well-trodden trails.

With two exceptions—Indians in Wisconsin who spoke Siouan and others between Lake Erie and the Hudson Valley who spoke Iroquoian—the people who worked these fields and followed these trails spoke some dialect of Algonquian, the most widespread linguistic family in North America. A hundred or so of their words (plus geographical place-names) have subsequently filtered down into our own vocabulary, including *hickory, hominy, moccasin, moose, succotash, terrapin, tomahawk, totem, wigwam, woodchuck.*

The home of the Woodlanders was a huge area between the Atlantic coast and the Mississippi River, extending about as far south as a line drawn through the northern border of present-day Tennessee and as far north as one drawn through the upper shore of Lake Superior. This vast expanse of land varied greatly from region to region, and the environment strongly influenced the character and culture of the Indians who lived in each section.

Among the fortunate were such tribes as the Powhatan, Delaware, and Montauk, who lived on the flat, fertile, breezy coastal plains. The ocean provided one of the world's richest fishing slopes, and to the west were hardwood forests teeming with game. Along much of the coastline, lush growing areas for the raising of corn and other crops could be created by clearing the trees. The clam beds of Long Island were yet another asset, and the many inland waterways made travel easy.

The harsh woods of the north—where mountains crowd close to a rocky shoreline, and the subarctic winds chill the air as early as September—sheltered seminomadic groups of Algonquians. Here corn would not grow, and such tribes as the Penobscot and Abnaki of Maine lived a hardy, wandering life in pursuit of deer, bears, moose, wild ducks, and fish.

Moose was probably the most important component in the diet of these cold-climate Indians. The chase, however, required skill and an understanding of the prey. Unlike buffalo, which travel in herds and are, therefore, subject to mass slaughter, moose are solitary animals and must be hunted individually. Hunters developed effective techniques for dealing with this phenomenon. An overhead snare, triggered by the ani-

A granite effigy of a bear, made some centuries ago by a Northeastern Indian, was unearthed in Salem, Massachusetts, in 1830. The stone's natural bearlike shape was modified only slightly by the carver to make it more realistic. Stones in the forms of animals or humans were highly valued as fetishes because they were thought to possess magic powers.

mal's weight, was one device used. When the moose was being actively hunted, it was attracted to the general hunting area through the use of a birchbark instrument that reproduced the moose mating call; this was especially effective during the rutting season in the fall. Then, to be able to approach the game closely enough to bring it down with an arrow, the hunter wore animal skins on his body and antlers on his head. Often hunting moose was easiest in winter when deep, soft snow covered the ground. The Indians, wearing snowshoes, could then run down the slow-moving animal.

Beaver also supplied food and, after the fur trade began with the Europeans, the pelts had great value as well. Beaver was hunted in several ways. Frequently, their dams would be broken up, and the hunters would club the animals to death when they came out of their shelters. Trapping was also employed along beaver trails and in the water near dams. Although dogs were used for tracking and hunting, they, along with porcupines, were sometimes part of the Indians' diet.

Fish were plentiful. Spears were used to take the larger species; weirs and birchbark nets brought in quantities of the smaller varieties. Shellfish and crustaceans abounded, and on occasion, seal meat found its way into the cooking pots of northern hunters. Ducks, geese, and partridge were among the birds readily available. Both meat and fish were preserved by smoking.

Because these northern peoples lived a seminomadic life moving seasonally to follow game, they required housing that was portable. They sometimes made tents of animal skins, but they preferred the wigwam. The wigwam frame consisted of four saplings bent toward a center; the covering was made by sewing long strips of bark together. Swamp grass provided an inside lining that kept out the cold and absorbed any leakage. Animal skins were hung at the entrance. Fir branches covered with moose hides were both floor and beds.

The moose was not only the main staple of the Indians' diet but the primary source of their clothing. In the making of jackets, some inventive tailoring was involved. Because of the long winter, sleeves were needed. Therefore, when the animal was skinned, the cut that began at the belly was extended to include the shoulder and forelegs, thus providing a sleeved garment requiring a minimum of sewing. A belt served the dual purpose of closing the jacket and holding up the moose skin trousers. During the relatively brief period of

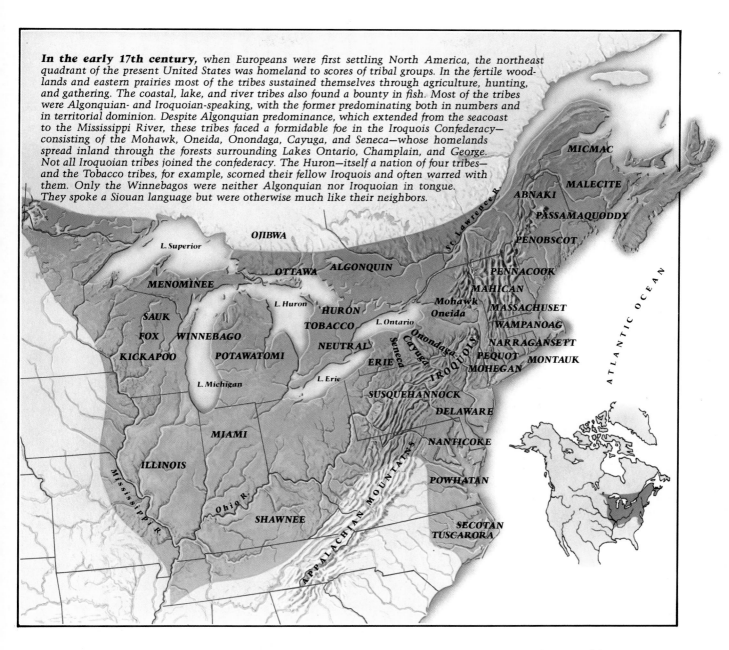

In the early 17th century, when Europeans were first settling North America, the northeast quadrant of the present United States was homeland to scores of tribal groups. In the fertile woodlands and eastern prairies most of the tribes sustained themselves through agriculture, hunting, and gathering. The coastal, lake, and river tribes also found a bounty in fish. Most of the tribes were Algonquian- and Iroquoian-speaking, with the former predominating both in numbers and in territorial dominion. Despite Algonquian predominance, which extended from the seacoast to the Mississippi River, these tribes faced a formidable foe in the Iroquois Confederacy—consisting of the Mohawk, Oneida, Onondaga, Cayuga, and Seneca—whose homelands spread inland through the forests surrounding Lakes Ontario, Champlain, and George. Not all Iroquoian tribes joined the confederacy. The Huron—itself a nation of four tribes—and the Tobacco tribes, for example, scorned their fellow Iroquois and often warred with them. Only the Winnebagos were neither Algonquian nor Iroquoian in tongue. They spoke a Siouan language but were otherwise much like their neighbors.

warm weather, both men and women wore skin loincloths plus lightweight deerskin shirts as protection against the sun. Most clothing was decorated with porcupine quills, eagle feathers, and shells. Both sexes wore large quantities of bead jewelery.

The area comprising present upper New York State, and descending on the west to the St. Lawrence Valley and basins of Lakes Ontario and Erie, was Iroquois territory. It was a terrain of dramatic contrasts: of low, luxuriant river bottoms and valleys cradled among mountains; of the five deep and parallel Finger Lakes, which seemed to have been gouged out of the earth by a giant hand; of maple trees that supplied syrup, of

marshes noisy with geese, and rivers filled with vast numbers of sturgeon, bass, and shad.

Along the present Canadian and American shores of the western Great Lakes, Algonquians were the majority of the population. Some—like the Ottawas and the Potawatomis, in the deciduous forests bordering Lakes Huron and Michigan, and the Sauks and Foxes to their west—were partly dependent on agriculture. The Iroquoian-speaking Hurons also lived here in a swath of farming country between Lake Simcoe and Georgian Bay, in modern Ontario.

West of Lake Michigan and to the south was a region half forest and half plains. This area offered its inhabi-

113

tants a delicious seed-bearing grass called wild rice, which grew thickly—as it still does today—in the thousands of lakes and ponds marking the retreat of the Wisconsin Glacier. Rice was harvested from canoes by the Menominees, the Ottawas, the Potawatomis, the Ojibwas, and the Siouan-speaking Winnebagos. During the summer when the fields had been planted, and in fall when the crops were in, some Indians would arm themselves and head south and west where buffalo populated the prairie.

Prior to the white man's arrival in Woodland territory, a chain of separate but interrelating Algonquian communities grew up along the Atlantic seaboard, from Chesapeake Bay to the Gulf of St. Lawrence. Some of these groups, which shared a common language and culture, never achieved more than local importance because of their disunity. Others, such as the Powhatans of Virginia and the Abnakis of Maine, consisted of numerous tribes formed into powerful confederations that dominated large regions.

When balmy weather arrived, Indians all along the seaboard turned to fishing and hunting, and in the southern regions, to the planting of corn. There was a regular flow of traders up and down the coast and from the inland areas carrying pouches of regional merchandise for barter. When a trader appeared at a village, he was usually greeted with warm hospitality that might include a welcoming embrace, a silent smoking session (mingling tobacco fumes symbolized the birth of friendship), and then a leisurely feast with much conversation.

In autumn this sociable life broke up. Among northern tribes, families resumed their nomadic ways and throughout the winter they pursued moose and smaller game into the snowy wilderness. The men of the south also went hunting in the fall, but their women stayed home and tanned hides, sewed clothing, and tended the children. Regularly, the hunters came back, hunched under the weight of venison sides and great sacks of furs.

Typical of southern, village-dwelling Algonquian tribes was the Delaware, or as they called themselves *Lenni Lenape*, "the People." The Delaware Indians may have numbered from 9,000 to 12,000 at the height of their prosperity, in the century before the white man came. They were spread out in a loose network of villages, each ringed with sovereign hunting territories. Their domains extended from the present state of Delaware to regions far to the north and west.

Their villages, always located on river meadows, were small, irregularly spaced groups of bark buildings. Some of these were round, domed wigwams; some were oblong and arched; and others were rectangular longhouses with pitched roofs. All possessed a gaping smoke hole in lieu of a chimney. Fires smoldered inside day and night. The only other opening was a low doorway covered with skins. *(continued on page 118)*

Early View of the Algonquian Tribes of Virginia

In 1590 the English got a realistic view of Indian life North America, thanks to the exquisite watercolors of John White, reproduced as engravings by Theodor de Bry with commentary by Thomas Hariot. White and Hariot had been participants in Sir Walter Raleigh's ill-fated attempt establish a colony on the North Carolina coast in 158 though both men returned to England before the colony mysteriously vanished. Through the work of White and Hariot Britishers gained some notion of Indian life, concepts the would color European perceptions for centuries. The India White depicted were of the Secotan tribe, an Algonquian speaking group. Although Raleigh's North Carolina colo did not last, the English settlement in 1607 at Jamestown Virginia, proved to be a secure foothold for the whites in the Middle Atlantic tidewater regions. The Indians contest growing white dominance, but intertribal rivalries usual prevented effective resistance. Scarcely half a century aft these paintings were done, the Algonquians had been push from this region by white settlers and the scenes depict here were but a memory. Quotes on the next pages are from Thomas Hariot's original text.

Having returned safely from a hunting or raiding expedition, these Secotans gather around a fire to celebrate and to g thanks to the spirits. The spirit world manifested itself in eve animate and inanimate object, and each spirit held great power—for good or evil—in the affairs of men. To show their gra tude and seek future benefit, these Secotans sing out the praise, shake gourd rattles, and toss pieces of that most holy plants, tobacco, into the fire as an offering. "If there is a sto on the waters," wrote Hariot, "they throw it [tobacco] . . . i the water to pacify the gods. Also when they set up a n weir . . . they pour [tobacco] into it."

A chief of a Virginia tribe (upper left) cuts a striking figure in his adornment of body paint. The necklace he wears may be made of pearls and copper beads, and at his wrists bracelets jangle. His hair is "cut from the top of the head to the neck in a coxcomb. One long bird's feather is tucked into the crest. . . ." The chief's only clothing is a deerskin breechclout, from which an animal's tail dangles. A deerskin apron is also the only garment of a chief's wife (lower left) whose face and arms are also adorned with body paint. The decorative sling she wears is made from beads of pearls and copper, the latter indicating that the Secotans maintained indirect trade relations with peoples hundreds of miles to the northwest. In her left hand she carries a large water gourd, and at her heels her daughter walks, fondling a doll given her by colonists. A typical village is the one above, beside the Pamlico River. Its multifamily houses are of arched saplings covered with bark and woven mats that could easily be removed to let in light. In the fields, ripening corn is protected by a human scarecrow who emerges from a platformed shelter to shout and wave his arms when birds approach. At lower left, a fire burns at the "place of solemn prayer," near a building sheltering the remains of departed chiefs. Nearby, celebrants dance amid a circle of posts elaborately carved with human faces while other villagers await their turn to join the dance. Still others crouch in the roadway to share a meal neatly laid out on rows of mats.

Algonquians of Virginia *(continued)*

A meal bubbles over a carefully tended fire as two Secotans prep[are] a savory stew of corn, meat, and fish. The great clay pot with [a] pointed base could withstand considerable heat. It is set up in a pile [of] earth, and the fire is built around it.

The manner of their fishing.

An evening's fishing expedition brings out four Secotans in a dugout canoe. Two of them pole while the others tend a small fire that will attract the fish. In the background, two tribesmen stand in the shallows with their spears. "As they have neither steel nor iron," wrote Hariot, "they fasten the sharp, hollow tail of a certain fish . . . to reeds or to the end of a long rod, and with this they spear fish both by day and by night." At left is a large reed weir that serves as an effective fish trap.

Secotan craftsmen burn out a log and scrape it clean with shells as they prepare a dugout canoe capable of holding 12 or more men. In the background, a tree is felled by burning it at its base. Later it will be stripped of bark and limbs, as is the trunk at left, before being hollowed.

A fisherman bends beneath the weight of his catch while anot[her] tends to a rack of fish already being roasted. So certain were the Se[co]tans of the sea's generous bounty that they made no effort to smok[e a] portion of their catch for future use.

During a twilight gathering Secotans from several villages meet at a circle of ceremonial posts for a ritual dance celebrating the harvest. "They come dressed in very strange fashion," wrote Thomas Hariot, "wearing marks on their backs signifying the places they come from. They meet on a broad open place enclosed by tall posts carved into faces resembling those of veiled nuns. Then, standing in a certain order, they dance and sing, making the strangest movements they can think of." Three young virgins, "their arms about each other," circle the center post. A shaman (left) wears a skin bag as a badge of office. Hariot called shamans "sorcerers . . . whose enchantments often go against the laws of nature."

Within a temple-wigwam the remains of chiefs are laid out. "When a chief died," wrote Hariot, "the skin is removed and all the flesh cut from the bones. . . . Then the bones, still held together by the ligaments, are covered. . . . They wrap each corpse in its own skin after it has been treated." Protecting the dead from harm is the crouching figure of a Kewas, a carved representation of a god. Beneath the platform is a deerskin, a resting place for the temple shaman who prays to the chiefs' spirits.

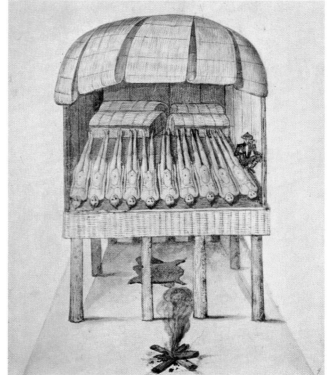

Families generally were outside in fine weather, cooking their food at a second fireplace by the door. They stored surplus food in silos dug deep into the cool earth, lined with marsh grass, and covered with insulating bark. Each village had a sweathouse beside the creek. Built of stakes and mud, it was low, windowless, and had a door so small even children had to crawl inside. Here, once or twice a week, men, women, and children took turns steaming themselves free of ailments and melancholy by pouring water on piles of hot rocks. When they could stand the heat no longer, they emerged and tumbled naked and glistening into the river. If it was winter, they rolled in the snow.

Clean and "purified" after their "saunas," the Delawares would spend hours restoring sweated-off body paint. The term *redskin*, applied by Europeans to Algonquians in general and the Delawares in particular, was inspired not by their natural complexion but by their fondness for vermilion makeup, concocted from fat mixed with berry juice and minerals that provided the desired color.

After using sharpened mussel-shell tweezers to pluck their heads bare except for a central cock's crest, the men would streak their faces and bodies with bright red ocher and bloodroot, as well as white and yellow clays. Women carefully rouged their cheeks, eyelids, and ear rims.

In summer Delaware children scampered about naked, the men wore only soft deerskin breechclouts, and the women, knee-length skirts and headbands of wampum. The Delawares were tall, lithe, and straight-featured with prominent cheekbones. In winter both sexes dressed more warmly, with fur shawls and robes woven of downy, waterproof turkey feathers.

Mysterious "Key" to the Origin of the Delawares: The Walum Olum—Legend or History?

"He created the sun and the stars of night."

"Those who were strong and those who had power came away, separating from those who remained living there."

"Things turned out well for all those who had stayed at the shore of water frozen hard as rocks, and for those at the great hollow well."

In 1836 a botanist from Kentucky named Constantine S. Rafinesque published a remarkable article entitled "The Walum Olum, or Red Score," in The American Nations *magazine. Rafinesque's translations of the Walum Olum purported to be the history of the Delaware Indians from earliest days to the arrival of the whites. But the Walum Olum remains to this day a subject of scholarly debate, and many experts have questioned its authenticity. The story was supposedly derived from a collection of sticks upon which the original pictographs had been etched.*

Rafinesque, a teacher of botany and natural science at Transylvania University in Lexington, Kentucky, obtained "some of the original Walum Olum (painted record)" in 1820 from a Dr. Ward of Indiana. "In 1822," Rafinesque continued, "were obtained from another source the songs in the original language . . . but no one could be found by me to translate them. I had therefore to learn the language . . . to translate them, which I only accomplished in 1833."

Copies of the pictographs made by Rafinesque unquestionably refer to people crossing "the water, over the frozen sea." This might well be an allusion to the Bering Strait land bridge. Others describe the munificence of Manitou, the Great Creator. Still others refer to specific chiefs and spirits, such as Grandfather of Boats. Altogether, the pictographs express a strong belief in a vast spiritual order and reflect a reverence for all life and all nature. However, no one knows if the Walum Olum dated back hundreds of years, were of 18th-century origin, or were merely a figment of Rafinesque's imagination. The author never produced the original sticks for scientific study and, if they ever existed, they have long since disappeared.

One theory is that the Delawares were, by the mid-1700's, a tribe in disarray and decline, having been among the first to feel the effects of the white man's culture, diseases, and rapaciousness. Forced from their homes along the Middle Atlantic Coast, the remnants of the tribe traversed the mountains and found temporary shelter in the Ohio Valley. There tribal leaders attempted to impose something of a cultural revival. The Walum Olum may have been part of an effort to revitalize the Delawares by the creation of an epic that traced, in fictional terms, the story of the tribe's migrations and heroic endeavors. Several of the copied pictographs, together with Rafinesque's translations, are reproduced at left and below. They recount the earth's creation, the departure of the peoples from Siberia, a golden age of peace and, finally, the coming of the white man to America's shores.

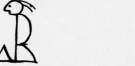
"When all were friends Wolf Man was chief; and he was the first of these."

"When Master of Boats was chief, they went after the Snakes in boats."

"...persons floating in from the east: the Whites were coming."

"...friendly people with great possessions: who are they?"

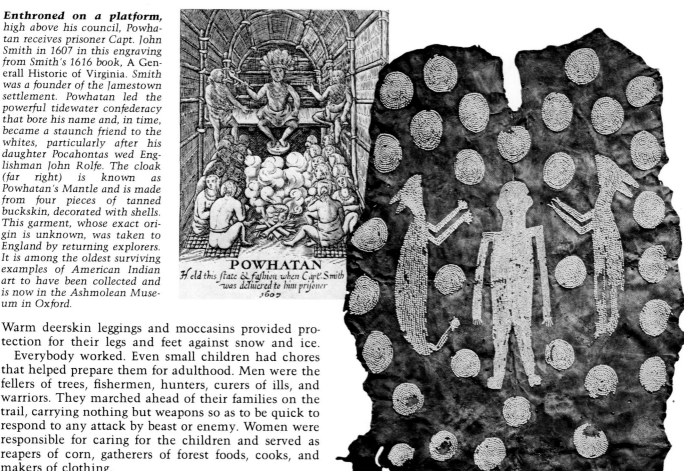

Enthroned on a platform, high above his council, Powhatan receives prisoner Capt. John Smith in 1607 in this engraving from Smith's 1616 book, A Generall Historie of Virginia. Smith was a founder of the Jamestown settlement. Powhatan led the powerful tidewater confederacy that bore his name and, in time, became a staunch friend to the whites, particularly after his daughter Pocahontas wed Englishman John Rolfe. The cloak (far right) is known as Powhatan's Mantle and is made from four pieces of tanned buckskin, decorated with shells. This garment, whose exact origin is unknown, was taken to England by returning explorers. It is among the oldest surviving examples of American Indian art to have been collected and is now in the Ashmolean Museum in Oxford.

POWHATAN
Held this ftate & fafhion when Capt. Smith was deliuered to him prifoner 1607

Warm deerskin leggings and moccasins provided protection for their legs and feet against snow and ice.

Everybody worked. Even small children had chores that helped prepare them for adulthood. Men were the fellers of trees, fishermen, hunters, curers of ills, and warriors. They marched ahead of their families on the trail, carrying nothing but weapons so as to be quick to respond to any attack by beast or enemy. Women were responsible for caring for the children and served as reapers of corn, gatherers of forest foods, cooks, and makers of clothing.

When a boy reached the age of puberty, he was initiated into manhood by a rite known as the Youth's Vigil. This obliged him to fast alone in the forest for many days in order to test his fortitude and make him feel the supportive, yet challenging, forces of nature. His fasting was supposed to bring on dreams and visions of supernatural forces that would guide and protect him throughout adult life. At puberty, youngsters became sexually active, but marriage was often delayed for some years. Weddings were casual. A couple simply set up a wigwam together. Often as not, parents arranged the alliance; there was no formal exchange of vows, simply a few ceremonial gifts from the young man to his in-laws. Divorce, too, was easy; the couple just parted. The woman, by custom, always kept both house and children. The family was the basic social unit, and inheritance was passed through the female line: from mother to daughter, or if she had no daughters, through her sister's daughters.

This matrilineal system determined the succession of tribal sachems, or chiefs, even though they themselves were invariably male. Rank passed not from a dying sachem to his son, but to a close relative in his mother's bloodline—a brother, perhaps, or the son of his sister.

Each sachem thus represented a family lineage: the Delaware nation consisted not so much of one large tribe as a loose federation of lineages. A Delaware sachem was a man of great influence and prestige, but he ruled by persuasion rather than by force. He performed a variety of ceremonial functions all year round, negotiated treaties on behalf of his lineage, and exacted blood money for relatives killed in battle—or paid it, if his warriors had struck at another lineage. His political power was strictly limited. The Delawares were a

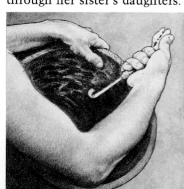

Indian art and white technology are combined in this 19th-century Abnaki "crooked knife" fashioned from a European metal file blade that was fastened to a wooden handle decorated with a carved beaver. The blade was tied to the handle with animal sinew, which also provided a grip for the craftsman who drew the blade toward him (left) when shaping wood. These knives became popular throughout the Northeast and Great Lakes area because they enabled Indian craftsmen to work rapidly.

119

Two women of a Massachusetts tribe tend kettles of boiling maple syrup in a sugar camp as other Indians gather birchbark buckets filled with raw sap. The trees were tapped in March by cutting a downward-slanting gash in the trunk. A spout was then inserted and a bucket placed beneath it to catch the sap. When sugaring was done, the Indians broke camp and stored their equipment. Among the tribes of the Northeast maple sugar was used as a seasoning for all kinds of foods.

strongly democratic people and conveyed their views to him through councillors. No declaration of war or treaty of peace could be concluded without a solemn assemblage of these tribal elders. They sat in a half-moon surrounding the sachem, ringed in a larger half-moon by their children, who were present to learn the ways of their tribe. Not until there was a chorus of approval from the adults did the sachem consider himself authorized to "take up" or "bury" the tomahawk.

Religion for the Delaware, as with most Algonquian tribes, revolved around the Great Spirit, a term that evoked creation, godship, and a host of spiritual forces inhabiting all things in nature. To a Delaware, those forces were everywhere, warming him, feeding him, healing him. The spirits listened to prayers and answered in the form of sunsets and snowfalls, favorable winds and spring rains. All things had souls. A twig, a stone had a life of its own, just as men, women, and animals did.

Old age was regarded as a high honor by all Algonquians, and death released the spirit into regions where pain, sickness, and sadness did not exist. The deceased was buried in a shallow grave, unconfined by any coffin, for the soul must be free to travel on the 12th day. In a world beyond the grave, the dead lived on, existing much as they had on earth, save for a freedom from the sorrows common to the living.

Embroidered with porcupine quills, this Pennacook pouch combines traditional design with decorations of European beads and iron bangles. The quills, colored with vegetable dyes, were soaked until flexible and wrapped around thread sewn to skins.

The Rise of the Iroquois

Of all the mysteries that enshroud early Woodland history, the most tantalizing is that of the Iroquois. How did that magnificent sisterhood of tribes—known as Romans of the New World for their political sophistication, and kinsmen of the wolves for their savagery—come to exist in the midst of the Algonquians, to whom they were total aliens? The Iroquois arose in present-day New York State during the 14th century A.D. Small, mutually hostile tribes at first, the Iroquois later became larger and formed a confederacy of five of their tribes that spread death and destruction throughout the Northeast. Their terrified victims were Algonquians and dissident Iroquois tribes who retreated on all sides. By the late 17th century, when commerce with Europeans was at its height, the Five Nation Confederacy was establishing a hammerlock on the fur trade, and Iroquois power was felt from Maine to the Mississippi River.

Archeologists still debate the origin of the Iroquois. One theory holds that the Iroquois were immigrants from north of the St. Lawrence River. Recent indications are that they were indigenous to upper New York State. During the 19th and early 20th centuries a few scholars believed the Iroquois came from west of the Mississippi. These scholars pointed out that the language of the Five Nations seemed somewhat similar to that of the Pawnees, whose historic homeland lay west of the great river. One Pawnee legend speaks of the Iroquois as a friendly tribe that, in the distant past, lived near them before moving east in search of independent territory. However, the majority of modern scholars has come to believe that the earliest Iroquois were indigenous Woodlanders.

Most anthropologists now accept the theory that a corn-growing people called the Owascos, who lived between A.D. 1000 and 1300 along the rivers and lakeshores of upper New York State, were Iroquoians. Archeological links between the Five Nations and this northeastern culture are much more impressive than the linguistic relationship with peoples across the Mississippi. But awkward gaps and inconsistencies still make both the "migrant" and the "indigenous" theories controversial. There—until conclusive evidence through excavations proves one or the other correct—we will have to leave the mystery and move on to a portrait of the Iroquois at the height of their political and military glory—about A.D. 1680.

The Iroquois were deeply appreciative of the land they inhabited. From the west bank of the Hudson River to the shores of Lake Erie, they lived in surroundings of great fertility and natural beauty. They divided this large rectangle into five north-south strips, one to a tribe. Each area was watered by its own lake or river system and governed by its own tribal council. The site of a council was symbolized by a ceremonial fire: the Iroquois likened the parallel plumes of smoke,

Twin human figures decorate this delicately carved 12-tine Iroquois bone haircomb made more than four centuries ago. Women used such combs for decoration as well as to keep their hair in place. These combs were common among the Iroquois long before the whites arrived. The clay and stone effigy pipes (below), also Iroquois-made, are about 600 years old. Some figures resemble humans (top row); others represent snakes, bears, and birds (bottom). The images usually faced the smoker.

streaming heavenward simultaneously, to a gigantic Longhouse. More than 200 miles from end to end, the Longhouse dominated the entire topography of upper New York State, just as much smaller longhouses dominated individual settlements and villages. The eastern door of this symbolic Longhouse was guarded by the Mohawk tribe and opened onto the Hudson Valley. The western door, protected by the Senecas, opened onto the Niagara River and game-rich lands to the west. Spaced out between these two extremities were the Oneidas, the Cayugas, and (right in the middle, about where Syracuse is now) the Onondagas. By the late 1600's, as other tribes were defeated by the Five Nations, the influence of the Longhouse spread over an enormous area, from New England to the Mississippi, and from Ontario to Tennessee.

Any eastbound wanderer crossing the Genesee River in present-day New York had first to "knock on the door" of the Iroquois Longhouse. It would be opened to him by the Seneca Indians, who in their prime about 1680 numbered some 5,000, including 1,000 of the most formidable warriors in America. Their territory extended as far east as the steep slopes west of Lake Seneca. (One of those hills, according to a legend, gave birth to the first members of the tribe: they have always referred to themselves simply as *Djiionondo-wan-enaka*, "People of the Hill.") Here was an aboriginal paradise of black, humus-rich soil, unlimited firewood, pine-scented air, and a thousand sparkling springs. At this time the Senecas occupied about 150 longhouses, mostly grouped into four main villages.

A typical settlement was located between the fork of two streams and protected from raiders by a high palisade. Such villages conformed to no set pattern but were built according to the whim of each community. Although the Senecas, like all Iroquois, were a sedentary people, their villages tended to "creep" up or down the river banks as they exhausted one farming area and moved on to clear another. They left behind a trail of bare, beaten earth and crumbling ruins.

Everyone lived in longhouses. Each was a rectangular structure of poles and sheeted bark. It measured 50 to 150 feet in length, depending on the number of families living inside, and 18 to 25 feet in width. Its high roof was arched and painted above the door. At each end was the crest of one of the eight Seneca clans: the Bear, the Wolf, the Beaver, the Turtle, the Deer, the Snipe, the Heron, or the Hawk.

In the shadowy, windowless interior a number of small fires burned, spaced out every 12 feet or so along a central corridor. The smoke curled up through open smoke holes. When there was heavy rain or snow, these vents would be partially or fully closed with sliding panels, and the longhouse would fill with eye-stinging smoke and a miasma of smells: soot, sweat, kettle soup, sweet grass, babies, bear's grease, and tobacco.

To left and right of the corridor were platforms piled with bearskin rugs. These huge bunks accommodated entire families. Here, snug under heaps of fur, men, women, and children would sleep together. On another platform above them they stored their heavier possessions: pots and kettles, cradleboards and weapons, while on the nearby walls and rafters hung braids of corn, strings of dried apples and squash, hanks of tobacco, and bundles of roots.

This family booth, which could be curtained off for privacy, was the quiet center of Seneca life. Although it was personal territory, its position in a communal dwelling symbolized the fact that each family was part of a much more important whole—the lineage that occupied the entire house.

Seneca kin relationships, as with all Iroquois tribes and a few Algonquian tribes, such as the Delaware, were determined by maternal descent. Supreme in every longhouse was the oldest woman, "mother" of the household in the sense that it exclusively belonged to her and her female relatives. When she died, the next oldest woman took over. All males left home as soon as

A longhouse rises in an early 17th-century Seneca village near L Ontario as some tribesmen build the framework of elm-wood po while others put on the facing of seasoned elmbark. When comple the house will be inhabited by many families of a single matrilinea the husbands having come from other longhouses, other clans. T typical Iroquois village was built on a rise near a river (upper rig used both for occasional fishing and canoe transport to nearby comm nities. A system of forest trails also connected the villages of the en Iroquois nation. When a village was begun, the land nearest the ri was cleared by burning the trees at their bases. This served seve purposes: an open area was created where raiders could be spott land was made available for cultivation; and wood was secured construction and fuel. Villages were surrounded by palisades, and this one a warrior stands guard while villagers carry on with peace pursuits. Here a woman dries deer meat on a rack, and nearby a w rior enters a low, domed sweathouse for steamy purification rites. N the palisade another warrior has just entered the village, a deer sl across his shoulders. He is walking toward a woman who is readyin fire for the next meal. Beyond the palisade, children romp while wo en haul water from the stream. In the distance, corn ripens in the s Such villages lasted 20 years at most. By then the land was exhaust and firewood was scarce. The village was then abandoned in stages a new community rose on a nearby hilltop.

they married and went to live in the longhouses of their wives. Conversely, when a woman married, her husband immediately moved into her longhouse.

The longhouse lineage of families was the basic unit of Seneca society. Lineages in turn built up into clans, clans into moieties (that is, half-tribes), and moieties into whole tribes. A young man had to marry outside his clan, preferably with a woman who had not even a distant blood relationship with his own mother and her female relatives.

Except for the men's weapons, clothing, and personal possessions, all property belonged to women, from the longhouse itself down to the farming tools. A wife was expected always to be well dressed, even if her husband was shabby. If he or any kinsman was killed in war, she was entitled to demand an enemy captive in compensation. Her kinsmen would then have to go out and take one, even if it meant starting another war. When the captive was brought, she was allowed to adopt him or consign him to torture or death as she pleased.

Rising to seniority in the longhouse, she gradually acquired considerable political power. Every one of the eight Seneca councillor-chiefs was appointed by the clan mother in consultation with other women of her clan, and should he fail in his duties, the same women could remove him from office.

There were sound, practical reasons why women had such control over property and politics. The Seneca was an ambitious, warlike tribe, eager to push its western door farther and farther toward the upper Great Lakes, thus gaining access to a wealth of beaver furs that white traders so coveted. Military expeditions were sometimes far-ranging, and warriors might be away as little as three days or as much as three months. When they returned, they were soon off on the chase, for they loved hunting almost as much as fighting. In between times many of the men would be off on trading expeditions. Though there were always some young men left behind to protect the village, most aspects of community life—looking after the old, caring for the young, and tending the crops—were left to the women. They planted, weeded, and harvested no fewer than a million bushels of corn a year as well as huge quantities of squash, beans, and sunflower seeds. What they could not eat fresh they stored in underground granaries. When their husbands returned from the hunt, bowed under the weight of deer, elk, and beaver carcasses, it was a time for feasting on rich, thick stews of meats and vegetables, hot corn dumplings, mushrooms, ash-baked apples, nuts, and berries.

This longhouse interior *shows the living quarters of two Iroquois families out of the dozen or more who shared the dwelling, which might be 100 feet long. Each family slept on a platform close to the earth and used part of a shelf that ran the length of the house for storage. Here such items as corn, tobacco, bowls filled with food, and skin robes were kept. Beneath the platform such other goods as snowshoes, bows, spears, and winnowing baskets were stored. Much activity went on in the central corridor. There cooking fires, each serving two families, were maintained, and women pounded corn into meal, as shown. Some privacy could be obtained by lowering curtains between the compartments.*

Perhaps the most important of a woman's responsibilities was to bear children, thus assuring the future of the tribe. When their time came, young Seneca women could be seen retreating into the forest. There, in the privacy of trees and shadow, babies were born, washed in spring water or snow, wrapped in furs, and carried back to the rejoicing village.

Two powerful influences worked upon the Seneca baby as his consciousness dawned: corn and womanhood. A soft compress of maize powder soothed the sting in the infant's navel, once the dried umbilical cord had been removed. Breasts swelling with milk nourished the child until it was three or four years old. Woven cornhusks provided a mat for sleeping, and the boy or girl played with dolls whose hair was made from the silk of the cob.

Because the father was frequently away, the mother was the primary source of wisdom, affection, and comfort. She was loving in her treatment but was careful not to spoil and "soften" the child. She encouraged a son to fight other boys with sham war clubs made from cornstalks and told him stories of the bravery of his ancestors. Both boys and girls were taught to eat sparingly and healthfully (gluttony was a sin: too many corn cakes dripping with maple syrup would bring on the bogeyman Longnose). Youngsters were toughened with regular baths of cold water. Should the child's nose bleed, the mother wrapped a ring of cornhusk around his finger; if intestinal worms troubled him, she brewed a purifying lye of corn ashes; when

This Iroquois pot *has a projecting collar with a figure motif. The deeply incised wide collar with its upward-turning points was a unique Iroquois design.*

he got filthy with dust, sweat, and bear's grease, she scrubbed him clean with dried corncobs.

From about his eighth year onward, the child became increasingly aware of his or her duties. A girl did light chores in the longhouse or went with older women to work in the fields; a boy was free to wander off into the woods for days on end—usually with a group of friends—living off berries and tubers and such small game as he could snare or shoot with his bow and arrow or with his blowgun. When he killed his first deer, unassisted, with bow and arrow, he could join adult hunting parties. During idle hours he was permitted to play with girls, often in openly erotic fashion.

When puberty arrived, a boy occasionally went back to the woods, this time in the company of an old man of the tribe. The boy was made to test his masculinity by bashing himself against rocks until he bled. He would have to besmirch his body with dirt or ashes and recount his dreams in great detail so that the old man could identify his "guardian spirit." Back in the village, the young adolescent would fondle some symbol of that spirit—a rock that looked like a deformed animal, a chunk of bone carved into a nightmarish face—and dream of the day when he would become a man and be off on the warpath, like all true men.

As "keepers of the western door" of the Longhouse, the Seneca tribe had a reputation for military ferocity equaled only by their eastern partners, the Mohawk. Seneca warriors, indeed, made up over half of the Iroquois fighting force—an army so terrifying it was called the Nation of Snakes by its Algonquian neighbors.

Before the formation of the league, Iroquois tribes were still living independently of one another, and Seneca warfare was largely a matter of private blood feuds carried on by an endless succession of small raiding parties. The victims were as likely to be fellow Iroquois as foreign Algonquians. Casualties were not very high

at first, because the purpose of an expedition was to settle minor scores. A brawl in some Cayuga village might end in the killing of a visiting Seneca; compensation in the form of a captive would then be demanded by his clan. In order to get such a captive, the Seneca raiding party might be obliged to kill three or four more Cayugas; whereupon the bereaved tribe would promptly send out its own raiding party, and so on. The net effect of these petty hostilities was gradually to escalate, decade by decade, the amount of blood spilled in every blood feud, until there were so many scores to settle on all sides that the tribes lived in a state of perpetual, debilitating war. The Iroquois were literally bleeding themselves to death. Meanwhile, their much more numerous neighbors, the Algonquians, inflicted a series of humiliating attacks upon them. The elders of the Five Nations grew increasingly worried. "We cannot restrain our young men," they complained.

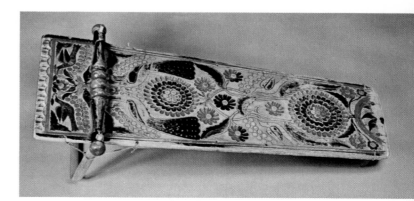

European missionary influence *is evident in this Mohawk cradleboard, its back covered with a festive floral motif of many hues. A turned wood cleat, resembling a chair round, supports a shelf that covered the baby's head, protecting the infant from injury should the cradleboard be dropped.*

125

A typical Seneca military expedition would begin with the thud of a hatchet into the village war post. This usually meant that a warrior had a score to settle somewhere and that all who wished to follow him might do so. Here, at last, was the chance for the impatient young man to test his valor. While he joined in the ceremonial war dance, his mother and sisters would prepare some battle rations—generally nothing more than a bearskin bag of dried corn flour mixed with maple sugar. (A handful or two of this nutritious powder, washed down with a gulp of river water, could keep him going all day.) Then, shouldering his weapons, he would fall in behind his elders, standing in single file. A farewell shout, lifted shields, an encouraging call of female voices; then the march would begin and soon the shadowy gloom of the forest would swallow up the men.

Approach like foxes, fight like lions, and disappear like birds—this was the fighting style of the Senecas and of all Iroquois warriors. Loping tirelessly through the forest on silent moccasins, the war party almost invariably had the advantage of surprising its victims. Weapons were light but murderous: bows and arrows; ball-headed clubs (tomahawks), some wickedly spiked with a tooth of flint; razor-sharp knives.

On long expeditions Seneca warriors were somewhat hampered by having to carry elmbark canoes, heavier and clumsier than the birchbark canoes of Indians living farther north. Elmbark, however, was highly workable and was readily available throughout the Iroquois domains. A canoe could be shaped in less than a day.

Before returning home from a successful raid, the war party would usually emblazon a tree in the enemy camp with its clan symbol, along with meticulous totals of men slain and captives taken.

En route to the village, the prisoner's wrists would be tied with a symbolic "slave band," and sometimes he would be beaten, bitten, pricked, and burned by his captors. War whoops announced that the expedition had returned home. Then, at the gates of the village, the captive would be forced to strip and run the gauntlet of villagers. A man who bore this beating stoically was often adopted by a family of someone slain in battle. Women and children taken in raids were almost always adopted.

But if the women were still too bitter about the death to grant mercy, the prisoner was doomed. Like all Indians in the area, he knew what to expect. Villagers poked him with red-hot embers, tore out his hair, tied cords around his body and set them to smolder, broke his bones, pulled out his nails, sliced off random chunks of flesh, and pulled out sinews. The victim was periodically revived from faintness by shocks of cold water. A brave captive was expected to meet such torture with silence or the singing of his personal songs. Only when he was near death was he killed. Sometimes bits of his flesh were eaten as a sacrificial rite: the

On the warpath, an Iroquois brave brandishes a traditio[nal] war club and an iron-bladed ax. In this somewhat fanciful dr[aw]ing by an 18th-century Frenchman, J. Grasset St. Sauveur, f[or] his book, Costumes Americaines, the warrior wears some cl[oth]ing—such as the ankle-high boots and the green stockings—[that] was not typical Iroquois dress. But the picture does convey [a] typical Iroquois' pride in his martial abilities. A young tr[ibes]man gloried in war as a means of proving his manhood [and] gaining prestige. In the hand-to-hand combat of intertribal r[aids] he was a skilled and merciless foe.

strength and wisdom of the slain victim, it was believed, flowed into those who had devoured him.

According to Indian mythology, the first Iroquois to express horror at the fraternal warfare among the Iroquois tribes was a holy man named Dekanawidah. Said to be born of a virgin mother in the mid-16th century (some accounts have him arising a hundred years earlier), he is alleged to have had a vision about 1570 in which he saw the union of the Five Nations. The Iroquois, he said, must cease warring upon one another and unite under the sheltering branches of a symbolic Tree of Great Peace.

A Mohawk named Hiawatha was so moved by De-

Warfare: A Way of Life for the Northeast Indians

At the time the Europeans arrived on America's northeast shores, they found warfare among the tribes was almost continual. Although confrontations were on a small, raiding-party scale, the rivalries among the peoples of the region were deep-rooted and intense. In general, this warfare had its origins in blood feuds avenging the death of one warrior by the death of another. The urging of a widow or a mother who had lost a son could rouse a clan to action, a local war chief would raise a raiding party, and then—bow and war club in hand—the braves would move stealthily through the woods and launch a surprise attack on a village of the offending tribe. In these raids people were slain, and captives and goods taken. The prisoners were sometimes tortured and killed, but often they were adopted into the captors' tribe to replace men who had recently died. The newly victimized tribe now had ample reason to seek its own revenge. In such circumstances the fur traders and settlers had little trouble using tribe against tribe to the advantage of the Europeans. An exception was the potent Iroquois League that united five tribes. The league was strong enough to dominate much of the Northeast and adept enough to use the conflicting ambitions of the French, English, and Dutch to maintain Iroquois power for many decades.

A clever adaptation by white traders was to combine the Indians' twin passions for smoking and war in a single implement. This 18th-century device, made in Europe, is both a war club and a pipe. The hollow handle is also a pipestem.

Two Woodland war clubs, formidable weapons for the close combat of intertribal raids, are each carved from a single piece of ironwood. The ball-like heads were highly efficient for splitting skulls with a single blow. The lower club, from the Great Lakes area, has an added feature that reflects the Europeans' presence. The ball head carries a sharp-pointed metal spike that made the weapon especially lethal.

kanawidah's prophetic words that he spread the message from one tribe to another, paddling and portaging his own white canoe across New York State. The Senecas, being the largest, fiercest, and most westerly of the Five, were among the last to yield to Hiawatha's diplomacy. But when all had agreed, each clasped the hands of the sister tribes "so firmly that a falling tree should not sever them." Thus was born the famous and formidable League of the Iroquois.

Whether or not the story is true, the strategic logic behind the movement is obvious. By warring incessantly on one another, the Five Nations were plainly doomed. It would be only a matter of time before Iroquois disunity ended in the destruction of the tribes. The success of the league was rapid and dramatic. Within 50 years (roughly the first half of the 17th century), the members had created the most powerful confederation of Indian tribes on the continent.

Basically, the league was an alliance of five nations, or states, speaking the same language and sharing common cultural traits. Each tribe was permitted to govern itself, with little or no league interference; but larger problems of government, such as dealings with other tribes, were decided by the Great Council that met annually at Onondaga, the principal village of the Onondaga tribe. According to tribal mythology, the meeting

Oratory—An Effective Weapon of the Iroquois League

The powerful confederacy of five Iroquois tribes was already in existence in the 17th century when the French, Dutch, and English began vying for the rich fur trade of upper New York, the St. Lawrence Valley, and the Great Lakes region. Standing athwart the major trade routes to the fur country, the confederacy's policy was to control the trade and, through shifting alliances with one white power or another, maintain, and even extend, the league's dominion over the northern Woodlands. Increasingly, at the annual Great Council of the league, discussion revolved around relations with the Europeans who sent envoys to the meetings. Council members held forth, to impress the whites with the power and unity of the five tribes. At such times, as indeed in all council discussions, oratorical skill was highly prized. In this excerpt from a 1684 speech by the Onondaga chief Grangula, the league answers the threats of a French representative who had come to warn that his nation would retaliate should the Iroquois continue their interference with the fur trade. But the Iroquois knew the visitor was bluffing, for the French forces had been decimated by epidemic. Though the speech has been translated into stilted English, it cannot fail to impress with its imagery and power:

"Onondio [a word for white]! I honor you. . . . My words make haste to reach your ears. Harken to them! . . . You must have believed when you left Quebec that the sun had burnt up all the forest, which renders our country inaccessible to the French. . . . Now you are undeceived. I, and the warriors here present, are come to assure you that the Senecas, Cayugas, Onondagas, Oneidas, and Mohawks are yet alive. . . . Hear, Onondio! I do not sleep. . . . Take care for the future that so great a number of [French] soldiers as appear there [in league territory], do not choke the tree of peace. . . . It will be a great loss, if, after it has so easily taken root, you should stop its growth."

The league sometimes sent out its own representatives to the whites. In the following speech, made in Montreal in 1694, the Onondaga representative, Dekanisora, warns his French hosts that the tenuous peace between them and the confederacy could quickly end should the French continue to raid Iroquois villages and attempt to build forts in the league's domains.

"Father [a French official] . . . We must tell you that you are a bad man. . . . You are still not to be trusted. We have had a war together a long time. Still, though you occasioned the war, we have never hated [you]. . . . You have almost eaten us up. Our best men are killed. . . . But we forget what is past. Before this we once threw the hatchet [symbol of war] into the river. . . but you fished it up, and treacherously surprised our people at Cadaraqui. . . . Then the hatchet was thrown up to the sky, but you kept a string fastened to the helve, and pulled it down, and fell upon our people again. . . . Onondio! We will not permit any [French] settlement at Cadaraqui. You have had your fires there thrice extinguished. We will not consent to your building that fort; but the passage through the river shall be free and clear [to permit the French to carry on the fur trade]. We . . . drive away all the clouds and darkness, that we may see the light without interruption."

Keeper of the council fire, Uthawah was a much respected councillor among his fellow sachems in the Iroquois League. He could do little, however, to stem the tide of white settlements on tribal lands. When he died in 1847, little was left of the once powerful league.

MOHAWK
Dekarihokenh
Ayonhwathah
Shadekariwadeh
Sharenhowaneh
Deyoenhegwenh
Orenregowah
Dehennakarineh
Rastawenseronthah
Shoskoarowaneh

ONEIDA
Odatshedeh
Kanongweniyah
Deyohagwendeh
Shononses
Dehonareken
Adyadonneatha
Adahoneayenh
Ronyadashayouh
Ronwatshadonhonh

ONONDAGA
Adodarhonh
Awennisera
Dehatkadons
Yadajiwakenh
Awekenyat
Dehayatgwareh
Ononwirehtonh
Oewenniseroni
Arirhonh
Oewayonhnyeanih
Thosadegwaseh
Sakokeaeh
Seawi
Skanaawadi

CAYUGA
Dekaeayough
Tsinondawerhon
Kadagwarasonh
Soyouwes
Watyaseronneh
Deyohronyonkoh
Deyothorehgwen
Dawenhethon
Wadondaherha
Deskae

SENECA
Skanyadariyoh
Shadekaronyes
Shakenjohwaneh
Kanokareh
Deshanyenah
Shodyenawat
Kanonkeridawih
Sagehjowa

The notched staff was used by a Iroquois sachem to list the members of the Great Council. The staff is divided into five sections—one per tribe—and pegs in each represent the various council members.

took place on a hill where stood the Tree of Great Peace, with an eagle in its upper branches. ("If he sees in the distance any danger threatening," Dekanawidah had promised, "he will at once warn the people of the league.") The Great Council Fire, symbolizing the confederacy, burned at the site. The ascending smoke would reassure the Five Nations and their allies that the council was in session and that their affairs were being looked after by responsible men.

Fifty seats of thistledown were traditionally spread beneath the tree for tribal representatives. Nine were allotted to the Mohawks, 9 to the Oneidas, 14 to the Onondagas, 10 to the Cayugas, and 8 to the Senecas. This allocation of seats had no relation to the size or power of any tribe and did not affect resolutions. All agreements had to be adopted unanimously by all representatives and all tribes.

Although there were 50 council seats, there were only 49 councillors; Hiawatha was regarded as so irreplaceable that no man was permitted to succeed him. Because he was a Mohawk, the vacant place was in that tribe's delegation. The other seats were owned by the clans and filled by male descendants, determined through the mothers of the original chiefs summoned by Hiawatha. Despite this law of inheritance, the men ruled at the discretion of the tribal matrons. These women nominated them, briefed them before each session, monitored their legislative record, and when necessary, removed them from office. On such occasion, and upon the death of a council member, the matrons might choose a successor too young to occupy the seat immediately; in this case a kinsman would act as his regent.

For all these feminine checks and balances, the actual business of government was a masculine affair. We may imagine a new Seneca councillor, just chosen for office, arriving at Onondaga for the start of the fall session in, say, the year 1644. He is greeted by his personal name, for he has not yet received the name that traditionally goes with his seat—for example, Sagehjowa, meaning "Great Forehead." He makes himself comfortable with a long cane pipe and waits for the proceedings to begin.

Before the council can be opened officially, a Condolence Ceremony is performed to mourn the loss of the recently departed and to "raise up," or install, the new Great Forehead, for the council cannot convene until the traditional requirement that all seats (except Hiawatha's, of course) be filled. During this preliminary, formal speeches are made and the names of all 50 original councillors are recited. No dancing or instrumental music accompanies this most solemn occasion. The ceremony lasts for an afternoon.

The next morning all members are formally sworn in, and the council gets down to the business at hand. A Seneca councillor reports that raids by the Hurons—Iroquoian cousins but bitterly hostile to the Five

Bedecked with feathers, this ceremonial Seneca headdress was made after the coming of Europeans, as its silver band reveals. Ordinary headgear offered a degree of protection from a war-club blow; the skin cap was reinforced with willow twigs.

Nation League—have grown in intensity. The Seneca speaks at great length, as is the custom, and he describes in graphic terms the suffering of his people at the hands of the raiders. He mentions the many Seneca warriors who have fallen protecting their homes or in retaliatory raids, and he speaks of young widows and fatherless children in words calculated to arouse both sympathy and desires for revenge among his audience. Finally, the orator appeals for unity among the Five Nations in a campaign of revenge that will, once and for all, properly chastise the upstart Hurons.

When the Seneca representative ends his oration, the representatives of the four other nations go off separately to discuss what they have just heard. Upon returning to the council, the most sagacious of the Mohawks arises to make his nation's views known. As if to add emphasis, he repeats much of what the Seneca orator had said, and then, in keeping with the consensus within the Mohawk delegation, he adds many choice tidbits of his own concerning the treachery and brutal actions of the Hurons and the need for a major effort to break their power.

Again the tribal representatives meet in separate caucuses, and when they return, an Onondaga rises to speak. Like the Mohawks and the Senecas, the Onondagas have long been appalled by Huron depredations, and the speaker adds his voice to the growing consensus for war. And so the council session continues for more than two weeks, until the representatives of every tribe have had their say and the feeling is unanimous that raids against the Hurons must be greatly increased and well-deserved punishment meted out to this outlaw tribe that dared to defy the Five Nations.

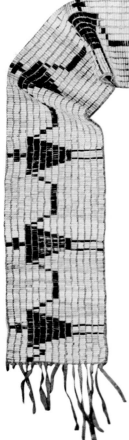

Wampum: Beads That Served Many Needs

By the time the Dutch occupied Manhattan in the early 17th century, the Algonquians and Iroquois of the Northeast were using wampum in their tribal and intertribal affairs. These white and purple disk-shaped beads, painstakingly fashioned from clamshells found along New Jersey and Long Island beaches, were strung together to be exchanged as gifts on ceremonial occasions, for gift giving—to accompany every sort of agreement and invitation, or to commemorate events—was a long-honored tradition.

The Indians never conceived of wampum as money nor, indeed, had any notion of currency at all. But not surprisingly, the European colonists, once they realized that the natives valued beads, adopted wampum as a medium of exchange in many of their dealings with the tribes. In fact, lacking gold and silver bullion to carry on their own affairs, Dutch settlers, for a time, used wampum as a form of currency among themselves. From the 17th century onward, a thriving cottage industry in wampum developed among the settlers. They sold most of the millions of beads they made to white traders, who in turn exchanged them for Indian goods, chiefly pelts. Because of their relatively sophisticated tools, white manufacturers were able to produce vast quantities of beads, all of them far more uniform in size and shape and lighter in weight than the traditional Indian products. In general, the tribes were eager to secure these beads, and the white traders were able to strike highly profitable bargains for themselves. These cylindrically shaped beads of white manufacture were often fashioned by the Indians into belts that commemorated important events in tribal history. In addition, Indians valued wampum as "good medicine," which calmed the contentious and consoled the bereaved.

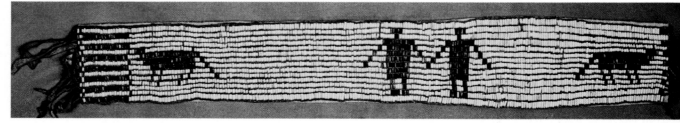

The Washington Belt *(top) is over six feet long and commemorates a covenant of peace between the original 13 colonies* *and the Iroquois League. The Wolf Belt (above) celebrated the friendly relations between white settlers and the Indians.*

Just before the council is about to adjourn, new fuel is added to the rising fever for war. A Pine Tree Chief, one of several famous Mohawk warriors to hold this title, suddenly appears. Though he is not a councillor, his reputation for courage and steadfastness gains him entry for the purpose of oration. He brings new and unwelcome news. The Hurons have just raided another Seneca village. Many warriors are dead, many women and children carried off captive. Surely the honor—and indeed the interests—of the Five Nations require an immediate response. As this Pine Tree Chief speaks, his audience remains silent, as is customary. But their expressions reveal that they are profoundly affected by

the catalog of horrors they are hearing about. (And when the council adjourns, they will carry home a unanimous decision for war, and war leaders among the tribes will raise raiding parties to scourge the Hurons with the wrath of the league.)

A few days later the Great Council Fire is banked and the speaker declares the session over. Councillors and observers collect into tribal bands and disperse in different directions.

As Great Forehead and his party journey west, somebody remarks: "See how the Great Bear drips blood." This is not a prophecy of doom, merely a mild comment on the fact that the leaves have changed color.

130

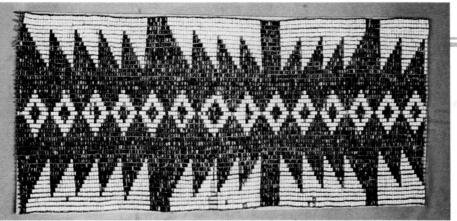

The Totadaho Belt, 14 inches wide and strung with commercially made beads, was woven sometime after 1755. The diamond shapes in the center of the belt are believed to represent the chain of human friendship. This wampum belt, the second widest in existence, was probably exhibited at the league's annual Great Council meetings.

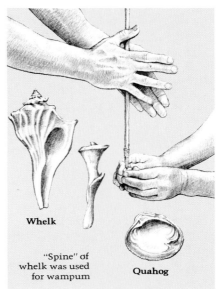

Whelk

"Spine" of whelk was used for wampum

Quahog

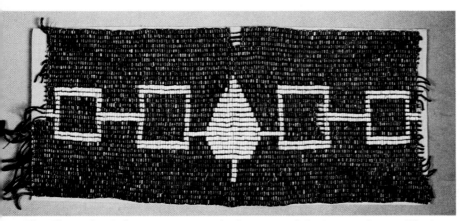

The Hiawatha Belt commemorates the formation of the Iroquois League. The interconnected squares, linked to a central tree, or heart, signify the unity of five Iroquois tribes. The belt was probably made after the arrival of Europeans; the beads are cylindrical, denoting manufacture by whites. Indian beads were usually flat.

Before mass-produced wampum was introduced by white traders, the Indians made their slender beads with painstaking efforts. The first step was to trim a shell by knocking off unwanted projections with a stone tool. Then, with one man holding the piece of shell, another man, using a sharp, slender drill, rotated the tool between his hands in a back-and-forth motion to create a hole. In the finishing process, bead-makers used sand to polish the rough, outer part of the shell. Shells from the quahog clam, the conch, and the whelk were highly valued. Finished beads, usually about one-tenth of an inch in diameter, were strung on sinews.

The Huron Belt commemorates the contract made in 1683 between the Jesuit missionaries and the Hurons for the erection of the first wooden church on tribal lands. The white cross on the purple ground represents loyalty to Christianity. The figures to the left of the cross are Jesuits; to the right, Indians. At the extreme right is the church with its enclosure.

Fall will soon be over; it is time for a man's thoughts to turn from politics to religion.

The world of the Iroquois was full of invisible spirits; earthly symbols of them were everywhere. Some of these were False Faces, demonlike spirits that could cause disease. Fortunately, their great power could also be harnessed and actually reversed by those medicine men who were initiates in the secrets of a False Face Society. They used the very forces that had caused the ailments to effect the cures.

To the Iroquois, the world in which they lived was one where the forces of good and evil were inherent in all of nature. It had been so from the beginning. To Great Forehead and his fellow tribesmen, human life began with a Sky-Woman who was pushed out of heaven. She landed on an island that had been created when a muskrat brought a bit of mud from under the sea and placed it on a turtle's shell. As the turtle grew, so too did the land to form an enormous fertile island for the Sky-Woman to live on. She had been impregnated by the Earth Holder before she left heaven and gave birth to a daughter. This daughter was herself magically impregnated and bore two sons, Great Spirit and Evil Spirit, but in bearing the latter the woman died. Though dead, her influence remained. From her head, Great Spirit fashioned the sun; from her body, the moon and stars. Not content with this work, Great Spirit turned his attention to the earth resting upon the turtle shell, and he made the seas, the rivers, the mountains and valleys, and finally man, the animals, and plants. Evil Spirit worked too, and from his labors came contention, strife, anger, and warfare, as well as creatures dangerous to all other living things. Obviously, two such opposite spirits could not live together, and so Great Spirit and Evil Spirit fought for two whole days. Evil Spirit was defeated and forced into exile in the netherworld, but his handiwork remained behind to bedevil the children of the earth.

The Green Corn Festival, which took place in late summer, celebrated the gift of corn. The first crop of corn was a beautiful sight, because it meant that the earth's fertility had not failed. The thanksgiving began with a day-long assembly summoned by the Faithkeepers, male and female dignitaries appointed for ceremonial duties by each tribe. With the people seated on both sides of the longhouse, a speaker expressed their gratitude to the whole pantheon of spirit forces—the earth, waters, herbs, grasses, saplings, trees, crops, animals, birds, thunder and rain, wind, sun, moon, and stars—and to the creator, the Great Spirit. Then the speaker would announce a list of forthcoming dances, beginning with the spirited, graceful Feather Dance. A great feast ended the first day's ceremonies.

The second day began with another speech of thanksgiving, followed by a dance that was constantly interrupted by more speeches expressing gratitude to the spirits. Singing was the major activity of the third day, solo performances by men who sang their personal songs of praise to the spirits. Finally, on the last day, a game of chance, known as the bowl game, was played, this too being part of the ritual. With its completion the celebration of the Green Corn Festival came to its conclusion.

Among other festivals were those held to give thanks for the Harvest (October), the Rise of the Maple (late February or March, according to sap levels), the Planting of Corn (May or June), and the Strawberry, first fruit of the season (June). Basically, they were similar to the Green Corn Festival in their expression of gratitude for the fertile earth.

But there was yet another and most awesome ritual, devoted to the supernatural world of dreams and visions: the Iroquois Ceremonial of Midwinter. Although details of the rite may have changed over the centuries, it is still primarily concerned with dreams, confession, and thanksgiving. The following description of a 19th-century Ceremonial of Midwinter would probably apply generally to one held by the Iroquois in the 1600's.

On the last day of the old year as calculated by the Iroquois (usually late in January or early in February), the ceremonial began with a ritual "naming of the babies." It was devoted to a recital of the names of babies born since the Green Corn *(continued on page 136)*

The False Face Society: The Power of the Supernatural

Among the many religious organizations of the Iroquois, t best known to Europeans was the False Face Society, whi was primarily concerned with curing ailments, particula those of the head, shoulders, and limbs. A toothache, a per tent nosebleed, a swollen ankle, and the like were all con tions amenable to the ministrations of society members. ceremonials, False Face members wore fantastic masks, su as those at right, which were endowed with curative powe By wearing the mask and practicing the proper rituals, th powers were transferred to the society members, enabli them to minister to the ill and injured.

Although society initiates were called upon to heal ma different ailments, their ceremony was essentially the sa whether they were treating an earache or a swollen joi Society members appeared at the patient's longhouse only invitation. The sick person usually had had a dream in whi a False Face appeared. This was a signal to call upon t society to effect a cure, though sometimes the dream was unclear that the afflicted first consulted a clairvoyant w informed the person that the dream was a summons to t False Faces. Clad in their magical masks, False Face memb arrived at the patient's dwelling and formed a circle arou him. Some members danced and shook their rattles; oth scooped up glowing embers from a fire and blew ashes at t patient. Once cured by such a ceremony, the patient hims automatically became a False Face member, and it was nec sary for him to secure a mask. Usually, it was the dream th had summoned the False Faces that provided the inspirati for the mask, and the new member might go out into t woods, find a suitable tree, and begin carving the face on t base of its trunk. If, however, he felt he did not have t necessary skill for the task, he would describe the features the mask to a carver who would then do the job. If the car began his assignment in the morning, the mask was color red; if in the afternoon, black.

As the face seen in a dream might take many forms, too did the masks. Features varied widely, and mouths, example, might be crooked, agape, straight-lipped, tongue p truding, smiling, or blowing. But despite varying physiogr mies, all masks were evocative of the original False Face supernatural being who had been punished by the Great Sp it for his boastfulness by being condemned to spend etern healing the sick.

The masks, however, were mercurial. They had to treated with respect, the owners feeding them corn mush a rubbing them with sunflower oil. A person who ridiculed mask courted almost certain illness, or if he left it lyi faceup, it would make fearsome noises. Similar rules su rounded the masks of the Husk Face Society, a smaller re gious group. Their masks, made of cornhusks, represented mythical farming people, and the masks themselves had t power of prophecy. It was during the Midwinter Ceremon that the Husk Faces held their ritual in which men and bo of the society performed dances and, through the medium their masks, predicted bountiful crops and the birth of ma children in the year to come. Unlike the False Faces, t Husk Faces were almost mute during their ceremonies a made only puffing sounds. Despite their differences, Fal Faces and Husk Faces, and indeed all other Iroquois religio societies, performed the same basic function: manipulati the forces of the supernatural to the purposes of the tribe the benefit of an individual.

This False Face mask, ornately adorned with long strands of horsehair and scowling eyes, is one of the oldest extant. Known today as the Joseph Brant Mask, it was taken to Canada by that Mohawk war leader who fought on the British side during the American Revolution. Brant and his followers settled in Canada in 1786 on land bought with British funds.

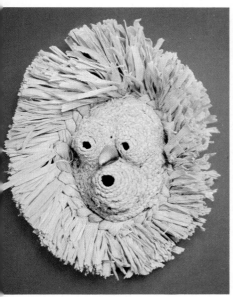

Made of cornhusks, this mask was worn by members of the Husk Face Society. The mask consists of individual cornhusk braids that were sewn together with husk fiber or twine into the form of a face. In the braiding process, two holes were left for the eyes and one for the mouth. A nose might be shaped from a husk or a piece of wood. The loose ends of cornhusk that surround the face represent hair.

A museum display of the work of several generations of mask-makers includes wood False Faces as well as a cornhusk mask and several masquettes (pole, far left). The miniatures were attached to larger masks or were charms to protect dwellings from witchcraft. The tree, with the mask still in its niche (right), shows an early stage in the process of mask-making. A man would find a healthy basswood, burn tobacco at its base, and offer prayers. Then he carved the face into the standing trunk. Only when the mask was near completion would he cleave away the sculpture to hollow it out and paint its features.

Marvelous Masks, Mysterious Cures

False Face Society members, their features obscured by extravagantly carved masks, practice their healing rituals on an Iroquois tribesman suffering from an intense headache. Surrounded by False Faces and observed by residents of his longhouse, where the ceremony takes place, the patient is having his head massaged by one society member while another blows ashes in his face. Nearby, another False Face scoops up a handful of ashes that he, too, will blow at the ailing man. Stationed around the longhouse are several other False Faces, one of whom guards the deerskin-hung entrance to prevent anyone from entering during the ceremony. Such an interruption at this stage would disturb, or perhaps even nullify, the healing process. Several of the False Faces carry mud-turtle shell rattles, like the symbolically decorated one below. These are filled with pebbles and are shaken to accompany the incantations that the society members chant to help drive out the spirit of sickness from the body of the patient.

Such were the powers of the False Faces that these ceremonies took but several minutes to complete, even for the most debilitating ailments. At the ritual's end the False Faces received their reward: a portion of precious tobacco and a platter of cornmeal mush, prepared in advance by the patient's grateful family who were certain that the rite would have its desired effect. As for the patient, presumably cured by the ceremony, he automatically became a member of the False Face Society, for all who were treated were obliged to join. In future ceremonials he will don a mask and help bring relief to others with ailments of the head and limbs.

Festival had been celebrated four months earlier.

Early the following morning two grotesque figures wearing shaggy buffalo robes encircled with braids of cornhusks came out of the longhouse to announce the new year. The children, far from being terrified, greeted them affectionately as "Our Uncles, the Big Heads." The Big Heads described the forthcoming festivities, the main purpose of which was the renewal of dreams.

For many in the village, this renewal was of surpassing importance, for it recalled days of illness in which signs had appeared to them in dreams. For example, four years earlier, the woman Winter Blossom had been ailing with an infected arm. Delirious with fever, she saw a False Face in a dream and then asked members of the False Face Society to dance for her. They did so, and she was cured. Now, every year at the Midwinter Festival, Winter Blossom requested the False Face Society members to repeat part of that curative dance. In this way the dream was renewed and the spirit that caused the infected arm was again warded off, preventing Winter Blossom from falling prey to the same ailment.

After the False Faces danced for Winter Blossom in her longhouse, they repeated the ritual in all of the

Seneca Big Heads, who announce the start of the Midwinter Ceremonial, trudge through the snow from longhouse to longhouse. Each Big Head carries a paddle to stir hearth ashes, a rite symbolizing the commencement of the new year.

other longhouses of the village. Indeed, for a period of days, the entire village and every longhouse echoed to the rhythm of dancing feet. Every society that had effected cures through their rituals renewed the dreams of those whom they had succored, repeating each dance over and over again as they moved from one longhouse to the next.

During the first day of the festival a second group of Big Heads visited the longhouses to stir the ashes of the fires. This symbolized the scattering of the Old Year Fire and the kindling of the New; also, their presence brought relief to any sick people in the house.

That same day a white dog—one of a breed symbolizing purity and kept especially for such occasions—was solemnly strangled. Its body was daubed with red paint, garlanded with white wampum, and then hung from a pole.

The following morning, the second day of the ceremonial, ashes were again stirred, this time first by Faithkeepers, then by ordinary people dressed in their best clothes. After thanksgiving songs in the council house, the dances for the renewal of dreams began. One man had once dreamed that the dream-guessing rite be performed. His request for renewal touched off a ceremony known as the great riddle. Those who had dreamed during the year gone by went from door to door hinting at their dreams in the form of riddles while listeners tried to describe the dream accurately. If someone guessed correctly, he was then required to satisfy the desire inherent in the dream, no matter how peculiar or extravagant.

"I seek that which bears a lake within itself," says one woman. Someone eventually guesses that the woman has dreamed about a pumpkin and hands her one. Had a pumpkin not been available, it would have been an extremely bad omen, for dreams expressed the desires of the soul, and such desires, unless fulfilled, could lead to misfortune.

On the third day of the Midwinter Ceremonial, the False Faces and other secret medicine societies continued their dream-renewal dances. The real fun, as far as youngsters were concerned, came now, when groups of youths, each accompanied by an old woman, roamed the village. In return for presents of tobacco, they would dance and sing; if no presents were forthcoming, they could steal whatever they might lay their hands on—an early form of trick or treat.

On the fourth day the village chief announced that the dream-renewal dances had ended. Everyone in the community then went to the council longhouse where various societies performed the dances for which

Equipment for an Iroquois game includes a decorated wooden bowl containing six peach pits, one side of each charred black, the other white. As played at the Midwinter Ceremonial, members from two moieties competed. The player rapped the bowl sharply against the ground, and if five or six pits turned up the same color, he scored and went again. If not, a member of the opposing team took his turn. Four clan symbols—bear, wolf, turtle, and deer—are on the bowl's bottom. They are purely decorative, serving no functional purpose.

Snowsnakes: A Seneca Sport of Strength and Skill

When the cold weather and its attendant snows settled upon the land of the Senecas, tribesmen gathered to play their favorite sport, snowsnakes. The game itself was deceptively simple—the goal being to slide a long, smooth stick along a trough in the snow farther than one's opponents. But expertise required not just strong muscles to start the stick on its course, but also an accurate eye and a great skill at placing the shaft properly in the trough so that it would travel a maximum distance. The game got its name from the flexible sticks that undulated in a snakelike fashion as they sped along the trough.

Snowsnake sticks might be as long as nine feet or as short as five, and were made from hickory, maple, or walnut. They were superbly designed for speed and, if skillfully handled, traveled their icy course with the velocity of a loosed arrow. To give a stick sufficient weight, its conical head was tipped with lead. Each shaft was about an inch wide at the crown and tapered off to less than half an inch at the tail.

To make a trough, the Senecas dragged a smooth-barked log lengthwise through the snow, repeating the process until the trench was about 1,500 feet long and 10 to 18 inches deep, its bottom and sides packed down into a smooth, icy surface. Any number could play the snowsnake game, either as individual competitors or as members of opposing teams. In addition to active participants, each side had snowsnake "doctors" who cared for the sticks, rubbing them with "medicine"—beeswax or animal oils—to reduce their friction. Contests were refereed by umpires who made certain that the rules of the game were strictly observed.

The game ended when every contestant had had his turn, and the distances were all tallied. Winners collected whatever had been bet on the outcome.

His snowsnake poised
for release, a Seneca makes a running approach to the trough and tries to maintain concentration in the face of heckling by members of the opposing team hoping to ruin his aim. If the player missed the trough or his shaft hit at an angle, he would be the target of a stream of good-natured abuse from the opposition.

they were noted. Some of these were medicine dances, but others might be an expression of exuberance. There were, for example, head-butting dances by the Buffalo Society; a Bear Society dance that climaxed in a feast of strawberry jam; a dance in which the False Faces appeared as clowns; and a dance by warriors of the Husk Face Society who were dressed in women's clothing.

The mood of the ceremonial turned solemn once more on the fifth day. Faithkeepers removed the body of the white dog from its pole. The remains were burned, and the soul of the dog ascended to the realm of the Great Spirit, to convey the villagers' thanks for the numerous blessings of the year that has gone by.

On the sixth day the Sacred Feather Dance was performed, followed by the Thanksgiving Dance. The last day of the celebration was taken up by the Rite of Personal Chants, in which each adult male sang his own song. Finally, there was the Sacred Bowl Game that everyone played until the contest was completed.

After a week of occult searching, dancing, games, general tumult, and fun, quiet gradually descended on the village. Now was the time to recall the skill of the dancers, the antics of the clowns, the personal chants, and all the other activities of the Midwinter Ceremonial. A new year had begun.

Peninsula Dwellers

Before European traders and missionaries gave the Hurons their insulting name (derived from the French *hure*, meaning "lout," or "ruffian"), these Indians called themselves the *Wendat*, that is, "Dwellers on a Peninsula." Their homeland in what is now southern Ontario, Canada, was indeed largely surrounded by water, being bounded on the west by Lake Huron and on the east by Lake Simcoe. A network of streams, rivers, and smaller lakes divided the area into fertile patches of land.

The 30,000 inhabitants of this tranquilly beautiful landscape were related linguistically and culturally to the Five Nations of upper New York State, but politically they were enemies. Like the Iroquois, the Hurons lived in longhouses; took their clan-affiliations from their maternal ancestors; grew crops of corn, beans, and squash; rubbed their skins with sunflower-seed oil; dressed in moccasins, leggings, and robes; and endlessly analyzed their dreams.

But there were differences as well. Because their territory was comparatively small, the Hurons lived close together. One ceremony unique to the Hurons was the ritual known as the Feast of the Dead. To the Hurons, death was such a catastrophe that the mere mention of it to those recently bereaved was regarded as a curse, terrible enough to make people come to blows. The dead themselves were believed to be equally sensitive about their loss of life and resented being separated from the community. Therefore the living, fearing the dead's power to cause illness, went to extraordinary lengths to make all corpses secure and comfortable. If,

for example, a fire broke out in the village, a man's first thought was to protect the graveyard, and only then his own house; to neglect that holy ground would be to run the risk of recrimination by angry ghosts. The remains of evening meals were left out for any hungry souls who might be wandering about.

The dead, it was believed, lived in a world mirroring that of the living. In that distant world, "life" went on much as it did on earth: the souls of men went hunting and fishing, while souls of women planted ghostly crops and suckled the souls of dead children.

But before leaving the earth for good, souls remained in the environs of their home village; so the Hurons built temporary cemeteries to accommodate them. Bodies were wrapped in beaver robes, placed in bark coffins, then elevated 8 to 10 feet above the ground on a framework of poles. Here they would await the next scheduled Feast of the Dead—which might not occur for 10 or 12 years. The infrequency of this ceremony, observed by all Huron tribes, only served to increase its solemnity. Its function was to console ghosts for the death they had suffered and send them off, happy and tranquil, to their villages beyond the place where the sun set.

Preparations for the feast might last for eight days. All bodies were removed from their coffins, and the bones of older corpses stripped clean of what flesh remained. The flesh was thrown into a fire, along with the sodden robes and mats that had wrapped the bodies. Then the bones were carefully washed and bundled up in fine new beaver skins. Fresh corpses were left intact. When all was ready, mourners hoisted bundles and bodies on their backs and transported them with great dignity to the village where the Feast of the Dead was to be held.

Feasting and dancing awaited the pilgrims at the host village. Meanwhile, in a field nearby, a pit was being dug, about 15 feet wide and 10 feet deep. It was surrounded by a semicircular scaffold and a platform, the former for the bundled skeletons, the latter for the bodies.

On the last evening of the ceremonial, when all the dead had been arranged around the pit and then festooned with presents, the mass grave was lined with beaver robes. Then the whole corpses were gently laid in place and covered with more beaver robes. That night the mourners camped in the field, warming themselves at great fires and feasting. At dawn a great cry of lamentation arose as the sacks of bones were emptied into the pit. Then

Elaborate designs on the Huron pouch (right) and moccasins (below) reflect European influence, but the embroidery techniques and decorative materials stem from the tribe's precontact past. Both items are made from black-dyed buckskin and embellished with colored hairs taken from the mane, cheeks, and rump of moose. In their natural state the moose hairs are about five inches long. They are white for most of their length but taper off to a black tip. Huron women traditionally used vegetable dyes that yielded bright, varigated colors. The hairs, once dyed, were stored in bundles according to color. When needed, each hair was moistened to make it flexible, and then three or four were sewn together with an awl and sinew, to make a single strand.

Life Among the Hurons: A French View

In the year 1615 the Hurons of Lake Ontario played host to a visitor from a distant world: Samuel de Champlain (c.1570–1635), explorer, cartographer, trailblazer, administrator, founder of Quebec, and loyal servant of His Majesty King Louis XIII of France. As the first Frenchman to reach Lake Ontario, Champlain was on a mission of great importance. He was to secure his nation's control over the Great Lakes country and, with it, a monopoly on the valuable trade in beaver pelts.

Pursuing this goal, Champlain spent five months among the Hurons and bound them to a firm alliance with France while he recorded their customs and made drawings on which these engravings are based. It was through his observations that his countrymen gained their first impressions of Huron culture. Thanks in part to the French alliance and French arms, the Hurons were able to act as middlemen in the fur trade and hold off their traditional enemy, the Iroquois League. But waning French influence and the rising power of the Iroquois League eventually sealed the Hurons' doom.

The living bear the dead to a common burial pit as part of the Hurons' Feast of the Dead. In his commentaries Champlain said that the Hurons believed this mingling of their relatives' bones obligated the tribesmen to live in a state of tribal unity.

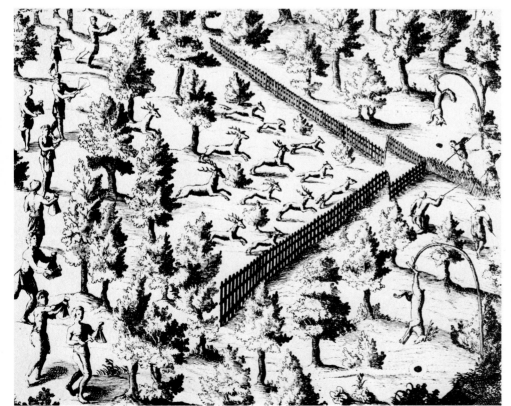

Protected by armor of wood slats, bow and tomahawk in hand, this Huron warrior is outfitted for combat in an engraving based on a sketch by Champlain. At left is the Frenchman's view of a deer hunt. Beaters drive their prey into a fenced enclosure where the animals may be easily dispatched by spear-wielding hunters. Other deer are taken with snares.

men, using poles, pushed and prodded the remains into an anonymous heap. When the pit was finally layered over with sand, poles, and sticks, the souls were at last free to journey to the west along the Milky Way.

The Lands of Wild Rice

The westernmost region of the Woodlands was often called the Lands of Wild Rice because of the self-sowing, seed-bearing grass that grew naturally along the shallow muddy shores of lakes, streams, and marshes as far west as the Mississippi Valley. This delicious grain played an important role in the diet of several western Algonquian tribes. In many instances wild rice was also used for barter with neighboring tribes who had no access to the marshlands where the grain grew.

In prehistoric times, however, the inhabitants of the Great Lakes area faced a far harsher environment. For a few thousand years following the final retreat of the Wisconsin Glacier about 8500 B.C., the landscape of

An Algonquian pictograph, probably centuries old, of a man, moose, puma, and canoes, decorates a cliff overlooking Hegman Lake in Minnesota. Pictographs are paintings, and the Indians used them as well as petroglyphs—images pecked, scratched, or abraded on stone—to record events or perhaps to prophesy hoped-for happenings. The red used in this pictograph was made from finely ground hematite, an iron ore, mixed with a binder of vegetable oils, blood, or egg white.

the Great Lakes region was cold, scrubby, and inhospitable. At least four successive hunting cultures roamed the region before wild rice grew there. The Paleo-Indians flourished between 10,000 and 7000 B.C., and their fluted, mastodon-killing spearpoints of flint mingled with the moraine of the retreating glacier. Next, between 7000 and 5000 B.C., came the Plano Indians with their nonfluted spearpoints for killing smaller prey, such as elk, bison, and caribou, and the Archaic Boreal Indians (5000–1500 B.C.) who, along with hunting, learned to make jewelry from local copper.

One early Woodland culture in this region, arising about 500 B.C., left behind the pots of fired clay and burial mounds throughout much of the region. By now the climate of the Great Lakes region was warmer, its soil deeper and more fertile. Corn arrived, by way of the Mississippi, Illinois, and Ohio Valleys, about A.D. 800, and agricultural villages were established along the banks of the three rivers. By the time French fur traders appeared in the 17th century, all of the tribes in the vast area between the west bank of Lake Huron and the east bank of the Mississippi were Algonquian, except for the Siouan-speaking Winnebago who lived along the western shore of Lake Michigan.

Although there were minor differences between such Algonquian tribes as the Menominee, Potawatomi, Ottawa, Ojibwa, Fox, Sauk, Illinois, and Miami, they all had similar cultures. Even the Winnebagos, save for their language, were scarcely distinguishable from their Algonquian neighbors. The primary difference among the tribes lay in their manner of securing food, but even this was merely a matter of degree.

Some, such as the Sauks, Foxes, Winnebagos, and Miamis, combined agriculture with buffalo hunting, and they staged mass forays onto the prairies for a few weeks each summer in search of the animals. In fact, the only tribes in the region that did not hunt buffalo were the Potawatomi and Ottawa. Their homelands were too far to the north and east to make the trek to the prairies worthwhile. In any case, the surrounding forests abounded with moose, mink, otter, bear, beaver, rabbit, wolf, and wolverine.

Although there were such differences in how neighboring tribes maintained themselves, all of these tribes of the western section of the Woodland were much alike in their domestic arrangements and religious beliefs. To one degree or another, all were seminomadic, though most roamed only within a radius of a hundred miles or so from their base villages to hunt. Close by these communities were cleared fields where the women planted and tended such crops as corn, squash, and tobacco. The last of these had profound religious significance throughout the region.

Tobacco, it was believed, was a gift from the spirits. To thank the spirits, the Indians made frequent offerings of tobacco. When, for example, a wild rice harvest was about to begin, a few pinches of dried leaf were

At a winter camp members of a Sauk band cope with their needs for food and clothing. Their shelter, a mat-covered domed lodge, is built for portability; when game in the area is exhausted, the band will dismantle the dwelling and carry it to a new site. Life revolves around the deer hunt. For the warrior at lower left, weighted down with a buck's carcass, the pursuit has been a success. The animal will provide both meat and clothing for the band. Near the lodge a woman prepares a deerskin for fabrication into leggings, dresses, breechclouts, and the like. Using a stone-bladed knife, she scrapes the hair from the pelt. Later she will turn the skin and scrape it free of fat. Next the pelt will be washed and then smoked, as at upper right, to make it flexible. Camp life ended with the arrival of spring, when the Sauks returned to their permanent villages on Lake Michigan's shore. The traditional summer house (photograph above), built of elmbark on supporting poles, dates from the 1880's, after the Sauks and the Foxes had been forced to relocate in Oklahoma.

tossed on the waters to ensure ample pickings. Or if a warrior encountered a misshapen boulder or a gnarled tree trunk in the forest, he sprinkled tobacco on the ground to ward off wraiths that might bring about misfortune.

In addition to its ritualistic use, tobacco was important in establishing relations between peoples. Invitations to a ceremony or feast were often accompanied by a pinch of tobacco, and peace treaties between tribes were sealed by the communal smoking of an ornate calumet: a long, feather-decorated pipestem attached to a carved-stone bowl.

Summer, for the Great Lakes tribes, was the time of return to the permanent (or semipermanent) villages. The weather was pleasant, the maple sugaring completed, and now the women sowed crops and tended the fields while the men fished and hunted small game in the surrounding forest.

This was also a time of the great religious festivals,

the ceremonies in honor of Manitou: the forces, present in all things animate and inanimate, that controlled the destinies of men. These forces were often beneficent, but their temperaments were mercurial, and they had the power to harm as well as to help. Therefore propitiation of the forces was necessary. By the early years of the 17th century a new ceremony, connected with the Midewiwin movement—dedicated to the warding off of disease, the prolonging of life, and the healing of the sick—had swept through the region.

The Midewiwin was the Grand Medicine Society and in theory, at least, was a secret organization. So great were the powers inherent in its rites that many of the tribes believed that membership not only cured sickness but granted the soul eternal life. Therefore it was hardly surprising that the healthy as well as the afflicted sought admission to the Midewiwin ceremonies. Often a dream or a vision commanding one to join was sufficient to ensure acceptance. Among some

141

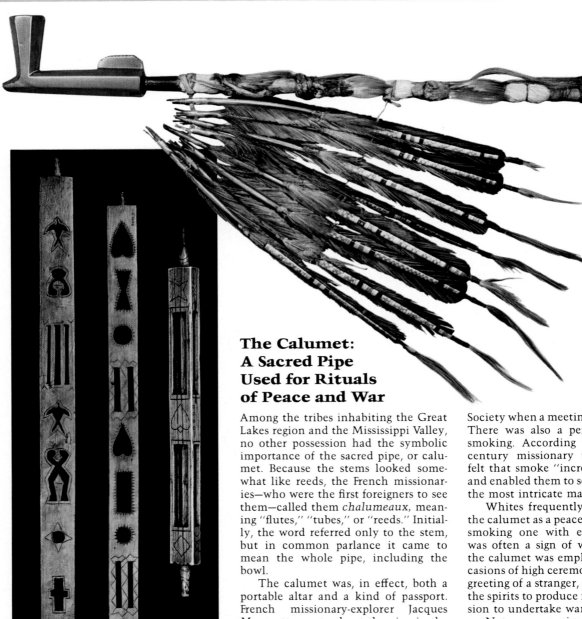

The Calumet: A Sacred Pipe Used for Rituals of Peace and War

Among the tribes inhabiting the Great Lakes region and the Mississippi Valley, no other possession had the symbolic importance of the sacred pipe, or calumet. Because the stems looked somewhat like reeds, the French missionaries—who were the first foreigners to see them—called them *chalumeaux*, meaning "flutes," "tubes," or "reeds." Initially, the word referred only to the stem, but in common parlance it came to mean the whole pipe, including the bowl.

The calumet was, in effect, both a portable altar and a kind of passport. French missionary-explorer Jacques Marquette wrote about the pipe in the mid-1600's: "There is nothing more mysterious or respected. . . . Less honor is paid to the crowns and scepters of kings. It seems to be the god of peace and war, the arbiter of life and death. It has to be but carried on one's person, and displayed, to enable one to walk through the midst of enemies, who, in the hottest of the fight, lay down their arms when it is shown."

The calumet probably acquired its symbolic importance because the Indians considered tobacco to have mystical properties. The Menominees, for example, included tobacco in their peace offerings, gave it to those from whom they expected favors and, accompanied by an invitation, presented it to the Medicine Society when a meeting was to be called. There was also a personal reason for smoking. According to another 17th-century missionary the Menominees felt that smoke "increased intelligence and enabled them to see clearly through the most intricate matters."

Whites frequently came to refer to the calumet as a peace pipe and, indeed, smoking one with erstwhile enemies was often a sign of warfare's end. But the calumet was employed on most occasions of high ceremony, including the greeting of a stranger, rites to encourage the spirits to produce rain, and the decision to undertake war.

Not every warrior had a pipe of his own, but chiefs often had several, some for personal use or for minor ceremonies, and at least one other, for particularly "strong medicine," that was smoked only when decisions of great importance were in the offing.

During such ceremonials the Indians usually sat in a circle and passed the calumet around, each tribesman taking his turn before offering it to the person on his left.

In almost every tribe that used the calumet, there was one pipe thought to be more powerful than any other. This was a tribe's most sacred possession, and a custodian of the pipes, a man conversant with all the rituals, guarded this calumet and directed its use.

Three carved pipestems—Ojibwa (left and center) and Winnebago—dating from the mid-19th century, reflect a high degree of craftmanship that is many centuries old. When fitted with tobacco-filled catlinite bowls, smoke passed down the stem through a zigzag channel that avoided the decorative cutouts. The channel was burned into the wood's pith with a heated copper wire. The 17-inch-long Potawatomi pipe (top) is of earlier origin and is decorated with quillwork and woodpecker scalps. Eight eagle feathers hang fanlike from the pipestem.

tribes, though, gifts to the society's elders were demanded as a price of admission. After initiation ceremonies, the new members were trained in various rites and the arts of self-healing, the teaching made graphic by pictograms incised on birchbark.

The most dramatic of the Midewiwin rites was the Grand Medicine Dance itself, when members of the society danced around a mat-draped lodge, chanting, working themselves into ecstasies, and throwing cowrie shells at initiates. These shells were thought to contain magical properties, and a candidate struck by a shell believed that it had entered his body. Immediately the Indian would fall into a trance, writhe in the dust, and finally go into a seemingly lifeless state. Then, as the magic began to work, the "dead" person stirred and arose, filled with new vitality and health.

Some of the rituals of the western Woodland tribes were solitary, and the most important of these was the vision quest. For a youth, the time of the first vision quest took place when puberty was beginning and he began to assume the stature of a man. To become a hunter and a warrior, he needed a guardian spirit. But to find this spirit, it was necessary to fast. The body, depleted through lack of food, became receptive to the spirits within the world of nature, spirits that appear in visions during dreamlike trances.

When a boy or his father believed the time was ripe, the youth was offered either food or charcoal at breakfast. If he chose charcoal, he rubbed it on his face as a sign that he would seek his guardian spirit. Then father and son left their wigwam and sought a likely place in the woods to build a rude shelter that would house the boy for as long as four days of almost total fasting. The shelter completed, the father returned alone to the village while the boy began his quest. As hunger sapped his vitality, the boy sat and waited, falling into a fitful sleep from time to time, until, in his deep reverie, the ardently sought guardian spirit came to him. The youth might dream of this spirit several times before he was certain that he had truly found his personal guide and protector. In some instances the spirit would confer un-

usual endowments—curative powers or the gift of prophecy—upon the youth. But in any case, the spirit that came during a boy's initial vision quest remained with him for life. Direct contact between spirit and warrior would periodically be renewed via additional vision quests.

Girls, too, might have visions of guardian spirits, although for them direct perception of the spirit world was not absolutely necessary. Among the western Great Lakes tribes, pubescent girls at their first menses went into a hut outside the village and, like their brothers, fasted and awaited the spirits. The girls sought divine aid in securing a good husband, health, and many children, and if a spirit actually manifested itself to the girl, she was doubly blessed.

Though women accepted menstruation as an unavoidable part of life, their monthly periods could be times of stress, as men looked upon menstrual blood as unclean, and the females were segregated. They remained in a separate shelter during their periods, for it was believed that if they touched the hunting or fishing tools of the menfolk, the quarry would smell the blood and keep their distance. And for a man to drink from a menstruating woman's cup or to share food with her was to invite misfortune. Sometimes this segregation was easily borne, for in the menstrual hut women could spend their time chatting. But at festival time, menstruating women keenly felt their disability, since it prevented them from partaking in the celebration.

Summer, the time of reunion, was also the season for war; not war on a large and bloody scale but, for the most part, raids on or small skirmishes with neighboring tribes. In this way young men proved their courage and took revenge for past

This Mide bag of otterskin, containing medicinal charms, a few migis shells, and herbs, is embellished with appliquéd beadwork, bells, and thimbles. It belonged to a member of the Winnebago Midewiwin Society, an organization of healers. This type of Mide bag was derived from a myth in which four spirit-beings, each carrying a live otter, suddenly appeared among the tribesmen and brought back to life a youth who had been dead for eight days. A Mide bag was highly prized by its owner and was buried with him.

143

Harvesting wild rice, as depicted by 19th-century artist Seth Eastman, requires a tribesman to maneuver the canoe and two women workers to gather the grain. Beating the stalks with paddles, the women garner about half of the rice grains, the rest falling to the bottom to germinate.

After harvesting, the rice was dried—by leaving it in the sun or by placing it on a scaffold over a slow fire. Then the rice was beaten to remove the tough hull and, finally, the grain was put into a birchbark tray and winnowed on a windy day. A favorite food among Great Lakes Indians, wild rice was served boiled with maple sugar or as part of a stew.

injuries. Men suffered and died in these encounters. But this was man-to-man or band-to-band combat and rarely, if ever, was there a wholesale bloodletting that left hundreds of women without husbands and their children without fathers.

"Wild Rice Men"

Summer was also life-giving, and no other Algonquian tribe greeted the season more enthusiastically than did the Menominee or, to use their full name, Meno-miniwok, meaning "Wild Rice Men." No other tribe ate such huge quantities of the "good grain" nor harvested it with such fervor. The Menominees relied entirely on the natural sowing cycle, but the mere act of gathering wild rice ensured propagation of the plant and thus a bumper crop for the next year.

In the late summer, when the wild rice stalks were almost ripe, the Menominees poled their canoes through the shallows to tie the tops of the stalks in bundles. Two or three weeks later, when the ripening was completed, the flotilla of canoes came again. Tribes of men and women drifted slowly through the reeds pulling the stalks over the gunwales of their small craft and beating the plants with sticks to release the seed-bearing husks. At least half of the husks fell into the water and sank to the muddy bottom, thereby renewing the cycle of growth.

Once ashore the harvest was threshed to separate seeds from husks. It was backbreaking work, but the results usually provided more than ample grain for the tribe's needs, and nothing was a greater goad to labor than the thought of a steaming dish of boiled wild rice seasoned with maple sugar.

The Menominees were medium-sized people with large brown eyes and light skins. Men wore shirts, breechcloths, and leggings of deerskin. Women wore deerskin tunics over shirts of woven nettles, buckskin leggings, and soft leather moccasins. Both sexes liked to decorate their clothes with beads, porcupine quills, and painted designs, and to wear jangling copper body ornaments. In summer the children went naked.

In the early 17th century the Menominees numbered approximately 1,900. They lived for most of the year in domed wigwams made of bent saplings covered with mats of reeds and cattails. In summer, however, the wigwams were too hot, and the tribe moved into peaked-roofed, rectangular houses whose higher ceilings and greater space afforded some relief from the heat.

These wigwams and houses were grouped into a number of year-round villages, with one main settlement near the mouth of the Menominee River, where it flows into Green Bay on Wisconsin's Lake Michigan shore. From the lake itself, and from nearby streams, the Menominees took various kinds of fish, although they particularly prized the large, sweet-fleshed sturgeon that abounded in the lake. These Indians employed just about every conceivable tactic for taking fish, using hooks, spears, large traps, and skillfully woven nets of bark fiber, for the women of the tribe were weavers of great renown. Throughout the western

A wood effigy bowl in the shape of a beaver is among the finest specimens of Kaskaskia craftsmanship. The Kaskaskia, once the leading tribe of the Illinois confederacy—which ranged from the Great Lakes south into present Iowa and Missouri—were noted for the quality of their wood carvings, many of which were used in medicine bundles. Their expertise with wood was excelled only by Indians of the Northwest Coast.

Woodlands they were famous for their supple bags of dyed vegetal fiber and buffalo hair spun into beautiful geometric designs. These bags, as well as other woven goods, were valuable items of trade, much sought after by the other Great Lakes tribes.

Next to wild rice itself, the Menominees probably prized maple sugar above all other foods. For them, as for their neighbors, maple sugar was both a food in itself and a seasoning. Children were often given medicine mixed with maple sugar to make the dose palatable, and the sweet was used with all manner of dishes, much as we might use salt.

The tapping of the maples came in early spring, just after the families returned from winter hunting. Whole villages of the Menominees made camp deep in the woods, and each family had its own stand of trees to tap. A gash was made in the trunk of each tree a few feet above the ground, and a cedar spout was hammered into the trunk. From this spout a trickle of sap would run into a birchbark pail set on the ground. After the trees had been drained, the sap was poured into larger birchbark containers, and hot rocks dropped in to bring the sap to a boil. The heat first reduced it to a syrup and then to a sugar. Only when each family had a year's supply of maple sugar did the band break camp and return to its permanent village where a portion of the harvest was consumed in honor of Manitou at a ceremonial feast. Another small amount of the sugar was taken to the grave sites of ancestors to "feed" the spirits of the dead.

Along the shores of Lake Michigan the Menominees came into close and constant contact with their neighbors, the Siouan-speaking Winnebagos, who lived in the deep-forested Door Peninsula that thrusts northward into the lake to form the eastern arm of Green Bay. Despite language differences, the two tribes had long been friends and allies, perhaps in part because they had a common interest in keeping the Sauk and Fox Indians to the south and west at bay. But also there was a mutually profitable trade relationship between the two tribes that lasted over many centuries. Although the Winnebagos prized wild rice, they harvest-

Fishing by torchlight—shown here in a painting by the 19th-century artist Paul Kane—was a common practice among the Menominee and other Great Lakes tribes. As fish are attracted to the surface by the light, tribesmen stand ready to spear them. Fish were an important food for the Great Lakes tribes, and they used nets and weirs, as well as spears, to make their catch.

ed less of the grain than did the Menominees. Both farming and buffalo hunting were more to the taste of the Winnebagos, and they cultivated quantities of tobacco, squash, beans, and corn, the last of these being a particularly important crop.

The Winnebagos consumed corn in a variety of ways—boiled, roasted, dried, and ground into a meal—but steamed corn was the favorite. This was prepared in a deep pit, its bottom lined with hot stones. Over this the Indians placed husks, then fresh corn, then more husks, and finally a thin layer of dirt. When all was ready, they poured water over the pit. The water seeped through the loosely packed dirt to the stones to create steam and cook the corn.

The Winnebagos skill in hunting and agriculture often provided them with a surplus of buffalo skins and dried tobacco and corn. They exchanged these products with the Menominees for wild rice and, sometimes, woven goods. Trade among these two tribes—and indeed among all of the peoples of the western Woodlands—was frequent. Until the height of the fur trade, there were no great expeditions with flotillas of canoes loaded to the gunwales. A Menominee family that was short of buffalo robes would merely paddle across Green Bay with a few sacks of wild rice and some baskets, spend a day or two in agreeable bargaining, and return home having made a satisfactory exchange.

During the course of the trading expedition, the Menominee visitors would find the surroundings wholly familiar. If the trading took place in the summer, the Winnebagos, like the Menominees, conducted all business out of doors. The long, airy summer lodges of the Winnebago, as of the other western Woodland tribes, were used primarily as shelters from rainy weather.

In spite of the fact that the housing was much alike, the way in which a tribe laid out its villages did have significance. Most of the tribes, including the

This Menominee sash was made from European wool, but the finger-weaving technique for creating the cloth was ancient. Before European traders appeared, the Menominees wove such sashes from the fibers of basswood or nettles, or from buffalo hair. No loom was employed. Instead, strands of yarn were tied at one end to a stick, the strands being interlaced with each other. The weaver moved downward from the top of the stick, carefully selecting his colors to produce the geometric designs. When the weaving was done, the loose ends were tied to make a fringe. These sashes could be worn as belts or as headdresses. Similarly made garters were used to secure leggings below the knee.

Winnebago, were divided into two groups, or moieties. Among the Winnebagos, Menominees, and Miamis, one moiety was composed of clans named after birds, the other after land and water animals. Each moiety was further divided into clans. The Winnebago sky moiety included the Thunderbird, War, Eagle, and Pigeon clans; the earth moiety, the Bear, Wolf, Water-Spirit, Deer, Elk, Buffalo, Fish, and Snake clans. Winnebago villages tended to be laid out according to moiety and clan lines, with perhaps half the village inhabited by the sky moiety and half by the earth moiety. Each clan had its own lodge, but through centuries of tradition, leadership of the sky moiety had come to reside in the Thunderbird clan; of the earth moiety, in the Bear clan. Tradition also dictated the roles of each of these two clans. The Thunderbirds were recognized as referees in arguments, and disputes between warriors were settled within the Thunderbird lodge. The hereditary Thunderbird chief was also chief of the village, and though his powers rested on personal influence and example, his counsel was always sought on matters of village or tribal interest. The Thunderbird lodge was also a place of sanctuary. No punishment could be meted out to a miscreant so long as he remained in the lodge.

The lodge of the Bear clan, on the other hand, was the place where justice was done, where executions and lesser punishments took place. The hereditary chief of the Bear clan in each village was also the local war leader, and it was from this clan that the warriors who policed the buffalo hunt were drawn.

Moiety, clan, and family relationships governed marriage among the Winnebago and the other Great Lakes tribes. Most of the tribes approved and even encouraged marriage between cross-cousins: a girl might marry the son of her father's (but not her mother's) sister; a boy, the daughter of his mother's brother. But all marriages had to be with members of the opposite moiety. This kind of cross-relationship extended to other activities as well. A youngster out on his first hunt or raiding party, for example, was likely to seek the protection and guidance of a maternal uncle. The uncle, for his part, took these tasks with the utmost seriousness, for in a sense he was the boy's sponsor, guiding him toward full membership in the tribe. Feats of bravery displayed by the boy brought honor to the uncle, while cowardice visited disgrace on the older man.

When a Winnebago warrior joined a raiding party, his foe was likely to be either the Sauks or the Foxes who lived along the western bank of Lake Michigan just south of the Menominees. There had been a time when the Sauks had shared the Door Peninsula with the Winnebagos. But their warlike ways had posed a serious threat to their neighbors, and together, the Winnebagos and the Menominees had pushed the Sauks off the peninsula. But the Sauks, along with their close allies, the Foxes, retained large territories southwest of Green Bay.

The Women of the Great Lakes: A Talent for Design

Long before the arrival of the Europeans, Great Lakes Indian women were masters of the art of decoration. They were especially skilled in the techniques of transforming such natural materials as porcupine quills, buffalo wool, and the fibers of basswood and nettles into a wide variety of elaborately decorated articles of clothing, sleeping mats, shoulder pouches, and storage bags.

When, in the 1600's, the French introduced beads, silk ribbon, and cloth, as well as European designs, these foreign influences provoked a radical change in the Indians' artistic conceptions. Traditional geometric patterns slowly yielded to the flowing and delicate outlines of leaves and flowers. The Indian women rapidly became proficient in the use of beads to decorate sashes, garters, headbands, and necklaces. They also made beaded strips to be fastened on buckskin or cloth. Such elaborately decorated clothing was not worn every day; it was saved for special occasions.

Flowers and leaves bordered with white beads embellish a Fox warrior's shirt (upper left). The European-made broadcloth as well as the hooks and eyes that were sewn on the top of the left shoulder were acquired by the Indians in exchange for furs. The storage bag (left) was made in the 1890's. It is woven with brightly dyed commercial yarn.

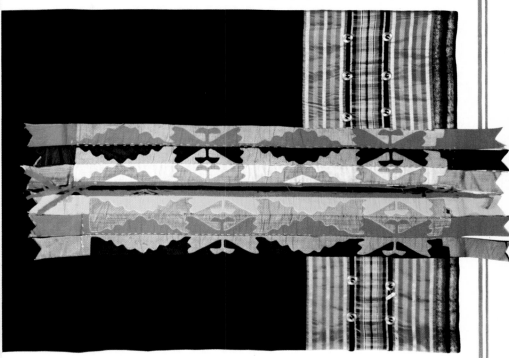

Panels of broadcloth, appliquéd with striped and plaid taffeta ribbonwork (above), were made to adorn the hem of a Fox woman's skirt or blouse. To make such decorative panels, the women cut mirror-image designs from one color of silk, sewed them on a silk strip of another color, and then sewed the finished appliqué on a piece of clothing. The Menominee beaded ornament (left), which hung from the shoulder, was worn purely for decoration. Some Indians wore as many as 12 of these accoutrements at a time. The beads on this bag were first strung and then woven on a loom and, finally, sewn on deep red broadcloth. Great Lakes Indians sometimes referred to these ornaments as Friendship bags, because they were often given as gifts or traded to Plains Indians for horses.

Like the Winnebagos, the Sauks and the Foxes—and the more numerous Miamis whose territories stretched from Lake Michigan's southern shores into present-day Indiana and Illinois—were hunting peoples. Each summer and fall they forayed out from their permanent forest villages onto the prairies to kill buffalo. During these trips their communities were all but deserted, for only a few of the young and healthy remained behind to care for the elderly and disabled, to guard the village from attack, and to prepare a welcoming feast for the returning tribesmen. The buffalo hunt was central to the Sauks and the Foxes, but they were farmers as well and, like their neighbors, they also harvested wild rice

and lived in communal houses during the summer. Throughout the area the affluent warriors occasionally married more than one wife. The Foxes called themselves *Mesh-kwakihug* (the "People of the Red Earth"), after the soil that, according to legend, gave them birth. The Sauks were the *Osakiwug* (the "People of the Yellow Earth").

During the 17th century Sauks and Foxes near Lake Michigan's southwestern shore represented a formidable military force. At the time, however, the threat they presented to the Menominees and Winnebagos was blunted by the preoccupation of the Sauks and the Foxes with incessant skirmishes with the Ojibwas.

Dressed in tribal finery, this member of a combined Iowa, Sauk, and Fox delegation to Washington in 1867 displays a fan-shaped roach on his head and a necklace of grizzly bear claws, signifying the warrior's high status. Roaches, ceremonial headdresses, were generally made of animal hair, as is the one directly below. When an occasion called for the donning of a roach, it was attached to the head with a roach-spreader, such as these at lower right that were carved from elk antlers. The actual fastening was done by pulling a scalp lock through an opening at the center of the roach and then through a hole in the spreader. Finally, a small wood peg was pushed through the braided lock to hold everything in place. Grizzly bear claw necklaces were highly prized and often passed on from one generation to the next. A warrior who obtained such a necklace by his own efforts—either by killing the dangerous animal or by slaying an enemy warrior who wore one—was especially proud. The one at left consists of 40 claws, each separated from the others by a bead. The claws are sewn to an otter fur base that ends in a lavishly decorated skin pendant.

Some of the ceremonies of the Sauks and the Foxes reflected the warlike attitudes that were common among Great Lakes tribes. Whenever a raiding party returned victorious from some foray, there was a *misekwe* ("scalp dance"). As the ceremony began, each warrior solemnly handed over the scalps he had collected to his clan chief. These grisly trophies, while indicative of a warrior's victories, were less important in establishing his status than acts of insolent bravery on the battlefield. To dart through a phalanx of foe to touch an enemy war leader with a hand or stick was the ultimate in courage. The brave who had shown such daring was rewarded with the highest honor, a new name, chosen by the commander of the expedition.

After the scalps were all collected, the dance began, and as each warrior circled the lodge, he lifted his voice in a chant that recounted his feats on the battlefield. "In this manner I clubbed him down," one might sing while chopping at the air. "He cried out and begged for mercy, but I had no pity for him!" Though this kind of self-praise was encouraged, exaggeration was scorned. A man who embroidered his account with fictional acts of valor was disgraced and viewed with contempt by his fellow warriors.

During the scalp dance each of the braves flourished his sacred war bundle, which was carried into every encounter. The bundle, made of animal skin, contained such charms and relics as tangles of weasel fur, a buffalo horn, rattlesnake rattles, and a string of human scalps. This pouch, symbolic of past victories and the ancestry of the warrior, was thought to have magical powers that protected the owner from harm. The pouch, a breechclout, and leggings were all the warriors wore into battle. All other clothes were left behind, for these were infused not only with their owner's own spirit but with the spirit of his tribe as well. Should the garments be captured and abused by an enemy, the entire tribe might suffer disaster.

As the 17th century entered its second decade, disaster indeed loomed, not just for the Sauk but for all of the Woodland tribes. But nothing so simple as captured leggings or shirts played a part in the threat. Instead, it came in the form of an alien people from beyond the sea who spread disease, disarray, and destruction among the Indians.

The European Conquest

The Europeans, who began arriving on the North American Atlantic Coast in the first half of the 17th century, came not as conquerors but as traders and settlers. In the north, in what is now Quebec, there were the French, whose interest was basically in the fur trade. Farther to the south, from Massachusetts to the Carolinas, there were Englishmen, some Dutchmen, and a scattering of Swedes, whose motivations ranged from a desire for religious liberty to dreams of riches in the form of precious metals. Of gold and silver there

were none, and soon even the most avid treasure seekers settled down to farming or fishing.

At first, contact between the Indian and the white man redounded to the benefit of both. The Europeans' muskets, brass kettles, sharp knives and ax heads, piercing needles and fishhooks helped the Indians to become more efficient hunters, fishermen, gatherers and workers of wood and metal. In exchange, the Indians introduced the newcomers to corn, showed them what berries and nuts were edible, taught them how to hunt down the game of the forests, and provided furs. But in essence the cultures were mutually exclusive and could not coexist for long. The white man wanted land—land that he could fence and put to the plow, land that would remain exclusively his for his lifetime and then be passed on to his descendants. In fact, many of the proprietors of the English colonies were granted huge parcels by King James I or King Charles II.

The Indians, of course, knew nothing of this disposition of their territories, nor did they adhere to the concept of private ownership of land. But so long as the white men were few in number and did not impinge heavily on tribal hunting grounds, there was relatively little trouble between the two peoples. But as each new European settlement grew and expanded, the Indian was faced with the choice of yielding to the white man and his superior technology or suffering destruction.

Almost from the first the white man drastically altered the traditional relationships among the tribes by ignoring some and favoring others with muskets and alliances in exchange for trade goods, chiefly furs. The first fur traders were the French, under explorer Samuel de Champlain. In 1608 Champlain, at the head of a small party, moved up the St. Lawrence in search of beaver pelts. The following spring he made contact with the Algonquin, the tribe that would give its name to a host of linguistically allied peoples. To curry their favor, Champlain joined the Algonquins in a raid against their traditional foe, the Mohawks of the Iroquois League. Thanks to the Frenchman's muskets, the Algonquins swept the field. But all unknowing, Champlain had made bitter enemies for France, the powerful Five Nations of Iroquois.

Seven years later Champlain was on the move again, this time deep into the unexplored regions around Lake Huron, where he lived among the Huron Indians for several months. Champlain's visit with the Hurons—an Iroquoian people who were nonetheless enemies of the league—convinced him that the future prosperity of New France lay in a firm alliance with this resourceful tribe. Strategically located between the eastern, western, and northern Algonquians, the Hurons had strong trading links with all. Soon the Hurons were acting as middlemen, channeling thousands of precious beaver pelts each year into the hands of the French and greatly enriching themselves in the process. In the Hurons, the French also believed they had an

Handicrafts Reflecting Two Distinct Cultures

Using materials native to their regions—moose hair, porcupine quills, birchbark, and skins—the Indians of the Great Lakes and Northeast evolved, over the centuries, highly stylized handicraft forms characterized by intricate geometric patterns. With the coming of the white man, the Indians began making such items for trade, but in so doing they often adopted European styles that not only pleased white merchants but evidently found favor among the tribes themselves. Traditional design motifs with their severe angularity slowly yielded to the circular patterns, often representing flowers, that the Europeans favored. And, as time went by, the Indians themselves came to appreciate the new motifs.

By the early 18th century scores of Indian girls in French-Canadian convents were turning out delicately wrought handiwork for the growing white market, an exercise that brought in much needed funds while providing the young women with a trade that would help equip them to live in a European-dominated society. The results of such endeavors are apparent in the handsomely intricate floral patterns, below and at right, that decorate a tablecloth. While European designs came to predominate, a market also existed among whites for traditional geometric forms, such as the decorated chair and container at far right.

Scenes of Indian life, such as this one portrayed in moose-hair embroidery on a birchbark tray, were popular among 19th-century buyers of Indian handicrafts. The Hurons, who made this handsome tray, lent a romantic aura to the hunt by surrounding the scene with a profusion of blossoms.

Exquisite Huron workmanship is shown in details (left and above) of an 19th-century tablecloth. The colorful and intricate floral designs of balsam fir, barberry, phlox, marguerite, clover, and other plants were created from moose hair and sewn on a felt base. Such patterns were popular with Europeans.

*This **18th-century chair** was made by Europeans, but the geometric design of porcupine quills on the back is the work of Micmac Indian craftsmen of Nova Scotia, who had few equals at working dyed porcupine quills into complex patterns. The birchbark container (below) is also quill decorated. The quills were pushed through holes in the bark, and each one was bent on the inside to hold it in place. Until the late 1800's the Micmacs used vegetable dyes to color the quills. Then aniline dyes with a wide variety of colors were adopted.*

ally who would hold at bay the Five Iroquois Nations, whose smoldering hostility to the French was now becoming manifest.

For their part, the Iroquois were fast learning to protect their own interests. By the 1640's they had made alliances with fur-seeking Dutchmen operating along the upper Hudson River. Now armed with muskets, the Five Nations ranged deep into the Woodlands raiding Huron villages. Because the Hurons were less well armed, they proved no match for the league, which in March 1649 administered a coup de grace.

It was then that Iroquois warriors launched an offensive against Huron settlements and in two days slaughtered all who had not escaped into the forest. Villages were laid waste, and the once mighty Huron nation utterly demoralized. Some survivors of the massacre fled farther to the west or north; others surrendered to their foes, and many were adopted into the league. Fresh from its victories, the league pressed its offensive, crushing the Tionontatis, or Tobacco Hurons, leaving but a few stunned survivors who, in the words of one witness, "sat silent on the ground, without raising their eyes, without moving and seeming hardly to breathe, like statues of stone."

Within a year the cornfields of the Huron homeland along Lake Huron's Georgian Bay were weeded over, while winds coursed through rotting longhouses that had once sheltered a nation of 30,000.

With its victory over the Hurons, the Iroquois League, although weakened by its own losses, became the most formidable Indian power in the Woodlands. For half a century it was almost a law unto itself, and such tribes that dared oppose it came to feel its wrath. Somewhat like the Romans of old, the Iroquois did not always destroy or scatter the Indians they conquered but often adopted them into the tribes of the league, thus swelling the numbers of warriors ready to do battle. And with their defeat of the Hurons, the Five Nations gained control of the fur trade, allowing the league to play the English off against the French, as representatives of both European nations scrambled for a major share of each year's harvest of pelts.

About 1722 the Five Nations of the league became six, after the Tuscaroras migrated into the shelter of the Longhouse, having been pushed inland and northward by the pressure of white settlement. By now Iroquois power extended as far west as Ojibwa country and as far south as Georgia. Even the once proud and self-sufficient Delawares paid tribute to the league.

Meanwhile, the strength of the English colonies, stretched along the Atlantic Coast, was waxing strong. If the French had crossed the Atlantic primarily for trade, most of the English had come to colonize. Once their coastal settlements were secure, they began moving inland to find new lands, sow new fields, and evict the Indians. Unlike the fur traders, who depended on Indians to trap beaver, the settlers had no interest in preserving any part of tribal society. On the contrary, the Indians were seen merely as an impediment to progress, an impediment that must, in time, be destroyed.

In the very beginning, there was no such intent. Without the aid of the Powhatans, the British settlement at Jamestown, Virginia, the first permanent English colony in the New World, would not have lasted through its first terrible winter of 1607–08. Similarly, the Pilgrim colony at Plymouth, Massachusetts, might have failed except for help from the Wampanoags.

Yet within several years of Jamestown's founding, relations between the colonists and the Powhatan federation had reached the breaking point. The major villain in the piece was tobacco, a crop that was enjoying immense popularity in Europe and one that the colonists saw as making their fortunes. The large-scale cultivation of tobacco required huge tracts of land, the more so because it wore out the soil at a prodigious rate. There was, of course, plenty of available land in coastal Virginia in the early 17th century, but it was heavily wooded. To the colonists it made perfect sense simply to seize the fields that the Indians had already cleared. Thus began the inexorable process of pushing the tribes farther and farther inland.

For a number of years the Indians contented themselves with occasional forays against the whites, but in 1622 the Powhatans struck with a fury born of despair. In one day they left 350 Englishmen dead and several settlements in ashes. The colonists, of course, responded in kind with their own unceasing campaign of terror, inflicting their wrath not just on the Powhatan but on all other tribes in the area. By the late 1640's tribal power along the Virginia coast had been broken forever, and most of the surviving tribesmen were either reduced to beggary or had fled.

The Tragic Pattern

What happened in Virginia was repeated time and again up and down the Atlantic Coast. In New England small-scale warfare culminated in the 1670's in King Philip's War, so named for a Wampanoag chief who allied his own tribe with the powerful Narragansett and for more than a year carried on a bloody campaign against the region's 50,000 white settlers. Though Philip proved himself a superb strategist, English numbers combined with those of their Indian allies, the Mohegans, brought about his total defeat in 1676.

Then it was the turn of the hapless Delawares, who were caught in a vise between the English on the coast and the Iroquois League inland. Rather than engage in hopeless combat, Delaware bands began in the early 1700's to drift westward "toward the setting sun." By 1742 they had settled beside the Susquehannocks, and a decade later they had joined the Huron survivors in eastern Ohio. By the end of the century the unity of the tribe had completely broken down, with individual bands of Delawares migrating into Spanish Missouri;

later others sought sanctuary on the cold plains of Ontario. Eventually, many of the Delawares found shelter in what came to be Oklahoma, which for many years the new United States would use as a dumping ground for Indians expelled from the East.

For a time the tribes of the western Woodlands fared much better, though they had to make room for tribes fleeing from the whites in the East. Most of the western Great Lakes tribes felt little pressure from white settlers until the last 15 years of the 18th century, and those as far west as the upper Great Lakes were mostly spared until well into the 19th.

During the series of wars between England and France in the 17th and 18th centuries, the Iroquois generally joined forces with the British, the Great Lakes Algonquian tribes with the French. When the British finally ousted the French from their American domains in the 1760's, a durable peace seemed at hand. But almost immediately after the French had been expelled, the Algonquian Ottawas rose in rebellion.

Though the rebellion was soon put down, the British Parliament, eager to pacify the Indians and maintain the fur trade, declared that the region west of the Appalachian crest was closed to white settlement. The colonists, however, had no intention of bending to London's authority, and even before the American Revolution began in 1775, hundreds of whites had migrated west to establish farms and settlements deep in Indian territory.

But greater tragedy for the Indians was in the making. When the American Revolution began, four of the six tribes of the Iroquois Nation, in keeping with their traditional ties, joined forces with the British. Led by a Mohawk chief whom the whites called Joseph Brant, hundreds of Iroquois marched with Loyalist guerrillas known as Butler's Rangers to lay waste to American settlements in western New York and Pennsylvania. In retaliation, George Washington dispatched an army under Gen. John Sullivan to rout the Indians and Tories, a campaign of pillage and arson that destroyed 40 Iroquois villages and most of the Indians' crops. Reduced almost to starvation, the Iroquois fought back with valor, but with the American victory over the British, Iroquois power was obliterated.

The peace treaty of 1783 that recognized American independence also conferred on the new nation a vast hinterland stretching west to the Mississippi. Here were the homelands of the Algonquian Miamis, Ottawas, Menominees, Illinois, Potawatomis, Ojibwas, Sauks, and Foxes, as well as the Siouan Winnebagos. Soon these tribes, too, would confront the white man's land hunger, and step by step they would be forced to yield.

The first Americans to arrive in the Great Lakes region of what came to be called the Northwest Territory were fur traders, who mingled with, and sometimes fought, the British and Canadian fur men who had long since established a footing in the area.

Sauk and Fox tribesmen, some of them obviously dismayed, strike a formal pose as Louis Bogy, commissioner of Indian Affairs, pretends to read from an 1867 treaty with Washington that seals the fate of the two tribes. Among the Indians are the Fox chief Chekuskuk (standing, third from left) and Sauk chief Keokuk (seated, second from left). The treaty, couched in befuddling legalese, specified that the tribes cede 157,000 acres of land along the Mississippi and Missouri Rivers in exchange for $26,574 and 750 square miles of land on a reservation in Indian Territory in present-day Oklahoma. The government obligated itself to establish a "manual labor school" on the reservation and to provide a physician and medicine "to promote the civilization of the tribe." Indians who refused to reside permanently on the reservation were barred from receiving any portion of the promised funds.

Of all the goods the fur traders brought in their baggage, the most destructive by far was alcohol. To the Indians, firewater was a magical potion that brought dreams resembling the much-sought-after visions. They would happily exchange a whole season's gathering of pelts for a bottle or two of rum. The white man's diseases, such as small pox and even measles, against which the Indians had built no natural resistance, were also devastating. Whole tribes were sometimes afflicted by raging epidemics.

But it was rum and whiskey that became a primary means of suborning the Indians in order to seize their lands. In the vanguard of land-seeking immigrants who poured into the Northwest Territory in the early and mid-19th century was the U.S. Army, together with a complement of Indian agents. Every means was employed, from flattery to force, to get the Indians to yield up vast stretches of their domains, and liquor eased the pangs of negotiation. Chiefs, or men the whites chose to call chiefs, were dined and wined, and their signatures or marks were secured on land cession treaties. Even though these "chiefs" rarely held leadership position in their own tribes, the whites chose to interpret their agreement as conferring legal title to the newcomers. When the tribesmen resisted, military power was employed.

All too typical was the fate of the Sauks and the Foxes. In 1804 representatives of the tribes were called to St. Louis, where federal agents plied them with alcohol and then secured their agreement to a treaty ceding all tribal lands east of the Mississippi. Not until 1829, however, were the two tribes forced across the great river, where for three years they led a hand-to-mouth existence. Finally, in 1832, about 1,000 tribesmen and women rallied around a 50-year-old warrior named Black Hawk, who promised to lead them back to their ancestral lands. Black Hawk sought no war. For some reason he believed that he could appeal to the conscience of the whites who now lived in western Illinois and they would return the land to his people. Instead a strong militia force was sent to expel the intruders.

Upon hearing of the whites' mobilization, Black Hawk realized that his cause was lost, and he made haste to seek negotiations for peaceful return of his people to the west bank. But the panicky whites fired upon his emmisaries. Now the warrior was enraged, and for three months he led raiding parties against white settlements, forays that took some 200 settlers' lives but cut Black Hawk's own fighting force in half. In August 1832, just as Black Hawk was leading the remnants of his party back into Iowa, a militia force caught up with him. Despite the warrior's attempts to surrender, the whites raked his party with gunfire, killing most of the fleeing Sauks and Foxes as they tried to swim across the Mississippi.

For all practical purposes, the massacre of the Sauks and the Foxes marked the end of tribal dominance in the western Woodlands. With the fate of Black Hawk's followers as an example, other tribes hastened to make whatever arrangements they could with the United States. In 1835 the Ojibwa, Menominee, Iowa, Sioux, Winnebago, Ottawa, and Potawatomi tribes, as well as the decimated and scattered Sauk and Fox, formally agreed that the United States might make "an amicable and final adjustment" of their various land claims. Less than a quarter of a century later, such "adjustments" had indeed been made, and the tribes had either been expelled to territories far to the west or restricted to cramped reservations within their ancient homelands. The era of the northeast Woodland Indian was over; the age of the farm and factory, the city and town, was coming into full flower.

THE GREAT PLAINS
Nomadic Horsemen

American buffalo again roam the Plains, as here in South Dakota, but their numbers are small when compared with the millions that once sustained the tribes, providing food and also hides for such items as the Blackfoot medicine shield (inset).

For most of the Plains Indians the buffalo supplied food, clothing, shelter, even fuel. But the white invasion wiped out the herds, and a way of life perished with them.

Early-19th-century explorers called the region the Great American Desert and described it as being unfit for settlement. The "desert," a wide swath of territory, extended all the way from northern Alberta and Saskatchewan south into Texas. Its eastern border generally paralleled the 100th meridian that cuts through present-day North and South Dakota, Nebraska, Kansas, Oklahoma, and Texas; its western border edged the foothills of the Rockies. Although there were variations—regions of woodlands along the riverbanks, the buttes of the Dakotas' Badlands, and the eroded slopes of the Black Hills of western South Dakota and northeastern Wyoming—the overwhelming impression was of a vast tableland of grass. This was shortgrass that pushed deep into the dense soil to soak up the limited moisture that the earth provided; in parts of this region the annual rainfall rarely exceeded 10 inches. But if the soil seemed useless for agriculture, the grasses of the High Plains were eminently suited to the grazing needs of vast herds of buffalo. The region had been their almost private domain for thousands of years.

To the east of the 100th meridian a different situation existed. For the most part the land was flat, like the regions to the west, but here rainfall averaged at least 20 inches a year. In this region the grass was tall, and once the steel-bladed plow, capable of turning the root-matted earth, came into use, agriculture was almost mandated.

But even in the western shortgrass country there were fertile regions beside the river courses. There were groves of oak, elm, willow, and cottonwood along the banks of the Missouri, the Platte, the Arkansas, the Kansas, and other eastward-flowing rivers. Both the forests and surrounding grasslands sheltered a wealth of game, big and small: bear, deer, antelope, rabbit, and a variety of waterfowl and game birds.

Centuries before the white man first came to the area, the grasslands were home to a number of nomadic bands that eked a sparse livelihood by hunting buffalo. Because these Indians knew nothing of farming, the hunt was literally a life-and-death matter. It was done on foot, for the horse had not yet been brought to the

155

New World. Life was marginal for these Indians, and starvation was a constant threat.

By about A.D. 1000, however, some of these peoples, especially those living along the middle section of the Missouri River, began to learn the rudiments of farming. The crops they were able to raise provided these Indians with means of supplementing their usual diet of buffalo meat and the wild-growing plants available.

When, in about the 13th century, new bands of Indians began populating the grasslands, they came not as nomads but as semisedentary villagers: farmers and gatherers who settled down upon the rich bottomlands along the river courses. They did foray out onto the Plains for the buffalo hunt but always returned to their settlements when the chase was finished.

Though the buffalo hunt was less vital to these settled people than to their predecessors on the Plains, it was still an activity of much importance. After the crops were planted but before they ripened, whole villages would virtually empty out, as men, women, and children moved onto the lands of shortgrass and then grouped themselves into small hunting units. In the balmy days of late summer or early fall, after the crops were harvested, a second hunt was organized. This time each band was larger than before, for the purpose

A **"medicine wheel,"** some six centuries old, is one of several that have been found in the eastern Rockies near the Plains from Wyoming to Alberta, Canada. Their function is a mystery. This construction, the most elaborate, is located on a plateau high on north-central Wyoming's Medicine Mountain of the Bighorn range. The circle of stones is about 80 feet in diameter; the "hub" is a cairn from which 28 unevenly spaced "spokes" project. Smaller cairns are located around the rim. Because its design bears a distinct resemblance to the floor plan of a medicine lodge, many anthropologists believe that it was used for religious rituals, perhaps early versions of the Sun Dance. Another view is that such wheels were made for astronomical sightings, to keep track of the directions of sunrises and sunsets. Thus it may have been a crude calendar, enabling the Indians to predict the time of the summer solstice.

now was mass killing. This was the season just after the buffalo's mating time, when the animals ran in huge herds, making themselves relatively easy prey for the Indians' tactics of wholesale slaughter.

If these twice-yearly hunts were eagerly awaited as times to gain new supplies of meat and skins, such expeditions were not without difficulty and hardship. Without horses to ride and pull supplies, the people were forced to move across the grasslands on foot, aided only by dogs, their sole domesticated animals.

Sometimes, when the bands went off in pursuit of buffalo, they tied packs to the dogs' backs, but more usually the animals pulled their burdens on a travois—two long poles, one end of each fastened to a dog's shoulders, the other trailing behind on the ground. Between the poles, baggage was lashed on a netlike frame. The first whites to witness this mode of transport were Spaniards who accompanied the would-be conquistador Francisco de Coronado onto the Plains in 1541 in a fruitless search for gold. In a letter home a Spaniard reported that he "saw dogs carry [the natives'] houses, and they have the sticks of their houses dragging along."

As the Indians traversed the grasslands in groups, the line of march was preceded by scouts who ranged far ahead on the lookout for both enemies and game. Flanks and rear were guarded by warriors carrying nothing but their weapons. In the middle were the women, toting small children on their backs and managing the travois. The dogs were not always satisfactory porters; they had to be kept well separated to prevent them from fighting. Given the slightest opportunity, a peaceful line of dogs would suddenly be transformed into a study of mayhem. Maintaining order among the belligerent animals was a time-consuming and often frustrating job.

During the actual hunt the Indians employed several methods to take their prey. One was to drive a buffalo herd over a cliff, so that the beasts were either killed outright by the fall or crippled and easily dispatched. The ancestral memory of these "buffalo jumps" still lingers. One Plains Indian, Old Fool Bull, reminisced in 1968: "In the ancient days, we had men who were 'buffalo callers.' According to legend, these were specialists who knew the beasts so well that they had almost become buffalo themselves. They dressed themselves in buffalo skins, and when they spotted a herd they positioned themselves at its head, walking before the chief bulls to lead them. Like the buffalo, they snorted and rolled in the dust, luring the herd ever onward to the edge of a cliff. There the callers suddenly disappeared under a ledge or in the brush. The other hunters, meanwhile, were coming up behind the herd. On signal, all roared mightily, stamped their feet and whirled torches over their heads to strike terror into their prey and set off a stampede. The buffalo in back piled into those in front, and soon there was a general rush over the cliff.

The Plains Indians, including Sioux, Cheyennes, Kiowas, Comanches, Blackfeet, and others who typified the hard-riding hunters and warriors of legend, were relative newcomers to the grasslands. Few, if any, could trace their ancestry in the region back more than several hundred years. By the 13th century successive droughts had driven many of the original inhabitants of the Plains into other regions, and the grasslands became an area of sparse population. Then, in about A.D. 1300, a population drift onto the Plains began that would last for half a millennium, as tribes from all four directions converged upon the region. A combination of factors were involved, including drought in the tribes' former homelands, increasing population pressure and, in later years, the coming of the white man whose land-hunger and guns forced tribe after tribe westward from their Woodland homes.

First to arrive on the Plains were probably the Pawnees, a Caddoan group that moved into Nebraska from east Texas in about A.D. 1300. They were followed by their linguistic cousins, the Wichitas. By 1400 the Mandans from the eastern prairies had settled into the upper Missouri Valley. As the map shows, other tribes followed.

Most of these tribes had been agriculturalists and, in their new homes, were at first semisedentary. But as horses from the Southwest became available in the 17th and 18th centuries, many, such as the Dakota Sioux and Cheyennes, adopted a nomadic life-style centered around buffalo hunting.

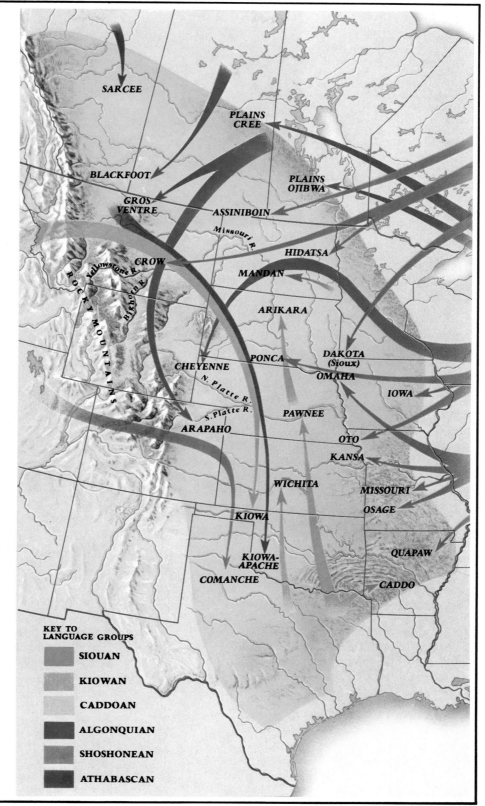

KEY TO LANGUAGE GROUPS

SIOUAN

KIOWAN

CADDOAN

ALGONQUIAN

SHOSHONEAN

ATHABASCAN

Vast herds of buffalo, like the one at right, were often hunted by bands of Indians who drove them off cliffs, killing hundreds at a time. But sometimes, in the days before the horse, two or three tribesmen might set out to bring down a solitary bull to supplement their families' meat supply. A favorite tactic for these small-scale hunts was for the tribesmen to disguise themselves in wolfskins (center). Being used to wolves, the animals took no notice as the hunters crept to within bowshot. In winter snowshoes were used to pursue the buffalo (far right). They were easy prey in deep snow because their immense weight made escape difficult as the hunters approached.

In this manner an entire herd might be slaughtered."

Another method was to trap buffalo by setting fire to the grass around a herd, hemming in the animals except for one passage left open as an apparent escape route. It was there, of course, that the hunters waited with their bows and lances.

A similar method was "the surround." Some 30 years ago a Blackfoot named Weasel Tail described this tactic much used by equestrian Indians as well as their foot-slogging ancestors. Here is an anthropologist's paraphrase of Weasel Tail's account:

"After swift-running men located a herd of buffalo, the chief would tell the women to get their . . . travois. Men and women would go out together, and approach the herd from down wind so the animals would not get their scent and run off. The women were told to place their travois upright in the earth, small . . . ends up. The travois were spaced so that they could be tied together, forming a semi-circular fence. Women and dogs hid behind them while two fast-running men circled the herd . . . and drove them toward the travois fence. Other men took up their positions along the sides of the route and closed in as the buffalo neared the . . . enclosure. Barking dogs and shouting women kept the buffalo [back]. The men rushed in and killed the buffalo with arrows and lances.

"After the buffalo were killed, the chief went into the center of the enclosure, counted the dead animals, and divided the meat equally among the participating families. He also distributed the hides to the families for making lodge covers. The women hauled the buffalo meat to camp on their . . . travois. This was called 'surround of the buffalo.' "

When Meriwether Lewis and William Clark crossed the Plains in 1804, they came into contact with numerous river tribes, among them the Hidatsa, Mandan, and Arikara along the Missouri, and they passed by the Pawnees' territory on the banks of the Platte. Though the river peoples had been in these general locations for centuries, they had not always lived on the riverways

of the Plains. The Pawnees, for example, had moved from present-day east Texas sometime about the 13th century. On their ancestral land they had been chiefly a farming people, and in their new homes they maintained their old ways. Probably drought, combined with population pressure, had forced the Pawnees from their ancient and once-fertile homeland onto the rich riverbanks of the Platte and its tributaries more than 300 miles away.

When the Pawnees moved north they found the Plains sparsely populated, for many of the nomadic bands had long since been driven from the central grasslands by drought. But the rivers began flowing again, at least in the eastern realm of the grasslands, and the earth offered promise of ample harvests. But why did the Pawnees move so far from their former domains? Certainly there was much fertile land closer to their old homes. One possible explanation for the tribe's long trek is that they sent scouts ahead, and these reported back that not only was the soil along the Platte and nearby streams rich, but that on the grasslands nearby the area the buffalo roamed in the tens of thousands. The setting seemed ideal for Pawnee settlements. In any case, by the 14th century the Pawnees' villages were strung out beside the eastern reaches of the Platte and its tributaries. There the Indians planted corn, squash, and beans, gathered and hunted in the woods along the river's edge and, during the summer and early fall, roamed the Plains in pursuit of buffalo.

For the Pawnees life in their new homes was secure, almost rich. The tribe grew prosperous, its numbers increased to such an extent that their few villages along the eastern Platte grew too crowded and new settlements to the west were created. By the mid-1700's the Pawnees' domain stretched all along the broad river that cuts through present-day Nebraska.

Within these villages the Pawnees lived in lodges built of logs and covered by layers of dirt and grass. As American pioneers would discover a century later, this sod construction was well adapted to Plains life. The

thick layers of tangle-rooted soil were excellent insulation, shielding the inhabitants from winter's bitter cold and summer's intense heat. But the log-and-dirt lodges were not particularly sturdy. The weight of dirt on the supporting timbers took its toll, and after a decade or so a typical lodge was near collapse. By then, however, villagers had exhausted nearby wood supplies; so rather than rebuild their sagging structures, they usually abandoned the settlement, moved upstream, and began a new community in virgin territory.

But wherever a village might be located, Pawnee life was governed by the cultivation of crops, particularly corn, and the herding habits of the buffalo on the nearby grasslands. Planting began in spring, usually early in May. The appearance of the first young corn shoots was a signal for vigilance. When the shoots were still small, villagers expended much time and effort weeding their plots—about one acre for a family of four—and guarding against such animal predators as gophers and

A Plains dog rests during a band's migration. Behind it is a travois—two long poles with a net stretched between them on which perhaps 75 pounds of gear was carried. Before the horse, the dog was the Indians' only beast of burden. But the animals were not very efficient. They constantly fought among themselves and darted off in pursuit of rabbits. Thus hunting bands could travel only about six miles a day.

rabbits that favored the tender plants. About a month later the corn had grown sufficiently tough, so that the animals no longer found it attractive, and the Indians could now allow nature to take its course while they left for the plains for the first of their two annual hunts. (Before the late 1600's, when the Pawnees first secured horses, hunting was done on foot.)

So numerous were the buffalo that the Pawnees could usually pick and choose among the animals. During this early summer hunt ambush was a favorite tactic, and the Indians would hide near river sites where the beasts were known to come to drink. When several buffalo appeared, the Pawnees would concentrate on shooting down young bulls and yearlings. The cows were just past their birthing season and offered little but tough meat and worn coats. Of course, if an opportunity presented itself for driving a herd over a cliff or surrounding it, the Pawnees would not hold back, but these tactics of mass killing were usually reserved for the fall hunt.

When the bands returned to the villages after the summer foray, the corn, squash, and beans were nearly ready for harvest. Now was a time of abundance. Buffalo meat was plentiful, and this was supplemented by antelope, deer, and elk. In the fields some women labored to bring in the produce, while others tanned skins to be made into leggings, tepee covers, blankets, and shirts. This was also a period of relaxation, of gossiping, and of games of chance and skill. Men were the usual players of these games in which skins, dogs, stored food, and clothing were wagered. Not surprisingly, there were disputes that occasionally turned into fights. Yet no matter how fierce the argument, how angry the participants, serious, long-lasting feuds rarely developed, for among the Pawnees there was a deep tradition of internal discipline and an almost instinctive understanding that survival depended on unity within each village.

Although the scattered settlements of the Pawnees constituted a tribe, there was little important contact among the communities. Each village was basically autonomous, governed by several chiefs as well as by priests who directed religious observances, shamans who cured the ill and prophesied the future, and notable warriors whose bravery had given them high status. There were, of course, many who fit into none of these categories. But an ordinary man could rise in the esteem of his fellow villagers and assume, by common consent, the role of a leader.

In large measure a Pawnee leader owed his status to the possession of a sacred bundle, a buffalo skin containing such items with supernatural powers as a pipe, pigments, tobacco, and corn. Although a bundle could be purchased, it was usually passed on from father to son. Its powers were derived from a star, under whose direction the bundle was assembled. Because the heavenly bodies played a dominant role in Pawnee religion, these gifts from above were held in awe.

Although Pawnee customs differed in detail from those of other river peoples of the Plains, in general the pattern of life was quite similar, revolving around farming and the hunt. If an 18th-century Pawnee, by some chance, were to wander hundreds of miles from his homeland in the Mandan country along the Big Bend of the Missouri, he would find there much that was familiar.

The Mandans came originally from the prairie lands along the Minnesota River. By A.D. 1400 they had firmly established themselves in large, palisaded villages along the upper Missouri. They were, perhaps, the first Plains tribe to be in frequent contact with whites, for French trappers as far back as the mid-18th century found shelter among them. From the first, Mandan customs, rituals, and habits deeply fascinated the Europe-

ans, who recorded in both word and picture a way of life that would vanish in the 1830's when the tribe was virtually wiped out by smallpox. The pictures on the following pages are part of that record.

Westward Movement

The Mandan and other tribes that settled along the Plains rivers from the 13th through the 16th centuries proved to be an advance guard of a flood of Indian peoples who would later work their way on to the grasslands. Increasing population in the Woodlands played a major role in these migrations, and by the mid-17th century the coming of Europeans became an added factor in determining the fate of many tribes. By then whites were firmly established along the eastern seaboard. Soon they would push inland, forcing the tribes to move ahead of them. But in the beginning there was little direct pressure from whites. Instead, the Europeans opened trade relations with local tribes, exchanging firearms for furs, and in a remarkably short time muskets found their way into the hands of numerous peoples of the interior. Those with firearms—several Algonquian tribes in Canada and the five nations of the Iroquois Confederacy—now had vast new power at their disposal and were able to seize great stretches of the Woodlands from peoples without guns.

Suddenly, the Ohio Valley and regions around the Great Lakes became the scene of incessant and one-sided warfare, with the tribes of the Iroquois Confederacy, in particular, raging through the forests to create mayhem. The peoples living in the prairie lands along the northern tributaries of the Mississippi—among them the Osage, Kansa, Omaha, and Missouri, all of them Siouan-speaking—found themselves displaced by tribes, native to more easterly regions, that were fleeing the well-armed Iroquois. Loading their boats with their possessions, these Siouan tribes floated down the Mississippi and thence onward to the Missouri as they searched out new settlement sites.

What they found in the Missouri Valley was an underpopulated region of rich soil. Here they could resume farming and establish villages along the Missouri River and its tributaries, the Osage and the Kansas.

Like the Mandan and Pawnee before them, these tribes quickly adapted themselves to Plains life. If the groves surrounding their villages were not as thick or as extensive as those in the Ohio Valley, the grasslands themselves offered an unparalleled opportunity to hunt buffalo, and the tribes became expert at their pursuit. Like the Mandans and Pawnees, these immigrants would vary their farming and gathering existence with the buffalo surround and the buffalo jump.

Not all the tribes from the Mississippi Valley went directly to the Plains. For the Dakotas, better known as the Sioux, and the Hidatsa-Crows, the journey lasted much longer and was indirect. Sometime before the 14th century these tribes (continued on page 166)

Setting off in bullboats, *Mandan women paddle across a river. The craft were made from buffalo hides stretched over willow frames. Light and sturdy, they could carry considerable freight and drew little water. To keep the boat from spinning, the buffalo's tail was left on with a piece of wood attached.*

Early Farmers of the Northern Plains

Four Bears, the last of the great Mandan chiefs, is the personification of martial qualities in this Catlin portrait. His quilled shirt, adorned with locks of hair, and his warbonnet bespeak his prowess as a warrior. He was also a noted religious leader and served as a negotiator in Mandan dealings with white traders.

Long before the white man or the horse arrived on the Plains, the Mandans and Hidatsas came to live along the Missouri River. From their villages, built atop rises, the men of these tribes conducted religious ceremonies, honed their martial skills, and formed hunting parties in summer to pursue the buffalo across the grasslands. Women descended from the villages onto the rich riverbank lands to cultivate corn, squash, sunflowers, and beans. When the land was exhausted and supplies of wood used up, these peoples moved on, up the Missouri. In the 400 years before white traders appeared, these tribes slowly migrated from the middle reaches of the Missouri into the North Dakota heartland.

In 1832 American artist George Catlin found the Mandans and Hidatsas living along the great bend of the Missouri. This energetic, self-taught painter was beginning the portrayal of Indians that was to be his lifetime concern. His deft, flowing style differed greatly from the work of another painter, Karl Bodmer, who saw the same tribes the next year. Bodmer was Swiss, classically trained, and meticulously realistic in his documentary paintings. In the combined works of Bodmer and Catlin a remarkably full view of these Plains farmers emerges.

From the earliest days along the Missouri the Mandans prospered, their surplus crops providing produce with which to trade with other tribes. When the first white man, French explorer and trader Sieur de la Vérendrye, arrived in 1738, the (continued)

Mandan lodges, compact as a honeycomb, are grouped around a village plaza. Each lodge housed several matrilineally linked families. The domed earth roofs were often used for dozing, courting, gaming, gossiping, and doing chores. The roofs also supplied storage space. There the women stored their round, lightweight bullboats, used on the Missouri for carrying trade goods to nearby villages. Poles on the plaza display scalp trophies and lengths of cloth obtained from the whites.

Early Farmers of the Plains *(cont.)*

Mandans numbered about 9,000. Nearby were the Hidatsa, a smaller tribe speaking a different language but living much like the Mandan.

By 1750 the Mandans were using both guns and horses, but they remained primarily a farming people. Two chiefs, one a warrior, the other a civil leader, led each village. Though the Mandans and Hidatsas were able fighters, both preferred peaceful relations with their neighbors, the better to carry on trade. After the Europeans arrived, the Mandans, in particular, maneuvered shrewdly to become intermediaries between the whites and the tribes farther west. Hide shirts and buffalo robes from the Plains changed hands for European cloth in barter sessions often held in Mandan villages.

But if the whites brought new prosperity, they also brought disease. La Vérendrye had hardly departed before smallpox struck the Mandans, the first of several epidemics. In the great epidemic of 1837 the tribesmen succumbed by the hundreds; only 125 survived. Among the victims was the Mandan chief Four Bears. As he lay dying, he gave voice to his bitterness at the whites: "Four Bears never saw a White Man hungry, but what he gave him to eat . . . and how have they repaid it! . . . I do not fear Death . . . but to *die* with my face rotten, that even the Wolves will shrink . . . at seeing Me, and say to themselves, that is Four Bears, the Friend of the Whites."

The Mandan woman Sha-ko-ka, *as portrayed by George Catlin, exhibits streaks of silver-gray in her hair, a common characteristic of the Mandans. Though admired for their charms, women were also prized for their hardiness. Farming, tanning, and even some heavy construction work were female tasks.*

Within a Mandan lodge, *Bodmer painted several Indians chatting around a firepit, the only light coming from the fire and its smoke hole. With their shields and weapons readily available and their horses tethered nearby, the men are ready for any emergency, such as a raid by bands foraying in from the Plains. Mandan men lived in their wives' lodges, bringing with them their few possessions—clothing, weapons, stallions, and geldings. The lodge, mares, colts, and dogs belonged to women.*

Triumphant Hidatsa warriors *are greeted by their women, who dangle scalps from poles as symbols of victory. If a single warrior was lost without the compensating deaths of enemies, this scalp dance was not performed. Instead, the war leader re-* *mained in mourning until the family of the victim forgave him. A second such loss cost the leader his position. The Hidatsas admired bravery, and a young man's first trophy of battle—a scalp or stolen horse—was celebrated by his family.*

Two Hidatsas *(above left) prepare to hurl lances in a game of hoop and pole, a favorite gambling activity. There were numerous variations of this game. In one, ac-cording to German naturalist Prince Alexander Philip Maximilian, who traveled with Bodmer, competing braves tried to hurl their lances through a rolling hoop.*

A Mandan fop, *in a Bodmer portrait, displays his blue-and-white bead choker and a variety of hair decorations, some of them bought from whites. According to Catlin such dandies, few in number, were much in evidence. Though scorned as "faint hearts" and regarded as drones, they prided themselves on their reputations for "beauty and elegance."*

In a final ordeal of the four-day Okipa ceremony, young Mandan tribesmen, supported by older warriors, race around a village plaza's central post, trailing buffalo skulls behind them. The Okipa, an annual summertime rite, was both a vision quest and a celebration recalling the creation of the Mandan people. During the ritual Okipa society elders, disguised as mythological figures, led young men into a round of tortures through which the youths, exhausted in mind and body, saw the visions that could shape their life goals and their roles within the tribe.

Okipa began with the arrival of Lone Man, who recited tribal myths, while Hoita ("Speckled Eagle") presided over ceremonies within the Okipa lodge. There young men fasted and prepared for the torture. After their backs, chests, and legs had been ritually slashed, the youths were skewered through the loose-hanging skin and raised toward the roof of the lodge (inset) on thongs attached to lengths of rawhide. There they hung until they fainted. Lowered to the ground in an unconscious or semiconscious state, they were now receptive to visions.

Meanwhile, outside the lodge, members of the Buffalo Bull Society danced around a ceremonial post, their frenzied weaving and stamping slowly building to the climax when they were joined by the vision-seeking youths. The ordeal ended when the youths were stripped of their buffalo skulls, their feat of endurance having ensured prosperity for the tribe in the coming year.

As farmers and nomads, the Hidatsas danced for both a plentiful corn harvest and a successful buffalo hunt during the Green Corn ceremony. Here chanting shamans stomp and warriors circle a cooking fire while carrying cornstalks. This ritual occurred when the first corn of summer ripened. The first ears were boiled, then removed from the kettle and placed on a scaffold above the fire as an offering to the spirits. After the ashes had been buried, a new fire was kindled, more corn boiled, and the entire village then shared in a feast.

Wearing buffalo masks, the men of a Mandan village act out the buffalo hunt. This Buffalo Calling Dance, a variation of a ritual performed during the Okipa ceremony, was held whenever hunger threatened a village. The dance, which might go on for days or even weeks—until a herd of buffalo was sighted—was intended to bring the animals onto the nearby grasslands. George Catlin reported that as a tiring dancer began to fall to the ground, another performer would draw his bow and shoot the man with a blunt arrow. The fallen dancer was then seized by the "bye-standers, who drag him out of the ring by the heels, brandishing their knives about him; and having gone through the motions of skinning and cutting him up, they let him off. . . ." When buffalo finally appeared, the hunters went in pursuit, while the other villagers consumed their remaining rations.

Old Bear, a Mandan shaman, poses in full regalia, "with medicine-pipes in his hands and foxes tails attached to his heels," wrote Catlin. Old Bear, dressed in a robe of white wolfskins and his body daubed with clay, took the role of Lone Man to preside over the Okipa ceremony. He was a healer of great repute and was called on in cases of extreme illness. For lesser ailments there were many shamans with the status of healers, among them numerous elderly women.

Wrapped in skins, Mandan dead lie on open scaffolds (background) built just high enough to be out of reach of animals. Relatives would visit these platforms to mourn, and when a body decayed, the skull was removed to join others in a circle. There friends and relatives would come to honor the dead and bring them food.

Comanches run down mustangs in this Catlin painting. One Comanche has already lassoed a wild horse, hobbled its front feet, and fastened a noose around its jaw. As the animal snorts and bucks, the Indian slowly advances. He places a hand over the horse's eyes, then breathes into its nostrils, actions calculated to help calm the animal.

moved into present-day Minnesota, Wisconsin, and Manitoba. There they thrived and multiplied, so much so that population pressure forced many bands westward. One element of the Sioux, known as the Assiniboins, pushed west to the edge of the Plains. Later other Sioux bands would find their way to the grasslands. As for the Hidatsa-Crow, they fell victim to pressure from more easterly tribes. In the 17th century fierce raiding parties of Crees and Ojibwas, armed with French guns, began attacks on Hidatsa-Crow communities, forcing the inhabitants to flee. Like other tribes, the Hidatsa-Crow found sanctuary on the edge of the Great Plains, and they settled in villages just beyond the Big Bend of the Missouri, several miles from the Mandan communities. Here the Hidatsa-Crows honed their skills as buffalo-hunters and farmers. In their new homes populations grew so rapidly that part of the tribe, the Crow, moved off far to the west and settled along the banks of the Yellowstone River.

There is not space to trace the migrations of all of the tribes that came to occupy the Great Plains. The story of the Cheyennes, the Gros Ventres, and the Arapahos was similar to those already mentioned, and population pressure forced elements of the Crees and Ojibwas out of their ancient homes onto the northeastern edge of the Plains. The Blackfeet, who may once have been inhabitants of the Hudson Bay region, moved westward onto the open country of Alberta as a result of population pressure. During the same general period tribes that had long lived in the Great Basin and later in the Rockies, such as the Comanche, migrated eastward and became Plains Indians. Here they came to mingle with peoples from the Woodlands and helped establish the classic Plains culture that would flourish for a brief time, only to flicker out with the arrival of whites. But in its moment of glory, this culture created the legend of the archetypical Indian, the buffalo-hunter celebrated in song and story.

Comanche Art of Horsemanship

Of all Plains warriors none excelled the Comanches as skilled horsemen. So close were the Comanche and his mount that one observer of Plains life compared them to the mythical centaur: "half horse, half man . . . so dexterously managed that it appears but one animal, fleet and furious." George Catlin, who painted the Comanches, described them as ungainly and slovenly on foot but said that they were transformed into the personifications of grace once mounted.

From the time a Comanche child—boy or girl—was four or five, he or she owned a pony. A boy, in particular, drilled day after day to hone his equestrian skills. Traveling at full speed, he at first picked up small objects from the ground; later, larger and heavier objects. Finally, he could swoop down along the flanks of his mount and sweep up the body of a man, a skill that enabled him to rescue a wounded comrade in battle. If the Comanche was a peerless rider, he owed much to the nature of his horse—an animal noted for agility, alertness, speed, and endurance. These horses responded instantly to touch or word and frequently could even anticipate their riders' commands.

Such magnificent animals were partially the result of the Comanches' skill as horse breeders. They used only the most responsive and fleetest stallions as studs. They also owned more mounts than any other tribe. One band of 2,000 Comanches had no fewer than 15,000 horses, and some war chiefs personally possessed more than 1,000. To the Comanches, like other Plains Indians, a horse was not only indispensable for hunting and combat but was also a form of wealth. In addition to breeding their herds, these Indians were expert at capturing and taming wild horses. However, the Comanches generally preferred to steal mounts from enemy tribes. Such raids not only secured already broken horses but burnished the Comanches' reputation as horse thieves, warriors, and the dominant equestrian people of the Plains.

Peoples of the Horse

The Indian, the Buffalo, and the Horse—in these words lies the essence of 18th- and 19th-century life on the Plains. When the edges of the grasslands were being populated in the 17th and early 18th centuries, the horse was the only missing element in the equation. Lacking the mobility the horse would give but enjoying the blessing of fertile soil along the river bottoms, the tribes had all settled down to a semisedentary life, punctuated by summer and fall buffalo hunts. But when these Indians secured horses, mostly in the 18th century, everything changed. For many of the tribes—among them the Sioux, Crow, Cheyenne, and Arapaho—village life suddenly seemed tame and dull now that they could ride with the wind, weave and dart among the herds of buffalo, engage in thrilling intertribal raids.

Even tribes that did not completely abandon village life became enamored of the horse and the freedom it provided. For the semisedentary Pawnees, Mandans, Hidatsas, and Arikaras, the buffalo hunt now assumed major importance. Where once they left their villages for only a few weeks, now they ranged the grasslands for far longer periods of time, returning home only at planting and harvest time and during the winter weather.

It is almost impossible to imagine the peoples of the Plains without mounts, so rapidly and expertly did they take to riding. The Plains peoples greeted the horse with something close to veneration, and because it replaced the dog as a porter, they called it Spirit Dog, Holy Dog, or Medicine Dog. Coronado had first brought horses to the grasslands in 1541, but fully two centuries would pass before the horse was a common sight throughout the plains.

The Southwest Indians, who were in constant contact with Spaniards since the close of the 16th century, were the first to own horses. In the beginning these Indians merely tended horses for the Europeans but,

167

inevitably, they came to own their own herds. By the early 17th century Plains tribesmen, foraying south on trading and raiding expeditions, had secured the beginnings of their own herds, and by 1770 just about every grassland tribe was well supplied with mounts. Not only did the Indians become expert riders, but they developed into peerless horse breeders as well. They practiced gelding to improve the stock, using only their best stallions for studs. By 1800 the original stock of half-Andalusian, half-Arab horses that the Spanish had brought into North America had evolved into the typical Indian pony whose shaggy coat and small stature did not suggest its actual speed and responsiveness. To the white man coming onto the Plains, these pintos, duns, and splotched cayuses appeared no match for their own heavy, grain-fed mounts; yet in battle or on the hunt the Indians' horses far excelled those of the Europeans.

A warrior kept his war-horse always tethered close to his tepee. He allowed no one else to ride it. He not only painted himself for war, but painted his pony, too, with a variety of multicolored designs, many of them symbolic of the feats of the owner.

To these painted symbols the Indian added rich adornments to his mount, tying eagle feathers to its mane or tail, fastening scalp locks to its bridle and, after trade with the whites began, red ribbons to its head. Such concern for a horse was fully justified; often its fleetness, endurance, and responsiveness spelled the difference between life and death. Before one battle a Sioux warrior named Siyaka dismounted and faced

his horse, saying: "We are in danger. Obey me promptly that we may conquer. If you have to, run for your life and mine. Do your best and if we reach home I will give you the best eagle feather I can get and the finest cloth offering, and you shall be painted with the best paint." Thus was a good war-horse honored.

During a fight many Plains Indians dropped down on one side of the mount, one leg hooked over the horse's back and an elbow resting in a sling that circled the animal's neck. This left the hands free for bow and arrow. Using their ponies as shields, they discharged their arrows over the horses' backs or from beneath their necks.

The horse also radically altered the lives of the Plains woman. Indeed, her value as a bride was calculated in the number of horses her suitor gave her father to win her. In the many tribes where women had owned their own travois dogs, it was only natural that they would later own their own horses. Blackfeet women boasted of their control over their own extensive herds and were eager to obtain new mounts through barter and inheritance. Hard-riding young Comanche women on horseback went antelope hunting with their men, successfully competing with them in bringing down game.

Horses had to be cared for, fed, and curried, and by and large the men did this. But when a tribe was on the move, the women did all the packing and loading. While on the trail they led the packhorses and kept the families together as their men rode guard or fanned out ahead in search of game or to spy out enemies. Moving

White Quiver, a Blackfoot warrior, returns victorious from a horse raid in this detail of a Charles M. Russell painting. Though White Quiver is clad in the white man's clothing, his horse bears traditional symbols of the prowess of man and mount. The symbolic hoof marks on the horse's neck refer to earlier successful raids, and the hand print on its flank reveals that its owner had killed an enemy in hand-to-hand combat. A Plains warrior gladly shared such honors with his mount and often painted his war-horse with the same colors and symbols he used on his own face and body. Several common symbols are shown below.

A horse might also wear an eagle's plume in its forelock. Its tail and mane could be trimmed and dyed, and a line of scalps was sometimes hung from its mane. All these were trophies or symbols of bravery.

 War party leader   Enemy killed in hand combat   Owner fought from behind breastworks   Hail   Coup marks   Horse raids   Mourning marks   Medicine symbol

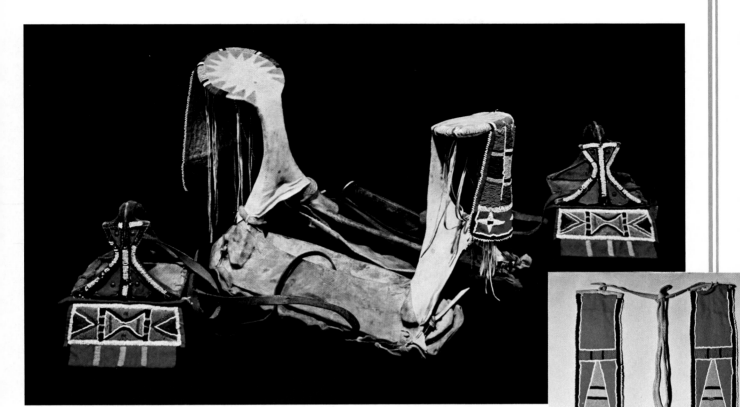

The Elegant Accoutrements of Crow Tribe Horses

The Plains Indians not only received the horse from the Spaniards but adapted Spanish design for much of the gear their mounts wore. Plains women, for example, rode in heavy wooden saddles reminiscent of the war saddles of the conquistadors.

Warriors, on the other hand, generally rode bareback, particularly when hunting or engaging in combat. Sometimes, however, they used small, flexible saddles of hide stuffed with buffalo hair or grass. Bridles were woven of buffalo hair or braided rawhide, and after trade was opened with the whites, steel bits were sometimes used to control and guide the mount. But more often a Plains Indian disdained the bit and achieved the same control with a rawhide thong fastened to his animal's lower jaw.

Among the most notable horsemen of the Northern Plains were the Crows. Only the Comanches, whose hunting grounds were far to the south, owned as many mounts. The Crows, a tall and strikingly handsome people, gloried in ornamenting their mounts with richly decorated saddles, bridles, collars, and blankets. Such superbly fashioned trappings were the work of the tribeswomen, whose skill at tanning and embroidering was unrivaled throughout the grasslands. Thanks to the talents of these women, the horses of the Crows were nearly as richly adorned as the mounts of knights in medieval Europe. Like the Comanches, the Crows were inveterate horse raiders and would take almost any kind of risk to increase the size of their herds. At times they would even swoop far to the south of their accustomed range to raid the much vaunted Comanches and make off with their superbly trained mounts.

The saddle and riding accessories shown above are typical of the finely wrought work of Crow women. The woman's saddle (top) resembles Spanish models, except that the pommel and cantle (backrest)—made from wood or horn—are much higher. The wooden saddle seat is covered with buckskin. To the left and right of the saddle are stirrups, made of cottonwood branches bent into U-shapes and fastened to level wood bases. The stirrups, like the pommel and cantle, bear ornamentations of beads formed into traditional Crow designs. The rosette (above left) is made from circles of yarn sewn on buckskin. It was fastened to the front of a decorated bridle. The suspender-like object (above), made of beaded buckskin and red trader's cloth, is purely ornamental. It was worn around a horse's neck, the square that joins both straps covering the animal's chest.

was a frequent occurrence, for a band stayed in an area only as long as its resources could support them. Often this meant breaking camp several times a month. The 19-century American artist George Catlin described a large group on the move:

"I saw an encampment of Sioux, consisting of six hundred lodges, struck and all things packed and on the move in a very few minutes. . . . At the time announced the lodge of the chief is seen flapping in the wind, a part of the poles having been taken out from under it; this is the signal, and in one minute, six hundred of them . . . were seen waving and flapping in the wind, and in one minute more all were flat upon the ground. Their horses and dogs . . . had all been . . . in readiness; and each one was speedily loaded . . . and ready to fall into the grand procession. . . . [On] the poles, [dragging] behind the horse, is placed the lodge or tent, which is rolled up, and also numerous other articles of household . . . furniture, and on top of all, two, three and even four women and children! Each one of these horses has a conductress, who sometimes walks before and leads it, with a tremendous pack upon her back; [at other times] she sits astride its back, with a child, perhaps, at her breast, and another astride . . . behind her, clinging to her waist with one arm, while it affectionately embraces a . . . dog-pup in the other."

Through most of the year the nomadic tribes formed relatively small bands that foraged and hunted on their own. But in the summer, just after the rendezvous for that most sacred of Plains ceremonies, the Sun Dance, hunting units of several hundred men and their families migrated together for the great annual surround.

This tribal hunt was a solemn affair, usually preceded by prayers and many rituals. On the trail and during the hunt itself, discipline was rigidly enforced by members of the various military societies who acted as police. They made certain that every hunter performed only his assigned task and did not attempt to hunt on his own. The group hunt was one of the few times when a warrior routinely submerged his own individuality, and those appointed as police had almost absolute authority. Often they were even granted the right to punish malfactors by whipping them or shooting their horses.

When scouts ranging ahead of the main party sighted a buffalo herd, the tribal cavalcade always stopped downwind from their prey. To compensate for poor eyesight, buffalo had an acute sense of smell, and they were constantly sniffing the air for the scent of danger. To prepare for the surround of the buffalo, the hunters normally stripped down to breechclouts and moccasins. Anything superfluous that might encumber the rider was left behind. The horses, too, were stripped of saddles and blankets. Going after buffalo, darting in and out of the herd and forcing the beasts into a circle where they might be picked off, was a risky business. Bows and arrows or lances continued to be used even after firearms were common among the tribesmen. The process of arming the muzzle-loaders was far too slow and cumbersome during the height of the hunt. Only

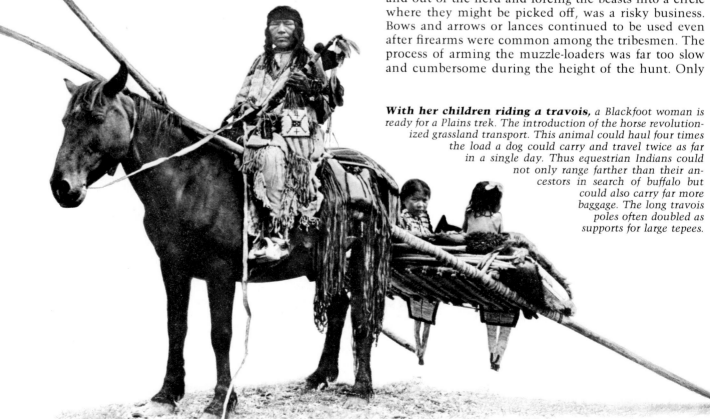

With her children riding a travois, a Blackfoot woman is ready for a Plains trek. The introduction of the horse revolutionized grassland transport. This animal could haul four times the load a dog could carry and travel twice as far in a single day. Thus equestrian Indians could not only range farther than their ancestors in search of buffalo but could also carry far more baggage. The long travois poles often doubled as supports for large tepees.

Personifications of grace in motion, *riders and horses close in on a buffalo herd in this Charles M. Russell painting. When a herd was sighted, riders set their horses off at a gallop across rough country, guiding them by knee pressure alone. Only when they were on the herd did the Indians discharge their arrows,* *leaving it to their mounts to dodge from the zigzag paths of wounded buffalo. Although a bull buffalo might weigh a ton and stand seven feet tall, it had amazing agility and endurance. Even with an arrow through the lung, it could run as much as a mile before collapsing.*

when breech-loading rifles became available in the mid-19th century did the Indians abandon their more primitive weapons for the buffalo chase.

The end of a successful hunt was an occasion for joy. When the hunters returned to camp, followed by the packhorses and the women who had helped with the butchering, the few people who had remained behind shouted their approval. Fires were burning, and meat racks stood ready. Some did not wait for the meat to be cooked but ate the livers and kidneys raw, flavored with drops of gall scooped up on a knife point. Sweet marrow also made for good eating, as did roasted intestines. But tongues and flesh from the hump were the morsels of choice, and after a hunt everybody feasted until sated. Even the dogs were quiet for once, having had their fill. Exhausted from the excitement, the Indians would fall to the ground for a few hours repose, only to be roused in the night by the beat of a drum calling everybody to a dance of celebration.

Killing his first buffalo made a boy into a man. One Sioux, Standing Bear, remembered the occasion well: "Everybody began to get ready. While one of my step-mothers was helping me, she said: 'Son, when you kill a buffalo, save me the kidney and the skin.' I didn't know whether she was trying to poke fun at me or to give me encouragement. But it made me feel proud to have her talk like that to me. My father told me: 'My son, watch the buffalo closely. If the one you are after is running straight . . . then you can get in very close. But if the buffalo is looking at you from the corner of its eye, then look out! They are very quick and powerful. They can get their horns under your horse and toss him high in the air, and you might get killed.' "

An old Indian once said that all his people ever needed for a good life was the buffalo; that this wonderful animal contained within its body everything the tribe needed, with the exception of water for drinking and lodgepoles for the tepee.

Cornucopia on the Hoof

The Indians literally lived off the buffalo. The skins alone had a wide variety of uses. At birth the Indian was often swaddled in the soft skin of a young calf; in death a buffalo hide became his shroud. Summer hides were scraped and sewn together to make tepee covers. Hides were used for inner curtains to keep drafts out of the lodge, while a single skin could be fashioned into a bullboat. Parts of the hides were made into drums and rattles, and the thick pelt from a buffalo's neck became a shield. Specially tanned, softened by repeated smoking, wetting, drying, and rubbing—hides were made into shirts, leggings, dresses, gloves, and moccasins. Skins taken in autumn and winter, when the hair was long and thick, served as blankets and wraparound, cold-weather robes. Tails made good fly whisks. Rawhide could be made into strings and lassos. When wetted and permitted to shrink in place, rawhide fastened stone heads to war clubs and arrow points to their shafts.

Buffalo hair also had myriad uses. Woven, it became strong rope; loose, it stuffed cradleboards, gloves, moccasins, saddle pads, and pillows; and tightly rolled, it became an excellent ball for a variety of games. The horns of a buffalo were fashioned into spoons and drinking vessels. The bones of buffalo were also put to use, becoming saddletrees and fleshing tools of various kinds. Ribs, tied together with rawhide, became sleds, while small bones were worked into knives and awls. Out of a buffalo's hooves and scrotum, rattles were made for religious rituals; in some rites the skull of the animal also played a major role.

Of course, buffalo meat was the center of the Plains Indians' diet. After a kill, when the tribesmen and women had had their fill of roasted meat and raw bits, the remainder could be dried on racks and made into jerky, or pounded together with fat and berries, a preparation known as pemmican, a concentrated, high-protein food carried by warriors out on the trail. Even the internal organs had their uses in Plains cookery. Before white traders introduced iron kettles, the buffalo's paunch served admirably as a cooking pot. It was large, leathery, and tough. To cook in it, the Indians suspended the paunch from four sticks and filled it with water, vegetables, and meat. Then hot rocks were dropped in to bring the water to a boil and cook the food.

With all the gifts that the buffalo bestowed, one can hardly wonder at the fact that the Indians revered this animal. Great tribal leaders took on names associated with the buffalo as a means of gaining added prowess in war and on the hunt. And all of the tribes held great religious ceremonies to honor this source of all blessings.

Without buffalo skins there could have been no tepees. Depending on the size of the dwelling and the size of the skins, 6 to 28 pelts made up a tepee covering. Not only was the tepee a movable home, it was also a sacred place. The floor of the tepee symbolized the earth on which the Indians lived; the sides, vaulting to a peak, the sky. The tepee's roundness was a reminder of the sacred life circle, which has no beginning and no end, and behind the hearth, in even the most modest of lodges, was an earth altar on which incense, in the form of fragrant sage or sweet grass, was burned. Here prayers were intoned.

An old lady on the Rosebud Reservation reminisced in 1970 about the tepee villages of her youth. "What a wonderful sight it was," she said, "on a dark night, the many tepees glowing faintly red from the fires within. Sometimes one could see shapes moving inside. These tepees were so alive, breathing almost with the blue-white smoke rising from them. How I wish I could see them again, but I still see them in my mind."

As a dwelling the tepee was well adapted to Plains life. It was sturdy enough to withstand the strongest of winds that sweep through the grasslands. Yet it was sufficiently light to be erected or struck in minutes, and the ease with which it could be transported made it ideal for nomadic peoples.

The tepee was a woman's castle. She made it, she put it up and, at moving time, she packed it on the travois. Among the Cheyennes a woman desiring a new tepee gathered her materials together, then requested the aid of a lodge-maker, another woman. Together the two women spread the skins on the ground and cut them to size and shape. Messengers then went out to call on a number of women to help sew the skins together. After the hostess served her helpers a meal, sewing began, followed by another repast. With concentrated effort even a large lodge could be put together in the course of a day. It was a joyous occasion for socializing, talking, and singing. While working, some woman might

Capped by a buffalo's skull, an outcropping of rocks was, in the minds of the Assiniboins, a lure to the herds. Like other Plains peoples, the Assiniboins believed that the power of the supernatural resided in all of nature's works. Thus a rock pile that even vaguely resembled a buffalo's form could be construed as having the power to attract the animals to its vicinity. The illustration is a lithograph based on a Karl Bodmer painting.

Sign Language: Common "Tongue" of the Plains

There were many languages spoken on the Plains, and they usually had neither vocabulary nor grammar in common. Yet people from tribes whose languages differed as much as Blackfoot from Mandan were still able to communicate through the universal "tongue" of the Plains: sign language. Little Raven, a chief of the southern Arapahos, once emphasized the importance of this form of dialogue: "I have met Comanches, Kiowas, Apaches, Caddos, Gros Ventres, Snakes, Crows, Pawnees, Osages, Arickarees [sic], Nez Percés . . . and other tribes whose vocal languages . . . we did not understand, but we communicated freely in sign language."

Though Indians of the same tribe might, on occasion, converse in the language of the hands, particularly if they did not wish to be overheard or were out of earshot of one another, sign language was particularly useful, of course, for intertribal discussions. Thus disputes could often be settled, alliances cemented, trade agreements reached through little more than a series of mutually understood gestures.

For all its usefulness sign language had obvious limitations. Communication was generally limited to simple, readily comprehended ideas, such as a Sioux' desire to exchange a couple of buffalo skins for a Mandan's surplus of corn.

When the fur-trapping mountain men came to the Plains area in the early 1800's, they soon picked up the rudiments of the Indians' sign language, a circumstance that enabled them to trade with the tribes for pelts. In later years soldiers manning forts on the Plains also learned the signs, making their dealings with the multitude of tribes much less difficult—at least in terms of basic communication—than they otherwise would have been. Some of the hand motions that formed the vocabulary of sign language are shown at right. These are all words for particular tribes, but oddly enough each tribal identification was preceded by the generalized sign for Indian.

Indian: Rub left hand, back and forth, twice

Cheyenne: Chop at left index finger

Comanche: Imitate motion of a snake

Crow: Hold the fist on forehead, palm out

Pawnee: Make V-sign and extend hand

Nez Perce: Move index finger under nose

Osage: Move hands down along back of head

Sioux: Hand across neck in cutting motion

recite the number of fine tepees she had made in the past, much as a warrior among a group of men counted his honors, or coups, in battle.

Sign Language

Among the Indians of the Plains, sign language played a major role in intertribal dealings. Hand symbols enabled tribes without a common spoken language to communicate with each other, and the quick, artful hand movements were as readily understood by the Kiowas in Oklahoma as by the Blackfeet, more than 1,000 miles to the northwest.

Art was also a bond of cultural unity throughout the grasslands. Painting and beadwork and porcupine-quill embroidery were at the heart of Plains art. An old Sioux woman, Leading Cloud, once said: "A good beader makes a good wife. I learned when I was ten. A girl who helped the grown-ups, who could tan and bead and quill well, was much honored. The men kept track of their brave deeds, and us women used to keep a record of our kind of 'deeds.' All girls and women had an elkhorn flesher. On one side they made black dots; on the other, red ones. Each black dot meant a robe tanned. Each red dot meant ten skins tanned or a complete tepee. They competed against each other. At Sun Dance time there were quilling contests. Grandmother's teeth were all worn down from flattening quills between her teeth. But she gained much honor from this work. That was her way of counting coup."

The most ubiquitous form of Plains art was painting. The Indians of the region decorated just about everything to which paint could be applied: containers, buf-

falo robes, hide tepee coverings, horses, and to their own bodies. These paintings served many purposes. Some were derived from visions and thus had supernatural powers. Others were a kind of signature or biography. A particular design on a robe might be unique to the person who wore it, while its trimmings could convey such information as the age of the owner, his marital status, and the specific feats he had performed on the hunt or in battle. Face and body paint served a dual purpose, the paint itself shielding the wearer from sun or wind burn, the design a kind of talisman protecting the wearer in battle or connoting his membership in a particular society. Finally, many tribes had ornately decorated hides displaying pictographs. These were, in essence, calendars that recorded, in pictorial form, the achievements and happenings in a particular year. By studying these hides a viewer—if he could interpret the symbols—might gain considerable knowledge of tribal history.

In general, the inspiration for the paintings of the Plains came from the environment in which the tribes found themselves. Not surprisingly, the animals of the grasslands, the topographical features of the region, the sky, the earth, and fellow Indians all formed part of the repertoire of tribal artists. Representational art was usually the preserve of men, while geometric patterns were often painted by women. Yet as abstract as a geometric pattern might be, it had a specific meaning and referred to particular animals, objects, or concepts. One school of opinion holds that the geometric forms were always conventionalized representations of the natural world, but another group of (continued on page 177)

The Buffalo: Source of Food, Clothing, Shelter, and Tools for Plains Indians

Although most of the young men are away on the spring buffalo hunt, there is much activity in this Cheyenne camp, established on a broad open area near both water and wood. The older men, too advanced in age to join the hunt, pass the day by smoking their pipes, spinning tales of past exploits, and gambling with dice made of buffalo bone. The children play games that sharpen the skills they will need in later life. Beside a miniature tepee covered with a buffalo skin, two girls pretend they are women and play at household chores. Acting out their future roles as hunters and providers for their families, boys run along a grassy open area, their toy bows at the ready to shoot down imaginary herds of buffalo.

Some of the women are out in the fields picking berries, used with buffalo meat to make pemmican, but most are busy within the camp refurbishing equipment after the long winter. Included in their many tasks are the making of parfleches—buffalo-skin containers to hold, among other things, dried buffalo meat (jerky)—and the tanning of buffalo hides that they will use for lodge coverings, blankets, robes, and other necessities. In general, it is the men who kill the buffalo but the women who process the carcasses, turning almost every portion of the beasts into food, clothing, shelter, and a host of other useful items.

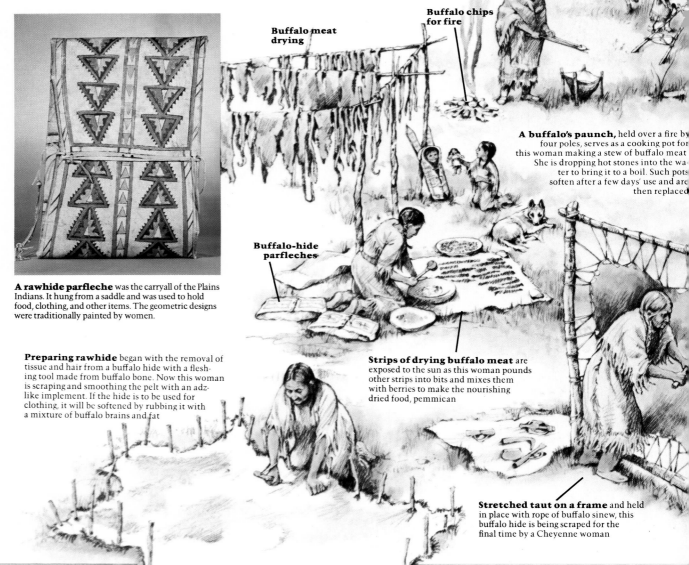

Buffalo meat drying

Buffalo chips for fire

A buffalo's paunch, held over a fire by four poles, serves as a cooking pot for this woman making a stew of buffalo meat. She is dropping hot stones into the water to bring it to a boil. Such pots soften after a few days' use and are then replaced

Buffalo-hide parfleches

A rawhide parfleche was the carryall of the Plains Indians. It hung from a saddle and was used to hold food, clothing, and other items. The geometric designs were traditionally painted by women.

Preparing rawhide began with the removal of tissue and hair from a buffalo hide with a fleshing tool made from buffalo bone. Now this woman is scraping and smoothing the pelt with an adzlike implement. If the hide is to be used for clothing, it will be softened by rubbing it with a mixture of buffalo brains and fat

Strips of drying buffalo meat are exposed to the sun as this woman pounds other strips into bits and mixes them with berries to make the nourishing dried food, pemmican

Stretched taut on a frame and held in place with rope of buffalo sinew, this buffalo hide is being scraped for the final time by a Cheyenne woman

A horseman approaches boys at play. The horse's bridle is of buffalo hair, the boys' bowstrings of buffalo sinew. Nearby, a buffalo-hide shield stands on a tripod

Men gambling with buffalo-bone dice

Rawhide hobble

Buffalo-horn bowl

A hired designer (standing) sketches in the basic figures on a tepee while the owner fills in the color with a buffalo-bone "brush"

Clothing made of buffalo hide and deerskin

In a working and gossiping session women cooperate in stitching up a buffalo-hide lodge cover. The standing woman is the lodge maker who supervises the work. She must be experienced and have a good disposition; for according to tradition, if she is bad tempered, the tepee's interior will always be smoky. As the women work, the hostess—the owner of the new lodge—feeds her guests generously. The women use thread made from tendons that run along the buffalo's backbone and legs. The tips of the threads are moistened to a point so that they can be slipped through the awl holes previously punched in the skin

Buffalo skins were sometimes used as "canvases" to record, in pictorial form, the outstanding events of a man's life. The hide at right is a kind of biography of Standing Buffalo, a notable Sioux war leader of the mid-1800's.

The Tepee: A Portable Home for the Plains Hunters

Long before the Sioux, Cheyenne, and other Plains tribes came to the grasslands, the tepee had been developed by the Indians of the northern forests. They used a pole frame to create the conical shape and then covered the skeleton with birchbark, caribou hides, or other materials.

The Plains Indians adapted this basic structure to their own environment and their own pattern of living. An adjustment in the framework was made to accommodate the strong winds of the region, and buffalo hides, sewn together, became the usual covering.

The tepee was an ideal dwelling for the Plains people. Like the buffalo they hunted, these Indians were constantly on the move. Their dwellings, therefore, had to be readily transportable. A tepee presented no problems. To move it, the ends of two of the tepee supporting poles were lashed to a horse. The other ends dragged along the ground, thus forming a roughly triangular frame, a travois, on which the buffalo covering and the family's other possessions were tied.

At the new campsite several long poles were bound together near their tops. The poles were then stood up and slanted outward from this center tie to form the outline of a cone. Other poles

were leaned against this framework to strengthen it, and a buffalo-hide covering, usually of 8 to 20 skins, was draped over the skeleton. The covering was joined near the top with wooden lodge pins, as shown below. An opening was left at the very top as a smoke hole; the entrance, with closable flaps, was at the lower part of this seam.

In hot weather, when cooling breezes were wanted, the flaps were left open and the lower part of the tepee

covering was rolled up, permitting the air to circulate freely. In winter an additional skin lining was added to the tepee covering, thus providing insulation. The fire that burned in the center of the floor kept the tepee warm as well as furnishing heat for cooking.

Because of the strong, prevailing winds that swept across the Plains from the west, a tepee was always set up with the entrance facing east. And the entire shelter was always tilted slightly toward the east to streamline the rear, thus lessening the wind pressure on it.

As shown in the illustration below, a typical tepee was crowded with hide bedding, a rug for the baby, willow-rod backrests, cradleboard, a suspended cooking bag, a supply of fuel, parfleches containing food, medicine, and other necessities, and similar household gear.

On the insulating lining of the tepee were hung sacred objects, weapons, shield, and other items. This lining was often painted with brilliantly colored designs that recalled past events in the lives of those who inhabited the tepee.

The Plains Indians had deep appreciation for the tepee. Secure, mobile, and comfortable, it was looked upon by these nomadic hunters as "a good mother" who sheltered and protected her children.

Smoke flaps can be adjusted to retain heat or to ventilate

Wooden lodge pins are removed to fold the tepee for traveling

Tepee poles. Three or four make the basic framework of the tepee. Long poles are prized where tall, straight trees are scarce. Same poles become the frame of the travois when traveling

Quiver with arrows. Arrows are striped with colored paint to mark ownership

Medicine bag. Special parfleche for sacred items that represent things seen in the owner's visions

Tepee lining. Additional layer of skin, often brightly painted

Parfleches are the closets and drawers of the tepee

Buffalo-skin bedding is rolled and stored during the day

Altar for burning sweet grass or other incense during ceremonial occasions

Firewood

Heated stones for cooking

Wooden bow is shaped by heating and bending. Bowstrings are made of sinew, rawhide, or twisted vegetable fiber

Shield. Some battle shields are painted with pictures from vision which offer spiritual protection. Highly decorated ones are too sacred for battle and can also endanger the bearer by calling special attention to his status

Backrest. The Plains family's easy chair

Cradleboard holds the fur-wrapped infant securely

Woman's sewing bag. Hide pouch holds awls, sinew thread, beads, quills, grasses, paints, small bones, and ermine tails

Buffalo-paunch cooking pot contains the day's soup of buffalo meat, wild turnips, and wild onions

An Indian camp at dawn was already a bustling place, as this 19th-century Jules Tavernier painting reveals. Smoke rises from cooking fires as families gather for the morning meal. At such a camp tepees were usually arranged according to relation- *ships, with newlyweds often erecting their dwellings near the lodge of one set of parents. The selection of the campground itself was up to the band's leader, whose decision depended on the proximity of buffalo, water, and grass for horses.*

experts believe that the patterns were conceived first and only later were the meanings imposed.

Color, too, was replete with symbolic significance, although this might vary from tribe to tribe. To a Crow black was the color of victory, while to a Sioux it symbolized night. Red was the hue of sunset or thunder for the Dakota Sioux. To an Arapaho red also meant man, or blood, or earth. To obtain their pigments the Plains Indians used a variety of natural substances. Blue, for example, could be derived from dried duck manure mixed with water, yellow from bullberries or buffalo gallstones, black from burnt wood, green from plants, and white from certain clays. These pigments were often mixed with water-thinned natural glues, which helped the colors adhere to the surfaces. Pigments were applied with various instruments—one "brush" per hue—made of chewed cottonwood, willow sticks, porous buffalo bone or, in later years, twigs tipped with antelope hair.

Of all Plains paintings the most spectacular were the murals on the lodges of tribal notables, such as chiefs and war leaders. The designs were directly derived from visions and, as such, the murals were endowed with supernatural powers. Though the owner of such a tepee may have employed a skilled craftsman to sketch and paint the design, the artist followed the most minute directions of his employer, for if the magic was to work, the instructions conveyed by the spirit in the vision had to be followed fully and faithfully.

As art was a part of everyday life, so too were games. Many of the sports for children were really educational, preparing the young for their adult roles. Boys had miniature bows, and at first they hunted only small game. When they had become proficient archers, they would join their elders in the buffalo hunt. Fleetness of foot was much prized among the young and old alike, and numerous running games and contests helped children develop speed and agility. When he was an old man, Crow chief Plenty Coups recalled the gamelike

training of his childhood: "I was playing with some other boys," he said, "when my grandfather stopped to watch. 'Take off your shirt and leggings,' he said to me. I tore them from my back and legs, and naked, except for my moccasins, stood before him. 'Now catch me that yellow butterfly!' he ordered. 'Be quick!' Away I went. . . . How fast these creatures are, and how cunning! In and out among the trees and bushes, across streams . . . the dodging butterfly led me far before I caught it. Panting . . . I offered it to grandfather, who whispered . . . 'Rub its wings over your heart, my son, and ask the butterflies to lend you their grace and swiftness.' "

Girls had games of their own and played with dolls and toy tepees, but they were welcome to participate in the more rough-and-tumble activities that the boys pursued.

Winter had its own amusements. Sioux Indian Standing Bear remembers the buffalo-rib sled made by his father many decades ago. "After all the meat had been cleaned from the bones," he said, "my father took six of the ribs and placed them together. He then split a piece of cherry wood and put the ends of the bones between the pieces of wood. The whole affair was then laced together with rawhide rope. . . . On top, father fastened a buffalo head. . . . This was my rib sleigh. After sliding down in the snow a few times, the bones would become smoother than most of the steel runners on the sleds of today."

Games were not limited to the young. "Older people," said Standing Bear, "had a game called the hand game. It was played after the manner of button, button, who's got the button?" The Plains Indians played this sleight-of-hand contest with two small objects—one marked, the other plain. One player concealed the objects in his palms; the other tried to guess which hand held the one that was unmarked.

The game sometimes lasted the whole night through. The player holding the markers did everything he could to confuse his opponents, while the songs accompanying the action grew more and more frantic. To addle their opponents during the game, men and women danced.

Another popular game—a favorite with women—was played with dice made from bones, beaver's teeth, or other materials. The Sioux painted and carved turtles, spiders, or lizards on the dice, and these were kept in a round basket. A woman grasped the basket, tossed the dice into the air, and caught them. Points were scored according to the designs facing upward, with different designs assigned different values. The women played sitting opposite each other and put counting sticks in the earth to keep track of points scored. Players wagered their hair strings and beaded chokers on the luck of the throw.

Games, like almost everything else in Plains life, were accompanied by songs. A song did not necessarily need words; it needed feeling. The high, trilling songs

of women inspired courage and excitement in their men. Plains life cannot be imagined without Plains music. "The throbbing of the drum," says Crow Dog, "is the Indian's heartbeat."

Songs fell into a number of categories: ceremonial songs, among them the Sun Dance and Ghost Dance chants; secular war and powwow songs; lullabies for infants; and funeral dirges for the dead. Music also played a role in romance. Flutes conveyed a young man's yearning for his beloved. These instruments were often carved in the likeness of an open-beaked bird's head and decorated with a picture of a horse, because this animal was believed to be a lover of great ardor. In the stillness of the Plains night the sound of the flute carried far. By playing a certain tune, known only to his beloved, a lover could convey to her a wide variety of intimate messages, such as: "I am waiting for you." "I am being watched." "Meet me at the creek tomorrow." "I will come again."

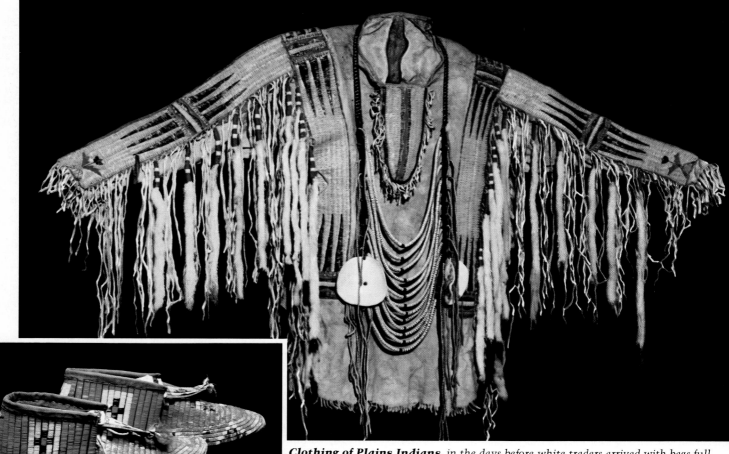

Clothing of Plains Indians, in the days before white traders arrived with bags full of beads, was resplendent with multicolored quillwork, as seen in the warshirt above and the Sioux moccasins at left. The dyed quills were sewn on or woven into the clothing by women, who took great pride in their quilling skills. Because porcupines were not often found on the Plains, the tribes of the region had to obtain the quills through barter with the Indians who lived in the woods to the north.

Using the White Man's Beads to Create Indian Art

When white traders introduced glass beads to the Plains in the early 1800's, traditional quillwork began to disappear. Unlike quills, which had to be dyed, the glossy beads came brightly colored, and they were easier to work with than quills. Three kinds of beads (right) were bartered by whites, who discovered that these baubles brought a much higher return in pelts than kettles, fabric, or guns. Pony beads, which were large and usually blue or white, were supplemented, after 1840, by seed beads. Their smaller size and wider range of colors permitted more elaborate designs. After 1870 translucent beads in still richer hues and more varied shapes became popular. Heavily beaded garments were worn only on ceremonial occasions, partly because of the weight. A shirt covered with beads might weigh as much as three or four pounds.

Pony beads 1800

Seed beads 1840

Medium-sized and faceted 1870

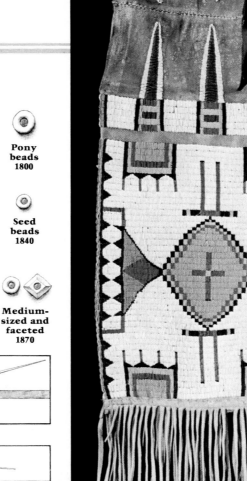

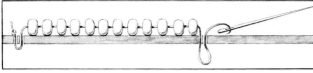

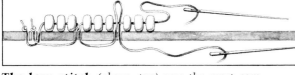

The lazy stitch (above, top) was the most common one used for Plains beadwork. This simple method of beading on buckskin involved merely the stringing of beads on a thread and tying knots at the ends. The strings of beads were then sewn on the hide. On the Northern Plains women often used the overlay stitch. It is like the lazy stitch except that a second thread crosses the beaded thread at intervals of two or three beads.

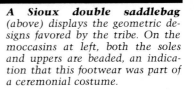

A Sioux double saddlebag (above) displays the geometric designs favored by the tribe. On the moccasins at left, both the soles and uppers are beaded, an indication that this footwear was part of a ceremonial costume.

There was more to courting, of course, than just flute playing. As the contemporary Indian Lame Deer explains it: "I have to tell you a big secret. Don't let it out. We, the warlike, he-man Sioux, are real bashful. Boys were shy, the girls even more so. In the old days, the girls were hard to get. They were always hiding their faces. If you screwed up your courage to talk to them, they didn't answer. If you came too close, they ran away."

Courtship had to be accomplished with a minimum of privacy. The young men waited near a stream hoping for an encouraging glance when the girls came to fill their water bags. "There was really only one way for the young folks to get together," says Lame Deer. "The girl had to stand outside her family's tepee with a big blanket. Her lover would come up and she would cover both of them. . . . Inside that robe they would put their faces close together and whisper to each other. The people pretended not see them. If a girl was pretty, there might be a stag line, three or four young bucks waiting their turn. It was all very innocent."

Among the Plains tribes chastity was carefully guarded. Girls were brought up to be good wives and good workers. Marriage was generally arranged by the parents with the help of go-betweens, but there was latitude for romance. A young man in love often prodded

Courting in a blanket, a thoroughly innocent practice among some Plains peoples, took place in front of a girl's family tepee once a maiden realized that she was being wooed. Too bashful to speak his mind, a young warrior might make his interest known by playing love songs on his flute, perhaps as the girl filled her water bag in a river. If the girl found the swain attractive, she would then invite him to stand with her in the privacy of her blanket. There they conversed softly, told each other of their feelings, and probably made plans for the future. This stylized version of blanket-courting was drawn by a northern Cheyenne in the 1870's.

his parents to take the necessary steps. On the other hand, a young woman whose parents wanted her to marry some famous and rich old chief could usually count on their daughter to be dutiful and accept the match without complaint. As in European societies love sometimes conquered all, even when a suitor could not secure the consent of his prospective in-laws. If the attraction between them was strong enough, the young people might ignore parental objections and elope. This they accomplished by disappearing into the grasslands for several weeks, then returning as man and wife. Though there might be considerable grumbling on the part of the old folks about this state of affairs, they usually came to accept the situation within a short time.

It is a widespread belief that Plains Indians bought their wives for a certain number of horses, but a woman was not considered a chattel to be purchased. It was customary for a bridegroom to give horses to the girl's family, but this did not mean buying her. In Plains society the gift of horses not only gauged a suitor's ardor for his love, but it was also the only way for a young man to prove that he was a fit husband. Success in horse raids was an indication that the youth would be a good provider.

The marriage ceremony was simple. Among the Cheyennes, for example, the bride was put on a blanket and carried to the lodge of her young man's father and left there. Sometimes a young couple had to live with in-laws until they had a tepee of their own, but given

Bead-covered amulets in the shape of a turtle (left) or lizard (right) were both symbols of longevity. The turtle held a child's umbilical cord. Such bags were attached to a cradleboard or worn around a child's neck to bring him good fortune.

the ease and rapidity with which the tepees were made, it was rare for the newlyweds to remain among their elders for a long period.

Marriage, however, was not always a one-to-one relationship among many of the Plains people. Buffalo hunting was an extremely dangerous enterprise, and a fairly large number of men were killed each year during the chase. Intertribal raids also took a heavy toll of men. Women, therefore, often far outnumbered men. To maintain the population under these circumstances, plural marriage for males was not only accepted but encouraged. A man might have two or even three wives.

But keeping up the birthrate was not the only reason for polygamy. Under the best of conditions a wife's workload could be crushing. If she happened to be married to a chief with obligations to provide lavish entertainment, her tasks could be almost overwhelming. With all the tanning, sewing, beading, cooking, packing, and unpacking to be done, many wives welcomed the help that a new member of the household would provide.

Girls married young and looked forward to becoming mothers. A woman gave birth in a tepee with the help of a midwife. She knelt during her birth pains, holding on to a stick driven into the ground before her. A clean piece of hide was kept in readiness to swaddle the baby. The infant's arrival was an occasion of great joy and celebration. The Omahas expressed this joy in a ritual chant that is one of the most evocative poems in Indian literature:

*Ho! Ye Sun, Moon, Stars, all ye that
    move in the heavens,
I bid you hear me!
Into your midst has come a new life.
Consent ye, I implore!
Make its path smooth, that it may reach
    the brow of the first hill!*

*Ho! Ye Winds, Clouds, Rain, Mist, all ye
    that move in the air,
I bid you hear me!
Into your midst has come a new life.
Consent ye, I implore!*

The newborn baby was rubbed with soft skins or, as among the Crees, dried off with moss. Its navel was disinfected with the powder of a puffball. In many Plains tribes the infant's umbilical cord was kept in a special beaded pouch. One of the grandmothers made such a container in the form of a sand lizard or turtle, "... because these animals are so hard to kill. A sand lizard, he loses its tail, it wiggles for a long time and grows another. Turtles grow very old. You kill a turtle and its heart goes on beating for days." Actually, there were always two umbilical-cord bags, but one was a decoy to attract the evil spirits. The other contained the cord, and this bag was hidden in the cradleboard and later in the toddler's clothing. A small child among the Sioux is therefore called "he who wears his navel."

The Plains peoples doted on children, seldom shouted at them, and rarely beat them. They gave the small ones a great amount of freedom, including the freedom to get hurt—and thereby to learn. The children lived within an extended family—grandparents, uncles, and aunts all assumed part of the parental role. Among the Sioux a child by tradition was provided with a second mother and father at birth, usually close friends of the family. In the words of author Mari Sandoz: "They avoided over-protecting the young and saved the eldest son from the mother's favoritism that could destroy the parents as well as the boy.... The second mother took over much of the small boy's care so he would never shame his blood mother by trailing at her moccasin heel, never bring the scornful whisper 'Little Husband! Little Husband!' as he usurped another's place in her attention and affection." Thus the children grew up, fitting themselves into the life stream of the tribe, without harsh discipline but without pampering either.

In many Plains tribes a girl's first menses was not marked by elaborate ceremonies, but in a few tribes—such as the Sioux—this was a time of great celebration. After her first menstrual period a girl's mother would inform the village crier so that he might spread the news far and wide and invite everyone to a feast to celebrate the beginning of womanhood.

All tribes, however, looked with awe and fear upon the menstruating woman, who was thought to be possessed by a powerful and dangerous spirit. In many tribes women were isolated during their periods. Thus, when a girl began her first menses, she was taken to a small shelter by her mother or an old woman, and there, for four days, she was instructed in making and beading moccasins or other traditional tasks for women. Among the Sioux the daughters of the rich marked the end of their first periods with ceremonial splendor. Friends of the family were invited to a lavish feast where all received gifts. Before the repast a shaman sang a chant to the powerful deity Buffalo Woman. Then the medicine man instructed the girl in her adult duties and, finally, he fastened an eagle plume to her hair as a symbol of her new status.

In Search of Visions

In most tribes the vision quest was a boy's initiation into manhood. What he experienced during this lonely vigil often determined the image he formed of himself

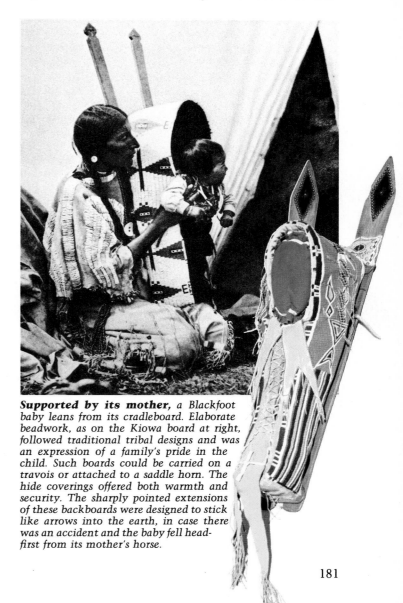

Supported by its mother, *a Blackfoot baby leans from its cradleboard. Elaborate beadwork, as on the Kiowa board at right, followed traditional tribal designs and was an expression of a family's pride in the child. Such boards could be carried on a travois or attached to a saddle horn. The hide coverings offered both warmth and security. The sharply pointed extensions of these backboards were designed to stick like arrows into the earth, in case there was an accident and the baby fell head-first from its mother's horse.*

Deerskin dolls with human hair were among a girl's favorite playthings. These two were made by Sioux women. To prepare for their future roles, young girls also played with toy tepees and travois and began riding ponies at about age five.

and his future role in life. At the heart of all Indian beliefs was the urge to find a mystical reality beneath the surface of life. As Crow Dog has expressed it, the Indian wanted "to see with the eye in one's heart, rather than with the eyes in one's head."

Experiencing a vision was an intensely personal event, a direct encounter with the Great Mystery Power that might appear in the most outlandish guise, such as a dwarf, a bird whose clapping wings made thunder, or even a mosquito. A vision quest, during which a boy "cried for a dream," was an initiation rite only in the sense that it was usually first undertaken at puberty. Unlike a girl's introduction to womanhood, which happened only once in a lifetime, vision quests were repeated again and again—as often as an individual felt the need for help from the spirit powers. This might be before a raid, or during a child's illness, or at a time of personal doubt. While women also went on vision quests, they did so less often and under less severe conditions than the men.

Among the Sioux, to seek a vision meant having to go naked, except for a breechclout and moccasins, to a lonely hilltop and staying there for four days and nights without food while crouched in a vision pit. One did not face this ordeal without help and instruction from a medicine man who invoked the spirits to bring the quest to a successful conclusion. "All the Powers of the world," the shaman might intone, "the heavens and the star peoples, and the red and blue sacred days; all things that move in the universe, in the rivers . . . all waters, all trees that stand, all the grasses of our Grandmother, all the sacred peoples of the universe: Listen! A sacred relationship with you all will be asked by this young man, that his generations to come will increase and live in a holy manner."

A vision quest was usually preceded by purification

in a sweat lodge. A sweat bath could be a ceremony in itself, but more often it was only the first step in a larger ritual. The sweat lodge was a small, beehive-shaped frame of willow sticks covered with buffalo skins. While the boy and his helpers sat naked in the darkness of this structure, rocks were heated outside and passed, one by one, into the sweat lodge while those inside prayed and sang. The entrance flap was then closed, and cold water was poured over the stones. In the enveloping cloud of steam the worshipers heard the voice of the spirit and felt its hot, purifying breath. The bathers then rubbed themselves dry with sage leaves, and the youngster now had to walk up to the hilltop.

The Sioux Lame Deer has described his first vision quest in the early years of this century: "There I was, crouched in my vision pit. I still had my boy's name, and let me tell you, I was scared. If I could endure it, if I got my vision, I would no longer be a boy, but a man. Blackness was all around me. It seemed to cut me off from the outside world, even from my own body. It made me listen to the voices from within me. I thought of my forefathers who had crouched here before me. . . . I felt their presence . . . as I cried out to the Grandfather Spirit until, at last, he granted me my dream." Given the emotional pitch at which a boy entered the vision pit, his overwhelming desire for a sign, and his mortification of the flesh through starvation and, sometimes, self-flagellation, it is not surprising that most were granted the visions they sought. And when the questor came down from his hill, a medicine man was waiting to interpret his vision. It would give clues

Under an instructor's watchful eye, a young Sioux practices with a small bow and arrow. Boys honed their hunting skills from an early age. They first shot at stationary targets, then began tracking down such small game as jackrabbits.

The Coming of Age of a Cheyenne Girl

No event in the life of a Cheyenne girl held more significance than the arrival of her first menstrual period. This meant that the time of womanhood had come and all the rights and privileges of that status—as well as its duties—were now hers. At the first evidence of her physical maturity the girl rushed to tell her mother the good news. The mother informed the father, and he spread the word among the people of the encampment. To celebrate the fact that his daughter was now of marriageable age, the father, if he could afford to make such a gesture, gave away a horse.

Among the Cheyennes, who held women in particularly high regard, a special ceremony accompanied a girl's first menses. After she bathed, older women covered the girl's body with red paint. Then, for a time, the girl sat before the tepee fire, a hot coal—sprinkled with sweet grass, cedar needles, and white sage—enveloping her in a cloud of purifying smoke. Then, clad in her mother's finest robe, much like the one at right, she departed for the menstrual hut. There she remained, in the company of her grandmother, for four days and received instructions from the old woman about her future duties as an adult.

From then on she would be isolated during her menses, for it was widely thought that contact with a menstruating woman was a portent of danger.

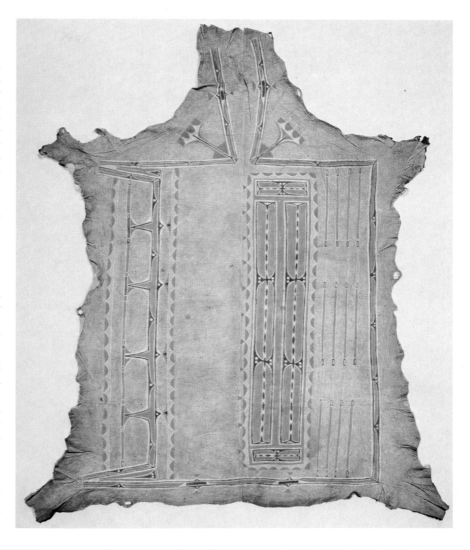

to the grown-up name the boy now received and would provide the youth with a protector from the spirit world. Through his vision the spirits had given the boy some of their power, and now he was ready to face life as a man.

In a sense life was one long ceremony that transformed day-to-day existence into a mystical adventure. The Sioux god was Wakan Tanka, the Grandfather Spirit, the Great Mystery Power without beginning or end. The Mystery Power manifested itself in the rays of the sun as well as in the crawling ant and the stinging mosquito. Sky, sun, and the winds were all part of the Great Spirit, though they were also gods in themselves. The religion of the Plains Indian was intensely personal, guided by voices heard, powers felt, and visions seen. His religion grew out of the soil on which he walked, and faith was intimately tied with every aspect of nature he experienced. A man might have power from an elk, which would make him a great lover. Or

his vision may have appeared as a bear, which would give him healing skills.

A Blackfoot returning from his vision quest made up his personal medicine bundle according to instructions received from the spirit. The bundle might contain certain pebbles with magical power, feathers, or tiny bags of herbs. If the bundle was lost or seized in a fight, the owner could remake it. Unless he voluntarily transferred the bundle, together with its power, it was his until the day he died. Some bundles were more powerful than others, especially those of great warriors and successful hunters who seemed always to have good fortune.

If he so desired, a man could approach the owner of such a superpowerful bundle and offer to exchange it for horses or other valuables so that he might benefit from its magic.

A central element of all Plains religion was the Sacred Pipe. Held aloft in prayer, it formed a link between man and the Great Mystery Power and expressed the unity between that supreme deity and Grandmother Earth. To the Sioux the red pipe bowl represented the earth; the stem, the soil's bounty; while the curling smoke, dissipating in the air, was the breath of the Great Spirit. Artist George Catlin, who painted many pictures of Indians, recounted the legend of a pipestone quarry that he visited in 1836: "The Great Spirit . . . called the Indian nations together, and standing on the precipice of the red pipestone rock, broke from its wall a piece, and made a huge pipe by turning it in his hand, which he smoked over them . . . and told them that this stone was their flesh, that it belonged to them all, and the war club and scalping knife must not be raised on its [the quarry's] ground." For many generations the quarry was neutral territory where hereditary enemies could meet in peace while digging side by side, their ancient quarrels set aside, at least for the moment. There was no prayer, no ceremony, without the smoking of a pipe. Especially revered were pipes belonging to a tribe as a whole.

Lame Deer was permitted to smoke his tribe's Buffalo Calf pipe many years ago and has described his feelings on the momentous occasion: "I held the pipe. I felt my blood going into the pipe. I felt it flowing back into me. I felt the pipe coming alive in my hand, felt it move. I felt a power surging from it into my body, filling all of me. Tears were streaming down my face. I knew that within this pipe was me. I knew that when I smoked it I was at the center of all things, giving myself

to the Great Spirit, and that every other Indian praying with this pipe would, at one time or the other, feel the same."

In every tribe there were persons with a gift for healing or prophecy—the medicine men. There were many different kinds, each with his own specialty. Some knew about herbs and the ways to use them in curing the sick. Others, such as the *yuwipis* of the Sioux tribes, performed healing ceremonies while wrapped up in blankets like mummies. Still others had stones with magical powers that helped them predict the future and locate game, missing things, or even lost people. In a special category were holy people, the seers, who were the keepers of tradition and directed the great rituals.

Indian medicine reached an impressively high level. The therapeutic properties of certain plants were well known, and these were used effectively. A variety of herbs were administered externally and internally to combat disease, to staunch the flow of blood, to speed up healing processes. Some medicine men were specialists in setting broken bones, and others knew of herbs that could induce abortion, though this practice was resorted to only in cases of absolute necessity, for throughout the Plains children were highly prized. A woman, too, might become a healer, and every tribe had women who were much sought after as midwives.

To the tribe's oldest and most respected holy men fell the task of conducting the Sun Dance. This was not only the greatest religious ceremony among most of the Plains peoples, it was a shared experience that

Within the confines of a sweat lodge, like the one above (shown without its skin covering), Sioux warriors began their vision-quest ritual. When a lodge was in use, its frame was covered and the rocks inside were heated. Water thrown on the hot rocks bathed the celebrant in purifying steam. His sweat bath completed, the warrior went to a lonely place to fast and, perhaps, to flagellate himself into a state of mind receptive to the coming of a vision. At left, a modern-day Sioux on a quest sits before a buffalo skull and prepares a fire of sweet grass. Its smoke will cleanse his soul.

maintained tribal unity among the many hunting bands. For the Sioux and, to a somewhat lesser extent, for several other Plains tribes, this twelve-day summer ritual was also a testimony to individual courage and endurance in the service of the Great Spirit. Through suffering, each participant in the Sun Dance achieved a personal communion with the spirit world and reasserted his identity as an Indian. Even today, among the Plains tribes, the celebration of the Sun Dance remains a vital reminder of an Indian's heritage, a link between past and present.

Like just about everything else associated with tribal life, participation in the often painful ceremonies was not compulsory, though almost all Plains warriors did join in. But men and women were free to go their own way, to reach their own accommodations with life, for the peoples of the Plains were no lovers of authority. They had no hereditary or elected governments, and in most tribes a chief had no power to compel or punish. A man might follow a leader into battle if he thought the leader's medicine was powerful, or he might stay home. Usually, even the title "chief" meant no more than the fact that the individual who held it was honored for his wisdom, his bravery, or his persuasiveness. In council, each man had the right to state his position for as long as he wished, which might be very long indeed.

In these unregimented societies a wide range of conduct was tolerated. If a woman threw her husband's belongings out of the tepee, that was her business. If a man decided to dress and act as a woman, that was his decision, and he was not ostracized for it. Indeed, such individuals were often looked upon with a mixture of pity and awe. Tradition was the key to tribal unity, and that tradition was freely and almost universally obeyed. Practically everybody was a member of some group, each with its own set of intricate rules, ceremonies, dances, costumes, and taboos that were strictly observed down to the smallest detail, even though this observance was voluntary.

Without a structured government the Plains Indians managed, nonetheless, to have a highly developed social system. Some tribes had clans tracing their descent from a common mother; others, from a common father. The Omahas, for example, were divided into 10 paternal clans. Besides these, the Omaha, like other

Crow medicine bundles *were often arranged on a tripod and placed outside the owner's tepee. This stand holds three bundles, all containing objects thought to have magical powers because they appeared in the owner's visions. The long-fringed bundle holds a sacred rock.*

Plains tribes, had societies, some open, some secret. The Omaha Thunder Society, for instance, was custodian of the tribe's two sacred pipes. Among the secret societies were the Bear Dreamers, who practiced sleights of hand and such tricks as swallowing long sticks; and the Buffalo Dreamers, whose members excelled in treating wounds.

While some tribes had no clans, practically all had military societies. Each tribe had from 4 to 12 of these groups, which played an important role in the life of the tribe. Military societies guarded the camps during periods of intertribal raiding, preserved order during the tribal hunt, took a foremost role in war, gave feasts and dances, organized games, transmitted tribal lore from generation to generation, and fostered a spirit of martial competition.

Military societies, in some tribes, were age-graded. Boys of a certain age group formed one society. After some period of time they "bought into" the society one step above them in age, purchasing their costumes, ceremonies, paraphernalia, and songs. Those replaced immediately bought into the society just above them. The Blackfeet, for example, had several age-graded warrior societies. The youngest group—with members as young as 15—was called the Doves. The next youngest was the Mosquitoes, for warriors between the ages of 19 and 23. Similar graded societies were common among the Mandans, Hidatsas, Arapahos, and Gros Ventres, while among the Sioux, Crows, Omahas, Cheyennes, and Assiniboins, nongraded societies were the rule. In these latter tribes a young man joined whichever society took his fancy or became a member by invitation. Often a vision told him which society to join.

Possibly the most prestigious and exclusive of warrior societies was that of the Kiowas' Principal Dogs, or Ten Bravest, limited to 10 warriors of surpassing courage. The Principal Dog leader was recognized as the bravest of the brave. He wore a long sash hanging from his shoulders to the ground. In battle he dismounted in the thick of the fray and anchored himself to the ground by driving his lance through the end of his sash. As he stood rooted to the ground, a target for scores of arrows, he urged his warriors on. He could not leave his post unless another member of his society pulled out the lance. Otherwise he fought valiantly in place until death or victory.

Some societies were composed of men who were too

old to engage in combat. The Sioux Big Bellies were one such group, whose members were chiefs, medicine men, wise men, and respected former warriors. Though their fighting days were over, the Big Bellies were much revered, both for their past prowess and their present wisdom. Some groupings were partly cults and partly military in nature. The "contraries," for example, whom the Sioux called *heyoka*, consisted of warriors who had all shared a vision of the thunder. To ignore this sign was to invite death by lightning. Contraries did everything backward. They rolled in the dust to "wash," and immersed themselves in water to "dry off," and they said "yes" when they meant "no" and vice versa. To obtain a service from a contrary you asked him for the opposite of what you wanted. In some tribes the contraries were among the bravest of warriors, and in battle there was nothing backward about them.

Performing warlike deeds of note was called counting coup, from the French word for blow or stroke. To be valid a coup had to be witnessed and sworn to by another warrior, and different values were assigned to different feats of courage. A minor honor might be the mere slaying of an enemy, while a major coup would be touching a live foeman during combat, rescuing a wounded comrade, or fighting staked to the ground in defiance of death. Thus it was that feats of bravery were much more highly prized than killing. War was viewed as a sport, roughly comparable to tournaments of medieval Europe. But though the game was played according to certain rules, it was a dangerous sport in which a man might easily be killed. All-out tribal wars

that endangered a nation's survival were extremely rare. Such confrontations happened more by accident than by plan. Even in the largest tribes the death of a young warrior was a serious matter. A war leader who lost a man also lost face and followers, no matter how successful his record. For the most part, warfare was a matter of small raiding groups of several men. There were no standing armies, no officers to give commands and be obeyed. Dreams and visions often told a warrior when to organize a raid, where to go and, among the Crows, even how many horses to steal. In combat there was no overall strategic view, only a contest in which to perform personal exploits.

This philosophy of war would put the Indians at a distinct disadvantage when fighting white soldiers who were much more concerned with destroying the enemy than with accumulating personal honors. It would only be in the very last clashes that the Indian leaders, such as Crazy Horse, were able to persuade the braves to concentrate on the business of destroying the soldiers rather than on personal glory. But even then warriors lost their lives in frenzies of reckless coup counting.

Plains warfare almost never involved blood lust or passionate intertribal hatreds. Prisoners might be abused and tortured, but sometimes they were adopted by their captors and spent their lives as free and equal members of the new tribe. Famous, but by no means unique, was the case of Jumping Bull. A group of Sioux warriors, the famous Sitting Bull among them, surprised a small band of Assiniboins in the winter of 1857. Among the attacked was Jumping Bull, then a mere 11 years old. At the height of the battle Jumping

The sacred stone quarry in present-day Minnesota, shown in this Catlin work (right), was neutral ground; no fighting was allowed. Here members of numerous Plains tribes came to gather the blood-red to pale-red stones for their pipes. Such stones, soft enough to be easily worked with a knife or hand drill, were found between layers of quartzite. (The stone is now called catlinite in honor of the artist who sent samples East for tests.) The pipe bowl below is probably of Sioux origin.

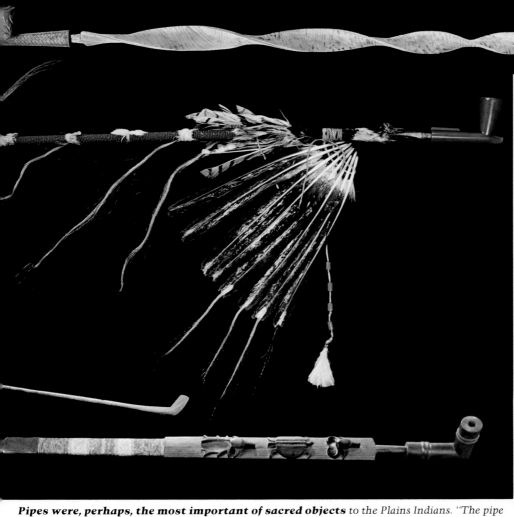

Pipes were, perhaps, the most important of sacred objects to the Plains Indians. "The pipe is us," said one Sioux. "The stem is our backbone, the bowl our head. The stone is our blood, red as our skin." George Catlin, that indefatigable recorder of Plains life, wrote of the great pipestone quarry in Minnesota: "Here ... happened the mysterious birth of the red pipe, which has blown its fumes of peace and war to the remotest corners of the Continent; which has visited every warrior, and passed through its reddened stem the irrevocable oath of war and desolation. And here also, the peace-breathing calumet was born ... which has ... soothed the fury ..." of the Indian.

Most tribesmen owned their own pipes, using them in religious ceremonies as well as for the sheer love of smoking. But the most elaborate pipes—some of them with delicately carved four- and five-foot-long stems, often decorated with fur, horsehair wrappings, and quills—were believed to have particularly strong powers. These were used only in ceremonies of the most sacred nature, such as the making of war or peace, the healing of the sick, or during rituals intended to ensure a successful buffalo hunt. Such pipes were highly revered, and their owners took every precaution for their safety. When not in use they were stored, together with other sacred objects, in elaborate containers.

In addition to highly prized catlinite, the bowls of pipes were fashioned from steatite, argillite, shale, limestone, or serpentine slate. Most pipestems were made from ash or sumac, soft woods with easily scraped out piths. After trade with whites began, Indians sometimes cleared the stems by burning the pith out with red-hot wires.

The two pipes shown above (top and center) are types that were used on ceremonial occasions. The one at bottom, though deftly carved, was for everyday use. Just above it is a pipe-shaped tamper; the bowl below is of catlinite with inlaid lead bands. At right is a quilled and beaded bag for holding a bowl and stem, as well as a supply of kinnikinnick, the smoking mixture that contained tobacco and such vegetable matter as sumac leaves and dried bark.

Bull held his ground, boldly defending himself with his small boy's bow. Seeing this display of courage, Sitting Bull dashed to the boy's side, shielded him with his own body, and shouted: "This boy is too brave to die. I take him as my brother!" After the Sioux returned to their camp, their young captive was accepted into the tribe as Sitting Bull's younger brother. For the rest of his life Jumping Bull remained his captor's loyal comrade, dying in a vain effort to protect Sitting Bull's life in 1890.

Magic and medicine played major roles in warfare. The Cheyenne chief whom the whites called Roman Nose had a warbonnet with magical properties that rendered him bulletproof, but there was a taboo connected with it. He was not allowed to take food with a metal implement. To do so would be to guarantee death in battle. Several days before an encounter with white soldiers he inadvertently ate food that had been touched with a metal fork. Although Roman Nose knew that to fight was to court certain doom, he did join the battle when a crisis developed and was promptly shot to death.

Women, too, played a role in warfare. They danced waving scalps, derived honors from their husbands' deeds, and publicly exhibited the men's shields and weapons. A woman's lamentations over a slain son was the most effective goad to a punitive expedition. Some

women even joined in battle. Among the Cheyennes old people still tell their grandchildren of Buffalo Calf Road Woman, the sister of Chief Comes-in-Sight. During the Battle of the Rosebud in 1876, Comes-in-Sight repeatedly charged the soldiers and counted many coups until his horse was shot out from under him. Suddenly, the warriors saw a woman galloping down from the hills right into the midst of the enemy. Heedless of the bullets flying about her, she made straight for the beleaguered Comes-in-Sight, slowing down only to permit her brother to jump on the horse's back. Together, brother and sister rode to safety as the braves cheered them on. Ever since, the Cheyennes have called this fight the Battle Where the Girl Saved Her Brother. Indeed, many Plains women made names for themselves as hunters and fighters, earning the right to wear an eagle plume, the symbol of courage.

The Coming of the Whites

The heyday of the Plains tribes was spectacular but relatively short-lived, lasting little more than a century. The white man's horse had made the period possible. The coming of the white man himself brought it to an inglorious end.

Some whites—mostly English and French—reached the eastern edges of the Plains in the mid-18th century in their search for beaver pelts to satisfy the European market for fur hats. But it was the Lewis and Clark Expedition of 1804–06 that generated great popular interest in the economic potential of the West.

From 1808 onward hundreds of trappers and traders poled up the Missouri River or rode out to the beaver-hunting grounds. In themselves, these trappers—known as mountain men—presented few problems to the Indians. Hard-bitten individualists with a desire to be free of civilization's constraints, the mountain men were, after all, not very different from the Indians.

Yet almost in spite of themselves, the mountain men were the precursors of white civilization, and with them came trading posts and whiskey. To be sure, such valuable items as knives, guns, blankets, and kettles were available at the trading posts. But even these useful objects, in a short time, led to a dependence on the white man's "convenience goods," undermining the Indians' self-sufficiency and creating the type called the Hang-Around-the-Fort Indian.

Though only a small minority of Indians were seduced by the kind of civilization the traders represented, the overall effects on Indian life were insidious. The availability of firearms, for example, artificially strengthened the tribes that secured them at the expense of the others, thus upsetting a balance of power. Even worse were the sicknesses brought by the traders—measles, diphtheria and, most dreadful of all, smallpox. Over the centuries whites had developed a degree of resistance to these ailments, but the Indians had none. Those whom the diseases *(continued on page 192)*

With ceremonial spear and rattle in hand, *a Blackfoot medicine man performs a healing ritual. He is wearing a bearskin that, as described by the artist, George Catlin, is adorned with "tails and tips of almost everything that swims, flies, or runs."*

The Sun Dance: A Plains Ritual in Praise of the Great Spirit

In the summer, when the chokecherries were ripe, the Sioux and other Plains peoples turned in supplication to the Great Spirit. Through awesome ceremonies that, in some tribes, included feats of endurance and acts of self-mutilation, the tribes gave thanks for the beneficence the Great Spirit had bestowed and asked its blessing for the year to come. In their celebration of the rites, which the Sioux called the Sun Dance and other tribes called by different names, the peoples of the Plains shared a unity of religious feeling.

Because the Sun Dance rites differed so widely, it is impossible to describe a typical ceremony. Among the Sioux, the entire ritual took 12 days. There was no rule mandating that the ceremony be held every summer, but it was a rare year when the Sioux failed to perform the Sun Dance. The festival was thought to ensure the well-being of the entire tribe while bringing singular merit to those warriors who volunteered to take part in its most physically painful aspects. Indeed, men who thought themselves particularly blessed by the supernatural during the past year, those who felt the need to experience visions, and candidates for the status of shaman were all likely to volunteer.

The first four-day period of the Sun Dance was a time of festivity, for this was the time of the summer encampment when the Sioux bands came together. Friends and relatives, separated through the long winter, sat about and swapped stories. Courtships began, and children romped freely. More relevant to the ceremonies to come, shamans selected assistants for the rites. Among these were the virtuous women whose task it would be to chop down the sacred cottonwood, around which the final parts of the dance would center.

During the second four days those who had volunteered to dance were segregated from the others and received instructions from the shamans on the intricacies and meanings of the ceremonies. Of these shamans, one was the Mentor, and it was he who would be in overall charge of the activities.

The last four days were sacred. The Sun Dance lodge, its dance bower and, most important of all, the cottonwood pole were the centers of attention. On the first of these sacred days a warrior was sent out to locate and "capture" a cottonwood of the proper height, a tree

A painted buffalo skull occupied a place of honor during the annual Sun Dance, the Plains tribes' famed ritual of sacrifice and thanksgiving. The skull's eye and nose cavities were often stuffed with grass, as a symbolic offering to the beasts whose presence was so crucial to the Indians.

with a long straight trunk that ended in a forked top. The cottonwood was chosen as the centerpiece of the ceremonial because its leaf was thought to resemble a tepee, and from this leaf the Sioux believed they had derived their dwellings. Upon discovering a proper specimen, the hunter marked its trunk with red paint and then returned to report his success. The Buffalo Dance was then performed to celebrate the blessings of home and human fertility.

On the second sacred day the virtuous women went on a ritual search for the tree the hunter had captured. Three times they pretended they could not locate the tree, and only on the fourth try did they make their find. Then a ceremonial procession to the tree took place. There were three ritual stops along the way for the purpose of chasing away evil spirits. On reaching the tree, four warriors, especially chosen for the task, counted coup on the trunk. Then, one by one, the virtuous women took turns chopping it down, the final blows being reserved for the one designated as the most virtuous of all. The felled tree was stripped of its bark up to the fork and then was borne back to the encampment on poles.

The third sacred day was taken up with final preparations for the climactic ceremonies. The trunk of the cottonwood was painted four different colors, one for each of the four sacred directions. Cutouts of a male buffalo and a male human were made, each with exaggerated genitalia, and these were placed in the fork of the tree, together with sacred objects. Finally, the pole was raised, and the men joined in a war dance around it and shot their arrows at the cutouts.

At last all was ready for the final day. At dawn the shamans greeted the sun; then the dancers were prepared for their ordeal. Each dancer was painted with colors and symbols relating to the degree of pain he had volunteered to suffer. After the audience entered the lodge, the dancers were given willow hoops—representing the four directions—and eagle-bone whistles that they would blow throughout the final dance. But first there was a repeat of the Buffalo Dance, followed by the ceremonial piercing of the ears of children. This latter rite was an initiation of sorts, representing faith in Sioux customs.

Now the great ordeal began. Some of the dancers had volunteered merely to fast and dance about the pole as long as they were able. Others had bits of flesh cut from their bodies, these bits being placed about the pole as sacrifices. Most honored were those who agreed to have skewers implanted through flaps cut in their skins. On some, the skewers were attached to buffalo skulls, and the dancers performed while dragging the skulls behind them. Other dancers had the skewers attached to the pole; still others were suspended from the fork of the pole via lines of rawhide tied to the skewers. They might hang for hours as warriors below danced about the pole, and through pain, each experienced a personal communion with the Great Spirit. The dance continued until the skin of each dancer ripped free from the skewers, marking the ceremony's conclusion.

The Sun Dance Climax: An Ecstasy of Pain

The climax of the Sun Dance among the Sioux goes forward under the direction of the Mentor (seated, extreme left), the medicine man who supervises the ceremonies. Suspended from the fork of a sacred cottonwood pole is one of the chief dancers. The pole is perhaps 30 feet high, and the warrior, who seeks a vision while giving thanks to the Great Spirit, is suspended by lengths of sinews attached to skewers beneath his skin. He has been hanging for quite some time and is in great pain. Yet he will continue to blow on his eagle-bone whistle until he faints. Even then he will not be cut down but will remain suspended until his skin rips free and he drops to the earth.

Meanwhile, two other warriors (upper right) are submitting to similar tortures only marginally less severe. Though their feet are on the ground, they too are attached to the pole in the same manner. While blowing their whistles, they rock backward and forward to increase the pain. Between them are a man and woman who have sacrificed bits of their flesh to the Great Spirit. This type of self-mutilation was the most extreme form of participation that a woman was permitted in the Sun Dance. As the warriors dance, they stare at the sun, the object of their worship, as long as they possibly can, through the roofless arena.

Another warrior (lower right) dances in place, the skin of his upper back rent by skewers from which hang four heavy buffalo skulls. He moves to the hypnotic beat of buffalo-hide drums pounded by the musicians at lower left, who chant the sacred songs of the tribe as they play their instruments.

Thus the Sun Dance draws to a close, ending when all the impaled dancers have ripped free of their skewers. Through their own sacrifices, their willingness to endure suffering as surrogates for the entire tribe, they have gained much honor among their people. They have helped ensure the Great Spirit's blessings—and hence prosperity—for the year to come. But there are individual rewards as well. Those dancers who have volunteered for mutilation and, in the agony of their pain, have passed into a semiconscious or unconscious state are most likely to have experienced visions of the spirits, thus attaining a personal communion with the world of the supernatural.

ravaged most were the Indians in closest contact with the whites, the semisedentary river tribes—Mandan and Arikara. After a series of epidemics in the first decade of the 19th century the Mandans were reduced in number from 3,600 to a mere 125 in 1837.

By 1840 the beaver was trapped out, and beaver hats had gone out of fashion. The day of the mountain men was over. Then came the forty-niners going to California, and settlers on their way to Oregon's rich Willamette Valley. At first they merely sought a road through Indian land. But soon settlers on their way to the Pacific discovered good black soil in parts of the Plains and saw no reason to go all the way to Oregon. Then prospectors discovered gold in Colorado and built their mining camps on Cheyenne land. And in the post-Civil War era the coming of the transcontinental railroads opened up the entire Plains region to millions of settlers. From 1850 on, the history of the Plains recorded an endless repetition of broken treaties and racial carnage. Forts were built to protect the settlers, and the Indians were bribed or forced to sign agreements they did not understand. If the leaders speaking for the tribes would not sign, a would-be chief, fond of whiskey, could always be induced "to touch the pen in the name of all."

Ironically, the real onset of the Plains Indians decline began with a sincere effort by the U.S. government to protect the interests of both natives and whites. By 1850 it was abundantly clear that thousands of whites would soon be traversing the Plains on the way to the West Coast. Already the gold strikes of 1848 in California had generated unprecedented traffic across the grasslands. In their desire to stock up on food, the forty-niners had slaughtered thousands of buffalo, while many herds were frightened away from their usual breeding and feeding grounds by the wagons along the trails. These developments worsened hunting for the Indians, who depended on buffalo for survival.

Perhaps believing that this invasion of their lands was only temporary, the Indians endured and did not strike at the wagon trains. But to Thomas Fitzpatrick, once a mountain man and in 1850 a government agent, it seemed certain that as white traffic increased and the slaughter of the buffalo grew, the Indians would indeed strike at their tormentors. "What then will be the consequences," he wrote, "should twenty thousand Indians . . . turn out in hostile array against all American travellers?" To head off a possible bloodbath, Fitzpatrick was authorized to call a meeting of Northern Plains tribes and work out an agreement guaranteeing free passage of whites in exchange for government annuities. In response, some 10,000 Indians, representing eight tribes, gathered near Fort Laramie, Wyoming, in September 1851. When the powwow ended after several days, it appeared that peace—not just between red man and white, but between tribes—was assured. Two

Magnificently bedecked, a warrior of the Hidatsa Dog Society (left) performs a ritual dance. His ceremonial headdress is a circle of magpie and turkey feathers surmounted by a single eagle plume. Each of the Plains military societies had its own distinctive songs, dances, ceremonial garb, and insignia, and its own set of taboos and obligations. The Hidatsa Dogs, for example, were "contraries" and did everything backward; thus, if a warrior was meant to attack in battle, he was told to flee. Pictured directly above are women of the White Buffalo Cow Society, a group found among both the Mandans and the Hidatsas. Wearing fezlike headdresses of albino buffalo skins and wrapped in buffalo robes, the women are performing a dance intended to lure the buffalo herds toward their village.

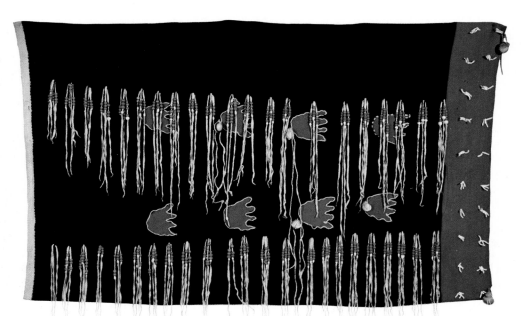

A Bear Society flag, made of cloth obtained from traders and appliquéd with designs of bear tracks, is typical of the insignias used by the Omaha and Pawnee Bear Societies. This flag was made about 1865.

These cults were elite societies; their memberships were restricted to men who had experienced dreams or visions involving bears and had thus acquired some of the supernatural power of those animals. Bearmen were esteemed for their abilities as healers and warriors, but among some tribes they were also feared. The Assiniboins, for example, believed that the cult members—like bears—were touchy and dangerous.

years later Fitzpatrick negotiated a similar treaty with several southern tribes.

Under the treaties the government would distribute thousands of dollars in trade goods every year to the tribes, while the Indians agreed to permit roads across their territories. In addition, each tribe vowed to hunt only within prescribed borders, thus not poaching on the hunting grounds of others. It was easy enough for tribal leaders to sign such an agreement, for they hardly understood its implications. Living up to the terms would have meant the immediate destruction of the Indians' whole way of life.

Under the treaties the Sioux, for example, would not be permitted to swoop down on the Crows in raids for horses, nor would the Cheyennes be allowed to scour the grasslands in search of buffalo. In fact, what the Indians agreed to was the establishment of vast reservations, one per tribe, reservations that could easily be reduced in size at the white man's convenience. And by agreeing to accept subsidies, the Indians unwittingly placed themselves in a position of supplicant to the U.S. government, turning over the responsibility for their own well-being to a fickle Congress in whose hands lay the power to appropriate or withhold the necessary funds.

Although the peoples of the Plains did not grasp the implications of the treaties, the government probably meant them no ill at this time. The government's policy was the eventual transformation of the Indian into a farmer or herdsman, a man indistinguishable from his white neighbors in everything but skin color. By urging the adoption of the settled agricultural life, the government believed it was doing the Indian a favor, for whites were totally ignorant of tribal culture, totally contemptuous of the tribesman's love of the freewheeling life of the Plains. And it was futile to insist, as the

government did, that every tribe elect a primary chief with powers to negotiate on the tribe's behalf. At the powwows the tribes were perfectly willing to put forward an array of chiefs to sign their marks on the pact, for after all, it was only the polite thing to do. But none of this altered the reality of tribal organization. No chief, however exalted his standing, could command the obedience of the tribesmen in a course they felt to be disastrous. Given all of these cross-purposes and misunderstandings, the pacts were doomed even as they were being signed.

Still it was not until 1854 that crisis came to the grasslands, and the cycle of terror and counterterror began in earnest. The cause of the first outbreak was nothing more than a stray sick cow, picked up and slaughtered by a hungry Sioux. Somehow the cow's owner heard of the animal's fate, and he demanded that the Sioux provide restitution in the sum of $25. The Indians offered $10, but the cow's owner refused to accept this; he insisted that the culprit be surrendered to the white man's justice. In this he was backed by a certain glory-hungry Lt. John L. Grattan at Fort Laramie. Unfortunately, Grattan was the kind of officer who exhibited more bravado than good sense. Bored and restless, he hungered for a fight, and so great was his contempt for the Indians that he boasted that he could secure the grasslands for the whites with a handful of men. With the incident of the cow as a goad, Grattan convinced his commander to give him 30 men to chastise the Sioux. He marched on the camp where the cow thief was said to be hiding, and after parlaying with the Indians and realizing that they would not hand over the man, Grattan orderd his command to open fire. Without warning, grapeshot and bullets tore through the tepees, mortally wounding a chief. Like a swarm of angry bees, the Sioux poured out

Counting Coup: Marks of Skill and Courage

In Plains warfare there was a strong element of gamesmanship: the greater the risks a warrior took, the more honor he brought to himself and his tribe. The final outcome of the battle or raid was less important than the courage displayed by individual participants. And nowhere was this attitude more apparent than in the custom known as counting coup (from a French word for "blow"). A Plains warrior scored a coup when he was able to touch an enemy with a coup stick (a long, slender branch), a lance, a bow, or anything else held in the hand. Because of the great risk involved, counting coup on armed foe was considered much more praiseworthy than simply killing him—especially if the killing was done at long distance with a bullet or arrow.

Coup could be counted on an enemy woman or even on a child. Some tribes counted the capture of an enemy's horses and the touching of an enemy tepee as coup, but the most honorable coups were those taken on an armed warrior in open combat. If a man wounded his enemy at a distance but was not the first to touch him, he did not gain a single coup. If he himself was touched by an enemy and lived to tell about it, he was greatly dishonored. In certain tribes a warrior could count three coups if he touched a living enemy and then proceeded to kill and scalp him.

A warrior who had counted coup was expected to describe his deed before the tribal council, whose members also sought corroboration from witnesses. If he was found truthful and worthy, he was awarded a coup feath-

A duel on horseback ends in sudden death in this watercolor by Charles M. Russell. The hand print on the vanquished warrior's horse indicates that he has killed an enemy in hand-to-hand combat. The feathers in his hair record coups counted on foes.

er—a tail feather of the male golden eagle, which was greatly admired for its courage and swiftness. Coup feathers were inserted singly or in groups at the base of the warrior's scalp lock. When he had won enough of them, he was allowed to wear them on a warbonnet.

The day a young man took his first coup was a great occasion, and every subsequent coup in defense of the tribe added luster to his reputation. He was expected to recount his exploits at dances and ceremonies and to shun the company of those less courageous than he, shaming them by his example.

Most honored of all was the warrior who, in counting coup, also captured his foe's weapons, horses, and ceremonial equipment. (The capture of an enemy's own coup feathers brought special glory to the victor and shame to the vanquished.) The medicine of such a hero was believed to be powerful indeed; he was honored with valuable gifts, and his counsel and leadership were eagerly sought.

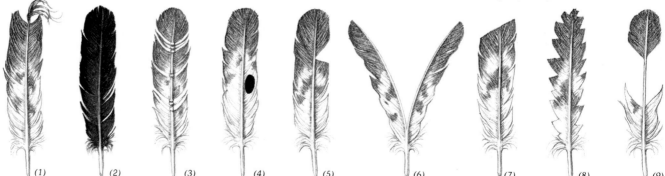

Feathers—notched, clipped, dyed, or otherwise altered—were used by the Sioux as symbols of specific kinds of exploits, or coups, as shown above. From left to right:
1) wearer's first coup—upright feather with horsehair tuft; 2) wearer wounded—upright feather dyed red; 3) wearer wounded but killed foes—upright feather with quillwork bands, one band per kill; 4) wearer killed foe—red spot on feather; 5) wearer cut foe's throat and took his scalp—notch in feather; 6) wearer wounded many times—split feather; 7) wearer cut foe's throat—top of feather clipped on diagonal; 8) wearer counted coup four times—serrated edge on feather; 9) wearer counted coup five times—sides of feather partially removed.

of their lodges and furiously attacked the hapless Grattan and his soldiers. In a few minutes it was all over, and the boastful lieutenant and all but one of his men lay dead. The sole survivor escaped to the fort but succumbed to his wounds several days later.

Thus began almost three decades of intermittent Plains bloodshed. In general, it would not be a war of massed armies and set-piece battles but rather a series of skirmishes, many of which the Indians won. But even victories could only delay the inevitable white triumph, for in the long run the whites had the organization, the weapons, and the manpower to work their will.

There would be little point in detailing the entire course of warfare between the Indians and the whites, for it would merely be a dolorous and repetitive tale of atrocity and counteratrocity. Yet certain engagements do stand out as archetypes of the bloody, merciless clash between cultures. Basically, the issue was simple enough. What the Indians had, the whites wanted—land for farms, mines for precious metals, unending miles of grass for raising cattle and sheep—and were determined to get through one expedient or another. In the white man's view the Indian was a savage, without the knowledge, good sense, or capability of putting his domain to acceptable use. To the Indian the whites came to symbolize everything that was rapacious, a deadly threat to his way of life. While knowing this, the Indian could still not truly comprehend the real nature of the threat he was facing. He tended to view the army as just another tribe from whom battle honors might be drawn and, in any case, his only real weapon against the intruders was personal bravery.

All too typical of the warfare that set the grasslands aflame was the so-called battle of Sand Creek, Colorado, in 1864, an engagement that was later and more accurately termed a massacre. During the U.S. Civil War (1861–65), army garrisons along the frontier were greatly reduced, and settlers were fearful lest the Indians take advantage of the situation. Every time a cow disappeared, it was assumed that the tribes—particularly the Cheyenne—were responsible. In retaliation for these often mythical depredations, Colorado volunteers, under orders to "burn villages and kill Cheyennes wherever . . . found," raided numerous Indian camps. Such provocations led the Cheyennes to respond in kind. Panic among whites reached a fever pitch in June 1864, when the mutilated bodies of a settler, his wife, and two young children were discovered and then exhibited in the small community of

Eagle-feather warbonnet displays the coup feathers won by its Crow owner. All Plains Indians understood the significance of other tribes' feathers, and in battle the bravest warriors usually sought an enemy who wore many such decorations.

Denver. Revenge became the watchword, and revenge the whites got, though the objects of their wrath, as so often happens, were not the perpetrators of the atrocity but a peaceful band of Cheyennes who believed they were living under the protection of the U.S. Army.

One of the chiefs of the Cheyennes was named Black Kettle, and he had long used his influence to press for peace and hold back the more headstrong warriors. That Black Kettle's pleas were often ignored was no fault of his, and in September 1864 he appealed to U.S. authorities to direct him and his 500 followers to a place of shelter. Ordered to camp beside Sand Creek, Black Kettle's band complied, and there they set up their lodges and for a few weeks lived in peace. And then, on an early November morning, the peace was suddenly shattered. The leader of the white forces was a former Methodist preacher turned soldier, Col. John M. Chivington, who, before the sneak attack on Black Kettle's camp, told his several hundred men to "Kill and scalp all, big and little; nits make lice."

Chivington, together with his volunteers, crept down upon the Cheyenne encampment in the predawn hours and surrounded it. Despite the early hour it was not long before the Indians were aware of the white soldiers, but Black Kettle assured his people that they were safe. Just to make sure he raised a

This war shield of thick buffalo hide was carried by the Crow chief Arapoosh at the time of the Lewis and Clark Expedition in 1804-06. It features a human figure representing the moon, which appeared to the chief in a vision.

A buckskin shield cover bears a decoration of feathers and a painting of a warrior, a design that appeared to the owner in a vision. Such a cover was not removed in battle, for its symbols were thought to be powerful medicine that helped protect the warrior in combat.

The Plains Indians' Accoutrements of War

Among the Plains peoples there were no standing arm[ies] commanded by all-powerful chiefs, nor were there wars [of] massive forces battling each other for territorial dominio[n]. Instead, warfare among the tribes was characterized by cou[nt]less hit-and-run raids conducted by small autonomous ban[ds] of warriors. Revenge, the capture of horses and, most of a[ll,] the accumulation of battle honors were the major reasons [for] combat. A raiding party was expected to fulfill its missi[on] without suffering any fatalities and, if faced with hopel[ess] odds, to pull out as quickly as possible. To do otherwise [in] such circumstances was needlessly to expend the lives of w[ar]riors, thus bringing grief to their families and weakening t[he] tribe as a whole. But once committed to battle, each warri[or] was expected to fight with all the skill and bravery at [his] command and to prove his worth by feats of daring. To sta[nd] amid the swirl of battle, yielding not an inch to surroundi[ng] enemies; to dash into a group of foeman and count coup [on] their bodies; to rescue a beleaguered comrade—these were [the] actions to be commended and honored with such symbols [of] personal courage as an eagle's tail feather or, among the Blac[k]feet, a white weasel skin. Such tokens of valor were far mo[re] precious than mere booty, for they set the warrior apart a[s a] man to be emulated by all.

Scalps, trophies of war, li[ke] the one at left, brought honor [to] the warrior who had tak[en] them. Their value, howeve[r,] varied from tribe to tri[be.] Among the Sioux and Crees, [for] example, a large collection [of] scalps was a mark of great val[ue.] But many tribes believed su[ch] trophies to be of far less wor[th] than the counting of coup on [a] foe or the capture of an enem[y's] horses.

A Crow or Sioux standar[d] (below) was carried in comb[at] by a warrior who rode next [to] the war leader. The standar[d] identified the leader in the co[n]fusion of battle so that his su[b]ordinates could locate him a[nd] receive orders. Its sharp poi[nt] also made it useful as a lance.

white flag together with the Stars and Stripes. Another chief, White Antelope, approached the troops to tell them that the Cheyennes were peaceful, but even before he could deliver this message, the volunteers opened fire on the village. Stunned by the slaughter he was now witnessing, White Antelope stood his ground, faced his tormentors, and sang his death song: "Nothing lives long except the earth and the mountains." Eventually, a bullet found its mark, and the chief crumpled dead on the ground. Many others died that day, most of them women and children. Altogether some 200 Indians were gunned down or clubbed and knifed to death, though Black Kettle himself escaped.

At first the engagement was hailed by the whites as a glorious victory, but slowly, as the facts came out, a wave of revulsion against Chivington and his men spread through much of the nation. Even the army's judge advocate general would call Sand Creek a "cowardly and cold-blooded slaughter." But out on the frontier, where Indians were considered a dire threat to white survival, many took a more charitable view of Chivington's action. The settlers believed that the Sand Creek Massacre had so demoralized the Cheyennes that they would not dare attack again. It was a forlorn hope, for the furious Indians of the Central Plains reacted to Sand Creek with bullets, arrows, war whoops, and bloody raids. Scores of settlers were killed, many more taken captive by revenge-seeking Cheyennes, and their Sioux and Arapaho allies. In the next four years the army was forced to expend hundreds of troops and some $30 million in campaigns to pacify the frontier.

On the Northern Plains, too, warfare soon became a way of life—and of death. In the Dakota country and the grasslands of eastern Montana and Wyoming, the

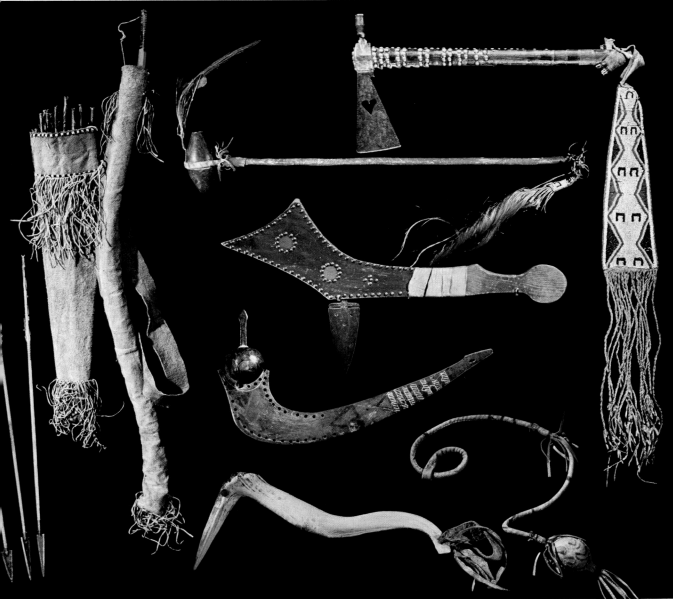

A well-armed Plains warrior would carry into battle several of the weapons shown above. Most important of all, of course, were his bow and arrows. Usually, he took about 20 arrows, like those at the extreme left, in a combination quiver and bow case (next to arrow) slung across his back. According to some observers, he could release arrows more rapidly than a white marksman could discharge the bullets from a revolver. From earliest childhood a Plains boy practiced with his bow, and by the time he reached fighting age, he had developed astonishing speed and accuracy in its use. Several types of clubs for close combat are shown above. They are, from top to bottom, a pipe tomahawk—more a ceremonial object than a weapon; a stone-headed, long-handled club, with feathers and scalp attached; a "gunstock" club bearing a knife blade; a ball-and-spike club, much like those of Woodland tribes; a slingshot club of rawhide, used to hurl a heavy stone; and a wickedly pointed club with a wristband of rawhide.

Sioux, under their great chief Red Cloud, were terrorizing settlers and soldiers alike. In 1862 a trailblazer named John Bozeman had opened a route through the Northern Plains and the Rocky Mountain foothills into the goldfields of Montana. Unfortunately, the Bozeman Trail coursed directly through much of the buffalo country, and by the mid-years of the decade Indian raids on white travelers were commonplace. To reach an agreement on the trail's use, the army called a council at Fort Laramie in 1866, inviting Red Cloud and several other Sioux leaders, as well as some northern Cheyenne chiefs, to attend. The Indians thought they had been called on to negotiate, but the army was prepared only to issue its demands for unquestioning acceptance. As the Indians and the white commissioners parlayed, Col. Henry B. Carrington, on his way to build forts along the Bozeman, appeared at Fort Laramie. When Red Cloud learned of Carrington's mission, he fell into a rage and shouted at the officers: "The Great Father sends up presents and wants us to sell him the road, but White Chief goes with soldiers to steal the road before Indians say Yes or No." This, in effect, was a declaration of war, and before 1866 was out, hard-

riding Sioux and Cheyennes had killed 150 whites along the trail that was now dubbed The Bloody Bozeman.

Warfare along the Bozeman reached a peak on December 21, 1866, when a small group of soldiers from Fort Phil Kearny, out on a wood-cutting detail, was ambushed by Red Cloud's warriors. The attack was just a ruse, intended to draw reinforcements to the scene of battle, and the army promptly fell into the trap. Leading the relief was Capt. William J. Fetterman, a fire-eater who, in an echo of Grattan's boast, had proclaimed: "Give me eighty men and I would ride through the whole Sioux nation." Like Grattan before him, Fetterman got his wish and, with colors flying, he and his command of 80 rode out of the fort to put down the Indians. But the attack on the woodcutters had been a feint, the attackers—two Arapahos, two Cheyennes, and six Sioux—mere decoys to lure the soldiers into ambush. With Fetterman's column on its way, the decoys retreated, the captain in hot pursuit along a trail parallel to the one the warriors were taking. Desultory fire was exchanged between the two galloping forces. To whet the captain's appetite, a few more Indians joined their retreating comrades. As the

A formal parade of Shoshoni Indians was a highlight of the 1837 Green River rendezvous of mountain men. Though these white fur trappers—who ranged through the West in the early 19th century—occasionally clashed with Indians, the mountain men were usually recognized by the Indians as kindred spirits, for these whites were almost constantly on the move, staked out no land claims, often wed Indian women, and were themselves sometimes adopted into the tribes.

warriors had hoped, Fetterman continued his pursuit beyond the point where he had been ordered to stop. In fact, he rode directly into the arms of the main Indian force. Within minutes Fetterman and his entire command were wiped out.

The massacre of Fetterman's force led the army to review its position on control of the Bozeman Trail. Several later battles with Red Cloud's warriors gave added urgency to the reassessment. And as the trail itself was becoming obsolete, thanks to a railroad being built to the south, the United States could afford a temporary retreat. In 1868 the government agreed to abandon the Bozeman, and Red Cloud rode in triumph through Fort Phil Kearny and then burned that hated symbol of the white man's dominance to the ground.

The Disappearing Buffalo

Red Cloud's victory soon proved to be in vain. No number of Indian triumphs over the soldiers could compensate for the depletion of the buffalo herds on the Plains. Indeed, in the Indians' dependence upon the buffalo for sustenance, the army had a far more powerful weapon than all of its ranks of bluecoats or its arsenals of repeater rifles and light artillery. If the buffalo were to disappear, the Indians would starve and the remnants of the tribes forced to accept whatever reservations the whites chose to put them on.

In 1800 there were an estimated 60 million buffalo on the Plains. Seventy years later the number had dropped to about 13 million, and by the turn of the century the herd had been reduced to fewer than 1,000 when the federal government began intensive efforts to protect these pitiful remnants and increase their population.

The slaughter had begun in earnest in the 1860's with the building of the railroads. Rather than import meat to feed the road-building crews, the railroad managers hired professional hunters to kill the buffalo. Once the lines had been laid, buffalo hunting became a great source of entertainment for sportsmen who went out West in luxurious railroad cars and from the safety of the slow-moving coaches banged away with rifles and pistols. "A uniquely American scene," reported one British traveler.

Finally, with the 1870's, professional buffalo hunting received new impetus when a Pennsylvania firm discovered that the hides could be commercially tanned and sold as leather. With buffalo skins selling for as much as $3 apiece, hunters took to the Plains with renewed zeal. Sometimes a small group of hunters could shoot and skin as many as 50 buffalo a day, and one hunter, accompanied by a band of professional skinners, claimed to have killed 1,500 in a single week.

The slaughter of the buffalo reduced tribe after tribe of Indians to penury. Where once they had known plenty, now they knew only starvation, and many were forced to settle on reservations that were little more than poverty-stricken ghettos. Still, in some places, the

A warrior fondles a gun, probably obtained from a white trader. *The earliest firearms the Indians obtained were muzzle-loaders. They were no match for the bow and arrow, for an Indian could shoot eight arrows in the time it took to load and fire a musket.*

Indians held to to their patterns of living, practiced their ancient rites and, whenever possible, scoured the grasslands for the dwindling herds. One area that remained to the northern tribes was the Black Hills of the Dakota country. These hills were sacred to the Sioux and several other tribes, and the government had promised they would remain inviolate. But in 1874 Lt. Col. George Armstrong Custer, known to the Indians as Long Hair for his flowing golden locks, commanded an expedition into the Black Hills and then reported there was "gold around the roots of the grass." Custer's report precipitated a rush of prospectors to the Black Hills in utter disregard for the Indians' treaty rights. The stage was being set for the Battle of the Little Bighorn, sometimes known as Custer's Last Stand.

The prospectors touched off a new wave of Indian resistance. Hundreds of Sioux and Cheyennes now forayed outside the various territories that had been assigned them in western Dakota and eastern Montana and Wyoming to raid white settlements, while the government organized punitive expeditions to round them up. By late spring 1876 some 12,000 Sioux and Cheyennes had assembled beside the Little Bighorn River to practice the ceremonials of their faith and hear calls to battle against the whites by war leaders Crazy Horse and Sitting Bull.

Of all the Indian leaders Sitting Bull was perhaps the most revered, for he combined the courage of a warrior

Mounted Sioux and Cheyenne warriors *swoop down on the 7th Cavalry during the Battle of the Little Bighorn on June 25, 1876. Little is known about this pictograph, painted by the* *Sioux Red Horse in 1881, except that it refers to one of the engagements on that fateful day when Lt. Col. George Armstrong Custer and his command of some 225 were wiped out.*

In Sitting Bull's grim features *many whites discerned the determination of the Indians to resist white domination. Born in 1831, Sitting Bull became chief of a major Sioux band, a warrior of great renown, and a man revered for his wisdom by thousands of Plains Indians. By the time of the Little Bighorn he was no longer an active warrior, but he was at the Indian encampment as leader of his band. There he had a vision of white soldiers falling into the Indian camp, a sign of the victory to come. After the battle Sitting Bull led his people into Canada but in 1881 surrendered to U.S. troops. He was killed by reservation police in 1890 when he resisted arrest on a charge of rebellion.*

Little Bighorn: Last Triumph of the Plains Indians

The day was June 25, 1876; the time: about 4 P.M.; the place: near the east bank of the meandering Little Bighorn River in eastern Montana. There, in a verdant valley, a force of U.S. Cavalry suffered one of the most crushing defeats of the Indian wars. It was beside the Little Bighorn that Lt. Col. George Armstrong Custer, recklessly impatient for combat, led his command of about 225 men of the 7th Cavalry into battle against the greatest assemblage of Plains warriors—between 2,500 and 3,000—ever to engage an army unit.

Custer had his orders—to scout out the encampment of various bands of Sioux and Cheyennes but to withhold offensive action until reinforced. Certain, however, that his approximately 600 men were more than equal to any force of Indians, Custer decided on the attack. Though faced with a powerful array, probably strong enough to defeat his entire regiment, Custer then proceeded to divide his command. He ordered Capt. Frederick W. Benteen, with about 120 troopers, to scout far afield—an instruction that defies rational explanation. Then he commanded Maj. Marcus A. Reno to take a similar number of men across the Little Bighorn and begin a diversionary attack on the Indian encampment from the south. Depleting his forces even more, he assigned 129 men to guard the pack train.

At about 2:30 P.M. Reno crossed the river, approximately three miles downstream from the encampment. Urging his men forward, they galloped toward the foe, only to meet a force of Indians rushing on horseback and foot to engage them. Reno, who had never before fought Indians, yielded the offensive advantage when he ordered his men dismounted to take up defensive positions. Beset by superior numbers, defense soon yielded to rout as Reno and his men abandoned the field—and their dead and wounded—and scurried across the river to dig in as best they could. For them the day's combat was virtually over.

Meanwhile, Custer was moving up the east bank to a point opposite the main Indian encampment. Evidently, he never made it across the river but came under an overwhelming attack on the east bank. By 4 P.M. his men were strung out in the open, as wave after wave of horsemen, under Gall and Crazy Horse, both repeatedly turned the bluecoats' flanks, cutting down scores with each assault.

Unable to retreat, Custer and his men fought with desperate courage. Later many of the Indians would report they had never encountered a braver foe. But for once the Indians adopted the tactics of the whites and generally ignored the quest for personal honors to get on with the grim business of inflicting maximum casualties. Long before dusk it was all over. Custer and his force were dead. It was the Indians' greatest and last victory. Soon the bands would be hunted down, destroyed, or led captive to the reservations.

with the wisdom of a sage. At 14 Sitting Bull had counted his first coup, and a decade later he had become a sash-wearer of the Strong Hearts warriors. In 1856, during a fight with the Crows, he had galloped far ahead of his own warriors and dismounted to face the enemy alone, taunting them with his war chant: "Comrades, whoever runs away,/ He is a woman, they say;/ Therefore, through any trials,/ My life is short!"

In spite of his many valorous feats Sitting Bull was not merely a war chief, for by his early thirties he was widely recognized as a prophet and holy man. At first he was not an advocate of war with the whites, for he hoped that they would leave his people in peace to follow the old ways and chase down the buffalo. Only when it appeared that the whites required Indian submission did Sitting Bull allow himself to become the personification of all Indians who refused to "walk the white man's road."

In the early summer of 1876 two columns of soldiers converged on the Sioux and Cheyenne holdouts in the Little Bighorn country. The army was conducting a dragnet operation that, so it was hoped, would scoop up the last of the renegades. One of the columns was led by Gen. Alfred Terry, and under him, Colonel Custer commanded the 7th Cavalry. Along the banks of the Yellowstone River, Terry, Custer, and a second column led by Col. John Gibbon joined forces and stopped to plan strategy. Terry would go off with Gibbon to outflank the Indians from the north; Custer, with his 7th Cavalry, would take up a position to the south of the Indian encampment and refrain from the attack until the units

under Terry and Gibbon were in their proper positions.

As Custer rode off with his men, Gibbon called after him: "Custer, don't be greedy! Wait for us." Long Hair called back: "No, I won't," an answer that could be interpreted in two distinctly different ways. In fact, Custer apparently had no intention of waiting. There was glory to be won, medals to be secured, promotions to be had.

He thirsted mightily for such recognition. Custer's military career had been a series of peaks and valleys. Although he was graduated last in his West Point class in 1861, his daring and combativeness brought him quick promotions during the Civil War, and he rose from second lieutenant to major general of Volunteers. When the war ended, however, the Volunteers were disbanded, and Custer returned to the rank of captain.

But because of his friendship with Gen. Philip Sheridan and President Andrew Johnson, Custer was soon elevated to the rank of lieutenant colonel and given a cavalry command at Fort Riley, Kansas. His career began to rise again as he scored a number of victories over the Cheyenne and other Plains tribes, only to fall once more in 1876 when he gave testimony, embarrassing to President Ulysses S. Grant, about corruption in the assignment of post traderships on Indian reservations. Grant stripped Custer of his command. Only after pleas from Custer's superior officers did the president relent and permit the troublemaker to take part in the 1876 summer campaign against the Indians.

Thoughts of burnishing his reputation must have been on Custer's mind when he came upon the Indians'

From the safety of a train excursionists fire away with six-shooters, repeating rifles, and any other weapons at hand to destroy a herd of buffalo. During the late 1860's and 1870's railway companies ran special trains for just such sport. Far more destructive, however, were the professional buffalo-hunters, who slaughtered the animals for their hides. In the decade that began in 1872, more than 1 million buffalo were killed every year. The skins were stripped and the carcasses left to rot. By the turn of the century there was scarcely a herd left on the Plains. Without buffalo to provide meat and skins, the Indians' way of life was doomed. Little wonder that Gen. Phil Sheridan remarked: "They [buffalo-hunters] have done more in . . . two years . . . to settle the vexed Indian question, than the entire regular army . . . in the last thirty years."

The Coming of the Ghost Dance: Renewed Hope for the Indians

When, in 1881, Sitting Bull and his band of Sioux surrendered to U.S. authorities, a chapter in the history of the Plains came to a close. Virtually all of the tribes and bands of Plains Indians were now confined to reservations where, as wards of the government, they were supposed to learn the rudiments of agriculture and, meanwhile, subsist on handouts authorized by Congress.

The Sioux, for the most part, were gathered on reservations in the Dakotas, on parched land that would have tried the skills of even the most expert agriculturists. And if the Indians could expect minimal bounty from the soil, they could anticipate little more from the government, for year after year Congress cut the allotments. At the same time other government agencies applied pressure to force the Indians to sell off so-called excess reservation acreage for as little as 50 cents an acre to land-hungry whites. For the Indians of the Dakota reservations the 1880's were a time of despair and near-starvation. Only the memories of the old days helped sustain them.

But in the midst of despair there came a new hope in the form of a messianic cult, the Ghost Dance. Far away, on a Nevada reservation, a Paiute prophet named Wovoka had had a vision. A new age would soon dawn for the Indians. The white man would disappear, all of the Indians' ancestors would be resurrected from the dead, and the tribesmen and women would live forever chasing down the new herds of buffalo that would reappear on the grasslands. Word of the new cult swept through the grasslands, particularly after a delegation of Sioux traveled to Nevada to hear these glad tidings from the lips of Wovoka. To prepare for the new age, Indians were to perform the Ghost Dance, a simple ceremony of chants and communal dancing heightened by religious frenzy in which participants might fall semiconscious on the ground and see visions of the world to come. Though the ceremony expressed distinct antiwhite feeling, it was harmless enough, for the message of the cult was one of peace. It forbade the taking up of arms, even against the white man.

On the reservations, however, the white officials looked upon the Ghost Dance with alarm, as a threat to their authority. In 1890, on the Pine Ridge Reservation, an Indian agent named D. F. Royer called for troops. And at the nearby Stand-

*A **Ghost Dance shirt** (above) was thought to make the wearer impervious to the white man's bullets. The painted figures were derived from the wearer's visions. Because dancers wore such shirts, many whites thought the ritual a war dance.*

ing Rock Reservation, another official, James McLaughlin, ordered the arrest of his most renowned ward, Sitting Bull, whom he thought to be the focus of the Ghost Dance agitation. In the predawn of December 15, 1890, 43 "metal breasts"—Indian police—descended on Sitting Bull's cabin and arrested him. As the old chief emerged from his dwelling, it is said that an aged woman taunted him to resist. Sitting Bull pulled free of his captors and announced that he would not go with them. A scuffle followed, shots were fired and, before the encounter was over, 14 people, including Sitting Bull, lay dead or dying. With the death of the old warrior and medicine man, panic overtook the people of the Standing Rock Reservation. Hundreds fled, and troops were sent out to round them up and return them to their quarters. The stage was set for the ultimate tragedy, the massacre at Wounded Knee (box, opposite).

Preparing for a new age of freedom and abundance, a circle of Arapahos performs the Ghost Dance in a painting based on photographs. Though much of the doctrine of the Ghost Dance cult was drawn from Christianity, many whites looked upon it as the work of demons and were determined to stamp it out, with force if necessary. There were, of course, exceptions to this view. Valentine McGillycuddy, once an Indian agent, was dispatched by the government to report on the Ghost Dance. "The coming of troops has frightened the Indians," he wrote. "If the Seventh-Day Adventists prepare . . . for the second coming of the Savior, the . . . Army is not put in motion. . . . Why should not the Indians have the same privilege?" Unfortunately, few heeded McGillycuddy's prediction that "If the troops remain, trouble is sure to come."

trail on June 24. Scouts reported the presence of a very large, hostile encampment, but when Custer went to look for himself, a thick haze obscured his vision, and he concluded that what he could not see was not there. Actually, Custer knew that beneath the rise where his men were making camp there were Indians, but he refused to believe that their strength was sufficient to threaten his command. Convincing himself that the Indians knew of his presence, Custer decided on an early attack, lest the enemy flee or strengthen their defenses.

At the Indian encampment Sitting Bull had had an omen. At a Sun Dance ceremony he had made a flesh offering of a hundred pieces of his skin and received a vision of soldiers falling into the camp circle. Victory would surely belong to the Indians.

It was midafternoon on June 25, 1876, when Custer and the Indians came face-to-face. Long Hair had split his command into three parts, leaving only 225 troopers under his direct control. Whether he planned, or actually even tried, to ford the Little Bighorn and attack the Sioux and their allies is unknown. But it was the Indians who quickly moved to the offensive, pinning Custer's men against the hills as hundreds upon hundreds of mounted warriors came swooping down upon Long Hair in swift, enveloping charges. In vain, Custer and his men tried to stem the tide, but the Indians swarmed through the regiment's defenses, cutting down the troopers in wholesale lots until the last white man had perished.

At the Little Bighorn the Indians had won their greatest military victory; but, like the Bozeman Trail triumph, this success too proved futile. Within weeks strong reinforcements of bluecoats were on the trail, harrying and hunting the starving Indian bands, forcing Sitting Bull and many of his followers into Canada. Resistance had become futile. Within five years there was scarcely a tribesman roaming free on the entire Plains. Even the redoubtable Sitting Bull was forced to surrender himself and his ragged band in 1881.

The great age of the Plains Indians had now come to a sorrowful close. Reservation life and, often, near-starvation would now be the Indians' lot. In the ensuing decades despair would lead them to a few, mostly feeble, efforts at resistance, but their captors proved far too strong for them. Only in recent years have these Indians of the Plains been able to renew their ancient culture.

Ghost Dance Aftermath: Slaughter at Wounded Knee

Sitting Bull was dead, the Ghost Dance cult was in disarray, and rumors spread through the Dakota reservations in mid-December 1890 that the government would take reprisals against the Indians. In fear for their future, about 400 of Sitting Bull's followers fled their homes to seek shelter among the Sioux under chief Big Foot at the Cheyenne River Reservation. Most never made it; they were talked into surrendering to the authorities at Fort Bennett. But a handful arrived at Big Foot's village. Soon it was surrounded by troopers, but because they were waiting orders, they made no immediate move to attack. Now fear spread among Big Foot's people, and on December 23, 1890, under cover of darkness, about 350 of them, with their chief, abandoned the village and set off toward Pine Ridge. The soldiers, with their arsenal of small arms and light artillery, followed in hot pursuit. On December 28 the Indians surrendered and, under the eyes of the soldiers, made camp at a place called Wounded Knee. The next morning the Indians received orders to hand in their weapons, but they refused. Soldiers began a search. There was a scuffle; a shot rang out. Suddenly the peaceful camp was transformed into a scene of horror. From the hills the troopers raked the Indians with their Hotchkiss guns and probably killed many of their own men caught in the crossfire. The Indians fought back as best they could, but it was an unequal battle from the start. In the heat of combat many of the soldiers—some of them from the 7th Cavalry, Custer's old command—went berserk, cutting down defenseless women with babes in arms as they tried to flee. In all, 25 soldiers were killed, 39 wounded, and at least 153 Indians—some say as many as 300—died. The military dead were buried with full honors, but days later a hired civilian crew dumped the bodies of the Indians into a common grave (below). One of the civilian workers remembered the scene: "It was a thing," he said, "to melt the heart of a man, if it was of stone, to see those little children, with their bodies shot to pieces, thrown naked into the pit." Wounded Knee marked the end of the Plains Indians' armed resistance, but the slaughter remains a symbol to the Indians of their treatment by whites.

THE SOUTHWEST
Planters and Herdsmen

The majestic Southwest offers spectacular beauty but little rainfall. Because of their centuries-old concern with rain for their crops, Indians have long placated the spirits that control the elements. The Hopi kachina doll (inset) represents such a spirit.

To survive in this beautiful but harsh land, the natives had to cope with broiling heat, intense cold, and little rainfall, but most of all with the greed of white invaders.

The American Southwest is a land of enormous majesty and spectacular contrasts—mountains and canyons, deserts and forests, rocks and groves, red cliffs and white ones, mounds of lava, and days of scorching heat followed by nights of bone-chilling cold. The air is clear and the sky usually cloudless: one can see for miles across the high, flat-topped mesas and strangely shaped buttes. It is the land of the Grand Canyon and the Painted Desert, of the Rio Grande and the Colorado River. High on its mountains are forests of yellow pine. Farther down piñons and junipers grow, and the deserts are dotted with sagebrush and prickly cacti. Small hoglike peccaries live here, together with Abert squirrels and jackrabbits. It is the land of the roadrunner, with its streaked brown plumage and long tail, and of the screech owl and the elf owl, which make their homes in hollows inside the giant saguaro cactus. The poisonous lizard called the Gila monster lurks in the desert lowlands, and the mountain lion claims the heights as home. For much of the year no rain falls, but when it comes, it often brings floods. In such a land the earth does not yield her bounty generously.

According to their lore, the Hopis have lived in this magnificent but arid country longer than any other people; in fact, the Hopi pueblo at Oraibi, Arizona, on the Black Mesa, is one of the two oldest continuously occupied settlements on the continent north of Mexico. This village was here nearly a thousand years ago, and even in those times, as today, the Hopis—whose name means "Peaceful Ones"—were following their tranquil way of life, raising crops in the dry soil and celebrating the year-long round of ceremonies that they believed ensured health and prosperity for all living things.

Even after centuries of close contact with the Spaniards, the Hopis remained a people of tradition, clinging determinedly to their old ways and old religion. They were the despair of the friars who had come to convert them and, although the Hopis were a basically peaceful people, they were a constant threat to the Spanish soldiers, ranchers, and administrators who wanted to make them serfs.

The Southwest *is the site of some of the best-preserved archeological remains in the United States. They offer evidence that the area has been inhabited for at least 6,000 years and that its early occupants had already learned to grow some varieties of corn and squash. This knowledge may have been introduced from Mexico, and it had a significant effect on the Southwestern peoples, enabling them over the centuries to transform themselves from nomadic hunters and gatherers into farmers who lived in villages.*

By the start of the Christian era this change had been completed, and four major cultures had emerged—the Mogollon, in the Mogollon Mountains, which stretch from present-day central Arizona into southern New Mexico; the Anasazi, in the area where Utah, Colorado, New Mexico, and Arizona meet; the Hohokam, in the southern Arizona desert and the Mexican state of Sonora; and the Patayan, in northwest Arizona and along the Colorado River (see map p. 53). All four groups were thriving by A.D. 700, and for the next four centuries their development con-

tinued, their villages growing in size and their cultural and social organization becoming increasingly sophisticated.

Then, starting about A.D. 1100 and lasting for the next 250 years, a series of disasters—probably droughts—took place that profoundly altered Southwestern life. The Mogollon culture disappeared entirely, although some of its elements were incorporated into Anasazi life. The other cultures remained alive but in very different form. The people abandoned their ancestral villages, some of them now grown to the size of small cities, and splintered into a number of different groups. They had already settled in their new homes when the Spaniards arrived some time during the 16th century. The map below shows the pattern of settlement the Spaniards found; it continues until today. The Apaches and the Navajos had not yet learned to farm, and they roved the mountains and the deserts hunting and raiding to find their food, often attacking the settled tribes. In the mountainous northwest were the Havasupais, the Yavapais, and the Walapais, whose culture was descended from the Patayan; to the south, near the Arizona-California border, were the Pimas and the Papagos, whose culture descended from the Hohokam. The remaining Southwest tribes—the Hopi in northeast Arizona, the Zuni in west-central New Mexico, and the Rio Grande people, along the valley of the Rio Grande River—were descended from the Anasazi. They differed in language, customs, and religious beliefs, but their common ancestry was clear in their dwelling places—apartmentlike stone houses built along rocky cliffs. Their villages, whose locations are shown on the inset map, were called pueblos by the Spaniards, and they closely resembled the much larger villages the Anasazis had built 500 years earlier.

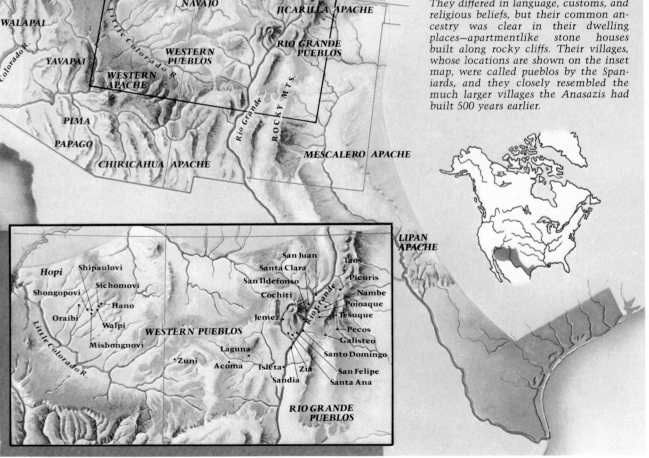

The arrival of the Spaniards in the 16th century is commemorated in this Navajo pictograph on the wall of Arizona's Canyon del Muerto. The pictograph, probably made after a sub- sequent Spanish expedition, shows a black-robed friar and his equestrian party. The horse, previously unknown in the Southwest, would add far greater mobility to the Indians' way of life.

Hopi villages, like those of their farming neighbors, were built on readily defensible mesas. These communities—called pueblos by the Spaniards, a name that remains—were made up of America's first apartment houses. They were built of stone and plastered with mud, and they all faced the streets and village plazas.

The Hopis, like other pueblo dwellers, did their farming on the flatlands where there were springs and water runoffs to irrigate the crops. But this location required a farmer to go down the paths of the cliff and walk perhaps as far as 10 miles to reach his land.

The most important parts of any pueblo were, and are, the kivas—stone-walled ceremonial and meeting chambers—that are often sunk deep in the ground in the village plazas. Although the Spaniards tried desperately to eradicate the kivas because of their spiritual importance to the Indians, 12 of these holy chambers remain in Oraibi. The kivas symbolize the World Below, from which come the spirits that are said to inhabit all things animate and inanimate. And it is to the World Below that the Hopis return after death.

Symbolic of the passage between the World Below and the earth itself is the sipapu, a stone-lined hole in the kiva floor. Through the sipapu came the original People from the World Below, and the kachinas still use this traverse when they come to the yearly ceremonies. Not every kiva has a sipapu, but each one does contain a dirt platform raised about two inches above the rest of the floor. Upon this platform some of the most important ceremonials take place.

To the east and south of the Hopis lived another Pueblo people, the Zunis, and east of the Zunis were the various tribes that made up the Rio Grande Pueblos. These people lived much as did the Hopis and, like the Hopis, were descended from the early people who came to the Southwest. Despite their common traditions, customs, and beliefs the various Pueblo groups spoke different languages.

Although the pueblo dwellers did some hunting before contact with Europeans, they were basically farmers, and for decade after decade the men tilled the fields, growing corn, squash, tobacco, and beans. Always, in the dry Arizona country, there was the problem of water for the crops. To overcome this shortage, a number of Rio Grande Pueblos cooperated in digging irrigation ditches that sometimes stretched for miles between the cultivated fields and the closest reliable streams.

The life of the Pueblo peoples was not isolated, however. They were occasionally raided by their Navajo and Apache neighbors in search of food, and from time to time the Pueblos would war among themselves. They also traded with one another along routes to the west and north. But on the whole the living pattern was tranquil and relatively stable. But as the 16th century moved toward its middle decades, newcomers arrived, and for the Hopis and the other peoples of the pueblos, life would never be quite the same again.

The Coming of the Spaniards

It all began in 1528 when a party of Spanish explorers, led by one Alvar Núñez Cabeza de Vaca, was shipwrecked on the Gulf Coast of Texas. During the next eight years Cabeza de Vaca and his dwindling party wandered through forest, mountain, and desert, crossing much of the Southwest as they sought some outpost of Spanish civilization in the New World. In the course of their trek Cabeza de Vaca and his companions—one of whom was a black man from Morocco named Estevanico—passed through territories no foreigner had ever seen before and heard rumors from the Indians they encountered of seven fabulously rich cities. When, at last, Cabeza de Vaca and his four surviving followers reached safety in Mexico, they passed on what they had heard, perhaps adding a few embellishments of their own.

Having already subdued the ancient civilizations of Mexico and secured an enormous wealth in gold, the Spaniards were now eager to seek new conquests, new hoards of treasure to claim, and new souls to save.

Thus it was that in 1539 a party of explorers led by Friar Marcos de Niza moved north out of Mexico into the uncharted deserts of the lands that would later be called Arizona and New Mexico. Somewhere in these harsh regions the friar believed that he would find the seven cities with their gold-and-silver-paved streets and jewel-encrusted dwellings. And to make certain that he would not go astray, he employed Estevanico as guide.

Ranging ahead of the main party, Estevanico and his retinue of Mexican Indians reached the Zuni pueblo of Halona. The first sight of these strangers on horseback must have stunned the Zunis. Were the visitors men or animals, or some strange combination of the two? And what of the creature at the head of the party, with his skin darker than any Indian's, in his bizarre attire that made him look like some grotesque bird of prey? Estevanico had deliberately clad himself in raiments intended to make him appear like a god. His body was decorated with feathers, and bells hung from his wrists and ankles. A greyhound ran on either side of his horse, and behind him came his company of Mexican Indians, now fallen from their past glory.

Estevanico's behavior was as terrifying and incomprehensible as his appearance. He demanded food and gifts and women, and threatened the Zunis with a terrible fate if they hesitated to obey. Perhaps such a creature was not human but the manifestation of evil incarnate. When the black man displayed a gourd rattle he had saved from his desert wanderings of years before, the object was instantly recognized as one belonging to another tribe. The Zunis, possibly angered by his casual use of a sacred object, ordered him away. Instead of leaving, Estevanico dispatched a messenger to Friar Marcos with the report that he had discovered one of the fabled cities. But shortly after the messenger left, the Zunis, their patience exhausted, loosed a flight of arrows at the black man, killing him and sending the Mexican Indians fleeing for their lives.

When word of Estevanico's fate reached Friar Marcos, he hastily beat a retreat to Mexico. But along the way he had caught a glimpse of the roofs of Halona in the rays of the setting sun. Bedazzled by the glittering reflections on the native stone, the friar became even more persuaded that the seven cities were both real and incredibly rich.

Their interest quickened by Friar Marcos' report, the Spaniards in 1540 mounted a more elaborate expedition, led by Capt.-Gen. Francisco Vásquez de Coronado at the head of 230 armor-clad horsemen and 62 foot soldiers. Also in the train were 1,000 Indians from Mexico and numerous priests, among them Friar Marcos de Niza who acted as the expedition's guide. Apparently, the Zunis had advance word of the Spaniards' approach, for when Coronado's force reached the pueblo of Hawikuh, they found only men—the women and children having been sent to the summit of Corn Mountain to hide until the intruders left.

The pueblo, a honeycomb of stone houses perched a forbidding cliffs, has been the home of the Hopis for over 1, years. Of all pueblos, Walpi—shown in the color photograp has the most spectacular location. It stands 600 feet above desert floor, where the Hopis grow their crops, and is reached a narrow, steep trail (above) cut into the side of a cliff. picture of the trail was made in 1901 by Adam C. Vroman, of the early photographers of Southwest Indians, who also t the picture of the plaza at the Mishonognovi pueblo (right) of the young Hopi mother bearing her baby on her back surrounded by children (far right). The Hopi man (top rig was photographed by Vroman's contemporary Edward S. Cu Both men admired the cultures of the Southwest and set ou record the ancient ways before they vanished.

These pictures form part of that record. The Hopi, with headband, earrings, and blanket, is dressed much as his rem ancestors would have been, as is the girl standing next to mother. Her double-whorled, squash-blossom hairdress is tr tional, signifying her marriageable status. The pueblo plaz Mishonognovi (immediate right) is also little changed from contact times. The attached houses have two stories, the sec set back from the first to form a terrace, reached by ladders, serves as an aboveground street. Adjacent houses in a row inhabited by matrilineally linked families.

In one respect this pueblo varies from tradition. House most such villages had neither doors nor windows, access to interiors being limited to holes in the roofs, also reached ladders. In the center of the plaza is a kiva, an undergro chamber of worship, from which a ladder extends. Though cred rituals were performed in the kiva, it was also a clubho for men, while the dwellings, which belonged to the wor were given over to domestic chores.

Hopi corn, fed by underground moisture, ripens on a patch of desert near the Oraibi pueblo. Though the plants are small, the corn is of a hardy strain that matures quickly and is not harmed by the extremes of desert temperatures. But the key to the corn's survival is deep planting. Using his digging stick, or dibble, the planter makes a narrow hole 12 to 16 inches deep. The damp subsoil at the bottom is loosened, 10 to 20 seeds dropped in, and the earth is packed down. The farmer then paces off five feet and repeats the process. Deep planting permits the seeds to receive the benefit of all the moisture in the soil, and shoots develop strong root systems, providing anchorage that protects the stalks from being blown away or washed out by storms.

Planting is done in April or May, and by September the slender ears are ready for harvest. Some of the ears are quickly consumed, some are kept for seeds, and others are stored for future use. Much of the corn is dried and pulverized into meal by the age-old method shown below. A Hopi girl uses a stone mano to mash the kernels against a rough slab called a metate, of which she has several. Each metate grinds the corn to a different degree of fineness.

When Coronado attempted to show peaceful intentions, the Zunis ignored him. Between the Spanish ranks and their own they drew a line of sacred cornmeal on the ground and warned the newcomers not to cross it. The gesture was useless, however, for even if the Spaniards had understood it, they would not have been cowed. As the invading army moved across the line, the Zunis let fly a rain of arrows. The Spaniards immediately replied with musket fire and swords, sending their adversaries into headlong retreat. The survivors fled to the mountains or to other pueblos to spread the news of the disaster.

The Spaniards had won this encounter, and the hungry army fed themselves with the Zunis' stores of corn. But the gold, silver, and jewels they had expected to find did not exist, and Coronado dispatched a message to Mexico's viceroy in which he bitterly noted that Friar Marcos "has not told the truth in a single thing he said."

The community of Hawikuh itself was a far cry from a fabled city. One member of the expedition described it as a "little, unattractive village, looking as if it had been crumpled up all together." Still, the Spaniards had come too far in search of their dream to give it up. While Coronado made camp at the Zuni peublo, he dispatched a group of horsemen under the leadership of Pedro de Tovar to scout out other settlements for possible plunder. At the Hopi pueblo of Awatovi, De Tovar and his men were met with resistance, which cost many Hopis their lives. Forewarned by this experience, the people of the next 14 Hopi pueblos that De Tovar visited met the strangers with gifts.

Disappointment for the Invaders

But from the Spaniards' point of view the entire expedition was a failure. The Hopi pueblos held no more gold than those of the Zunis. Finally, the Europeans left the area, pushing eastward into the pueblos of the Rio Grande and thence northward and still farther east, into the Great Plains, searching now for still another fabled city, Quivira. When Quivira, too, proved to be a will-o'-the-wisp, the Spaniards became discouraged and returned to Mexico, leaving the pueblos in peace for almost 40 years. In 1580 desire for land, workers, and souls to save sent the Spaniards on another expedition northward.

Now that they had established contact with the Indians, the Spaniards began to send Christian missionaries to the pueblos. From that moment conflict became inevitable. The Indians' religion was at the center of their lives, and they were not prepared to abandon it. Moreover, the Spaniards treated them with contempt and hostility. They requisitioned the corn and set their horses to pasture in the cornfields. The Europeans put the Pueblo men to forced labor and sexually abused the Pueblo women. Those who dared resist Spanish power were flogged, burned at the stake, garroted, or taken into slavery. And those who denied the white man's religion suffered equally brutal treatment. One Hopi man, discovered by a friar in "an act of idolatry," was first beaten in public, then taken into the church and beaten again. Then his body was smeared with turpentine and he was set afire. Yielding to brutality, many of the Pueblo peoples formally adopted Christianity.

A severe drought began in 1660. Year in and year out the rains did not fall, the crops failed, and famine spread over the land. At times, hunger was so great that the people were forced to eat hides. Bitterness grew. In the past, individual pueblos had attempted to rise against the white man, but every rebellion had been crushed. If the invaders were to be driven from the land, it was clear that the pueblos must act together.

The Successful Revolution

In 1680 the Indians finally achieved unity of purpose and action. It was the year of the Pueblo Revolution, perhaps the most spectacular and successful act of defiance that Indians anywhere would ever accomplish in their relations with Europeans. The leader of the revolt was Popé, a medicine man from one of the Rio Grande Pueblos. On his back Popé bore the marks of Spanish whips for his refusal to adopt Christianity, and in his heart he nourished a bitter hatred for the Spaniard and all his works. From Taos, a pueblo where resistance had always been strong, Popé sent out a group of runners to all the villages scattered along hundreds of miles of desert and cliffs. Each runner carried a knotted cord, the number of knots indicating how many days were left before the uprising.

But two of the messengers were captured, and on August 9 word was sent to the Spanish governor that "the Christian Indians of this kingdom are convoked, allied and confederated for the purpose of rebelling, abandoning obedience to the Crown and apostatizing from the Holy Faith. They plan to kill the priests, and all the Spaniards. . . . They are to execute this treason . . . on the 13th of the current month."

Frantically, the Spaniards made ready to crush the rebellion expected on the 13th. But when the Indians had learned of the capture of the messengers, the date of attack had been moved forward two days. When the people of the pueblos attacked on August 11, the Europeans were unprepared. Within a few days some 400 Spaniards lay dead, and scores of pueblo churches and ranch houses were in flames. Then on August 14th a strong force of Indians laid siege to the Spaniards' provincial capital, Santa Fé. For almost a week the battle raged. The Spaniards were routed, and Santa Fé lay in ruins. Nowhere in the Pueblo country was there shelter for the Europeans, who were forced to retreat southward to El Paso.

But 12 years later the white men returned to the pueblos of the Zunis and the Rio Grande. But the Hopis would not submit. So (continued on page 214)

A Ritual to Bring an Abundant Harvest

Central to Hopi life is the belief that all things in nature have specific roles to play in maintaining the world's equilibrium. The Hopis' role requires them to keep good hearts and observe complex rituals. Failure in these duties upsets nature's delicate balance and causes calamity.

Of the many rites the Hopis observe, the Snake Ceremonial is one of the most spectacular. The pictures of the ceremony shown here were taken in the early years of this century, before photographers were barred at such events. The rite is held in late August and is meant to bring rain that guarantees a good harvest. The snake, with its zigzag movements, symbolizes lightning and its accompanying rain.

The entire ceremony, conducted by the Snake and Antelope religious societies, lasts for nine days. For the first few the men prepare themselves—praying, fashioning prayer sticks, and setting up altars within their kivas. Then each morning for four days members of the societies go into the desert to capture snakes, both poisonous and nonpoisonous, which are placed in the kiva. On the eighth day there is a symbolic marriage between a girl representing a Snake virgin and a youth representing a Snake Hero.

Also on the eighth day the men of the Antelope Society perform, dancing around the plaza while holding the earliest fruits of the harvest—melons, squash, and bean vines. The stamping of their feet is to draw the attention of the gods.

On the ninth day—the most dramatic of the colorful Snake Ceremonial—the reptiles are brought from the kiva where they have been washed in water and dried in sand. The snakes are credited with the ability to tell if a man has a truly pure and fearless heart, and after their ceremonial baths the creatures drape themselves over the bodies of the most worthy men to sleep. This climactic day ends at sunset when the Snake men dance as the Antelope men chant. While dancing, the Snake men pluck the snakes from the *kisi*, a bower that has been built for them, and carrying the reptiles in their mouths, they circle the village plaza.

Finally, the snakes are taken back to the desert and released to spread the word of the Hopis' prayers and intercede with the spirits to bring the much-needed rain.

Ritually prescribed clothing, body decorations, and religious objects are used during the ceremonies. The feathered headdress and the kilt (above) are worn by Snake priests, such as the one at right. The snake theme, symbolic of lightning, is painted on the celebrant's kilt and appears again on the snake stick (above left) from a kiva altar. Additional regalia includes shell necklaces, foxskins suspended from the backs of kilts, turtle-shell rattles worn below the knees, bags of sacred cornmeal and, most important of all, a "snake whip," made of eagle feathers. The whip is used during dances when the snakes are carried by men. The reptiles are thought to be terrified of eagles, and the touch of the feathers is usually enough to stupefy a snake and keep it from striking.

Joining with the Snake men in the celebration are members of the Antelope Society (below). The Antelope dancers wear kilts and sashes embroidered with traditional designs. The bodies of the dancers are painted ash gray, and white zigzag lines course down their upper arms, chests, backs, and legs. One of the dancers stamps on a wooden board placed over the sipapu, a hole in the ground that represents the entrance to the underworld where the spirits live. At the extreme left is the kisi, the bower in which the snakes are kept until they are needed in the ceremonial.

Climax of the Snake Ceremonial

occurs when the dancers, members of the Snake Society (right and above), have made four circuits of the village plaza. Now each dancer picks up a snake from the kisi. Members of the Snake Society now dance around the plaza, holding the reptiles in their mouths. Each dancer, such as the man at far right, is accompanied by a guard, or "hugger," carrying a snake whip. The hugger carefully watches the reptile and is ready to stroke it with an eagle feather to keep it from biting. When the circuit of the plaza has been completed, the dancer removes the snake from his mouth and places it on the ground. Then a third man, a gatherer, shown near the snakes (above), quietly approaches and deftly picks up a reptile that he drapes over his arm or hands to one of the Antelope men, who are standing in a long line and chanting an accompaniment to the dance.

The procedure is repeated until all the snakes have been taken from the kisi, danced with, and gathered up. At this point the chief Snake priest traces a circle of sacred cornmeal on the ground, and within this circle the gatherers place the snakes. This dance is the last great ritual of the Snake Ceremonial. Soon the snakes will be returned to their desert homes, and the Snake men will swallow an emetic, causing them to vomit and thus purify their bodies.

passionate was their commitment to their traditions that in 1700 they again rose up in an act that was both tragic and desperate. In one pueblo, Awatovi, the Spaniards had managed to establish a mission and convert 73 villagers. When the other Hopi pueblos heard of this, they ordered the missionaries out, but the Europeans refused to go. Under cover of darkness the men of the other pueblos struck. They swept down on Awatovi, setting fire to everything that would burn and smashing everything that would not. Worst of all was the killing. Christian and non-Christian alike were victims. Before a day was out, nearly 700 bodies—of men, women, and children—lay in the smoldering ruins.

By now the Spaniards had begun to learn from their bitter experiences. They no longer made any serious effort to convert the Hopis. Still, the Hopis' resistance to the white man did not abate. Even three-quarters of a century later when a Franciscan missionary, Friar Francisco Garces, made his way into Oraibi, traveling alone and seeking only to be friends, the villagers would not speak to him, or give him shelter in their homes, or sell him corn. For two nights they permitted him to sleep in the streets. But on the morning of the third day a deputation of chiefs ordered him to leave the pueblo, and a crowd of silent villagers escorted him to the edge of the mesa. The date of this quiet declaration of independence was July 4, 1776.

The World of Oraibi

Oraibi was located atop the mesa, and to reach the farming and hunting areas the men had to make their way down 600 feet of steep cliff, along narrow trails cut into the crevices and breaks in the red-brown sandstone. Once in the desert, some farmers still had long walks ahead of them. Each household grew its own crops—corn, beans, squash—on plots assigned it by the village chief. Every household had several fields for each crop. The Hopis' irrigation system was rudimentary, and basically they depended on the uncertain rainfall and seepage from the mesa slopes to water their crops. Thus they had to sow seeds in several carefully selected areas to be reasonably certain that some plants would survive and grow. A trip to tend and weed the scattered fields could take an entire day.

The men also hunted. Their quest was as much for clothing materials as for food, even though much of the Hopis' wardrobe was made of cotton. The men's short kilts and the women's calf-length blankets, which they wore draped under the left arm and tied to the right shoulder, were of cotton cloth. But the leggings worn by both sexes were of deerskin, and the men frequently used deerskin for their breechclouts. Rabbit fur was favored by men for the headbands that held down their bangs and for tying the long hair gathered in a knot at the backs of their necks.

The hunt was a sacred act as well as a search for food and clothing. Hopi legend gave the animals an equal place with man in the plan of creation, and animals' lives could not be taken without the appropriate rituals and propitiations. A man who wanted to organize a hunting party first descended into the kiva to make his prayer offerings to the patron deities of the game. Thereafter, the village crier called out the details of the event to the entire pueblo—when it would take place and what animal would be hunted—so that any men who wanted to could join. Then the entire hunting party retired to the kiva to make prayer offerings and to smoke the ritual pipe, blowing the smoke in the direction they planned to take: the fumes would, so tradition told them, confuse their prey and make it easier to catch. Now the hunt had been sanctified, and it could begin.

The game sought was deer. The time for hunting rabbit would come later, when the crops were in full bloom and no longer needed care. The hunting party moved across the desert quietly, seeking out its prey. For a long time they found nothing. Then, suddenly, a deer appeared, and the hunters crept toward it, forming themselves into a circle, surrounding the animal, and shooting their arrows at it. As the wounded deer darted this way and that, searching frantically for safety, the hunters closed in to club the dying animal.

A few of the older men, no longer up to the rigors of farming or of the hunt, had remained in the village while the others were away. But their age did not keep them from working. Weaving was men's work among the Hopis, and it was up to every man to supply all his family's clothing. The men gathered the cotton, carded it, and spun it into thread; the women dyed it in bold colors—yellow, orange, green, black, and red—extracted from native plants. The younger men usually did their weaving in the winter, when the fields lay fallow. But the older men could work at the craft at any time of year. Tall looms were all over the village—hanging from the inside walls of the kivas and from both the inside and outside walls of the houses. On a summer day such as this one, it was much more pleasant to work outdoors. The weaver could feel the warm sun on his body and watch the bustling streets of the village around him, where children were playing and a number of women were cooking in the open-air ovens.

Other women were on the roofs busy at basketry. Basketmaking was a woman's task, and women of different pueblos fashioned their baskets by a variety of weaving methods. Here at Oraibi, baskets were often woven of wicker, a form of weaving for which this pueblo was famous. The weaver first laid one group of sumac twigs side by side and then placed a similar group at right angles over it. Then she wove the supple branches of a desert plant called rabbit brush in and out among the overlaid twigs, giving form to the vessel as she wove. Some of the strips of rabbit brush were dyed the same colors that were used for cotton. With this assortment of materials the basketmaker was able

Surrounded by bowls and plates, the master Hopi potter Nampeyo displays the best of her work in 1901 for Adam Clark Vroman, photographer of Hopi life. Among the most delicate of Nampeyo's designs is the large bowl in the arrangement at right. Resolved to rebuild the tradition of Hopi pottery, Nampeyo taught her skill to her daughters. The small, double-spouted wedding vase at immediate right was made by her daughter Fannie in 1975, and the pot at the far right, fashioned by Nampeyo herself, was painted by her child Annie. The daughters, in turn, trained their own children. The exquisite bowl at the front and center of the arrangement is the work of Nampeyo's granddaughter Leah, who is now passing on the skills to her children.

A Renaissance in Hopi Art Generated by the Work of a Master Potter

It was the summer of 1895 when American archeologist–anthropologist J. Walter Fewkes—to whom we owe most of our knowledge of Hopi life before contact with Europeans—began excavating the remains of the pueblo of Sikyatki, in northeast Arizona. According to Hopi accounts the village was destroyed during a dispute, probably over land and water rights between its residents and those of the pueblo of Walpi, a few miles away. By Fewkes' calculations the disaster that struck Sikyatki took place in the 14th century, at a time when the Hopis were producing, as he put it, "the best painted ware of prehistoric North America." The forms were simple, functional, and elegantly proportioned. The designs, painted in red, brown, and black on light yellow-brown clay, some-

times covered both insides and outsides of the pieces. These patterns were bold, lively, and rich with symbolism.

Among Fewkes' assistants at the excavation was a Tewa Indian whose wife, Nampeyo, was part Hopi. As a child Nampeyo had learned the potter's art from her grandmother, and she was highly accomplished in the making of contemporary Hopi pottery. But when her husband brought home shards of Sikyatki pottery, Nampeyo immediately realized that the bowls and pitchers she made were markedly inferior to those fashioned by her remote ancestors. Determined to restore Hopi pottery to its ancient beauty, Nampeyo began visiting the excavation site and studying the pottery forms and designs found there so that she might duplicate them. At

first her pieces were entirely imitative, but soon she allowed her imagination to take over. "I used to go to the ancient village . . . and copy the designs," she once said. "But now I just close my eyes and see designs and I paint them."

Thanks to the patronage of Fewkes and others, Nampeyo and her work soon became well known in the world outside the Hopi domains. In 1898 she and her husband journeyed to Chicago to demonstrate her pottery-making techniques at an exposition. Thereafter, for some 15 years, she worked at other expositions and major fairs. By 1915, however, Nampeyo's eyesight began to deteriorate, and by 1920 she was nearly blind. Though she could no longer paint, she still shaped pottery while her daughters decorated the wares.

Acoma, New Mexico (above), is possibly the oldest continuously inhabited settlement in the United States. The Acoma Indians had the same ancestors as other Pueblo peoples but speak a language common to only a few pueblos. They also have a distinctive pottery-making style. The bowls are unusually strong yet thin-walled, their surfaces satin-smooth and gently and evenly curved from base to rim. Acoma pottery is highly decorated, either with geometric or representational forms. Shown here are 19th-century examples of both decorative styles.

to weave intricate designs rich with symbolism into her work.

Basket-weaving provided many of the necessities of daily life: containers for corn, trays and platters, the hampers in which the crops were carried from the fields, the headguards at the top of the cradleboards in which all Hopi infants spent the first three months of their lives. Basketry had its place in ceremonial life, too: specially designed plaques and baskets formed an important part of the three religious ceremonies—Lakon, Marau, and Owaqlt—that were controlled by women.

Roofs were also used for pottery-making, another woman's task. The potter dug up the clay from a large deposit nearby. Then she carried the clay back to the village, where she soaked and kneaded it until it was the right consistency, sometimes adding specks of sandstone for strength. When the mixture felt right to the touch, she was ready to begin. First she patted the circular base into shape, then she rolled small lumps of clay back and forth between the palms of her hands until they formed long coils. These she laid one atop another, shaping the vessel as she went and pinching and smoothing the seams between coils until they disappeared. When she had finished, she set the pot to dry. Later she would fire it, and it would then be ready for use.

Women were at work on still another roof, spreading ears of corn in a long row to sun so that they would remain dry and safe from ground insects. This corn had been harvested the year before. Every household tried to keep at least one year's supply of corn in reserve in case the next year's harvest should be poor. One room in every house was piled high with neat stacks of ears, in all the brilliant colors of the Hopi

corn—white, red, and yellow, and a purple so dark and gleaming that it seemed almost black.

Although the men planted and harvested the crops, they belonged to the women, who owned the seeds of everything the Hopis grew. Women also ground the grain and cooked the food. Along a wall in one of the rooms of every house were the metates—the grinding boards—stone slabs fixed slantwise into stone-lined troughs sunk into the floor. A household had at least three metates, each of a progressively smoother texture, and the corn was passed from one to the next until it had been ground as fine as possible. Every day, in one house or another, the women and girls of the family knelt at the trough, scooping up the corn, spreading it on the metate, and rubbing it vigorously with the mano, the oblong grinding stone. They talked and sang as they worked, and occasionally they patted some meal on their faces to absorb the sweat.

Once the corn was ground to the desired fineness, it was placed on a flat basketry tray and shaped carefully into a conical heap. Now it was ready to be turned into piki, the paper-thin bread that was the Hopis' staple. Piki could be eaten by itself, but it was most delicious when dipped into a stew made of squash, beans, wild sagebrush, milkweed, watercress, and some dandelions. When hunting was good, rabbit or deer meat was added to the pot.

Piki was made from a thin batter of cornmeal, water, and wood ash, and baked on a greased slab of sandstone, called a duma, heated from below by a fire. The baker would dip her hand into the batter and quickly spread it over the stone. In a moment the piki was baked, ready to be lifted off the stone between thumb and forefinger and rolled into a cylinder that soon became so crisp it crackled when eaten.

A Skilled Potter, An Ancient Art

Santana Antonio (right), one of the most skilled of Acoma's potters, learned her art in school from a white teacher who had made an intensive study of traditional techniques and designs. Santana's work, therefore, is a modern variant of an old tradition. She begins by soaking dried clay to a proper consistency, then mixes it with ground fragments of ancient pots, before rotating it swiftly in her hands to shape a base.

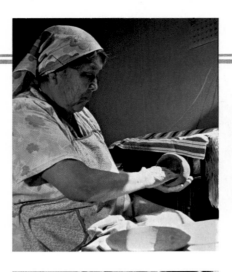

Next she rolls chunks of tempered clay into long, thin coils that will be used to form the sides of the pot.

Now she joins a coil to the base, smoothing the juncture with her fingers and a paddle and thinning the walls.

As new coils are attached, Santana forms the pot, deftly pressing it into the graceful shape that yields maximum strength.

After the shaped pot has partially dried, Santana scrapes its surface with a sardine can to give it uniformly thin walls.

She applies the slip—a mixture of clay and water—then rubs the pot to a high sheen with a smooth piece of flint.

Traditional designs, modified by Santana's imagination, emerge from her yucca-strand brush and black paint.

Finally, she adds color to the design, polishing each section with a rag. The yellow-orange color is traditional at Acoma.

When the pot is completed, Santana lets it dry for several days before firing it. The firing oven (left) is built on a layer of dried cow or sheep dung and topped with old pottery fragments on which the new pot is placed. Additional fragments are then placed around the pot, and then more dung is added to cover everything (above). The fire is usually set in the morning, when winds are minimal and will not fan the flames unevenly or make them too high. Still there is a risk, and Santana is nervous on firing day and watches the fire for about an hour and a half. When the fire is reduced to ashes, it is knocked apart; the pot emerges and is set aside to cool. It will probably be used for storage of corn, flour, or water. If used for water, the thin, porous walls will permit tiny amounts of moisture to seep through and evaporate, thus lowering the temperature of the liquid inside.

It took great skill to bake piki—to know just when the duma and the grease had reached precisely the right temperature, and to spread the grease and the batter so quickly that the cook would not burn her hand. It took a proper duma as well, made of a special sandstone brought from a quarry more than 10 miles from the community. The duma was smoothed by grinding with coarse gravel. Then it was polished with cottonseed oil, heated and seasoned with piñon sap and then treated with an oil. Her duma was one of a woman's proudest and most valued possessions, to be handed down from one generation to the next.

Far down the street other Hopis were busy adding a new room onto one of the dwellings. The men had already done their part of this task. They had brought the stones—quarried from the mesa—and the heavy wooden roof beams to the building site. They had also performed the rituals that consecrated the new addition, sprinkling sacred cornmeal to mark its outline and placing eagle feathers at the corners of the house. Then the men dressed the stones and set them in place, while the women filled in the chinks between them with mud. When the walls had reached their proper

Zuni pottery, painted in red and black on a white background, has several characteristic motifs. The deer, white-rumped and with a red "heart line," is among the most popular with collectors.

height, the men heaved the roof beams into place. Women then plastered the inside walls with mud and finished off the roof, covering the beams with grass and brushwood and a final coat of mud.

The Spaniards had introduced the Hopis to one innovation the Indians found acceptable. Before the Europeans came, a Hopi home had only a ventilator shaft in the wall or a hole in the ceiling as a vent for smoke from an indoor fire. Now the Hopis made chimneys, knocking the bottoms out of cooking pots and piling them one atop another. The pots were fixed together with a mud plaster, and the finished chimney inserted through one of the two holes in the roof. The second hole served as an entrance: Hopi dwellings had no windows or doors to the outside; one entered through the roof.

The kivas were the men's domain, the houses were the women's. Just as they owned the seeds, the women owned the dwelling places—and they ruled them. Among the Hopis, descent was reckoned through the mother. Children—boys and girls alike—belonged to their mother's clan, and men moved into their wives' homes when they married. In every house were moth-

The pueblos are the homes of several different peoples with varying pottery styles. The double-spouted black wedding jar (above left) comes from Santa Clara; San Ildefonso is represented by the large water vase bearing a bird design, the prayer-meal bowl with a serpent motif, and the geometrically decorated plate to its right. A Laguna potter made the rounded bowl in the rear; the one in front, with its fanciful animal forms, was made at Tesuque; and the two with birds and flowers come from Zia.

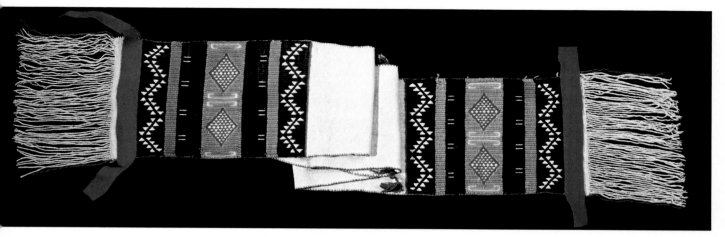

ers, daughters, granddaughters, and all their husbands and children. Hopi households were always overflowing their space, and more rooms were constantly being added. This particular room was being built because one of the women of the household had recently given birth and the house was already overcrowded.

The birth had occurred three weeks earlier. From the moment she knew she was pregnant, the young mother had prepared herself with great care. Daily, she had prayed to the sun, and all during her pregnancy she had worn her hair loose and carefully kept it free of knots, just as she had been careful to see there were no knots in her clothing. A knot would "tie up" the baby she bore inside her. She had been careful, too, never to look at a snake or even think of one, lest the baby be twisted inside her and come into the world feet first.

With all these precautions she felt no fear when her labor pains began. Then, accompanied by her mother and other clan women, she retired to a room in the house, taking some sacred cornmeal with her. There she prayed until, with the assistance of her attendants, she brought her baby into the world. The grandmother severed the cord. This birth had been especially joyous: the baby was a girl—another woman to carry on the line. Her father would not see her until she was 20 days old. Until then—and possibly for as long as 40 days—he would sleep in his kiva. But the father's mother was introduced to her grandchild very early. Once the maternal grandmother had finished her chores, the paternal grandmother arrived to wash the baby's head and to take charge of preparations for the naming ceremony and the feast.

These events took place 20 days after the baby's birth. That morning, at dawn, the new young Hopi was set properly on the Road of Life, symbolized by the cornmeal that the father sprinkled in a path as the naming party carried her to the edge of the mesa. There her father's mother and her mother prayed over the child, presented her to the rising sun, and bestowed a name on her.

Hopi children were loved and cared for, but they were not coddled. Laziness was a disgrace, and although the children had ample time for play, they were introduced to adult work at an early age. Small boys

A Hopi weaver (below) *plies his craft on a loom suspended from a high beam in his home. This type of loom is mostly used to make such items as wool or cotton blankets or the larger articles of clothing. For smaller items, such as the intricately patterned ceremonial sash above, or belts, garters, and headbands, the weaver uses a special loom that is also suspended from a high beam, but the other end is attached to his waist, forcing him to sit in one position while working in order to keep the device taut. Among the Hopis the only weaving done by women is the fashioning of rabbit-fur robes.*

accompanied their fathers on the long trip down the cliffsides and were taught to farm and hunt. At home the boys learned to weave. Small girls helped their mothers—taking care of infants and learning how to grind corn, bake piki, weave baskets, and make pottery.

When they were eight or nine, both boys and girls were initiated into the mysteries of religion as members of Kachina cults. Sometime between the ages of 16 and 20 girls passed through a four-day ceremony of grinding corn in a darkened room, from which they emerged with their hair in two fat buns above their ears—the squash-blossom hairdress that signified they were of marriageable age.

The boys' puberty ceremony was more elaborate, involving tests of strength and courage as well as a mock battle between some of the grown men and the initiates. In this encounter the youngsters were always victorious, their triumph symbolizing their readiness for full tribal membership.

An adolescent boy could now sleep in the kiva and, if he so chose, leave it during the night, wrapped in a blanket and bound for a dumaiya—a tryst with the girl of his choice. Silently, while everyone else in her house was sleeping, he would make his way down the ladder and creep to her side. If she liked him, she would welcome him into her arms, where he could remain until shortly before the household awoke. All Oraibi's young people had dumaiyas—usually with more than one partner. Sometimes, of course, a girl would become pregnant. There was, however, no shame attached to her condition. She had only to choose her favorite among her several lovers, name him as the probable

This Hopi tray, bearing the image of a kachina doll, is used to hold food. It was made by wrapping stems of Hilaria grass with thin strips of yucca leaves. The yucca was also used as thread to sew the concentric coils together.

father, and the two would be married. Parents objected to these practices only if they considered the dumaiya partner an unsuitable candidate for marriage.

One stricture was inviolate, however: the boy and girl should never be members of the same clan. Mating with someone in the same maternal line of descent was sacrilege—a sacrilege so serious that the thought of it should never even cross young people's minds.

Once the match had been decided on, the girl went to the boy's home, to remain there for three days and demonstrate such household skills as grinding corn for her prospective mother-in-law. As the girl worked in the house, a mock fight went on just outside. The boy's paternal aunts pelted his mother and sisters with mud and taunted them for permitting this snip of a girl to carry off their nephew. The next day, with the taunting continuing, the girl came out of the house. Together, bride and groom had their hair washed in a single basin, a ceremony symbolizing the mingling of their lives. Then the two young people made their way to the edge of the mesa to solemnize their union by offering prayers to the sun. When they finished praying, they returned to the groom's house, where the bride's mother dressed the girl's hair in the braids, the style she would wear all her life except during pregnancy.

For the next several weeks the couple remained in the groom's house, while the young man, helped by his friends and family, wove a marriage costume for his bride. He spun the cotton and then wove it into two blankets and a white-fringed belt, and made his wife a set of white leggings and a pair of white moccasins.

The squash-blossom hairdo (left), symbol of female maturity, is worn by marriageable Hopi girls. But before they are permitted to assume this coiffure, they must demonstrate their mastery of women's skills by grinding corn into meal for four days. Then their hair is arranged in the squash blossom, a style that takes much dexterity to produce. First the hair is brushed and parted in the center (near right) and separated into two long locks, each of which is then wound over a U-shaped bow (center). A complex series of steps follows in which separate locks of hair are interwoven. The entire process is time-consuming. Often it can take as long as an hour before all of the strands of hair are in place, as in the picture at the far right.

A Hopi dwelling *has a single room divided into storage (left) and work areas (right rear), while the smooth, clay floor serves for sleeping. The walls are of adobe; the ceiling, of brush, grass,* *and mud supported by heavy beams. Though wood is scarce in the Hopi area, such beams last for centuries. When a Hopi builds a new home, he often salvages the beams from the old.*

Only when the costume was finished did the couple move away from the boy's house to the one they would occupy for the rest of their lives—the home of the bride's mother.

The girl wore her marriage costume as they walked to her house. She wore it once again during the first summer of her life as a married woman, when she watched the dance of the Niman Kachina—the first important ceremonial she was permitted to attend after her marriage. But when the Niman Kachina dance was over, she laid the marriage costume away in a basket. She was never again to wear it—until her burial.

For the Hopis, death was part of the recurring cycle of life—another emergence from one world into the next—and the ceremonies that accompanied it were the simplest of all the Hopi rituals. A man's body was wrapped in a deerskin, a woman's in her marriage costume, and a cotton mask, symbol of the rain cloud, was laid over the face. Then the body was placed in a sitting position, with the head bowed between the knees. The corpse was carried out along the mesa to the spot

221

where a rude grave had been dug. No one spoke as the body was lowered into the grave, as a bowl of food was placed on a nearby rock, and as the burial party made its way back to the pueblo. For four days the women of the household mourned, visiting the grave daily and placing bowls of food and feathered prayer sticks on it. Then the women returned to their lives in the village, and the soul of the deceased emerged into the World Below—there to live among the kachinas.

In the World Below, where they lived for half the year, the kachinas were pure spirit. But during the six months they were on earth—from the winter to the summer solstice—they assumed material form and inhabited the bodies of the kachina impersonators. Whenever the impersonators wore their kachina masks and costumes, these men—for the impersonators were never women—felt themselves to *be* kachinas, imbued with the qualities of these supernatural beings including all their power to intercede on behalf of the Hopis with their gods. It was always important for a Hopi to "keep a good heart"—to have only pure thoughts and to avoid quarrels—but it was essential when he was taking the part of a kachina. To be in any way immoderate or intemperate at that time, or to fail to observe the ritual fasts and the ban on sexual activity, would be to violate a sacred tradition.

Hopi children learned about the kachinas early in life. Among their most precious possessions were wooden kachina dolls, carved, painted, and costumed by the men. By the time they were old enough to toddle, the children had been introduced to kachina impersonators—beautiful ones who gave them presents when they were good, frightful-looking impersonators who threatened them when they were bad. But not until they were about eight and were initiated into the Kachina cults did the children learn who the kachinas really were. The initiation ceremonies were held during the Powamu (February) festival.

The children sat on the floor of a kiva, the boys on one side and the girls on the other, and the Powamu (Kachina Chief) chanted a long song that told the story of the Hopis' emergence from the underworld. After being sprinkled with water, each child was touched by the chief four times with ears of corn.

Terror in the Kiva

When the last child had been thus blessed, the ordeal began. The ritual began with a terrible noise from above the kiva—a frightful, eerie howling and a great rattling of the cover over the kiva entrance. Then the ladder leading into the kiva began to tremble violently, and one by one three grotesque figures carrying yucca whips made their way down it. The first was Angwu-shahaií, the Whipper Mother Kachina, wearing a turquoise helmet mask, her face an inverted triangle and her ears two black crow wings. Behind her came the two whippers, the Hu' kachinas, their bodies painted black with white dots. They wore only red kilts and black masks fitted with carved horns, bulging eyes, bared teeth, and long black-and-white-striped beards.

One by one the children were led by their ceremonial sponsors—usually family friends who were not members of the clans of the true mother and father—to the center of the kiva, to stand on a sand painting of these very kachinas. The whippers, urged on by the Whipper Mother, took turns flogging the boys and girls. Each child received four lashes. When all initiates had undergone this ordeal, the Hu' kachinas whipped each other as the children watched. Then the Kachina Chief gave presents of cornmeal and sacred feathers to the boys and girls and, that rite completed, all went home to an elaborate feast.

The next morning brought the initiation to a close. At daybreak each child prayed to the sun, and each was given a ceremonial name. Then all the children were taken back to the kiva for the climax of the ceremony—the moment they were permitted to learn that the kachinas inhabited the bodies of ordinary men. There in the kiva, as they watched in astonishment, the Powamu kachinas danced for them—unmasked. Now that they knew this holy secret, which they were sworn never to reveal, the boys had the right to become kachina impersonators themselves one day.

Just as the women dominated the Hopi households, the men dominated the religious and ceremonial life of the village. Because religion was at the very heart of all Hopi activities, the men were also responsible for the

A variety of Hopi musical instruments includes a pebble-filled gourd rattle (lower left) and a three-piece device consisting of a lamb's scapula, a notched stick, and a hollow gourd. To produce a resonant, rasping sound, the scapula is rubbed on the stick held against the gourd. The wooden bull-roarer (upper right) produces a moan when twirled in the air by its string. Such instruments are used to accompany chants and dances.

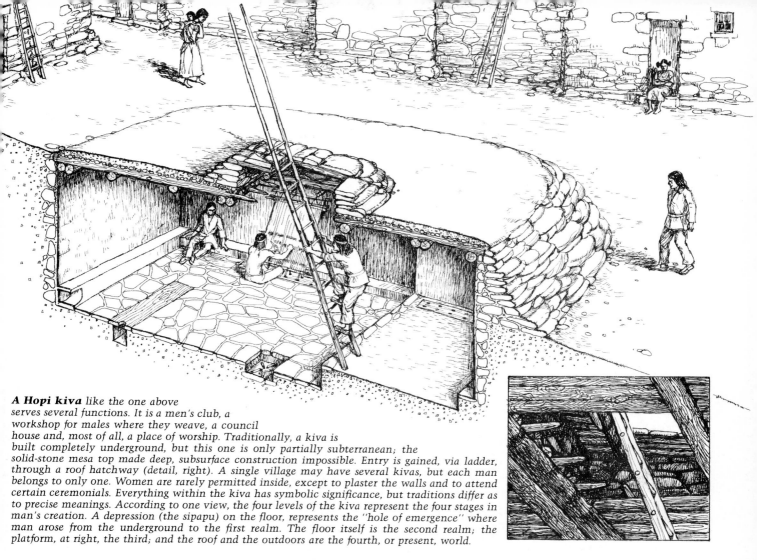

A Hopi kiva like the one above
serves several functions. It is a men's club, a
workshop for males where they weave, a council
house and, most of all, a place of worship. Traditionally, a kiva is
built completely underground, but this one is only partially subterranean; the
solid-stone mesa top made deep, subsurface construction impossible. Entry is gained, via ladder,
through a roof hatchway (detail, right). A single village may have several kivas, but each man
belongs to only one. Women are rarely permitted inside, except to plaster the walls and to attend
certain ceremonials. Everything within the kiva has symbolic significance, but traditions differ as
to precise meanings. According to one view, the four levels of the kiva represent the four stages in
man's creation. A depression (the sipapu) on the floor, represents the "hole of emergence" where
man arose from the underground to the first realm. The floor itself is the second realm; the
platform, at right, the third; and the roof and the outdoors are the fourth, or present, world.

organization of projects that involved the entire pueblo. The chiefs of the kivas and of the many religious and healing societies were all men, as were the ceremonial and religious chiefs of the clans.

The clan was the fundamental unit of pueblo society. Every aspect of village life was organized around it, from living arrangements to the most sacred ceremonies, and it was to the clan that every Hopi felt his deepest loyalty. The mother-daughter households were, in fact, clan households, and a man's true home was not his wife's house, where he lived, but the house of his mother, from whom he took his clan membership. Moreover, he owed more responsibility to his sister's child than he did to his own: he and his sister's child were members of the same clan, while he and his own child were not. When a chief died or became too old or sick to carry out his responsibilities, the office went to a member of his clan, selected by a council of the heads of ceremonial associations.

The senior chief of the village presided over the Council of Chiefs, which guided the affairs of the pueblo. That man was the chief of the Bear clan. According to legend, the Bear clan had been the first to arrive at the mesa on which Oraibi was built. The other clans came later—the Badger, the Parrot, the Eagle, the Snake, the Antelope—each bringing its sacred objects

and its special powers, as important to the rest of the village as to the clan in whose control they lay.

The Badger clan, for example, assumed particular importance at the time of Niman Kachina in July. The badger is associated with roots, medicine, and plant growth, and the medicine chiefs who danced in the ceremony were Badger clansmen. But the Badger clan's importance did not give it control of the Niman ceremony. Each kiva in the village took its turn at sponsoring the yearly dance.

The first steps were taken long in advance of Niman, at the time of the winter solstice in December. At that time the kiva chief and his most trusted associate retired to the kiva to prepare themselves spiritually for the great events to come. They carried a heavy responsibility. The fate of the entire village might be determined by the care and devotion with which Niman was carried out. For four days they smoked and prayed and carefully fashioned the many prayer sticks necessary for the ceremony.

The next important step came in early spring, when the men of the village went to gather the eaglets that would be sacrificed at the end of Niman. They had already scouted the cliffsides to find the eagles' nests and had planted prayer sticks near them. These sticks were requests that the noble birds come willingly to the

223

A theatrical set forms part of the Horned Water Serpent Dance ("Palulukonti"), a Hopi ceremonial performed to ensure rain for a good harvest. The props include a screen ornately decorated with symbolic figures and designs. Projecting from the screen are several effigies of horned water serpents. They are fashioned from wooden hoops covered with cloth and are manipulated from behind by unseen men. These men cause the serpents to "dance" and knock over the plants in a miniature cornfield in front of the screen, an action symbolizing the ripeness and abundance of the harvest. Meanwhile, two men in clowns' masks entertain the audience. A third celebrant, dressed in the costume and mask of Ha-hai-i-wuh-ti, the mother of all kachinas, feeds sacred cornmeal to the snakes.

village, there to live happily until their spirits were released. Now that spring had come, the men again scaled the steep cliff ledges to capture the eaglets. These they brought back to the village, where they tied them by one foot to special platforms built on the pueblo roofs. Daily, young boys fed the birds on lizards and mice caught in the desert below the pueblo.

There was another daily task, this one performed by the Sun Watcher, who observed the course of the sun as it traveled northward past Oraibi to Towaki, the Summer Sun House. When it reached this point, the summer solstice would have arrived, and with it the time to begin Niman—the celebration of the return of the kachinas to the World Below. As this day neared, the pace of preparations quickened. From then until

Blowing smoke on prayer sticks, *a Hopi Antelope priest makes a sacrifice to the spirits. A prayer stick ("paho") consists of two bound stakes, one representing a female, the other a male. A human face is often painted on one end of the stick.*

the night immediately preceding the dance, the men spent all their nights in the kiva, smoking, praying, practicing their songs, making prayer sticks, and decorating their kachina masks.

Any of the hundreds of Hopi kachinas could take part in Niman, but the Hemis Kachina—the Far Away Kachina—was most likely to be chosen, both because the name described the realms to which the kachinas were now returning and because its mask and costume carried all the symbols of rain and a bountiful harvest. The mask had white dots on it, signifying rain, and was painted blue and yellow for the sun and the clouds. The top of the mask was a terraced wooden tablet, its top cloud-blue and decorated with tufts of wild grass and eagle-tail feathers to symbolize the sun. At the bottom of the tablet, just above the kachina's face, a rainbow was painted along with a butterfly or a frog. Around his throat the Hemis kachina wore a ruff of spruce branches. There was more spruce at his wrist, at the belt of his kilt, and on his blue armbands, and he carried a twig of spruce and a downy feather in his left hand. He wore no clothing save his kilt and moccasins, and his entire body was blackened with burnt corn as a prayer for rain to wash off the black. The only decorations on his body were the white marks of brotherhood—two on his back and two on his chest.

The Hemis Kachina-Mana, who represented the female spirit, also took part in the ceremony—though the male always took her role. Her mask was orange, and her hair was dressed in the squash-blossom whorls of a Hopi maiden. Under her white blanket she wore a black one, on her feet were white buckskin moccasins, and in her hands she carried her musical instruments—a gourd, a notched stick, and the scapula bone of a deer.

Now that the masks and costumes were ready, the

sacred spruce had to be gathered and brought back to the village. On the 18th day of Niman, three days before the ceremony, runners were selected to make this pilgrimage. Each was given special prayer sticks to carry with him, for the journey was long and full of spiritual danger. It involved much more than merely cutting down the trees. The men had first to go to Kisiwu, the Spring in the Shadows, which was hidden in a cave atop a rocky ridge about 20 miles from Oraibi. It took a full day of exhausting travel to make the journey across the sands and rocks. When the men arrived, they made camp for the night.

The next morning, after placing prayer sticks beside the stream, they made their first approach to the spruce trees that dotted the side of the ridge. Standing in front of one of them, the leader of the expedition announced its purpose. "*Salavi*," he said, "we have come to get your leaves for our clothes, so come with us," and he and his companions blessed the tree and planted prayer feathers in payment. Then they gathered the necessary boughs and shrubs. Carrying the greenery with them, they returned to the spring to discover, by examining the prayer sticks they had left there, whether things would go well or ill for their people. If the prayer sticks were still standing firm and straight, the omens were good for the village, but if any of the sticks had fallen, the future was ominous. The men who had made the prayer sticks had not kept a good heart, and their impure thoughts could endanger the entire village. (When the pilgrims returned to Oraibi, they would speak to these men so that they could correct their ways.)

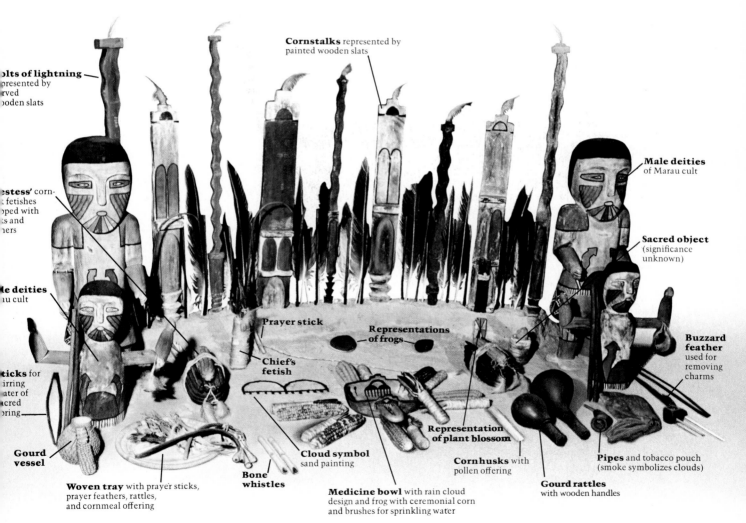

Bolts of lightning represented by carved wooden slats

Cornstalks represented by painted wooden slats

Male deities of Marau cult

Priestess' corn-ear fetishes topped with sticks and feathers

Sacred object (significance unknown)

Male deities of Marau cult

Prayer stick

Representations of frogs

Buzzard feather used for removing charms

Sticks for stirring water of sacred spring

Chief's fetish

Representation of plant blossom

Gourd vessel

Cloud symbol sand painting

Cornhusks with pollen offering

Pipes and tobacco pouch (smoke symbolizes clouds)

Bone whistles

Woven tray with prayer sticks, prayer feathers, rattles, and cornmeal offering

Medicine bowl with rain cloud design and frog with ceremonial corn and brushes for sprinkling water

Gourd rattles with wooden handles

An altar of the Hopi Marau Society, like the altars of the tribe's other cults, displays symbols associated with rain and nature's abundance. Traditionally, these symbols—such as the wood slabs representing corn stalks; the zigzag sticks, lightning; and the figures, deities—were placed on a bed of cornmeal on which a design of a rain cloud had been drawn. Celebrants offered up prayer sticks, tobacco smoke, and cornmeal to the spirits. The rattles were used in ritual singing and dancing.

225

Then, carrying the boughs and the shrubs in sacks, the party started on the long and difficult walk to Oraibi, arriving late in the day before the Niman dance. The spruce shrubs would be planted in the plaza, and the branches prepared for the kachinas to wear.

Now the kisonvi—the plaza in front of the kiva—had to be prepared for the ceremony. The men painted their bodies with ritual markings, donned their kachina costumes, and then went out to the plaza to lay paths of sacred cornmeal and place prayer sticks in honor of the sun. They also dug holes in which to place the sacred trees. (Toward the end of the Niman dance they would remove these trees and use them in the ceremonial.) All this accomplished, the men quietly left the village and made their way to a shrine a short distance off. For the rest of the night they prayed and smoked. Before dawn they had donned their kachina masks and were ready to begin.

A Vital Ceremony

By dawn the plaza was already massed with people. It had not been easy for anyone to sleep that night. Niman was a crucial time for every Hopi: the whole of the harvest depended on it. As soon as the first rays of light appeared, the kachina procession began its march toward the village. The Kachina Chief was at its head and behind him were two members of the Powamu kiva who had been designated Fathers of the Kachinas. Then came the long line of kachinas, single file, unearthly in their majesty. The Hemis kachinas came first, 30 or more of them, in their kilts and gorgeous masks, with rattles in their right hands and rattles tied to their knees. Then came about eight beautiful "maidens"—female impersonators in the roles of the Hemis kachina-manas. Silently, the kachinas arranged themselves on the plaza—first the long line of Hemis kachinas and behind them the shorter line of kachina-manas. The Powamu Chief went from one to the next, blessing each with sacred cornmeal taken from a sack around his neck. Then the Kachina Chief spoke to them, encouraging them in their holy work, and the leader of the dancers, standing in the middle of the first line, shook his rattle—the signal for the dance to begin.

Now the two lines began to move and to turn, each dancer stamping his feet, shaking his rattle, and singing the special songs composed for the occasion. Each line moved separately, the kachina-manas turning in the opposite direction from the kachinas. The dance was repeated many times throughout the day.

When the kachinas had entered the plaza, they had brought their presents with them—the first ears of corn, fruit, basketry plaques, bows and arrows, kachina dolls, and trays heaped high with piki, made in all the rainbow colors of the Hopi corn. In the afternoon they distributed these gifts.

After the third dance had reached its conclusion, one of the Kachina Fathers (continued on page 230)

Kachinas: Deities and Guardians of Pueblo Life

At the center of Hopi and Zuni spiritual life are the kachi supernatural beings with vast powers to confer prosperit the form of abundant harvests. For part of the year the chinas live as disembodied spirits in their own land in vastnesses of the San Francisco Peaks of Arizona. But w the winter solstice comes, they leave their homes and tr to the world of mortals, to take up residence within the ies of men, remaining there until the Niman Kachina fes in July.

In their corporeal manifestations the kachinas bring n needed rain, present gifts, and provide entertainment fo Indians. Because of their vast, life-or-death influence the affairs of men, kachinas are honored in ceremony a ceremony. Masked dancers, the kachina impersonators, believe themselves to be the embodiments of these spiri belief shared by other members of the tribe—lead the cele tions. In addition, wooden dolls, fashioned in the nesses of kachinas, are distributed to the children. These not meant to be playthings but objects to be treasured studied, enabling the young to learn to identify the n different kachinas and the roles they play.

Zuni kachina dolls *(above) are usually taller and thi than the Hopi dolls and are unable to stand without sup Shown here (left to right) are Wakaci Koko in a cow's Long Nose Ogre, and Shalaco Hemucikwe holding a bow.*

Kachina monsters (left) appear for the annual chastisement of children. The leader, Soyoko (fourth from right), dressed in a hideous mask and dark robe, carries a crook and a huge knife. Another menacing figure, in a black, long-billed mask, acts as her assistant. At each house they demand food from the children within, threatening to eat them if they do not comply. Though the monsters are appeased and, therefore, do no harm, they leave behind frightened children. Also in the group are two long-billed kachinas with saws that they scrape on house walls, and two Heheya kachinas carrying lariats to rope anyone refusing their demands.

A display of Hopi kachina dolls illustrates their varied forms. Sio Calako (inset, left) is derived from a Zuni kachina, a giant spirit nine feet tall. Tcutckutu (inset, right) is a clown noted for his gluttony. The others (left to right) are Tawa, associated with the sun; Natashka, who helps discipline erring children; Eototo, Chief of the Kachinas; Angwusnasomtaqa, the Crow Mother, whom some Hopis revere as the mother of all kachinas; and Ahote, a singer of sacred songs.

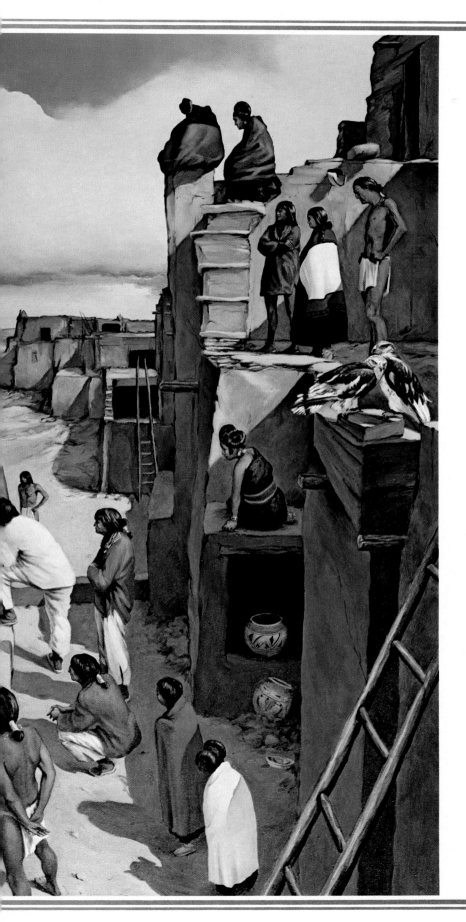

A Hopi Ritual to Bring the Rains

As clouds gather over distant mesas, bringing a promise of rain, members of the Hopi Hemis kachina cult perform the final ceremony of the Niman Kachina. This annual 16-day festival begins 5 days after the summer solstice and marks the departure of the benevolent, rainmaking kachinas to their mythical home in the San Francisco Peaks of Arizona. When the sun sets, they will leave the pueblo, not to return until the winter solstice, when they will once more live for six months among mortals.

Facing the spectators assembled on the dwellings are some of the officials of the ceremony. Behind them are two rows of kachina impersonators wearing masks. Though kachinas are of both sexes, their roles are always taken by men. The kachinas in the ornate wooden masks have rattles at their knees, carry spruce twigs and rattles in their hands, and are decorated with feathers and painted rainbows, all symbolic of rain. The female kachinas (last row) are less ornately attired and carry instruments for producing a resonant sound.

At this moment of the ceremony the kachinas have just finished their last dance, a foot-stomping, rattle-shaking step-in-place to bring cloudbursts. Now the kachinas must be blessed, given gifts, and sent on their journey. The kachina chief (between the two rows of impersonators) will approach each kachina, sprinkling him with sacred cornmeal, which is a prayer for rain, growth, and abundance. Another official, the Powamu chief (at far right, holding a bowl), will then spatter the kachinas with medicine water that connotes lifegiving rain. Then the tobacco chief will blow smoke at the kachinas, the smoke representing clouds. After these symbolic gestures have been made, the head women of the Kachina and Badger clans (first row, wearing squash-blossom hairdos) will bestow their blessings on the kachinas.

As the sun sets the final act occurs. The kachina fathers, standing by a kiva entrance, deliver their farewells to the departing spirits: "Around here our crops, our plants, are growing poorly. You will come soon to bring them drink. When they have drunk, when their children have grown . . . when . . . the little ones taste them they will surely be happy. Therefore, you will come soon to bring us drink."

spoke a farewell to the spirits now about to descend into the World Below:

"Now we have finished the day. This morning I told you that we were to have a good time here for this one day, but at the sunset you must go home to your parents as I promised you. Now the time has come, the sun has reached its place and I am tired, and you too may be tired.

"When you go home and get to your parents and sisters and the rest of your relatives who are waiting for you, tell them all the words that I am going to tell you. Tell them that they should not wait, but let them come at once and bring rain to our fields. We may have just a few crops in our fields, but when you bring the rain they will grow up and become strong. Then if you will bring some more rain on them we will have more corn, and more beans, and more watermelons, and all the rest of our crops. When harvest time comes we will have plenty of food for the whole winter.

"So now, this will be all," he concluded. "Now go back home happily, but do not forget us. Come to visit us as rain. That is all."

The leader of the dancers shook his rattle, a sign that

This carved buffalo head, *its beard of horsehair, was an altarpiece in a Zuni kiva. It appeared during the Shalako ceremonial inaugurating the new year.*

he accepted the Kachina Father's words. Silently, the kachinas and the kachina-manas formed into a line and walked through the narrow streets of the village to the edge of the mesa. Then they descended the mesa and vanished from sight.

The next day the final act of Niman was performed. The chiefs of each clan at Oraibi ascended to the roofs of the houses, where the eagles were tethered, and quietly snuffed out each bird's life, smothering it with a blanket. When its body became cold, each chief plucked the feathers of one of the eagles to use in prayers to the sun and in the making of prayer sticks. Then the birds were buried with sacred cornmeal, tobacco, piki, and prayer feathers in the eagle burial ground on the outskirts of the village. Each grave was marked by stones with a stick erect among them— the ladder on which the proud spirit of the eagle would descend into the World Below.

Now, after the months of preparation and the meticulous enactment of the rites, the Niman Kachina was completed. For the Hopis there was only the fervent hope that the spirits in the World Below would be pleased. If there was ample rain for the crops, the Hopis would know they had found favor with the spirits.

Wood and stone fetishes, such as these hanging from a storage pot (center), represent animals and plants sacred to the Zunis. The Zunis believed that animals and plants had the power to act as mediators between man and the forces controlling the universe. These powers also resided in representations of the living things, fetishes the Zunis decorated with symbolic markings as well as animal sinews and feathers. When fetishes were stored, offerings of cornmeal were regularly dropped into the storage pots.

A Zuni man prayed to his personal fetish before hunting, and every year an elaborate festival, the Day of the Council of the Fetishes, was held in the kivas. The fetishes were taken from their storage pots and arranged before an altar. For several hours the men chanted before the representations, after which the people participated in a great feast.

The Havasupais have made their home on the floor of Cataract Canyon, in present-day Arizona, for at least 900 years, living in peaceful isolation and adopting only those "modern" improvements—such as the wooden house in this photograph—that seemed to them to enhance their way of life. The tribe has always been small, numbering only 34 families in 1776.

People of the Blue-Green Water: The Canyon-Dwelling Havasupais

The land of the Havasupais, nestled deep in Cataract Canyon, a side branch of the Grand Canyon, is spectacularly beautiful and, unlike most of the Southwest, extremely fertile, thanks to the Colorado River. The river gives the Havasupais their name, for in their native tongue it means "People of the Blue-Green Water." Yet, according to legend, the Havasupais did not always live in their present home. They say that once they dwelled to the south and east, but warlike tribes drove them from their ancestral home and, eventually, they found refuge in the high-walled canyon. But all that was a long time ago. Archeological evidence indicates that the Havasupais have occupied Cataract Canyon since about A.D. 1100.

Their closest relatives in the area are the Walapais and the Yavapais, with whom the Havasupais share a common language. But unlike the Walapais and the Yavapais, who traditionally lived primarily by hunting and gathering, the Havasupais have long been farmers, irrigating their fields with water from the river and cultivating a wide range of crops—beans, squash, melons, sunflowers, corn, and tobacco. The Havasupais learned to farm from their neighbors to the south, the Hopis. Only late in the fall, after the harvest was in, did the Havasupais leave the security of their valley and climb the precipitous sandstone walls of the canyon to winter on the juniper-and-piñon-studded plateau. Here game was far more plentiful than in the valley, and the men hunted, stalking deer, antelopes, mountain sheep, wildcats, and mountain lions with bow and arrow. They also participated in relatively large hunting drives to chase down and kill rabbits.

Although the Havasupais did spend a portion of each year on the plateau, it was the valley they thought of as their true home. There they had their permanent dwellings—some of them rock shelters, dug out of the canyon walls; others, thatched and dirt-roofed houses, either circular or rectangular and built on a framework of poles. There, too, they had their sweat lodges—small, domed structures that served both as baths and as clubhouses. When there were no chores to do, the Havasupais could sit for hours in the sweat lodges, playing games and gossiping. Gossip was their most aggressive occupation, as important to Havasupai life as war was to some other tribes, for though these Indians had six hereditary chiefs, not one was a war leader. The Havasupais simply had no interest in combat and, fortunately, the steep walls of their canyon protected them from unfriendly tribes.

Life in the village was easy and informal. When a couple wanted to marry, for example, the young man simply moved into the home of the girl's family. In time, when children began to arrive, the husband would build a home near his parents, for it was from his father that he would inherit the land that afforded them their living.

Religion, too, was a relatively casual affair, though the men would neither hunt nor plant without first offering up prayers. Three times a year there were ceremonial dances, one of which was much like the Hopis' Kachina ceremonies. But the most important Havasupai celebration was primarily a social event. At harvest time they held a great dance to which neighbors from the area were invited. To the sound of chanting, stamping feet, drum beats, and the like, both the harvest and the Havasupais' skill as farmers were celebrated, the musical events being interrupted now and again with speeches by the chiefs and visiting dignitaries.

A **Pima basketmaker,** shown in this old photograph, uses an ancient coiling technique, winding willow around cattail. The designs were made from strands of devil's-claw plant. Some baskets were so large that weavers climbed inside to finish the interiors.

The Pimas and Papagos: Farmers of the Desert

Southern Arizona, near the present-day Mexican border, is the ancestral home of two closely related peoples, the Pimas and the Papagos. Because the Pimas' homeland, along the Salt and Gila Rivers, is more hospitable to man than the Papagos' domains deep in the desert, the two tribes exhibit some major differences in their ways of life. The rivers make irrigation possible, and the Pimas inherited a knowledge of irrigation farming from the two tribes' common ancestor, the Hohokams, who were using river water to irrigate their fields more than 2,000 years ago. Thus the Pimas were able to live in permanent villages the year round, where they raised crops of squash, corn, and beans. The Papagos, with no such water resource, were obliged to live as seminomads. They spent the summers in their "field villages" in the desert, where heavy rainstorms provided water that they collected in ditches to use on their crops of pumpkin, beans, and corn. In winter the Papagos moved to their "well villages" near springs in the mountains. There they depended mostly on the hunt for food.

In both tribes men were the farmers, women made pottery and baskets. Papago women also spent much time foraging the desert for seeds and other wild foods to eke out their scanty crops.

The settled life-style of the Pimas enabled them to develop a more complex social and political system. Each village had a chief, responsible for communal activities associated with farming and for organizing defense against Apache raiders. Village chiefs also elected a tribal chief from among themselves. Though the Papagos also had village chiefs, these had less authority, and as each village was autonomous, there was no chief for the tribe as a whole.

In several respects, however, there were great similarities in the ways the Pimas and Papagos lived. Both tribes were divided into two clans: the Red Ant and White Ant peoples among the Pimas; the Coyote and Buzzard among the Papagos. Children took clan membership from their fathers and, as marriage was permitted within the clan, many families in both tribes were composed entirely of members of one clan. The tribes shared two principal deities, Earthmaker and Elder Brother, and in every Pima and Papago village one man, designated Keeper of the Smoke, was ceremonial chief. Similarly, every fourth year both peoples held a harvest festival, the Viikita, in which the main performers were masked dancers and sacred clowns. But reflecting their constant need of water, the Papagos also had special rainmaking rituals. They made regular pilgrimages across the desert to the salt flats along the Gulf of California, where they prayed to the rain spirits that dwelt there, asking these deities to follow them home. And they held an annual summer ceremony that reached its climax in the ritual drinking of wine made from the fermented juice of the giant saguaro cactus fruit. The Papagos drank until they were reeling drunk, believing that this altered state of consciousness purified mind and heart, thus encouraging the rain spirits.

The giant saguaro cactus (above), native to Arizona, is especially prized by the Papagos for its sweet, fleshy fruit, which grows high on the trunk. It is eaten fresh or dried, and sometimes the dried fruit is ground into a powder and mixed with water. The fresh fruit is eaten raw as a candy, or boiled down into jam and syrup, some of which is later fermented to make a ritual wine. The men maintain a constant and careful watch over the fermentation process, and every night villagers dance and chant to ensure that the wine will be good.

To this day gathering the fruit remains primarily women's work. The Papago woman in this modern photograph uses a long pole called a kuibit—made from dried saguaro ribs—to knock down the ripe fruit. The fruit is gathered in a basket like the one below and taken back to the village to be eagerly devoured by young and old, who have patiently waited all year for this late spring and early summer harvest.

Sheep graze under the watchful eye of a Navajo herder. Although sheep were usually the property of Navajo women who, together with children, tended them, an old man, like the one above, might be pressed into service as a shepherd. The sheep flocks were driven to the mountains for summer pasturage, then to sheltered valleys late in the fall.

People of the Way

From birth to death the Navajo people walk along a tortuous path laid out for them by supernatural beings, the Holy People. That path is both perilous and rewarding, for to stray from its narrow confines is to invite the wrath of the spirits, while to maintain a steady course is to ensure one's harmony with the universe and its supernatural forces. Good health, contentment, and a measure of prosperity are the rewards for following the Holy People's way. Sickness, death, bad luck, and grief are the punishments that the spirits exact for the slightest wayward action or expression. To ease their passage down this difficult way of life, the Navajos sing. Good-luck songs ward off danger while the people work in the fields or in the family dwelling place, which is called the hogan. There are ceremonial chants to cure the sick and restore their harmony with the universe, and other hymns to mark important milestones between an infant's first laugh and the ripeness of age.

The songs of the Navajos express their vision of the world and the traditions that guide them through their lives. The core of their beliefs and hopes is embodied in their celebration of a young girl's transition into womanhood, when the Navajos sing of the "door path" that will be hers:

The door path of hogan God
The door path made of afterglow,
The door path made of yellow corn
The door path made of all kinds of jewels,
The door path made of gathered spring waters
The door path made of corn pollen,
Now it is a door path of long life
and everlasting beauty.

This is the road, the road.
This is the road,
The road which is blessed, the road
which is blessed.

If the song is a promise, it is also a strongly implied threat, for the road of life is blessed *only* when the individual adheres to the many ancient rules of the Navajo faith. The Navajos are a people who live in an awareness of the catastrophe that will befall them should any of the hundreds of strictures on day-to-day living be ignored or violated.

It is said by the Navajos that man came into existence after the Holy People ascended to the surface world through the Hole of Emergence. Upon the surface world the Holy People created the mountains, the mesas, the deserts, the life-giving springs, and all of the animals and plants. Among the Holy People were the Hero Twins, born of Changing Woman and fathered by the sun. The Hero Twins journeyed across the surface world, slaying monsters and littering the landscape with fallen carcasses. But some monsters—Poverty, Hunger, Old Age, and Dirt—were spared the Twins' righteous fury to play their part in the human scheme.

When the Hero Twins had completed their task, the Holy People held a great conclave, during which they created the Earth Surface People and taught them exactly how they were to build their houses, find food, marry, protect themselves against disease, and contend with the perils of daily life. Thus armed with a code for living, the Earth Surface People wandered about in scattered bands until they came together in the region that the Navajos regard as their homeland.

When the Earth Surface People first came upon this

233

land of the Navajos, it was an awesome sight. The vast severed head of Big Monster lay where the Hero Twins had flung it, and the blood had dried into fields of lava. Winged Cliff Monster had become, in death, a lava rock. Four sacred mountains rose to mark the cardinal points of the Navajo country that lies in present-day northwestern New Mexico and northeastern Arizona. A peak, one not positively identified, in the San Juan range of southwestern Colorado is the north point; Mount San Mateo (later renamed Mount Taylor) is the south; a peak, probably Pelado, is the east; San Francisco Mountain, near Flagstaff, Arizona, is the west.

Latecomers to the Area

Although the original myth suggests that the Navajos can trace their ancestry in this region back to time immemorial, there is little basis for this concept. Many archeologists believe that the Diné ("The People"), as the Navajos call themselves, did not arrive in their present homeland until perhaps the late 15th century. Even the name "Navajo" (generally meaning "Takers From the Field") was given them by the Tewa, a Pueblo people of the Santa Fe region.

Who, then, are the Navajos? Where did they come from? The primary clue lies in their speech: Athabascan, closely related to the languages of the hunters of northwestern Canada. Splitting off from these bands at a date as yet unknown, The People migrated to the south in small groups of nomadic hunters. Their ranks, in time, were swelled by other wanderers to form, between the four great mountains, the loosely affiliated but culturally similar groupings that came to be called Navajos.

They had few possessions when they came to Dinétkah ("Home of the People"), a land of towering peaks, grasslands, deserts, and blood-red canyons. The People's way of life, when they first appeared in the Southwest, was simple, being limited to hunting, trapping, and camping in transitory shelters made of brushwood, skins, and leaves. One can only guess at their wonderment and awe when they first laid eyes on pueblos—towns built on mesa tops, vast cliff houses, and multi-tiered cave-homes located high on canyon walls. The People must have gazed in wonder at the fields of corn, beans, and pumpkins. What probably most impressed The People were the blankets of cotton, baskets, pottery, turquoise beads, and tools to tame the soil.

The Navajos pounced on these treasures. In raid after raid they seized looms, pots, baskets, blankets, and agricultural tools. Women were taken as well. But all was not warfare. As the Navajos settled down in the Southwest, they opened their eyes and ears to the wonders around them and adopted many Pueblo practices, beliefs, and a large part of their mythology, molding them to their own uses. In later years, when the Pueblo peoples were battling with the Spaniards, many of the Pueblos fled to Navajo lands to live among these less sophisticated Indians and teach them such crafts as weaving and pottery-making. Soon The People were wearing blankets they had made and growing their own corn.

Although village life held no appeal for the Navajos, they needed permanent settlements now that they were tillers of the soil as well as huntsmen. Acknowledging neither central authority nor tribal community, they built their homes in small, family-sized groups, each cluster miles away from its neighbors.

If Pueblo influence added much to The People's culture, so too did that of the Spaniards. The Navajos watched, fascinated, as the 16th-century Spanish colonists moved into the Pueblo lands with their impressive train of goods-laden carts and herds of sheep, cattle, and horses. In lightning raids upon the fledgling Spanish settlements, The People made off with fresh spoils: knee breeches, silver baubles, and—best of all—numerous sheep and horses.

With considerable foresight the Navajos refrained from eating the sheep they stole, unlike the neighboring Comanches and Apaches, who also delighted in raids on Spanish holdings. Instead, The People used the sheep to build up herds for future meals and a self-perpetuating supply of wool. Their women learned to shear, spin, and dye this new material, and wove it into blankets and breechcloths. But sheep require grazing land. As the herds grew over the decades, Navajo families drifted westward in search of grass, and Navajo dwellings grew farther and farther apart. Many families built two or more hogans, and moved from one to another as weather and the needs of the herds dictated.

The Power of Navajo Women

Within this developing Navajo society, women held a pivotal position, for the thread linking related family groups together was the matrilineal clan. By the 19th century, and perhaps much earlier, there had come to be about 60 clans. A child belonged to its mother's clan and, if a girl, inherited property through her. Sheep, in particular, were passed on from mother to daughter.

When a man married, he moved into the home of his wife and became the overseer of her goods. But he would never own this property, for according to Navajo custom it all had to be passed down from his wife to his daughter and then to her daughter in an unbroken line.

In fact, when a man married, his primary responsibilities remained with his mother's clan, to which he belonged. Although he assumed responsibility for his wife and children, his major obligations were to his sisters and their offspring. Thus a man, even when he was not out hunting or raiding, might not be found within the hogan of his wife. In many instances he would be many miles away, looking after the needs of his sisters and their children. And it was his sisters' children, rather than his own, who would be his heirs.

This old-style Navajo hogan (above) exhibits the classical conical shape. Built of timbers and poles covered with bark and dirt, it seems almost a random construction but is both waterproof and well insulated. Of newer design is the six-sided hogan built of logs chinked with mud. The interior of one is seen at right. Instead of a smoke hole over an open fire, this hogan boasts a chimney and wood stove.

A Day Among the Navajos

In the early 19th century there might well have been a woman called Sweet Water, married to a man known as Spotted Horse. These would not have been their real names, for a person's true name—his secret, or "war," name—had to be used very sparingly. It was part of an individual's personal power and must be saved for use as a verbal talisman in times of danger. Therefore, The People referred to each other, in day-to-day talk, by innocuous names descriptive of their nature, their looks, or their possessions.

It is a summer night, and Sweet Water and her four children lie asleep on sheepskins spread on the dirt floor of their hogan. Their bodies are arranged about the circular dwelling like the spokes of a wheel, feet pointing toward the firepit in the center of the floor. The baby, called Tooth Lost, sleeps snugly in her cradleboard close to Sweet Water. Nearby is the girl Gray Eyes, the oldest at 13, and the two boys, Crystal Boy and Little Horse, aged 9 and 7 respectively. Their father is away, advising his sister in some problem with her children.

The moon illuminates a complex of scattered structures in this family community: several hogans, each separated from the others to ensure privacy, but all within shouting range; storage dugouts; a brushwood sheep corral; and a sweathouse set well away from the hogans beyond the garden plots. The garden contains not only corn, squash, tobacco, and beans, whose cultivation the Navajos had long since learned from the Pueblos, but also such foreign crops as wheat and melons. The Navajos have adopted these European plants from the Spaniards and made them their own.

When the sun throws its first beams through the open entranceway of Sweet Water's hogan, the young family stirs and rises. From a second hogan emerges Sweet Water's brother, Tall Singer. He is a visitor whose wife lives, as wives do, in her mother's establishment, but he will be here a long time because he has come a great distance to see his sister and her children. He is particularly well suited to give them guidance and instruction, for he is a shaman, or medicine man, of great wisdom. Sharing his hogan is another and even more respected man: Che, Sweet Water's clan father; not her real (continued on page 238)

The Intricate Designs of Navajo Weaving

The Navajos, world famous for their skill as weavers, owe much to the Spaniards, who introduced sheep to the inhabitants of the Southwest, and to the Pueblo Indians, who taught them the techniques of the craft. In fact, the loom that the Navajos have used for centuries is derived from the Pueblo prototype. After the coming of sheep, the Navajos eventually adopted the white man's shears for clipping and his toothcomb card for straightening the tangled wool fibers. To spin the wool, however, Navajo women still use a traditional spindle, consisting of a disk on a wooden shaft, on which they twist and pull the fibers until they have strands of the proper thickness. The strands are then dyed with the desired colors.

A Navajo loom *makes use of two trees as supporting posts. Vertical warp threads run between horizontal bars at the top and bottom of the loom. Weaving from the bottom up, the woman interlaces the colored weft threads that carry the design across the warp.*

 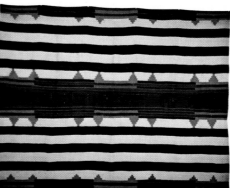 

A gradual evolution of Navajo design *in chiefs' blankets is evident in these three woven between 1840 and 1875. The oldest (left) bears simple stripes that yield to slightly more complicated variations in the next oldest (center). Finally, by 1870, motifs had evolved to include diamond shapes (right), although the traditional design of wide and narrow stripes was also retained.*

A riot of angular patterns *characterizes these Navajo serape-style wearing blankets from the mid-19th-century Classic period. By then the Indians were using imported materials. The blanket at right is made of silk; the other, from bayeta, a European flannel fabric. Because the bayeta came as finished cloth, the Navajos had to unravel the material before using it.*

A late-Classic serape of the 1870's features bold, eye-catching crosses, some of which are framed in larger crosses in contracting colors. Unlike many of the contemporary blankets in which several types of wool, including yarns imported from Europe, were combined, this one was made only from homespun.

A dazzling array of diamonds in this blanket of the early 1870's marks a transition between traditional banded designs and the more variegated patterns of the late 1800's. The Navajos' desire to attract white buyers for their woven goods helped generate a broadening of design concepts among the weavers.

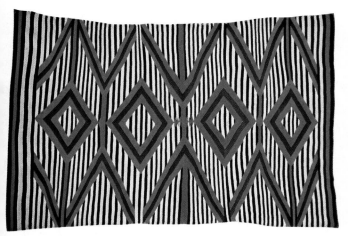

A child's blanket (left) combines the traditional Navajo design of bands with a variety of complex patterns. The weaver used both coarse handspun and fine machine-made yarns in the creation of this cloth for some fortunate youngster.

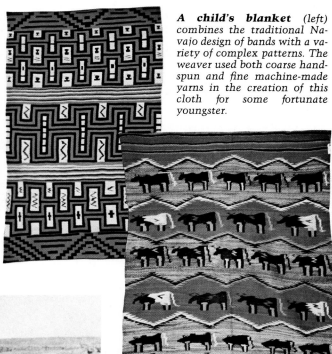

Like the op art of today, this "eye-dazzler" design of the late 1880's creates the illusion of form and color in motion. Such patterns, which were extremely popular, made use of commercial yarns colored with aniline dyes of brilliant hues.

Pictorial rugs like the one above became popular in the 1880's among white buyers. Merchants at Navajo trading posts encouraged the weavers to spend their time fashioning floor coverings and wall hangings for the export market. Using machine yarn, the craftsmen produced a variety of pictorials featuring such untraditional motifs as cows, birds, houses, and even trains.

To flatten a blanket, which is curled when it comes off the loom, a Navajo woman buries the cloth in damp sand. In a few days the blanket is ready for use.

father, but an old man of her clan who came many months ago and is welcome to stay for as many more months as he wishes. He is going blind, but he retains much of his power because of his wisdom and his knowledge of the chants and medicine lore that are so valuable to his people. Also, he is not so blind that he cannot chop wood.

In a third hogan are Sweet Water's mother and her two unmarried daughters, Sweet Water's younger sisters. When they marry, their husbands will join them in new hogans near the mother—but not too near, for Navajo tradition forbids the meeting of a man with his mother-in-law. This is one of the Navajos'strongest taboos, and a young man will go any lengths to avoid gazing on or speaking directly to his mother-in-law. To do otherwise would invite blindness.

Sweet Water begins the day by sprinkling sacred corn pollen on the poles of her hogan. This is a gift to the Holy People and shows that her first waking thoughts are of them. Early-morning rituals completed, Sweet Water then takes the sheepskin bedding outside to air. She hopes in this way to reduce the number of lice in her hogan. But past experience has taught her that she will soon have to abandon her house to the insects and move into a new dwelling. Meanwhile, Crystal Boy and Little Horse have run to the corral to let out the sheep and drive them to pasture, for tending the flocks is a traditional task for small boys. Later in the day the boys will gather firewood for the cooking and night-warming firepit. Meanwhile, women and girls share the household duties. It is women's work to clean the hogans, butcher sheep, gather the crops, cook the meals, and weave.

Basket in hand, Sweet Water gathers the vegetables needed for the next few meals. The family settlement is quiet when she returns. Tooth Lost is sleeping; Gray Eyes and the women are singing softly as they sit in the open air carding the wool they washed yeterday and dried before the sun went down. Sweet Water joins the group and begins to weave.

For her dyes Sweet Water has used indigo obtained from an itinerant trader, extracts from wild goldenrod, orange hawkweed, sorrel root, sumac, and the yellow-gold flower of the rabbit brush. Adding red to her design, she weaves in bright thread unraveled from the scarlet bayeta, or baize, cloth used by the Spaniards and Mexicans.

In the late afternoon the weaving stops. By the time the boys and the old man have driven the sheep back into the corral and Tall Singer has tethered his horse after rounding up the strays, Sweet Water will have prepared a meal of mutton, squash, and corn. There will also be a fried bread, airy and crisp, a favorite dish of The People.

Gray Eyes spreads a sheepskin, wool-side down, on the ground, and she and her brothers place bowls of food on it. The whole family sits down, cross-legged, and eats from the communal bowls, dipping up meat and gravy with the bread. "May I be lively, may I be healthy," they murmur as they end their meal.

It is night again. The family members enter their respective hogans, not pausing to undress before lying down on their sheepskins with their feet toward the fire. Whoever gets up before the others awaken will take great care not to step over a sleeping person; such an act might unleash dreadful luck.

The Holy People

Among the many forces threatening the Navajos are the Holy People themselves, the strange and powerful spirit-beings who travel on the wind and on sunbeams, on rainbows, thunderbolts, and lightning flashes. Though they have created The People, the spirits are not always benign and must be continually propitiated by ritual acts and offerings, lest they use their power to harm humans. Among the Holy People only Changing Woman, the Earth Mother, is always benevolent. It was she who taught mortals how to live in harmony with nature; she who built the first hogan out of turquoise and shell; she who gave The People the gift of corn.

The other Holy People, however, are mercurial and capricious. The sun, whose rays bring life from the soil, may at any time disappear from the sky, causing the fields of corn and squash to wither and die. Spider Woman, who taught the Earth Surface People how to weave; Spider Man, who warns of coming danger; and the Hero Twins, who slew the monsters—all require never-ending praise and supplication to keep them from turning against and harming The People.

In addition, there are many lesser but still threatening divinities, such as Big Fly, Corn Beetle, Gila Monster, Big Snake Man and Crooked Snake People, Wind People, Thunder People, Cloud People, and Coyote, the trickster. Each being or group of beings has its own power, which it can use for good or evil. Every Navajo knows that the goodwill of all the Holy People must be retained or, if lost, regained.

Even more fearsome than the Holy People are the chinde, the ghosts of Earth Surface dead. These manifestations are wholly evil and cannot be propitiated. Even if the ghost is the departed spirit of a loving and beloved human being, it is feared and loathed, for not the whole spirit but only the evil part of the dead person returns to the place of dying to torment the living for some oversight or insult. So malevolent are ghosts that The People have an intense abhorrence of death, dead bodies, and the places where death has occurred. Often the ailing and aged are moved from their hogans to die in a shelter outside the dwelling area. If a person dies inside a hogan, the body is removed through a hole broken in the northern wall, the direction of evil; and the hogan is often burned to the ground.

Ghosts always appear at night in the shape of an owl, a coyote, a semihuman figure, or sometimes an amor-

Navajo Dry Painting: Art as a Remedy

Unlike the shamans of many other American Indian tribes who treated the symptoms of disease with herbal preparations—many of them highly effective—Navajos concerned themselves with treating what they considered to be the causes of ailments: the spells of witches, ghosts, Holy People, or the effects of contact with non-Navajos. To exorcise the evil magic that had caused the sickness, Navajo shamans conducted elaborate ceremonies. One of the most common of these rituals was and is the construction of dry painting—designs made up of ground minerals or vegetable matter laid on a bed of sand. The paintings, which can take as many as 15 men up to a full day to complete, fall into literally hundreds of categories, depending on the nature and source of the spell. If, for example, a Navajo blames his ailment on contact with someone outside the tribe, the dry painting Enemyway might be performed as a cure.

When someone falls ill, like the baby in the photograph at right, a special shaman, the Singer, and his helpers are summoned to the family hogan. They load blankets with clean sand and spread it on the hogan floor to make a uniform background for the dry painting they will compose. After smoothing the sand, the shaman and his assistants begin the design, using white, red, yellow, black, and blue powders made from ground sandstone, charcoal, gypsum, and ocher. The shaman or his assistant begins the dry painting by picking up a small amount of the desired color in his hand and, using his thumb and forefinger as a siphon, trickles the material onto the sand, forming the design as he works. The process is repeated with the various powders until the painting is completed.

The dry painting at right portrays a figure known as the Slayer of Enemy Gods, a benevolent war diety whose weapons are lightning bolts, which he stands on and holds in his hands. When the shaman and his assistant have completed the picture, the mother, holding her sick infant, sits on the design so that the healing power inherent in the work will be transferred to them. The shaman shakes a rattle, prays, and chants. In a curing gesture he will touch both mother and baby with his hands.

When the ceremony is finished, the painting is immediately destroyed, but each person in the hogan is permitted to help himself to a pinch of colored powder that now has healing powers. A person with a headache may touch some of this powder to his head, others will place it in fetish bags to be used in future ceremonies for curing illness. Finally, what remains of the painting is swept up into blankets and dumped nearby, to the north of the hogan.

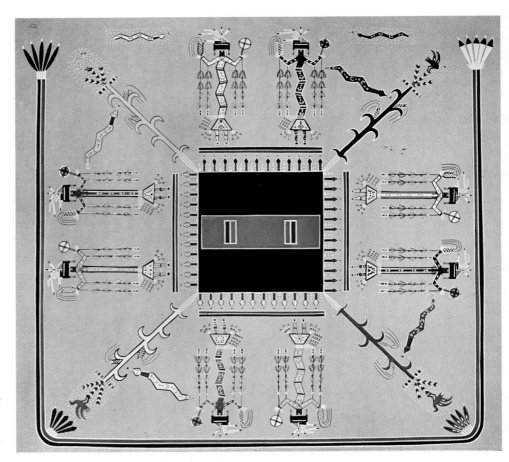

Powerful magic is created by this Navajo Grinding Snakes dry painting that is among the most rarely composed works of the Singer's art. The painting is made only for a young man or woman of a wealthy family and is part of a nine-day ritual called Male Shootingway. As befitted the complexity of the composition, the Singer who fashioned this painting—to appease the powers of thunder and lightning—received an unusually high fee for his services.

The black square at the center represents a metate; the blue bar outlined in yellow, a grinding stone or mano. Twelve snakes border each side of the square. They symbolize the 12 brothers who had magical hunting powers. A stalk of corn, surmounted by a bird, extends from each corner; the corn represents bountiful harvests; the birds, spirits that bless the food. Arrowsnake People are positioned on the four sides of the square and carry corn and baskets in their hands. Small snakes near the Arrowsnake People are positioned as guards.

phous pitch-black form in the gloom. These malignant spirits are likely to run across the paths of traveling people and terrify their horses; or to mutilate their livestock; or to leap upon the living to claw at their clothing or throw dirt in their faces; or to inflict the dreaded ghost sickness, which no but a skilled shaman can cure. Always the appearance of a ghost is a certain portent of disaster.

As if the Holy People and ghosts were not enough, the Navajos must also contend with witches. These are living Earth Surface men and women who practice their evil craft for personal gain. Among their more offensive habits are incest and the eating of human flesh. Anyone may become a witch, for there are few qualifications other than a strong stomach, greed, and envy or hatred of others more fortunate. Usually, witches combine desire for vengeance with desire for wealth. During the daytime they are indistinguishable from other Navajos, unless their incestuous practices are notorious; and when roaming at night, as they often do, they dress in the skins of wolves, bears, foxes, or coyotes.

An easy way for a witch to gain wealth is to rob a grave, an act abhorrent to the normal, death-fearing Navajos. A more subtle method, which may be employed by a witch who is also a shaman, is to make a person ill and then treat him at an exorbitant price. A witch may even cause the victim's death and then seize his livestock, crops, and other property.

Enchantment by spell is a common means of inducing illness. The witch need only procure a strand of the victim's hair, a smear of his excreta, a fingernail paring, or a shred of clothing, then bury it in a grave and utter an incantation over it. If the victim's secret name is known to the witch, the spell is even stronger.

Equally effective is a dose of "corpse poison," a powdery, pollenlike substance made by pulverizing the dried flesh and brittle bones of corpses, preferably young ones. This preparation is surreptitiously introduced into the person's food or furtively blown into his face at a social or ceremonial gathering. Every Navajo carries a small bag of gall medicine—a preparation made from the gall bladders of mountain lions, bears, eagles, and skunks—whenever he thinks he might encounter strangers or be in a crowd. At the slightest suspicion that he has been exposed to corpse poison, the Navajo quickly swallows some of this preparation, a quick-acting antidote.

Sometimes, however, even the most careful precautions are of no avail against a witch's power, and the victim may contract lockjaw, waste away, or suffer from bouts of pain or fainting fits. In this case there is nothing to be done but call in a medicine man to hold a curing ceremony.

There is scarcely an act in Navajo life that does not have an accompanying protective or curative rite. The longer, more elaborate rites are, in fact, ceremonials, encompassing a complex of rituals. Each major rite is based on a myth, and each takes the form of a chant that not only relates the myth but applies directly to the occasion or reason for the ceremony. From the many hundreds of songs in the Navajo repertoire, several major ceremonials emerge. The songs are not always chanted in their entirety, for not every occasion demands a "sing" lasting for five to nine days, but even minor rituals are accompanied by songs from the appropriate myth.

The Blessing Way chant, for example, reenacts the grand conclave of the Holy People at which the Earth Surface People were created and mortals were taught how to live in equilibrium with their world. It is a chant sung to ensure health and harmony in family life. Holy Way, in turn, is sung to propitiate the Holy People when it appears they have been offended, while Evil Way is a chant for counteracting witchcraft.

Observance of custom and ritual begins for a Navajo while he is still in the womb. A Blessing Way song is sung for an expectant mother when she is about to give birth. At a difficult delivery all the woman's female relatives and friends loosen their hair to "untie" the baby. If this does not help, all tethered and hobbled horses and sheep in the vicinity are released to run free. In truly stubborn cases a medicine man may be summoned to give herbal drinks to the laboring mother and coax the baby along with an eagle feather while singing a Blessing Way chant.

The baby's arrival is greeted with much rejoicing. The woman who grasps the emerging baby has the privilege of being the first to bathe it. Later she will be the one who kneads and molds the infant's face and body, "shaping" it to be comely and well made. First, though, the baby must be placed in a ritually prescribed position at its mother's left side and its head anointed with corn pollen.

The father makes the cradleboard in which the child will spend many months of its early life, and when the baby is placed in it a special chant is sung:

I have made a baby board for you, my son (daughter),
May you grow to a great old age.
Of the sun's rays have I made the back
Of black clouds have I made the blanket
Of rainbow have I made the bow
Of sunbeams have I made the side loops
Of lightning have I made the lacings
Of sun dogs have I made the footboard
Of dawn have I made the covering
Of black fog have I made the bed.

A Nightway mask, used in a nine-day Navajo healing ceremonial, represents a female deity. It is usually worn by a small man or a young boy who impersonates the female spirit. At the actual ritual, however, male and female deities are represented in equal numbers.

Sometime after his seventh birthday each Navajo child is initiated into adult life via the Yeibichai ceremony, similar to the Hopi Powamu rite, which is performed for the same purpose. The Yeibichai—representations of the Holy People—are much like the kachinas, from which they are derived, and to the children involved in the ritual, an encounter with these creatures with their fierce masks and ear-shattering screams is a terrifying one. Perhaps as many as 50 boys and girls, all from neighboring compounds, participate in the initiation, which takes place in a clearing or a sheltered gully.

The Holy People, one man and one female impersonator, are represented by masked male dancers who prance about in a menacing manner while uttering unearthly falsetto cries. The white-masked goddess figure marks each of the boys with sacred cornmeal, after which the black-masked god lightly whips them with a rod of bound-together yucca leaves. Then the goddess applies the sacred meal to the girls; and the god, now without his whip, presses ears of corn against the markings made by the goddess.

It is a frightening ritual for the youngsters, for they have no idea what the dreaded Holy People have in store for them. But then comes a joyous surprise: the deities remove their masks, and the children realize that the dancers are not, after all, the supernatural creatures they have feared from infancy but human beings like themselves. Before the ceremony ends each child is permitted to wear one of the strange masks himself so that he may gaze upon the unmasked mortals as if through the eyes of the Holy People. The youngsters are then gravely warned to breathe not a word of their experience to the uninitiated.

The onset of a girl's puberty is the proudest of all occasions for her, one celebrated by family and friends in a four-day ceremony called Kinaldá. At the beginning of the series of observances the maiden has her hair ceremonially washed with soap made from the yucca plant and is cautioned about the many things she must not do or eat during this period. Every day at dawn during her first menses she runs toward the east, each morning a little farther. Other girls, younger, are permitted to run with her, but must be careful not to pass her so that they will not grow old before she does.

Each day, too, the girl undergoes a molding rite, lying on a blanket in front of the hogan door while an older female relative or friend kneads her body to make it as shapely as that of Changing Woman. For three days out of the four, bedecked in her finest jewelry, she diligently grinds corn on the family metate until, exhausted, she can grind no more. On the fourth day older women mix the ground corn into batter to make an enormous cake—sometimes as much as six feet across if the young one has labored well—which they bake in a heated earth pit near the hogan. Portions of this corncake are distributed to all the assembled guests; and on that night, the fourth, there is singing until dawn. By the fifth morning the girl is considered a woman, ready to marry and start her own family.

The Navajos impose one major restriction on the choice of marriage partners: marrying within one's own clan or the clan of one's father is strictly forbidden, for this is considered incest. Young boys are not permitted to dance or even walk with some female members of their mother's or father's clan. But marriageable youths meet many suitable partners at ceremonial dances and feasts. Courtship is a simple matter of a suitor's giving horses to the girl's family.

If he is acceptable to the young woman and her immediate relatives, he moves into her family's enclave. He then builds his own hogan that is consecrated in a Blessing Way rite. In song and prayer the couple and the family call upon the Holy People to "let this place be happy" and smear corn pollen on the hogan poles.

With the responsibility of adulthood and marriage comes a sharpened awareness of the many acts that are forbidden because they invite disaster and the many others that should be performed to ensure health, safety, and prosperity. As carefully as a Navajo will avoid his mother-in-law, he avoids a lightning-damaged tree, or traveling alone at night, or eating raw meat. He must also refrain from killing snakes, bears, coyotes, or birds that feed on pests. He will not, if he can possibly help it, permit any kind of beast to cross his path, for the animal may be some evil creature in disguise. A woman weaving a blanket should never quite complete the border design; unless she leaves a spirit path through it to the edge, she may entrap her soul.

Stones from a sweathouse, if placed in fields or orchards, are considered safeguards against frosts. A man on a journey is wise to add pebbles and bits of shell or turquoise to trailside mounds begun by those preceding him along his route. These offerings bring good luck not only to the traveler but to members of his family, wherever they may go.

It is also advisable to bury the dead with their possessions so that they will be content in their graves and not come back to haunt the living. If any occupant of a hogan repeatedly has nightmares of illness, deformity, or death, he can only suspect that dissatisfied or vengeful ghosts are entering the home. The family then will have to destroy the hogan and move to a new one.

Yet in spite of all these and countless other precautions, misfortunes still occur: crop failure, a fall from a

An Apache fiddle, or "the wood that sings," was probably modeled after violins that white settlers brought to the Southwest. The sound box is made out of a hollowed-out yucca stalk, and a peg is used to tighten the single sinew string. Holes near the top of the fiddle help modulate the sound. The instrument is played with a bow.

The Apaches: Huntsmen and Warriors of Desert and Mountains

Like the Navajos, the Athabascan-speaking Apaches were arrivals in the Southwest, having drifted down from t Canadian homeland about 500 years ago. Unlike their Na cousins, however, most Apaches did not settle down to come primarily herders and farmers. Instead, for centu they zealously maintained their reputation as ferocious riors and raiders by striking hard, time and again, at the ious Pueblo tribes to kill and loot.

Loosely organized into bands of hunters and raiders Apache tribes or groupings shared a common language. the cultural traits they came to exhibit varied widely f band to band depending, in large measure, on the partic region each group roamed and the customs they borro from the peoples with whom they came into contact. Jicarilla Apaches, of present-day northern New Mexico, example, adopted many of the characteristics of the Pl Indians and became buffalo hunters, but they also did s farming, having learned the rudiments of agriculture f the Pueblos. The Lipan Apaches, on the other hand, did l farming, preferring to engage in hunting, gathering, and ing throughout eastern New Mexico and west Texas. Yet other group joined the plains-dwelling Kiowas to become Kiowa Apaches. The Mescaleros of south-central New M co, so known for their appetite for the mescal plant, l exclusively by hunting, gathering, and raiding, while Chiricahuas, who ranged through southern Arizona and I Mexico, achieved a reputation as the fiercest of all Apac Finally, there were the Western Apaches, of east-central zona. These included the White Mountain, Cibecue, San los, and Northern and Southern Tonto subdivisions. T farmed more extensively than the others and were clo linked in language and culture to the Navajos.

Apaches had no central tribal government. The b. within each tribe had headmen, whose positions were m tained through their persuasiveness and warlike prov Each band was made up of a number of extended fami and together they loosely controlled a region. Yet even wi the bands there was little organized government, and war were free to carry out raids on their own.

Peculiarly, for so militant a people, the Apaches h horror of death. Enemy scalps had to be purified in smok make them safe and, when a band member died, he quickly buried, his dwelling and possessions burned. T the mourners purged themselves in sagebrush smoke moved away from the immediate area to escape harm f the ghost of the deceased.

Surrounded by a variety of baskets made by the women, an Apache family relaxes outside its wickiup, a dwelling made of slender poles covered with brush and grass. Apache women made little pottery, but they excelled in basketwork. The two-foot-high San Carlos basket (left), used for storing food, is an example of their work. To make such a container, three willow rods were bundled together, as illustrated in the cross-section at far right below. These rods were then wrapped with a thin strip of willow that was also used to join the coil with the top rod of the coil immediately below. To create a dark pattern against the beige background, black strips from a plant called devil's-claw were substituted for the willow.

The Apaches: Huntsmen and Warriors (continued)

Clad in the rainments of mountain spirits, *known as Gans, these Apaches perform a ritual thought to cure an illness or ward off evil powers. Though he does not appear in this picture, the entire ceremony is under the direction of a shaman, who selects and supervises the costuming of the dancers whose body paint, kilts, black masks, wooden swords, and spectacular wooden-slat headdresses are all symbolic of the Gans. As the costuming proceeds, the shaman chants his prayers to the spirits whose aid he seeks. Although Apaches recognize numerous denizens of the supernatural world, they have a supreme diety, known as Yusn, or Ussen—the Giver of Life. It was from this godhead that all life was generated, both in the visible and the unseen, supernatural world. Throughout their lives Apaches appeal to Yusn's spirit creations for help in coping with such everyday problems as drought, illness, and shortage of game. Not all ceremonials, however, are serious in nature. At a puberty rite, for example, the Gans appear in full regalia, but their purpose is merely to entertain the celebrants. To the white men who first encountered the Apaches, the flamboyant costumes worn by the Gans impersonators, particularly the arresting headdresses, were all redolent of Satan, and the newcomers incorrectly looked upon the Apaches as devil worshipers.*

Near exhaustion *from dancing through the night, an Apache girl kneels on a sacred deerskin during a ceremony marking her coming of age. Such puberty celebrations—as much social as religious in nature—are usually communal affairs marking the transition to womanhood of several girls who recently had their first menses. The ceremonies last for four days (four being a magic number), during which ritual chants and dances are punctuated with feasting, entertainment, and gift-giving.*

During the ceremonies each girl is attended by an older woman, who advises her on the duties and privileges of womanhood. Equally important is the Singer, who supervises the construction of the tepee where the ritual songs are chanted and leads the singing. Each evening the Gans (left), representing the mountain spirits, entertain guests with dances.

The celebration reaches a climax on the fourth day, when the girls run a race between a basket containing sacred objects and the ceremonial tepee. Four times they run, and each time the basket is placed closer to the tepee. The race is to ensure that the girl will be strong and a good runner and will "have a good heart"—that is, be brave. After the races the ceremonial tepee is dismantled, and the girls return to their own homes to observe four days of taboos associated with their status. Finally, the observances come to an end; the girls resume normal activities, but now they are considered eligible for marriage.

horse, disease among the sheep, the illness of a child. Then it is necessary to divine the cause of the affliction and combat it with the proper ceremonial.

Treating the Sick

Let us see what necessary steps are taken by again observing the family of Spotted Horse and Sweet Water.

Crystal Boy, Sweet Water's older son, has been ill for many days. Pains and fever have been racking his young body, and the gentle hands of his mother have been able to do nothing for him. But news travels fast, and others have come from far away to help the boy. His father, Spotted Horse, has ridden swiftly home, bringing with him an old man gifted in divining.

After a time of purifying, the old man rubs pollen on Crystal Boy and on his own right arm. Offering prayers and songs to Gila Monster, the diviner slowly passes into a trance, and then his hand and arm begin to tremble violently. By the manner and direction of the movements of his hand, he discerns the nature of the youngster's ailment and determines the cure: ghost sickness, to be treated by the curative chant called Evil Way. The ceremonial will last nine days and will call for dry paintings to be created on the floor of a hogan especially blessed and cleansed for the occasion.

There is no doubt in Crystal Boy's mind that the old man is right, for one evening when his younger brother had run on ahead and he himself was late in driving home the sheep, he had seen a dark and ugly shape among his flock. The next day a sheep died.

After the old man's diagnosis, a medicine man comes to the dwelling place of Sweet Water and Spotted Horse to treat the boy. He is a man who has studied his craft under older medicine men for more than 20 years and brought it to near perfection in several more years of constant practice. People for many miles around hold him in great esteem for his fine voice and excellent command of every word and detail of the most complex of chants.

It is now late afternoon on the eighth day of the treatment. For four days Crystal Boy has purified himself by taking emetics and sweatbaths; for the last four days the medicine man has been supervising the creation of dry paintings depicting the figures in Evil Way myth. For eight days there has been chanting. Colored dusts—made from clay, crushed flowers, ocher, vegetables, and pollen—trickle through the fingers of the dry painters to complete the prescribed pattern.

For long moments there is silence. Then, at the direction of the medicine man, Crystal Boy, who has been sitting to the south of the painting, moves to sit on the design. It is the last of a series of four dry paintings; all the previous ones have been destroyed at sundown of the days on which they were made. Outside the ceremonial hogan the women go about their tasks, anxious for news but busy gathering and preparing extra food for the final day.

The singer resumes his chant and gives the boy a herbal infusion. Then he dips his fingers into water, touches all parts of the painting, and takes dust from those parts to rub onto the shoulders, back, abdomen, limbs, forehead of Crystal Boy's aching, feverish body— to bring the boy in tune with the meaning of the painting and transfer its power to him.

Crystal Boy, half-hypnotized, listens to the chant and follows it in his mind. But he is not altogether concentrating on it, for he is young and he knows that his ordeal will soon be over. Tonight the last dry painting will be swept up and buried in four separate places to keep it safe from harmful influence; and tomorrow, the ninth day, many friends will come on horseback from afar to make camp, build fires, cook sumptuous meals, and prepare for a night of dancing, festivity, and the final sequence of the chanting. By then he surely will be well.

Drowsily, he moves his lips in imitation of the singer's chant. The spirits of the song and the dry painting penetrate his being. Confidence surges within him. His pains and fever are fading; already he feels better. The words and cadences of the chant permeate his body and soul and seem to come from within, saying:

> Happily I recover.
> Happily my interior becomes cool,
> Happily my eyes regain their power,
> Happily my head becomes cool,
> Happily my legs regain their power,
> Happily I hear again!
> Happily for me the spell is taken off!
> Happily may I walk,
> In Beauty, I walk!

The White Invasion

Until the mid-19th century, when white people began to swarm through Navajo territory, European influence on The People had been, on the whole, more beneficent than destructive. Scattered as they were through lands that few Spaniards wanted, the Navajos were largely left to their own devices.

Life was especially good for The People in the years following Mexico's declaration of independence from Spain. If Madrid's ability to protect its colonists in New Mexico and Arizona had been slight, Mexico's military presence in these territories was practically nonexistent, and the Navajos and their neighbors, the Apaches, were able to pillage Mexican towns and ranches at will. But these days of easy conquest were not to last. In 1846, as a result of the outbreak of war with Mexico, the United States took possession of present-day New Mexico and Arizona and soon made it clear that raids against settlers would no longer be tolerated.

Heavily armed garrisons were established on Navajo soil—alien and hostile presences infinitely disturbing to The People. Whites, on their way to California after the great gold strikes of 1848, swarmed across the land,

Geronimo: A Man of Peace Who Became a Great Warrior

Of the many Apache warriors whose names were anathema to Mexican and U.S. settlers along the border regions, few were so feared as the man they called Geronimo. Yet nothing in this man's early life suggested that he would become an outstanding warrior. Born among the Bedonkohe Apaches in 1829, he was called Goyanthlay—One Who Yawns—a name suited to his easygoing nature. At 17 he married and for the next decade lived in peace. But in 1858 Mexican troops murdered his family, an act that transformed Goyanthlay into a man of vengeance. It was during a battle with Mexican troops in 1859 that he was given the name by which whites would henceforth know him. For unknown reasons the Mexicans nicknamed him Geronimo (Spanish for Jerome), and as Geronimo he became the scourge of the mountain and desert areas along the Mexico-Arizona frontier.

In the 1860's Geronimo, having left his own band to marry and live among the Chiricahua Apaches, fought alongside Chief Cochise in engagements with the U.S. Army. But when Cochise made peace in 1872, Geronimo led renegade Chiricahuas on numerous raids into Mexico and Arizona. Arrested by U.S. authorities in 1877, Geronimo and his Chiricahuas were confined to the San Carlos reservation—aptly called, by one white, Hell's Forty Acres—where they tried, for the next four years, to farm the parched earth. In 1881 Geronimo resumed raiding on both sides of the border, only to be tracked down by Apache scouts loyal to the United States and recaptured by Gen. George Crook. It was not long, however, before Geronimo and his band were at large once more, striking terror into the hearts of Mexicans and Americans alike.

Troops under Gen. Nelson A. Miles pursued him into Mexico, but for months Geronimo slipped from their grasp. Finally, in 1886, Lt. Charles Gatewood and a party of five ran him down and talked him into surrendering on the promise that the warriors and their families would not be separated in captivity. The promise was immediately broken. Geronimo and his men were imprisoned in one Florida camp, their kinfolk and other peaceful reservation Apaches in another. Though Geronimo's warriors were eventually united with their families and sent to live in Alabama, the Apaches suffered in the damp, unfamiliar climate, and by 1890 about 25 percent of them were dead.

In 1894 all surviving Apaches were dispatched to Fort Sill, Oklahoma, and there Geronimo attempted farming for a time. But with the army's permission he turned to selling souvenir bows and arrows and pictures of himself at expositions and fairs. In 1905, at the special request of President Theodore Roosevelt, he was brought to Washington to ride in the inaugural parade. Geronimo's last years were spent at Fort Sill under the watchful eyes of federal troops. He died there in 1909.

Geronimo (right), his son (second from left), and two other Chiricahua warriors strike a martial pose in 1886, shortly before they surrendered to federal troops.

helping themselves to Navajo firewood and shooting Navajo game. The People retaliated with swift and bloody raids against the invaders, who in turn called upon the U.S. Army and local militia for protection. From time to time peace would be restored through negotiations and treaty, but such respites were always short-lived because of misunderstandings and broken promises on both sides.

So the Indian raids continued, building to a crescendo during the early years of the Civil War when Navajo territory was practically denuded of soldiers, whose services were needed on the battlefront. Taking advantage of this opportunity, the Navajos swooped down upon American and Mexican settlements in the Rio Grande Valley to kill and loot without mercy. By 1862 the whole future of white settlement in the Southwest was imperiled, forcing the United States to take action. The man placed in charge was Col. Christopher ("Kit") Carson, long famous as a hunter, trapper, scout, fur trader, and guide, but now serving as an Indian fighter with the New Mexico Volunteers. Carson's orders were to drive The People out of their homes to a 40-square-mile reservation of wasteland called Bosque Redondo, on the Pecos River in eastern New Mexico.

In the summer of 1863 Colonel Carson, having already herded a band of Apaches into Fort Sumner in

Bosque Redondo, marched against the Navajos at the head of the 1st Cavalry of New Mexico Volunteers. Cooperating with the soldiers was a band of Ute Indians, who served as guides and trackers. Carson's plan of attack was simple. Rather than war directly on the Navajos, who were scattered throughout a wide area and would disappear into the landscape at the approach of troops, he decided to destroy their lands, crops, and sheep herds, thus starving The People into submission.

Month after month Carson kept his men and horses well fed on corn, beans, squash, and pumpkins grown by the Navajos and burned whatever was left. Whenever the Volunteers came upon a flock of sheep, they ate to surfeit. Those sheep they could not eat were either slaughtered and left to rot or were driven to army outposts. Navajo horses were also killed in large numbers, and hogans, corrals, and storehouses were burned.

To supplement his scorched-earth campaign, Carson waged a form of psychological warfare that had telling effects. Through released captives, he was able to get word to the scattered and starving bands of Navajos that if they surrendered they would be fed and clothed, then escorted to a new home in Bosque Redondo. There they would learn new methods of farming and become self-supporting. But for those who refused the government's offer, there would be only death, either from starvation and exposure or in battle.

Hundreds had already succumbed to Carson's promises and threats when, in January 1864, the colonel, leading about 400 militiamen, trapped hundreds of Navajos who had sought shelter in their sacred Canyon de Chelly, a narrow gorge between sheer cliffs. While part of his force stood guard atop the steep canyon walls to prevent retreat in that direction, another group of soldiers moved quietly into the gorge's only open end. In a sudden attack the soldiers moved forward, killing and setting fire to stores as they advanced. Caught completely by surprise, the Navajos were pressed into an ever-narrowing cul de sac where they could do nothing but surrender.

The defeat of the Navajos at Canyon de Chelly marked the real end of the campaign. Over the next months thousands of emaciated Navajos came out of hiding to throw themselves on the mercy of the U.S. government, which imprisoned them temporarily at Fort Defiance in Arizona. But if The People hoped for kindness, they were to be deeply disappointed. At Fort Defiance they were fed little and clothed less. Then, in March, began the time of exodus and exile that the Navajos would remember as the Long Walk: a 300-mile journey across mountain and desert from the fort in Arizona to Fort Sumner in Bosque Redondo, 180 miles southeast of Santa Fe.

The first convoy of captives left on March 6, 1864. There were 30 wagons and 400 horses for 2,400 people. Only the very young, the very old, the very sick, and the disabled were permitted to ride. The rest walked.

The weather was bitterly cold, and many of the ill-clad, underfed exiles died along the way.

By December 1864 more than 8,000 Navajos had made the Long Walk to Fort Sumner. There they found nothing but new calamities. Driven from their vast holdings of mountaintops, mesas, and valleys, they were now crammed into 40 square miles of flatland already occupied by Apaches. Firewood was scarce, the alkaline waters of the Pecos River made them ill, and nowhere were there wild nuts, tubers, and berries such as grew in their homeland. Because there was no material with which to build shelters, many of the Navajos were forced to live like gophers in holes gouged out of the ground. Where once they had owned numerous sheep, their herds were now cut to a bare minimum, for the plan of the government was that they should become farmers, not sheepmen. But in Bosque Redondo not even corn would grow.

During their first three years in captivity The People tried to make the best of their situation and each spring planted crops, but caterpillars and floods destroyed all hopes for a harvest. By the fourth year the Navajos were in utter despair, and that spring they did not even attempt a planting but subsisted as best they could on the scant rations provided by the government. They yearned for the pastures and familiar fields of their homeland and recalled with bitterness and longing the days of their freedom.

An Expensive Government Blunder

For the U.S government, too, the attempt to settle the Navajos in Bosque Redondo was proving a costly failure. Gen. William T. Sherman, sent to investigate the Navajo situation, reported that the cost of keeping these Indians in poverty was as great as if they had all been put up at an expensive New York hotel. Finally, in 1868, the government signed a treaty with The People granting them a reservation of 3.5 million acres—half in northeastern Arizona, half in northwestern New Mexico—that was within their traditional homeland, and late that year the survivors went home.

When the Navajos returned to their homeland, they found everything destroyed, and for years The People had to exist as best they could as hunters and gatherers. When, at last, they were able to resume farming and herding, their land was struck by prolonged drought. It was as if the Holy People, ghosts, and witches the Navajos so feared had combined forces to destroy them. Calamity piled on calamity. In the 1880's their best land was taken and granted to the Santa Fe Railroad, and soon white settlers were crowding around the edges of the reservation, bringing with them diseases and alcohol to plague the Navajos.

Yet The People survived and in time came to prosper once more. They once again were able to move along "a door path of long life and everlasting beauty"—along the road that is blessed by the Holy People.

Jewelry of the Southwest: A Heritage of Exquisite Design

Hand-polished shell beads and the luminous blue-green stone turquoise have long been the hallmarks of Southwest Indian jewelry. Since precontact days Pueblo and particularly Zuni artisans have been fashioning works of stunning beauty with little more than these raw materials and primitive tools. The fetish necklace at left, for example, is the work of a modern Zuni craftsman, but its design of birds and other animals carved from stone and interspersed with beads of shell reflects motifs that date back centuries. Although many basic designs of Southwestern jewelry have changed little for hundreds of years, a new element was added in the mid-19th century when the Navajos—who had come late to the jewelry craft—learned the art of silversmithing from the Mexicans and passed on the skill to the Hopis and Zunis. Suddenly, silver became the material of choice but, because the raw metal was in short supply at the time, craftsmen at first used U.S. dimes and quarters, which they pounded into ornate shapes. Then, when the U.S. government forbade the practice of mutilating money, the Mexican peso was used instead, until traders made silver slugs and, finally, sheets of silver available.

Today the silverwork of the Southwest tribes is world famous. Particularly favored are Navajo "squash-blossom" necklaces, bracelets, and concha belts. Competing with them in popularity are Zuni stone and shell jewelry and Hopi jewelry boxes, buckles, and bracelets of silver cutouts overlaid on a dark background.

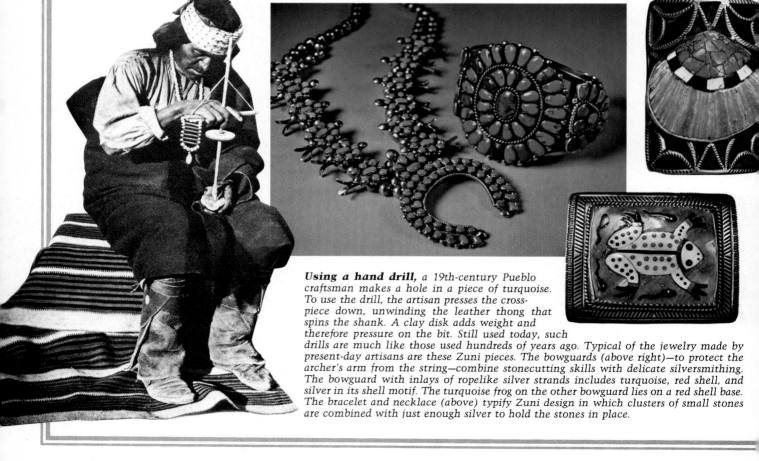

Using a hand drill, a 19th-century Pueblo craftsman makes a hole in a piece of turquoise. To use the drill, the artisan presses the crosspiece down, unwinding the leather thong that spins the shank. A clay disk adds weight and therefore pressure on the bit. Still used today, such drills are much like those used hundreds of years ago. Typical of the jewelry made by present-day artisans are these Zuni pieces. The bowguards (above right)—to protect the archer's arm from the string—combine stonecutting skills with delicate silversmithing. The bowguard with inlays of ropelike silver strands includes turquoise, red shell, and silver in its shell motif. The turquoise frog on the other bowguard lies on a red shell base. The bracelet and necklace (above) typify Zuni design in which clusters of small stones are combined with just enough silver to hold the stones in place.

Using tiny saw blades, Hopi craftsmen cut intricate patterns in sheets of silver to make the bracelets and buckles shown above. The sheet is then fastened to a base of copper, jet, or oxidized silver. The backing, showing through the openings in the design, creates an eye-pleasing contrast of dark against light.

Hammered shells of silver formed into a concha belt are displayed by a Navajo artisan. Silver conchas were once worn in back suspended from a lock of hair, but today they are often used as belts. Typical of Navajo silverwork are the so-called squash-blossom necklaces at left. Actually, this is a misnomer; the flower-shaped beads represent young pomegranate fruits. The naja, or "crescent," is sometimes made to be worn separately. Also typical are the simple stamped patterns that characterize some Navajo silver bracelets, such as the one at left, below.

Foragers and Gatherers

Beneath towering, snow-capped mountains, *the parched soil of the Great Basin supports only spindly growths. Here desert foragers wandered in a constant search for food. Always they carried pine-gum-coated basketwork bottles (inset) filled with precious water.*

Generally peaceful peoples, the Indians of the Great Basin, California, and the Plateau lived in environments ranging from the bitterly hard and barren to the richly bountiful.

The Great Basin

Few regions on earth are more inhospitable to man than the western desert known as the Great Basin. Through much of the year a merciless sun in a cloudless sky parches the land. The midday air shimmers from the reflected heat of sand and rock. Because rainfall is sparse, everything that lives in the region—plant or animal—must be capable of surviving with a minimum of water.

The Basin, encompassing some 200,000 square miles, lies between some of America's highest and most rugged mountains—the Sierra Nevada on the west, the Wasatch on the east. A part of the Snake River watershed serves as a northern boundary, and the southern perimeter is the north edge of the Mojave Desert and the watershed of the Virgin River. Most of the Basin is in present-day Nevada and Utah.

Since the beginning of the Pleistocene epoch a million years ago, the great range to the west has determined the desert character of the Basin by blocking most of the eastbound rain clouds. And, before the coming of the white man, the mountains also isolated the Basin's Indian inhabitants from outside contact.

The aboriginal desert-dwellers were themselves widely scattered: Shoshonis in the northeast, reaching as far as present-day Wyoming; Northern Paiutes (also known as Paviotsos) in the west and northwest; Southern Paiutes (also known as Chemehuevis), ranging from Utah across Nevada's tip to the Mojave Desert, and Washos near Lake Tahoe, where California bends around Nevada. Shoshonis and Paiutes were linguistically related, but neither understood the other's language. The Washos were of other stock. But all the tribes were alike in adjusting to the desert.

White pioneers en route to California goldfields in the 1850's were appalled by the Desert Indians, who went about nearly naked, subsisted on such strange, unappetizing foods as insects and rodents, and seemed to live in a society wholly without structure.

But what the transients did not see was that the

Great Basin was diverse and supportive for those who could acclimate to its rigors and discern the pattern of its ways. Primitive as the Indians may have seemed, they had lived and even thrived in their environment for 10,000 years by observing and respecting nature's cycles and processes. Although natural caprices, such as a meager crop of piñon nuts or a periodic scarcity of rabbits, could 'work hardships, there were always enough edible plants and animals to sustain the Basin's population. But even in the best of times life was spent wandering the valleys and hills, from one oasis to another, in a never-ending search for water, firewood, and food.

Search parties were usually small, often no more than a few related families whose needs would not exceed the minimal sources of supply. While buckberries might be ripe (and gathered before birds picked the bushes clean), or duck eggs found, or fish caught, or rodents trapped, or roots dug, seeds gathered, and insects caught, the harvest was rarely adequate for large numbers of Indians. Only when nature was prodigal with fish, locusts, rabbits, or the like did Indians come together in large communal bands. On these occasions, not only was there food enough for feasting but for a cache to be put aside against the pinch of winter as well.

Thus the desert's rhythms governed virtually all aspects of Indian life. The people were primarily foragers and gatherers, rather than farmers or hunters, because the Basin had insufficient rain to support agriculture, and hunting was usually minimally rewarding. Clothing as well as diet reflected the paucity of large game. Such animals as the deer and the antelope that furnished Plains Indians with food and their handsome buckskins were scarce, widely scattered, and difficult to stalk in the Great Basin. Small game, such as rats, lizards, and jackrabbits, provided most of the meat rations for the Basin Indians.

Rabbits—Suppliers of Food and Clothing

The jack (actually, a hare—*Lepus californicus*) was a particular target whose pelt was as important as its flesh. Cut spirally into continuous strips and twisted into ropes, the skins were then sewn together to make a cloaklike blanket for winter wear. A man's robe required as many as 100 skins; a child's, 40. For greater density and warmth, each strip was sometimes wrapped around a core of fiber—yucca, cedar, or nettle. Finished robes were left outdoors on a freezing night to

A vast land of desert and salt flats intersected by mountains, the Great Basin—some 200,000 square miles—is one of the most resource-poor areas in North America. From its eastern border—the Wasatch Range—to its western—the Sierra Nevada—the region presents a picture of almost unrelieved grimness. Yet here lived many groups of foragers—Paiute, Ute, Gosiute, Shoshoni, Bannock—who for centuries wrested a living from the inhospitable environment. They moved with the changing seasons, scouring the land for anything edible: seeds, berries, nuts, roots, bulbs, lizards, rats, rabbits, snakes, insects and, occasionally, antelopes, sheep, and deer.

Rocky Mountain sheep *cavort in a petroglyph, or carving, on a boulder in California's Coso Range at the western edge of the Great Basin. Probably of Paiute origin and possibly hundreds of years old, this petroglyph, like most others, was a device to secure the spirits' aid in hunting. Throughout the Coso Mountains that overlook the Mojave Desert, there are hundreds of such petroglyphs. Some of them are quite ancient; others—which depict hunters on horseback—date from post-contact times. To make such illustrations the Indians pecked against the boulders with a harder stone to incise the hundreds or even thousands of dots that formed the pictures.*

kill off lingering fleas. Animal skin might also be worked into moccasins, or tree bark coarsely woven into shoes, but usually Basin Indians went barefoot.

Because they were nomadic people who remained in one place only as long as they could fill their bellies, the Shoshonis and Paiutes built only rudimentary shelters wherever they happened to camp. Their customary structure was like a cone without a top. A circular framework of willow poles was set up, and then bundles of tule reeds, standing on end, were slanted toward the center and bound to the frame. The round top of this abode was open to the skies, but this was a minor problem in a region where the annual rainfall is only five to seven inches.

Disposable Housing
Huddled together inside around a fire with bright stars overhead, they were cozily sheltered from the chill night winds. And invariably, when a group broke camp, it abandoned the flimsy structures to the weather or the next group that happened along.

The people of the Basin were equally casual about social organization because their principal unit, the foraging family, was too small to require much structure. Only in large tribal groups did hierarchy, rank, precedence, and protocol find expression in the roles of chief and war leader, in ordeals and initiations, in secret or mystical societies, in ordained positions, such as seating in a lodge, and in other ritual stratifications.

"Shoshoni" and "Paiute" are primarily anthropological designations. Even in the aggregate, neither group had much sense of tribal identification or allegiance. The Northern Paiutes alone recognized 23 divisions of their clan, but their colloquial names associated them not with each other but with the most important item of their diet—Ground Squirrel Eaters, Trout Eaters, Nut Eaters.

In the self-sufficient family unit there were no titular leaders. The counsel of a grandfather, wise in the old ways, might be sought on occasion. An experienced or charismatic man might, by common consent, act as the group's head in the solution of a collective problem.

When independent families joined together, a new social or political structure might be required to direct the more complex activities of the larger group. Leaders of communal antelope or rabbit drives, having already demonstrated their abilities, might transfer their authority to other areas: dances, ceremonies, defense against marauders. On the other hand, by exercise of a primitive form of democracy, followers were free to withdraw their support from one chief and shift it to another or to choose among competing leaders. No one held power permanently. A dance chief, a rabbit boss, or a war chief served only as long as his expertise was needed. Further, a leader, leaving a large group to rejoin his basic family unit, might be respected as an honorable elder but otherwise carried no status with him.

The Modest Role of the Shaman
Even the role of the shaman was modest. He was neither an augur nor a diviner, only a healer. His knowledge was thought to be imparted by animal spirits—eagle, bear, owl, snake, antelope, mountain goat—that appeared in dreams. Anyone visited by such dreams could become a shaman, and unless called upon for a curing ritual, he lived like his peers and was shown no special favors.

Although survival required the Basin Indians to utilize all resources that came to hand, the people of the Basin did not consider themsevles preeminent. Sky above and earth below were to be shared with everything that existed, even as the spirits decreed. All of creation, animate and inanimate, was imbued with supernatural power, *puha*. For whatever the Indians took from the earth, they felt obligated to return something, if only symbolically: for a root dug up, a bead or a

stone put back. And they prayed to the spirit of the mountain for a share of the piñon nuts growing on its slopes or for a drink of the life-giving water from its tumbling brooks.

Each season, the people knew, had its rigors and rewards, times when the *puha* was beneficient, times when prayer was unavailing. Winter was the hardest time. Storms blasted the desert. Snow fell. The cold bit through the furriest rabbitskin cloak. Often an extended family would elect to camp beside a marsh where sea blite seeds and plots of late-blooming nut grass could still be found to supplement the dried food laid by at harvest time. Seeds and piñon nuts could be stewed with dried fish heads and entrails in the large watertight baskets that served as cooking pots. Fire-heated rocks dropped into the mix cooked the stew without burning the basket.

Game was scarce in cold weather. Kangaroo rats,

A Paiute encampment *(above) on an arid northern Arizona plateau was photographed about 1875 by John K. Hiller, who also took the picture (top) of the woman weaving a basket. Because the Paiutes were nomadic, they built only these crude,* *open-topped conical structures of brush or reeds placed over a frame of willow poles. Such dwellings contrasted sharply with the Paiutes' highly developed basket-making skill. For example, the pitch-coated jar in the top picture was able to hold water.*

field mice, muskrats, gophers, and ground squirrels were in underground hibernation. Fish were safe under a lid of ice. Men had to hunt long and hard for the stray bird, the occasional rabbit. Sometimes they lost out to that other mighty hunter of rabbits, the coyote, but killing that animal itself was taboo because of its mystical significance to all Indians of the Great Basin.

Women spent the cheerless gray days in companionable work. Sagebrush and cedarbark were pounded to shreds and woven into sleeveless pullovers and pants for the men or into blouses and skirts for women. Cattails and tule rushes were woven into all-purpose mats. The slender cattail leaves were braided into thongs, and *weepah*, the "milkweed plant," was twisted into twine. With chokeberry wood frames and supple twigs, the women constructed cradleboards for their babies. Softly tanned, hard-to-come-by antelope hide was the covering. Now, too, was a time for weaving the Paiute baskets whose artistry and utility brought Navajos from present-day Arizona eager to trade.

At evening, warmed by hot food, a fire, and the close, familiar touch of the clustered family, people joked, laughed, and recounted the day's doings. Or they turned to the Teller of Tales for a story. In his repertoire were all the myths of the Paiutes: the creation of the world, the distant time when men and animals could talk together, the magical adventures of Coyote and how he made the lifesaving theft of fire when mankind seemed doomed to cold and darkness for eternity.

A Change of Seasons

The first sign of winter's retreat was the emergence of ground squirrels—an important source of fresh meat. Next was the return of migratory waterfowl—Canada geese, mallards, pintails, canvasbacks, and in the shallows avocets, curlews, and killdeer. To attract birds to within shooting range, the men fashioned excellent decoys by wrapping small bundles of tules in the plumage of skinned ducks. Large sheaves of tules were bound into raftlike boats for cruising the marsh to net ducks and search for eggs.

The first tender shoots of the cattail were another harbinger of spring. Women waded into the chill waters of the marsh to gather the edible white-green spears; by fall these reeds would be tough enough to make rope.

As the weather became warmer, the various bands moved onward. No one area could sustain them for

Piñon pines (above) on the Great Basin mountains provided the Paiutes with a most-prized food. In autumn the cones (below) ripened and released nuts that the Indians ground into a paste for soup.

long, and the complex geography of the Great Basin creates variable life zones. Far from being a bowl, the Basin floor is ridged by eroded mountains that are as much as a mile higher than the valleys between them. In prehistoric times the Basin was filled with the waters of melting ice age glaciers—a huge inland sea, some 9,000 square miles in extent, that contemporary climatologists have named Lake Lahontan. But the intense heat eventually evaporated most of the water, leaving only a few shrunken lakes and a few streams fed by runoff water from the Basin ridges. Water also seeps into the brackish cattail and tule marshes, but a few paces beyond these oases the desert presses in.

From the hot valley floor to the cool, flattened tops of the Basin ranges there are several distinct levels of climate in which plant species ripen progressively. A shoot or berry coming to fruition in the hills already will have gone to seed in the valley.

So the wandering continued. Here watercress. There thistle and clover. One day a field of seeds and—good luck!—the rabbits feeding on it. Another day the leaves of the squaw cabbage or the red berries of desert thornbush.

Hunters, ranging far and wide for game, might find an unexpected flourish of mustard seeds or medicinal herbs, a tangle of firewood, a skein of fibers for weaving, or flakes of flint or obsidian for arrowheads. Word was relayed back, and the group headed toward the treasure.

Punishing Weather

There were disappointments as well, for everything was at the mercy of the weather. Last year a pond or stream was filled with water and seemed a permanent source of supply. This year there might be only a dry bed. A flash flood racing over the flats could create a lake ankle-deep and miles wide, a gleaming puddle drowning vegetation yet too transitory to cultivate the valley.

As the weather moderated and mild winds riffled cottonwoods and willows, it was important for a band to be located beside a valley lake or stream. For now came the fish, spawning runs of cutthroat trout, schools of darting silver shiners flickering in the shallows, and the ugly black species of sucker known as cui-ui. In a good year they were numerous beyond counting and could be hooked, speared, netted, or clubbed. A fisherman would toss his catch to the women on the shore, who gutted and split it, preserving the

The Northern Paiutes—The Endless Search for Food

For the Northern Paiutes of the Great Basin, life's yearly cycle was dictated by the search for food—for the nuts, berries, roots, seeds, small game, and fish on which the people lived. Each food had its season and its place. Winter was the season for desert game and for the fish found in the marsh ponds. Spring brought roots, plants, seeds, and fowl and the start of the great spawning runs of fish at the mouths of the rivers that cut through the terrain. Summer was the time of ripening—of desert seeds, rice grass, and berries; the time when ducks were fat. Autumn brought a journey from the blistering heat of the shadeless desert and marshes to the cool, invigorating air of the forested plateau and hills where the pine nuts were ready for harvest. Then down to the desert again for the late autumn hunt for rabbits.

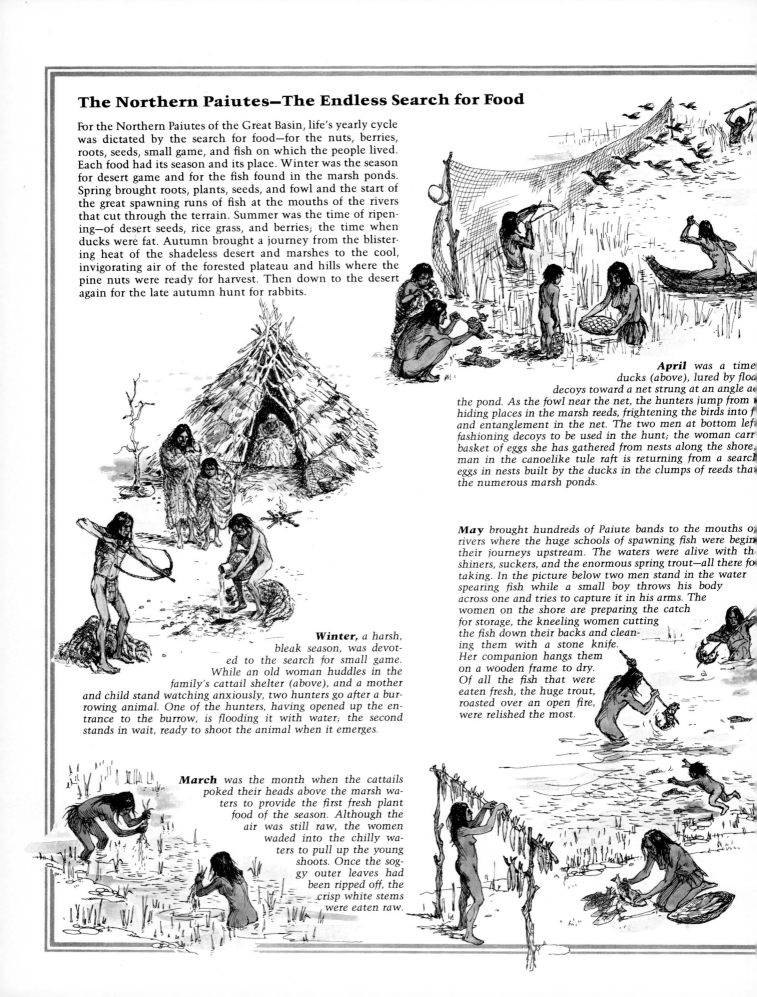

April was a time [...] ducks (above), lured by floa[...] decoys toward a net strung at an angle a[...] the pond. As the fowl near the net, the hunters jump from [...] hiding places in the marsh reeds, frightening the birds into f[...] and entanglement in the net. The two men at bottom lef[...] fashioning decoys to be used in the hunt; the woman carr[...] basket of eggs she has gathered from nests along the shore, [...] man in the canoelike tule raft is returning from a searc[...] eggs in nests built by the ducks in the clumps of reeds tha[...] the numerous marsh ponds.

May brought hundreds of Paiute bands to the mouths o[...] rivers where the huge schools of spawning fish were begin[...] their journeys upstream. The waters were alive with th[...] shiners, suckers, and the enormous spring trout—all there fo[...] taking. In the picture below two men stand in the water spearing fish while a small boy throws his body across one and tries to capture it in his arms. The women on the shore are preparing the catch for storage, the kneeling women cutting the fish down their backs and cleaning them with a stone knife. Her companion hangs them on a wooden frame to dry. Of all the fish that were eaten fresh, the huge trout, roasted over an open fire, were relished the most.

Winter, a harsh, bleak season, was devoted to the search for small game. While an old woman huddles in the family's cattail shelter (above), and a mother and child stand watching anxiously, two hunters go after a burrowing animal. One of the hunters, having opened up the entrance to the burrow, is flooding it with water; the second stands in wait, ready to shoot the animal when it emerges.

March was the month when the cattails poked their heads above the marsh waters to provide the first fresh plant food of the season. Although the air was still raw, the women waded into the chilly waters to pull up the young shoots. Once the soggy outer leaves had been ripped off, the crisp white stems were eaten raw.

July, the height of summer, brought the Indians rice grass, which the women harvested, threshed, and ground (right). They gathered it in huge armloads from the semidesert regions where it grew and carried it to threshing pads made of sunbaked earth. Here some women, like the one at far right, singe off the grass stems and, using a winnowing basket, separate the edible black seeds from the chaff. Next, as can be seen at lower left, another woman uses a mano and metate to husk and grind the seeds into a coarse meal.

September was the happiest month of the year. It was the time to gather the pine nuts that grew in profusion on the scrubby, round piñon trees (left) dotting the sides of the hills. The boys climb the trees to shake down the cones in which the tiny nuts are found; the men beat the branches farther up, hooking the cones with twigs lashed at an angle to long wooden poles. The women gather the cones in coarsely woven winnowing baskets, like the one at far right, to remove the stray twigs and needles from the harvest before loading it into huge conical burden baskets. Young girls carry the baskets back to camp, where older women husk the nuts.

November was the time to leave the hills for the desert, where the rabbit drive (below) was held. Although both men and women participated in this activity among some Paiute groups, in most the hunt was the exclusive reserve of the men. First cord nets—about three feet high and often lashed together into lengths as great as half a mile—were strung to enclose a semicircular area. Then piles of brush were stacked at either end of the net. Now the hunt could begin. The young men, armed with sticks and bows and arrows, form a moving fence, driving the rabbits toward the nets and killing them, when possible, as the creatures run. The older men hide near the nets and then slaughter the animals caught in the webbing.

pink flesh for winter by smoking and drying. If the run was meager, faces were grave; there would be hungry days ahead, and the hunters redoubled their efforts, hoping for a windfall to make up the difference.

The short green spring gave way to a long brown summer. By midyear, heat held the desert in its grip. Sentinel cactus, gray-green sagebrush, and greasewood bushes stood impassive in the gritty drought, and the air was abuzz with insects. Locusts, caterpillars, the big crickets later called Mormons, plus their chrysalides and eggs—all were part of the Indian diet, raw or roasted. Ants were roasted and ground with tiny seeds into a nutritious flour. A plague of grasshoppers was welcomed. Flushed by beaters into a wide firepit, they were scorched and ground into flour to make porridge. Everything that fed on insects, such as birds and chuckwalla lizards, was eaten as well.

Summer Harvest

At the height of summer, rice grass seeds and the yellow pollen of cattails were harvested. Mixed with water, this combination made a dough for appetizing bread cakes the children loved. Roots and bulbs—bitterroot, camass, sego lily (now Utah's state flower), and yampa—were dug, dried, and made part of the winter ration. And whenever the Indians found one of the 300-odd remedies they knew for human ills—mentzelia seeds for reviving the sick and aged, for example, or cinnabar for calomel to relieve a balky liver—it was carefully collected for future use.

Cottontail rabbits were especially plump at this sea-

son. They were shot with bow and arrow or trapped, along with robins and flickers, which also went into the pot. Magpies, however, were not eaten but were treasured for their iridescent feathers. Appliquéd to women's skirts, they would brighten the piñon nut dance in autumn.

Summer berries ripened and were gathered amid clouds of mosquitoes. Daubed with mud to forestall bites, the pickers loaded their baskets with elderberries, chokeberries, currants, and buffalo berries.

Perhaps once every eight years, depending on the mysterious cycles of abundance and scarcity, there might be signs of enough pronghorn antelopes to call for a drive. This was the responsibility of an antelope shaman well versed in charms and incantations. He was the one who picked the time and place for the drive and the direction in which the herd was to be driven into the corral, or killing pen. Such strategic considerations might, indeed, seem to require magic arts, for the beautiful little animals are easily frightened and capable of a getaway speed of 60 miles per hour. Even for the horse-riding Shoshonis of the eastern desert, this was a challenge. For the Paiute on foot, hunting antelopes was an exercise in patience, stamina, and guile. Fortunately for the hunters, pronghorns are insatiably curious, and the antics of a clever shaman—waving an unusual branch or wiggling his fingers from cover—could immobilize a herd until encircling hunters could guide it to destruction.

Pronghorns were prime trophies. The supple, tan-and-white hides were soft to the touch and had many

Clad in her rabbitskin robe, a Paiute woman sits by her Great Basin shelter. *Rabbitskin garments were essential to the Paiute and other peoples of the Great Basin, for with deer, antelopes, and mountain sheep in short supply, rabbits were the only reasonably certain source of warm clothing. Most of the skins were taken during the autumn rabbit hunts when thousands of the animals might be slain during a single drive. As many as 40 skins were needed for a child's robe, and 100 for a full-grown man's. A highly successful hunt was required to outfit an entire group. After each animal was skinned, its pelt was cut spirally into a long ribbon and then twisted in such a manner that the fur side was out. The ribbons, like the one above, might stretch as long as 15 feet. Finally, after the skins had dried, they were woven together on a simple loom made of willow sticks.*

Guided by the Shoshoni woman Sacajawea (*standing in canoe at right*), *members of the Lewis and Clark Expedition encounter Chinook Indians at Gray's Bay on the Columbia River on November 8, 1805. The painting by C. M. Russell, based on* the journals of Lewis and Clark, shows Sacajawea using sign language to communicate with the Chinooks. The Indian woman, who had been taken captive as a child, had long lived among the Mandans on the eastern edge of the Plains.

uses; the meat, cut into strips and jerked (cured and dried in the sun), could be stored for the winter.

Autumn was the zenith of the Northern Paiutes' year. When rose hips ripened in the valleys, the wandering families knew it was time to come together and ascend the mountain slopes where the piñon nuts grew. Groups came from all directions. Months had passed since last meeting, and there was much news and gossip to exchange. Children had been born. Some old people had died, animals had been slain, unusual weather encountered, hardships endured. A shaman had healed a woman sick unto death. The reunion also provided an opportunity for courtships among the young men and women eager to find mates during the annual reunion.

But the collection of food was the primary purpose of the gathering, and scouts were soon dispatched to locate the best stands of pine. The piñon pine was a capricious tree, yielding a heavy crop of nuts one year, then nothing for three or four. The scouts might have to travel 50 miles to find a grove with enough nuts to sustain the united families.

This year the news was good: the scouts returned with sample boughs whose cones were bursting with nuts. The site, the scouts announced, was a two-day walk south and east. The Indians broke camp, carrying their belongings in baskets. Precious water was carried in jugs coated with pitch to prevent leaks, and nourishing cattail seeds were packed in baskets of such fine mesh no seed could escape.

Prayers and Thanksgiving
Their first sunrise amid the pines was spent in prayer. The first day's harvest was dedicated to the ritual piñon prayer dance that began in the evening at sunset and lasted through the night. A wise woman, blessed with special powers, exorcised any ghosts that were about, and then nuts were scattered on the ground in gratitude to the earth for its bounty. The dancers circled the campfire with a shuffling step, praying for rain to keep the nuts from drying and singing songs of thanksgiving.

Cone collecting began at first light as entire families

Striking a heroic pose, *Gov. Caleb Lyon of the Idaho Territory presents a treaty to local Indians in the spring of 1866. Like many other pacts, this one called for the settlement of the Indians on reservations in exchange for government annuities. Though this particular agreement was shelved, similar treaties* were made with most of the tribes of the region. Often the government failed to keep its end of the bargains. One Shoshoni chief, Washaki, complained: ". . . we are sometimes nearly starved, and go half naked . . . do you wonder . . . that we have fits of depression and think to be avenged."

swarmed through the groves. Lengths of willow, lashed together to make a 15-foot pole, were wielded by the men to slap boughs and shake the cones from their moorings. Small boys went aloft to knock cones free by hand. Soon cones, bearing nuts the size of olive pits, littered the ground. Young women filled their *kawans*, conical burden baskets, and carried them back to camp where the older women pried the nuts from the cones. To free the meat from the hard shells, the nuts were roasted on a *yattah*, a flat winnowing tray made from peeled willow twigs. Hot coals were placed among the nuts, and all were flipped and shaken until the kernels were free. Skill was needed to avoid burning the *yattah*. After a second roast, the nuts were ground to a paste and boiled in a cooking basket to make a creamy soup.

Harvesting a good crop of nuts could keep a band together for several weeks and sometimes months. But work was not all-encompassing. There was time for naps at midday when the sun was high and warm and for the excitement of gambling.

Perhaps the most important function of the piñon nut harvest was to give the assembled families an opportunity to strengthen the network of relationships that bound them together. Marriages of young people renewed the promise that the Paiutes would perpetuate themselves. Family ties were made doubly strong when there were multiple marriages—brother and sister pairing off with sister and brother, or a man taking two sisters to wife. A rich man might well support more than one wife, and by wedding sisters he could be reasonably sure his wives would be compatible and his fireside harmonious.

Occasionally, a woman took two or more husbands. Women were often scarce, and a man might prefer to share a wife than have none. Desert women were valued and respected. Aside from their roles as companion and mother, their foraging and gathering made them the principal providers. They were clever weavers and as capable as men of becoming shamans.

Assemblies also were times to choose leaders, if needed, and to settle differences. Among Basin Indians the custom was to resolve problems reasonably, nonviolently, by discussion between the families involved. Even in cases of wife-stealing or witchcraft, the two most common serious crimes, the parties to the case sought equity without punishment. For casual misbehavior, the sharp tongue of gossip was an effective restraint.

At first snowfall in the mountains the Indians returned to the desert floor. Again an advance party was sent out, and they reported that the long-legged, black-earred jackrabbits were abundant. The band now deferred to the orders of the rabbit boss for organizing a drive. The jack was the source of both meat and fur, and single animals were hunted throughout the year. But when the rabbit population flourished—like all forms of desert life, it fluctuated from year to year—the Jackrabbit Eaters prepared for a massive kill.

As with other drives, the hunt was essentially a surround, with beaters herding the quarry toward waiting lines of clubbers. Crucial to the success of the drive, however, were the rabbit nets, the Indians' most valuable equipment. Nets were woven from fibers of Indian hemp, or dogbane, which grew in the moist soil along the banks of streams. The cordage was chain stitched in a loose mesh just large enough to catch a fleeing jack behind the ears as it tried to force its way through. Nets were several feet high and as much as 500 feet long. A good one became an heirloom, carefully maintained and passed down from generation to generation.

The nets were set at intervals in a narrow canyon, or sometimes in a wide semicircle on the desert flats, depending on where the rabbits were and how the drive captain thought it best to approach them.

The Rabbit Hunt
On an auspicious day the beaters fanned out over the desert, then doubled back behind the rabbits. On signal all the men began running and yelling to flush the jacks from their feeding places. The fastest hunters could overtake a jack, which was fast afoot but short of wind and inclined to run in spurts, but most men concentrated on channeling the darting prey toward the nets. At each net clubbers lay in wait, leaping to the attack as the rabbits were snared in the mesh or skittered back and forth seeking an opening. Those that escaped one net were usually snared in the next or the one beyond, and slain. By midday hundreds of carcasses littered the desert floor.

Some meat was sun-dried and then cached in grass-lined storage pits that were topped with grass, brush, and stones to discourage the keen-nosed coyotes. The remainder of the catch was skinned and boiled for immediate consumption. Nothing was wasted; even the bones were pulverized for soup.

The rabbit drive ended the community of families for the year. Winter neared, and smaller units were more self-sufficient in survival. As a family made its way toward a hilly site with a supply of firewood, they knew the work of the long summer would now sustain them. Dried fish, rabbit, and jerky were piled on willow racks. Piñon nut flour, dried berries, seeds, weaving fibers, and medicines were plentiful. Under lowering skies they prepared to live through the cold days ahead and await the coming of spring. `

This early-20th-century basket by a Washo weaver named Datsolali uses three fibers: willow for the background and western rosebud and bracken fern root for the intricate colored pattern.

The Discovery of Gold
Ten thousand years of Basin life were disrupted with the discovery of gold in California in 1848. Prospectors led the way; settlers followed. And when gold and silver were found in western Nevada as well, Virginia City became a hub of commerce and the frontier vanished. In a dismayingly short time the Indians' precarious dependence on nature's cycles was broken. The stands of piñon trees were ruthlessly leveled for fuel. Horses and cattle grazed and trampled the Indians' seed plots. White man's diseases, for which Indians had no immunity, weakened and killed them by the thousands. Cholera alone took 2,000 lives.

Paiutes, hearing that whites were coming, fled in panic, often burying their children up to the neck and piling sagebrush around their heads to hide them from the invaders. These Indians made no attempt to fight the whites. Among the Paiutes there never had been honor or glory in combat. Nomads for whom one piece of ground was much like another, they had no territorial imperatives. Men were never judged by their performance in battle and were therefore not much inclined to wage war. Even the appearance of hostile Indians prompted them to take cover and avoid conflict.

As wagon traffic intensified and ranches spread over the West, western Shoshonis and Utes became bedraggled pillagers on the outskirts of white settlements, begging or stealing to survive. Wilderness bands occasionally defied the white man, but their resistance to his blue-clad cavalrymen was futile.

In 1863 the United States government laid claim to the Basin without formal treaty or payment. The Indians were consolidated on reservations. By 1874 most of the Great Basin bands earned wages as housekeepers or field hands, and only vestiges of their customs and traditions survived.

Hopes for the Future
Today, more than a century later, some 4,200 Shoshonis, Paiutes, and Washos live on 15 reservations and in 10 small "colonies" that were established in 1934 to shelter indigent Indians working in white towns. Paiutes want to develop tourist facilities on their 475,000-acre reservation. Utes on the Uintah and Ouray Reservation in Utah hope that oil and natural gas will be found in their million-acre domain. The children of Great Basin Indians now go to public schools or government boarding schools, where they are taught skills far removed from the survival arts of their grandparents. That vulnerable life-style was blown away in the dust of wagon wheels, the smoke of miners' fires.

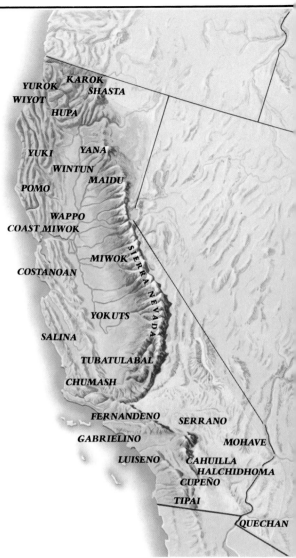

The rock-strewn coast (above) at Point Lobo in San Francisco Bay and the rolling, oak-tree-studded landscape of the Russian River region (top) illustrate two of California's many natural environments. The waters around such places as Point Lobo were teeming with crustaceans, fish, and sea mammals. There was a wealth of salmon, sturgeon, perch, and trout in the many nearby rivers. With a rich food supply at hand, the Indians in such places—most of them along the central and northern coasts—became fishermen. In the lush valleys between the Sierra and the coastal ranges, the land was rich in deer, elk, rabbits, nuts, berries, and fruits, providing the natives with more than ample sustenance. But not all of California was so well endowed. In the sun-baked deserts of the extreme southeast, rainfall averaged but two inches annually. Here the Indians, like those of the Great Basin, wandered the area in small bands and subsisted on piñon nuts, mesquite beans, snakes, rodents, and insects.

Favored by a mild climate and an abundance and variety of foods, the native peoples of California flourished and may have numbered about 133,000 when the Europeans arrived. California was also a land of wide cultural diversity where some 100 tribes and bands spoke numerous dialects of several language groups. In the northwest, Athabascan-speakers adopted some elements of Northwest Coast culture: plank houses, dugout canoes, carved figures. Shoshonean-speakers in the south were influenced by Arizona and New Mexico tribes. But the Penutian-speakers in central California were isolated from eastern contacts by the Sierra Nevada. Most central Californians were fishermen, hunters, and gatherers, and were among the least warlike of all Indians. Exceptions were the Mohaves and Yumas, who were both agriculturalists and warriors.

Indians of California

Almost everything the Great Basin lacked, California had. The climate was benign. The rain that was withheld from the Great Basin by the Sierra Nevada fell generously on the western slopes of the mountains, swelling California's rivers and streams and nourishing the land. Food, plants, and animals were varied and abundant. Raw materials for fashioning shelter, clothing, tools, weapons, and other necessities were plentiful and easily obtained.

This rich and spacious environment accommodated an exceptionally large Indian population. There were perhaps as many as 310,000 of them by the time white man appeared. These Indian tribes differed from one another in size, appearance, and language, but because of their shared geography many of the cultural patterns they developed were similar.

Like all American Indians they had broad, heavy faces, dark complexions, brown eyes, and straight black hair. But aside from these generally prevailing characteristics, variations in physical type were considerable. The Mohaves of the lower Colorado River valley, for example, were among the tallest people on the entire continent; the Yukis of the northern coast were among the shortest.

A Land of Many Tongues

In speech there was even greater diversity: more than a hundred distinct languages and dialects were spoken. Those who used Penutian, Hokan, and Shoshonean were most numerous. The Penutians extended over the largest single area—central California—while Hokan-speaking people were scattered in small pockets from present-day Oregon to Mexico. Athabascans, Algonquians, and Yukians—relatively few in number—were concentrated in north-central and northern California. This mix suggests that California was populated by immigrant peoples unrelated by language and that, as small groups became separated in the vastness of the territory, isolation fostered divergences in dialects.

Overall, however, California's Indians had more similarities than differences. They ate the same kinds of foods, gathered and prepared in much the same way. Their homes and dress were much alike. They followed the same pattern of social organization and held similar religious beliefs. Basket-weaving was the main artistic expression for all the peoples.

Wild plants and fish—especially the migratory salmon that could be smoked for year-round use—were sta-

*This **Chumash polychrome** pictograph has been partly destroyed by time and erosion. The figures may represent mythical or religious beings or strange objects seen in dreams.*

ples for almost all groups, but deer, elk, smaller game, and birds were hunted as food in lean seasons of the year. Hides were worn as clothing or as robes for winter warmth. Most of the time, however, men went naked, while women wore a two-piece garment serving as skirt and apron. Dwellings were of a simple design and construction, and built to shelter a single family.

The family was the basic social unit: seven or eight people—parents, children, and several adult kin. An aggregation of families—related through the male line—settled together and made up an independent village. And if there were an outlying satellite village or two, the whole—a hundred persons or so—formed a loose, largely unstructured association.

But these small, self-contained groups had no sense of identification with or allegiance to a large tribal organization. Custom and tradition defined the boundaries of their living space, and generally they operated within it, sharing common rights to all it contained.

A Peaceful People

Whether nature's bounty made it unnecessary to seize or defend territory, or whether their temperaments were unusually pacific, Californians rarely waged war. Conflicts were normally on a small scale, arising out of a feud or as an act of vengeance, and were usually settled by negotiation. There was no real hierarchy of leadership. A hereditary headman normally served as a functionary in village affairs, but his authority was slight.

Perhaps the predominant figure was the shaman, and in some areas this was more likely to be a woman than a man. California Indians put great store by the shamans' curative powers, believing that they were bestowed through a spirit helper.

The course of Indian life in California flowed gently, and differences between "tribelets"—a term coined for these small units—were mostly matters of area and local custom. In the north were groups influenced by the rich culture of the Northwest Coast. In a broad central zone were the most populous and typical of the native societies.

Although California's natural abundance made food gathering sure and easy, and there was, therefore, ample time and opportunity to evolve toward a more complex society, the culture of these Indians did not change substantially over the centuries. Perhaps, in the long quiet days before the disruptions of the white man, responding to the rhythms of a blessed land seemed life enough for those who enjoyed this bountiful existence.

Southward, in the area of the Santa Barbara Channel, were the Chumashes, who were among those North American Indian groups adept at ocean fishing. There were land-bound Chumashes as well, living north and south of the channel, from the coast eastward to the mountains. They were linked as members of the Hokan linguistic family yet isolated by differences in dialect. They decorated their bodies distinctively, using various designs as a form of identification. Earrings, nose plugs, and necklaces of shell and stone were also among their personal adornments.

Even the seagoing Chumashes—some six to seven thousand people on the mainland and the channel is-

A soapstone pipe, carved in the form of a killer whale, was called a cloud blower by the Chumashes, whose shamans smoked it during certain rituals.

lands—had a seasonal pattern of existence similar in most respects to the other California Indians sharing a like geography and climate. Oak trees provided a mighty harvest of acorns; deer and smaller game were hunted for winter meat and hides. Villages were often large, with more than 1,000 inhabitants who lived in dome-shaped houses. Each village had one or more sweathouse, a ceremonial area for religious functions, and a cemetery. The people were excellent basketmakers and proficient workers in wood and stone.

But in their saltwater fishing, they were unique. Great beds of kelp provided a rich marine environment in the channel that harbored some 125 species of fish, including yellowtails, bonitos, albacores, and tunas, and attracted numerous species of sea mammals—seals,

Maidu tribesmen (above) gossip on the roofs of their semi-underground houses in their village of T'seno in the Sacramento Valley. This village consists of a scattering of dwellings, each 20 to 40 feet in diameter. The opening in the center of each roof does double duty as a smoke hole and an entryway. Near the houses are barrellike structures for storing acorns, a major part of the Maidu diet. The drawing at left depicts the interior of a hut of the neighboring Patwins. Long poles support the earthen walls and ceiling, and poles also form the frame of a bed. On the floor one woman (rear) pounds acorns into flour and another boils mush. Behind the cook are several duck decoys made from stuffed duck skins.

The Mohaves: Desert Warriors and Farmers

Among the peoples of Carlifornia, those settled along the lower Colorado in the southeast portion of the region were unique in several respects. They identified strongly with their tribes, they were the only Indians in the area to rely on farming, and war was a major element in their lives. Perhaps archetypical of these riverside peoples were the Mohaves. Their homeland in the desert that bears their name was subject to great extremes of heat and cold, and their clothing reflected their environment: narrow breechclouts for men and simple aprons for women during the excessively hot days. At night and during the cold season, men and women alike wrapped themselves in rabbitskin robes.

The Mohave settlements, too small to be called villages, were scattered near the banks of the lower Colorado. The warm-weather abodes were simply open-sided, flat-roofed shelters that shaded people from the sun. In colder months they moved into low, rectangular structures supported by four posts and covered with arrowweed and sand.

That life was possible at all for the Mohaves was owing to the annual flooding of the lower Colorado, a circumstance that created a narrow swatch of green through the dismal surrounding landscape. Along this fertile fringe the Mohaves farmed, growing corn, beans, pumpkins, melons, and in postcontact times, a little wheat. These crops provided half their food. The rest

The Mohaves' dress and body tattoos are shown in this painting by H. B. Mollausen, an artist who accompanied an 1857–58 expedition to the Colorado River.

came from hunting rabbits and other small desert game, fishing, and gathering such wild growths as mesquite beans, screw beans, and piñon nuts.

When not farming, hunting, or gathering, the Mohaves were likely to be at war. For some—a special class of about 40 or 50 men called the Kwanamis—warfare was an obsession. But their influence among their fellow tribesmen was pervasive. When the Kwanamis spoke for war, the others followed, and as the warrior class cared only for honors in battle, combat was an almost incessant part of Mohave life. Usually the enemy was one of several fellow Yuman-speaking peoples, though the

Yuma tribe itself often allied itself with the Mohaves. A Mohave raiding party, which might include only several of the Kwanamis among a few dozen combatants, was divided into three elements: archers, clubbers, and stickmen (who carried lances).

One other element of Mohave life is worthy of note. They were a people of great curiosity and loved to travel. Often travel was linked with trade, but sometimes they journeyed hundreds of miles because, in the words of anthropologist A. L. Kroeber: ". . . they were as eager to know the manners of other peoples as they were careful to hold themselves aloof from adopting them."

otters, dolphins, whales, and sea lions—some of which used the islands as rookeries. Shores, shallows, and tidal basins could also be dredged for mussels, abalones, oysters, scallops, and clams.

The Chumashes fished from 25-foot canoes made of fitted driftwood or pine planks sewn with fiber cordage and caulked with asphalt. They were double-ended, looked somewhat like a dory, and were similarly swift and skittish. But a crew of three or four, using double-bladed paddles, could take them well out to sea in fair weather.

Fishing was best from late spring to late summer, when fish schooled and mammal herds congregated. Equipment was simple but effective: tridents, toggle harpoons, and nets woven of sea grass with stone balls to weight them. In confined or still waters, traps were used, or soap plant was put into the water to stupefy the fish and make them easy to catch.

Seals, valued primarily for their pelts, were hunted

cooperatively by groups of men. The strategy was to get between a herd and the open sea, startle the animals with sudden screams, and lance or club them as they fled shoreward in panic.

Of all of California's Indians, none enjoyed a more comfortable life than the many inhabitants of the territory's well-wooded, well-watered central zone. And of these fortunate people, none were more affluent than the Pomos living north of San Francisco Bay. Ranging from the coast to the Sierra Nevada foothills, with the great Central Valley between, the region offered an environment with a moderate year-round climate and an abundance of food plants, game, and useful raw materials. It amply supported some 75-80,000 people.

The Pomos, perhaps 8,000 in all, were a Hokan-speaking people scattered in some 50 self-sufficient communities throughout the area. These Indians were typically dark-skinned, stocky, with large, heavy faces and a tendency to become fat with age. They were noted for their

265

Conical dwellings (above), one of several kinds of habitations used by the Interior Miwoks, had a framework of poles, bound together with vine stalks and covered with brush, grass, or tule. The tribesmen also lived in lean-tos of bark slabs and in semisubterranean houses. Miwok women used rocks like these in California's Indian Grinding Rock State Park (upper right) as mortars. They chipped holes in the boulders, filled them with acorns, and used stone pestles for grinding.

basketry, which was among the finest ever created by any aboriginal people, for their "minting" and use of money, and for the associated talent of counting.

A few Pomos were coastal people, living amid fog and incessant wind from the shoreline cliffs to the crest of the first inland ridge. They were cut off from the majority of Pomos by a forest of giant redwoods. More than a third of all Pomos lived farther inland in the Russian River valley.

Still farther east was Clear Lake, some 150 square miles of fresh water, teeming with fish and a haven for waterfowl. On the banks of nearby streams, rather than at the lake's edge, was the largest concentration of Pomos. Despite the many differences generated by these various environments, the three Pomo groups were culturally homogeneous.

Food From Oaks

For the Pomos, like most other Californians, acorns were a dietary staple, especially those of the white oak—the most common of California's seven species. The huge fall harvest was an important event. Gathering was largely women's work, although men and boys helped by climbing the great trees and shaking or knocking nuts loose. Thereafter, the acorns had to be dried, hulled, and pounded into flour, then placed in a sandy basin and leached with hot water to remove the tannic acid that makes them bitter. The acid-free meal was boiled in a tight-meshed basket and emerged as a mush that was served at each of the day's two meals. Acorn meal could also be baked into an unleavened bread.

But there was great variety in the Pomo diet. Fish was readily available. Seeds, berries, roots, bulbs, and tubers were dug or gathered. The tender shoots of many plants were eaten as well as the blossoms of springtime clover. Deer, rabbits, and gamebirds—including ducks and geese around Clear Lake—provided meat.

The Pomos were capable hunters with bow and arrow, and masters at herding deer into a corral for slaughter. The Pomos were also adept with snares and traps, at shooting from blinds, and at bagging waterfowl from tule rush boats with slings and nets.

A Bountiful Region

The certainty that food was ample and easy to come by determined the course and pattern of the Pomos' life. They built substantially and settled in more or less permanent locations. Even the simple homes of the coast Pomos—slabs of redwood bark piled against a centerpost to make a conical, single-family tepee—were more elaborate than anything that would be found in the Great Basin. As for the Russian River and Clear Lake groups, their pole-frame-and-thatch structures were up to 30 feet long and housed several families.

These were the living quarters of the women and children, the places where food was cooked and eaten and property stored. The largest and most important building was the dance house, or "singing lodge," a circular pit up to 60 feet across with an earthen roof. Here the men assembled to confer on village affairs or to conduct ceremonies from which females were excluded.

Like most Californians, the Pomos had no overall political or tribal unity but lived independently in some 50 local groups, each made up of 75 to 300 people. An average community of 150-200 lived in a main village with one or two outlying settlements. The extent of each group's area was known and respected, and its resources were communally owned and utilized.

Authority was vested in the village males. The meager powers of the hereditary headman were largely ceremonial: to welcome, to preside, to mediate. It was also his prerogative to deliver public lectures: advice on moral behavior, a recital of customs, reminders, instructions, exhortations. The oratorical style was loud, repetitive, emphatic, and rhythmically jerky.

As elsewhere in California, the single family was the basic social and economic unit. Unattached kin were included, and several closely related groups might share a home. Children were wanted and welcomed. During pregnancy the mother's diet and behavior were strictly regulated to ensure safe delivery. Birth usually took place in the family dwelling. A shaman—among the Pomos, a male—was consulted if labor was difficult.

Postnatal care was also rigorously prescribed. The umbilical cord was buried, and the mother was placed in a sweat room to aid recuperation. Even the father had to observe certain disciplines: he had to undergo the couvade—a male approximation of the female experience. When his wife was about to give birth, he remained indoors, in confinement, for some days and did not hunt, gamble, or travel for a month.

Children were casually and indulgently raised, and education was largely imitation of the elders. At the onset of puberty Pomo girls were considered contaminated, placed in isolation, and restricted in activities,

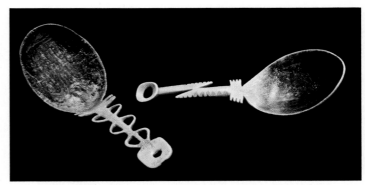

Spoons for eating acorn gruel are carved from elk antlers. The one on the left was made by a Yurok craftsman, the other by a Karok. Fine workmanship and ornate decorations were the hallmark of even their most common utensils.

somewhat like a new mother. Unlike other groups, Pomos held no public ceremony to honor the event.

Marriage was negotiated by older women—usually maternal aunts—but did not involve bride purchase. The couple's wishes were duly considered: the young man indicated the woman he wanted to marry, and she had the right to accept or refuse the proposal. Blood relationship was the only taboo. Gifts were exchanged only as a pledge of goodwill between the families. Responsibility in marriage was divided traditionally. The man hunted, fished, built the home, made his gear. The woman gathered all edible plants, cooked, tended the children, and wove baskets. The Pomos regarded their

Purifying acorn flour, a Pomo woman kneels before a sand-banked leaching pit and pours hot water on unrefined meal to leach it of its tannin, a bitter tasting substance that causes indigestion. The hot water washes the tannin through the meal and is then absorbed in the sand base of the pit. The woman pours the water over a bundle of bullrush twigs to lessen the force of the water and distribute it evenly over the flour. The fire at the woman's right is used to heat stones that she will grasp with the wooden tool (in front of the pit) and place in the water basket to her left. To grind acorns into meal, the Pomos used a flat stone as a mortar and surmounted it with an open-ended, woven cone (inset). A second stone served as a pestle. The cone permitted a woman to grind many acorn kernels in a single operation, and the high sides of the basket-like cone acted as a shield to keep the flour from blowing away. Grinding was often the work of the elderly.

The Superb Basketry of California Tribes

Perhaps because their environment offered life's necessities virtually for the taking, the Indians of northern California were never compelled to develop a sophisticated technology to exploit their surroundings. All of them were hunter-gatherers, living in small villages and using only the simplest tools and techniques to obtain the things they needed in their daily lives. In one respect, however, their technology was remarkably advanced. They were highly skilled at basketry, using the reeds, grasses, barks, and roots they found around them to fashion articles of all sorts and sizes—not only trays, containers, and cooking pots, but hats, boats, fish traps, baby carriers, and ceremonial objects.

Of all these experts, none excelled the Pomo—a group of small tribes who lived on or near the coast. They made baskets three feet in diameter and others no larger than a thimble. The Pomos were masters of decoration. Some of their baskets were completely covered with shell pendants; others with feathers that made the baskets' surfaces as soft as the breasts of birds. Moreover, the Pomos made use of more weaving techniques than did their neighbors. Most tribes made all their basketwork by twining—the twisting of a flexible weft around a stiffer warp. Others depended primarily on coiling—a process in which a continuous coil of stiff material is held in the desired shape by a tight wrapping of flexible strands. Only the Pomos used both processes with equal ease and frequency. In addition, they made use of four distinct variations on the basic twining process, often employing more than one of them in a single article.

In other tribes basketry was exclusively women's work, but among the Po-

A California basket-maker gathers tule along the edge of a pond. Tule, a tall reed found only near water, is too heavy for use in fine basketry, but the Pomos used the material for other purposes. From one of the two tule species they made coarse twined baskets and boats. The other was used for such items as house thatch and mats.

mos, men also participated. Men made relatively simple articles, such as mats, fish traps, and baby carriers, while Pomo women concentrated on more complex and delicate work. Although a wide variety of materials was available, the Pomos used only a few. The warp was always made of willow, and the most commonly used weft was sedge root, a woody fiber that could easily be separated into strands no thicker than a thread. For color, the Pomos used the bark of redbud for their twined work and dyed bullrush root for black in coiled work. Though other materials were sometimes used, these four were the staples in their finest basketry.

If the basketry materials used by the Pomos were limited, the designs were amazingly varied. Every Pomo basket-maker knew how to produce from 15 to 20 distinct patterns that could be combined in a number of different ways. Superstition surrounded the way the patterns were used. No Pomo basket-maker would ever run a pattern completely around her work. She had to leave a break in it somewhere, lest she lose her sight. Nor would she fail to use the quills of the yellowhammer for a few of the wrappings in her coiled work if she were doing it during her menstrual period, for the quills were a charm against the accompanying evil.

Plain twining employed weft threads twined together across each of the stiff warp strands. This simple variety of basket weaving was used by all the Indians of northern California; only the Pomos used the techniques shown in the other drawings.

Three-strand braiding was a Pomo technique used primarily for basket bottoms and borders. It involved the continuous braiding of three weft strands in such a way that each strand passed under two warps and over one in an alternating pattern.

California basketry, above and right, exemplifies the wide variety of uses to which basketwork was put and the diversity of shapes and decorations produced. At right is a Pomo coiled gift basket decorated with shells and the feathers of several kinds of birds. Above are examples of the work of six California groups. At the front is a Yokuts gambling tray on which several other baskets rest. Included is a lidded Hupa trinket basket (bottom left), next to which is a round Hupa hat. Behind these, on its side, is a conical Washo basket partially within a Wintun berry basket. At upper left is a Washo winnowing tray, beneath which is a Tulares ceremonial basket and another richly decorated Pomo feather basket.

Lattice twining made use of rigid core pieces placed both horizontally and vertically, around which two weft strands were twined. This extremely tight weave was used for cooking, winnowing, and parching baskets and for storage ware.

Three-strand twining, used on basket sides, employed three weft threads, two of them passing over each warp element and one passing under, as shown above. For basket bottoms the Pomos sometimes used a six-strand twining method.

women more highly than did most California Indians.

Weaving was a skill at which Pomo women were unexcelled. They used more than 30 plant materials, employed a number of weaving techniques, and were superbly artistic in their designs and ornamentations.

Pomo men were noted for the manufacture of money, of which they were the major purveyors in central California. They were uninterested in the dentalium shell currency so highly valued by others; the Pomos made both magnesite cylinders and discoidal clamshell beads.

Magnesite, a creamy white mineral with a texture like meerschaum, was ground into cylinders one to three inches long, drilled, baked (to infuse color), and polished. They were extremely valuable and bargained for individually. The clamshell beads were rounded, sanded, bored, and strung, their value depending on size, thickness, and degree of polish. Treasured antique strings gained an inimitable gloss. Because the beads were cheap and numerous, the Pomos had to become adept at large computations. They did not know division or multiplication, but they could add their beads in string units up to 40,000. Money was used in trade, for funerary offerings, and as payment of reparations between feuding families.

The Marts of Trade

Villages enjoying a surplus of raw materials, foodstuffs, or artifacts were usually willing to trade such goods for things they lacked. Some trading expeditions ventured hundreds of miles away from home, but most transactions took place between neighboring units of the same tribe or with an alien but friendly tribe nearby.

In the northwest the Hupas of the lower Trinity River traded principally with the Yuroks, who lived along the coast near the mouth of the Klamath River. The Hupas exchanged acorns and other inland foods for seaweed (a source of hard-to-find salt), dried fish, and other produce of the sea. Even the dugout canoes the Hupas used were acquired from the Yuroks. Made from half a redwood log, and thus round-bottomed and square-ended, the craft was nonetheless stable and could carry a large crew and more than a ton of cargo.

Inland and coastal people were natural trading partners. In spring, when the air lost its dampness and turned balmy, groups from the interior began making their way to the shore. Sometimes an all-male trading party went on a mission. On other occasions an entire village made an outing of the bartering sessions. Camping on a beach, the visitors surf-fished and collected shellfish among the rocks. Pomos from the interior journeyed to the coast for seafood once or twice a year, while coastal Pomos went inland at the time of acorn harvest. Visitors usually were free to gather what they came for, as long as they had the courtesy and good sense to ask the locals' permission. At such times, trade became incidental.

Occasionally, however, territorial rights were violated. The Chumashes, for one, were aggressive in defense of their boundaries and did not take lightly the trespassing of strangers on their hunting or collecting grounds.

That Invaluable Asset: Salt

Some groups were the fortunate possessors of an unique resource, such as the salt deposit owned by certain northeastern Pomos. The salt crystallized each summer from brackish groundwater seeping from a particular acre. Visiting Indians were welcome to partake of this treasure, but the Pomos wanted presents or payment in return and would fight anyone who tried to steal salt.

Magnesite had both decorative and monetary value. Obsidian, a stone that would hold an edge, was in demand for arrowheads, cutting tools, and weapons. For their commodities the Clear Lake Pomos traded with northern groups for arrows, sinew-backed bows, and iris fiber cord for deer snares; with coastal people for mussels, seaweed, and seal furs; with southerners for clamshells from which to make money beads.

Other tribes also traded their surpluses, sometimes raw materials, sometimes finished goods, such as cooking pots, arrow straighteners, tanned skins, or paint.

Frequently, goods would be purchased rather than bartered. The Hupas in particular used for money the thin, tubelike dentalium shells that came to them through intertribal trade. Unfinished dentalium shells were a trade item that originated west of Vancouver Island, far to the north, and were exchanged many times before reaching the Hupas.

The trade system had its limitations. In lush California needs were simple and easily satisfied. There was no transport except backpacking. Loads were

Elkhorn purses were common among northern California tribes. The purses shown here (clockwise from upper left) are from the Karok, Yurok, and Hupa tribes. The string of dentalium shells, which were widely used as a medium of exchange, were obtained from a northerly tribe, the Tolowa.

A Passion for Games and Gambling

Like almost all North American Indians, those of California were inveterate gamblers as well as enthusiastic participants in games that stressed skill, strength, endurance, and chance. Particularly popular among the Mohaves was the hoop-and-pole game, which required both an excellent aim and judgment under pressure because participants bet heavily on the outcome. A hoop was rolled and a player slid a pole along the ground, hoping that the hoop would fall on top of it when it stopped rolling. Variations of this sport were also played by the Luisenos, Diegueños, Maidus, Pomos, Shastas, and Modocs. Most of these tribes also competed in a game that involved catching a ring or loop on a stick.

Ball games were also popular among many tribes. The Pomos played a variety of lacrosse in which they propelled a ball down a field with a netted stick. The Miwoks and Yokuts engaged in a similar sport, except that the stick ended in a loop instead of a net. Among the Mohaves, shinny—a game that involved batting a small block of wood with a curved stick—was a popular pastime.

The lack of flat spaces in the rocky northwestern region limited the playing of field games. But one favorite amuse-

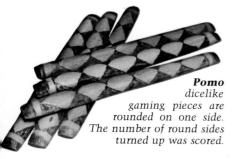

Pomo *dicelike gaming pieces are rounded on one side. The number of round sides turned up was scored.*

ment involved throwing two blocks of wood—tied together with sinew—with a shinny stick. As the blocks could not be thrown very far, the game could be played in a small clearing. In the south and along the coast, however, a kind of soccer was highly popular, and players could use only their feet to propel a ball down a large field.

In most areas dicelike counting games were played exclusively by women. The counters might be walnut shells, as at right, sticks (left), acorn cups, split acorns, or mussel shells. Whatever the game, it was almost always an occasion for gambling by both contestants and spectators. Among men throughout the region, the favorite betting activity was a guessing game involving objects hidden in the hands (above), a contest of wits that could go on for days while fortunes in shells, bows, skins, and baskets were wagered.

The hand game, a favorite gambling entertainment among many Indians, is underway in this Maidu lodge. One player holds a marked and an unmarked bone and rapidly switches them from fist to fist. He then challenges his opponents to guess which hand holds the marked bone. Bets were high in this contest.

A counting game, popular among Yokuts women, was played on a basketry tray with eight walnut shell halves filled with pitch and inlaid with bits of abalone shell. Two teams of two women faced each other across the tray, and one woman tossed the shells. A fifth woman kept score with sticks. Points depended on how many shells landed pitch-side up when caught on the tray.

whatever expeditions on foot could haul over the mountains to isolated communities. And communication was thwarted by the babel of unintelligible languages.

Still, traveling afield to trade was a project eagerly undertaken for adventure as well as profit. It offered new sights and new sounds, the pleasure of seeing old friends, and the excitement of meeting strange, new people. It was little wonder that trading expeditions returned in triumph, the men as full of stories as their packs were full of goods, or that villagers turned out en masse to celebrate the homecoming and enjoy the wondrous tales of far-off lands.

The Religions of California

For California Indians religion was a varying collection of beliefs and observances. In most instances it accounted for the Creation of the earth, perpetuated mythologies, identified supernatural spirits and defined relations with them, celebrated ritual events, and certified shamans.

The Luisenos of southern California had perhaps the best-developed conception of how life began. Mother Earth and Father Sky emerged from the original void, and from their union plants, animals, and man were born. In contrast, the Hupas, in the northwest corner of the state, had no notion of a Creation. They believed

271

that the world always had existed as it now was and that the human race had simply sprung into being.

The Pomos' concept of the universe involved three coexisting worlds. The two upper ones were the abode of Madumda, the Creator, and his brother. Lowest was the earth, whose people had been made from feathers and sticks, and animated by Coyote, a clever and ingenious figure that was sometimes equated with Madumda.

The realm of the supernatural was complex. Most important to the Pomos was Kuksu, healer of the sick and, some said, ruler of the dead. He was a figure of ceremonial importance. But others—Sun-Man, Thunder-Man, the devouring scourge Gilak, or the bearded dwarf of the Hupas who ruled the vegetable world—existed but had little impact on the affairs of men.

Of far greater consequence were the numerous local spirits domiciled in mountains, boulders, trees, caves. Benign spirits could be prayed to for success in one's ventures, but others were evil and their habitations places to be avoided.

The forms and purposes of rituals varied from group to group, but they were alike in that the ceremonies involved and were performed by men only. The White Deerskin Dance and the Jumping Dance were the principal ceremonies of the Hupas and Yuroks. Each rite continued for 10 days and sought to revitalize the world for the year ahead and avert illness and misfortune. For the Hupas, who put great store by personal wealth, the ceremonies were an opportunity for display. The dancers required elaborate regalias—albino deerskins, red woodpecker scalps, and the like—and important families took pride in supplying them from their treasures.

The frenetic Ghost and Kuksu ceremonies of the Pomos were unique in being the only ones in which spirits were impersonated. Both were initiations of youth into the secrets of male society and took place over a period of days in the dance house, hidden from the eyes of women. The Ghost dancers disguised themselves as spirits of the dead. They ate fire, handled rattlesnakes, stomped the ominously resonant foot drum, and twirled the bull-roarer, or thunderstick, a device that makes a great noise when whirled through the air. The Kuksu dancers masqueraded as the spirit itself, enacted mythological dramas, and ritually slew and than later revived the initiates.

Luiseno and other southern California youths were initiated to manhood in a lengthy sequence of ordeals and ceremonies. Most important was drinking a Jimsonweed potion to induce visions from which one acquired his personal guardian spirit. The creator of this ritual was said to be Chungichnish, a powerful deity that prescribed

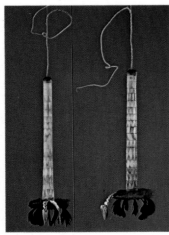

Elaborate jewelry, denoting wealth and status, was an important element in the dress of northern Californians. The Hupa woman at left is bedecked with shell necklaces, and shells also cover her fringed skirt. At far left above are the tassels worn at the ends of a belt by a Wailaki shaman during curing ceremonies. The tassels are made of abalone and clam shell beads and tufts of deer hair. Below them is a pair of earrings once worn by a wealthy Pomo woman. The rods are engraved crane leg bones, decorated with quail feathers; the pendants, which hung in front of the woman's shoulders, are fashioned from abalone and clam shells.

the codes of behavior and also punished transgressors.

Other rituals of importance to California's Indians did not involve or propitiate spirits, but celebrated circumstances of life or of the season. Among such rites were dedications of salmon from the first run of spring and acorns from the first harvest of fall; an observance in honor of girls arriving at adolescence; war and victory dances; and death ceremonies to free the spirit of the deceased and keep it from returning as a ghost.

Shamanism, although essentially the medical art of curing disease, was rooted in magic and mysticism because of the belief that illness had supernatural causes and because shamans had spirit allies. In central and southern California shamans were men, and their curative powers were acquired supernaturally in a trance or dream. The Pomo shamans encountered a spirit animal or being; the Luisenos saw a deity, a monster, or a heavenly phenomenon.

Women as Healers

Among the Hupas, the healers were women. They had no guardian helper but gained power by learning to control "pain" that was given by a spirit or a ghost and taken into the body in a dream.

A shaman medicine bag contained such talismans as coyote feet, dried lizards, snakeskins, a rattle, colored pebbles, obsidian, a thunderstick, and odd or misshapen natural objects. These were amulets of power, and a child unfortunate enough to stand in the shadow of a bag might die. Doctoring paid well. Shamans were people of consequence, and their fees were high. But if the patient failed to improve or died, the shaman paid a penalty: he had to refund the fee.

The Atypical Hupas

The Hupas—probably never numbering no more than 1,500—lived in California's mountainous and remote northwestern corner, where the Trinity River flows swiftly through evergreen forests to meet the Klamath. They were broadheaded, muscular, of medium height. All had long hair, the men's worn in two bunches in front of the shoulders, the women's in two rolls. The

A cloak, made from a whole bearskin (above), *completely covered the body and head of the Pomo bear doctor who wore it. Bear doctors, who carried horn daggers, were feared by the Pomos, who considered them capable of performing evil magic.*

ears of both sexes were pierced. Men's beards were plucked, and women's chins were tattooed with three vertical stripes for beauty. The Hupas spoke an Athabascan language, fished for salmon, gathered the ubiquitous acorn, and resembled other California tribelets in dressing minimally, living in small villages, and centering male life around the sweathouse.

They differed from other California Indians, however, in reflecting the distinctive culture of the Northwest Coast (see next chapter). This influence was particularly notable in the Hupas skilled use of wood and their determination of status on the basis of personal wealth.

Their homes were sturdily built of cedar planks on frameworks of poles and beams. The craftsmanship was exceptional, considering the limitations of their tools.

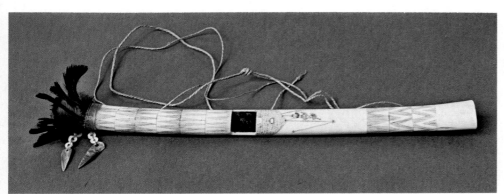

A bone whistle, with a figure of a deity engraved on it, was used by a Pomo medicine man during a curing ceremony. The deity, sometimes known as Big Head, was believed to live in a large house at the south end of the world. The figure on the whistle stands atop such a house. The medicine man effected cures by dancing around his patient, prodding the sore spot with a feather-tipped staff, and blowing the whistle, whose sound supposedly represented the speech of the deity.

273

The Patwin's Hesi Ceremonial: A Dance for Food and Fortune

From October to May the Patwin Indians of California's Sacramento Valley held a series of sacred ceremonials and dances designed to bring health and prosperity, to cause the rain to fall, and to ensure a plentiful harvest of wild crops. All the ceremonies were conducted by the members of the Kuksu cult, a secret society of males that played a major role in the practices of many central California tribes. The rituals and activities of the Kuksu varied from one tribe to another, and by the end of the 19th century many original forms and much of the significance of the rituals had been lost, even to the Kuksus themselves. The causes were partly white influence and partly distortions introduced by the Ghost Dance movement that swept Nevada and California in the 1870's (see the Great Plains chapter). But in their original forms, the importance of the ceremonies was great, for the rites were believed to provide protection from catastrophe—possibly even the disintegration of the earth itself.

Like secret societies among other Indian groups, the Kuksu made use of disguises, both as a way of concealing the identities of its members from the women and children of the tribe and as a means of transforming participants in the ceremonies into the spirits and deities whose parts the members played. These disguises took the form of elaborate feather or grass headdresses large enough to cover the face and sometimes the body as well. Some of the most impressive of these feathered masquerades were used during Hesi, the four-day dance that ushered in the ceremonial cycle that lasted intermittently from fall to spring. People from several villages usually assembled at a host community for Hesi. The visitors did not arrive until the second day of the ceremonial; the first day's dances were performed by men of the host village with only local people in attendance.

The sacred dances of the Hesi were led by a man representing Moki, the most important and highest-ranking spirit in the Patwin pantheon. Although the role endowed the performer with much honor, many Kuksus who were qualified to impersonate Moki shrank back from the challenge, for they believed that any mistake in their performance would bring about their death. No such fear was attached to another principal role in Hesi—that of Tuya, the Big-Headed dancer, nor was there fear of the role of Chelitu, another Patwin spirit, who danced unmasked.

Hesi was not a group performance. Each of the Tuyas performed separately or with a Chelitu, whose primary function was to direct the movements of his Tuya partner. In the painting at right, a portion of the ceremonial is in progress. The spectators are arranged in rows behind the dancers. At the far left is Moki, his entire body concealed beneath a feathered cloak. He has just returned to the dance house after calling in a Tuya and a Chelitu to perform. At the center of the picture is the Tuya, disguised by his huge headdress of feathers and painted willow rods. Two long bands made from the quills of the yellowhammer hang from a stick at the back of his headdress, and he wears a feathered skirt and carries a rattle in each hand. The Chelitu (far right) wears a headdress of magpie feathers and a pair of yellowhammer quill bands. In his left hand he carries a bow; in his right, arrows in a quiver made from a whole foxskin. As the Chelitu dances he signals the Tuya, thus directing his partner's movements. Accompanying the dancers are two drummers (extreme left) who pound out a steady rhythm on a foot drum, and two singers and a chorus who chant ancient and sacred songs.

Renewal Rituals of Northern California

Each year the Hupas, Yuroks, and Karoks of northern California held their World Renewal ceremonies, a series of rituals to "firm the earth" and ensure good fortune. The time when these rituals were conducted varied from group to group, as did their length and the specifics of the rites that were performed. But all were alike not only in their purpose but in their general form. They were divided into two parts—a highly sacred one involving only a few people and a festive one with many participants and a large audience. In the sacred rites a specially designated man, who had prepared himself through a series of purification rituals, traveled—often with several assistants—to a number of prescribed locations. At each he carried out a particular rite that would ensure nature's renewal. In the festive part that followed, two dances—the Jumping Dance and the White Deerskin Dance—were always performed. The dancers were often outfitted by wealthy tribesmen who proclaimed their status by the lavishness of the costumes they supplied.

A Hupa obsidian knife bearer displays a ceremonial blade across his chest for his role in the White Deerskin Dance. His costume includes a headdress of sea lion teeth and a necklace of dentalium shells. Together with another knife wielder, he danced for the other celebrants, crouching, blowing a whistle, and brandishing his blade, a major status symbol among northern Californians.

White Deerskin dancers prepare to perform, in this photograph taken in the late 19th century. The two obsidian bearers are in the front. The others wear costumes that include civet cat or deerskin aprons, dentalium shell necklaces, and tall headdresses made of several feathers. Each dancer carries a pole around which a whole deerskin is draped—the head stuffed and decorated with woodpecker scalps, the body and legs hanging loose. Although gray, black, or mottled deerskins could be carried, white ones were the most desirable. They were the rarest and therefore the most valuable—the best evidence of their owners' wealth and status in the community.

Lacking axes, they felled trees with fire and split planks from logs with antler-horn wedges and stone hammers. Cedar also was used for furniture, utensils, and storage chests. Bows were made of hardwoods. Elkhorn was converted into spoons (for men only; women used mussel shells) and money boxes; bone was the material for harpoons and awls, and stone for arrowpoints and tools. The women were versatile basket weavers, though less skilled than the Pomos.

Although Hupa communities existed without formal government authority of any kind, their interpersonal relations were governed by a complicated code requiring compensation for injuries done. No matter how mild or how heinous the offense—from public insult to murder—there was a fine whose payment would set things right. The social standing of the aggrieved party was a factor in determining a just settlement. Terms were negotiated by a mediator who haggled with both sides until agreement was reached.

Even war could be settled in this manner. The Hupas abhorred bloodshed, but if conflicts did arise among feuding individuals or families, go-betweens sought to minimize the fighting and make peace by payment of reparations for death, injury, and the destruction of property. Payment could be made in dentalium shell money or in slabs of obsidian, woodpecker scalps, or

Jumping dancers line up before their performance. Like the White Deerskin dancers, the performers wear civet or deerskin aprons and a profusion of dentalium shells around their necks. But the headdress (below) is different, and the dancers carry tubular baskets that they shake as they perform the crouching, leaping movements characteristic of the ritual. Both the White Deerskin and the Jumping Dances were repeated many times over a week or more, with new participants joining each performance.

Wealth and status—either his own or his sponsor's—are evident in the ornaments worn by this Hupa Jumping dancer. The woodpecker scalp headdress itself is evidence of substantial means, but the huge and elaborate shell necklace is even more impressive. Aside from demonstrating status, the display was thought by the Hupas to indicate concern for the well-being of the community.

This woodpecker scalp headdress for the Jumping Dance has about 50 scalps on a band of deer fur taken from the animal's belly.

deerskins of unusual color, all of whose value was enhanced by rarity.

Like the Northwest tribes, the Hupa were obsessed by personal wealth and social status, but stopped short of the potlatch, the ostentatious giving away of one's property. Wealth was to be accumulated, guarded, and bestowed intact on children. Wealth was for display and relinquished only for the most significant transactions: a bride's price, a shaman's fee, or a compensatory fine.

The Hupas, and their neighbors the Karoks and Yuroks, were unique among California Indians in establishing a social pecking order based on the value of one's possessions. Deference was paid to the wealthy man who was identifiable in any gathering by the kinsmen and hangers-on in his entourage—and perhaps even by a slave, a man indentured for nonpayment of debt. As in other societies at other times, the rich man's words were welcomed as wisdom, and lesser men were pleased to heed his advice and run his errands.

Theoretically, it was possible for any Hupa to better his station, but in fact, it was difficult. Because wealth was harder to accumulate than to inherit, most Hupas remained at the level of their parents.

Coastal Indians encountered the white invaders first. In A.D. 1542 galleons appeared, emblazoned with the cross, and from them debarked men of Spain, swarthy,

Christianized Indians at California's Carmel Mission line up to greet the visiting Frenchman, the Count de La Pérouse, and his party in 1786. These Indians had been coerced by Spain into leaving their rich hunting and fishing grounds and living within the mission, where they labored in the fields and were taught religion.

"Seven hundred and forty persons of both sexes, including children," wrote La Pérouse, were lodged in some 50 huts "as wretched as can be met by any people . . . it hurts us to say it but the resemblance to a slave colony is so great that we have seen men and women loaded with irons, others in stocks and, finally, [some were subjected to] the blows of the whip."

clad in steel, and bearing firearms. They were cruising northward from Mexico, exploring the edge of New Spain, seeking China. In the Santa Barbara Channel they found the Chumash Indians.

Spain's only interest, and that a fleeting one, was to find a suitable spot for a harbor where galleons, making the journey between Mexico and the Philippines, might refit and resupply. Only in the mid-18th century, when it appeared to the Spanish government that either Britain or Russia might contest Spain's claim to California—and thus threaten the far more valuable empire farther to the south—was serious action contemplated to tighten Spain's hold on the region.

The method chosen to achieve this was the mission, an institution that served several purposes, all of them

aimed at strengthening Spanish control. The arrival of missionary priests, together with soldiers to protect them, gave Madrid a physical presence on the land. And through the conversion of the Indians to Roman Catholicism, a religious buttress would be built against the influence of Protestant Britain and Orthodox Russia. Also, as the Indians were weaned from their hunting and gathering ways and adopted the lives of peasants, a native labor force would become available for the future development of California.

It was not until 1769 that the first mission was actually established on California soil, but in the years that followed a string of these settlements was built along the coast. With each new mission, the traditional way of life of more and more tribes was threatened. Though the Mission Period would last only 65 years, this proved to be ample time to accomplish the almost total destruction of Indian cultures in California.

Paradoxically, everything presumably done for the benefit of the Indians undermined their culture and alienated them from traditional ways. Their nakedness was clothed. Their diet was changed. They became susceptible to alcohol. Hunters and gatherers of food, they became cultivators of mission farms. People with no domesticated creature save the dog, they were instructed in tending mission flocks and herds. They surrendered their religions to Christianity, their languages to Spanish, the independence of village life to the congestion of mission communities.

The Luisenos were thoroughly transformed by 1798, when some 3,000 of them were working as peons on the farms and cattle ranches of a huge Franciscan mission. Whatever they gained from acquaintance with European arts and crafts they lost in the disruption of their mode of life. Their crowded enclaves were swept by epidemics of previously unknown diseases, and they died in appalling numbers.

Modoc warriors, shielded by boulders at their camp at northern California's Tulelake, hold off units of U.S. Cavalry in 1873. Despite the army's advantage in men and weapons, the Modocs held out for months before being forced onto a reservation.

End of the Mission Period

When Mexico won independence from Spain in 1821, the power of the Church was broken as well. In California, now a Mexican province, the Mission Period came to an end. After a lifetime of dependence on the padres, however, the mission Indians were devastated by freedom. There was no longer a Luiseno culture to return to. Promises of land grants were not kept. The Indians were shunted to government tracts or were hired on as ranch hands at low pay. Many became vagrants.

Annexation of California by the United States in 1846 was followed by a never-ending stream of white settlers whose occupation of the territory completed the dissolution of Luiseno society. The few who survived were settled on tiny reservations in 1870. The Chumashes, among the first to be exposed to the missionaries, were similarly destroyed by disease and culture shock. By 1850 they were in decline; by 1875, near extinction.

The fortunate circumstance that Spain failed to colonize north of San Francisco enabled the Pomos to escape the mission experience, and they flourished intact until the gold rush that began in 1848. But they were powerless to withstand the overwhelming energy of U.S. expansionism. Although gold fever subsided in a few years, land fever remained rampant. The Pomos were dispossessed, became prey to disease and starvation, were indiscriminately shot and killed.

The government attempted to relocate Russian River and Clear Lake Pomos on a reservation in 1856, but after 12 years the experiment was declared unsuccessful. By then, of course, no Pomo lands remained. As elsewhere, the Indians became dependent on white society for a livelihood.

The Fortunate Hupas

The Hupas had the good fortune to live in a nearly inaccessible valley. Trappers, following the course of the Trinity River, discovered them early but did not stay. The Spanish and the Russians never found them. Gold brought whites and Chinese to the upper Trinity in 1850, but the gravel was soon worked out. Settlers followed the miners, however, and clashes with the Indians led to stationing troops in the area to keep order. Congress then made the entire Hupa territory a reservation in 1864. White settlers were compensated and moved out. Thus Hoopa Valley has remained Hupa.

Not surprisingly, the Hupas are among the most numerous of all California Indian groups. Their life-style has changed; the old ways have largely died out, but at a pace that has permitted a comfortable adjustment. The Hupas are self-sufficient. They have become farmers or stock raisers, or found jobs in the lumber or construction industries. Most of all, they have retained within themselves the feeling of being Hupas.

Ishi, the Last of the Yahis

In August 1911 a 54-year-old Yahi Indian, the last of his extremely primitive and isolated tribe, left the foothills of northern California's Mount Lassen and walked to Oroville, many miles away. There the near-naked and starving Indian was jailed, not for any crime but for safekeeping while the authorities tried to decide what to do with this living vestige of a culture long gone. The sudden appearance of the Indian caused a sensation, nowhere more so than among the members of the University of California's anthropology department. There two anthropologists, T. T. Waterman and Alfred L. Kroeber, had been trying for years to track down a member of the Yahi tribe—if any were still alive. The two professors quickly made arrangements to take charge of the Indian. Ishi (the Yahi word for man), as they named him, was taken by train to San Francisco, where his custodians provided him with a sunny bed-and-sitting room in the museum. Here they spent countless hours in his company learning all they could about Ishi's language and beliefs. During a joyous camping trip to his former home in the wilderness, they witnessed how Ishi coped with his environment and watched as he made a salmon harpoon (above), snared deer, and shaped juniper wood for a bow.

Ishi, in turn, adapted well to his new environment. He learned some 600 English words and overcame his fear of crowds, for in the wilderness he had probably never seen more than 30 people at any one time. Everything about San Francisco—from trolley cars to roll-up window shades—fascinated him, and he, in turn, was a source of wonder to hoards of museum-goers who thronged to see him and watch as he made arrowheads. After Ishi's death from tuberculosis in 1914, his friend and protector Alfred Kroeber said of him: "He was the most patient man I ever knew . . . he had mastered the philosophy of patience, without trace either of self-pity or bitterness to dull the purity of his cheerful enduringness."

The Columbia River, *seen here as it courses around Blalock Island—along with the Fraser, Thompson, Okanogan, Deschutes, Umatilla, Snake, and a host of smaller streams—was all-important to the well-being of the Plateau peoples. These rivers,* *which teemed with salmon, trout, and sturgeon, supplied the staple food for a population of about 200,000. The Columbia and its tributaries were also waterways for trade; natives traveled by dugout canoes hollowed from the trunks of trees.*

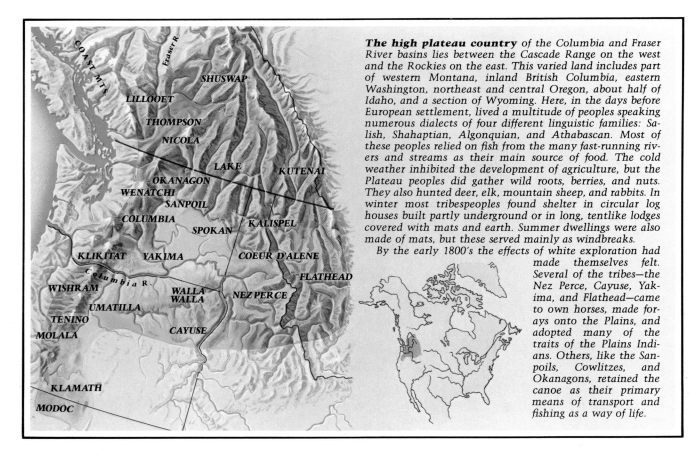

The high plateau country *of the Columbia and Fraser River basins lies between the Cascade Range on the west and the Rockies on the east. This varied land includes part of western Montana, inland British Columbia, eastern Washington, northeast and central Oregon, about half of Idaho, and a section of Wyoming. Here, in the days before European settlement, lived a multitude of peoples speaking numerous dialects of four different linguistic families: Salish, Shahaptian, Algonquian, and Athabascan. Most of these peoples relied on fish from the many fast-running rivers and streams as their main source of food. The cold weather inhibited the development of agriculture, but the Plateau peoples did gather wild roots, berries, and nuts. They also hunted deer, elk, mountain sheep, and rabbits. In winter most tribespeoples found shelter in circular log houses built partly underground or in long, tentlike lodges covered with mats and earth. Summer dwellings were also made of mats, but these served mainly as windbreaks.*

By the early 1800's the effects of white exploration had made themselves felt. Several of the tribes—the Nez Perce, Cayuse, Yakima, and Flathead—came to own horses, made forays onto the Plains, and adopted many of the traits of the Plains Indians. Others, like the Sanpoils, Cowlitzes, and Okanagons, retained the canoe as their primary means of transport and fishing as a way of life.

Indians of the Plateau

If an 18th-century student with an aversion to extensive travel had wanted to observe the varying Indian civilizations of the Plains, the Great Basin, California, the Subarctic, and the Northwest Coast, he could have enjoyed the convenience of a survey course simply by living with the different tribes of the Plateau. Their culture was essentially a patchwork quilt with the pieces provided by the neighbors. Political and social structures, religions, dress, customs, housing, occupations—all reflected the regions bordering the Plateau.

The boundaries of the Plateau were roughly the Rocky Mountains on the east, the Cascade Range on the west, the upper reaches of the Fraser River on the north, and a line about midway through today's Oregon and Idaho on the south. The region included parts of Washington, Montana, British Columbia, and a wedge of Wyoming as well.

The two great arterial rivers, the Columbia and Fraser, and their tributaries were the pulse of life for this landlocked region. They were avenues of travel and trade, and in season, they were the source of food in the form of the ubiquitous salmon. Their hospitable banks provided homesites for innumerable small villages. The Columbia, on its tortuous 1,200-mile journey to the sea, passed through the territory of some 30 tribes speaking the dialects of four major linguistic families.

The first Indian immigrants, drawn to promising fishing sites along the Columbia River, arrived toward the close of the last ice age. A favored camp was the grand Dalles-Deschutes area of the Columbia River valley. Located near the present town of The Dalles, 150

"She Who Watches," a mythic female chief, was depicted centuries ago on a cliff over the Columbia River. In legend, the woman was turned to stone and told to watch over her people forever.

miles from the coast, a basalt channel squeezes the swelling Columbia into boiling rapids, eddies, and waterfalls for a distance of 15 miles. The Dalles features the richest salmon-fishing on the river and boasts a continuous archeological record starting about 9000 B.C.

Leaf-shaped Cascade projectile points, recovered from the deepest excavations here, are a key artifact identifying what archeologists dub the Old Cordilleran tradition. From riverbank landings Old Cordilleran fishermen flung fiber cord nets, weighted with grooved stones, to collect salmon. They also jabbed bone-barbed harpoons into thrashing fish trapped within stationary weirs planted in the river bottom. And with stone wedges they split cedar poles to rig the fish-drying racks that lined the shore. Old Cordilleran stone-tipped arrows and spears brought down buffalo in the Fraser Canyon. Their digging sticks uprooted such nutritious plant foods as wild carrots and potatoes.

After 4000 B.C. the Old Cordilleran world was superseded by a fresh influx of Indian groups who brought new languages, tools, and traditions. By the time of European arrival more than two dozen separate tribes roamed throughout the Columbia Plateau. Although these peoples shared general cultural adaptations in religion and community life as well as fishing and hunting habits, each had evolved its own subtle character.

As the desert floor of the Great Basin lifts northward into the Plateau, the Shoshonean-speaking world yielded to Indian groups who spoke languages of Penutian stock. Ancestoral speakers of the widespread Penutian tongue, Shahaptian, probably trickled into the region about 6000 B.C. By the time of Lewis and Clark's epic journey through this territory in 1805, the major Penutian tribes were the Cayuse, Klamath, Nez Perce, Umatilla, Walla Walla, and Klikitat.

North of the Penutian stronghold, the Plateau stretches from eastern Washington up into British Columbia where it is broken by low-lying hills, sliced with winding river and lake valleys. In this middle Columbia region flourished the most representative of Plateau peoples, the Interior Salish-speaking tribes. Their ancestors, who probably had arrived soon after 1500 B.C., introduced burial mounds, beaten copper objects, polished stone tools, and effigy figurines. These Indians emerged as the Coeur d'Alene, Flathead, Kalispel, Spokan, Wenatchi, Thompson, Shuswap, Lillooet, and Columbia tribes.

The massive flow of the Columbia eventually turns again, a meandering route southward through the present-day state of Washington, and soon after merging with its largest tributary, the Snake, curves westward. This is the final quartering shift in direction until the stream empties into the Pacific at Astoria. For this last long stretch the Columbia serves as the border between present-day Washington and Oregon. The Salish language was left behind. Here, south of the Columbia in the Snake River basin, Shahaptian dialects were spoken by Cayuses, Walla Wallas, Umatillas, Yakimas, Klikitats, and others.

As with the tribes in the Great Basin and California, most of the later Plateau groups had few, if any, political ties outside their immediate communities. The leaders were not so much all-powerful overlords as hereditary headmen who guided tribal councils in deciding such matters as when and where to move camp and the naming of feast days.

Most Plateau peoples spent summers in lodges constructed of bullrush mats layered over cottonwood

Salmon hang on racks to dry *at a Chinook encampment near The Dalles on the Columbia River in an 1843 painting by Paul Kane. The Chinooks, whose territory included The Dalles—an area of impassable rapids—specialized in two activities: salmon fishing and trade. A group of tribes rather than a single entity, the Chinooks were the middlemen of the Northwest, and within their domains all manner of goods—fur pelts, canoes, dried salmon, candlefish oil, baskets, dentalium shells, and even slaves—changed hands. The Chinooks were also a people noted for their horn carvings, much sought by other tribes in the region. The bowl at right, with its excised geometric decoration, was carved from the horn of a bighorn sheep; the spoon below it, made by the Wishram, the easternmost Chinook tribe, was carved from mountain sheep horn.*

frames. In winter the Indians lived in semiunderground earth houses, entered by way of a notched log ladder emerging through a central roof opening. Early spring found them combing the ground for wild carrots, wild onions, bitterroot, and above all, camas root. The starchy bulb of the camas, a variety of lily, was second in importance only to salmon in the Plateau diet. When the plant's sky-blue petals had withered, women dug out the camas bulbs with willow digging sticks. The bulbs were eaten raw, roasted, or pulverized into cakes that were then boiled. Fish, berries, and wild game rounded out the common Plateau diet.

The Plateau's Thriving Trade

Thanks to the Columbian and Fraser river systems, trade thrived throughout the Plateau. Dugouts bearing enterprising Chinook merchants from the west came to The Dalles with sea otter pelts and decorative shells. Coastal Salish arrived to do business with their Interior Salish linguistic cousins; along with material goods, they passed on their typically Northwest Coast love of wealth, status, and power. Plateau traders paddled their yellow pine and black cottonwood dugouts downstream to barter their deerskins, Indian hemp for basketmaking, and bitterroot. The bargaining was conducted in the Chinook jargon, a mishmash of Salish, Nootka, and Chinook words that served as a general language. Overseeing this native commerce were the

Chinooks, who shrewdly controlled the flow of wares and even exacted tolls from river traffic.

Cultural influences inevitably accompanied trade to the Plateau. From the Plains and the Great Basin in the early 18th century came the horse—some 200 years after its introduction by the Spaniards. It was a curious adoption for salmon fishermen and root gatherers, but the well-watered grassland areas of the middle and upper Columbia Basins were ideal for horse-raising, and a number of tribes took to it eagerly. The Yakimas developed large herds. The Nez Perces became perhaps the most expert horse breeders of all North American Indians. The Cayuses, whose name whites used for all Indian ponies, became preeminent horse dealers. The name of the famous breed, Appaloosa, was derived from the Palouse River Indians of the Washington-Idaho border who bred the animals.

The economic value of the horse was soon established. A flourishing exchange of horses for slaves sprang up between the peoples of the Plains and the slaveholding tribes of the Northwest Coast, with the Plateau dealers serving as middlemen.

282

From the Blackfeet of the Plains, the Nez Perces and Coeur d'Alenes adopted a more structured tribal organization. Unlike most other tribes of the Plateau, with their decentralized small villages and casual attitude toward community property, the Nez Perce and Coeur d'Alene had a possessive view of territoriality. Strangers were barred from tribal hunting and gathering grounds, and trespassing was regarded as an offense.

The Plains concept of winning personal honor (coup) in war also found favor among these tribes, as well as with the aggressive Shuswap, Thompson, and Lake who frequently raided their more peaceable neighbors. The Plains use of buckskin shirts and breeches, of skin coverings for tepees, of leather parfleches (pouches), and of feathered headdresses spread first to the Kutenai and Flathead, the easternmost Plateau tribes, and later to a number of groups farther west.

From the Northwest Coast came the custom of flattening heads (by pressure bindings beginning in infancy) and of piercing noses as enhancements of personal appearance. Where local flora permitted, shredded-bark clothing was copied. Chinookan tribes practiced the potlatch—the ceremonial festival at which lavish gifts were given away to enhance the status of the hosts. Along the lower Columbia some Plateau tribes instituted slavery.

Perhaps least affected by these social modifications were the Sanpoils of the middle Columbia, within the curve of Big Bend of the Columbia River, and their nearby neighbors, the Nespelems, Chelans, and Colvilles. Located in the geographical center of the Plateau, the Sanpoils lived in cultural isolation that made them unaware of, or uninterested in, most alien notions. Even the horse was sparingly used. The bounty of the stream provided for most of their needs.

The Sanpoils numbered perhaps 1,600 and lived in some 30 villages located on both sides of an 85-mile stretch of the Columbia. Three to five families—30 or 40 people—made up an average small village. A large one, at an exceptionally good section of the river for fishing, might number several hundred inhabitants.

Village life was governed by two principles rarely practiced by any society at any time: social equality and pacifism. The Sanpoils were the more unusual for being completely at odds with the influential Northwest Coast tribes with an elaborate and inflexible system of social rankings, and with the Great Plains Indians with their glorification of war.

For the Sanpoils, equality went along with personal

A flattened forehead is created by pressing a board against the padded skull of this Cowlitz infant. Several Plateau tribes used this procedure, but oddly enough, the Flathead—misnamed by early French fur trappers—was not among them.

independence. They abhorred the idea of slavery even as they disdained the pointless accumulation of wealth and the elevation in status it conferred in other societies. Well-paid shamans might accrue riches, but they earned respect for their healing powers, not for their affluence. All adult residents of a village—men and women alike, and even newcomers—automatically enjoyed the rights of citizenship: membership in the general assembly, voting, holding office, participating in all activities. Every man was eligible to be chief, and selection was made by popular vote on the basis of moral character. Even the quest for supernatural power through a guardian spirit was open equally to men and women.

Villages had traditional hunting grounds, root fields, and fishing stations, but strangers were welcome to use them as guests, and all shared in community harvests regardless of their contribution to the effort. The communal salmon catch was divided equally among fishermen and nonfishermen. The rewards of a hunt were shared by all members of the hunting party.

Individual effort was acknowledged and did not go unrewarded, and certainly there were personal possessions. But with everyone assured the necessities of life, few had any urge to be acquisitive. Stealing was almost unknown.

Maintenance of peaceful relations with other tribes and social harmony at home were, perhaps, the fundamental motivations of Sanpoil life. The people avoided conflict with neighboring tribes no matter what the provocation. The Sanpoils nursed no grudges, fanned no feuds. More remarkably, they accepted attack without retaliation. There were no reprisals for raids by Shuswaps, Lakes, Coeur d'Alenes, or other hostiles. Even loss of life went unavenged. The principal role of every Sanpoil chief was serving as peacemaker. "Our children are dead and our property is destroyed," one chief counseled. "We are sad. But can we bring our children to life or restore our property by killing other people? It is better not to fight. It can do no good."

Seasonal Patterns

As did most North American Indians, the Plateau peoples structured their lives around the seasons and the availability of food. For the Sanpoils, the only excitement during the endlessly overcast cold seasons were the laborious treks on snowshoes to nearby villages for all-night get-togethers. There they gambled, sang the guardian spirit songs, and witnessed marvelous shamanistic performances. The "time when buttercups bloom" (March) could come none too soon.

The arrival of warmer weather saw a spree of spring activity. Everyone slept outdoors. Along the sandy riverbanks women hunted for the earliest roots, eagerly yanking out wild onions even though they were not yet fully grown. Occasionally, they lucked upon prickly pears and would burn off the spines of the cactus and roast the fruit on the spot. The men plunged into the underbrush to hunt for rabbits and wildfowl and groped in the still-freezing shallows for freshwater shellfish.

In April, "the time when leaves come out," the village leader announced the season's major relocation. They would head for the summer village site along the Sanpoil River. Bidding farewell to the lame and old and those chosen to care for them, the villagers launched themselves into summer's strenuous food-gathering.

Before settling into the large summer encampment, however, they split up into fast-traveling bands of four and five families. Fording the Columbia, they dispersed farther south into the root-digging plains. Wielding their serviceberry and willow digging sticks with antler crosspieces, the women harvested wild plants: camas, cous, bitterroot, wild carrot, tiger lily, sunflower, bracken fern, and dogtooth violet, among others. Then

Spears in hand, Colville Indians fish for salmon swimming upstream at Kettle Falls on the Columbia. Fish that could not be speared were trapped in weirs, such as the one at the base of the falls. During the May-to-November fishing season, the Indians of the Plateau made camp beside the rivers and lived in mat shelters like the Chinook lodge at right. In most years the catch was sufficient to permit storage of large numbers of fish.

The "X-ray" style was a distinctive art form developed by the Washo and Wishram tribes of Oregon. This small wooden statue is about 12 inches high and shows the characteristics of this mode in which the underlying skeletal structure is both revealed and exaggerated. The ribs and facial bones are especially pronounced, giving the viewer the impression of seeing through the flesh. Almost all the artworks of the two tribes employ this style. Smaller X-ray images, including animal as well as human subjects, were used in basketry designs and appeared as well on bowls, spoons, and a variety of objects carved from wood and horn. The statue shown here was found on Upper Memaloose Island in 1905.

all returned north to the new camp. About early May the first white sturgeon, weighing up to half a ton, began tempting Sanpoil fishermen. Each day incoming families busily set up new summer mat lodges until upward of 400 people were in residence.

At familiar spear-fishing sites, where fish had to navigate extremely narrow passages, the rapids were redug to a depth of three feet and strewn with white quartz to better outline the flashing salmon and steelhead trout that would soon arrive. A succession of these reliable locations for thrusting the three-pronged Sanpoil harpoons were established for different times during the spawning run. The fragile bridge, from which the men precariously leaned over the torrential waters when spearing fish, was repaired with willow shoots. Huge, communal weirs—actually two open-willow fences spanning the river—were set up. Fish heading for an upriver spawn could just make it through the lower grid but were penned in at the upper one.

Until August everyone's days were feverishly active. The women gathered the glistening mounds of fish piled up alongside the weirs and spearing platforms and began drying the catch, a process that took from 10 to 14 days. Each week the drying racks grew longer along the riverbanks. Meanwhile, new faces continuously showed up in camp. Gambling and trading filled the intervals of rest from working the streams. The starry summer nights were lively with bright campfires, visiting between friends, and ardent courting.

As the spawning fish thinned out in September, the men took movable nets farther up and down stream in a last-ditch effort to secure the winter's food supply. The women made final foraging jaunts into the lower mountains to collect such fall fare as the spindle-shaped root known as masawi and Hawthorne berries. By now the sun's heat was lessening daily, and the last of the salmon haul had to be smoked in special huts.

About mid-October the Sanpoils returned to winter camp. Frost shone on the ground each morning as the last elevated storage platforms were packed with tule bags bursting with dried salmon. While the men cut massive piles of firewood and repaired roofs, the women made fresh sleeping mats and cushioned the house floors with new rye grass.

Then the severe midwinter months set in. Except for occasional deer-hunting expeditions, the weather forced people inside. Women wove baskets and mats and sewed deerskins into leggings and shirts; men gambled at the stick game or dice. The most welcome interruption came about the time of the winter solstice. For the two midwinter months of "time that it snows" and "time that it gets cold" the Sanpoils gathered in different communal houses to conjure up their guardian spirits. Dancing and singing went on for days on end. These were also occasions for shamans to announce curing visions and perform such feats as exiting from the dance house to reappear as a grizzly bear, then come back minutes later in human form again. The guardian-spirit ceremonies boosted morale and made it easier to endure the long wait for spring.

The Trading Tribes

Trade brought considerably more variety to the lives of the more enterprising tribes, such as the Klamath, Cayuse, Walla Walla, and Nez Perce. The annual visit to The Dalles for business and pleasure, for example, was the exciting climax of the summer. And at first the coming of the white man to the West Coast only swelled The Dalles' variety of goods and profits. After

Baskets were a speciality of the Plateau tribes. The Interior Salish basket at right exhibits a decorative form unique to the Cascade region: imbrication. It involves facing each horizontal row with bark strips arranged in such a way that a shinglelike surface is formed. The basket's core of cedar or spruce root is held by interlocking loops of flexible fiber, as shown below left. Before each row of loops is pulled tight, a strip of cherry bark is woven through. Sometimes the bark is faced with a piece of dyed grass (below right).

Clad in a typical Plateau costume—*a beaded dress and a fezlike basketry hat—this Cayuse woman carries both beaded and cornhusk bags. Her dress was made from two deerskins, to which a fringe was added. The woman's hat, the basketry bag in her left hand, and the bags above, all bear traditional geometric designs, but the bag the woman holds in her right hand has a floral pattern, indicating European influence.*

1775 European vessels began docking at Nootka and Makah Indian settlements along the coast; soon thereafter steel knives, guns, and beads made their appearance at The Dalles. Traders added French and English words to the Chinook jargon. When Lewis and Clark appeared at The Dalles in 1805, they discovered tribes who had never laid eyes on white men carrying articles of European make.

By the early 1840's the horse had given greater mobility to the Plateau tribes, and the Walla Walla, Cayuse, and Nez Perce were riding from eastern Washington to trade with Indians at Sutter's Fort in California. The Plateau Indians also detoured south of San Francisco to mine cinnabar, from which they made sacred red paint. Their visits to the Plains also increased. The full inventory of resplendent Plains horse gear—saddles, martingales, cruppers, and mountain lion saddle blankets—was adopted by the Nez Perces, Flatheads, and Kutenais. Now Plateau shirts and leggings were of Plains cut, with richly decorated beadwork. Plains-style parfleche storage bags became as numerous as the traditional Plateau woven containers. In 1806 Lewis and Clark had counted only one buffalo-hide tepee in the Nez Perce camps; a few years later the traditional mat-roofed lodges had virtually been replaced by skin tepees.

Just as this prosperity began to crest, however, a pincer movement of white expansion began boxing in the Plateau peoples. Although the full impact of white domination would not be apparent until the 1830's, there were signs a half century earlier of the agony to come. In 1782 a party of Sanpoil traders returned home after a lengthy trip through the Cascade Mountains. Along with bundles of coastal goods, they brought back smallpox. Within the year almost a half of the tribe had died from the disease.

In 1792 an American seafarer named Robert Gray sailed up the Columbia River. Then, pressing in from the east, the Corps of Discovery expedition led by Lewis and Clark in 1804—06 broke ground for later fur trappers and traders. Guided by the famed Shoshoni woman Sacajawea, as well as friendly Nez Perces, the explorers spent time with all the major Plateau tribes. Along with alerting the young U.S. government to the region's vast economic potential, the Lewis and Clark journals contained glowing descriptions of the local Indians' hospitality.

In the years immediately following Lewis and Clark's momentous journey, frontier trade created a mutually beneficial relationship between white man and Indian. But then, in 1829-32, the Chinookans were exposed to white diseases, and almost all perished. A decade later white settlers reached the Willamette Valley in Oregon via the recently opened Oregon Trail. Ranchers, farmers, railroad hands, and townsfolk poured into the Northwest. The territorial governments began hungrily eyeing Indian lands.

Between 1843 and 1852 the Washington territorial governor, Isaac Stevens, conducted a marathon series of treatymaking sessions with the Plateau peoples. Cajoling, bribing, and threatening them, he managed to negotiate 52 treaties by which the natives of Idaho, Oregon, and Washington lost 157 million acres of land. Most of these documents called for concentration of Indian tribes on reservations often in forced proximity with unfriendly Indians. Seething resentment over these treaties and the infractions of agreements that began almost before the ink was dry touched off a number of Indian insurrections.

The first blood had been shed a few years earlier. In 1836 Dr. Marcus Whitman established a Christian mission near Walla Walla along the Oregon Trail. He was described as "holding a Bible in one hand and a whip in the other," and his mission became a major overnight stop for frontier travelers and settlers. When the local Cayuse Indians could abide its presence no longer, they rebelled, with Chief Tamsuky as their leader. Whitman, his wife, and 12 other whites were killed. Stunned, the settlers formed a vigilante army. Five Cayuses were hanged to appease their fury.

Governor Stevens' handling of the 1855 Walla Walla Treaty council was particularly grating to the Indians. The Yakimas, complaining that he had bought off their leaders, recruited allies among other tribes and

Chief Joseph of the Nez Perce led 600 of his tribe in a 1,600-mile fighting retreat against U.S. forces. After 13 battles in 1877, he was forced to yield when only 30 miles from sanctuary in Canada.

launched a bloody war. Under the leadership of Chief Kamaiakian, the fighting went on for three years and spread to the Pacific Coast before federal troops brought the rebellion under control.

Of the Plateau wars the most renowned was the final conflict, the short-lived 1877 Nez Perce war. In the last of the 370 treaties the United States signed with Indians, the Nez Perces had been pressured into signing away their beloved Wallowa Valley in Oregon and relocating in an uncongenial site in Idaho. Just before the removal was to take place, several Nez Perce horses were stolen, and the patience of the younger warriors ended. They killed 18 settlers in retaliation, and the war was on. Led by Chief Joseph, the rebellious Nez Perces outmaneuvered the pursuing troops in a 1,600-mile running duel, and were only 30 miles from the Canadian border when they were finally captured. There Joseph made a surrender speech: "I am tired of fighting. . . . It is cold and we have no blankets. The little children are freezing to death. My people, some of them, have run away to the hills and have no blankets, no food. No one knows where they are—perhaps freezing to death. I want to have time to look for my children and see how many of them I can find. Maybe I shall find them among the dead. Hear me, my chiefs. I am tired; my heart is sick and sad. From where the sun now stands, I will fight no more forever."

A mounted party of Nez Perce, 2,500 in all, form a serpentine column as they gather for a parlay with Gov. I. I. Stevens of the Washington Territory in May 1855 in an unfinished watercolor by a government artist. During this meeting the Nez Perce and other Plateau tribes ceded some 60,000 square miles to the United States at an average price of about three cents an acre. That July, Stevens acquired another 25,000 square miles from the Flathead, Kutenai, and Upper Pend d'Oreille tribes. The governor was less successful in his dealing with the Blackfeet, who, in October 1855, refused to sell off their lands. By then, several tribes were in rebellion. Two decades of intermittent warfare followed. Not until 1878 was the army successful in forcing the last of the Plateau tribes to relocate on reservations.

THE NORTHWEST COAST
Traders and Fishermen

Dotted with islets, surrounded by hills, *British Columbia's Pender Harbor typifies the environment of Northwest Coast peoples. The Kwakiutl mask (inset) celebrates the spirit of the sea from which the Kwakiutls garnered a wealth of fish and sea mammals.*

In this bountiful land the natives developed a sophisticated culture, a flourishing economy, outstanding art, and the amazing custom of potlatching to display status and wealth.

The Tlingits, Kwakiutls, Chinooks, and other peoples of the Northwest Coast believed the salmon to be a race of immortal men who lived in houses beneath the sea during the winter and, in the late spring, assumed the form of fish, swarming up the rivers in huge numbers to offer themselves to humans for food. But this self-sacrifice did not destroy the salmon-men. The fisherman had merely to strip the flesh from the fish and throw the bones back into the rivers. The bones would then be carried out to sea, to be reborn as men and live in their underwater dwellings until the next spring, when they would again become salmon.

The annual salmon run must have seemed miraculous. During the early summer, when salmon from the Pacific Ocean were fighting their way to freshwater spawning areas, the rivers were filled with masses of squirming, struggling fish. But this abundance was not limited to salmon. The ocean and the region's countless rivers teemed with life. There were halibut, trout, cod, herring, and smelts. There was also the eulachon, or candlefish, so called because it was unusually rich in oil; when the fish was dried, a string run through it would burn like a candlewick. In the Pacific Ocean, not far from dry land, whales, hair seals, sea lions, porpoises, and sea otters abounded. On the shore at low tide, clams, mussels, and sea urchins were there for the taking, and on the shore itself were the eggs of seabirds.

The deeply wooded mountains that abutted the narrow beaches were havens for animal life—for deer, elk, mountain goat, wolf, grizzly bear and black bear, and such smaller animals as beaver, marten, and land otter. But the rugged terrain made game difficult to hunt; the woods were dark and deep, and the mountains, which rose to heights of 18,000 feet in some places, were craggy and precipitous. Hunting was usually restricted to the winter when snow drove the animals from the mountains to the lower coastal areas. Basically, the people directed their lives toward the ocean and its bounties, building their villages on the shores of the mainland and on the mountainous offshore islands, creating, in the process, a culture unique among all the native Americans. The Northwesterners had virtually

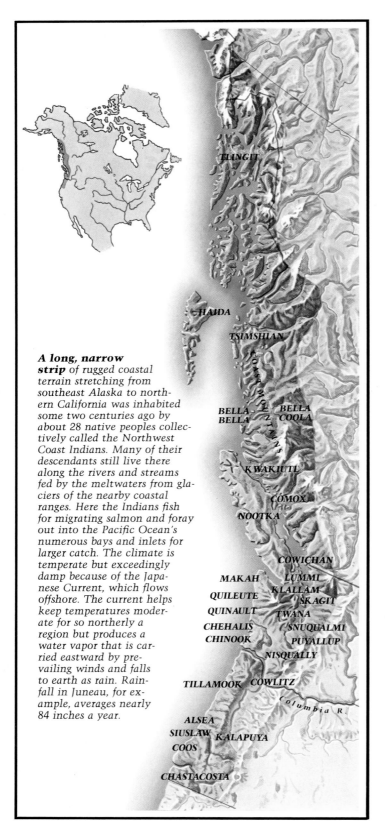

TLINGIT

HAIDA

TSIMSHIAN

A long, narrow strip of rugged coastal terrain stretching from southeast Alaska to northern California was inhabited some two centuries ago by about 28 native peoples collectively called the Northwest Coast Indians. Many of their descendants still live there along the rivers and streams fed by the meltwaters from glaciers of the nearby coastal ranges. Here the Indians fish for migrating salmon and foray out into the Pacific Ocean's numerous bays and inlets for larger catch. The climate is temperate but exceedingly damp because of the Japanese Current, which flows offshore. The current helps keep temperatures moderate for so northerly a region but produces a water vapor that is carried eastward by prevailing winds and falls to earth as rain. Rainfall in Juneau, for example, averages nearly 84 inches a year.

BELLA BELLA   BELLA COOLA

KWAKIUTL

COMOX

NOOTKA

COWICHAN

MAKAH   LUMMI

QUILEUTE   KLALLAM   SKAGIT

QUINAULT   TWANA

CHEHALIS   SNUQUALMI

CHINOOK   PUYALLUP

NISQUALLY

TILLAMOOK   COWLITZ

Columbia R.

ALSEA

SIUSLAW   KALAPUYA

COOS

CHASTACOSTA

no agriculture. Other than the ocean's seaweed, about the only edible plants native to the region were the many varieties of berries, wild celery, and roots. Agriculture has always been considered a precondition for the development of a complex culture. Yet the Northwest Coast Indians, who planted only tobacco—and little of that—achieved a culture that was not merely complex and sophisticated, but affluent. In their relatively high living standards, the grandeur of their arts, the excellence of their technology, and the success of their trading methods, the Indians of the Northwest Coast were unrivaled by any people north of Mexico. They were also unrivaled in their concern for rank and wealth and in their profligate generosity.

The people of this region exploited the waters and their riches with such success that they had to give only a few months every year—from the middle of May until the middle of September—to the task of providing themselves with a year's food supply and a considerable surplus for trading. Drying and smoking preserved the fish for an almost indefinite period. Thus, for well over half the year, the people were free to pursue other interests—the trade that converted the surplus catch into other kinds of wealth; social rank that sprang from wealth; the arts and ceremonies in which rank and wealth could be lavishly displayed.

The most important and unusual of these ceremonies was the potlatch—an institution that stood at the very center of Northwest Coast Indian life and that had no exact counterpart in any other known culture. The potlatch was a ceremonial feast of several days duration, with guests often numbering in the hundreds, many of them making a journey of several days to attend. On such an occasion the host announced and validated his claim to a title or a name—or some other symbol of personal rank and family worth—by a lavish distribution of gifts to each of his guests. It was no mean feat to accumulate enough possessions—and possessions of sufficient quality—to give a proper potlatch, one that would reflect real honor on the host and would confirm his right to all the glories he claimed. Therefore, the people of the Northwest Coast devoted at least as much of their considerable energy and enterprise to the pursuit of these luxuries and the honors associated with them as they did to the tasks of subsistence.

The origin of these Indians is as obscure as the origin of the potlatch. Very little is known about the earliest inhabitants of the area, nor do we know when people first began to build permanent settlements along the 1,400 mile stretch of coast and islands in which the potlatch culture flourished—an area that runs from Yakutat Bay in the Alaska panhandle to Cape Mendocino in northern California. We know that people lived there more than 10,000 years ago. Among the archeological remains that have been found in the region are stone tools which are at least that old. And harpoons have been discovered that indicate there were fisher-

Thousands of candlefish dry on racks in a Tsimshian village in British Columbia. These small marine fish, related to the smelt, were highly prized for their oil, which was used to flavor halibut, salmon, clams, and roe. Candlefish, as the name implies, were also a source of artificial light for these Indians. After drying, their carcasses were threaded with wicks and, when lighted, the oil within the fish produced a steady flame. At potlatch feasts hosts traditionally threw vast amounts of candlefish oil on the fire to flaunt their wealth.

Cedar trees abound along the Pacific Northwest Coast and have long been a source of raw material for local Indians. As shown above, sleek dugout canoes were made from the trunks, and strips of inner bark were twisted into string and then woven into mats for a summer fishing shelter. Bark was also woven to make clothing (left). Chests (right), so tightly constructed they could be used to store fish oil, were yet another use of cedar.

A search for the past is made at the site of Ozette (above) and its archeologists' camp. Students (far left) use garden hoses to spray away mud beneath which they have found such objects as the wooden, three-foot-high dorsal fin studded with sea otter teeth (left) and the owl's head (below). The fin sculpture was probably used in some kind of whaling ritual.

Uncovering the Mystery of a Long-Buried Village

It was a summer night about 500 years ago when the inhabitants of Ozette—a small Makah Indian village on Washington's coast—fell victim to sudden disaster. From the hills behind the village thousands of tons of mud cascaded down to bury many inhabitants, their houses, and all they possessed beneath a deep blanket of ooze.

For half a millennium part of Ozette remained buried. Then, in 1966, a team of archeologists, under the direction of Washington State University's Dr. Richard D. Daugherty, began excavating the site. What had been a tragedy for the people of Ozette proved to be a treasure trove for the diggers. Because the mud that doomed the Indians sealed their artifacts in an almost airless environment, many objects, particularly those of wood that are normally subject to rapid decay, were uncovered in pristine condition. These have provided a wealth of information about the lives of those pre-Columbian Northwest Coast people.

By 1977 about 65,000 artifacts, including several wooden houses, had been freed from the mud. To remove the outermost layers of mud, seawater is pumped through the site, then workers employ the gentler spray of garden hoses to wash off the last layers. Among the many fascinating objects found were harpoon heads, shafts, and killing lances used to hunt whales.

men on the coast some 5,000 years ago. But nothing more is known about the ancient Northwest Coast culture or how it developed. The area is not a favorable one for archeology. For the people of the Northwest Coast wood was the easiest material to come by, and they used it not only for houses but for many other utilitarian and artistic purposes. But wood disintegrates relatively quickly, especially in a damp climate, leaving few clues for the archeologist.

The most fruitful archeological work in the region has been done at Ozette village, on the tip of the Olympic Peninsula in Washington, where an extraordinarily rich find was made. Already, complete wooden houses, with much of their associated paraphernalia, have been dug out virtually intact from under layers of earth. The houses and other artifacts were preserved because they lay in the path of an unusually dense mud slide that blocked out most of the air, thereby preventing oxidation. The Ozette village finds prove beyond a doubt that the Northwest Coast Indians had a highly developed culture long before the Europeans arrived. But the remains may date back only about 500 years—hardly long enough to give us any clear idea of how that culture developed or who the original inhabitants of the region were.

Europeans did not even become aware of the Northwest Coast Indians until a mere 35 years before the American Revolution, and that first contact was no more than fleeting. It occurred during the summer of 1741, when an expedition headed by the Danish explorer Vitus Bering set sail from Siberia under the auspices of the Russian crown, seeking to discover whether a land bridge existed between Kamchatka Peninsula, on the southern tip of Siberia, and the American mainland. There were two ships in Bering's expedition—the *St. Peter*, which was under his command, and the *St. Paul*, commanded by a Russian, Capt. Alexei Cherikov. During a storm the two ships became separated, Bering's moving northward, Cherikov's heading farther east. While Cherikov's ship was riding at anchor off Chickagof Island, the crew saw two canoes with Indians in them. But that brief view was as far as things went. Cherikov could not put in to shore: the *St. Paul* was too large to navigate the narrow inlets, and he had already lost the two boats he had with him that were small enough to make a landing. The first had vanished after setting out to explore the shore, and the second was lost trying to find the first. The disappearance of his small boats, and what Cherikov considered hostile gestures made by the Indians toward his ship, led him to believe he was in dangerous territory; so he returned to Siberia.

For Bering, the voyage was equally fruitless. It was also to be his last. His ship had dropped anchor considerably farther north, off Kayak Island, and he had sent the German-born naturalist Georg Wilhelm Steller ashore to make a survey. Steller found a hut on the island in which he left some gifts—tobacco, cloth, iron knives, iron pipe, and an iron kettle. But he saw no one, and when he returned to the *St. Peter*, Bering decided to set sail for home. He had found no evidence of the land bridge, and he was ill. But on the return trip the *St. Peter* was wrecked on one of the islands between Alaska and Siberia, and Bering died there.

The crew members who survived, however, made the discovery that was responsible for bringing Europeans in the thousands to the Northwest Coast. While the men were repairing the vessel, they kept themselves alive by eating the meat of the sea otters they found in abundance off the shores of the island on which they had been wrecked. After the sailors had made their ship seaworthy, they returned to their homeland, taking with them some of the animals' sleek, lustrous pelts. From that moment the rush was on—at first by the Russians, and then by the Spanish, the British, the French, and later the Americans, all of whom were eager both for the Indians' riches and their territory.

By modern standards, "rush" is perhaps the wrong word. News traveled slowly in the 18th century, and Russian adventurers had been exploiting the Alaska fur trade for more than 30 years before word of their activities reached King Charles III of Spain. His country had long since established a foothold in the New World, and he was determined to prevent other nations from staking out claims anywhere else in western North America. In 1773 he ordered a sea expedition northward from Mexico, authorizing it to take title to all lands south of latitude 60° N—the latitude of Yakutat Bay. Juan Josef Perez, who led that expedition, claimed the land for the Spanish crown.

When his ship anchored off the Queen Charlotte Islands, he also did some trading with the Haidas. An account of this event, written by Juan Crespi, the chaplain of the expedition, is one of the first reports we have of the Europeans' view of the Northwest Coast people. Like practically everyone who followed him, Crespi was struck by the natives' skill at trading. Although he did not entirely approve of their business methods, his report indicates that his party and the Indians dealt amicably with one another and that the Europeans were, on the whole, favorably impressed. "At latitude 55°," he wrote, "Perez treated with the Indians and saw that they were cheerful, robust, with beautiful eyes. . . . They bartered sea otter, bear and wolfskin for knives, glass beads and the like and were so tricky that it was necessary to give them the stipulated trinkets in advance and when they left they were accustomed to demand more, threatening not to fulfill the contract agreed upon."

Hot on the heels of the Spaniards came the British to stake their claim. In 1778 the British explorer Capt. James Cook, one of the first men to circumnavigate the globe, sailed east from Hawaii toward the Canadian coast, dropping anchor off Vancouver Island, in Nootka

Nootkas roast fish *over an open fire in this painting by British artist John Webber, who visited these Indians in the company of Capt. James Cook in 1778. Houses such as the one shown were multifamily dwellings. Each family had its own space for sleeping and storage along the walls. The huge carved figures—family emblems—were thought by some of Cook's men to be idols, but the captain reported that the Nootkas held these carvings "very cheap" and would sell them for a bit of iron or brass.*

Sound. Cook had a scientist's objectivity and an ability to look with sympathy at a culture different from his own. His observations about the Indians were straightforward and unbiased. He appears to have gotten along very well with them: he was invited to see several villages and to visit with the villagers inside their homes. But not all the members of his expedition had his detachment, and some of them seem to have been prepared to dislike the Indians before they knew anything about them. Here is a diary entry made by one of his midshipmen:

"In the Canoe that first came Along side was a Man that stood up and held forth a long while—at the same time pointing to the Sound as if the ship should go further Up—his oratory did not seem to me the best in the world and he appeared to Uter [sic] with much difficulty: on his head he wore a kind of hat . . . in the shape of a buck's head; after having finished his harangue he presented it to Sale as well as several other things, which at once convinced us they were no novices at that business, in return for his hat he had a large Axe and left us quite content."

The "harangue" was undoubtedly a speech of welcome—protocol for ceremonial occasions among all the Northwest Coast Indians—and what seemed to the Englishman difficulty in speaking was probably nothing more than evidence of one of the differences between the English and Nootka languages.

Misinterpretations like these undoubtedly played a part in the difficulties that began to develop between the Europeans and the Indians—difficulties that sometimes led to serious quarrels. But despite the problems, the Europeans' territorial ambitions and the profits there were to be made from the fur trade brought more and more of them to the Northwest Coast—especially since it seemed to them that, in trading, they were getting far better than they gave. The glass beads and iron knives with which they bartered were trinkets, while a single fur pelt was worth more than $100. For the natives, who were as eager as the Europeans to continue trading, exactly the opposite was true. Furs were readily available, while glass beads and iron knives were rarities and therefore valuable—not merely as symbols of wealth, but also as trade items to be used with other native groups. Moreover, iron knives were far more effective than knives made of stone, bone, or wood—the materials most easily available to the natives.

But although the trade between the two peoples was mutually beneficial, the more contact they had with one another, the worse their relationship became. We have no way of knowing which of the two was initially responsible, but there is no question that the Europeans did their share to make things difficult.

A Clash of Cultures

In 1786, when the French explorer Count Jean François de La Pérouse arrived at Lituya Bay to deal with the Tlingits, the relationship between the Europeans and the Indians had deteriorated so seriously that the Frenchman had not a kind word to say about them.

"Some of the Indians were continually about our ships in their canoes," he wrote, "and spent three or four hours before they began to barter a little fish, or two or three otter skins, taking every opportunity to rob us, catching at every bit of iron that could easily be carried off, and examining particularly in what way they could deceive our vigilance during the night. . . . Whenever they assumed a smiling and cheerful air, I was sure they had stolen something. . . . Their arts are considerably advanced and their civilization in this respect has made great progress; but in everything that polishes and softens the ferocity of manners, they are yet in their infancy. . . . I will admit, if you please, that it is impossible for a society to exist without some virtues; but I am forced to confess that here I could not perceive any."

Certainly, he was unable to see the irony of his words. His description of his own behavior suggests that the Indians would have had to be extremely naive to expect friendship from him or his men, or to soften their "ferocity of manners" in dealing with the Europeans. "We never landed," wrote La Pérouse, "except in force, and armed. They greatly feared our muskets, and eight or ten Europeans together were sufficient to awe a whole village."

Indeed, the enmity that developed between the Europeans and the natives was itself a kind of irony. Despite the enormous differences in their beliefs and backgrounds, the two shared many basic values and attitudes—from their passion for trading and their overriding concern with material wealth to the taking of slaves. Like the Europeans, the Northwest Coast Indians were competitive and aggressive, and frequently warred with one another and with the people farther inland for economic gain. And, again like the Europeans, they often made slaves of those they conquered. The two peoples were also similar in their concern with rank and status and in their acceptance of hereditary privilege. The European nations had their monarchs, their nobles, and their commoners, and although by this time the rigid rules of the divine-right monarchies were beginning to come under severe attack, rank was still an important part of the organization of society. The natives, too, organized their society around a ranking system—one so strict that in it no two persons ever had exactly the same status. Except for slaves, who were lumped together at the bottom of the social structure, every person was classified on an individual basis. For example, it was important for husbands and wives to hold ranks as nearly equal as possible, but even in marriage, one spouse was rated above the other. In this respect the Indians' system was far more rigid than the Europeans'.

But in another, the native system was more flexible. Among the Europeans, rank was almost entirely determined by heredity: titles and status were not earned but inherited. Among the Indians, an individual's forebears had the greatest influence on his or her rank, but wealth was also an important factor. And wealth was something that could be acquired by skill, hard work, shrewd trading, or success in war. So, although it

always helped to be born into a high-ranking family, it was possible for a person to advance in standing through his or her own efforts.

This ranking system operated throughout the region: within the villages, where the highest ranking individual—usually, although not always, a man—was the acknowledged leader; among the various villages of the same group; and among the different groups. The leader of one Tlingit village, for example, could outrank all the other Tlingit leaders. But because wealth was such an important aspect of rank, even these standings were not permanent. Anyone with any claim to high rank was always striving to move up the ladder—to acquire more wealth and more honors and, thereby, more status.

To the people of the Northwest Coast, rank and merit were virtually identical: rank was merely the public expression of the individual's qualities as a human being, and the effort to demonstrate rank was, therefore, the effort to become a better person. It was the competition this concept generated that gave the region's life its unique flavor, creating a culture that placed an enormously high value on the acquisition of wealth and an equally high value on the profligate dispensing of wealth in the potlatch.

Riches From the Water

Fishing was the major source of this wealth, and no period was more important to the Northwest Coast people than the months of the salmon run, which began in late spring. As the fish left the ocean and began their swim up the freshwater streams to spawn, men and women from all over the region gathered along the riverbanks to gather their annual harvest.

For many of the peoples, especially those from the southern part of the coast, the taking of the first salmon was followed by a rite of thanksgiving to the race of

This carved Tlingit pipe portrays a myth concerning a sea monster that controlled the waters of Lituya Bay. For Tlingits the pipe also recalls the drowning of French sailors in 1786. The Frenchmen, under the command of mariner-explorer Count de La Pérouse, were lost when the small boats from which they were making a reconnaissance of the bay overturned in a riptide. The pipe shows the chief monster (right) and its slave (left) creating great waves that swamp the helpless craft. When the Tlingits returned the bodies to La Pérouse, the Indians were fired on, the Frenchmen believing that the natives had murdered the crew members.

immortal men who had turned themselves into fish to feed humans. Without acknowledgement of their gifts, they might not return the next year.

The first salmon caught had to be taken to a specialist in charge of the ritual. Although details of the ritual varied from group to group, the specialist always treated the salmon with reverence. In some villages he sprinkled it with eagle down and placed it on a special altar, with its head pointing upstream to show the rest of the fish the direction to swim. Then he spoke to it as he would to any guest of high rank, and when the elaborate speech of welcome was finished, the rest of the assembled villagers joined voices in a chant. Now the fish could be cooked, and the chanting continued until it was fully roasted. Finally, everyone was given a small piece of its flesh to eat. That concluded the ceremony: the salmon had been honored and the men were free to begin fishing.

All the people of the Northwest Coast used weirs—latticeworks stretching across the river—to make their fishing easier. The weir permitted the water to continue flowing while it held the fish in a limited space. Once the fish were confined, they could be taken in any one of several ways. A man might use a harpoon—a wooden shaft up to 16 feet long with a barbed bone point fitted over one end. The point was firmly attached to the shaft with a strong leather binding.

Or the fisherman might use a dip net—a bag of netting suspended from a Y- or V-shaped wooden frame. But probably the most efficient technique was trapping. Several different kinds of traps were used, but all were latticework and designed to take advantage of the difficulties the salmon faced in their upstream struggle against the strong current. Once the fish had been diverted by the weir, for example, they could be forced into the funnel-shaped entrance of a boxlike or cylindrical trap.

Once the fish were caught, the women's part of the work began—drying the salmon, which was highly prized for its meat. In one method of preparing the fish for drying, the women removed the head, tails, and fins, slit the belly open, and placed the carcass on its back on a wedge-shaped wooden block. There they cleaned out the entrails with a crescent-shaped bone knife set in a wooden handle, and then hung the fish on a drying frame.

The eulachon was especially rich in oil, but rendering it was a slow task. The fish was left to rot for several days, then mashed and put into a canoe partially buried in the sand. Then the canoe was about half filled with water. Meanwhile, large stones were heating in a fire, and when they were sufficiently hot, the women picked them out with long wooden tongs and threw them into the canoe. Gradually, the water reached the boiling stage and the fish began to cook. As the oil accumulated on the surface of the water, the women ladled off the oil and poured it into large wood-

Salmon: The Basis of an Economy of Abundance

Without the salmon, the people of the Northwest Coast could never have established or maintained their affluent way of life. It was not the only fish in the region, nor the only one that the Northwest Coast people caught and ate, but the life cycle of the salmon differed from the others' in a way that made bountiful—even extravagant—salmon catches regular, predictable events. All Pacific species make their river runs for their spawning areas in the summer. All spawn in fresh water, in the river of their birth, swimming upstream from the ocean in schools so huge that the waters are packed with them. Thus the people always knew when the salmon were coming and where they would be: all they needed to do was be there to catch them and to take a quantity sufficient to provide a year-round supply of food. Every summer the people would move from their winter villages to temporary camps on the riverbanks, where the men fished and the women cleaned and preserved the catch, to keep the fish edible over the winter months. Every family—all those who lived in the same winter house—worked for itself, and there were clearly established rights to specific fishing grounds. The most desirable were those where the king salmon spawned.

The ceremonial mask at right was made by the Nootkas to represent the superhuman power that first brought the salmon to their land, the west coast of Vancouver Island. The mask, carved from red cedar, with a headdress of eagle and woodpecker feathers, has eyes and mouth that can be made to move. The seven salmon that hang from it are also made of carved and painted wood. Because of the importance of the salmon to Northwest Coast life, the fish often appears as a motif in the art of the region.

en boxes. As the oil cooled, the impurities settled to the bottom, and again the top was ladled off and transferred to another box. The amount of oil thus gathered was substantial, easily enough to fill cooking, seasoning, and medicinal needs for the rest of the year with a surplus for trading.

Spring was also the season to fish for herring and eulachon and the time to take herring roe by setting long rows of hemlock branches in places where the fish were known to spawn. Normally, the herring deposited their eggs, encased in a gelatinous covering, on seaweed, and anyone who saw a piece of roe-covered seaweed would certainly gather it in. But the hemlock

Weirs and traps like those shown
above were among the most common means
of catching salmon as they fought their way upstream. The weir—a fencelike wooden enclosure across the
entire width of the river—prevented continued upstream swimming by those salmon
that entered its gates. There they could either be speared at leisure or were swept by
the current back into the traps at the side of the entrance. But many of the fish were
speared before they had a chance to enter the weir, for Indians stood in the water
near the entrance and killed the salmon as they approached. The fish were taken
with leisters, spears with three prongs. A salmon run is shown at right.

branches were longer and wider, providing more space
for eggs. In addition, the branches were heavier, and
the fishermen weighted them at both ends to keep
them from floating away. The branches could also be
placed in convenient places where the roe could be
easily harvested.

Although spring and summer were the most important fishing seasons, some was done during the winter,
both because reserves occasionally became low and because a change of diet from dried to fresh fish was
welcome. So the men took their canoes into the ocean
to angle for halibut and cod, using a line to which was
tied a carved hardwood hook with a bone barb.

Skilled Work With Primitive Tools

The varied and fanciful carvings on the hooks were
merely one example of the Northwest Coast Indians'
extraordinary skill in working wood with relatively
primitive tools. The woods most commonly used in the
region—red and yellow cedar—are fairly soft and pliable, and therefore easy to work with. But until the
arrival of the Europeans there was little iron, and therefore no nails with which to hold things together and no
metal axes to use in felling the trees. Yet with drills
made of bone or stone, and wedges made of hardwood,
and with an array of stone tools—adzes, chisels, knives,
and the large hammers called mauls—the people of the

Northwest Coast were able to bring huge trees down and to construct from their trunks and branches objects that were as beautiful as they were useful.

The canoes, on which they relied so heavily, showed especially fine craftsmanship. Most of the Northwest Coast canoes were dugouts—carved from a single log. But they were also made in many different shapes and sizes, depending on the purposes to which they would be put—whether they would be used for travel on the river, along the coast, or out at sea; whether they were to accommodate 2 men on a fishing trip or 50 in one of the so-called war canoes, which measured up to 65 feet in length. These larger craft were used not only to transport war parties but also to take the households of high-ranking men and women on ceremonial trips to great potlatches. But whatever the size of the canoe or the purpose for which it was used, it was the product of a few men's craftsmanship from start to finish. All the men along the Northwest Coast knew how to work with wood and were proficient carpenters. But the making of a canoe called for special skills and the use of ingenious techniques. After the hull had been sanded and polished, decorations were often added—paintings, or carvings, depicting honors associated with the family of the owner.

In the building of an exceptionally large canoe to be used mainly for ceremonial purposes—a specialty among the Haidas, who excelled in canoe-making—an additional step was necessary before the final polishing and decorating. A carved figure, elaborately decorated with clan symbols, was erected at the prow and at the stern. These pieces were sewed to the hull with spruce twigs drawn through carefully drilled holes.

The Northwest Coast people used their woodworking skill to make almost everything they used. They ate from large, elegant, troughlike containers made from hollowed-out logs. Although those used for everyday purposes were simple and undecorated, the huge bowls used at feasts and potlatches were intricately and elaborately sculpted. The wooden storage boxes, in particular, reflected a high degree of skill in

Halibut-fishing tackle of the Tlingits included this elaborately fashioned hook (right) and an elegantly carved club. Because a halibut might weigh 400 pounds, it had to be stunned while being landed, lest its thrashings capsize the boat.

carpentry. A few were made simply by hollowing out blocks of wood and fitting covers to them, but most were made in a much more sophisticated manner. All four sides were produced from a single cedar plank, carefully grooved along three lines. When the plank was made pliable by steaming, it could be bent into an open-ended box with three seamless joints. The fourth joint, where the ends of the plank met, was sometimes sewn and then made watertight with a clamshell paste. Other craftsmen preferred "spotting": the face of one of the ends was coated with pigment and then pressed against the other end to form a bond. Sewing reinforced the joint. When the bottom was added, grooved around the rim so that the sides fitted firmly into it, and all the bottom joints were reinforced with pegs driven into carefully drilled holes and then sealed with paste, the boxes could safely be used both as storage containers for fish oil and as cooking utensils in which fish and berries were boiled by the usual method of adding red-hot stones to water. Nor were these the only purposes to which the boxes were put. They provided storage space for practically everything the people owned—from their everyday clothing to their ceremonial garments, from their trinkets to the masks and rattles they used at great potlatches.

There were other uses for the tree: the bark and roots were used in weaving and basketry. Weaving was women's work, and after they had taken long, narrow strips of bark from the red cedar and had discarded the coarse outer skin, they used the softer inner bark in several different ways. They split it into strips and wove it into matting, or beat it until it was shredded and then rolled it, by deft movements of the hand against the thigh, into long, flexible fibers to be woven into winter clothing.

The roots of spruce trees—washed, partly dried, then washed again, and split into strips—provided another article of clothing: conical basketwork hats—so finely woven that they were waterproof—were worn as protection against the rain. These hats were often made in the north and traded to the southern groups for other goods.

A Nootka chief's hat of tightly woven twined fibers celebrates the whale hunt in its ornate design. Such headdresses made effective rain hats.

Man Against Whales: A Perilous Pursuit in Canoes

Among the North Pacific Coast peoples only those of Vancouver Island and the Olympic Peninsula—chiefly the Nootkas and Makahs—were true whale-hunters. While other tribes were content to butcher an occasional beached whale, these peoples actively pursued the giant mammals from canoes.

Such a pursuit was led by a chief harpooner, a man of great repute who inherited his position from his father. When a whale was killed, it was towed to the village beach for butchering by the assembled tribespeople. Because of his rank, the chief harpooner always received the choicest piece of blubber from the whale's back. The rest of the animal was distributed among the villagers. Virtually every part of the animal was used. The meat and the skin, a highly regarded delicacy, were eaten; the sinews were braided into rope; the intestines were used as containers. Most important of all was the oil extracted from the blubber.

Carved wooden effigies and human skulls lend their mystical powers to a whalers' shrine near a Nootka village. Here Nootka fishermen practiced rituals intended to cause dead whales to drift ashore, thus obviating the need for the tribesmen to pursue the beasts at sea.

Armed for the hunt, *a Makah whaler (left) displays his lethal spear, an 18-foot-long wooden harpoon. The razor-edged blade is made from mussel shell, and it is backed by protruding sharp bone spurs. Attached to the harpoon by lines of sinew are large sealskin floats. During a hunt, like the one above, the chief harpooner stands in the bow of the lead canoe. He is about to thrust his weapon into a gray whale, already wounded by a harpoon point imbedded behind its flipper. When the harpoons are implanted, their floats are thrown over the side. They impede the whale's movements and, when the creature finally dies, they will keep the carcass afloat. While the paddlers and helmsman in the lead canoe struggle to steady their boat, other canoes approach, each bearing a harpooner making ready to help finish off the great beast.*

This Nootka canoe (above) was used for inlet fishing or open-sea whaling. The basic steps of canoe-making are shown at right.

The Dugout: Seaworthy Boat for Seafaring Peoples

The societies of the Northwest Coast were dominated by the sea. The Pacific Ocean and its innumerable inlets were both hunting grounds and arteries of trade. Therefore it is not surprising that the Northwest Coast peoples became expert canoe builders, for it was the canoe that was their primary means of transportation, both for people and freight. The craft they made were dugouts, usually fashioned from a single cedar or redwood log. But depending on the functions for which they were intended, canoes varied in design and degree of seaworthiness. Those intended for use in protected areas, such as Puget Sound, were relatively fragile. But the Nootkas, however, who traveled the open sea in search of whales, required sturdier craft that combined speed and maneuverability with a structural integrity sufficient to withstand the buffeting of high waves. Because of their sturdiness, Nootka canoes were highly prized throughout the seaboard, bringing high returns in trade items. But the recognized masterpieces were the Haida canoes. Their large, elaborately decorated craft were used as both ceremonial and war canoes. To own a Haida canoe was to proclaim one's exalted rank.

After felling a red cedar and clearing the trunk of branches, this Nootka craftsman splits the log lengthwise, then turns it roundside up. Here he uses an adze and wooden wedges to begin shaping the bottom.

The basic canoe form begins to take shape as the craftsman smooths down the bottom and chips away at the sides to achieve the proper thickness. When the Nootka artisan is finished with this detail work, the bottom of the boat will be about two fingers thick.

A stylized w[olf] appears ready to spring from the prow of a Ha[ida] canoe built about 1882. Behind the wolf is an ela[bo]rate abstract carving, perhaps representing a wh[ale]. Throughout the Northwest Coast, Haida canoes were esteem[ed] and the demand for them was great. They often measure[d] feet in length and were 6 or 7 feet wide in the center. Such a craft co[uld] carry about 60 warriors or their equivalent weight in merchand[ise]. Though the hull was carved from a single log, the projecting bow and st[ern] were separately made and fitted so perfectly that the joints were scarcely visi[ble]. The high bow and stern offered protection from waves. The elaborate orname[nts] were usually family crests and indicated the owner's rank.

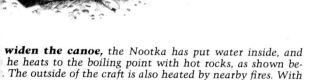

ng mauls and wedges, *the craftsman clears away the ex-
wood from the canoe's interior, a tedious and strenuous
. As he hollows out the boat, the Nootka is careful to shape
sides to the desired thickness: one finger's
th at the top, two fingers' at the
om.*

widen the canoe, *the Nootka has put water inside, and
he heats to the boiling point with hot rocks, as shown be-
. The outside of the craft is also heated by nearby fires. With
wood softened by hot water and fire,
d thwarts are placed inside to
den the interior.*

ving carved the high bow and stern pieces, *the canoe-
er is now putting the stern piece in place. It is securely
ched to the boat with cedar-peg dowels or
ings of slender spruce branches. The fit is
xact that the seal is watertight,
n though no caulking is used.*

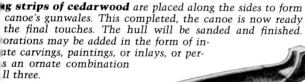

g strips of cedarwood *are placed along the sides to form
canoe's gunwales. This completed, the canoe is now ready
the final touches. The hull will be sanded and finished.
orations may be added in the form of in-
te carvings, paintings, or inlays, or per-
s an ornate combination
ll three.*

Nowhere on the Northwest Coast was pottery made: where others relied on vessels made of clay, the Northwest Coast people used wooden boxes and baskets. And here again their extraordinary technical skill was evident. Like their wooden boxes, their baskets were so expertly made that they were leakproof and could be used as containers for liquids.

A Forest-and-Sea Existence

The people's dependence on the forest and sea would have been immediately evident to anyone visiting one of their villages, whether it was small, with no more than 50 inhabitants, or large, with a population approaching 1,000. Whatever its size, every visible structure was made of wood, and the entire village was oriented toward the water, whether a river, a quiet bay, or the ocean. A large village might stretch for up to two miles along the beachfront, its one or two rows of gabled wooden houses all facing the water. Drawn up on the beach were the canoes, covered with cedarbark matting or with boughs to protect them against the weather. In the back of the houses were other wooden structures: drying racks for fish, sheds that served as smokehouses, and storage sheds in which the preserved catches were kept. Some groups built special huts for women in childbirth, for girls undergoing their lengthy puberty ritual, and for all females during their menstrual periods. Wooden shelters for the ashes of the cremated dead were usually built near the houses, while shamans' graves were placed some distance from the village on a cliff overlooking the water.

The living quarters were imposing. In the north a house of average size measured about 30 by 45 feet, and some shelters in the south were more than double that size. All of them were built for multifamily use. There is even evidence of houses 1,000 feet long, built to accommodate an entire village. In the northern gable type, large, thick beams served as framework for the walls, and long ridgepoles ran from front to back, supported at either end by a post. All these elements were securely and precisely fitted by mortising. The sidings and the gabled roof were of overlapped planking to keep the building weatherproof. There were no windows: ventilation was provided by a hole left in the roof, which could be covered, when necessary, by a sliding wooden panel. If the principal resident of the house was of particularly high rank, that fact was immediately obvious in the massive poles in front of the building. These posts, which were elaborately carved and painted, were not merely for esthetic effect. Like the decorations on canoes and boxes, those on the posts proclaimed honors associated with the family history. They were, in other words, announcements of rank.

Even if rank did not announce itself outside, it was always in evidence inside, both in the arrangement of the living space and in the amount of internal decoration the house contained. In the houses of men and

women of the highest rank the interior posts were as elegantly carved as the ones at the door. In the center of many houses was a kind of sunken living room that was surrounded on three sides by wide ledges with wooden floors. This center section, with a firepit in the middle, provided communal living space and the cooking area. The broad ledges were partitioned with wooden walls or curtains—according to the affluence of the residents—to provide private living quarters for each family. The ledge along the back wall was the place of honor, reserved for the highest ranking resident and his family, although, if the house was very large, the family next to his in rank might have their living quarters there too. Along the side walls, in descending order or rank, were the living quarters of the other families—the highest ranking nearest the back wall, the lowest ranking nearest the entrance.

For the Tlingit people in particular the rules of residence for each house were strict and specific. All the Tlingits, in whatever village they lived, divided themselves into two major groups—one called the Eagles, the other the Ravens—each of which was subdivided into several clans. All the men who lived in a given house had to be of the same clan, a requirement not made of the women. Thus all the males living under one roof were related as brothers, nephews, uncles, or cousins. Marriage between two Eagles or two Ravens was strictly forbidden.

The children in the house had their mother's clan affiliations. The Tlingits, like their immediate neighbors, reckoned descent matrilineally, and although a father felt affection for his children, his ties to his sister's children—all of whom were members of his lineage—were in many respects even stronger. His sister's children, not his own, would inherit his wealth and family honors. Indeed, his sister's sons would come to live at his house when they were about 10 years old,

and his sons at that same age would leave their home and join the household of his wife's brother.

A child's education consisted largely of watching and imitating adults. But some of his most important lessons were learned by listening. As soon as a boy or girl was old enough to understand, the time had come to learn the family's history. Over and over, mothers and grandmothers recited the clan story—a long and detailed account of its wealth, its honors, and the glorious deeds that had been performed by its members. The lesson of clan loyalty and the stories of clan accomplishments could never be told too often: they were drummed into children's heads until they knew them by heart, for clan loyalty was the deepest loyalty any Tlingit had. In the rare event of a quarrel between a man's clan and his wife's, neither could remain neutral. The man would support his clan, and his wife and children would be on the other side.

Along with being indoctrinated with family history, the children were taught proper behavior, for with all their competitiveness and eagerness for rank and wealth, the Tlingits had a strict, even puritanical code of personal behavior and morality. Girls—especially of high rank—were expected to be chaste at marriage. Boys were expected to know and carry out their responsibilities to others. Boys and girls alike were taught that hard work, thrift, strength, and bravery should be their goals. They were always to treat others with respect and to maintain an air of quiet dignity. Quarreling and

Plank houses varied in design according to tribe, as these four examples show. They ranged from the simple shedlike Coast Salish style to the partly underground dwellings of Chinooks and Kalapuyas.

[H]aida winter village on [the] Queen Charlotte Islands stretches [alon]g a narrow beach that is hemmed in [by f]orested mountains. Each large cedar-plank [hous]e shelters several matrilineally linked families. Ris[ing a]bove each house is a frontal post with carved figures that [are e]mblems of the people living within. To provide for a growing [popu]lation, new houses are rising (top right and right). Behind the main [row] of houses are several huts. Some of these shelters are for menstruating [wom]en; others are for the ashes of the dead. While some of the Haidas are [busy] with construction work, three villagers are returning from a fishing [expe]dition. A portion of their catch will be placed on one of the many [driftwoo]d racks in front of the houses. Scattered about the beach are canoes, [the l]arge ones reserved for transporting notables.

This winter house, 50 feet square, provided shelter for some half-dozen related Haida families. With the only ventilation coming from the smoke hole, the communal fire, set in the middle of the cedar-plank floor, provided considerable heat within the windowless house. The fire, of course, was also used for cooking, and here a woman roasts fish while nearby another weaves a basket, a man carves a wooden box, and children romp.

On all four sides of the floor is a broad raised platform, its outer edge serving as a passageway around the house. Set into the platform are the private sleeping compartments of the families. These are arranged according to status. The place of honor (upper right)—opposite the doorway to the outside—is reserved for the house chief. His quarters are flanked by two carved posts that relate the history of the Eagle moiety, to which the chief and all adult, free, male residents belong. The compartment is set off by an ornately decorated screen. Less desirable are those compartments of the high-ranking families, though these too have places of honor, adjacent to the chief's quarters. They have partitions of wooden panels that are far more substantial than the simple woven mats that form the walls of the compartments of the lowest ranked families. The slaves' quarters, near the doorway, are not shown.

creating difficulties should be avoided at all cost.

Every adult taught these lessons, but they had a special importance when they were taught by the house chief. On chilly winter evenings he would gather the children of the house around the firepit, and although it was important for all the youngsters to learn and to take his words to heart, it was most important for the children of the highest rank, for they were the ones who would have the greatest responsibilities when they grew up.

As the children neared adolescence, these lessons began to take on a more concrete and personal form. No longer was it a matter of merely listening to tales of the clan's great heroes and their honors or of heeding exhortations on self-discipline and restraint. Now it was important to demonstrate that one had all the Tlingit virtues. By this time a boy was living in the house of his mother's brother, no longer under the care of his own indulgent parents, but of an uncle whose responsi-

bility it was to be a strict disciplinarian. Even on the coldest winter days his uncle would wake him before daylight and stand waiting on the shore as the boy waded into the frigid water up to his neck and stood there stoically until his uncle gave him permission to come back. Nor was this the end of the ordeal. Once he was on dry land, his uncle whipped the boy's cold, wet skin with alder boughs. All this had a purpose—to make him strong, to harden and to purify him so that good fortune would be his lot.

He also began to learn in earnest the skills he would need as a man: how to hunt and fish and work with wood. He was assigned specific jobs to do. It was his daily task, for example, to gather and chop the wood for the firepit before daybreak and to build up the house fire, so that it was burning brightly when everyone else awakened. This chore would remain his responsibility for a long time. Nor did the cold water plunges cease as he grew older. He would take one every morning, not only for the sake of cleanliness but for its purifying effects, especially so when he was about to undertake a dangerous task, a trip into the forest to hunt or across the mountains on a trading journey to the interior.

The most important lessons his uncle taught him related to his clan. The boy had already learned from his mother and grandmother something about his clan's traditional rights and prerogatives that could be exercised only by its members. Only the members of his clan could sing certain songs, do certain dances, tell certain legends. Only they had the right to use depictions of certain animals and supernatural creatures. Only they could give certain names to houses and canoes—and to people. He had to know in detail what all these intangibles were, and his uncle's lessons were a kind of advanced course in this field. But his uncle's teachings also had more practical aspects. Each clan in the village retained certain territorial rights, which others infringed upon at their peril: to fish in particular sections of the river; to hunt in specific areas of the forest; and to use certain routes on trading trips inland. All these were paths to wealth and thus to rank, and it was important for the boy to know in detail all his clan's exclusive privileges and protect them.

The Transition to Womanhood

For the girls the first menses marked the beginning of a long and trying indoctrination that lasted anywhere from a few months for girls of low status to two years for those of the highest rank. For all that time they were shut away in a special hut behind the house, seeing only one another and their mothers, grandmothers, and paternal aunts. The first eight days were the most difficult, and a girl's conduct during that period was an omen of her future life. She was supposed to sit as nearly immobile as possible for the whole time and to rub her lips and face with a hard stone eight times each day. She could have no food or water until the end of the fourth day, and then she had to fast again until the end of the eighth. Failure to observe any of these rules would destroy her character. If she did not rub the stone across her face and lips, she would grow up a gossip—and therefore a troublemaker; if she broke her fast, she would grow up a glutton or a thief—or worst of all, a loose woman. If she became any of these things, she would bring disgrace not only on herself but on her entire clan.

The rest of the period of seclusion, devoted to mastering adult skills, was far less difficult. The girl sewed and did basketry—crafts she would need as a wife and mother—until the time finally came for her to return to life in the village. This return was the occasion for a feast given by her father. Moreover, now that she was a woman, the time had come for her to wear a labret—an elliptical plug of wood or bone that was inserted in a slit cut into her lower lip. It was also time for her to

The totem pole has come to be, in the minds of many Americans, a symbol for all northern Indians and Eskimos. In fact, such heraldic monuments with their fantastic animal figures are native only to the peoples of the Northwest Coast, where the art of totem-pole sculpture still flourishes. An Indian who wanted one of these elaborate sculptures bearing his accumulated family crests often hired the services of a skilled carver who fashioned the pole from the trunk of a cedar tree.

Among the Northwest Coast tribes the Haida are especially known for their carving skill, as the examples here reveal. The 37-foot-high house post (left), now a museum piece, has an entryway at its lowest level and originally stood in front of a Haida dwelling. Among the figures on the pole are Thunderbird, Sea Grizzly Bear, Raven, and three watcher guardians. The sculptures above stand close together at the Haida settlement of Skidegate, on the Queen Charlotte Islands. Many of these poles proclaim the importance of the families that owned them. Others are mortuary poles, fashioned to hold the ashes of the deceased, while still others are "shame" poles, carved and erected to embarrass a person who did not pay his debts or broke his word.

Fantastic Carvings of Northwest Indians

Among the least understood aspects of Northwest Coast Indian life are the wooden figures carved in deep relief on poles. Whites thought them to be objects of religious veneration but, in fact, they have nothing to do with religion and certainly were never worshiped. Instead, the animal representations are family heraldic symbols, quite similar to those found on European coats of arms. Northwest Coast Indians thought their clan lineages to be connected with certain animals that had performed miracles or feats of heroism. Thus a totem pole displaying a bear, a raven, and a beaver is a form of mythic clan history and a proud assertion of lineage. Unfortunately, many 19th-century missionaries misinterpreted the meaning of the poles and, believing them to be objects of pagan worship, destroyed many of the best examples.

A bear is the chief design element in this carved Tsimshian headdress. The three potlatch rings show that the original owner was a man who had given away much wealth and was therefore of high status. The significance of the five hands is unknown.

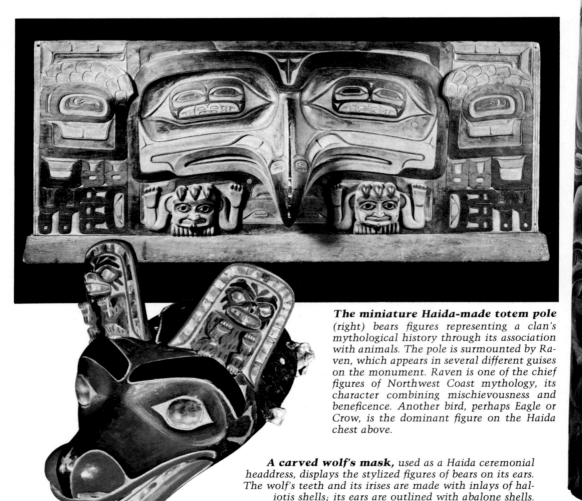

The miniature Haida-made totem pole (right) bears figures representing a clan's mythological history through its association with animals. The pole is surmounted by Raven, which appears in several different guises on the monument. Raven is one of the chief figures of Northwest Coast mythology, its character combining mischievousness and beneficence. Another bird, perhaps Eagle or Crow, is the dominant figure on the Haida chest above.

A carved wolf's mask, used as a Haida ceremonial headdress, displays the stylized figures of bears on its ears. The wolf's teeth and its irises are made with inlays of haliotis shells; its ears are outlined with abalone shells.

receive her first tattoo. Both men and women were tattooed, and the girl's first tattoo—of her family's crest and placed on her hand—was done at this time.

While she was in seclusion, arrangements were probably already under way for her marriage. Among the Tlingits, choosing a spouse was not a personal affair between two young people, but a method of achieving greater rank and wealth and of consolidating relationships among the clans. Therefore marriages were usually arranged by the young peoples' families. Some kinds of matches were especially desirable. If a boy married his mother's brother's daughter, for example, he would acquire as a father-in-law the man from whom he would one day

Symbols of wealth and status adorn *the headgear of this Haida tribesman. Surrounding the carved family emblem are ermine, feathers, and sea lion whiskers.*

inherit. If he married his father's sister's daughter, his wife would belong to his own father's clan.

Like virtually everything else in Tlingit life, the procedures surrounding marriage arrangements involved displays of wealth and generosity. The boy's mother or his maternal uncle offered the girl's mother as many and as valuable gifts as the family could afford. In a few days she made her response: if the gifts were accepted, the marriage would take place. Now the girl's father

made his gifts to the groom's family—again, as generous as he could afford—to signify the high value he placed on his daughter.

The wedding took place in the house of the bride's father, where she waited hidden in her family's quarters until the guests had assembled and the groom had entered to take his seat near the center of the floor. Then, to the accompaniment of songs and dances, the guests spread a bridal path of fur. Shyly, eyes cast down, the bride emerged to take her place next to her husband-to-be. She and he sat quietly throughout the festivities that followed, and they were not permitted to share in the wedding feast. A few weeks later, if they had the wealth, the groom's family gave a feast for the family of the bride. This completed the formalities and sealed the match. Although man and woman were already living together, a wealthy couple was not considered truly married until the return feast was given.

Childbirth was surrounded by many of the same rules and rituals as those that accompanied a girl's first menstrual period. Again she was secluded in a special hut and attended only by women: her husband was not permitted to see her or their new child until they left

A Kwakiutl maiden stands amid her kinfolk in a canoe bringing her to the village of her intended husband. Among the class-conscious Northwest Coast Indians courtship was permitted only between persons of the same rank, and marriages were usually arranged by families. Exchanges of gifts between the families of the bride and groom demonstrated the wealth of each.

the hut—at least eight days after the baby's birth. Before that time arrived, the mother had already chosen a name for her baby—one that was associated with her lineage and her clan and had been held by one of her ancestors, now reborn in this small, new body. For although the Tlingits were not a deeply religious people, they believed in a great cycle of death and rebirth. Just as the salmon returned to life each winter after having offered themselves to the people for food during the previous summer, so human beings, after death, became incarnate again as babies.

Even so, death was an awesome event for the Tlingits. The dead—especially those of high rank—deserved honors, and when a chief or his wife died, the body was dressed in ceremonial robes and placed in a sitting position against the back wall of the house, where it remained, surrounded by his or her treasures, for several days. During this mourning period close relatives cut their hair short and blackened their faces. At night clansmen and other villagers gathered at the house to chant ritual dirges.

The spirit world was pleasant, but the ghost of the dead faced a long, difficult journey to get there. To make the trip comfortable, the mourners provided food, dressed the deceased for travel, and cremated the body to keep it warm. A funeral pyre of fragrant cedar was built behind the house, and once the body was deposited on it and the fire was lighted, the circle of mourners slowly and somberly broke up, and eveyone left. After the fire had burned down and the corpse had been consumed, the charred bones were taken from the ashes and carefully wrapped in cloth. Then the bones were placed in a carved wooden box, which was set inside a grave house near the village.

Supernatural beings were everywhere in the world of the Tlingits, taking on many different forms. There was the Thunderbird, for instance, who lived atop the highest mountain peak, with a lake on its back and lightning as its pet, and who, merely by flapping its wings, could bring on thunder, lightning, and drenching rain. There was the Land Otter Man, a fierce-looking creature who stole people away, deprived them of their senses, and turned them into land otter men who tormented humans. Raven, the Trickster, was a major supernatural being. In the long repertoire of stories about him, which detail his clever exploits and his skill at outwitting others, is one involving his uncle Nasca-

A feathered headdress is both a badge of office and a symbol of power for this Nootka female shaman. Among the tribes of the Pacific Northwest Coast male shamans outnumbered female, but the latter were generally thought to be as powerful.

kiyel, who created the world. According to this tale the world was without light until Raven managed to get into his uncle's house and steal the sun from a box where it was kept. Raven, who had been white until that time, made his escape through the smoke hole and has been black with soot ever since.

Witches—seemingly ordinary men and women who possessed the power to bring disease and death—were a constant threat. When the witches wanted to harm a person, they would obtain something closely associated with him—a hair, a fingernail, spittle—and bury it near a grave house. Promptly, the victim would fall ill and might even die. Indeed, the Tlingits believed that all illnesses had supernatural origins. Spirits stole away peoples' souls or caused their bodies to be invaded by foreign objects. Therefore, illnesses could be cured only by supernatural means.

The Powerful Shamans

It is not surprising that a special group of men and women—the shamans—should have existed to cure diseases. The shamans had power to perform other extraordinary feats as well: to bring good or bad weather; to assure an especially heavy run of salmon; to ferret out witches; to bring success in war. Although the shamans charged for their services and thus could become relatively wealthy, they seldom stood high in the ranking system and usually came from the less prestigious branches of a lineage or clan. But because of their control over the supernatural, their influence was enormous. Like the village chief, the shaman was respected. But he was also held in awe.

Although the ordinary person could never achieve the supernatural powers of a shaman, all the Tlingit men strove to acquire guardian spirits. To this end the males purified themselves with cold-water baths; flagellated themselves with birch boughs; fasted, purged themselves, and at times abstained from sexual activity to make themselves pleasing to the spirits and to attain control of one in particular that would act as a protector. If a man was lucky, he might even have a vision and be seized by a spirit, which would thenceforth become his guardian. But shamans would always far exceed ordinary men and women in controlling the spirits.

Even when they were not performing cures or otherwise exhibiting their extraordinary skills, the male and female shamans were intimidating in appearance. Shamans never cut their hair— *(continued on page 312)*

The Occult Arts: A Route to Wealth and Power

Among the Northwest Coast peoples shamans, who might be either male or female, were regarded with both awe and respect, for it was the shaman—whose supernatural powers were derived from association with personal guardian spirits—who could control the weather, bring success in war and hunting, predict the future, and most important of all, cure illnesses. Although shamans might amass considerable wealth through fees for effecting cures, their position, oddly enough, was not inherently one of the highest status. Most shamans—now often called Indian doctors—inherited their roles but, before taking up practice, each was required to serve an apprenticeship or endure a time of solitary fasting when a spirit would appear to confer its powers.

As the shaman used his powers to cure, so his adversary, the witch, used his to cause illness. The witch was thought to practice his evil craft in secret, to strike down those who displeased him. It was the shaman's job to neutralize the evil power of witches and to point out the evildoer for possible punishment. In some tribes the shaman did not work a cure himself but forced the witch he held responsible to withdraw the magic that had caused illness. In others, the shaman cured and also accused someone of witchcraft so that the tribe or clan might deal out retribution. So great was the power of a shaman—particularly among the Tlingits, Haidas, and Tsimshians—that even after death his body was treated in a special manner. Unlike ordinary persons, his body was not cremated. Instead, he was buried at a site he had chosen. As the power of the spirits remained within the body, people passing the grave took extraordinary precautions not to offend, walking by with faces averted while throwing offerings toward the site.

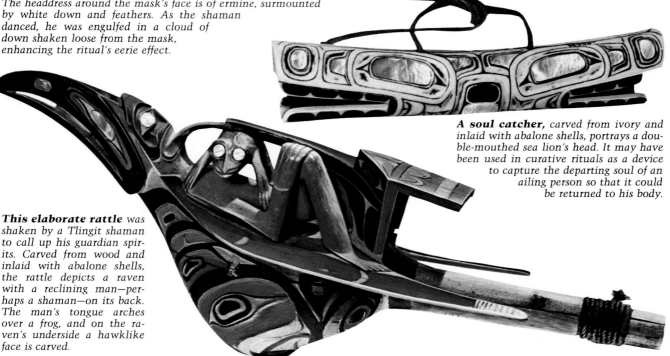

This awe-inspiring mask, *representing one of the shaman's guardian spirits, was worn by a Tlingit shaman during curative rites. Usually, such masks were worn on the forehead or crown. The headdress around the mask's face is of ermine, surmounted by white down and feathers. As the shaman danced, he was engulfed in a cloud of down shaken loose from the mask, enhancing the ritual's eerie effect.*

A soul catcher, *carved from ivory and inlaid with abalone shells, portrays a double-mouthed sea lion's head. It may have been used in curative rituals as a device to capture the departing soul of an ailing person so that it could be returned to his body.*

This elaborate rattle *was shaken by a Tlingit shaman to call up his guardian spirits. Carved from wood and inlaid with abalone shells, the rattle depicts a raven with a reclining man—perhaps a shaman—on its back. The man's tongue arches over a frog, and on the raven's underside a hawklike face is carved.*

Masks for Northwest Coast Storytellers

Among the peoples of the Northwest Coast—particularly those of the central region, such as the Kwakiutls and Bella Coolas—masks were an important element in their rich ceremonial life that revolved around secret societies. Carved from wood, ornately painted in many hues, and often topped with human hair or feathers, the masks represented spirits or creatures drawn from mythology. No two masks, even when they portrayed the same spirit, were completely alike. Each represented the owner's interpretation of a story connected with the figure. This story was told, at least in part, by the wearer during a ceremonial. But rarely, if ever, did he relate the full tale, for only he was privileged to know it. Thus the meanings behind many masks were lost when their owners died.

Masks that date from the early 20th century are often less precisely carved than those made earlier. By then artists had come to rely more on paint for characterization. With features only sketchily carved, such masks could be used to represent several figures, the old paint being washed away and a new coat applied to depict a different spirit.

Storytelling masks, such as these, once served as props in tale-spinning. They are all Tsimshian, except for the fantastic Kwakiutl work directly above, which combines human and birdlike characteristics. The beak of this creature is in two parts, each hinged, so that during a ceremonial the owner might hide the human face behind it and then at the proper moment fling open the beak—which would spread out like wings—to reveal the fierce-looking visage. The mask at top left has similar attributes. Though the woman's face is immobile, the birdlike ornaments hanging from her braids have "wings" on hinges so that the figures themselves could be hidden or revealed according to the dictates of the tale. The striped and spotted woman's head at left is of a much simpler design. But the mask at right is a study in complexity. It shows a human figure astride a raven that sits upon the forehead of a man.

presenting a mythical being that de-
nded from the sky to live in a lake, this 19½-
h-tall Cowichan mask was worn by a person
xalted rank. When worn in ceremonies, the
sk was encircled with a ruff of white feathers
l adorned with sea lion whiskers. Cowi-
n masks, like those of the other Salish
ples, were distinctive, being more ab-
ct than the masks fashioned by
er groups of the Northwest
ast.

e spirit of the sun is the central motif in
s Bella Coola mask worn during the group's
ter ceremonials. Such disk-shaped masks,
ved from different levels of a block of wood to
ance the three-dimensional effect, were com-
n among the Bella Coolas. Though the sun
s one of the most popular themes on Bella
ola masks, figures symbolic of the moon,
ds, or even flowers were also favorite motifs.

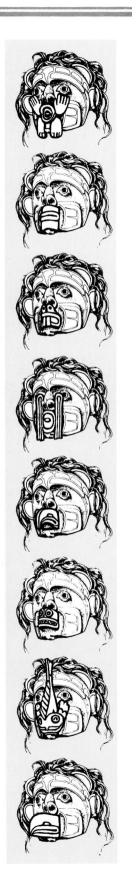

A Kwakiutl Echo mask with interchangeable mouths
(beneath the mask) was used to represent several different
figures, depending on which mouth was used. The basic
mask depicts the spirit Echo, said to have the ability to imitate the sounds made by any creature. During the course of
the ceremonial telling of Echo's tale, the wearer would hide
his masked face beneath the folds of his cloaklike blanket
and surreptitiously replace Echo's mouth with the mouth of
the creature the spirit was imitating at the time. Each one of
the mouths is equipped with a wooden stem at its back, and
the wearer clamped his jaw down on it to hold the mouth in
place. At right are eight different characters that could be
portrayed by the wearer. They are (top to bottom) Echo itself, a human being, a beaver, an unidentified figure, Eagle, a
bear, a sculpin (a type of spiny fish), and Raven.

lest they lose their power—and never combed it, but wore it in a wild tangle. And when they *were* performing a cure, the effect was truly electrifying. Although the cure took place in the patient's house, it was always a public exhibition. The huge room was dark, lighted only by the fire at its center, next to which the patient lay. Around the room his housemates and relatives were ringed, singing to the beat of a drum placed near the entrance. Then the shaman, masked, dressed in a special blanket, and carrying a rattle, entered and began his curing work. Each Tlingit shaman had a number of different masks, each representing a different spirit, and he or she might use several of them in the course of treatment, depending on the shaman's sense of which spirit would be most effective at a given time.

The shaman commenced his cure by running rapidly around the fire in a crouched position, shaking his rattle, and singing to the steady beat of the drum until his spirit helper entered him. Then, when he had learned from his spirit the cause of the patient's illness, the shaman would attempt a cure. Sometimes he would bend over the prostrate body to suck out the object that had caused the disease, either by placing his lips against the patient's body or by using his special bone tube. At other times he would give medication.

When he was exhibiting his skills merely to advertise his prowess, the shaman performed even more miraculous feats—swallowing sticks and knives and vomiting them up, singing power songs, falling down in a faint so convincing that he appeared dead and, after lying motionless on the floor a while, springing in a frenzy back to life—sometimes even stepping into the firepit and walking, barefoot, across the burning embers.

Among the peoples of the upper reaches of the Northwest Coast, religion tended to be a relatively private affair in which a shaman interceded with the spirits on behalf of clients. There were few rituals that involved groups of people, few ceremonials of a primarily religious nature that were intended to spread awe or fear of the supernatural world.

But farther to the south, in the region around Vancouver Island, and particularly among the Kwakiutls, religion was highly formalized. Religious societies—each with its own complex ceremonials and each divided into subgroups—held powerful sway over the minds and emotions of initiates and noninitiates alike. Indeed, these societies were closely bound up with status. Membership was generally limited to the men and women of the tribal aristocracy whose wealth enabled them to pay the required fees and to host potlatches that membership in the occult groups entailed.

Among the Kwakiutls there were three secret religious societies, each with its own subgroups that united people of similar rank and wealth. The Nutlam, or Dog Eater Society, was dedicated to the spirit of the wolf, thought to be the chief enemy of dogs. The Society of Those Descended From the Heavens celebrated

The Frightening Apparitions of the Kwakiutl Hamatsa Dance

Unlike more northerly tribes whose religion is a personal mostly informal affair, the Kwakiutls have elaborate sac rituals enacted by secret organizations. The order of high rank is the Shamans' Society's Hamatsa (Cannibal Danc membership in that group is eagerly sought by men and w en who aspire to a lofty station.

The Hamatsas hold their ceremonial annually. It is a ual of conjury and drama, calculated to impress nonmemb with the power of the order while initiating novices into group. In the course of the performance the novices—wh bodies have supposedly been taken over by cannibal spiri scream, leap about, engage in apparently cannibalistic a and inflict wounds on the other participants. All this occ to the accompaniment of rites intended to pacify the spi performed by fantastically costumed and masked soc members. As the ceremony progresses, carved birds strings—manipulated by men hidden above the beams of ceremonial house—swoop over the audience, strange vo howl from beneath the floor, and dancers disappear and appear in puffs of smoke.

The affair is all carefully staged. The dim lighting perr props to be obscured and lends a mysterious and ghostly ment to the proceedings. The viewers are as much an a ence for a magic show as attendants at a ritual.

Possessed by a cannibal spirit, a Hamatsa novice is re for the rite of purification. His bulging eyes and vacant exp sion are indications of his possessed state. The hemlock bou on his head and wrists will remind the audience that he been in the forest for several days, a prisoner of evil spirits.

Arrayed in traditional costumes, members of the Shamans' Society pose for a photograph in a large building used for the initiation rites of the Kwakiutl secret societies. The Hamatsa, representing the Cannibal Spirit, stands in front of the left-hand post. A cedarbark ring around his neck is evidence of his exalted position. The Cannibal Spirit is surrounded by his retinue, many of them creatures noted for their bloodthirsty natures. Among these birdlike spirits is the Crooked Beak of Heaven, whose appetite for human flesh is insatiable. Then there is the straight-beaked Raven (thick bill), which devours the eyes of the Cannibal Spirit's victims. In the supernatural world the straight-beaked Raven and Cannibal Spirit live together. As fearsome as any in the group is the Hoxhok, which has a straight, thin bill. It is well adapted to cracking human skulls and sucking out their brains. Yet another associate of Cannibal Spirit is Grizzly Bear (at right of the center post). With a swift swipe of its sharp claws it disembowels unwary humans.

Not all of the members of the Shamans' Society represent such terrifying spirits. The woman just to the left of the center post symbolizes the weather. And near the far right (wearing horns) is the figure of the Mountain Goat Spirit, symbol of the mountain climbers. Grizzly Bear lopes about threatening all with its claws and fangs. The Hamatsa Spirit itself leaps to and fro, pretending to take bites from the flesh of members of the audience. The birdlike creatures whirl their cedarbark skirts, wave their arms, and clack their beaks in a menacing way.

Shortly after the Hamatsa Dance is over, members of the order often give a potlatch. Here they make restitution for any property that was destroyed during the dance, and people who had been wounded while watching or participating in the ceremonial are paid with gifts.

Malevolence incarnate is the role of this bird-spirit participant (below) in the Hamatsa ceremony. The figure represents the Hoxhok and may have once been decorated with wooden skulls to emphasize the creature's evil nature.

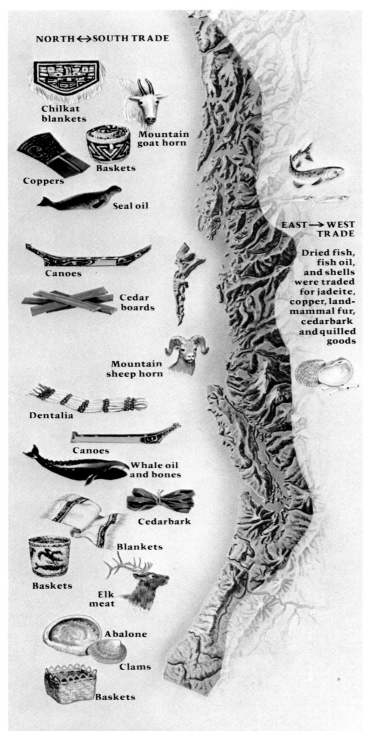

NORTH ⟷ SOUTH TRADE

Chilkat blankets

Mountain goat horn

Baskets

Coppers

Seal oil

Canoes

Cedar boards

EAST → WEST TRADE

Dried fish, fish oil, and shells were traded for jadeite, copper, land-mammal fur, cedarbark and quilled goods

Mountain sheep horn

Dentalia

Canoes

Whale oil and bones

Cedarbark

Blankets

Baskets

Elk meat

Abalone

Clams

Baskets

Outstanding traders, the Northwest Coast Indians amassed prestige-conferring wealth. Because the coastal peoples had an abundance of necessities, seaboard trade centered on luxuries. The Makahs and Nootkas of the south-central part of the region offered whale products, for example, in exchange for the ceremonial canoes built by the Haidas of the Queen Charlotte Islands. Slaves—the ultimate proof of wealth—were a major item in coastal trade. There was also much trade with the tribes of the interior, the Tlingits acting as middlemen.

the spirits of the sky, such as the star and the bird. Finally, and best known, was the Shamans' Society, whose ranks were limited to shamans. The most prestigious of its members formed a subgroup, Hamatsa, or Cannibal Dancers.

Normally, membership in one of these societies was inherited, though a child did not automatically assume a position in the society of a parent. There were no clans such as existed among the peoples farther north, and a man or woman was free to confer society membership upon anyone of his or her choosing. A member might pass on the honor to a son, daughter, son-in-law, niece, or nephew. A member could even sell the privilege to the highest bidder. Such an eventuality could occur when a man fell upon hard times and was approached by a newly rich tribesman seeking to confirm his status through membership in a secret religious society.

Another—and grimmer—means of securing membership was to murder an initiate. All privileges, all rights to ceremonial participation, were then automatically transferred from victim to killer. In the rare instances when murder was employed, the killer would usually choose as his victim a society member who lived in a distant village. Distance made retribution difficult for the murdered man's family. At the same time the killer was careful not to select a victim of higher rank than himself. In the world of the Kwakiutls, as with other Northwest Coast tribes, status was power and to slay a superior was to invite terrible retaliation.

Fall and winter were the times of the great Kwakiutl ceremonies. By autumn fishing had ceased, and dried fish and berries had been packed away, and the tribesmen and women had moved from their summer camps back to their permanent villages. Now was the time for the secret societies to begin preparations for the great ceremonials. These rites would reinforce the status of the members by regenerating awe among the poor—who formed the audiences at the rituals—at the power of both the spirits and their human intermediaries.

In essence, all of the ceremonials of the three societies served the same superficial function—to initiate new members—and all played out the same theme in the form of a drama. The novice was "kidnapped," his soul taken over by one of the spirits of the society to which he would belong. During the ceremonial the novice was "found" by the society members. Their dances and rituals calmed the spirit within the novice and returned the person to his former self.

In the frenzy of dancing, chanting, screaming, and mock combat of the performance, the power of the spirits was celebrated. Society members appeared in fearsome garb representing those spirits. Their clothing, elaborate headdresses, grotesque masks and paraphernalia were all calculated to impress the audience—and themselves—with the group's capability of influencing the supernatural creatures. At the same time the

dances were a form of dramatized warfare, rituals that
extolled the combative ardor of the participants. This
ardor was made manifest through rites in which blood,
usually from knife wounds, was drawn from the dancers and sometimes from members of the audience as
well. The chants, too, acclaimed bloodshed and mayhem, as in this portion of a Cannibal Dancer's song:
"I went all around the world to find food.
I went all around the world to find human flesh.
I went all around the world to find human heads.
I went all around the world to find human corpses."
Important in the performances were magical tricks,
carefully arranged in advance, that seemed to lend substance to claims of occult powers by society members.
During the Hamatsa ceremony, for example, a woman
member might publicly proclaim her supernatural powers and ask another to behead her, run a spear through
her body, or dismember her. Although minor wounds
might actually result from these magical enactments,
sleight of hand and other deceptions were employed to
create the illusion of mayhem. The woman seemed to
be beheaded and, indeed, a head was produced. It was
not, of course, the woman's own but a carefully carved
replica in wood. Yet it was all so realistically done that
even though the audience might know, in one part of
their minds, that no beheading had taken place, their
eagerness to believe permitted them to accept image for
reality. And when the woman reappeared, "restored"
to wholeness, audience and participants alike gasped at
the power of the spirits and the wonders they could
perform.

Yet such acts, however wondrous, were really supplements to the main event: the initiation of the novice.
In a typical Hamatsa ceremony the prelude to the ceremonial began when the novice appeared to become ill

and then was "kidnapped" by the Cannibal Dancers
garbed in the rainments of spirits. The society members secreted their charge in the woods, and there for
several days they taught him the rituals, dances, and
chants of the Hamatsa. He also learned to act as if he
were possessed by the spirits and to pretend to eat the
human flesh that these specters required for their nour-
ishment—an act so repulsive to the Kwakiutls it indicated, through its very loathsomeness, immense spiritual power.

When the actual ceremonial began, the Hamatsa performed the dances that were supposed to lure the novice from the hands of his captors. As if in reply to their
beseechings, the novice appeared—in the midst of a
puff of smoke—through the roof of the house where
the ceremony was performed, or in some other seemingly magical manner. Clearly, by his frenzied actions,
he was possessed. He danced about, screamed, hurled
imprecations at the audience and his fellow Cannibal
Dancers. To calm the raging spirit within, he was
offered the "flesh of a human"—usually the burned carcass of a bear or a wooden dummy in the form of a
man. The novice ate and danced, disappeared and reappeared. Intervals of calm alternated with periods of
great frenzy. Eventually, after several reappearances,
the ministrations of the dancers began to work; the
hysteria that had characterized the novice slowly yielded to tranquillity. But the spirit within had not been
exorcised. Instead, it had been brought under control,
to remain with, and grant great powers to, the new
member as long as he belonged to the Hamatsa.

With the appeasement of the spirit the new member
was formally inaugurated into the Cannibal Dancers
division of the Shamans' Society. All present witnessed
marvelous events, and the power of the Hamatsa spirits

315

was affirmed. Shortly after the novice was admitted, he or members of his family gave a potlatch at which gifts were distributed, particularly to those who were injured or insulted during the initiation ceremonies. The various societies performed throughout the winter, but with the coming of warm weather preparations began for the forthcoming migration of salmon. In May the people abandoned their permanent villages to return to their fishing stations.

Successful Middlemen

The Kwakiutls bartered their surplus fish and oil, but trading was not nearly as important to them as it was to the Tlingits. For the Tlingits trading was the economic cornerstone of their life. Although they bartered their own goods with Eskimos to the north and the inland peoples to the east, the Tlingits were primarily middlemen in trading, serving groups to the north, south, and east. Because the Tlingits had a direct route to the interior, for example, they received the wares of the people farther south and exchanged them with the Athabascan Indians to the east for copper, caribou skins, sinew to be used as thread, lichen with which to make dyes, and other goods. As the most northern of the Northwest Coast peoples, the Tlingits served the same function between the Eskimos and the other groups.

A trip to trade with the Athabascans was a major undertaking, requiring a walk of several days in each direction. The trails were clearly marked, and they had been laid out to provide the easiest possible traveling. Even so, it was an arduous journey—across rushing rivers, through dense forests, and up and down precipitous mountainsides. Moreover, the bundles the men carried on their backs—held in place by straps across their foreheads and their chests—often weighed as much as 100 pounds. In winter, when the entire countryside was deep in snow, the trading trip was a true test of strength and endurance. The large snowshoes the men wore helped keep them from sinking into the snowdrifts, but they were an additional burden.

Before leaving on one of these expeditions, the men bathed, fasted, painted their faces, and invoked their guardian spirits to ward off danger. Once they set out, the party marched steadily from dawn to sunset, stopping only to kill small game for food and to place bits of dried salmon in caches so that it would be there for them to eat on the return journey. Bears were a constant threat to these caches, but the men burned off the

Weaving a Chilkat blanket from goat's wool is a project that can take a skilled Tlingit woman as long as six months to complete. At her side is a board painted by her husband or father detailing the composition she faithfully follows. Because the design is symmetrical, only half of it need be painted. In addition to paying for the weaving, the husband or father must gather the goatskins and provide the loom needed for the blanket. Before she begins weaving, the woman must spin the goat's wool and cedarbark fiber into yarn. Then she separates the yarn into four batches, one to be left white, the others to be dyed black, yellow, and blue-green, the last the most favored of colors. The bags hanging from the loom are for holding the ends of the warp wool, thus keeping them from dragging on the ground and becoming soiled.

A Chilkat blanket and a Chilkat dancing shirt, *woven from cedar-bark fiber and mountain goat's wool, were among the most treasured objects a Tlingit could own. They were made by Tlingit women according to designs composed by their husbands or fathers, each design depicting, in a highly stylized form, some animal with which the owner's clan was associated. Several common symbols to be found on Chilkat garments are shown below. The Tlingit who could afford to pay his wife or daughter the high fee normally charged for weaving a Chilkat blanket or shirt was indeed a genuine Ankawoo, a wealthy person worthy of great respect. Such garments might be handed down by the owner to his relatives within his clan or might be used as a funerary object and allowed to disintegrate at the owner's death. In addition, they were flaunted by hosts and guests alike at potlatches. The potlatch host who cut up his Chilkat robe or shirt and distributed the pieces among his guests was engaging in a spectacular form of conspicuous consumption and drew great honor from the act.*

Chilkat blankets are still being woven by Tlingit women and are as highly prized as ever. For a time, after the arrival of whites, relatively inexpensive versions were made as trade items. Often inferior imported wools were used and shortcuts taken in the weaving methods. In recent years, however, the weavers have reverted to the finest traditional homespun and the age-old weaving methods. Because of the demand for them among local tribesmen, these blankets and shirts are rarely available on the open market.

A human face
symbolizing the
body of a bird

A bird's feet in
stylized form

The tail of
a bird that
is attached
to a wing
form

Head of a
brown bear

A bear's fore-
legs and paws

A frog's head
that is associated
with a bear

The weaving technique used by the Haida basket maker at left is called plain twining (diagram above). The basket's warp strands are formed by uprights of spruce root. These are bound together by a double weft: two strands of spruce root entwined around each warp, one passing from front to back of successive warps, the other from back to front. Patterns were often made by a relief design woven on the finished surface.

A Haida weaver uses a pole as a simple but serviceable workstand as she rotates the basket she is working on. A stone on top keeps the basketwork in place.

Tlingit baskets, such as these above, are all made from thin strands of split spruce roots and dyed grasses, and were used for storage and berry picking. To obtain the desired colors, various natural dyes were used. Black was made from a mixture of mud from sulfur springs and hemlock bark boiled in salt water. For red, the Tlingits steeped grass stems in an alderwood bowl containing urine. Yellow was obtained by soaking grass in a solution of moss and water, while blue-green was created by boiling hemlock bark and iron oxide in urine. Though geometric designs predominate here, the basket at far left is adorned with whales and bears, the one next to it displays a face, and the largest basket has a design including whales and stylized eyes. Basket weaving was usually done when it was raining, for at other times the materials dried out.

grass around the places where they hid their food, thus creating a scent that masked the smell of the salmon.

Except for such brief stops, nothing interrupted the march, and the men went steadily on—fording rivers and forming human chains where the currents were particularly swift, zigzagging up and down the mountains, keeping a wary watch for the dangers in the forest. By the time the Tlingits reached a campsite at dusk, they were glad to divest themselves of their heavy packs and rest for the night. Along the trail were designated meeting points. When the Tlingits arrived at one of these spots, they sent up smoke signals to notify the Athabascans of their presence.

For the Tlingits coastal travel was easier physically than travel inland, but the actual trading with their Northwest Coast neighbors demanded far more shrewdness than did dealings with the relatively unsophisticated Athabascans. In encounters with the people to the south, the Tlingits had to employ all their trading skills to derive maximum advantage from their unique position as middlemen. They were bartering the goods obtained from the Athabascans for southern merchandise, part of which the Tlingits would retain, while the remainder would be used for further trading with the Athabascans. The southern groups were well aware of the demand for their products and bargained hard.

Wrapped twining (above) was the weaving technique used to make the tightly constructed Makah basket at right. The structural elements are made from relatively stiff spruce roots. These are held together with an interlacing of flexible dyed strands of the same material, pulled very tight for a close weave. The major design element is a stylized wolf's head, one of the favorite motifs among Makahs.

The Haidas, for instance, supplied the Tlingits and their trading clients with war canoes and with smaller canoes that were especially graceful and elegantly decorated—appropriate vessels for people of high rank. The Tsimshians provided horns of mountain sheep, from which Tlingit craftsmen carved elaborate ceremonial spoons. From the shores of Vancouver Island, which abounded in a small mollusk, the detalium, the Nootkas and the Kwakiutls collected and traded the shells, which were prized throughout the region for their decorative value. And the Nootkas, the most intrepid of all the Northwest Coast people in braving the open ocean, supplied the bones and oil of such deep-sea mammals as the whale and the porpoise.

The only unique Tlingit-made items that had value in trade were spruce-root baskets and the magnificent fringed robes, known as Chilkat blankets, that were used up and down the Northwest Coast for ceremonial purposes. These blankets, with their intricate and tightly packed designs in tones of yellow, blue, black, and white, were made of yarn spun from goat's wool reinforced with yellow cedarbark string. The men made the looms on which blankets were woven—simple, three-sided wooden devices in which the bottom end was left free. To guide them as they worked, the weavers referred to wooden boards on which were painted the traditional patterns. It took a woman half a year or more to make a Chilkat blanket—long months to spin the yarn and dye it and to weave the robe.

The Slave Trade

But there was also a dark, tragic aspect of trading between the peoples of the Northwest Coast. Human beings were the merchandise—men, women, and children captured from the poorer and weaker tribes in the interior and farther south along the California coast. Slaves were an extremely valuable property that only men and women of high rank could possess. Slaves were coveted not merely because they performed most of the menial tasks of the household, but even more because they were constantly visible evidence of their owner's rank

A Klallam woman weaves a Salish blanket while another (background) spins fleece into yarn in this painting by Paul Kane. Though mountain goat's wool was used, some of the yarn might have come from the coats of white dogs, like the one shown, bred specifically for that purpose.

A Cowichan spindle whorl of wood bears a design typical of the tribes of British Columbia's south coast: a human figure in the fetal position. This disk, eight and a half inches in diameter, was used on a long spindle for spinning yarn. Other spindle whorls were made from bone or antler.

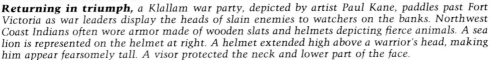

Returning in triumph, *a Klallam war party, depicted by artist Paul Kane, paddles past Fort Victoria as war leaders display the heads of slain enemies to watchers on the banks. Northwest Coast Indians often wore armor made of wooden slats and helmets depicting fierce animals. A sea lion is represented on the helmet at right. A helmet extended high above a warrior's head, making him appear fearsomely tall. A visor protected the neck and lower part of the face.*

and wealth. Slaves lived with their owners' families, sleeping in their houses, accompanying them on their fishing and trading expeditions, and relieving them of the backbreaking, tedious tasks that men and women of lower rank had to perform for themselves—from chopping trees and carrying the huge trading bales to gathering berries and cooking the family food.

The slaves who were obtained by trading had little hope of gaining their freedom, and even that hope must have been weighted with a strong element of fear. A slave might be set free at an especially elaborate potlatch. Or release from bondage might come when the owner gave a feast honoring his children when their ears were pierced for earrings; on such an occasion custom dictated that for every child honored a slave must be freed. But regardless of the celebration, "freedom" often had a fatal meaning: the slaves were as likely to be killed as let go. The death of slaves was, in fact, mandatory when a wealthy family completed a new house. According to legend, when slaves were killed, their bodies were thrown into the holes that had been dug to receive the great carved doorposts. Both freeing slaves and killing them were, of course, the ultimate proclamations of their owner's rank and wealth: only those of the very highest status and the most enormous riches could afford to give up such valuable property.

Although the Tlingits acquired most of their slaves through trading, a few came to them through raiding—either between two groups of Tlingits or between the Tlingits and their Northwest Coast neighbors. For a Tlingit to be taken into slavery as a war captive was a disgrace to the entire clan, and a slave so taken was ransomed as quickly as possible. In trading for slaves,

the Tlingits haggled, as they haggled in all their business transactions. But ransoming a member of the clan who had been taken into slavery was an entirely different matter. One could never get the best of the bargain. The disgrace could never be wiped out and never forgotten; it would remain a permanent blot on the clan's history, to be told in shame to the children. But a generous—even extravagant—ransom offer was at least an announcement of the captive's worth and of the clan's honor, and it helped, therefore, to assuage at least part of the humiliation.

Most of the ransomed captives were women and children: men taken in raids were usually killed. And small wars occurred along the Northwest Coast with some frequency. The Northwest Coast people raided for wealth and, indirectly, rank, taking by force the goods and honors that belonged to their neighbors.

Such conquests usually took the form of night raids, carefully planned and carried out with the utmost stealth. The village chief himself might draw up the battle plan and lead the raiding party, but most often he gave the task over to a war leader, who had inherited his title and had been taught his skills and responsibilities from an early age.

Preparations were long and arduous; scouting had to be carried out, weapons made, and tasks assigned. The warriors hardened their bodies and their spirits by icy baths in nearby streams and by flagellation in front of the blazing fire of the firepit. They abstained from sexual relations with their wives—often for as long as a year if they expected the battle to be particularly difficult. They and their wives made wooden images of the enemy, on which the warriors practiced their skill with the clubs, bludgeons, and daggers they would use on the raid. And the men had already cut special supports for the war canoes—crossed beams placed under bow and stern—and had tied up their paddles, which would not be untied until the war party was ready to leave. When that time came, the warriors and their wives exchanged the images each of them had of the enemy— the women handing theirs to the men as the boats were launched, the men tossing theirs back to the shore after the canoes put out. It was crucial for every woman to catch the image her husband threw her: if she did not, the raid would bring his death.

Chiefs and war leaders usually protected their bodies with elkhide armor and breastplates made of wooden rods bound together with sinew. The warriors wore no special clothing. For them, speed and agility were essential, and the heavy garments would have impeded their movements. The only step they took to protect themselves was to knot their long hair, normally worn loose, on top of their heads so that their enemies could not get hold of it during the battle.

Because surprise was vital to success, the war party beached its canoes some distance from the village to be attacked, and in the dark of night the men advanced cautiously and stealthily across the beach and into the forest to approach their target from the rear. Each man knew precisely what he was to do: which house he was to attack, which resident of the house he was to slay, and where in the house his intended victim had his living quarters. All this information had been learned in advance; no responsible war leader would undertake a raid until he knew every detail both of the village layout and of the arrangement of living quarters within each house. And if he did not know these things from his own experience or the experience of others in the raiding party, he made it his business to find out, asking cautiously worded questions of neutrals who could be counted on to know.

When the silent warriors had crept, one by one, through the doorways of the houses they were to attack, they took up their battle stations and waited for the war leader's cry—the signal for the carnage to begin. And carnage there was—even the men who were not designated targets were clubbed and beaten to death. When the bloody work was over, other tasks remained to be done: looting the houses of their treasures and, sometimes, burning them; tying up the captives; and

This Kwakiutl "slave killer" with a stone blade could be used in combat as well as for the execution of a slave.

beheading those who had been slain. The Tlingits scalped their victims; the other Northwest Coast people brought the severed heads back home with them and displayed them on tall poles in their villages.

Even more frequent than raids were feuds provoked by insult. Among the Tlingits, for whom clan loyalty was the basis of the social order, an attack on one member of a clan was an attack on all the others. The only way the group as a whole could maintain peace was to take a life for the life of any one of its members who was murdered by a member of another clan. But because the clan was highly structured, with each person occupying a specific place in the ranking hierarchy, account had to be taken of the rank of the murdered person. Adequate vengeance could not be achieved merely by taking the life of the murderer. The life that was taken in retaliation had to be of the same worth as the life that had been lost—especially if the victim had been a man of the highest rank. The ideal solution was self-sacrifice: for a man of equal rank among the murderer's clansmen to make a voluntary offer of his life to the clansmen of the murdered man. A party of the offended clan would come to his village and wait on the beach as, dressed in his finest regalia, which displayed all the trappings of his rank, he ceremoniously left his house and moved toward them, performing the dance that was the most honored of all the dances of his clan. The murdered man's kinsmen stood motionless, waiting until he was no more than a few yards from them. Then they loosed their arrows at him.

This ideal was not always honored, and sometimes bloody feuds developed that went on for many years. But even when the act of self-sacrifice was observed and appropriate vengeance had been taken, the affair was still not over. There had to be an exchange of payments between the two clans, as tokens of the value of the lives that had been lost.

The Potlatch Ceremony

The interconnected themes of rank and wealth that ran through all of Northwest Coast life were nowhere more dramatically expressed than in the great ceremony of the potlatch. Here, in an elaborate display of getting and giving, the two were inextricably intertwined. At a potlatch the host acquired rights that spelled rank and status by giving gifts that were evidences of wealth,

A Lavish Feast to Display Wealth

No occasion was more important among Northwest Coast Indians than the potlatch, a mammoth feast given by a house of one clan to honor the house of another. Such affairs offered the hosts an opportunity to display their wealth—thus confirming their status—through the lavish dispensation of food and gifts to the guests. A potlatch was usually held in the house of the hosts, its nominal purpose to celebrate the marriage of the house chief, to inaugurate a new clan house or to mark the death of an old house chief and the accession of a new one.

In the painting at right, a Tlingit potlatch is in progress within a house of the Eagle moiety. The guests, who may number several hundred, are all members of the Raven moiety. Shown is the raised platform at the front of the house on which the Eagle house chief (center left)—who is the principal host—and the most-honored guest (center right) are seated. Behind them is an ornately carved red cedar screen bearing the emblems of the Eagle moiety. More of them are carved into the totem poles flanking the platform. Although the potlach is given in the name of the principal host, all members of the house have contributed portions of their wealth to make the affair a success, for rarely does a single individual, however rich, have the resources to host a potlatch on his own.

Like the most-honored guest, the principal host is garbed in a valuable Chilkat blanket. Both men wear hats surmounted by potlatch rings, each ring representing a potlatch the wearer has hosted. Next to them stand their primary advisers, also dressed in finery that befits their high status. The host's adviser holds a carved piece of metal called a copper—a piece of engraved metal—that will be given to the most-honored guest. Throughout the days of the potlatch, gifts will be showered on all guests, each present suitable to the station of the recipient.

At the far right of the platform are three performers from the ranks of the guests. Two of them hold a blanket emblazoned with the stylized figure of a raven, and partially hidden by it a dancer in a raven costume performs. At the far left are two performers of the hosts' house who will act out a legend of the Eagle lineage. During the entire potlatch Eagles and Ravens will alternate in providing entertainment.

and the guests acknowledged the validity of the host's claims by accepting the gifts that were bestowed on them.

The potlatch served this same purpose all along the Northwest Coast, but its procedures varied from one group to the next, and each group saw the event in somewhat different terms. For the Tlingits, who believed in a great cycle of death and rebirth, the potlatch was part of a mourning ritual for a dead chief. Mourning was part of the Tsimshian potlatch, too, but the emphasis was placed on the new chief, now formally inheriting the dead one's honors and rank. And the Haidas, like the Nootkas, the Kwakiutls, and the Bella Coolas, used the potlatch to celebrate the heir presumptive—the child or young man who would one day inherit the rank and honors now held by a living chief.

Yet although one individual held the central place of honor, nowhere was the potlatch solely the expression of that individual's importance, and nowhere was it an individual's undertaking. The decision to hold a potlatch was usually made by the highest ranking man in a house in consultation with other members of the clan. But everyone participated in its preparation and in carrying it out. Everyone, even the lowest ranking individual, gave gifts. The potlatch was a clan event—an expression of the clan's pride and unity that gave all its members an opportunity to share in the glories of the group. In a culture that emphasized competition and rivalry, the potlatch was an expression of cooperation.

It could take years to prepare for a potlatch. There might be several hundred guests present, and the festivities might go on for 10 or more days—and it was the hosts' responsibility to feed and house all these people for the entire period. Simply to prepare the necessary food and housing was a monumental task. Moreover, there had to be gifts for every single guest—and gifts appropriate to his or her rank. It was easy for a wealthy man to accumulate enough cedarbark blankets for low-ranking guests, but even such blankets were difficult for a poor man to acquire. And the gifts that were merited by a man of high rank—a canoe, perhaps, or a robe made of marmot pelts—represented years of hunting, fishing, and trading for even the wealthiest chief. Finally, ceremonial masks and garments had to be readied and ceremonial songs and dances rehearsed until they could be performed impec-

"Coppers," engraved metal plaques such as this three-and-a-half-foot-high Haida specimen, were the most valuable gifts that a potlatch host could present to a guest. By giving copper, the host flaunted his wealth and honored the recipient.

cably. All these things took time. And it took time, too, for the host to prepare himself spiritually for this great event. For a full year before the potlatch, he bathed daily before dawn and ate and drank only sparingly, and in the last days before the potlatch, he fasted completely and refrained from sexual relations with his wife.

The guests were invited long in advance by a special messenger. They too had important parts to play in the potlatch and needed time to prepare themselves. They would be expected to perform—both the traditional songs and dances of their lineages, and new ones composed especially for the occasion. Their performances, too, had to be impeccable. At many potlatches—indeed at all the potlatches the Tlingits held—guests were invited from two different clans, each of which tried to outdo the other in singing and dancing.

The arrival of the guests was itself a spectacular event. They came by water, the highest ranking chief in his elaborately painted and decorated war canoe, which was surrounded by the smaller vessels that carried the men and women of lesser rank. As the craft neared the shore, the entire party joined in chanting a special song. On the beach in their finest regalia were the hosts, whose highest ranking chief greeted the guests with a welcoming speech.

In the first days there was feasting. Etiquette demanded that the guests do more than eat. They were expected to gorge themselves—eating salmon and drinking its oil until they became sick. Along with the feasting, there was singing and dancing by both guests and hosts. The audience was ranged in rows on the ledges that lined the walls of the great house, everyone carefully placed in order of rank. The center of the floor was given over to the performers, whose songs and dances recalled and reenacted ancient myths and family sagas. All the performers were magnificently attired, and the principal dancers often wore elaborate hats representing the legendary figures.

For the Tlingits, these first days were most joyous. The later part of the potlatch was a somber occasion, a commemoration of death and a ceremony of mourning, at which the hosts spoke and sang of their sorrow. Every gift actually bestowed on a guest at the potlatch, every morsel of food a guest consumed, had its spiritual counterpart: to the Tlingits, everything that was given to the guests was also given *(continued on page 326)*

Dressed for a potlatch,
Tlingit residents of Klukwan's
Whale House (top) pose before
the ornately carved screen behind which
the house chief lived. A huge ritual mask is at the right
of the man in front. Many of the items on the platforms are serving vessels
associated with the feasting that was part of every potlatch. Hosts at these
affairs were expected to supply more fish, seafood, meat, seaweed, berries, and
fish oil than the hundreds of guests could eat, and the guests, in turn, honored
their host by consuming as much as humanly possible. Because a potlatch
could last as long as 12 days, the amount of food offered and consumed was
truly prodigious and required serving vessels of gargantuan size, such as the 14-
foot-long "woodworn" dish (upper platform). The fish-oil dipper (immediate
left) is made from mountain goat horn, while the two vessels directly above
are of handsomely carved wood inlaid with beautiful shells. Both bowls display, in stylized form, the fearsome features of bears.

325

to the dead. Through the centuries these dead, and their ancestors before them, had accumulated family honors—crests, songs, dances, names, titles, legends—which had increased in number and value through the years as successive heirs had made their contributions to the family's glory and worth. Now these honors were to be assumed by the living—but only after the host displayed them to all the guests so that all should know and recognize the merit of the lineage. Dirges were sung; lineage dances were performed; long speeches were made in praise of those who had died.

Finally, the time came for the distribution of the gifts. Among the most important were the pieces of copper that the Tlingits called bones of the deceased, which were given to the highest ranking guests. These fragments were taken from great plaques—some of them three feet long—that were particularly valued along the Northwest Coast. Then the rest of the gifts were shown and given out, and each was described in loving detail—its worth, its history, its special meaning. Each recipient offered thanks, and when no more gifts

remained, the highest ranking guest made a final speech of gratitude. He thanked the hosts not only for the gifts they had given, but for the honor they had bestowed on their guests by permitting them to see all the great lineage heirlooms and introducing them to the new holders of these important privileges. That marked the end. The chief host now had the right to all the rank he had claimed: that right had been acknowledged by his guests' acceptance of his gifts.

European Influence

The arrival of the Europeans brought change to all the institutions of the Northwest Coast. The potlatch was no exception. In earlier days potlatches were rarely held: even the wealthiest and highest ranking chief could not afford to give more than a few in his lifetime. He might hold many feasts to mark important events and to display his wealth, his rank, his generosity—and his superiority to others. But these were not true potlatches. Especially in the north, among the Tlingits, the Haidas, and the Tsimshians, the potlatch was always a

Thousands of trade blankets, *piled inside a Kwakiutl house during a potlatch, draw an admiring audience. At one such affair at the turn of this century, the host gave away 18,000 blankets to his guests. A host might also establish his prestige by encouraging the wholesale destruction of his property. The Kwakiutl figure (left) symbolizes this destruction by averting its face and shielding it from the devouring flames.*

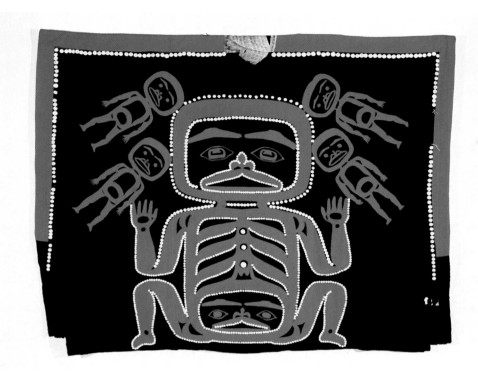

Tsimshian button blanket combines European materials with a traditional design that shows a family crest in red flannel. Both the design and the blanket itself are outlined by hundreds of small iridescent buttons, each sewn on with sinew. Such garments began to be produced in the early 19th century, the materials being secured by exchanging pelts—sea otter, land otter, mink, marten, and beaver—with Hudson's Bay Company traders. Originally, brass buttons were used for the trimmings, but these were quickly replaced by mother-of-pearl when the latter became available. As with the Chilkat blanket, ownership of a button blanket confers status. But because button blankets are easier to make, they have a wider distribution. Even so, the fabrication of a button blanket requires considerable labor and patience. A European visitor to the Northwest once counted the buttons on a single blanket: the total was 2,998.

commemoration and therefore a serious affair—not solely a display of self-aggrandizement, but a statement of group loyalty and of respect for group history and tradition. Both past and present were important.

With the coming of the Europeans, however, the potlatch often became a travesty of its earlier self. A number of factors brought about this transition. The white men, with a rich, flourishing market for sea otter pelts and other furs, brought undreamed-of prosperity to large numbers of natives of the Northwest Coast. Also, the Europeans had great quantities of mass-produced goods for barter. For example, the Hudson's Bay Company, which for years largely controlled the fur trade, used blankets for trade. But unlike the native cedarbark blankets, which were handmade, those of Hudson's Bay had been produced cheaply and in huge quantities on the mechanized looms of Europe. Thus even low-ranking guests at a potlatch could be given blankets, gifts once reserved for only the high caste. The same was true of factory-made cloth, tin pots, zinc-lined wash boilers, and other items. Potlatches became more and more elaborate for many of the native groups. Another element in the change was cultural and psychological. The Europeans needed a peaceful situation for profitable trade, and therefore they sternly put down any warring between the natives. The potlatch then became the Indians' outlet for aggression.

By the second half of the 19th century many potlatches had so far departed from their original mold as to become little more than opportunities to shame a rival. Insults were hurled; songs and dances became angry and menacing. Bitter competition now seemed to overwhelm every other aspect of the proceedings. And many people became enmeshed in a never-ending series of debts. Each potlatch called for another in re-

turn: more lavish and—at least in the eyes of the Christian missionaries—more wasteful, savage, and heathen. In 1884 the government of Canada, in whose territory many of the Northwest Coast people had their ancestral homes, outlawed the potlatch, and in 1895 the statute was amended to become even more severe. The natives protested, and in their protest were supported by the American anthropologist Franz Boas, an early student of the Northwest Coast culture. But despite continuing protest and several legal battles, the law remained. The potlatch was driven underground, but it continued—and every year the number of arrests increased. By the 1930's, however, even some of the missionaries—at whose instigation the antipotlatching laws were originally passed—had begun to realize the futility and foolishness of trying to use the law to destroy an institution whose roots went so deep. When the Canadian code of law was officially revised in 1951, all mention of potlatching was dropped.

The antipotlatch law had already been passed when Franz Boas first requested permission of a Kwakiutl council to study the people's way of life. The answer the chief gave him is eloquent testimony to the strength the ancient culture retained long after the white man had come and to the people's devotion to that culture.

"We will dance when our laws command us to dance," the chief said, "we will feast when our hearts command us to feast. Do we ask the white man, 'Do as the Indian does?' No, we do not. Why then do you ask us, 'Do as the white man does?' It is a strict law that bids us dance. It is a strict law that bids us distribute our property among our friends and neighbors. It is a good law. Let the white man observe his law, we shall observe ours. And now if you are come to forbid us, begone; if not, you will be welcome to us."

THE SUBARCTIC
People of the Caribou

The Canadian forests, dotted by glacial lakes, were home to Subarctic nomadic hunters whose lives were tied to migrations of moose and caribous. The caribou, the beaver, and the dangerous bear are shown on the birchbark basket (inset).

Except for the few weeks of summer, the Indians of the Subarctic faced weather that was a constant foe. Only raw courage and great ingenuity enabled them to survive.

On the brow of a stony hill overlooking the vast, lonely lands of the Athabasca Delta in northern Canada is a stone monument with a bronze plaque commemorating the founding here, some 200 years ago, of a place called Fort Chipewyan. To the east the great expanse of Lake Athabasca, once a major source of whitefish for ancient Indian bands, gleams like molten silver. Behind the hill along a rutted, gravel road is an Indian village, its cabins bleak in the wan light of the midwinter Subarctic sun. There is a post office, a Hudson's Bay Company store, a café-bar, and a huddle of whitewashed cabins and trailer homes that serve as a hotel. An elderly, propeller-driven aircraft, bringing mail and an occasional passenger from Edmonton, lands at the local airport three times a week. Down the road is an old Catholic mission with a beautifully carved and painted church and a school for Indian children. That is all there is to the town. At night, when a husky chained in a backyard howls at the moon, wolves answer from the sparsely wooded hills just beyond.

Fort Chipewyan is not a lively tourist attraction, but it is a very good place to sit and think about the Indians. They have lived here for a very long time—long before the Yankee trader Peter Pond came and established the fort to which the Chipewyan Indians gave their name. They saw the fur trade wax and wane: Fort Chipewyan was for years the northern terminus of the fur traders' canoe route into the deep forests where the fur-bearing animals lived. This village was the jumping-off place for most of the pioneering expeditions that opened up northwestern Canada: Alexander Mackenzie's epic journey north to the Arctic Ocean in 1789; Simon Fraser's heroic conquest of the mountain pass and river system that finally brought him to the Pacific Ocean in 1808.

The Chipewyans saw all this happen and, to some extent, participated in it; but they knew this Subarctic land as their mother long before the white men came. As members of the Athabascan-speaking family of tribes, their ancestors in all probability crossed the Bering land bridge from Asia about 12,000 years ago, following the game on which they lived. As the ice age glaciers receded, hunters spread out and dispersed into many different bands that, in time, occupied the American Subarctic. Athabascan-speaking peoples, such as the Kutchin, Slave, and Dogrib, lived in the west, while groups, such as the Cree and Naskapi, who spoke Algonquian, occupied the east. The Chipewyans finally found their niche in a roughly diamond-shaped area some 500 miles across and about 600 miles from north to south, a region where the forest begins to give way to the tundra that is also the home of the caribou.

This is a very special place to live, combining, as it does, elements of two distinct environments, each in its own way as harsh as the other. Northward stretch the Barren Grounds, mile after mile of treeless land, sometimes rolling, sometimes flat, dotted with lakes and small ponds, laced with streams and rivers. In the short summers—they begin after the ice breakup in June and are already waning by early September—the tundra bursts briefly into bloom, attracting caribous but also clouds of mosquitoes and blackflies. Winter is a time of savage, unremitting cold, when lakes and rivers freeze to a depth of five feet or more and constant winds drift and comb the snow to the density of hard-packed sand.

South of the tundra lies the great boreal forest, which stretches unbroken from the Atlantic Ocean to the Rockies, a world of pine and spruce glinting here and there with the twinkling leaves of aspen and shimmering with the pale white of birch trees. Birchbark was an Indian staple, used for everything from cooking vessels to canoes. The forest was an abundant provider of this and other necessities in all but the winter months. Life was always difficult in this part of the world,

but in the bitterly cold winter survival was a desperate, never-ending struggle.

Even the strongest of men might have recoiled from such a challenging dwelling place and pushed on to find an easier living. But the Chipewyans, relatively recent arrivals in the New World, successfully adapted to their region. Some of the southern bands even developed a way of life that fitted into the fur-trade economy, which became the dominant factor in their lives after the Europeans came.

The Chipewyans' creation myth tells something about their basic character as a people. In the center of their primordial world they saw a woman who lived in a cave and subsisted on berries. To her one day came a doglike creature that at night crept into the cave and slept with her. She dreamed that in the night this creature turned into a handsome young man with whom she made love and thereby became pregnant.

Then there came to her a giant of a man, so tall that his head reached almost to the clouds. This man was the Creator: he outlined lakes and rivers with a stick and caused them to fill with water, and he made forests grow and mountains rise. He tore the doglike animal into many pieces: the internal organs he tossed into the water where they turned into fish; the flesh was torn into bits and pieces and flung into the fields and woods, bringing forth the caribous, moose, wolves, and other animals. The skin, which was shredded and flung into the air, turned into birds. Before the giant departed, he told the woman that she and her offspring need never fear deprivation, since they would have the power to kill all these animals for food, clothes, and shelter

Rock paintings of animals and Manitous are found throughout the Subarctic. The painting at right was made about 1810; the others are prehistoric and have not been precisely dated. The one at left is of an elk; the other two, which derive from myths and visions, are more difficult to interpret. The Cree painting (center) may depict the Thunder Manitou. The dominant creature at right may be the Great Manitou, together with the Snake Manitou. Five men in a canoe are also shown.

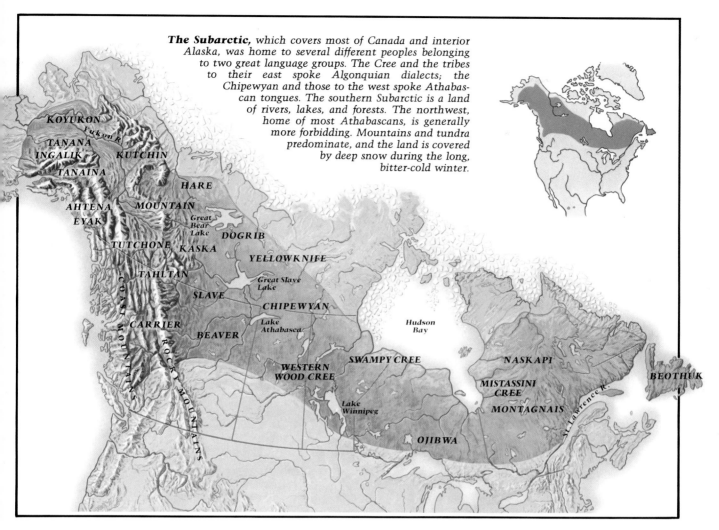

The Subarctic, which covers most of Canada and interior Alaska, was home to several different peoples belonging to two great language groups. The Cree and the tribes to their east spoke Algonquian dialects; the Chipewyan and those to the west spoke Athabascan tongues. The southern Subarctic is a land of rivers, lakes, and forests. The northwest, home of most Athabascans, is generally more forbidding. Mountains and tundra predominate, and the land is covered by deep snow during the long, bitter-cold winter.

when they needed to, and it was his command that the animals all multiply and so assure a constant supply. So saying, the giant vanished mysteriously and was never seen again.

This legend reflected the Chipewyans' way of life. They were hunters whose primary source of food, clothing, and most of the necessities of life was the caribou. They killed indiscriminately; had not the Creator assured their Mother that there would always be an abundant supply of animals? If there were no caribous to be found, the Indians caught and ate fish, with which the lakes and rivers of their land abounded: trout, whitefish, pike. They were a proud people, self-sufficient to the point of arrogance in their relationships with outsiders. When the first white men came, they found the Chipewyan tough and haughty men to deal with, a tribe that looked down on white men because they did not have the good fortune to be Indians.

Unlike most other Indians of the Subarctic, the Chipewyans had a special relationship with dogs. The creation myth of the Chipewyans told them that their race had been sired by a dog, and so they felt a close affinity with the animal. Dogs were well fed and cared for, and when the Indians changed their campsites in

the winter, the heavily laden toboggans were usually pulled not by the dogs but by the women.

Women were subservient to men in Chipewyan family life. While the menial nature of their role appears to have been exaggerated in some early accounts, there is no doubt that the life of Chipewyan women was not an easy one. They were the haulers of water, the makers of fires, the preparers of food, the scrapers of skins, and the doers of all the other lowly tasks of camp life. They accepted their status submissively; any show of spirit brought beatings. At meals, women were not allowed to sit with the men and were fed only what the men did not eat; if no food was left over, the women went hungry.

The caribou was the pole around which all Chipewyan life revolved. These animals, which migrated seasonally in enormous herds, provided the Indians with food and the basic material for clothing and shelter. And of all the tasks that fell to the Chipewyan woman, none was more burdensome than the processing of caribou skins after the hunt. She skinned the animal and hauled its hide to the campsite; she butchered it and prepared its parts for cooking or for drying to store against lean times; and when the hide was pro-

331

The Caribou: A Vital Subarctic Resource

The caribou, a large deerlike animal that usually roams the Subarctic in great herds like the one shown above, provided many of the people of the region with virtually all the necessities of life. They ate its flesh, made tools and weapons from its bones and antlers, and converted its skin into clothing and shelter. Caribous travel 400 to 500 miles every year, migrating from the forest to the tundra in herds that can number 100,000 in the late spring soon after the calving season.

In winter, when a herd was dispersed, a man often hunted alone, tracking a single animal or ambushing it by luring it within his range with a decoy. But most of the time caribou hunting was a communal endeavor in which a large group of men cooperated to take a number of animals from a herd. One technique was to chase them into water, where men in canoes could spear them. But the most widely used technique was to drive the animals into a surround—a series of wooden posts arranged to form a large open-ended circle. The largest surrounds, which measured up to a mile and a half in diameter, were permanent structures; smaller, temporary ones were also used.

A Naskapi ceremonial m... (above) and the bag at right on... opposite page are both made of c... bou hide. The skin of the mask ... bears the animal's hair; the top of ... bag is dehaired and tanned. The ... ting that forms the bag's body ... gives it strength is babiche—pa... tanned skin cut into strips.

cessed, she sewed it with primitive tools into garments, tent covers, or blankets for the family.

Skinning a caribou with a copper or stone knife was not a simple task, but it was probably the easiest step in the processing of a hide. Once the skin had been removed from the carcass, the inside had to be scraped clean of any clinging flesh. A caribou leg bone, broken across to provide an oval cutting surface with a somewhat serrated edge, was used for this job. Now the cleaned hide was softened in water, dried, and then the inside was dressed with a paste made of partially decomposed caribou brains. After drying, the inside was given a second scraping, this time with hoe-shaped

copper blade affixed to an antler handle. Finally, the hide was made soft and pliable by long hours of hand massage.

An extra procedure, the removal of the hair, had to be carried out when the hide was to be made into leggings, skirts, and certain other articles of clothing. The tool used was a two-handed scraper, made from a caribou leg bone split lengthwise. After draping the skin, hair side out, on a slanting support, the woman pulled the scraper against the grain of the hair. When the hide was bare, it was usually smoke-cured.

The tools and household utensils used by the Chipewyans were often beautifully made and served

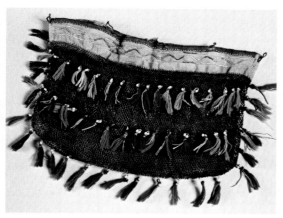

Men's caribou skin clothing (above) illustrates stylistic differences between two Subarctic groups at opposite ends of the continent. The coat at left, shown in a back view, was made by the Naskapis of eastern Canada. It has a fitted waist and three triangular inserts that give the skirt its flare. The outfit at right was made by the Kutchins of western Alaska. The trousers and moccasins are made in a single piece and, like the shirt and mittens, are decorated with beads, red ocher, and dentalium shells that were obtained through trade. Throughout the Subarctic women made the clothing and performed the laborious task of tanning the skins. First they scraped the hide on both sides until it was completely free of flesh, fat, and hair. They also removed the animal's brain and kneaded it into a smooth, thick paste, which was then thinned down with water. After the skin had been washed, this mixture was rubbed into the hide and left to dry. This started the softening process. The skin was washed again, wrung out, allowed to dry, and scraped once more with a stone stool. Still it was not considered soft enough. Once or twice again it would be rubbed with paste, washed, stretched, and scraped. Usually, it was then sewn into a bag and smoked over a fire to give the skin its characteristic golden color.

their purpose well. Copper was the only metal they worked, and from it they fashioned knives, arrowheads, lance points, and scraping tools. While most copper was hammered cold, there is evidence that some groups softened the metal by heating it. They did not know the art of smelting nor did they pound out pots that could be used for cooking. Cooking was usually done in containers, made either of birchbark or skin, that were filled with water. Hot stones were then dropped in until the water boiled. The containers were folded and sewn with caribou sinew. The women did not have needles; the sewing was accomplished with bone or copper awls, used to make holes through which

the sinew was threaded. Most women carried with them a skin bag that served as a sewing kit and contained an assortment of awls and lengths of sinew.

The tools used by the men were equally simple. Their most important and most valued implement was a crooked knife made of a copper blade fastened to an antler handle. They also fashioned axes from copper, attaching the blades to handles of wood or antler. Copper was used as well to make awls, drill bits, points for chipping holes in the ice for winter fishing, arrowheads, spearheads, and spoons. The copper, which was almost pure, was pounded into an approximation of the shape desired—in some instances the metal was

An Ojibwa camp on Lake Huron, *as depicted in the mid-19th century by Canadian Paul Kane, is a cluster of birchbark wigwams with frames of sapling. The time is summer, and a* *woman stands near her wigwam pounding seeds, probably for a gruel. Near one of the beached birchbark canoes a few men converse as a dog digs in the earth.*

probably heated first—and then further hammering provided a sharp edge. The Indians also knew how to keep the edge sharp by honing it with a stone tool.

The most likely source of copper for the Chipewyans was the deposits along the Coppermine River. The Chipewyans probably mined considerably more copper than they needed; there is evidence that the metal was a sought-after item of trade throughout the Chipewyans' home territory and far beyond.

Like almost all Indian hunting tribes, the Chipewyan were nomadic, following the caribou on its seasonal migrations between forest and tundra. This pattern contrasted sharply with that of the Ojibwas to the southeast, and the difference clearly illustrates how important the game and their habits were to a peoples' pattern of life.

The Algonquian-speaking Ojibwas inhabited the territory of present-day Ontario, Minnesota, northern Wisconsin, and northern Michigan—much of it the typical north woods country of the "land of 10,000 lakes." In pre-Columbian times, long before the loggers came, there were great coniferous forests, with huge trees towering a hundred feet into the air, their upper

An Ojibwa woman, *portrayed by George Catlin, holds her baby in a cradleboard. Though her costume is traditional in design, the material is European.*

branches overlapping in a canopy so dense that almost no sunlight penetrated to the forest floor. As a consequence, there was little of the shrub type of undergrowth favored by deer. Game in the deep woods was a mixture of woodland caribous, moose, and bears. Unlike the Barren Grounds caribou, these animals were not present in huge herds, but there were many smaller groups of them throughout the region.

The Ojibwas, therefore, did not move with caribou herds; only the hunters and traders were prodigious travelers. The men hunted in small bands, leaving their wives and children in temporary or semipermanent encampments, and were gone for days at a time, returning to camp only for brief rests before setting out again. These long, solitary journeys, especially those through the heavy storms, snow, and ice of winter, induced a way of thinking that focused Ojibwa mythology and religion on the large game animals. But beaver and other small game were also important food sources, and after contact with the white man and his rich market for fur animals, the trapping of beaver, marten, muskrat, and other fur-bearers become central to the Ojibwa economy.

334

Elegant Sewing, Weaving, and Embroidering With Quills

The porcupine, found in all but the most northerly parts of the Subarctic, provided many of the people of the region with one of their most valuable decorative materials: quills. Every porcupine has more than 30,000 of these darts, some as long as five inches and as thick as an eighth of an inch. When a porcupine was killed, the women pulled out the quills, sorting them by size, washing and then drying them, and dying them with colors obtained from bloodroot, wild plum bark, blueberries, and other plants. Next they were softened, either by soaking them in water or holding them in the mouth. Some quills might then be flattened into ribbons by pulling them between fingernails or teeth. This done, the quills were ready to be worked—sewn, woven, or embroidered on a base material. The 18th-centruy cradleboard decoration at right reveals how elaborate quillwork could be. The cover is composed of two separate panels, each produced by wrapping quills around a series of parallel thongs in such a way as to interweave them. Quill-wrapped thongs connect the panels and form a bottom fringe. The design shows mythical thunderbirds—which always traveled in pairs—with zigzags of lightning shooting out of their eyes.

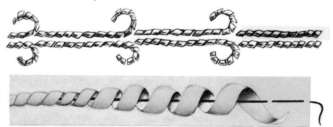

Sewing, the most common method of working with quills, is shown above. The softened and flattened quills are wrapped around thread, and the thread, when sewn on skins, holds the quills in place. Traditionally, a sharp thorn or bone splinter was used as a needle. Sewing could produce curves, like those in the topmost diagram, and geometric forms.

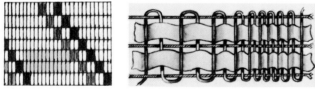

Weaving is the most difficult technique. The warp threads are stretched parallel to each other on a loom, and as the weft threads are laced in and out, flattened quills are worked over and under the weft. The weft threads are packed together (right above), making a beadlike surface (left).

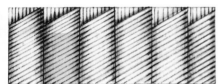

Embroidery was a common technique for decorating birchbark. The quills were put through holes in the bark with a satin stitch (right) to form the design.

There was ample room for all, and one hunter seldom found himself competing with another. In most areas there would be at least one stream, pond, or lake that provided fish to supplement the diet of an Indian family. During the winter the women would chip through the ice and set nets low in the water. The nets could be raised to bring up the catch, and then lowered again. The trees in the hunting territory supplied the materials—in the form of wood, bark, and roots—for most of the things the Indians needed, from wigwams to snowshoes to cooking pots.

The game provided all the rest. The meat and fat were used for food. The bones were used for making implements. From the hides the women sewed clothing, using tendons for thread. The stomachs were made into cooking utensils, and some of the glands were used as medicines. There was little waste in the Ojibwa economy, simply because there was not enough to waste. Maximum use had to be made from what each hunter brought back to camp.

By late March the southern Ojibwa family was ready to leave the winter camp and head for the groves of sugar maples. (The hunters of the Barren Grounds, to the north, such as the Chipewyans, enjoyed no such nutritional treasures.) Sugar-making was an annual event, a winter's-end pause in the migration to the summertime village. Family groups might meet at a river or lake where fish and other foods were in plentiful supply.

Although these summer gathering places were true villages in the social sense, they had no political or tribal character: the residents were usually autonomous family units, most of them related. A small village might be composed only of related families; in larger ones, some families might be distant relatives or only invited friends. By long custom the locale of the village belonged to its regular occupants; if it was situated on a lake, the lake "belonged" to each family, but also to the village as a whole.

Summer was a beautiful time in every way for Ojibwa families—a reward for their survival through the rigors of winter. Berry picking, storytelling, games, and visits alternated with the tanning of hides and construction of canoes. There were puberty rites to be observed, dances to be attended, religious ceremonies to be held. Such activities took place at other times of the year as well, but they were especially pleasant during the warm months.

The end of summer was signaled by the ripening of the wild rice in the lakes and, from the end of August to about mid-September, all efforts were directed to the wild rice harvest. By the end of September the families began the trek back to the winter hunting area. The staple foods were in, the winter's clothing made; now the long winter awaited, with its rigors and its uncertainties, its darkness and its bone-chilling cold.

The life-style of the Athabascan-speaking

The Midewiwin That Healed With Natural and Supernatural Means

One of the most important institutions in Ojibwa life was Midewiwin—the Grand Medicine Society—a group of men and women skilled in the arts of healing. Both contact with the supernatural powers—the Manitous—and herbal medicines were employed. The path to membership was long and arduous. The aspirant had first to serve an apprenticeship, paying a Mide master for instruction in the secrets of herbal cures and in the myths and rituals that evoked the Manitou powers. Then came an elaborate multiday initiation rite that tested the novice's abilities. Only thereafter was he or she permitted to practice the healing arts. This first initiation might be only a beginning. There were four ranks of Mide, the highest of which required four separate apprenticeships and four initiations, each more demanding than the previous one. Few attained this eminence, and those who did were regarded with special awe, as their enormous power enabled them to do evil as well as good.

Most Mides were guided to their calling by visions or the wish to reverse bad fortune or ill health. Particularly among the Ojibwas, participation in a Mide initiation was thought to bring good fortune and long life. The Midewiwin was also found among other eastern Subarctic peoples, notably the Cree, but none were more influenced by the Grand Medicine cult than the Ojibwas.

A Midewiwin rite reaches its climax within the Midewiwin lodge as a novice—supported by his mentor and an assistant—kneels before a Mide officer to be symbolically shot with cowrie shells from a medicine sack. Through this ritual the novice will gain supernatural powers. When the medicine bag is aimed at him, the novice flinches, then collapses, apparently dead. Suddenly, however, he recovers, his restoration to life made manifest by his coughing up of the cowrie shells that had supposedly entered his body. Now the novice has new powers that he demonstrates by aiming his own medicine bag at the other Mides.

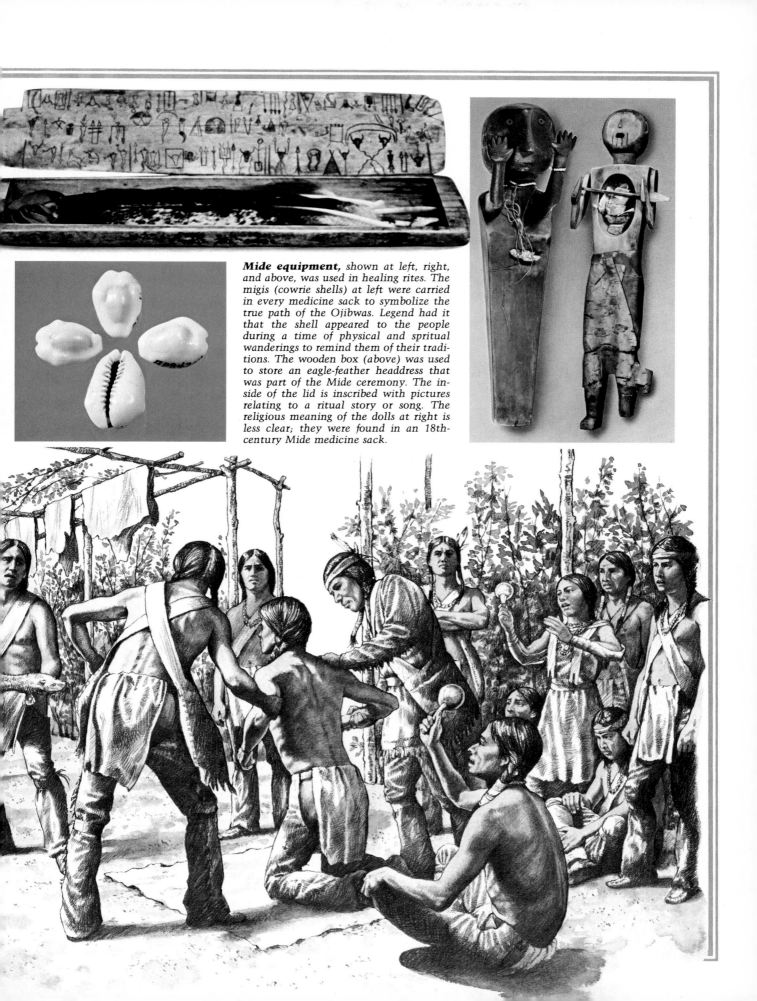

Mide equipment, shown at left, right, and above, was used in healing rites. The migis (cowrie shells) at left were carried in every medicine sack to symbolize the true path of the Ojibwas. Legend had it that the shell appeared to the people during a time of physical and spritual wanderings to remind them of their traditions. The wooden box (above) was used to store an eagle-feather headdress that was part of the Mide ceremony. The inside of the lid is inscribed with pictures relating to a ritual story or song. The religious meaning of the dolls at right is less clear; they were found in an 18th-century Mide medicine sack.

A domed winter house (left) of the nomadic Kutchins was both easy to construct and light enough to be struck and carried from place to place on a toboggan or sled. Built on a frame of dried, bent poles and covered with tanned caribou skins sewn into two sections, the house was protected from winds by banks of snow piled around it. All peoples of the Subarctic carried food with them in winter, storing it in caches when they made camp. A platform cache (above) kept the food safe from animals.

Chipewyans in their northern territories was in many ways sharply different from the Algonquian-speaking Ojibwas. The Chipewyans had to be true nomads to follow the caribous on their seasonal migrations between the forest and the tundra. The structure of their society as well as of their dwellings reflect this need for mobility. The Chipewyans had no permanent buildings, even though there were certain campsites to which they might return year after year. The basic social unit was the family, and the family was in all ways self-sufficient. The camp was organized around the family dwelling, in which the cooking fire always burned, and apart from a few seasonal occasions, such as the caribou migrations, these camps usually stood alone in the woods.

The family dwelling of the Chipewyans was a variation of the familiar tepee. A framework of poles was set in a circle, tied loosely together at the top, and then covered with caribou skins—sometimes as many as 70—sewn together like tarpaulins. A smoke hole was left at the top; inside, the fire, first lighted with sparks struck from iron pyrite, was always kept burning. Fresh spruce boughs covered the floor and were in turn covered by caribou skins. Inside the tepee the family sat crosslegged or reclined; the haze of smoke that always hung in the upper part of the structure encouraged staying outdoors as much as possible.

Chipewyan food centered on the caribou, and the meat was usually boiled. Their gourmet delicacies were the head and fat from the back. Grubs from under the caribous' skins were sometimes consumed as well. The Indians also cooked and ate the caribou's stomach, contents and all. They prepared this dish by adding to the fermenting lichens inside a mixture of shredded fat,

meat from the tender parts of the animal, blood, and the heart and lungs cut up into small pieces. The stomach and its contents were cooked by roasting it over a slow fire.

The Chipewyans also used pemmican. The word itself comes from the Cree language and probably means "substitute grease." The Chipewyans prepared it from sun-dried, lean meat cut into strips (it might also be dried by a fire). The dried meat was then pounded to a powder and mixed with fat. The resulting paste was stuffed into caribou intestines. In this manner a highly concentrated food could be easily carried on long journeys; it was the staple of the Chipewyan hunter.

There were virtually no plants in the Chipewyan diet. Lichens were eaten only as part of the contents of a roasted caribou stomach, but the Indians are also known to have eaten moss, which might be prepared as a soup or used as a seasoning.

There was nothing in a Chipewyan campsite that was not functional. These Indians knew no luxuries; they had only a subsistence economy, and the campsite reflected this fact. It was a working place, and evidence of the work being done was everywhere to be seen. Caribou hides hung drying in the sun; beaver pelts, stretched on wooden frameworks, were propped against trees to dry; tripods of poles were scattered about, with skin bags hanging from them—bags that held dried caribou meat, yellow globs of fat, and smoked or sun-dried fish. A canoe might be under construction, its shape staked out on the ground, with spruce frames being installed while, nearby, women sewed long strips of birchbark into pieces, the seams covered with pine pitch heated on the fire and mixed with fat, to cover the frames. Young boys made bows and feathered arrows while girls worked on caribou skins; there could never be enough skins to keep Indian bodies warm in the biting, bitter, winter cold.

If it was a summer camp near a lake, nets would be everywhere in evidence, hanging up to dry. The gill net was the type most commonly used, its mesh large enough to let a fish's head pass through but small enough to entangle the gills when the fish tried to withdraw. Mesh gauges for various sizes of fish would be lying nearby, used constantly as guides by the women as they wove the nets of thin strips of unprocessed caribou hide or willow bast. When the net was finished, wooden floats were attached at regular intervals along the top to keep it afloat, while stones tied to the bottom ensured that it would hang vertically in the water. Nets like these were set across narrow streams or at certain places on lakes where fish were known to be particularly numerous. Pike and whitefish were the species most often caught, although others would be taken in their season.

The Chipewyans felt a supernatural association with fish that was reflected in many ritual practices. Each net had its own personality for them, and no net was ever joined to another for fear the nets would be jealous of each other and so spoil the fishing. Charms were attached to each corner of the net to give it special powers to attract and hold fish. Fishhooks, too, often had charms attached; the hooks themselves were made of antler, bone, or carved from wood. When a new net or hook made its first catch, the fish was boiled and its skeleton was removed intact and burned.

Sometimes the Chipewyans built brush weirs across a stream and caught the fish penned behind them with dip nets. Poles from such weirs have been found embedded in the mud, and traces of stone traps built in rivers have also been found—traps that channeled the fish toward a pen from which they could not escape. Fish were also killed with barbed arrows, and they were even speared from canoes by hunters while they waited for caribous to swim across a lake or river.

Hunting was, of course, the principal occupation of the Indian male: it was up to him to provide enough meat and hides to keep his family fed and clothed. Because the caribou was the prime source of everything they needed, the Chipewyan, like other Athabascan tribes, governed their lives by the pattern of the animals' seasonal movements. In the spring they followed the caribous' northern migration to the Barren Grounds, where the cows dropped their calves; in the autumn they gathered at various places along the forest's edge to intercept the animals as they migrated southward to the deep woods.

Summer and winter were the times when the Chipewyan tribes stayed the longest in one place, and campsites were chosen with an eye to emergencies. The best spots were those where alternate forms of sustenance were available should the caribou hunting

prove unexpectedly poor. A winter camp, for this reason, was usually set up close to a lake or river known for its good fishing. Winter dwellings varied among the Athabascan tribes, but all were built with the certain knowledge that during the winter temperatures would fall to as far as −70° F. Thus the Kutchins, in the north, built domed tents for the winter but added a second layer of caribou skins with the hair left on for extra warmth. In northernmost Alaska winter homes were dug partially underground, with central hearths that provided warmth as well as cooking fires. The deep snow served as an excellent insulator against the bitter cold.

For the Chipewyans the tepee covered with caribou skin was the standard dwelling the year-round. With snow piled deep on the outside of the skin covering and a fire burning brightly in the tent, the indoor temperature was probably fairly comfortable. Winter clothing helped the inhabitants to keep warm—a tailored

Kutchin hunters, sketched by Alexander Murray in the mid-19th century, show one effect of European influence: the gun carried by the man at left. But the bow and arrow were still widely used, and as the picture shows, the hunters had not yet exchanged their traditional skin garbs for woolens.

slip-on dress with long sleeves and an attached hood; trousers fastened with a drawstring and usually with moccasins attached. Under this outfit the men wore a breechclout and, if the weather was extremely cold, an old set of summer clothes as well. Mittens were attached to a length of braid that went around the neck so they would not be lost if the wearer had to take them off. Sometimes an outer cloak of caribou or rabbit skins was worn. Caribou-skin boots with soles of moose hide came into use at a later time, probably having been adapted from the Eskimo footwear that, at the time of contact with the white man, was already being used by the Koyukon groups of northwestern Alaska.

Winter was often a time of privation. Sometimes it even became a time of starvation. Every Chipewyan family had its store of dried meat, pemmican, dried and smoked fish, but the family head also counted on being able to supplement this diet with fresh meat or fish from time to time. Here the hunters did not rely entirely on their bows and arrows; they also set deadfalls and snares for rabbits, ptarmigans, and other small game. They might find a bear hibernating in a cave or under a fallen tree; if so, it was killed and butchered. Caribous and moose were tracked down on snowshoes and dispatched with bow and arrow.

Surviving the Winter

If the campsite had been chosen carefully, at a place where wandering caribou could be spotted and near a lake that could provide fish, a few Chipewyan families might be able to last out the entire winter in a single spot. Usually, however, they moved at least once or twice to new hunting grounds. If the hunting was known to be good, a corral might be built to entrap caribou, and snares set for hares and ptarmigans.

But fresh game was always hard to come by in the north woods, and when food supplies ran low, starvation was imminent. If all else failed, the family might subsist for as long as possible on moss, berries, and other edible plants. As a last resort they ate their skin clothing. The journal of Richard King at Fort Resolution in the early 1800's gives a poignant description of one starving Chipewyan band:

"The feeble gait of the torpid and downcast father—the piercing and sepulchral cry of the mother—the infant clinging by a parched mouth to a withered breast, faintly moaning through its nostrils—the passive child, calmly awaiting its doom—the faithful dog, destroyed and consumed—the caribou robe dwindling almost to nothing—can give but a very inadequate idea of their suffering."

In the utmost extremity the Chipewyans might eat their own dead or even kill the weakest member of the band in order to stay alive themselves. But cannibalism was not a general practice, nor was it undertaken lightly.

But if winter was sometimes life-threatening, spring was a time for joy and release. Then the caribous migrated northward to the Barren Grounds, and the Chipewyan bands met at certain places on the forest's edge to intercept the animals. The journey to the hunting grounds was often made by many families at once. Samuel Hearne, an 18th-century explorer, reported seeing a party of some 200 people gathered for the trip.

On the Trail

When moving, the women did most of the chores, but children and even dogs were sometimes pressed into service. The members of the band literally carried the whole camp on their backs, with the women shouldering loads of up to 140 pounds. Women and girls pulled toboggans, dogs trotted alongside loaded with caribou skins and tent poles, and children, if too young to help, kept up as best they could. The men, meanwhile, ranged through the woods searching for game.

These journeys in the early spring were usually made when snow was still on the ground, which meant that snowshoes were needed. Snowshoes were made of birch frames, steamed and bent to shape, with wooden crosspieces across each frame. Depending on their use, they might be rounder in front for traveling over fresh snow—or small and slender for use on already traveled trails. The snowshoes were laced with babiche, strips of dehaired caribou hide, passed through predrilled holes to form a distinctive, crisscrossed pattern. Building the frames was the men's work; the lacing was done by the women. Equipped with the proper type of snowshoes, a hunter could jog along over deep snow for hours, easily keeping pace with a floundering caribou.

When the edge of the forest was reached and the Barren Grounds lay before them, the character of the Chipewyan spring migration changed. Out on the treeless tundra the snow melted earlier than in the depths of the thick woods, and snowshoes and toboggans could be put away. But now the load-carriers had increased burdens to bear. Meanwhile, the men were always on the hunt for food, and as spring wore on, the abundance of game increased. Flocks of migratory waterfowl were killed with arrows as they passed overhead. Musk-oxen and fish were also part of the spring diet.

Certain places at the edge of the woods or along a river were known to be caribou crossings, and here Chipewyan bands gathered in large numbers. This meeting was one of the few truly social occasions in the year, and newly arrived families might find as many as 600 people already encamped. Families or groups of families that had not seen each other for months were reunited, and these reunions followed a set pattern that was characteristic of the Chipewyan culture.

There were no loud cries of greetings, no enthusiastic, happy embraces. Instead, two solemn groups would seat themselves at a considerable distance apart and

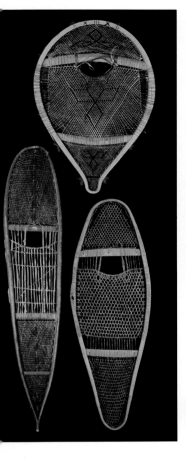

Snowshoes and toboggans *were used for winter travel by Subarctic peoples like the 19th-century Ojibwa family above. Most groups in the northern region preferred long, narrow snowshoes, like the one at the extreme left, made by the Kutchins. The wider one next to it was for a Naskapi child. Most southern groups used round snowshoes like the topmost model. Snowshoe frames were made from spruce, birch, or willow, the webbing of partly tanned strips of skin. Toboggans, like the one below, were used to haul supplies. They were sometimes as long as eight feet and were occasionally pulled by dogs, as above. But people also had to carry supplies.*

maintain a long period of silence. Finally, an elder in one group would speak of the deaths, illnesses, famines, and other misfortunes that had been visited on the family since the last reunion. His account was met with sympathetic cries from the other group. Now a speaker from the second family would give his account, and the first group would voice its condolences. Only when this ceremony was completed would the two families come together for greetings and the exchange of presents.

The climax of the spring meeting came with the arrival of the caribou. Once the first herds appeared, they streamed by for days on end. Like the buffalo on the Great Plains, the caribou migrated in huge numbers, and the Chipewyan hunters took what they needed. After they had accumulated as much meat as they could possibly carry, the hunters continued to kill but took only the skins, long bones, fat, and tongues, leaving the rest of the carcasses for the wolves and other carnivores.

Chipewyan hunting equipment was simple, efficient, and suited to the game. The bow used for hunting caribou was made of birch, rounded and tapered at both ends, and strung with babiche. The arrows had three split feathers fastened to the shaft with sinew; the points were of stone or bone, and unbarbed. For birds or hares, a different point was used: blunt, heavy, designed to stun rather than kill. Fish were shot with barbed points.

Through the summer the Chipewyans followed the caribou as the herds wandered through the Barren Grounds. In the fall, during the rutting season, hunters sometimes attached lengths of antler to their belts, which would clash together as they walked. If a lone bull were nearby, he might be deceived into thinking that the noise was made by two other bulls fighting over a cow; he would then rush toward the sound, thinking to make off with the cow, only to run straight into the arrow of the hunter.

At the time of the migrations and at regular crossing points of caribou on rivers and lakes, the Chipewyans made elaborate preparations to catch large numbers of the animals. They built corrals—converging lines of brush stuck in the ground that led finally into a large, round enclosure from which there was no escape. When the trap was full, the confused animals, milling around in panic, could be easily dispatched with arrows or spears.

Sometimes, along the way to the corral, the Chipewyan hunters might string a stout snare between two conveniently placed trees so that an animal seeking to escape would be caught by it. The same methods of catching large numbers of caribous were used at the time of the fall migration when, once again, many families would meet at the caribou crossing places.

An indispensable aid to hunting in spring, summer, and fall was the birchbark canoe. These were usually built in the spring. The Chipewyan canoe looked quite

Birchbark: Material of a Hundred Uses

The white birch, also known as the canoe or paper birch, dots the forests of the northern United States and Canada. For the peoples of the region—especially the Algonquians of the east—the bark of this graceful tree was a vital resource. It was used to make such large items as canoes and wigwams, and such smaller ones as cooking pots, dishes, and needle cases.

In addition, birchbark played a major role in the artistic and cultural lives of the tribes. Used as a paper—for pattern cutting, painting, and drawing— it was both a means of decoration and a surface on which to record dreams and rituals. Such chronicles helped the peoples pass down their ways of life through the generations.

The bark of the birch grows in a series of layers—white on the outside, darker farther in. In late winter and spring the darker, inner layer is coated with a brownish deposit. It was then that the Indians peeled the bark from the trees, using knives and wooden wedges to remove it in sheets as large as eight feet long by three feet wide. Once the outer layers of bark were removed, they were separated into sheets of various thicknesses, depending on the purposes for which each of the sheets was intended.

The inside of the bark layers generally became the outside surface of the object being made, because bark tends to curl back on itself once it has been peeled. This surface was also the one that most readily lent itself to decoration. Its brownish coating, which contrasts with the yellow backing, is easy to remove. By selective scraping, brown on yellow designs—some realistic, others symbolic—were formed.

White birches (above) have lost some of their bark, making the tree vulnerable to weather, insects, and fungi. The bark, however, is resistant, making it a sturdy material for fashioning such objects as the mocock, the container shown at right, used for both solids and liquids. It was made by cutting the birchbark to a pattern, folding it to shape, and sewing it with spruce root. If used to hold liquids, the seams were smeared with pitch.

different from the Algonquian craft, which had the familiar shape still used in modern canoes. The Chipewyan type was short—about 13 feet in length— with the greatest width toward the stern. A single paddle propelled the canoe, which was often used in hunting caribou as they swam across a lake or river, and in pursuit of water birds during the molting season, when they could not fly.

The conditions under which the Chipewyans lived— frequently on the move, constantly searching for game, and rarely with enough food to sustain them for more than short periods of time—determined the social organization of the people. Such circumstances discouraged

the formation of large, interdependent groups. In times of crisis a small, self-sufficient band could survive more readily then a large, unwieldy group of people. Thus the social organization of the Chipewyan, like that of most of the Subarctic Indian tribes, had the basic simplicity of people who live very close to the land on a bare subsistence level.

In such a society cooperation was vital. Each member of the family—including small children—knew and abided by the duties imposed by the requirements for survival. The family leader was the father, the bearer of the primary obligation for its welfare. There was little tribal sense among the Chipewyans, although they did

signs by biting birchbark are still
~~ma~~de by Subarctic Indian women, such as
~~th~~e one below. This skill has been passed
~~down~~ from generation to generation. Delicate
~~an~~d elaborate symmetrical patterns, as
~~sh~~own above, are produced by taking a
~~thi~~n sheet of bark about four or five inches
~~squ~~are, folding it several times, and biting
~~int~~o it with the canine teeth, according to
~~a~~ design the artist has visualized in her
~~mi~~nd's eye. Held against a light, the out-
~~lin~~e of the design is clearly visible. Al-
~~tho~~ugh bitten designs are sometimes used
~~as~~ patterns for other decorations, they are
~~usu~~ally made purely for esthetic purposes—
~~for~~ the pleasure that the craftswoman de-
~~riv~~es from creating and looking at them.

Birchbark cutouts at left
were made by Ojibwa women
in the shape of animals, people,
and objects that were familiar
in everyday life. Every Ojibwa
woman had her own supply of
such cutouts, both because she
derived pleasure from making
them and because they were
used as patterns for decorations.
Placed on other birchbark objects, like the mocock on the
opposite page, the cutouts outlined a design made on the
material itself. Placed on moccasins, they served as patterns
for decorative beadwork. In precontact times the operation involved two steps: first, using a
sharp fishbone to outline the
design with a series of tiny
holes in the bark; then, cutting
the bark with a knife. After the
arrival of the Europeans, the
women began using scissors.

A memory scroll (above) was inscribed on birchbark by an apprentice Mide to help
him learn the sacred songs and stories performed at the Midewiwin rites. The symbols
stand for entire sequences of a story or song. Because an individual invented his own
notational system, each scroll could only be understood by its maker.

have a concept of territory. With no real tribal society,
they had no tribal leader. The need for a solidarity
beyond the family level arose only in answer to threats
from outsiders. In response to such danger they might
seek and find a unifying leader.

But organized warfare was rare for the Chipewyan,
and indeed for any of the Athabascan tribes. They
knew nothing of such large-scale military operations as
those conducted, for example, by the Iroquois. The
Chipewyan and other Athabascan tribes did have a traditional hostility toward two enemies: the Eskimos to
the north, and the Cree Indians to the south in the
great boreal forest around Lake Superior. The reasons

for this hereditary enmity lay in the Athabascan religion. The Athabascans believed that the shamans, or
medicine men, of the Eskimos and the Crees had the
power to send disease by supernatural means among
the Athabascan tribes.

Like many other Indians, the Athabascans held that
the destiny of each individual was controlled by his or
her own personal spirits. The shamans could control
these spirits, and so it was not far-fetched to believe
that a hostile shaman might use his powers to make an
enemy ill. No other explanation for illness was credi-
ble, because only the aged could contract diseases from
natural causes. A spread of (continued on page 346)

The Birchbark Canoe: A Triumph of Indian Technology

Among the Algonquian peoples of the eastern Subarctic, whose lands were dotted with lakes and rivers, the canoe was indispensable. It took them to their hunting and fishing grounds and on trading expeditions; it carried them from camp to camp; it even provided shelter: on long trips they slept under it when it rained. As the drawings at right show, the characteristic shape of the craft varied from group to group, both among the Algonquians and among those of the Athabascans who built bark canoes. These variations were, in part, related to the kinds of waters on which the canoe was used. Canoes with low ends were more efficient in calm waters than those with high ends, which offered greater wind resistance. Canoes with high bows and sterns gave protection against waves in rough waters. Practical considerations also helped dictate the shape of the gunwales and the overall size of the vessel. Small, light canoes were best for navigating rapids; larger ones, for open waters on which cargoes of trade goods were transported.

But despite these differences, construction methods (opposite page) and materials used were much the same. The choice of materials was particularly important. The paper birch provided the best bark for the skin of the canoe. The material is relatively unblemished; it is resinous and therefore does not stretch or shrink; it can be peeled off in large sheets; and its grain runs around the trunk, thus making it easy to sew the sheets together along the length of the canoe. The white cedar, which splits easily and cleanly, was the tree of choice for the framework. For the same reason, hard maple was preferred for the paddles and the thwarts that held the gunwales together. The black spruce also played an important role. Its roots were used to sew the bark sheets together, and its resin provided a waterproof coating to smear on all of the seams.

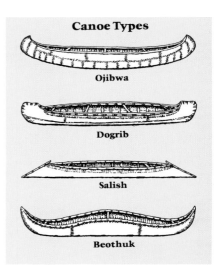

Canoe Types

Ojibwa

Dogrib

Salish

Beothuk

A canoe race between Ojibwas (right) was painted by George Catlin. Such races, Catlin wrote, were one of the Indians' favorite amusements, and "a great concourse . . . had assembled to witness" this one. The contestants propel their craft from a standing position while spectators in canoes cheer them on. Light canoes were always used for racing because they moved, according to Catlin, with "wonderful velocity."

A birchbark canoe, built in the 1950's by two eastern Algonquians from Quebec, was constructed according to traditional methods shown on the opposite page. The high bow and stern suggest that this type was used in rough waters.

1. The first step in building an Ojibwa canoe was to lay out the gunwales, fashioned from white cedar wood. Root lashings of black spruce were used to bind the ends together, and white cedar crossbars were inserted to stretch the gunwales to the proper shape. This completed, the basic frame was then moved to the building site—a clear, flat space, preferably well shaded. Here the canoe-makers pounded stakes into the ground along the outside of the gunwales, as shown in the sketch above.

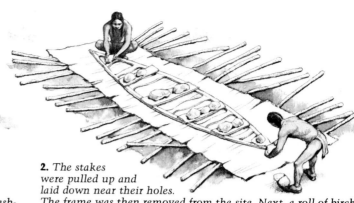

2. The stakes were pulled up and laid down near their holes. The frame was then removed from the site. Next, a roll of birchbark was unrolled, white side up, on the building site. The frame, weighted down with stones, was now brought back and carefully positioned on the bark, using the stake holes as guides. If, as occasionally happened, the roll of bark was not wide enough, it might be pieced out at this stage, or the builders might wait until later.

3. The bark outside the frame was slashed so that strips could be turned up to reveal the stake holes, into which the stakes were again driven. Then pairs of stakes on opposite sides of the frame were tied together, and small stakes were set inside the frame to clamp the bark in place (insert).

4. The canoe-builders removed the stones and then raised the gunwales to their proper height, resting them on poles placed underneath the crossbars. It was now that the women, as shown above, took over to lace the bark skin around the gunwales. First they punched holes in the bark with their awls, then they wrapped the bark around the gunwales and laced it in place with the split roots of black spruce. These roots, sharpened at the ends, were water-soaked to keep them flexible.

5. The canoe was set, bottom up, on wooden horses, and the women repaired such parts of the underside as needed patching. They added more root lashings to bind the ends of the craft together (inset). Then the canoe was turned rightside up on the grass. Black spruce gum, heated to a thick syrup, was used to waterproof the seams and cracks.

6. Finally, the men sheathed the inside of the canoe with white cedar strips laid lengthwise edge to edge. These were held in place by ribs—bow-shaped strips of cedar that ran across the bottom of the craft and up the sides, as shown above. During this operation the bark was kept moist so that it would not split while these wood elements were added. The outward spring of the ribs helped keep them in place, but the inner framework was made more rigid by sewing the ribs to the gunwales with spruce root.

The Cannibal Monsters of the Canadian Forests

The Windigos—superhuman, evil giants—were dreaded by all the Algonquian peoples of the Subarctic. Different groups called these monsters by different names, and some described them as being made wholly of ice, while others said that only their hearts were of ice. But all agreed that they were the most dangerous and terrible of spirits. Windigos arose in the deep forests in the dead of winter; they stood 20 to 30 feet tall; their lipless mouths contained great jagged teeth; their eyes rolled in blood; and their footsteps in the snow were soaked with blood. They hissed with every breath, emitting sounds that could be heard for miles around, and their howls were so eerie that people's knees became weak as they tried to run away. The Windigos were as strong as they were frightful. They could disembowel a man with a sweep of a clawlike hand. And they were friendless, enemies to each other as well as to man. When two Windigos met, they battled to the death, the winner eating or burning the loser.

Worst of all was the fate the Windigos dealt to human beings—their most sought-after prey. The Windigos either devoured their victims—every hunter who failed to return from a trip into the forest was presumed to have perished at their hands—or took possession of them, so that they too craved human flesh to eat. These men and women—now Windigos in appetite if not in appearance—were almost as much to be feared as the monsters themselves. They became violent, sometimes indulging their gruesome appetites, sometimes becoming so frightened by their own actions—or impulses—that they begged to be killed. Because curing anyone possessed by a Windigo was extremely difficult, the death plea was often honored.

Clearly, the Windigo legend grew out of the somber realities of eastern Canadian Indian life. The dense forests contained many real dangers. Food in winter was often in short supply and starvation was always a possibility, one that might be eased by resort to cannibalism, however much the Indians abhorred this practice. Although Windigo psychosis—the belief that one has been possessed by a Windigo—was relatively rare, some 70 cases have been documented since it was first observed in the 17th century by French Jesuit missionaries. The details of some of these cases are unknown, but it was established that men tended to be afflicted with Windigo psychosis more often than women. Of the 70 cases recorded, only 10 of the victims recovered, while 33 of the human Windigos were executed in order to save the other tribe members from them, for victims of the Windigo psychosis did indeed crave human flesh. Forty-four of them committed acts of cannibalism—and of these, 36 killed and devoured members of their own families.

illness among the younger members of the tribe *had* to be the work of evil shamans. The Athabascans' shamans, therefore, were engaged in a constant struggle to ward off the evil machinations of hostile shamans in either the Cree or the Eskimo camp. From time to time this internal need to avert evil erupted into punitive raids against the enemy.

Because they were not a warlike people, the Athabascans' raids as well as their response to enemy incursions were usually hastily improvised affairs. Samuel Hearne once witnessed such a raid by Chipewyans against the Crees. He described it as more of a confused melee than a prepared attack, and elaborate taboos were observed afterward to placate the guardian spirits of the enemy who were killed.

Scaling the Social Ladder

Only an extraordinary man could rise to a position of prominence among the Subarctic tribes. History does record a few, however, among them a man named Matonabbee who supported six wives and nine children. With a family that size Matonabbee had to be an unusually good provider, and to be a good provider he had to be an excellent huntsman and have the spirits on his side. All these prerequisites Matonabbee fulfilled, but the real source of his strength lay in his special relationship with the spirits.

Such a man could have his pick of marriageable maidens and thus strengthen his position even more with influential members of the tribe. Marriage was a simple affair, with no special rites or ceremonies: the marriage was announced and the couple began living together. They might be given clothing and household utensils by friends and relatives, and they might exchange gifts between themselves—a shirt sewed by the bride for her husband, a canoe he had built for her. If the groom prospered and his reputation grew, he might take other wives and thus gradually assume a position of preeminence among the tribe.

Female virginity at the time of marriage was important among many of the Subarctic tribes, and parents were careful to prevent premarital intercourse by their daughters. When a girl had her first menses, it was one of the most important milestones of her life, because it signified that she was now ready for marriage, and the occasion was therefore marked with considerable ritual and ceremony.

Unless the family was traveling, a girl having her first menses was taken to a small hut some distance—as much as half a mile—from the family dwelling, and there she lived in seclusion from 10 days to a month; the length of time varied among local tribes. She was taken care of by older women, and in some tribes she wore at all times a menstrual hood of soft caribou or moose skin, decorated with porcupine quills and a fringe. If she had to leave the hut for any reason, she was not allowed to walk on any hunting trails for fear she might contaminate them, and she walked always with her head down. She wore gloves because she was not allowed to touch her body with her bare hands, and used a tube made from a swan's leg bone to drink from the special cups and bowls that were provided for her. In each succeeding menses she was similarly banished but then only for the duration of her period.

When a girl married, her husband moved in with her family; in some tribes he might even move in before the marriage—at the time his bride-to-be was in seclusion with her first menstruation. When she became pregnant, she worked as usual until she felt her time had come. Birth was as simple an event as marriage. At the onset of labor the mother-to-be was taken to a small tent or brush hut at some distance from the camp. Another woman or a midwife attended at the birth, which was accomplished in a kneeling or squatting position, sometimes with the pregnant woman holding on to a horizontal bar suspended above her. Like all Indian women, she enjoyed little recuperation time after giving birth.

Peter Fidler, a surveyor for the Hudson's Bay Company, describes how a woman bore a baby boy right on the trail in 1792:

"March 13. Moved NNE 2 miles & was necessitated to put up short of where we intended to go on account of [a] deceased man's wife being delivered in the Track when hauling a very heavy sledge. The other women wished to erect the small tent for that purpose but she was too quick for them. She had a

A veil mask of caribou skin, like this one, was worn by a Naskapi girl during her first menstrual period. A number of taboos surrounded menstruating females. They wore special gloves as well as masks and were segregated in special huts.

boy.... [The next day she] took her heavy sledge to a drag as usual the same as if nothing had happened to her. She sleeps in a small brush hut not having permission to come into the Tent along with the men & other women."

Under more normal circumstances the new mother would remain apart from the rest of the tribe for about a month. Other women would take care of her, but she saw no men, and even the new father did not see his child until his wife's period of isolation was over.

During its first year an infant was carried on its mother's back under her skin robe. The baby was held in place by a harness lined with a padding of moss that served as a diaper.

Apparently the lives of Subarctic children were happy and uncomplicated. Boys were favored over girls, but both sexes were shown affection and treated as adults by their elders. A strong sense of individual worth had to be inculcated in a child from the start if

he or she was to assume and carry out successfully the responsibilities of adult life.

There were a few games to lighten the daily round. Most popular was a hand game in which each contestant began with an equal number of counters. A player would hide his hands behind a curtain and conceal a chip in his left or right palm. He would then show his fists to his opponent, who had to guess in which hand the chip was concealed. When one player had won all the counters, the game was over.

For a girl childhood usually ended at about age 12, for it was then that she would generally be married. Her husband might be twice her age and, frequently, he was a cousin on her mother's side of the family. Because of the bride's tender age, there would probably be no offspring for at least a couple of years.

Although the family was the cornerstone of Subarctic culture, the ties of marriage were not strong. Among some Athabascans a wife could be wrestled for by any man who chose to challenge the husband, and if the huband lost, the woman had no choice but to follow the winner, regardless of what her own feelings might be.

The rules of wrestling were simple: the first man to throw his rival won. Men cut their hair short and greased their ears to make these favorite grabbing places less vulnerable during a match. Although a man might have a number of wives, he was likely to be fiercely jealous of their sexual loyalty. On occasion, two men might trade wives for a night, but the arrangement had less to do with sexual variety than with economic realities. The two men were thus pledged to each other for friendship and assistance, and if one of them died, the other would take care of the widow and her children.

The lot of the aged among many of the Subarctic Indians was difficult when the group was close to the limits of subsistence. When an aging person was no longer able to carry out assigned responsibilities, he or she was simply dropped from the ranks of those who were useful and hence entitled to their share of food and wordly goods. The aged were not killed; they were simply ignored. They had to scrounge for their food from what was left over after the others of the band had eaten; they slept on the outer edges of the sleeping place around the fire in the tepee. When, in times of severe shortage, the band broke camp to move on, the aged were simply left behind. "They are dead," the younger members of the family would say.

Eskimo Influence

Some of the Subarctic tribes, such as the Ingalik and Koyukon of Alaska, were influenced in many ways by the Eskimo cultures immediately adjacent to them—a fact that is reflected in the semiunderground construction of sod houses and in the use of sleds rather than toboggans. Modes of life also varied according to environment. In the western regions, with their great boreal forest, mountains, broad rivers, and wide swamps, there were different sorts of game and hence different ways of hunting, although the bow and arrow, spear, and knife were in general use throughout the region.

In other parts of the Subarctic there was a far greater variety of animals than those the Chipewyans knew. In such regions Indian bands hunted moose, grizzly and black bears, rabbit, porcupine, beaver, muskrat, and ground squirrel. Mink, marten, lynx, and otter were hunted when other game was scarce. Wolves, however, were taboo for the hunter everywhere; like the dog, the wolf was considered to be the brother of man. In the Yukon and northern Alaska, Indian hunters pursued Dall sheep; in British Columbia and the southern Yukon region, mountain sheep, elk, and deer; fish, especially salmon, were taken in the extreme west.

In the northeastern part of the Subarctic region, on the edge of the boreal forest in what is today the Province of Quebec, lived the Algonquian-speaking Naskapis whose lives, like those of the Chipewyans, revolved around the seasonal migrations of the caribou. The Naskapis inhabited an area of northern Quebec covering about 100,000 square miles, much of it taiga, the swampy coniferous forest that, at this point, begins almost imperceptibly to thin out, finally becoming the treeless tundra.

Like other Subarctic peoples, the Naskapi tended to be nomads. They were few in number. Their total population appears to have been less than 1,500 divided into small bands, each with its own cycle of following the caribou to the edge of the forest, but seldom beyond. The Naskapis were more woodland Indians than roamers of the tundra, and this fact had some influence on their way of living, notably in the winter, when the forest was buried in snow and temperatures of –60° F were relatively common.

Their dress was not as warm as that of other northern tribes, in part, no doubt, because they lived differently. In their tepeelike homes a wood fire was kept burning constantly when they were encamped, and with caribou skins providing the tent covering and fir boughs piled deep inside, their abodes were kept reasonably warm. When they were outside, the Naskapis were usually on the move, wandering hundreds of miles in the course of their annual migration, so that loose clothing permitting freedom of movement was preferable to heavier clothing worn primarily for warmth.

They were expert workers of caribou hide, soaking the skins so that the hair could be efficiently removed, then curing them with rotted brains and massaging them until they were as soft and supple as any cloth. From these skins the Naskapis made moccasins and knee-length, form-fitting coats with flared hems that were worn by both men and women. In the cold season some added fur leggings. As winter head covering they

Hunting moose in winter, in a painting by Catlin, captures the drama of the pursuit across the snowy fields. In winter moose travel in small groups of three to five, moving with difficulty through drifts that often come as high as their bellies. The hunter, wearing snowshoes, moved much more easily. Windy, sunny days right after a snowfall were best for hunting. The wind deadened any sound the hunter made, while the fresh snow, crusted by the sun, outlined the animals' tracks. Moose were also hunted during the rest of the year. In the fall mating season the hunters often used a birchbark moosecall, like the one below, to lure an animal into the open where tribesmen lay in wait.

wore hoods, usually of caribou skin with the hair turned inward for extra warmth. Hide mittens completed their cold-weather garb.

The Naskapis were highly skilled in woodworking. For summer travel they made birchbark canoes, from which they also hunted caribous as they swam across lakes and rivers. Canoe travel was far preferable to tramping through the swampy woods, and it was also far more likely to be free of the pestiferous swarms of mosquitoes and blackflies that appeared in the summer.

For winter travel through the deep snow of the woods, the Naskapis made snowshoes, wider than those used by Indians of the tundra and closely woven with strips of babiche. The babiche was laced on when wet, so that when it dried the snowshoe was tight and light, enabling the wearer to travel across deep, soft drifts without sinking into the snow.

Though caribou was their mainstay, the Naskapis also hunted such smaller animals as beaver, otter, porcupine, and ptarmigan, which were available the year around. In the spring lake trout became an important food. But even so there were times when no game at all could be found, and then starvation

A bear's skull (above) was thought by many Subarctic peoples to possess the same powerful spirit the animal had in life. Bear skulls were often honored with decorations, and a hunter always apologized and explained his need for food before hunting a bear.

stalked the deep woods and often entire families died. Like other tribes, the Naskapi had a horror of cannibalism, and in their mythology there existed a monster called the atsan that kidnapped people and ate them. The atsan was similar to the Windigo of the Athabascans and was believed to be the reincarnated one who had eaten human flesh.

One of the most interesting aspects of the Naskapis was their relationship with the Eskimos, with whom they lived in close proximity. Just as with the Chipewyans, the Eskimos were regarded as hereditary enemies. While there was a certain overlap of hunting territories, the Indians rarely went far into the tundra, nor did the Eskimos ever venture far into the woods. Yet raids did take place.

When there were clashes, the Eskimos were almost always the losers. The Indians usually attacked by night, having observed the Eskimos from afar, and when they overwhelmed an Eskimo camp, they usually killed everyone in it. Occasionally, however, an Eskimo girl or woman would be spared and taken away as a wife.

The Naskapis considered the Eskimos to be animallike because they ate raw meat and fish; the Eskimos, on the other hand, ridiculed the Indians as having louse eggs growing in their hair. Each side accused the other of smelling bad, and the Indians disapproved of the Eskimos because they used dogs to pull their sleds.

Like most tribes throughout the Subarctic region, the Naskapi were also fishermen, particularly when game was scarce. Because they had no metal, all of their implements, including fishing gear, were made of stone, bone, or antler. They smoked both fish and meat by hanging them over a fire. The only way they cooked was by smoking, boiling, or roasting. Often they simply threw a fish or small animal directly on the fire.

The End of the Beothuks

In 1829, with the death of a woman named Shawnawdithit, an entire people—the Beothuks of Newfoundland—ceased to exist. She had been the last survivor. It is not known how long Newfoundland had been their home or where they had come from, for their language and customs differed sharply from their Eskimo and Algonquian neighbors. And no one knows how many Beothuks were living in Newfoundland in 1497 when Britain's explorer John Cabot made landfall on the island. But it was from that moment their problems began. In the 16th century many were sold into bondage by European slave traders. In the 17th century they were harried and killed by English and French fishermen, because the Beothuks, having no concept of private property, stole from the Europeans. The Beothuks were also set upon by the Micmacs of Nova Scotia, whose assaults were encouraged by the bounty the French had placed on Beothuk scalps. By the mid-18th century only 27 Beothuks remained.

The Beothuks were a migratory people who wandered in small bands, hunting deer, caribous, and small game on land, and seals and whales at sea. They were excellent archers, spearmen, and harpooners, and according to one observer, they built fences as tall as 10 feet to divert herds of caribous into areas where they could easily be taken. Like the Algonquians, they made extensive use of birchbark, using it to fashion their containers, cooking vessels, wigwams, and canoes. These canoes had a unique shape: the gunwales rose to sharp points amidships, so that from the side the craft looked like a rather flat "W." Deer and caribou skin provided the Beothuks' clothing, which, like their bodies, was dyed red with a mixture of ocher and seal fat. Some experts believe that phrases like "red Indian" and "red man" first came into being when whites encountered the ocher-dyed Beothuks.

Little is known of the Beothuks' religious beliefs. Shawnawdithit spoke of a creation myth that described men and women as arising from arrows stuck in the ground.

Most Subarctic tribes also did some fishing, and their methods were generally the same or similar to those of the Chipewyan. Notable exceptions were the tribes of Alaska, the Yukon, and British Columbia that had the good fortune to live in regions where the salmon ran. Salmon was as dependable a source of food as caribou.

The arrival of the salmon on their annual return to their spawning grounds was celebrated by some tribes with a "first salmon" feast, at which the first fish caught was divided among all members of the band. Catching, cutting, and drying fish was a major occupation among the western Athabascans. The summer camps were equipped with fish-storage caches, drying sheds, drying racks and, in some cases, permanent fish traps made of stone at special places along rivers. Salmon nets of willow bast rolled into twine were made by the women. The nets were tended by the men in canoes, who clubbed the salmon and then brought them ashore where they were filleted and hung on the racks to dry. Egg sacs, borne by female salmon, were left attached to the fillets and dried along with them. Later the eggs would be used in soups or mixed with berries and fat and served as a special delicacy.

The woodland Indian bands of the western Athabascan regions supplemented their meat diet more often than did the Chipewyans with berries and other plant foods. Rhubarb, licorice plants, wild onions, and birch and willow leaves were also part of the diet, and in some places various dishes were flavored with the sap of birch and willow trees.

As all over the world, different places bred different customs. Most Athabascans lived and traveled in family groups, but some Alaskan tribes as well as the Chilcotin and Carrier of British Columbia were village dwellers. The Koyukon, by contrast to other Athabascan groups, claimed property rights to particularly favored fishing or trapping areas; elsewhere, territoriality, if it existed at all, was flexible enough to permit even members of neighboring bands to hunt in tribal territory, although they usually asked permission.

The Coming of Spring
Probably the closest that any of the Athabascans ever came to our modern, romantic notion of early Indian life was when spring came. With the arrival of longer and brighter days, the men, women, and children of these groups could leave their dark winter dwellings and, with all their gear piled on sleds or toboggans, depart for their spring camping grounds. Along lakes and streams where muskrats abounded, the Koyukons, Ingaliks, and some of the Kutchins set up brush huts or skin tents, and then men, women, and children set to hunting and trapping the animals.

Muskrat meat was the most important food to these Indians in the spring. Muskrat meat was eaten either boiled or roasted, and the surplus was dried for later use. The skins were carefully treated to make clothing

The Decline of the Subarctic Culture

In 1670 the British crown granted a charter to "a Company of Adventurers of England," declaring the group to be "the true . . . Lordes and Proprietors" of much of present-day Canada. Thus was set in motion a chain of events that would radically alter the lifes-style of the native peoples of the Subarctic, destroying their old culture without providing a workable substitute.

Like the other Indians of North America, the Subarctic peoples had been self-sufficient, making their own tools, hunting, gathering food, and trading with one another on a simple barter basis. The Hudson's Bay Company—as the proprietors called themselves—changed all that. Its primary concern was to acquire furs for the European market, and to that end it set up trading posts throughout the Canadian wilderness. There Indians could exchange pelts for such European items as muskets, powder, wool blankets, glass beads, and metal knives, hatchets, and kettles—all of which the tribesmen were most eager to obtain. Hunting, once a matter of subsistence, became a commercial activity, and Indians began to focus on the animals whose pelts the white traders wanted—chiefly beaver. As trapping was the most effective way of catching beaver, hunting increasingly became an individual enterprise rather than the communal endeavor it had been when large game like caribou was the target. Competition soon developed, leading to destructive rivalries among tribes and even within tribes. As the supply of beaver in one area was depleted, the trappers moved on to another, to poach on territories within their neighbors' traditional domains. The Crees, especially, moved into the lands

Wool blankets, copper pots (above), bolts of material and muskets (right) were among the items offered by the Hudson's Bay Company to Subarctic Indians in exchange for pelts. The Indians found such items to be more useful than their own handicraft products and quickly became dependent on the company's merchandise. In the drawing, made in the mid-19th century, of a Hudson's Bay trading post, Indians crowd the doorway to gain access while two customers carefully examine a musket, presumably offered by the trader in barter for their catch of beaver skins.

of other tribes, using guns to gain entry.

Moreover, the old nomadic life-style was almost entirely abandoned, and many traditional skills were lost. As the Indians became dependent on the Europeans for kettles, blankets, and beads, they stopped making their own utensils, fabrics, and decorations. And instead of migrating in pursuit of animals, they settled down in permanent villages near the trading posts, where the women and children lived all year while the men went off for extended periods to trap.

For as long as the supply of beaver held out, the Indians prospered as they never had before. But by the beginning of the 19th century beaver had become virtually extinct in many areas of the Subarctic, a circumstance that not only destroyed the trappers' livelihood but upset the ecology of the whole region. With the ancient traditions gone and the beaver depleted, poverty became the Indians' lot. They could not even take up agriculture, for the climate and soil of their Subarctic homeland were not suitable. Other problems arose. Alcoholism, fueled by the white man's whiskey, grew rife, and epidemics of such European diseases as smallpox and typhus decimated the tribes. Like the beaver he hunted, the Subarctic Indian became an endangered species.

---

for winter, and the tough sinews were saved for sewing.

At such times, when the snow was melting and the summer heat and mosquitoes and blackflies had not yet arrived, a family encampment of one of these tribes presented an idyllic picture. Released from the rigors of winter, even the adults were gay. It was a time to build canoes and make birchbark baskets.

Flocks of wildfowl flew overhead, their lonely honking a welcome sign that the winter was over. They were caught with snares or occasionally shot down with arrows. Bears coming out of hibernation were killed, both for the meat, which is particularly good at such a time, and for their skins. As with the Chipewyans, the bear

was a ceremonial animal, but in these regions the taboos were less strict, and bears were hunted regularly.

For thousands of years before the coming of the Europeans, a vast network of trade existed among the Subarctic Indians. Because of the need for tools and weapons, such hard stones as flint and quartzite were among the main items of exchange. Quartzite from Labrador, central Quebec, and other places, for example, was bartered throughout the region. Copper, of course, was also an important trade item, sometime traveling as nuggets of pure ore, sometime manufactured into knives and other implements.

All this was to change with the coming of the white

man and the tools and weapons that he brought with him. By contrast to the regions farther south, in the present United States, the changes among the Indians of the Subarctic were seldom violent and never involved organized warfare with the white settlers.

Nonetheless, the Indians of the Subarctic knew that their ancient way of life and many of their treasured traditions were disappearing beyond recall and that nothing they or anyone else might try to do could stop this inexorable process.

The change came in two stages, and the first stage lasted for a very long time. Its agent was the French-Canadian or British fur trader, who came by canoe with trade goods supplied by the Northwest Company or the Hudson's Bay Company—iron kettles, knives, blankets, guns, and ammunition. The first fur traders appeared in the north woods and lake country of southern Canada in the mid-1600's. They were followed by the trading companies that, in the next two centuries, wove themselves into the very fabric of Indian society. Where the companies established trading posts, Indian settlements gradually took form.

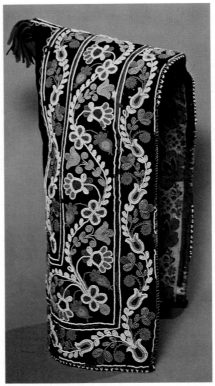

A man's hood, made of wool and decorated with beads and ribbons, dates from the late 19th century. By this time Ojibwa and Cree art was heavily influenced by the teachings of French missionaries and by the use of European materials.

Government Influence

The second stage of change began shortly after the turn of the 20th century, and its agent was the federal government of Canada. What the trading companies had begun with their trade goods and trading posts, the government made permanent. And if Indian life and culture are still in the process of slow change in the Subarctic regions, it is now only in the direction of further acclimatization to the white man's ways.

The fur trade, because it was so closely related to the ecology of the region, did not at first greatly influence the Indians' lives. Indian bands had been trapping fur-bearing animals for centuries for their own use; now they simply trapped more for white people far away across the seas whom they would never see but whose demands for furs seemed to be insatiable. At the trading post the Indians could look over the goods the white man was willing to give in exchange for the many furs they brought, and to get what they wanted. The Indians' lives accordingly became somewhat easier. Now there was a sharp knife of hardened steel to skin a caribou and an iron pot that could be hung directly over a fire for cooking. With woven blankets readily available to provide warmth, there was no long-

er the need for the laborious task of processing hides.

But on the whole the social patterns of the Subarctic tribes changed relatively little as the fur traders moved among them, spreading their influence farther and farther into the interior. The traders were not interested in changing Indian lives; they wanted only furs. And they got them. But as the Indian hunting bands increasingly adapted to a way of life that centered around hunting and trapping fur-bearing animals, subtle changes did occur in their way of life, at first so quietly that they were scarcely noticeable.

One was the slow development of territoriality in hunting grounds and trapping areas. Previously, in the loosely knit social organization of the various Athabascan tribes, there were no strictly defined areas given over to specific hunting groups. There were vague understandings that such and such a group usually went back year after year to such and such a place. But now distinctions grew more rigid. One reason for this was the emergence of local leaders who took the initiative in trading for the band as a whole. At the same time there developed a tendency for several of the small, family-type bands to coalesce and form larger, more effective hunting and trading groups. This, in turn, brought with it the gathering of such groups with their families and their belongings around the trading posts. And because there were fewer trading posts to be used as rendezvous points than there had been summer fishing grounds where the tribes foregathered, the yearly cycle of events was slowly changed as well.

In a subsistence economy, in which the food supply was preeminent among the Indians' concerns, fish had alternated with caribou as the mainstay of the diet; the times of fishing and the times of caribou migration dominated the Indian calendar. But by the beginning of the 20th century food could be obtained in quantity by trading furs for it, and so one of the final bastions of the old life fell. Instead of their seasonal trips to the hunting and fishing grounds, the bands now had only to make the journey to the Hudson's Bay Company store, where all of their needs could be filled.

To effect such slow and basic changes in the lives of the Subarctic tribes took almost two and a half centuries. And by the end of this time the second great agent of change, the Canadian government, was ready to step in. In 1905 a treaty was signed with the Crees of the

James Bay area and with the Ojibwas of the Albany River. Another quarter-century was to pass before this treaty was extended to the rest of the northern tribes of Ontario. While the treaties left the Indians with certain lands of their own in exchange for lands freely ceded to the government, there were other provisions, in the form of services by the government to the Indians, that had much greater impact and more far-reaching consequences on their lives.

One of the first of these was the education of Indian children, a policy that, of course, was in direct contradiction to the cultivation of the old tribal traditions. By the 1940's some children were removed from the villages and sent to residential schools. This policy has since been changed, and schools are now provided directly for the villages concerned. Another important service was medical aid for the Indians, either in the form of direct aid by establishing doctors, nurses, and hospitals in the villages or transporting the sick to places where such services were available.

Probably the most important and far-reaching change was brought about by the various welfare services offered to Indians throughout the territory of the Athabascan tribes. The Canadian government's Indian Affairs Branch offers direct aid to destitute Indian families, which removes any incentive the family might have for providing its own subsistence as in times past. There are, furthermore, a number of other welfare measures for all Canadians: family allowances, widow's allowances, and old-age pensions.

The effect of these measures can be seen today on the streets of such remote northern villages as Fort Chipewyan. A few of the men still hunt and trap in the rich marshlands of the Athabasca Delta, but their numbers dwindle each year. The family dwelling is no longer the nomadic tepee; it is more likely a wooden cabin or a prefab, brought up the Athabasca River from Fort McMurray at the railhead by barge in the short summer season. No longer does family life revolve around the migration of the caribou; these days it is the arrival of the monthly welfare check that is awaited with impatience.

However, it would be wrong to infer from this sad picture that the Chipewyan and other Athabascan Indians have arrived at a dead end. The Indians of the Subarctic regions have been existing in this habitat for a long, long time. In their myths and their traditions is a history that extends back unbroken to a journey from a far country across a land bridge that sank without a trace into the Bering Sea, leaving them cut off irrevocably from their Asian origins. Their new homeland was, according to the seasons, bountiful or almost barren of natural gifts. Survival itself was proof of courage and ingenuity. Their evolution as Americans since their first contact with the white men is a chapter in their lives that is fascinating to all who are interested in the history of North America. Sturdy as these Indians have proven themselves to be, there is no reason to believe that this chapter will be played out by them entirely as wards of the U.S. and Canadian governments. As one anthropologist put it: "Underneath the sometimes distasteful appearance of undigested borrowings lie innumerable unsuspected remnants of ancient thought which are responsible for the behavior and point of view so alien to a European mind." Those remnants of ancient thought will make themselves heard again.

The surrender of Chief Poundmaker and his Cree followers in 1885 to Gen. Frederick Middleton is shown in this painting by Canadian R. W. Rutherford. The ceremony marked the end of one of the very few wars between Canadians and Indians. Hostilities came about after dominion authorities announced plans to build a coast-to-coast railroad. To prevent this invasion, Poundmaker joined forces with a group of métis—people of mixed Indian and French-Canadian blood—who also opposed the railroad, and together they waged war under the leadership of the métis Louis Riel. Evidently, Poundmaker was uncertain of his course, and after one battle he permitted surrounded Canadian troops to withdraw in safety. And after Riel's makeshift army was decisively defeated, Poundmaker surrendered.

THE ARCTIC
Dwellers in an Icy World

An icy sea off northwest Greenland, swept much of the year by sub-zero gales, reflects the bleak world of the Eskimos. They lived mostly on seal and caribou, and the decoy helmet (inset) was worn to attract seals, used for their skins, oil, sinews, and meat.

For thousands of years the Eskimos have survived in this cruelest of environments. Here is the story of how they have wrested existence from a frozen land at the top of the earth.

For up here where we live, our life is one continuous fight for food and for clothing and a struggle against bad hunting and snowstorms and sickness. That is all I can tell you about the world, both the one I know and the one I do not know."
—*Told to Knud Rasmussen by an Eskimo woman, 1923.*

In many ways the Eskimos were the most remarkable of all the aboriginal peoples of North America. They inhabited the harshest natural environment on the face of the earth—the desolate lands by the Arctic Ocean. There, with incredible tenacity and ingenuity, they fashioned a way of life from meager resources of snow and stone, animal skin and bone.

The Eskimos, who probably never numbered more than 90,000, migrated over vast distances. From the eastern tip of Siberia, where a handful of Eskimos can still be found, across Alaska and northern Canada, to Labrador and Greenland, Eskimo territory stretched more than 5,000 miles. Over such an expanse the fur-clad nomads encountered craggy coasts, rushing rivers, and jutting mountain ranges. But the Eskimos' major homeland was the tundra—rocky, rolling plains bearing little vegetation other than moss, lichen, and low-lying bushes. There were no trees except in the southern areas; most of the Eskimos lived north of the tree line.

Covered with snow and ice for much of the year, the topsoil of the tundra thawed during the brief summer. But the water could not drain away because of the permanently frozen subsoil—permafrost—that lies beneath the surface in the Arctic. So, in the summer, the tundra became a marshy, mosquito-infested quagmire.

North of the tundra and the glacier-scored coast lay the Arctic Ocean, abode of the seal, walrus, and whale—and the main hunting ground of the marine Eskimos. Hunting and killing these mammals was essential for survival. They provided the Eskimos with food and the skins for clothing and sometimes summer tents. From their skin, bone, and sinew, the Eskimos crafted tools and utensils, weapons and ornaments.

In the winter the ocean froze to a depth of six or seven feet, and the Eskimos hunted seals through the sea ice. Hours of daylight were short. Temperatures averaged well below zero, often falling as low as -50° F. But with the coming of summer and the longer hours of sunshine, the ocean ice cracked into pieces along the coastline, and huge floes were borne away by the ocean currents.

How the Eskimos came to this inhospitable part of the world—and why they remained there—has puzzled many students of their ways. Some, such as the late Danish writer Peter Freuchen, believed they once lived farther south but were driven into the icy north by more aggressive Indian tribes. But most scholars now are convinced that the Eskimos had their origins in eastern Asia. Physically, they resemble some Asian peoples. Their bodies are stocky and short-legged; their heads are marked by prominent cheekbones and straight, black hair; many Eskimos' skin has a yellowish tint; their eyes are narrowed by the fleshy lids and epicanthic folds common to some Asians.

Archeological finds in Alaska have demonstrated almost conclusively that the Eskimos made their first appearance in North America about 3000 B.C. Earlier emigrants from Siberia may have come to America across a then existing land bridge between the continents. But when the Eskimos began to arrive, the land bridge no longer existed, and the likelihood is that they came in their skin boats or even on ice floes. They were the last of the Asian aboriginals to cross into North America.

As the Eskimos, by boat and sledge and foot, spread across the Arctic over the centuries, some groups abandoned a few of the ancient customs and adopted others to meet new conditions. The Eskimos of southern Alaska, where timber was plentiful, came to live in wooden houses. Other Alaskan Eskimos lived in semiunderground houses with wooden frames and sod roofs. Those who had contact with the Indians learned to make woven baskets and elaborate ceremonial masks. Some Eskimos even took on such Indian customs as having chiefs and waging war against rival bands.

At the other end of the geographic spectrum, many of the Greenland Eskimo groups were exposed to Norse settlers in the Middle Ages and to Danish colonizers from the early 18th century onward. Some lived in

A masklike carved ivory ornament, probably a grave marker, is one of many artifacts found at the Ipiutak site, Point Hope, Alaska. The site, several hundred miles north of the Bering Strait, dates from about A.D. 300 and is the largest Eskimo settlement ever uncovered in the Arctic. Here were more than 600 semiunderground houses and a three-mile-long cemetery. Many of the graves displayed elaborate ivory carvings that closely resemble those found on the Asian side of Bering Strait, indicating an infusion of Siberian forms. More astonishing is their close resemblance to Chinese carvings of the Shang Dynasty, evidence that the influence of ancient Cathay stretched northward to Siberia, thence eastward to Alaska.

rectangular houses of stone and turf with gut-skin windows that admitted at least a little light.

Of the Canadian groups, the Caribou Eskimos of the Barren Grounds to the west of Hudson Bay departed from Eskimo ways by leaving the sea and becoming an inland people. The poorest of all Eskimos, they managed a bleak existence by hunting caribou and fishing in the freshwater lakes. The Copper Eskimos in the region around Coronation Gulf in northwest Canada clung to most Eskimo patterns, but instead of using stone or bone to make their tools and weapons, they used the copper nuggets they found in great profusion.

To a striking degree, however, the far-flung Eskimos kept to old patterns. Life was organized around the hunt and around the need to survive in a harsh environment. All Eskimos shared an unshakable belief in the supernatural, and their daily lives were directed by concerns over human and animal souls, good and evil spirits, ghosts, monsters, and deities. They believed in innumerable taboos, which, if broken, could bring down the wrath of the spirit world. All Eskimos relied on shamans, half priests and half sorcerers, to protect them and the community against the unpredictable whims of the supernatural world.

Over the extended area inhabited by the Eskimos, only one language—with minor local variations—was

Ivory goggles, made from the tusks of sea mammals, were fashioned hundreds of years ago by a Thule hunter, an ancestor of modern-day Eskimos. Such goggles were used to ward off snow blindness, caused by the sun's glare reflected from the snow.

spoken. In the early 1920's Knud Rasmussen—an Eskimo-speaking ethnologist born in Greenland of Danish and Eskimo forebears—had no difficulty in communicating with any of the local groups as he traveled from Greenland across Canada to Alaska. They called themselves simply *Inuit*—"The People." The name Eskimo, meaning "raw flesh eaters," was bestowed on them by the Algonquians and adopted by the world at large.

Eskimos have been bracketed by scholars into three major groupings: the Alaskan Eskimos (including the Yuits of Siberia and the Mackenzie Eskimos of northwestern Canada), the Greenland Eskimos, and the Central Eskimos. Among the Central Eskimos were such groups as the Netsilik, the Iglulik, and the Aivilik. Until the early part of the 20th century these Central Eskimos were relatively uninfluenced by European culture and the white man. They kept the traditional Eskimo

ways longer than others, and for that reason the Central Eskimos and their way of life are emphasized in this chapter. With their dog teams, snow igloos, and kayaks, the Central Eskimos were the intrepid "hunters of the northern ice" of popular imagination.

Most of the Central Eskimos lived in a region close to the Arctic Circle, where the climate required the use of both winter and summer hunting techniques. Always haunted by fear of starvation, the Eskimos went where the game was available. Essentially nomadic, they did not lead a highly developed village life or evolve political structures. Perhaps more than any people on earth, they moved with the seasons.

The Long Winter
For the Eskimos, midwinter in the Arctic presented nature at its most demanding. A feeble sun barely rose

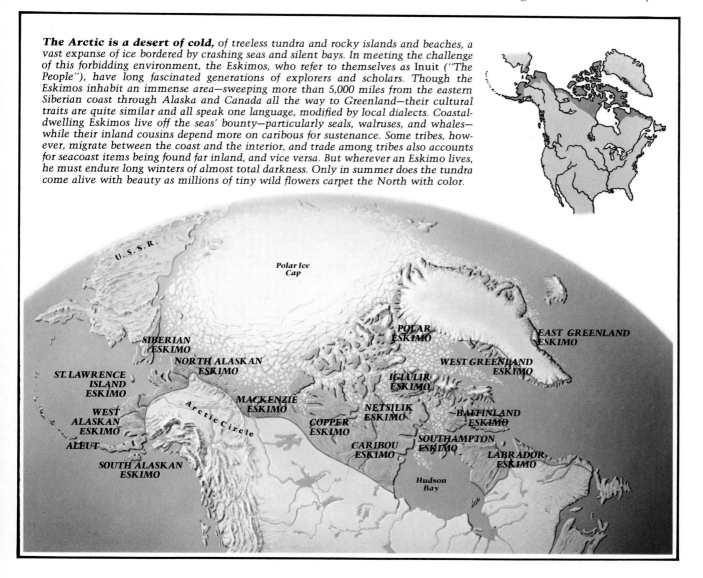

The Arctic is a desert of cold, of treeless tundra and rocky islands and beaches, a vast expanse of ice bordered by crashing seas and silent bays. In meeting the challenge of this forbidding environment, the Eskimos, who refer to themselves as Inuit ("The People"), have long fascinated generations of explorers and scholars. Though the Eskimos inhabit an immense area—sweeping more than 5,000 miles from the eastern Siberian coast through Alaska and Canada all the way to Greenland—their cultural traits are quite similar and all speak one language, modified by local dialects. Coastal-dwelling Eskimos live off the seas' bounty—particularly seals, walruses, and whales—while their inland cousins depend more on caribous for sustenance. Some tribes, however, migrate between the coast and the interior, and trade among tribes also accounts for seacoast items being found far inland, and vice versa. But wherever an Eskimo lives, he must endure long winters of almost total darkness. Only in summer does the tundra come alive with beauty as millions of tiny wild flowers carpet the North with color.

U.S.S.R.

Polar Ice Cap

POLAR ESKIMO

EAST GREENLAND ESKIMO

SIBERIAN ESKIMO

NORTH ALASKAN ESKIMO

WEST GREENLAND ESKIMO

ST. LAWRENCE ISLAND ESKIMO

IGLULIK ESKIMO

WEST ALASKAN ESKIMO

MACKENZIE ESKIMO

NETSILIK ESKIMO

BAFFINLAND ESKIMO

Arctic Circle

COPPER ESKIMO

ALEUT

SOUTHAMPTON ESKIMO

CARIBOU ESKIMO

LABRADOR ESKIMO

SOUTH ALASKAN ESKIMO

Hudson Bay

above the horizon for a few hours; the rest of the day was twilight and darkness. A bone-numbing cold froze the sea solid, often to a depth of six feet or more. The tundra itself was frozen hard, piled deep with drifting snow, and whipped by gales and blizzards. The caribous and the migratory birds had long since gone south. Now it was time for the Eskimos to head through the tundra to the seal-hunting places on the thick sea ice.

Getting to these sites was often a punishing experience for the small groups of Eskimos and their dog teams. The men often had to help pull the heavily laden sledges through the snow. The women usually walked ahead of the dogs, shouting signals back to them. But frequently the women, too, had to help with the pulling. Often progress was agonizingly slow, with men and dogs gasping for breath as they pulled the sledges up icy inclines through blinding snowstorms. Sometimes the trails were blocked and had to be dug out, and sometimes a smooth crust of snow concealed rocks and fissures that smashed the runners of the sledges.

With the sledges piled high with almost everything the Eskimos owned, only the smallest children were allowed to ride. The old people stumbled along behind the rear of the sledges, legs aching, falling farther and farther behind. Often the main party reached its destination for the day and had completed building its camp of snowhouses before the elders straggled in from the trail.

"I am old and I am tired, and my knees are open with sores," old Amusa told her son Apitok. "I cannot go on, so you must build me a snow hut." Once before, Apitok had refused a similar request by his mother. But others in the caravan were hungry and eager to reach the sealing grounds. So now, without a word, Apitok cut a trench in the snow about the length of old Amusa. He lined it with caribou skins and helped his mother to sit down in the trench. Then Apitok built a little igloo over Amusa and placed a small amount of food inside. He took his knife, cut a block of snow, and walled up the entrance with it. No one spoke a word. It was time to begin the day's travel, and the group moved on. From time to time Apitok stopped to smooth over their tracks so that death could not follow them.

Finding the right place to hunt the seals was all-important. Eskimos usually had favorite sealing grounds in the many ice-covered bays and straits along the Arctic coast, and they returned to them year after year. But the exact location of a sealing campsite depended largely on where the Eskimos found large numbers of seal breathing holes in the ice. But finding these holes was rarely a simple matter of sighting them. Usually they were hidden under a light covering of snow.

Seals swam beneath the ice in winter, but as air-breathing sea mammals, or *puiji*—"those who show their noses"—they needed a number of widely spaced breathing holes in the sea ice. And so, as ice began to

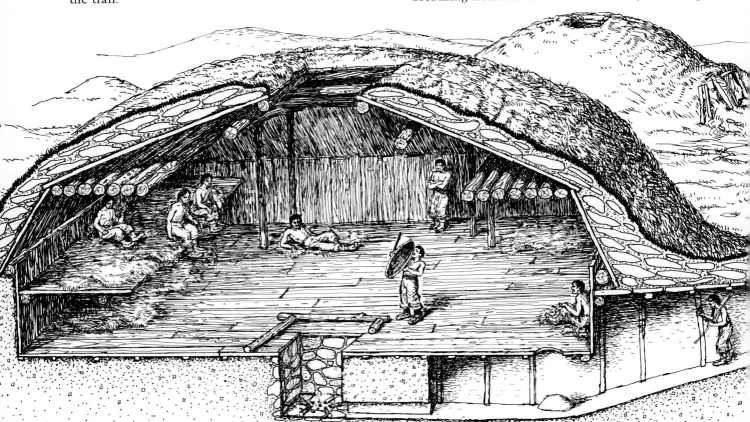

form in the autumn, a seal scratched holes through the undersurface with its sharp claws. As the sea ice gradually thickened, the seal kept its breathing holes open, clearing away new ice as it formed. By midwinter, even with the ice many feet thick, the seal still had kept the holes open through the ice to the surface. Every 15 or 20 minutes the animal rose to one of its breathing holes and gulped in the icy winter air through the snow cover.

After choosing a likely place, the Eskimos built their camp. With long, thin probes of caribou antler they poked through the soft top snow cover to locate a layer hard enough to make good building blocks. To create their igloos—in this case snowhouses—the Eskimos first removed the soft snow with shovels made of antler, sealskin, and sinew. Each man then drew a large circle in the snow with his antler snow knife (pana). The circles, each 9 to 15 feet in diameter, roughly outlined the floor space the Eskimos envisaged for their houses.

From inside the circle the igloo-builder carved into the hard-packed snow with his knife. Working along the inner edge of the circle, he hewed out rectangular blocks about 20 by 24 by 4 inches. Around the ledge he thereby created, the Eskimo placed one block after another in an ascending spiral. Each higher row extended a little farther inward. Each block was tamped against the preceding one, locking the two together. The ascending spiral gradually closed in to form the igloo's characteristic beehive shape and dome. The snow igloo was one of the architectural wonders of primitive man.

As the Eskimo man fashioned the shell of the igloo, his wife, working outside, shoveled loose snow over the walls to fill any cracks or holes. When the main shell was finished, he then built a rounded porch for an entryway and dug a long, low corridor beneath the snow to an opening on the surface. This entryway usually opened to the south, thus avoiding the fierce north wind. A ventilation hole was cut in the roof of the igloo, and a rectangle of clear freshwater ice—often carried along from the autumn hunting grounds—was installed as a window. The Eskimo, working steadily, completed his basic igloo in little more than an hour.

Inside the igloo the man also built a sleeping platform of packed snow. The platform, which was two or three feet above the igloo floor, was to be used by the Eskimo's family for eating and sitting, as well as for sleeping. In another corner of the igloo the Eskimo finally built a "kitchen table" of snow blocks.

The wife now took over the job of getting the interior in order. She placed her flat, soapstone lamp on the kitchen table, pounded a piece of frozen blubber with a mallet made of musk-ox horn until the fat was softened, then placed the dripping piece of blubber on the back half of the lamp. As its oil spread, she placed wicks of finely chopped dry moss all along the edge of the lamp and then lighted the fire with hot embers she had brought with her. Soon the entire row of moss wicks was ablaze; the blubber melted even faster, and the lamp gave off a smooth, smokeless flame. The heat melted the inner surface of the dome slightly, but the

The sod dwelling, rather than the snowhouse, was home for the Alaskan Eskimo. Domed-shaped, built on a frame of driftwood or whale bone, and covered with layers of sod, these houses were partially underground and consisted of one large room—for sleeping, eating, and other activities—that was entered through a long passageway, also built partly under the surface. Aside from permitting access to the central room, this passageway was also used for storage and sometimes as a kitchen. The semi-subterranean structure of the houses as well as the layers of sod on top provided excellent insulation. Thus a stone lamp was all that was necessary to keep the central room of each house reasonably warm. Light from outside entered the sod house through a hole cut in the wall, and this was covered either with a sheet of clear ice or a piece of sea mammal intestine. In the typical Alaskan village, like the one shown, all houses were grouped around a larger structure called a kashim. This was a combination men's club and ceremonial center which women rarely entered.

The Snowhouse: A Temporary Winter Dwelling

Contrary to popular belief, only certain Eskimos built snowhouses, and even these peoples did not use the shelters as permanent dwellings. The snowhouse was used exclusively in the central Arctic, and there only as a temporary base during the winter seal-hunting season. As these drawings of a Netsilik snowhouse show, its construction was fairly simple. The blocks of which it was made held together only if they came from a layer of snow that had fallen in a single storm and had frozen into a solid sheet. The builder's first task was to find such a layer, by testing the snows with an antler probe about four feet long. Once he found the cohesive level, he cleared away the surface snow with his shovel and, with a snow knife, drew a circle anywhere from 9 to 15 feet in diameter, to outline the house. Standing inside this circle, he cut the blocks—each about 20 by 24 by 4 inches—and placed the first row along the round outline. Each of the succeeding rows is set progressively farther in, and the blocks are pressed together to ensure a close fit. As he worked, his wife plastered the exterior with fine, soft snow. When the last small block at the top had been laid in place—about an hour later—the man cut a hole in the wall about two feet from the bottom, through which his wife entered after handing in the family belongings. Now he closed the hole and dug another, connecting the house to the porch he now constructed. At the other side of the porch—domed, like the house—he built a corridor, into which he cut the door to the outside. Next, he hacked out a ventilation hole in the ceiling and, a few days later, cut a window in the wall and inserted a pane of clear, freshwater ice to admit light.

A snowhouse at night glows with the light of a pressure lamp used by contemporary Eskimos on northern Hudson Bay. In earlier times the lamp was made of stone and burned seal oil.

Cutting blocks for a snowhouse, the builder stands inside the circle that outlines the dwelling to be constructed.

Placing blocks in ever-shorter, spiraling rows, he creates the characteristic dome-shaped snowhouse shelter.

Finishing the house, the builder sets the last blocks in place as his wife plasters the exterior wall with soft snow.

Moving into the house, the wife hands the family goods in through a hole her husband has cut in the snow wall.

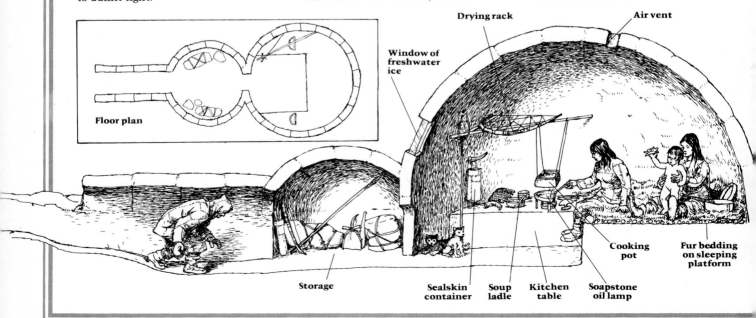

Floor plan

Drying rack

Air vent

Window of freshwater ice

Storage

Sealskin container

Soup ladle

Kitchen table

Soapstone oil lamp

Cooking pot

Fur bedding on sleeping platform

dome did not drip. Instead, a thin film of meltwater flowed down the walls, where it froze. A thin crust of ice thus formed over the inner surface of the igloo, locking the blocks even more firmly together and solidifying the entire structure.

Near the burning lamp the Eskimo woman set up a clothes-drying rack of antler and caribou-skin thongs. She hung her ladles, dipper, and sealskin containers on sticks jabbed into the ice walls, and she suspended a soapstone pot directly above the lamp flame. Frozen fish or caribou meat, brought along on the trek from the south, was thrown into the pot, and the smell of cooking food soon filled the igloo. The Eskimo woman then put the sleeping platform in order. For insulation against the moisture of the snow, she sometimes arranged a layer of caribou ribs or waterproof sealskin. Then she spread out the mattress of caribou skins, the bottom one with the hair facing downward, the top one with the fur facing upward. On top of all this she placed a blanket of finer skins. The woman stored extra skins, frozen blubber and meat, and extra equipment in the snow porch.

Outside in the snow the boys played noisily, and the men completed the building of the camp. They erected a snow platform high enough to keep dog food out of the reach of the strong, ever-hungry huskies. Sometimes they built a small, round toilet igloo and a large snow structure, also in typical beehive fashion, for a ceremonial, or dance, house.

When the camp was completed, it was time to plan for the seal hunt. Most winter camps housed 50 or 60 people, and of that total there were—including the older boys—perhaps 15 hunters. As a rule, Eskimos did not have chiefs, but there was an acknowledged leader of the winter camp, the Umealiq. He was usually the oldest of the capable hunters, a man whose judgment and experience commanded respect. All the hunters gave their views, but it was up to the leader to decide when—and exactly where—to hunt the seals.

It was the morning of the first seal hunt, and Apitok was eager to begin. His wife, Moraq, had reminded him several times that their supply of frozen meat was running low. Now Apitok ate a good meal of cooked caribou meat—the last food he was likely to have until he returned that evening. After the meal Apitok put on his heavy outer clothing and footwear. He collected all the equipment he would need for the hunt, placing the smaller articles in the squarish, fox-fur hunting bag he would carry on his back. He examined his favorite sealing harpoon to make sure that the shaft of antler was still strong and the head of chipped flint was sharp. Most important to all, before leaving the igloo, Apitok hung around his neck a stone amulet that brought luck when hunting seals through the ice. Twice he chanted a special charm dedicated to the seal: "Beast of the Sea! Come and place yourself before me in the dear, early morning!"

Each Eskimo hunter had a dog on a leash as he set off on foot through the snow. As the group approached the agreed-upon sealing place, each man moved off in a different direction. The smooth snow made the breathing holes difficult to find, but the huskies—with their keen sense of smell—could sometimes sniff them out. When a dog smelled a breathing hole, it would stop and either lie down or turn around in place. At that, the hunter would signal to the others, who rushed to the scene. All of the Eskimos then began to thrust their probes into the snow, and the one who actually located

The warm atmosphere of a snow igloo belies its frigid appearance. Though the stone lamp, which the woman above is tending, provides the sole artificial source of heat and light, the body heat of family members helps maintain room warmth, as does the natural insulation provided by the snow blocks themselves. Within the igloo, quarters are crowded, but family cama-

raderie, mutual affection, and a respectful attitude toward the rights of each inhabitant help create a feeling of spaciousness. Each person has a private area, however small, and etiquette requires that those in a contemplative mood be left alone. But mostly the ambiance within a snowhouse is friendly, no more so than at night when a family beds down (above) and talks.

The Many Tactics of Eskimo Seal-Hunters

Next to the caribou, the seal has been the Eskimos' primary source of sustenance. From its flesh comes meat; its skin provides clothing and sled runners; its oil, fuel for lamps.

Two species of seal are hunted: the bearded seal, which at maturity may be seven feet long and weigh 600 pounds; and the more common ringed seal, a third the weight but with a more supple skin.

Before guns became available, Eskimos usually hunted seals with harpoons from kayaks. Curiously, the prey sometimes cooperated in its own destruction. The seal is an inquisitive creature and often swam to within easy harpoon range of the kayaks. When it finally sensed danger, it became paralyzed with fear, thus making itself an even easier target.

There were other means the Eskimos use to hunt seals. In the spring, when the animals were sunning themselves on ice floes, some Eskimos hid behind blocks of ice (ice blinds) that they pushed forward until they reached striking distance. Then, before the animals could escape by plunging into the water, the hunters would rush from behind the blind and kill the seals. At other times, when the sea was frozen over, seals were, and still are, taken with harpoons thrust through ice holes (right) or, more rarely, with nets lowered beneath the ice (far right).

When a seal is killed, it is not immediately butchered. First the spirit of the animal is offered a drink of fresh water, and mittens are placed on the carcass. The hope is that the seal's spirit will report its good treatment and encourage other seals to make themselves available as prey.

Ice-hole hunting is a common method the Eskimos use to take seals during the long, virtually sunless winter when temperatures frequently fall as low as -50° F. The task is arduous and uncomfortable and requires great patience. First, the Eskimos must find the seals' breathing holes in the ice, where the creatures come many times a day to take in air. For sniffing out these holes, the Eskimos' well-trained dogs are invaluable. Once a hole is found, the Eskimo explores its shape with a probe, for the seals make the holes in the thick ice with a variety of subsurface patterns and a hunter must know the characteristics of the angles so that he can take proper aim with his harpoon when his quarry appears.

This done, the hunter crouches over the hole and sets up two uprights—one on each side of the hole—as a harpoon rest (shown above). He lays his harpoon across the rest, and from the center of the shaft he dangles a length of sinew into the hole. Attached to the sinew is a feather that rests on the hole's outer edge. When a seal approaches, the moving water beneath the hole agitates the sinew, which in turn causes the feather to shake, thus alerting the hunter to the prey's presence. Now the Eskimo moves quickly, seizing his harpoon and plunging it through the hole into the body of the seal

below (shown above). The head of the harpoon remains imbedded in the seal, but the hunter removes the shaft. If the Eskimo has been lucky and aimed well, he will have dealt the animal a mortal wound. Unable to swim away, the seal thrashes about beneath the surface as the hunter chips away at the edges of the breathing hole to enlarge it. It is through this hole that he drags the creature to the surface and kills it. At day's end, all of the hunters in the band take their catches to camp for butchering.

---

the opening was entitled to hunt the seal that used it.

The lucky hunter brushed the soft snow away from the hole and used an ice pick of hard bear bone that was fixed to the shaft of his harpoon to enlarge the opening. The Eskimo then removed the chopped ice from the hole with a scoop made of musk-ox horn. He took his breathing-hole searcher—a long, thin, curved length of caribou antler—and poked around beneath the surface. He could thus judge the contours of the seal's tunnel to the surface and the direction in which he would have to strike. The hunter then covered the hole with snow and poked a small hole in it with his probe. Then he inserted a small piece of hard caribou

sinew into the hole. The caribou sinew was attached by a finer sinew thread to a white feather, which sat directly atop the small hole. When the seal swam to the surface, the agitation of the water caused the feather indicator to vibrate—thereby alerting the hunter.

With his indicator in place, the Eskimo stuck two harpoon rests of antler and fur into the snow near the breathing hole, placed his harpoon on the rests, and began his wait. Patience was essential. Sometimes the hunter made a snow block to sit on, but often he would put his fur bag on the ice and stand on it to keep his feet from freezing in the sub-zero cold. Hours might pass, but the Eskimo kept his eyes fixed on the feather,

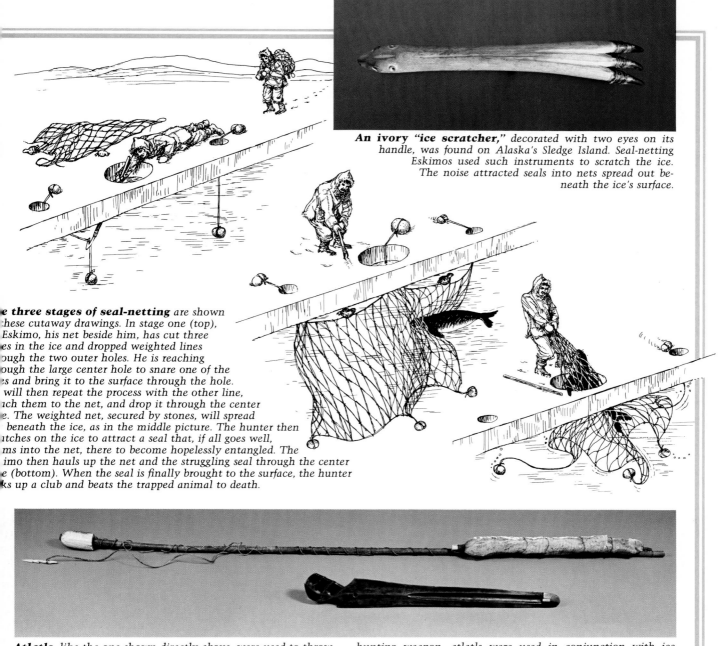

An ivory "ice scratcher," decorated with two eyes on its handle, was found on Alaska's Sledge Island. Seal-netting Eskimos used such instruments to scratch the ice. The noise attracted seals into nets spread out beneath the ice's surface.

The three stages of seal-netting are shown in these cutaway drawings. In stage one (top), an Eskimo, his net beside him, has cut three holes in the ice and dropped weighted lines through the two outer holes. He is reaching through the large center hole to snare one of the lines and bring it to the surface through the hole. He will then repeat the process with the other line, attach them to the net, and drop it through the center hole. The weighted net, secured by stones, will spread out beneath the ice, as in the middle picture. The hunter then scratches on the ice to attract a seal that, if all goes well, swims into the net, there to become hopelessly entangled. The Eskimo then hauls up the net and the struggling seal through the center hole (bottom). When the seal is finally brought to the surface, the hunter picks up a club and beats the trapped animal to death.

Atlatls, like the one shown directly above, were used to throw a spear (top) by Eskimos in the days before harpoons. As a seal-hunting weapon, atlatls were used in conjunction with ice blinds, behind which hunters crept up on their prey.

waiting for the signal that the seal was at the breathing hole and the moment to strike had come.

At last it came. In an instant the hunter seized the harpoon, thrust it downward into the breathing hole with all his strength, deep into the body of the seal. The Eskimo quickly withdrew the shaft, leaving the head—to which a line of sealskin thong was tied—buried in the animal. As the stricken seal desperately flailed about below the ice, the hunter sometimes let out a bit more line. But soon the seal lost strength, and its resistance ended. The Eskimo then enlarged the breathing hole with his ice pick and hauled the seal out onto the ice where it was killed.

In some parts of the Arctic other techniques were used in winter sealing. When the ice was not too thick, some Alaskan Eskimos would bore four small holes in the ice around the breathing hole. Then they would lower a tough net of whale bone strips through the breathing hole, attaching its four corners to lines slipped through the small holes. The Eskimos would try to attract the seal by scratching gently on the ice with a strip of whale bone, imitating the sound of a seal's claws on the ice. If the hunter was successful, the seal would swim over the suspended net to reach the hole. After breathing at the surface, the seal would dive steeply—and become entangled in the net. Then the hunter

A strenuous kickball game, a favorite among all Eskimos, was sketched by an Alaskan artist in the 1890's. Although this is essentially a team sport, each player tries to maintain personal control of the ball as long as possible, and only when pressed severely, as at left, will he kick it to a teammate. No points are scored. The sole objective is to keep the other side from getting control of the ball. Most often the game is played by men, frequently teams from two ceremonial houses. It is not unusual, however, for women and children to join the fray. One observer in the Hudson Bay area wrote that the game "calls out everybody, from the aged and bent mother of a numerous family to the toddling youngster. . . ." The typical ball (inset) is a soft, leather-covered sphere about five inches in diameter and stuffed with caribou hair or a similar material.

hauled up the net and killed the seal with a blow on its head.

While the men were hunting, life in the camp went on at a normal pace. The women busied themselves around their igloos, drying clothes, chewing on boots to soften them, and taking care of the infants. They took sealskin bags and went out to collect old sea ice. Old ice became largely desalinized and was melted and used for drinking water. Girls of 10 or over regularly helped their mothers, often hauling their baby brothers or sisters around on their backs.

The women, along with their children, also visited each other's igloos. During the summer the Eskimos were separated into smaller bands, and the winter camp was the time to exchange stories and gossip. Even in the coldest weather the children played outside, the boys shooting with small bows and arrows or sledding in the snowdrifts, the girls playing house or hide-and-seek. On particularly bitter days the children moved their games into the large ceremonial igloo. In the evening, when the returning hunters were spotted on the horizon, women and children gathered to meet them and learn how the day's seal hunting had gone.

The dead seals, which had been dragged back to camp by the dogs, were taken to the igloos of the Eskimos who had killed them. There the seals were butchered by the wives of the hunters according to strict rules. In order not to offend the soul of a dead seal, the Eskimo wife covered the igloo floor with a layer of fresh snow. The animal was laid on its back atop the fresh snow, and—since even the souls of the dead might be thirsty—the wife poured some water into its mouth. This was supposed to guarantee future luck in sealing, because the soul of the animal would report to other souls of seals how respectfully it had been treated. When the souls reappeared in other seal bodies, the Eskimos reasoned, they would have little cause to resist being killed by the hunters.

In butchering, the wife first skinned the seal, taking care not to damage the skin. Using a semicircular ulu, or women's knife, she removed the layer of blubber and then cut the meat and remains of the carcass into exactly 14 carefully defined pieces. Most of the pieces, along with portions of blubber, were then given to "sharing partners"—those with whom there was a standing agreement for mutual sharing of game killed—a kind of insurance against the uncertainties of the

The spirit of friendly competition *characterizes these Eskimo women as they play* nugluktaq, *a game in which each tries to be the first to poke a stick through the hole of a twirling spool. As in other Eskimo games, players must walk a fine line between healthy competitive spirit and over-aggressiveness.*

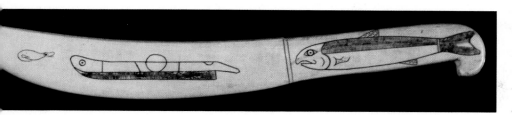

hunt. As soon as the wife completed distributing the seal, she prepared the evening meal for her family.

Apitok was in high spirits, as he always was when he came home from a successful hunt. He himself had killed two seals, and the other hunters had also made some kills. "I am a poor hunter," he laughed. "I have forgotten how to kill seals." Moraq and the other women in the igloo giggled at Apitok's mock humility. They passed around pieces of cooked seal meat, the men and boys sitting on one side of the igloo, the women and girls on the other. Then someone crawled into the igloo. It was Ugak—an orphan adopted by Apitok and Moraq years ago and now a young man of mercurial temperament. He had spent very little time at the hunting grounds that day—and now he had returned to the igloo without a seal. Moraq handed him some meat. Ugak ate it with relish, but he sat alone and did not join in the family gaiety.

For the most part Eskimo family life was warm and varied. Eskimo parents doted on their children, and the younger among them were treated with great tolerance. It would take a major mistake—like breaking a soapstone lamp—to warrant a cuff on the head. This easy-going attitude toward youngsters also applied to adopted children—and there were many of them among the Eskimos. As elderly women often adopted a young child, whom she would call her walking stick. This expressed the hope that one day the adopted child would take care of her in her extreme old age.

Among some Eskimos sex was no mystery. All members of a family slept together on the sleeping platform, and children witnessed sexual activities at an early age. Sometimes, at play, young Eskimos would imitate the sexual antics of their elders. Other groups were more reticent and had a separate room or closet for sexual relations.

Ties between Eskimo fathers and sons were particularly strong. The fathers made miniature sleds and harpoons for the boys and encouraged them to play at hunting. Sometimes the fathers would help their young sons snare seagulls. Once a bird was captured, a boy would play with it for hours on end. Sons watched their fathers and imitated them, and by the time they were 10 or so, the boys began to go along on hunting trips.

Eskimo girls were closer to their mothers. At an early age they helped gather moss or attend to light household chores. Later on they cared for infants and sewed skins for clothing. Eskimo girls married early, and it was rare to find one unmarried after the age of 15 or 16. There was no marriage ceremony for most Eskimos. The girl simply gathered up her belongings and moved into her new husband's igloo.

The immediate family—father, mother, and children—was of fundamental importance. But to the Eskimos it was also essential to maintain the widest possible network of kinship. Often, two or more blood-related families lived in the same crowded igloo. There might be three generations living in the same shelter—grandparents, husbands and wives, and assorted children. In addition, the Eskimos maintained ties with cousins, nieces, aunts, and uncles. Eskimos believed they needed a large number of allies not only in the struggle against nature but also in the event of conflict with other Eskimos.

Working a sealskin with an ulu, an Eskimo woman scrapes away hair and blubber. The ulu, a semicircular blade with a wood or horn handle, is a multipurpose tool. It is also used to cut leather for sewing and meat for cooking. Ulu blades once were made from slate, as at left, but in modern times metal blades have been substituted.

The more allies an Eskimo had, the safer he felt; and so he looked beyond his kindred and formed a rich variety of partnerships. They existed between members of the same winter camp, and they existed between Eskimos in different bands. The sharing partners of the sealing season were usually chosen by a male Eskimo's mother shortly after his birth. She tried to find 12 of them, and each was assigned to a particular part of the seal. Then, when the boy grew to manhood and began to kill seals, his wife carefully gave the prescribed part of the butchered animals to each sharing partner. A sharing partner who received the lower belly of the seal was referred to by the hunter as "my lower belly." Sharing was generally a friendly arrangement, and it made the Eskimos feel safer, less concerned about possible starvation in lean seasons.

Among some Eskimo groups an individual's name was of great importance to him, because he believed that names had souls, souls that acted as guardian spirits. And so, between Eskimos with the same name (men's and women's names were interchangeable), there existed a special bond. The "name partners" felt a special kinship for each other, and they would exchange gifts, usually identical objects or objects of equal worth, such as knives, harpoons, and lamps.

Of all the curious Eskimo alliances the most complex was the male "song partnership." Song partners were usually close friends. During part of the year the men might travel to different hunting grounds. But when they came together in the winter camp, they would meet in the ceremonial house. As other men in the camp pounded drums and danced, the partners sang, one after another. Often they sang old Eskimo chants, but sometimes they would inject a bit of fun, belittling the partner's hunting ability or sexual potency.

But usually song partners would decide to put on a more elaborate display of their friendship. Each would compose a new song and then teach it to his wife, who was to do the actual singing. A meeting would be arranged at the ceremonial igloo, and from all over the winter camp Eskimos came and crowded into the building in a festive mood. The partners rubbed noses and embraced each other. One of the wives began to sing, and the other Eskimo wives would join in the refrain. As the wife sang, the Eskimo husband danced slowly around the igloo, beating on a drum and occasionally crying out a high-pitched "ai-ai-ai." When the song was over, the Eskimo turned the drum over to his partner, who then danced and drummed while *his* wife sang.

So close was the bond between song partners that they often swapped wives, a practice common to nearly all Eskimo groups. Sometimes the exchange lasted for only a night or two, but often it lasted sporadically over a lifetime. The wives were usually consulted, and they usually agreed. But whether or not they agreed, Eskimo wives did what their husbands told them to do.

Moraq was unhappy. Last night, when Apitok came back from the cermonial house, he told her that Tallerk, the wife of his friend Navik, would be moving into the igloo for a while. Moraq did not mind that too much, because Tallerk was her good friend. But Apitok also told her that she must go and live with Navik, and she did not like Navik very much. He was a strong man and a great hunter, but he used coarse words and boasted loudly of his sexual powers. When Moraq told her husband that she did not want to go to Navik, he slapped her hard on the side of the head, knocking her onto the sleeping platform. This morning, before Apitok left for the sealing place, he reminded her of the

Ivory buttons, at left, and the needle case, below, were made by Alaskan Eskimos. The buttons, which come from Cape Nome and date from the late 19th century, were originally used on men's clothing. Only an inch long, they are carefully carved to represent a man's face. The ivory of which they are made came from walrus tusks and was carved with a metal blade that was probably obtained from the Russian fur traders who thronged Alaska at that time. The needle case, which is about six inches long, comes from the Kuskokwin River region. The geometric patterns on the body of the case are characteristic Eskimo decorations. The fish head at the end of the case is, however, only one of several animal representations that were commonly used. Often walrus and seal heads were depicted, and just as this case takes the general form of a fish, others with walrus or seal heads were made in a more bulky shape that gave the overall impression of the animal's body.

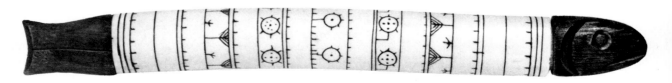

Eskimo Marks of Beauty—Tattoos and Labrets

Although the Eskimos never developed a tradition of decorating utilitarian tools and weapons—perhaps because the rigors of nomadic life left no time for concern about the appearance of such handiwork—the people had a strong esthetic sense about themselves and the way they looked. Their clothing was often handsomely decorated, and both sexes adorned their persons in a variety of ways. In virtually all groups the women's faces were tattooed. Their bodies were also tattooed, and some women wore nose rings and chin or lip labrets. The men were seldom tattooed. Instead, they wore lip labrets. These plugs, which were made from such materials as shell, ivory, sandstone, and wood, also served as evidence of wealth and were sometimes used in trading transactions. Facial decorations were occasionally applied during childhood, but they were more commonly associated with the arrival of puberty. In northern Alaska they were signs that full adulthood had been achieved. Here a boy could not begin to wear labrets until his father had decided he was ready to assume all the responsibilities and

prerogatives of manhood—not only to hunt and fish with his elders but also to marry if he chose. The boy himself made the first labrets he wore—small round plugs called *tuutoks* that were placed in his lip immediately after it was pierced in a simple private ceremony during which he was expected to show no sign of pain. For the girls of northern Alaska, facial tattoos were a sign of eligibility for marriage, and the girls were eager to have them applied as early as possible, despite warnings from their elders that they might thereafter be pursued by men they did not like. The tattoos, which were made by an older woman, usually a relative, consisted of a series of parallel lines that ran from the center of the lower lip to the top of the chin. Girls were not expected to be stoic during this painful process, which involved passing a needle and thread through the soot of an oil lamp and then pulling them through the young woman's flesh.

A young Nunivak woman, photographed by Edward Curtis, wears a variety of beaded facial ornaments: a nose ring, long, dangling ear pendants, and a chin labret—strings of beads plugged into slits cut into the skin below her lower lip. For dances and ceremonial occasions, Nunivak women wore special earrings and nose rings made of ivory and cloth.

Labrets and facial tattoos, shown in the drawing at far right, are characteristic of those worn by the Eskimos of northern Alaska. The women's tattoos ran from the lower lip to the chin; the men wore two labrets, one at either end of the lower lip. In some groups boys began wearing labrets in childhood, starting with small round ones like the one at near right and graduating to larger oval kinds.

exchange. Tallerk would come to his igloo before he returned from the hunt, and she must be in Navik's. The matter was settled. Now, sadly, she placed her knife, some utensils, and her needle case in a sealskin bag, crept out of the igloo, and trudged across the camp toward Navik's igloo.

Over the centuries the Eskimos had to endure many periods when the sealing was bad and other game was scarce. Whole communities starved to death, and some survived only by practicing cannibalism. A shaman told Rasmussen the following story:

"Once when there was a famine, Nagtok gave birth

to a child, while people lay around her dying of hunger. What did the child want here? How could it live, when its mother, who should give it life, was herself dried up and starving? So she strangled it and allowed it to freeze and later on ate it."

Infanticide was widely practiced among the Eskimos, particularly in hard times. Girls were valued less than boys because they would not grow up to become hunters and providers of food. Usually, it was the father who decided that a baby girl must be killed, but it was the mother who actually did the deed. Sometimes she simply placed a caribou skin over the infant's face until she stopped breathing. Or the mother laid the infant in

The Dog and Sled: Tundra Transportation

Though numerous Indians, particularly those of the Subarctic, employed toboggans for winter transport, the Eskimos developed a true sled—a platform of crosspieces raised off the ground by two runners. The best sleds were made of wood, but except in the Hudson and Davis Straits regions, where driftwood was plentiful, Eskimos were often forced to use other, heavier materials: whale bones for the runners and caribou antlers for the crosspieces. And when bone was in short supply, a skin tent was sometimes cut in half, the two pieces rolled up and frozen, and then used as serviceable runners. Among the Netsiliks frozen fish—laid overlapping, end-to-end—were often used to fill the interiors of skin runners. When spring arrived, making sledding impossible, the fish began to thaw, and the Netsiliks unwrapped the fish and ate them.

The sleds were pulled by teams of huskies; a lightweight wood sled needing only 6 or so of the animals, while the heavier skin and bone models required teams of as many as 16. Each team had a lead dog, the smartest of the lot, that was both feared and respected by the others. Its job was to direct the team according to the verbal orders of its master and the signals of the whip. When warm weather turned the tundra surface to marshes, the Eskimos put aside their sleds, and the dogs were left free to forage.

The husky, the Eskimos' only domestic animal, performs two vital functions. Not only does it pull sleds, but it uses its keen sense of smell to find seals for hunters.

Before beginning a winter journey, Eskimos polish the surfaces of their sled's runners, as at left. The runners are long strips of baleen or ivory lashed to the sled. These are covered with a preparation of frozen clay and moss, and then made slick with a rubbing of ice. The purpose, of course, is to cut down friction and improve the sled's gliding ability. The wood sled being loaded (above) is a central Arctic type, which can be anywhere from 5 to 15 feet long and several feet wide, depending on the weight and bulk of the cargo it is meant to carry. This sled is backless, but backs are often used in other areas. In the east dogs are hitched in a fan-shaped formation, as shown above, but among western Eskimos a long, single trace of dogs is preferred.

the entrance to the igloo, and there the baby screamed until she froze to death in the snow.

In killing off so many infant girls, the Eskimos created great social problems for themselves. Competition for the limited number of marriageable women was intense and often violent. To guarantee that their sons would have wives when they grew up, mothers would seek out the mothers of newly born girls. If a match was agreed upon, a small gift was made to the girl's mother and the eventual marriage was almost a certainty.

Still many boys did not have promised wives, and when they reached adulthood there were few women available. Sometimes these young men would hear of nearby tribes that practiced infanticide to a lesser degree and therefore had more marriageable women; so the men would set off on wife-hunting expeditions across the snow. Some of the young men were lucky enough to find an unattached woman in their own camp—a widow, perhaps, or a woman who had abandoned her husband or had been abandoned by him. The more aggressive of the young unmarried men stole other men's wives, often by outright force. A wife was an Eskimo's most valuable possession, and wife-stealing often touched off violence, murder, and family vendettas that lasted for years. On rare occasions the stealing of a man's wife by an Eskimo from another camp led to something resembling warfare between the camps.

Many Eskimo camps apparently seethed with hostility and aggression. Wife-stealers were hated, wife-exchangers grew jealous, unmarried men envied the married, poor hunters were despised and ridiculed, shamans were feared, and nonkinsmen were viewed with the deepest distrust. During the long, dark winter on the ice, nerves grew taut, and malicious gossip pervaded the camp. Fistfights erupted for trivial reasons, property was destroyed out of malice, and shamans summoned the spirit world to harm their enemies. "If he tries to take my wife he will look up at the sky," one Eskimo would threaten. (To "look up at the sky" meant to lie dead on the ice with one's face upturned to the sky.) On occasion, Eskimos murdered their neighbors with sharp snow knives—usually by surprise, from behind. Sometimes the murderer, fearing revenge, left the camp and sought refuge with relatives in a nearby tribe.

There were no laws to punish wrongdoers among the Eskimos. But there were a number of accepted ways for an aggrieved Eskimo to get some satisfaction. Often an Eskimo who believed he had been wronged would challenge another Eskimo to a fistfight. These were carried out in a carefully prescribed way. The two men stripped to the waist and faced each other. Only one blow could be delivered at a time, and no defense was allowed. The challenged man was allowed to go first, and then the two fighters took turns, pummeling each other with punches to the neck and temple. This went on until one man gave up or was knocked out. And when the fight was over, the quarrel that had started it

was regarded as settled. In some tribes ear-pulling or nose-pulling contests between adversaries served the same purpose as the fistfight.

Another way of settling a dispute was the "song duel." Like the songs exchanged by friendly song partners, these also took place in the ceremonial house and were attended by all the adult Eskimos in the camp. But in the duel the songs were far from friendly. One Eskimo would accuse the other of all manner of things, from being henpecked and a poor hunter to incest, bestiality, and murder. The adversaries used all their guile and wit to win over the audience, and the Eskimo who gained the greater approval for this performance was regarded as the winner of the duel. No other verdicts were rendered and no punishments were meted out, but the adversaries had unburdened themselves of their complaints and that often satisfied them and averted violence.

Ugak, the adopted son of Apitok, was challenged to a song duel. The challenger was Kuliut, and in his song he accused Ugak of many misdeeds. He commented scornfully on the young man's lack of hunting skill, telling how Ugak had actually let a seal escape after he had got his harpoon into its side. Kuliut also suggested that Ugak had stolen some frozen meat from his igloo—a serious charge among the Eskimos. Kuliut's sarcastic song was well received by the other Eskimos. Ugak, when his turn came, produced a clumsy song, accusing Kuliut of lusting after his own sister and—even worse—of laziness on the hunt. In the end it was plain that the Eskimos favored Kuliut, and they did not speak to Ugak. In a rage, he went back to Apitok's igloo, wrapped clothes and tools in a sealskin tent, and collected his weapons. Then, without a word, he left the igloo and the camp and disappeared into the snowy wasteland.

In most cases punishment for misdeeds was strictly a family affair, and often it took the form of banishment from the community for a time. In some cases, however, the Eskimos did go as far as to sanction execution. Mental derangement was common in the Arctic, and sometimes a seriously disturbed person would come to be a menace to his family and other people in the community. A shaman might misuse his powers and cause illness and injury through his black arts. On such occasions the relatives of the one perceived to be dangerous would meet and discuss his fate. If they agreed that the situation was serious enough, they would decide to kill him—either by stabbing or strangling. The execution was always carried out by a close relative so there would be no cause for revenge.

If the natural world of the Arctic was harsh and demanding, the supernatural world was no less threatening, no less real to the Eskimos. Faced with so much that they could not explain, the Eskimos evolved a rich array of other-world spirits and deities. They were extremely credulous people. "It is said that it is so," they would explain, "and therefore it is so."

With local variations Eskimos all across the central regions of the Arctic told the story of Sedna and how the world came to be. The following is a version Eskimos passed down through the centuries:

"Once there was a beautiful girl named Sedna, who married a seagull and went with him to the country of the gulls. But once there, Sedna was wretched, and she called out to her father to come and rescue her. The father went to the land of gulls, killed the seagull husband, and fled the land of the gulls in his boat with Sedna. The other gulls were sad, and they continue to mourn and cry until this day. They flew after Sedna and her father and caused a great storm to threaten the boat. Hopeful of appeasing the birds, the father flung Sedna overboard. She clung to the edge of the boat, but the father cut off the first joints of her fingers, which became whales when they fell into the sea. When Sedna still continued to hold on to the boat, her father cut off the second joints, which swam away as walruses. Then he cut off the stumps of the fingers, and these became seals.

"The storm subsided, for the gulls thought Sedna had drowned. But Sedna took up an abode in the bottom of the sea. There she became the sea spirit and mother of the sea beasts. She sent out the animals that served to nourish mankind, or she withheld the supply, causing want and famine. When the people on earth displeased her by their behavior or by breaking taboos, she punished them with starvation."

To many Eskimos, Sedna—called Nuliajunk by some—was the supreme deity. But other powerful gods also inhabited their universe. Narssuk was a gigantic baby who was the master of wind and snow, and he despised mankind. A more agreeable deity was Tatqeq, or the moon spirit. It he wished, Tatqeq could bring good fortune to the hunter and fertility to women. Eskimo women did not sleep exposed to the moon if they did not wish to become pregnant.

Among the Alaskan Eskimos, Sedna was less important than Moon Man (a version of Tatqeq). Moon Man ruled the skies and the souls of game animals and human beings. Among the Caribou Eskimos, who were almost wholly dependent on the antlered animal for

A naturally waterproof parka, sewn from strips of seal intestines, kept the kayak-borne Eskimo dry in rough seas. When maximum protection was needed, the parka was worn with a hood, and the skirt of the jacket tied to the rim of the kayak opening. This Alaskan parka, with its low neckline, reflects Russian influence. The Russians, in turn, copied the use of sea mammal intestines for clothing.

survival, the principal deity was Mother of the Caribou.

In addition to the gods, hosts of other supernatural beings and spirits populated the Eskimo universe. Of greatest importance were human souls, which inhabited the body, animated it, and gave it personality. Human souls might get lost or be stolen by some evil shaman, thus causing disease or madness. When that happened, the Eskimos would ask the help of a friendly shaman in finding the soul and returning it to its proper place.

After death, human souls lived on. If the proper death taboos had not been observed, those souls could turn into wicked spirits, which lurked about the camp and took terrible vengeance on the living. But if the proper taboos had been observed, the souls would go to live peacefully in one of three Eskimo afterworlds. Two of these, the first, high in the sky and the other, deep within the earth, were beautiful lands of continual pleasure. Only the souls of brave hunters and women with large and beautiful tattoos were admitted. The third afterworld was just below the surface of the earth, and it was there that the souls of lazy hunters and women who could not endure the pain of tattooing were sent. It was an ugly place, where the souls were idle, melancholy, and hungry; the only food these unhappy souls got to eat were butterflies.

An Eskimo's name was also thought to have a powerful soul with the power to protect its bearer from harm. Therefore, many Eskimos sought added protection by taking a variety of names. There are records of Eskimos who had dozens. When a newborn baby cried, the Eskimos believed, it was crying out for an additional name or for a name other than the one already bestowed on it. Another name must be quickly given.

To the Eskimos the souls of animals, particularly of game animals, were also of extreme importance. When a hunter killed an animal, respect had to be paid to the soul of the dead beast, and strict taboos had to be observed. "Thank you for coming," an Eskimo wife would say to the lifeless head. "You must be thirsty." Then she would trickle a little water into its mouth. If everything was done correctly, the animal's soul was pleased, thereby assuring that it would reappear again in another animal body someday and again allow itself to be killed by man. If, on the other hand, the taboos were violated, the animal soul could become enraged

Returning from the hunt, Eskimos head for harbor. The most distant kayak tows two inflated bladders, used to buoy a harpoon line and keep the carcass of a sea mammal afloat.

Kayaks: The Eskimos' Swift Hunting Craft

Like the snow igloo, the kayak has long been considered a hallmark of the Eskimos. Only those Eskimos of the deep interior do not use these sleek, speedy, lightweight craft that skim silently through the water, allowing the hunter to stealthily approach his sea mammal prey.

In general, kayaks are one-man craft, though the Nunivak Island type takes two men, back to back, in a single cockpit. Kayaks, rather like covered canoes, vary somewhat in shape and weight according to local conditions. In areas where the waters are usually calm, a typical kayak is designed for lightness—both for portaging between watercourses and for paddling—and maneuverability. Obviously, such a craft is ill-adapted to rough seas, and a kayak for use in such waters is heavier and larger.

Whatever the design, the kayak's skeleton is of driftwood (usually fir, pine, spruce, or willow), and the preferred covering is sealskin or sea lion skin, with the fur removed. Skins are well soaked, then stretched over a frame, and sewn together with sinew. Seal oil is used to make the covering waterproof. The usual method of propelling a kayak is with a single or double-bladed paddle, the latter being employed when speed is important. Sometimes kayaks are lashed together for hauling cargo, and among some Alaskans two kayaks are linked in a parallel formation and fitted with a mast and sails. The resulting design is similar to that of a twin-hulled catamaran, a craft with good maneuverability and remarkable stability in rough waters.

The kayak is so swift, maneuverable, and relatively safe that its use has been widely adopted by American sportsmen for activities as varied as fishing and rapids-running. Among the Netsilik Eskimos, the shallow drafts of these vessels make them useful for caribou hunting at the animals' water-crossings. When a herd enters the shallows, waiting Eskimos paddle swiftly to confront them, spears at the ready. Women and children on shore act as beaters.

To make waterproof seams on the skin coverings of kayaks, Eskimo women overlap the skins, sewing a double row of stitches with sinew thread. The first line of stitches is sewn from the outside, along the outer edge of the overlap. This close stitch (far left) is called silalik *("takes the weather"), and it produces a waterproof seam. When all outside stitching is completed, the women reinforce the seams with a second sinew binding of whipstitches, as at near left.*

Ceremonial masks *were important elements in Eskimo festivals, both religious and secular. In general, masks that realistically portrayed humans or animals were worn during secular dances, while the more abstract and stylized kinds had religious significance. Masks were based on visions seen by shamans, but often they were fashioned by carvers working under the direction of a medicine man. Only the shaman who had seen the vision ever knew the precise meaning of his mask, but others had a general idea of its significance, for each mask represented the spirit of the creature it depicted. Though many spirits, whether of animals or of forces of nature, were depicted in highly stylized human forms, other forms, such as the round mask bearing several concentric circles (second from left), were complete abstractions. The complex mask at top depicts the spirit of a shaman sitting astride a beaver's spirit. The one at right represents all seals—living and dead—but the significance of the mask at far left is unknown.*

Finger masks (right) were used by women dancers at ceremonials, while the men wore face masks. Often the finger masks were replicas, in miniature, of the human or animal images worn by the men. Decorations around the finger masks included, as above, fur and feathers, though caribou hair was also commonly employed. As the women danced, the flow of fur and feathers attached to the masks accentuated the movements of the hands. Most masks were made of driftwood—usually cottonwood or spruce. Where wood was in short supply, Eskimos frequently used whale bone as a substitute, as in the one at left.

and turn into a fiend that would bring terrible misfortune down on the entire community.

In the Eskimo mind, demons of all sorts also lurked across the Arctic wastes. Some of these were giants; others, dwarfs. Some were relatively genial, but others were fearsome, bloodthirsty maneaters. A demon also might look exactly like an ordinary human being, a situation that made Eskimos all the more suspicious when they encountered strangers on their travels.

Clearly, the Eskimos needed help in coping with the world of the supernatural, and so, over the centuries, they evolved a bewildering variety of rituals and taboos. Many of these had to do with their chief preoccupations—hunting and game animals. Mixing the flesh of land and sea animals in a meal, or using the same weapons to kill them, was taboo. It was taboo for dogs to chew on the bones of a whale or the antlers of a caribou. The division of the world into land things and sea things was so deeply ingrained in the Eskimos that it was even taboo to cook caribou meat over a fire of ocean driftwood. Many taboos concerned the polar bear, whose soul was reckoned to be extremely dangerous. When a bear was killed, the skin had to be hung inside the igloo for five days—the length of time that the bear's soul remained on the tip of the spear that killed it. On the skin of the dead bear the Eskimos hung presents in an effort to pacify its soul.

Dead seals, too, were treated with the utmost respect. It was strictly taboo to place a seal's dead body on a dirty igloo floor and to do other work while an unbutchered seal lay in an igloo. It was taboo to have old blubber in the igloo when a freshly killed seal was brought in. Seal meat could not be cooked over anything but a blubber lamp. And if the Eskimos changed sealing camps in the winter, they would arrange the skulls of seals that had been killed so that they faced in the direction of the new campsite. In that way the friendly souls of those dead seals might follow the hunters and bring them good fortune.

Among the Eskimos childbirth was also surrounded

*This **abstract mask** from the lower Yukon is one of the most celebrated pieces of Eskimo art, though its function was religious rather than esthetic. The mask is basically of wood, but other materials are also used. The bow, for example, is strung with a seal thong, and the two faces are linked with baleen.*

A moon goddess mask of Alaska's Unalit Eskimos depicts the features of a real woman whose beauty is enhanced by facial tattoos and a lower lip ornament. The rings around the mask may represent supernatural worlds. Masks representing the sun and moon deities are common among Eskimos, but this mask is unusual because the moon is depicted as a woman.

by taboos. The expectant mother was not permitted to remain in the igloo, because she was deemed to be unclean. Instead, the woman was isolated in another, small igloo, where she delivered the child herself. After the birth the woman was moved into a larger, but still separate, igloo for a month. During that time she was not allowed to engage in sexual activities or eat the meat of animals caught by hunters other than her husband. For a whole year after giving birth, a properly trained Eskimo woman was expected to eat only late at night or early in the morning. She also was not allowed to eat raw meat and had to keep her drinking bowl bottom-upward when she was not using it.

When an Eskimo died, it was extremely important for the whole camp to heed the taboos, lest the dead person's soul cause great harm to befall it. For four or five days, the Eskimos believed, the soul remained in the dead body. During that time members of the dead Eskimo's family could do no work, and others in the camp could not comb their hair, cut their nails, feed their dogs, or clean their soapstone lamps. When the mourning period had come to an end, relatives

Among the oldest Eskimo masks yet found, this one from the Canadian Arctic dates back about 1,000 years, evidence of the antiquity of the art in the North.

placed the body on a sled, drove far away from camp, and left the corpse on the ice.

The Eskimos also placed great faith in amulets—objects endowed with supernatural power that helped them on the hunt, assured them good health, and propitiated the spirit world. Usually, the amulets were small objects: stones, teeth, miniature knives, pieces of animal skin. When the Eskimos traveled, the amulets—sometimes dozens of them—were attached to their clothing. These amulets, which increased in power as they got older, had very specific functions. A small piece of polar bear bone, for example, was expected to make its owner invisible when stalking the caribous.

Every Eskimo had intimate ties with the spirit world, but those with the strongest links with the supernatural were the shamans. Respected and feared, these priest-sorcerers were sometimes called upon by the community at large to divine the reasons for a scarcity of game animals or to predict weather conditions for an important hunting season. If the game was scarce, a shaman might go into a trance and travel to the bottom of the sea to visit Sedna, in hopes of getting her to release the game animals. Or, if he wished, a powerful shaman could unleash the fury of the supernatural world against the community or against individual enemies.

Shamans usually were hunters, husbands, and members of the camp. But it was clear to the other Eskimos that they were men with special powers. They could speak in a secret tongue passed down from shaman to shaman since ancient times. They were entitled to wear a special headdress and belt. Most important of all, each shaman possessed a *tunraq*, a protective spirit that helped him in his supernatural calling.

Among other things the shamans were healers. Eskimos worried continually about injury, disease, and the mental disorders brought on by their constant concern about survival. Such misfortunes, they believed, were caused by a failure to observe the taboos, by magical attacks by hostile shamans, or by the theft or loss of their souls. Disease induced by an enemy shaman could be cured by a more powerful shaman. He was able to find the soul stolen by the wicked shaman and return it to the sick Eskimo, thereby effecting a cure.

The best shamans were intensely theatrical, and many of their activities were carried out before audiences, either in their own igloos or in the ceremonial house. Sometimes the shamans employed trances, ventriloquism, and slight of hand in their performances. It was customary during these sessions for apprentice shamans to help create the proper air of mystery by moving objects about on unseen strings in the dim light. In pursuit of psychological healing, or of harnessing the forces of nature and the supernatural, the shamans had many arcane tricks at their command, and they did not hesitate to use them to full effect on their credulous fellow Eskimos.

For days Apitok had felt weak and downcast. He returned Tallerk to her husband and brought Moraq back to his igloo, but her familiar presence did not make him feel any better. So he went to Kamjuq, a most powerful shaman, who told Apitok that an evil spirit had invaded his body. Now, in the ceremonial igloo, as Apitok and a dozen other Eskimos peered through the semidarkness, Kamjuq crouched in a corner under a caribou skin. Suddenly, a torrent of strange words came from his mouth and then a frightful howling. Then something began fluttering around in the dark, and the Eskimos whispered to themselves that the shaman's tarnaq had somehow sucked the evil spirit out of Apitok's body and that the spirit was now trying to escape. "Wait, wait," they cried out to it as Kamjuq woke from his trance and sprang to his feet.

A healing ceremony *is conducted by an Eskimo shaman, who bangs on a tambourine and invokes the spirits while the patient and his family await a cure. The Eskimos believed that most illness was caused by the loss of one's soul, and it was the function of the shaman to retrieve it and thus restore the victim to health. Here the shaman kneels by the entrance well of the patient's house, a pair of mittens dangling from his legs. One sign of the spirits' presence would be the disappearance of the mittens into the well. Should that occur, the shaman will engage in a seemingly fierce struggle to retrieve the mittens, which will presumably hold the patient's soul. Or the shaman might fall into a days-long trance, at the end of which he would be in possession of the soul. A cure brought a shaman almost any fee he demanded.*

Cornering the spirit, the shaman uttered some secret charm, then took his snow knife and began to lunge and slash. The spellbound Eskimos heard the evil spirit shriek with pain and then gasp in a final spasm. As Kamjuq's wife lighted one of her lamps, the exhausted shaman put down his knife and displayed the blood of the dead spirit on his hands. All the Eskimos praised Kamjuq, and Apitok promised to kill a seal for him. With the wicked spirit no longer in his body, Apitok felt as strong and cheerful as ever.

As the winter progressed, the Eskimos would often exhaust one sealing site and decide to move on to another, sometimes a considerable distance away. But first they repaired their sleds or built new ones for the journey. Driftwood was scarce in many Eskimo areas, and so they often fashioned the sled runners out of sealskin wrapped around frozen fish or wood and tightly bound by sealskin thongs. Crossbars were made from caribou antlers and fastened to the runners with heavier thong. Once the frame was ready, the Eskimos made a thick paste of earth and decayed vegetable matter. They smeared this mixture a few inches thick on the underside of the runners, smoothed it, and then let

it freeze solid. The Eskimos then rubbed a piece of wet bearskin over the mud layer, creating a hard, thin layer of ice that enabled the sled to glide smoothly over the snow. The mud "shoes" on the runners would last for months, but the ice glazing soon wore off and had to be renewed each day.

When the sleds were ready, the teams of huskies were assembled. The same hardy breed of dog was used all across the Arctic. Among the Greenland Eskimos and the Central Eskimos each dog was hitched to its own trace, so that the team spread out fanwise in front of the sled, with the lead dog—usually a female—in front of the others. The western Eskimos favored one long trace, to which the dogs were yoked in pairs.

From time to time the strong, tough huskies shared in the dangers of the Eskimos' everyday life. Traveling from one sealing site to another, for example, the Eskimos sometimes detected polar bear tracks. The Eskimos respected these fierce creatures, but they also prized their meat and skins highly; so they almost always dropped their other pursuits and tracked the polar bear. When they found it, the Eskimos unleashed their dogs, which rushed furiously at the bear from all sides, howling and snapping. The bear took vicious

The Bladder Dance, *part of which is depicted in this model of carved ivory, is one of the many Eskimo ceremonials intended to propitiate the spirits of the animals and thus ensure successful hunts. This dance, performed by male Eskimos who live beside the Bering Sea, honored sea mammals, whose meat, skin, blubber, and other parts were vital to the survival of the people. The festival, which sometimes lasted more than a week, took place in the men's ceremonial house—the kashim. The scene shown here would have occurred near the ceremonial's end and involves the honoring of sea mammals through the ritual handling of their air-inflated bladders. The animal's soul was said to reside in the bladder.*

During the ceremonial period the men and boys who took part kept themselves pure by avoiding women and taking sweat baths each day. Though the ritual did involve some singing and dancing, the sound was muted, for loud or unpleasant noises were believed to disturb the souls of the animals. The festival neared its conclusion when the bladders were collected, deflated, and returned to the waters—their natural habitat. A display of gymnastics and an exchange of gifts ended the rite.

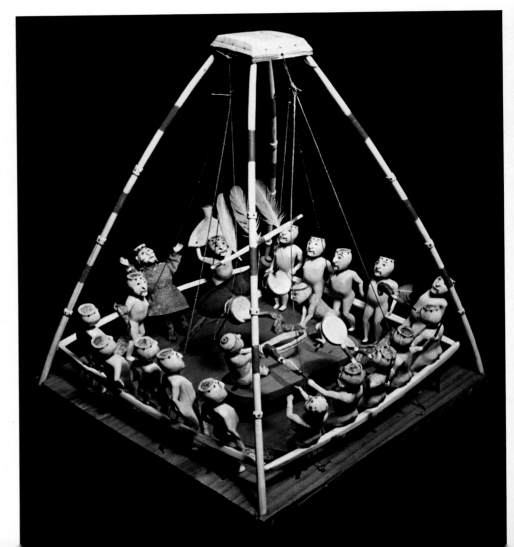

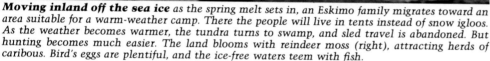
Moving inland off the sea ice as the spring melt sets in, an Eskimo family migrates toward an area suitable for a warm-weather camp. There the people will live in tents instead of snow igloos. As the weather becomes warmer, the tundra turns to swamp, and sled travel is abandoned. But hunting becomes much easier. The land blooms with reindeer moss (right), attracting herds of caribous. Bird's eggs are plentiful, and the ice-free waters teem with fish.

swipes at its tormentors, but the dogs were quick and usually avoided its murderous claws.

As the dogs kept the bear at bay, the Eskimos planned their strategy. If they had with them the kind of heavy spear used to hunt musk-oxen, they would try to wound the bear mortally from a distance. If not, they had to attack the awesome beast at close quarters with their lighter sealing harpoons or bows and arrows. These fights were extremely dangerous, and often the Eskimos ended up with deep scratches or more severe wounds. But they were tenacious hunters and, if necessary, they would fight on for hours. In the end the bear usually was killed, its meat was shared, and the skin was kept by the hunter judged to have delivered the fatal thrust—a reward for his valor.

Spring Hunting

Toward the end of the winter the days lengthened as the sun rose higher and brighter above the horizon. In some areas small animals, such as white foxes and squirrels, began to reappear. The Eskimos caught them with simple snares or crude traps—resembling miniature huts—made of flat stones. Seal meat bait was used to lure the animal inside; then an Eskimo, who was hidden nearby, shoved a stone trapdoor closed on his prey.

At this time of the year the Eskimos—weary of eating seal meat—cut holes in the sea ice and fished for cod and other Arctic fish. Or if they were close to the craggy cliffs where seagulls nested, they hunted these birds and their eggs. Always quick to devise new hunting stratagems, the Eskimos sometimes built little igloos, which they constructed with especially thin ceilings.

They placed a bit of seal liver on top of the igloo as bait and then went inside to sit and wait. When a seagull landed to snatch the bait, the Eskimos would thrust their hands up through the ceiling and grab the bird by the legs.

In the early days of spring many Eskimos remained on the ice and continued to hunt the seals. But it was not as difficult as it was in the dead of winter. Toward the end of March the seals would dig their way through their breathing holes and come up on the ice to give birth. The baby seals had not yet learned to swim; so the Eskimos simply caught them by hand on the ice.

About the beginning of May the snow igloos began to melt and drip, forcing the Eskimos to remove the roofs and drape sealskins over the top of the buildings. This type of dwelling, half ice house and half tent, was called a *karmaq*. In the early summer the Eskimos dismantled them and moved off the melting ice onto firm land. The snow was also melting, and patches of exposed tundra could be seen. The large winter camp, a necessity because many hunters were needed for effective midwinter seal hunting, broke up, and smaller camps of sealskin tents dotted the coastline.

From their new camps the Eskimos continued to hunt seals until well into June. There was no longer a snow cover, and the breathing holes were clearly visible. Women and children with sticks would stand over some of the holes and frighten seals back underwater when they came up to breathe. Since the seals needed air, they eventually surfaced at holes where hunters were waiting with their deadly harpoons. As the days grew warmer, the seals made hunting even easier by

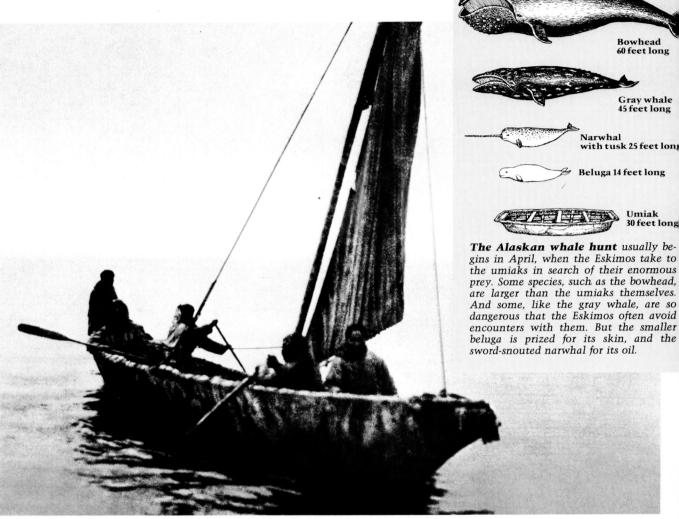

The Alaskan whale hunt *usually begins in April, when the Eskimos take to the umiaks in search of their enormous prey. Some species, such as the bowhead, are larger than the umiaks themselves. And some, like the gray whale, are so dangerous that the Eskimos often avoid encounters with them. But the smaller beluga is prized for its skin, and the sword-snouted narwhal for its oil.*

Bowhead
60 feet long

Gray whale
45 feet long

Narwhal
with tusk 25 feet long

Beluga 14 feet long

Umiak
30 feet long

An all-purpose craft—*cargo carrier, passenger boat, and hunting gig—the open-decked umiak is sturdier and larger than the kayak and therefore suitable for major migrations and the hunting of whales and walruses. The typical umiak is 20 to 30 feet long and is made from seal or walrus skins—waterproofed with seal oil—sewn over a whale bone frame. The umiak combines speed, maneuverability, and lightness with considerable strength, and the flexibility of its skin helps protect the craft from floating ice. The boat is usually rowed, but occasionally a sail, as above, supplements the efforts of the oarsmen.*

coming up on the ice to bask. When hunters spotted a basking seal, they had several ways of stalking it. The simplest was to inch across the ice behind a blind covered with clean white polar bear skin until close enough to strike. Other Eskimos tried to imitate the movements and the sounds of seals. They dragged themselves across the ice, using their hands and legs in flipperlike gestures. And they scratched on the ice with their knives to imitate the sound of a seal clawing on the ice. Some Eskimos even made guttural, seal-like noises. All the while they were creeping closer and closer to the seal. When they came close enough, they would jump to their feet, rush at the seal, and harpoon it before it could disappear down its breathing hole.

Along the Labrador coast, and especially in northern Alaska, spring was the time for the most exciting and

perilous event of the year for the Eskimos—the great whale hunt. When the warming temperatures caused the ice along the coast to break up, leaving lanes of open water, the bowhead whales began their annual migration to the north. They were huge beasts, 60 feet or more in length and weighing up to 60 tons. In preparation for their coming, the Eskimos mended their umiaks—boats made of skin and whale bone that were large enough to carry a dozen or more people. The wives sewed waterproof suits of walrus skin for the hunters, and in the ceremonial houses the hunters chanted songs urging the whales to come and be killed by their harpoons.

When the spouting whales offshore were sighted by the Eskimos, the men hurried to launch their umiaks. Each boat was manned by six paddlers, a harpooner standing in the bow, and a crew leader who sat in the stern maneuvering the boat with a steering paddle. The crew leader was also the owner of the umiak, and he was expected to outfit the boat and provide the lines, weapons, and whale-hunting amulets that hung along the gunwales. Around his neck the owner-steersman wore the skin of a raven, beak pointing downward toward the whales. To increase the chance of success, the owner usually gave the crewmen permission to sing his personal whaling songs, which he had obtained by inheritance or by purchase. These chants not only summoned the whales but weakened them for the kill.

As the whales dived, the crewmen in the lead umiak paddled furiously and sang, while the crew leader steered them toward the place where he expected a whale to surface the next time. When the whale broke water, the paddlers edged the umiak to within a few feet of the mighty animal. Then the harpooner, using every bit of his strength, plunged the weapon into its side. As the head of the weapon sank deeply into the whale, the wounded animal began to thrash furiously in the foaming sea. The line, which was attached to the harpoon head, whizzed overboard, carrying drags of inflated sealskin along with it. The whale dived, but the Eskimos followed its underwater course, and when it surfaced again, the harpooner was ready for another thrust, and another. Finally, exhausted by its wounds and the steady tug of the sealskin drags, the whale no longer had the strength to dive.

With the leviathan now resting quietly on the surface, the Eskimos paddled up to its side. The harpooner lifted a heavy, stone-pointed lance and stabbed it into the whale's side, searching for the kidneys, heart, or lungs. This was the most dangerous time of the hunt, since the whale thrashed convulsively as the lance pierced its vitals. Eskimos were poor swimmers; so the paddlers maneuvered carefully to keep from being overturned. The death throes continued, the whale began to spout blood, and soon it floated dead.

As the crewmen shouted in triumph, other umiaks

The ungainly looking walrus, *whose nature is usually placid, can turn aggressive when attacked. A mature male may be up to 12 feet long and weigh 3,000 pounds. It uses its tusks to uproot clams and other shellfish on the sea bottom.*

converged on the spot to help with the job of towing the mammoth catch to shore. Sometimes it took long, hard hours of paddling to reach land, where the entire camp came out to help drag the giant carcass onto the ice for butchering. The head was severed, and—just as with the butchering of seal—the wife of the victorious hunter politely offered it a drink of water. She also urged the soul of the dead whale to return to the land of the whales and tell its fellows how decently it had been treated. After butchering, the tons of whale meat were distributed among the camp members in an atmosphere of jubilation. Much of the meat was buried in storage pits dug into the permafrost, while the blubber, or whale fat, was made into oil or saved for trading later in the year with inland Eskimos for caribou skins or furs.

In some parts of the Arctic, Eskimos also hunted the small white whale, or beluga, an animal 14 to 16 feet in length. The most fearsome denizen of the western Arctic was the orca, or killer whale. Because of its ferocious qualities, the orca often appears in Eskimo folklore. Although the Eskimos were courageous and determined hunters, few believed it worth the risk to attack the "tiger of the sea."

In June the Pacific walrus, a formidably tusked sea mammal of more than two tons in weight, began to crowd the waters off Alaska. About the same time the slightly smaller Atlantic walrus appeared off the Labrador coast and around Baffin Island. These powerful beasts were herding animals, and often the Eskimos would find large numbers of them basking on some rocky promontory or ice floe.

When the Eskimos spotted a walrus herd, they would creep as close as possible without being seen and then rush at the herd with their harpoons. It was not a

Alaskan baleen trinket baskets *decorated with ivory are made for the tourist trade, for these materials are usually thought too valuable for domestic use. The baleen comes from certain species of whales. They have baleen plates instead of teeth and use the plates to filter plankton and crustaceans from seawater. Eskimos separate the bristly plates into strands for weaving.*

one-sided struggle. Usually placid animals, the walruses became dangerous when attacked. Their sharp tusks, normally used for uprooting mollusks on the ocean floor, were lethal weapons. Sometimes these mighty creatures knocked or dragged Eskimos into the water and then turned on them furiously. On occasion the Eskimos used their kayaks to hunt walruses. But this was even more dangerous. The enraged animals often attacked the slender boats, charging them head-on, piercing their skin covering with their tusks and sending boats and Eskimos to the bottom.

To the Eskimos walrus hunting was well worth the risk. The meat was usable, the hide could be made into many articles of clothing, and the tusks provided ivory. From this, the Eskimos made many things, from knives and snow goggles to combs and labrets—the ornamental plugs worn beneath the lower lip by Alaskan Eskimos.

Summer Campsite

During the early summer the Eskimos gladly turned from hunting whales, walruses, and seals. The winter campsites dissolved into family groups; solitary hunters and traders drifted away on their own. Some Eskimos remained near the Arctic coast; the more enterprising moved farther inland for caribou and fish. Over parts of the tundra, brightly colored flowers bloomed; waterfowl swam in the lakes; rabbits, owls, and ptarmigans displayed their brown summer coats.

Moraq was happy, as she always was when the warm weather came and the family prepared to leave for the summer campsite. While Apitok fished or repaired the bone and wood frame of their kayak, she spent her days mending their summer tent by patching new sealskins over the worn spots.

Moraq spent hours sitting in the sun with her friends as she made waterproof sealskin boots and dog packs. When Apitok finished his work on the kayak's frame, she covered it with fresh sealskins. She took great care in this work, for the kayak was one of their most precious possessions. It was, in fact, one of the necessities for survival. It had to be ready for occasional use during the summer and—later on in the year—for hunting the caribou. In a few days time she and Apitok and a group of close relatives would be ready to start the inland trek; so Moraq sang softly to herself in the patch of flowers near the tent.

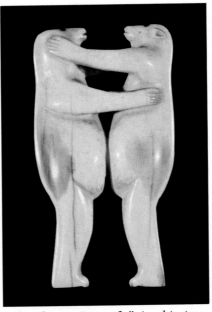

Polar bears "wrestle" in this ivory carving from coastal Alaska. This piece dates from the late 1800's, but carvings in bone and ivory go back much further. Carved figures of men and animals served as personal charms to bring luck in hunting and other endeavors.

With the snow cover gone on the tundra, sleds were no longer of use. In most cases the Eskimos left them behind, along with other winter equipment, in caches along the coast. The caches were built of stones on cliffs or offshore islands, where they would be easy to find in the fall and be secure from animal predators. Once these things had been done, the Eskimos strapped their summer equipment on their backs and headed inland on foot. Men, women, older children, and dogs—all were heavily burdened and sank into the muddy earth at every step.

In some parts of the Arctic, if the migration took place along a stream, the Eskimos eased their travel by taking their umiaks along. Summer clothing and equipment were piled on the boat, while the dogs trudged along the banks and pulled it forward with long, animal-skin thongs. Sometimes, during the summer migration, Eskimos paddled part of the way along streams in their kayaks. But usually the one-man boats were loaded with equipment or things to trade, making them exceedingly difficult to maneuver in the swift currents.

In most cases the Eskimos on the inland trek headed for a known fishing site, a place on a stream or river where the salmon ran in abundance during the summer. These places might be only a few miles inland, but often they were at great distances and took many days to reach.

After arriving at the fishing site and setting up tents, the Eskimos looked to their stone weirs. These were dams built across rivers at shallow, stony spots. Their walls, rising a foot or two above the water, slanted inward from the shore, forming a roughly V-shaped funnel. At the tip of it was a small opening, through which fish swimming upstream would enter a rounded basin, also built with stone walls.

These weirs were maintained from year to year, but during spring, when the river ice cracked, stones shifted and were carried away by the currents; so the first Eskimo men to reach the weirs in summer began to repair them, standing up to their waists in ice-cold water, laboriously finding, carrying, and setting in place new stones. The men worked quickly, since the weirs had to be ready for the first salmon run, about the first or second week in August.

Often only one family might camp at a fishing weir, but sometimes they were joined by other families.

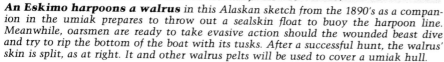

An Eskimo harpoons a walrus in this Alaskan sketch from the 1890's as a companion in the umiak prepares to throw out a sealskin float to buoy the harpoon line. Meanwhile, oarsmen are ready to take evasive action should the wounded beast dive and try to rip the bottom of the boat with its tusks. After a successful hunt, the walrus' skin is split, as at right. It and other walrus pelts will be used to cover a umiak hull.

The Walrus Hunt: Hides, Ivory, and Dog Food

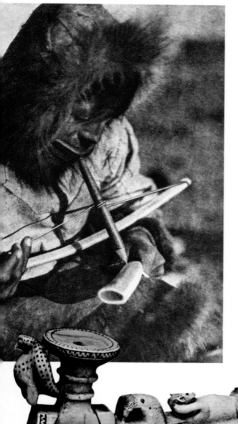

The huge Pacific walrus and its smaller Atlantic cousin are major objects of the hunt for Eskimos living along the Arctic coast from Alaska to Greenland. The animals, which travel in herds, appear in June with the northward movement of ice floes. During their annual migrations walruses do very little swimming; instead, they hitch rides upon the floes. In July and August, when the floes drift near the coast, the Eskimos pursue their lumbering prey. Traditionally, most of those walruses taken were dispatched by harpoon-wielding hunters in umiaks. Today guns are used. After the kill the women butcher the walruses.

Except for walrus flippers—which are allowed to ripen before cooking—the meat is usually not used as food for humans. But the flesh is stored and fed to the dogs, an important use considering the scarcity of meat in winter and the indispensable value of sled dogs. The teeth of walruses are carved into fish hooks, the bones are fashioned into harpoon parts, and the hides are invaluable as covering for umiak hulls. Of particular worth are the ivory tusks. Walrus ivory, with its hard marbled core and outer layer of enamel, is difficult to work, but its luster has long attracted Eskimo craftsmen. Before carving, they soften the ivory in urine, then score it until a suitable piece can be broken off. Traditionally, ivory carvings were simple, but with the coming of whites a considerable market has developed for elaborate scrimshaw work.

A mythical bird, perhaps the Raven, stands guard on the bowl of this ivory pipe from Alaska. Fashioned from a single walrus tusk, the pipe is elaborately decorated with carved animals and engraved hunting scenes. Various tools were used to make this pipe, but the most ingenious was the bow drill (left, above). The artisan uses his mouth to hold one end of the shaft, which he rotates with a bow, leaving one hand free to hold the ivory.

Standing beside a weir along the Arctic coast of Canada's Northwest Territories, a group of Eskimos plunge their spears into migrating Arctic chars, salmonlike fish. The weir, built across a stream, consists of two stone dams, a lower one with a small opening to allow the fish to get through, and an upper dam, completely closed. As the chars swim upstream, they are trapped as soon as they pass into the weir. During the late summer migrating season a single Netsilik family might catch 2,500 pounds of char, much of which would be split and then dried in the sun (top). These fish were taken with special spears called leisters, carried by the two men at right. The leister has a central bone point and two flanking barbs. The point spears the fish, and the barbs prevent its escape.

These Eskimos might be from widely scattered groups, but often the males had partnership relations, including summer wife-swapping. Each of the families had its own tent, pitched next to the river so the Eskimos could keep a close watch on the fish basin. As they waited for the salmon to start running, the men made certain that their leisters, the ingenious devices the Eskimos used to spear fish, were in sound working order. These weapons had long wooden shafts, at the end of which two prongs of musk-ox antler were tightly fixed. Each prong had a tiny hook of sharp bear bone. Between the prongs, set directly in the end of the shaft, was a needle-sharp tine of bone. When in use, this tine would sink into the fish, while the two prongs grasped it and prevented it from escaping.

When the Eskimos saw a school of fish heading to-ward the basin, the men quickly took off their trousers. Then they tied their sealskin boots around their legs just below the knee. This was to keep water that did get into their boots from splashing out again, since it became warmer than the river water and served as an insulation. The men assembled in front of the tent of the headman, usually the oldest capable hunter in the camp. When the entire school of fish was in the basin, the headman gave a signal. The men rushed to the shore, picked up their leisters, and waded into the river.

The first man to reach the basin sealed it closed with a large rock. Then all the men climbed into the basin and lunged furiously with their leisters. Gripped in each Eskimo's mouth was a long needle of bone, to which a sealskin thong was attached. As soon as a fish was speared, the Eskimo pulled it off the leister, skewered it with the needle, and strung it securely on the thong. The jabbing, the removing, and the skewering were done swiftly, and in an hour a fisherman often caught 50 or more salmon.

When they had speared all the fish, the Eskimos pulled them ashore and laid them on the ground in front of their tents. The wives then cleaned the fish with their sharp ulus, laying most of them out to dry in the warm sun.

The summer was a happy time for the Eskimos. The weather was clement, the food was abundant, and the anxieties of the midwinter were all but forgotten. The men found time for playing games with the children and making toys. Women gathered heather and prepared community banquets. They and the small children sat separately from the men. The pieces of fish, sometimes cooked, sometimes raw, were handed around from person to person. Each Eskimo would take a bite, then pass the fish along to the next person.

Flocks of ptarmigans, a low-flying Arctic bird, would sometimes flutter nearby. The Eskimos, especially the boys, would hunt them with bows and blunt arrows. The adult Eskimos killed the ptarmigans simply by flinging handfuls of stones at them. These birds were a minor part of the Eskimos diet, but they were esteemed as a delicacy and added variety to the summer fare of fish.

At all times of the year the taboos were remembered and observed. It was taboo to work in the fishing camp next to the river, because the hunting site was regarded as a holy place. Mending the leisters and the sewing of skins had to be done at a different location—an area nearby called the working place.

In some areas the Eskimo men went off on trading trips, leaving their women and children at the fishing camp. At some camps nets of whale bone were used instead of weirs. The nets were simply stretched across the river or stream, and while the men were away, the women hauled in the catch, cleaned it, and stored it in holes dug in the permafrost.

The men, meanwhile, walked or kayaked to settlements where inland Eskimos would be eager to trade. At some of these places the Eskimos from the Arctic coast traded whale blubber or oil for caribou skins. A piece of driftwood suitable for the frame of an umiak or the shaft of a lance was exchanged for a dozen wolverine skins. Nuggets of copper were traded for flintstones or wild ducks preserved whole in seal oil.

Among many Eskimos the end of August was the time to close the summer camp. The salmon no longer ran in great numbers, and the Eskimos spent their time making caches of fish. The sides of the caches were built of large boulders, arranged in a roughly oval shape. The floors were covered with a layer of gravel, on which the fish were neatly laid, all facing the same direction. Once full, the caches were covered with

heavy stones. They pressed down heavily on the fish, leaving no room for hungry foxes or other animals to get at the store. It was important for these caches to be secure from predators, for in the winter, if the seal hunting was going badly, the Eskimos would return to these caches of fish to avert starvation.

The Caribou Hunt

Once again the Eskimos prepared to take to the trail. They talked of the coming hunt for the caribou, that large North American relative of the reindeer, and of the best tactics for killing large numbers of them. During the summer months the caribou herds split into smaller groups that grazed over wide areas of northern Canada. Not until September did they come together into large herds again and begin their southern migration. This was the best time to hunt caribous. They were fat from summer grazing, and their new hair was short, making the skin just right for fashioning into winter clothing.

Just a few days before the Eskimo disbanded their summer camp, Ugak—the adopted son of Apitok and Moraq—returned from the tundra. He was gaunt and sullen, and he refused to tell Apitok where he had gone after leaving the winter camp in disgrace. Moreover, the young man was stranger than ever. He glared at the other Eskimos, clenching his fists and muttering threats.

The hunter Ootah, a friend of Apitok, came to see him in his tent. Ootah told him that neither he nor

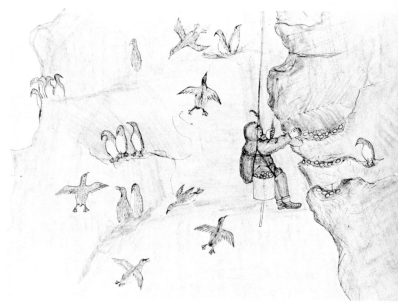

Suspended along the side of a cliff, an Eskimo gathers eggs from the nest of a guillemot in this fanciful sketch of the 1890's. Though the Eskimos liked eggs and went to great trouble to raid nests, they had little use, in general, for the meat of fowl. Only the ptarmigan and owl were hunted for their flesh.

An Eskimo family and their leashed pack dogs travel across the tundra to a summer fishing camp. At times the tundra becomes so swampy that dogs and people alike sink several inches into the mire, making each step a trial.

the other Eskimos trusted Ugak and did not want him to come along on the caribou hunt. Apitok was aware of Ugak's curious behavior. But he was, after all, a member of his family. Apitok remembered the many happy times when Ugak was a boy, following him around the camp and imitating his every move. He promised Ootah that he would talk to Ugak and make him mend his ways. Ootal was plainly dissatisfied, but because Apitok was a great hunter and a wise man whose opinion must be respected, Ootal reluctantly agreed that Ugak could join them on the hunt.

Expert and ingenious hunters, the Eskimos devised many ways of killing the caribou. Like other primitive people, they dug pits along paths that their prey was known to travel. They planted sharp knives in the pits, then covered them over with roofs of earth, moss and, sometimes, snow as a camouflage. But this was a rarely used method. The important ways of hunting the caribou were on foot with bow and arrow, and in kayaks with a spear.

When they were stalking the caribou, the Eskimos carried along sealskin quivers. In them were bows made of musk-ox horn, antler, and sinew, as well as arrows with wooden shafts and long bone points. Once they sighted some caribous, the huntsmen maneuvered carefully toward the animals, taking care not to startle them with sudden noises. They also tried to stay downwind of the caribous, because these animals had an extremely keen sense of smell and could easily pick up the pungent odor of Eskimos.

The hunters tried to find cover behind rocks or clumps of grass. Sometimes they would wait for hours, concealed, hoping that the caribous would wander within range of their arrows. If no cover existed, the Eskimos tried to imitate the caribous and thereby lull them into a sense of security. The hunters walked bent forward from the waist, trying to look from a distance like caribous. They held their bows and arrows upright to look like antlers and pretended they were grazing.

All the time the Eskimos moved closer to their prey, until they were close enough to let their arrows fly.

In some hunting situations the Eskimos divided themselves into beaters and archers. The beaters, howling like wolves, drove the frightened animals down a narrow valley. The archers crouched behind stone walls; as soon as the caribous drew close enough, they stood up and released a barrage of arrows. In another commonly used tactic a band of Eskimos would leap out of the woods, uttering loud shrieks and driving the animals onto the thin autumn ice cover of a lake. As the heavy animals galloped across the ice, it often gave way under their weight. When they struggled on the breaking ice, the Eskimos slew them with arrows or their heavy spears.

Eskimos took their kayaks along with them during the caribou-hunting season. They knew where the herds habitually swam across narrow lakes on their southward migration, and so they set up camp near one of those caribou crossings. Camps were located on high points, from which the Eskimos could watch the lake shores. When they saw a herd begin to wade into the water, an older huntsman gave the signal for the hunt to begin. The Eskimos rushed to the shore, climbed into their kayaks, then paddled furiously toward the swimming animals.

Maneuvering their narrow vessels close to the terrified beasts, the Eskimos thrust their spears at the animals' buttocks or kidneys. Many of the caribous were killed or wounded in the first fierce onslaught by the fleet of kayakers, but some managed to swim back to shore. There the Eskimo women and children howled

like wolves, frightening the caribous back into the water to face the kayakers once again. If the herd was a large one, a fast, skilled man could kill as many as 10 caribous in a single hunt. After it was over, each Eskimo gathered the caribous he had killed, tied their antlers together with thong, and towed the bodies to shore.

Unlike the sea mammals, the caribous were butchered by the men, as soon as they dragged them ashore. The Eskimos skinned the animals carefully and handed the hides and sinew over to the women, who took them off to dry near the camp. Then the hunters carved up the carcasses and carried the meat, along with marrow bones, back to their tents. The family was always waiting. The children were treated to the caribou's eyes, which they ate greedily. Men and women cut off pieces of raw meat and gulped them down. In the evening the entire camp came together for a community meal and gorged themselves on cooked caribou meat. Especially prized was the green, half-digested vegetable matter from the stomach of the caribou.

For Central Eskimos the caribou-hunting season lasted but a few weeks, and so the hunters had to be persistent. It was absolutely essential that each hunter kill enough caribou to provide the skins he, his wife, and his children would need for new winter clothes. These caribou skins were also used for mattresses and blankets, as well as for trading with other Eskimos encountered on the year's migrations. By the end of September the caribou-hunting season ended. The lakes and rivers were frozen solid, and the herds had disappeared toward the south. It was time to leave and move northward toward the Arctic coast.

Apitok did his best to get Ugak to stop behaving hostilely toward the other Eskimos. But warnings did no good. During the caribou hunt Ugak shot an arrow dangerously close to Ootah, though there was no animal nearby. Even worse, Ugak attempted to puncture Navik's kayak with his spear while the two were closing in on caribou on the lake. This was serious. Navik was a poor swimmer and might have drowned if his kayak had been sent to the bottom. At the end of the day's hunt Navik gave Ugak a severe and humiliating beating in a fistfight. Then the unhappy young man ran off, cursing, threatening to kill Navik and his whole family in their sleep.

To most of the Eskimos it was clear that Ugak was seriously deranged. The evening before they departed from the caribou-hunting camp, Ootah, Navik, and three other hunters invited Apitok for a talk on the high rocks outside camp. They told Apitok that Ugak had become so dangerous that he would have to be killed. And the execution, according to Eskimo custom, would have to be done by Ugak's closest of kin: Apitok.

The words of the other Eskimos did not surprise Apitok, for he had come to the same conclusion; so he nodded in agreement, examined the point of his snow knife, and went directly to Ugak's tent. Ugak was there, pacing up and down, grimacing and muttering. Apitok did not hesitate. In an instant he reached Ugak and thrust his knife three, four, five times into his breast. A little later, Ootah and Navik came and helped Apitok carry away the body of his adopted son and leave it on the tundra.

On a caribou hunt Eskimos use a common tactic to drive the animals into an ambush. Having spotted the grazing prey, women and children howl like wolves and wave their arms to frighten the caribous onto a narrow strip of ground between water and a ledge. Scarecrowlike objects of stone and turf have been placed strategically to keep the animals on course. At the end of the run hunters in shallow pits wait with their bows.

Practical Eskimo Garb

The two prime requisites for clothing among the Eskimos—protection against the bitter Arctic cold and pliability to facilitate movement—were carefully combined in all their wearing apparel: boots, mittens, pants, and parkas. The most commonly used materials for such garments were seal and caribou skins, though the hides of birds, ground squirrels, hares, and hoary marmots, as well as sea mammal intestines, were also used. Sealskin clothing, because of its natural water-resistance, was preferred for wear during the rainy season and on seagoing hunts. But for winter wear caribou skin was the material of choice. Though it is less durable than seal, it is softer and lighter, and because the individual caribou hairs are hollow and trap body heat, these hides provide more warmth than do sealskins.

In their details of style and decoration Eskimo clothing varied from one group to another, but in the basic design, particularly of the parka, all followed the same general pattern. The skins—one for the front, one for the back, and one fashioned into the two sleeves—were cut to follow loosely the contours of the body, but the garment was pulled tight at the waist to prevent updrafts of air. The backs of parkas worn by women with very small children were usually much wider than the fronts. This permitted a mother to carry her baby strapped securely inside the garment. There the infant, completely covered, was kept warm in even the most bitter weather. The general loose-

This Eskimo woman's costume of caribou skin has an appliquéd front panel of different colors. It fits loosely, except at the neck, wrists, and hips, thus retaining body heat and helping to keep the wearer warm in sub-zero weather.

ness of the parka, in addition to allowing free movement, provided another layer of insulation in the form of body heat. When only one parka was worn, the hair side was always against the body. Some Eskimo groups wore both an inner and outer parka, the inner being sleeveless—a kind of vest—again with the hair side in, the outer one worn with the fur side out.

Most parkas, both inner and outer, were hooded, and the hoods, which could be thrown back, were often trimmed with decorative bands of wolverine and fox fur.

Autumn Life

In the late fall the weather became bitter cold, freezing the lakes and the rivers and coating the tundra with a layer of hard frost. It was still too early for sealing; so the Eskimos lived on their caches of fish and caribou meat, and they fished the lakes and streams across the Arctic. Because the salmon and lake trout did not concentrate in large numbers in the fall, the 20 or so Eskimos of the caribou-hunting camp split up into smaller family groups, which tried their luck at scattered fishing spots.

The snow was not yet deep enough for building igloos, so the Eskimos shivered in their sealskin tents. With typical inventiveness, however, some Eskimos built more comfortable houses out of ice. The lake ice in the autumn was six or seven inches thick, and the Eskimos used their ice picks to carve out slabs and drag them ashore. Eight or 10 such slabs, welded together by wet snow, formed the walls of a hut. Tent skins were

used for roofs, giving the Eskimos a snug, warm shelter.

In order to fish through the lake or river ice, the Eskimos chopped round holes through to the water below. They fished with lines of plaited sinew and ivory lures, sometimes shaped like small fish. With his left hand an Eskimo jiggled his lure in the water; with his right hand he held his leister ready for the kill. When he saw a fish approach his lure, the Eskimo swiftly impaled it on the leister and hauled it up through the hole.

In some parts of the Arctic large herds of musk-oxen roamed, and in late autumn the Eskimos in those areas hunted the shaggy, horned animals. When the Eskimos found a herd, they unleashed their dogs, which rushed the beasts and circled them. Under attack, the male musk-oxen formed a protective circle around the females and the young. The males had formidable horns, but they were peaceful animals and rarely charged their attackers. The Eskimos stood at a distance from

The variagated styles of Eskimo clothing are illustrated in this museum display drawn from seven different Inuit groups. The two mannequins at far left are of a northwestern Alaskan man and woman, both wearing garments of caribou skins. Among this group, parkas are quite long and complex in cut and decoration. They reach to the knees and end in rounded flaps often trimmed with fur. Caribou is also the basic material used to make the ornate ceremonial costume of the Copper Eskimo to the right of the couple, the long parka of the Caribou Eskimo next to him, and the clothing of the man and woman in the center. That man—the figure in the rear—is also a Copper Eskimo, but he wears everyday garb. The woman in front of him comes from western Hudson Bay and wears boots typical of the region. Her pant legs have large pouches that function as pockets. The three figures at right wear clothing made of a variety of skins. The man at far right is a Polar Eskimo. His parka is made from fox fur, his trousers from the skins of polar bears. To his right is a woman from western Greenland. Her clothing is of sealskin, as is that of the Iglulik man to her right. Most of the work related to making clothing was done by women. The woman at left is scraping a sealskin with a stone or bone to soften it for clothing.

the cornered animals and shot arrow after arrow into their sides. When a musk-ox was wounded badly enough, the Eskimos would close in and kill it with heavy spears.

As autumn deepened, the women busied themselves sewing the coats, trousers, stockings, and boots that the family would need for the winter. Both men and women had to have two layers of each item of clothing, an inner one to be worn with the hair facing the body, an outer one with the hair facing outward. Over the stockings and boots the Eskimos also wore fur "shoes" with two layers of soles. When completely dressed for the midwinter sealing, the Eskimo hunters wore four layers of caribou fur on their feet. Putting together this large winter wardrobe took many hours of sewing. But functionalism was not enough. The Eskimo women took the time to decorate many of the outer garments with borders and designs of white fur.

During the fall the Eskimos usually camped close to the Arctic seacoast. Their bands grew larger once again, in preparation for the trek to the midwinter camp on the ice. While the sewing work was being done, it was strictly taboo to do any hunting at all. Many of the men traveled back and forth between the camp and the caches of fish and caribou meat they had stored in the interior. The men also repaired their sleds, mended the dog harnesses and lines, and made certain the many tools and weapons were in good working order. In the evening the Eskimos gathered for community meals and songfests. If they had sufficient food, they postponed their move onto the ice as long as possible. But by December of most years the Eskimos left their coastal camps and headed toward the uninviting sea ice.

Over the years Moraq had become used to the movement from campsite to campsite. But as she walked ahead of the dog pack and sled, she thought of the happy days at the stone weir and the flowers that cov-

Aleut baskets, such as these, are widely considered to be among the most superb examples of the weavers' art. Noted for their delicacy in both design and fabric, and their workmanship—as many as 40 stitches to the inch—such baskets were traditionally made from a type of rye grass that grows on Aleutian Island beaches. The women dried the grass, split the stems with a fingernail, and then trimmed the fibers to the thinness of sewing silk. To make patterns, the women dyed some of the stems and worked them into the design. They also employed "false" embroidery for decoration.

A wood hat, once worn by an Aleut noble, was made by steaming and bending a thin board, then sewing it at the back. It is decorated with beads and sea lion whiskers.

The World and Ways of the Aleuts

Stretching some 1,000 miles south and westward from Alaska's southwest coast is the Aleutian archipelago, nearly 100 treeless islands—fogbound, cold, and damp. For several thousand years these dismal patches of earth, set in the inhospitable North Pacific waters, have been home to the Aleuts. They are a people originally from the Asian mainland who managed, over the centuries, to adapt themselves to the rigors of the Aleutian environment. Short, round-faced, and plump, the Aleuts speak a language related to that of the Eskimos, with whom they share numerous characteristics. Like many Eskimos, the Aleuts traditionally derived much of their sustenance from the sea, in the form of seals, sea lions, whales, and sea otters. But to supplement their sea mammal diet, the Aleuts also hunted birds, trapped fish and shellfish, and gathered roots and berries. Living in a world of scarcity, they became experts at deriving maximum benefit from the scanty resources that nature provided. Fur, skin, sinews, intestines, and bone—all found their way into Aleut clothing, houses, boats, tools, or weapons. Waterproof parkas, for example, were fashioned from seal intestines. Even bird skins—tanned in urine—were used in numerous items of clothing.

Again like the Eskimos, the Aleuts used stone lamps for lighting and heat. They also hunted from kayaks. But being an island people, the Aleuts tended to be somewhat more settled than most Eskimos. Though they sometimes established fishing camps at some distance from their villages, the villages were permanent homes, nurturing generation after generation within their confines.

These villages were generally situated along the coast, and within them the Aleuts lived in large communal houses called *barabaras.* These were partially underground and roofed with driftwood or whale bone covered with sod. In their social organization the Aleuts were closer to the Northwest Coast Indians than to the Eskimos. Like the Indians, the Aleuts lived within a highly rank-conscious society. Each island and village had chiefs, the *toyons.* They were persons of wealth and social stature. Chiefs consulted with "honorables," the local nobility, and in concert they ruled over the commoners and slaves, the latter usually orphans or captives taken in interisland raids. Slaves, dentalium shells, amber, and highly decorated clothing were all signs of wealth and, hence, power, and when a rich man died, his favorite slave was often killed and buried with him.

As among numerous native Americans, kinship was normally accounted in matrilineal terms, and boys were trained by maternal uncles. When a young man married, he lived for at least two years with his wife's parents.

In the 1740's the traditional life of the Aleuts received a blow from which it has yet to recover. Russian sea otter traders occupied the islands. More than a century of oppression followed, the Russians enslaving the Aleuts. Thousands died as a direct result of Russian brutality; thousands more succumbed to the white man's diseases. By the time the United States took over the islands in 1867, the native population had dropped from more than 15,000 to 2,500. Today there are about 3,300 Aleuts, but only about half of them remain on the islands.

ered the tundra in summer. Now everything on land and sea was frozen solid and covered with many feet of snow. The wind-whipped snow stung her face, but Moraq trudged on. She could hear Apitok urging on the dogs and occasionally flicking at one of them with his whip. In a few more hours they would stop and build an overnight igloo camp. Tomorrow morning they would set off again in the freezing twilight. In a week's time, perhaps, they and the other Eskimos in their party would reach a sealing site on the ice and build their camp. The long winter would begin again.

Coming of the White Man

The way Apitok and Moraq lived—the traditional Eskimo way of life—endured for 30 centuries. The Eskimos hunted the same animals in the same seasons. They generally followed the same customs and believed in the same supernatural beings. Their technology, as expressed in tools and weapons and building and sewing, remained little changed from ancient times. Generation after generation faced the same hardships in the struggle for survival in the Arctic. The Eskimo way of life was influenced only slightly by the Indian cultures to the south. But it was to be drastically altered by the advent of Europeans and Americans.

The earliest of the Europeans to encounter the Eskimos exerted little lasting influence. After Eric the Red visited Greenland in 982 or 983, many Norsemen went to settle permanently on the island. They soon came to know the Eskimos, whom they called Skraellings, and probably intermarried with them over the years. But as time went on, friction developed and the two groups clashed violently, with the Eskimos emerging victorious over a dwindling number of Norsemen. By the late 15th century few pure-blooded Norsemen remained in Greenland, and they were soon to be submerged in the Eskimo culture. In 1578, when British explorer Martin Frobisher visited the island, he found no Norsemen, only Eskimos.

As early as the 16th century the more adventuresome European fishermen worked the banks off Newfoundland, encountering Eskimos in Labrador and on the shores of the St. Lawrence Gulf. Frobisher found them on Baffin Island, and subsequent British explorations discovered Eskimos along Hudson Strait and at Hudson Bay. Finally, in the mid-17th century, the Hudson's Bay Company—under a charter issued by England's King Charles II—established the first permanent European base in the Eskimo heart-

An Aleut commoner, as seen by a member of Capt. James Cook's expedition in 1778, wears a headdress that the captain called a "snouted" visor. Cook wrote copiously on the Aleuts' lifeways.

land. In 1721 the Danes embarked on the colonization of Greenland, and today the island is an integral part of the kingdom of Denmark. The people, who call themselves Greenlanders, are largely of Eskimo extraction and speak both Danish and Eskimo.

Far to the west, the Russians expanded across Siberia in the 17th century and finally pushed up against the Eskimos. Vitus Bering, a Danish naval officer in the service of Czar Peter the Great, reached the south coast of Alaska in 1741, finding the remains of their camps but no Eskimos. Reports of the abundance of fur-bearing animals in the newly discovered lands swept across Russia, and by the middle of the 18th century trappers had hopped from island to island in the Aleutian chain until they reached the American mainland. In their pursuit of the animal pelts, especially those of the sea otter, the Russian trappers raped, murdered, and enslaved the native peoples. In a matter of a few years the Aleuts, a people closely related to the Eskimos, were almost exterminated. The more numerous Eskimos were also cruelly oppressed by the trappers.

The Russians did not explore the Arctic coast of Alaska. But in 1778 Capt. James Cook sailed through Bering Strait and followed the coast some distance to the northeast. Not until the 1826 expedition of Britain's John Franklin and Capt. F. W. Beechey, however, did white men find the northern Alaskan Eskimos in the area around Point Barrow. Farther east, along the Arctic coast of Canada, Alexander Mackenzie discovered a large group of Eskimos. But most of the Arctic coast of Canada—the homeland of the Central Eskimos—was still an unknown land to the white man.

Not for long. The British were eager to find a northwest passage across the Arctic from the Atlantic Ocean to the Pacific in order to shorten the route from Europe to east Asia. Consequently, they mounted a series of expeditions to the Canadian Arctic. Sir John Ross spent the winters of 1829-33 in the region around the magnetic pole, and there he discovered the large Netsilik group of Eskimos. Ross lost one of his ships owing to severe ice conditions, thereby providing the Eskimos with an unexpected bonanza of wood and iron. In 1833 Sir George Back traveled along the river that now bears his name and encountered the inland kinsmen of the Netsiliks. Sir George Simpson explored the territory now called Simpson Peninsula, and in 1845 a large expedition led by Sir John Franklin sailed for the Canadian Arctic. The ships arrived near King William Island in 1847-48 and became locked in the ice. According to the Eskimos the crew finally abandoned the ships; one by one the 129 officers and men, including Franklin, died of starvation.

The intrusion of the white man into the Arctic made a strong impact on the Eskimos and their way of life. By the early years of the 19th century the Eskimos had begun to trade their skins, fur, and whale oil for metal knives, kettles, and guns. And after 1848, when commercial whalers descended on the newly discovered Arctic whaling grounds, the influence of the white man spread swiftly.

The whalers were avidly interested in baleen, which was made into buttons and corset stays in Europe and in the United States and which commanded high prices on the market. Soon hundreds of whalers plied the Alaskan coast, far outdistancing the Eskimos in the competition for the bowhead whale. The whaling crews mingled freely with the Eskimos, trading repeating rifles and ammunition, as well as tobacco and whiskey, to them for furs, ivory, and the company of their women. Whaling and trading stations were established along the Alaskan coast, and both inland and maritime Eskimos flocked to work as deckhands or guides. An Eskimo could make $200 for the six-week whaling season, enough money to see him through the year with some comfort.

The Eskimos took to the repeating rifle with enthusiasm, a development that was to have a profound impact on their traditional way of life. No longer did they have any need for harpoons and spears. Nor did they need their kayaks to hunt the caribou at the crossing places. Now they could kill as many caribou as they wished from a distance. All their complicated sealing techniques also became unnecessary. The Eskimos could now shoot the seals and walruses on the ice or in the water. In a matter of a few years the Eskimos killed so many game animals that the animal population across the Arctic suffered a sharp decline.

So did the Eskimo population, for along with his advanced technology the white man brought such diseases as measles, small pox, and influenza. The Eskimos had little resistance to these new maladies, and so they fell ill and died at an alarming rate.

Eskimo cultural life also underwent a drastic change. Hunting with rifles made the Eskimos far less dependent on cooperation with their fellow hunters and encouraged individual effort at the expense of community activity. Whiskey also had a disruptive effect on family and group life, and along the whaling coast the sight of drunken Eskimos became commonplace.

In the latter part of the 19th century—particularly after the purchase of Alaska by the United States and a growth of concern in Canada about its northern peoples—the pace of change in the Arctic quickened. To replace the depleted caribou, the United States imported 1,250 reindeers from Siberia between 1892 and 1902.

Siberians and Laplanders were brought over to America to instruct the Eskimos in the art of reindeer herding. For a time the reindeers flourished mightily in the New World, and by 1932 more than 600,000 of them were being herded by the Eskimos.

Increasingly, Eskimo life was shaped by the desires and whims of the outside world. In the early decades of this century the fur of the white Arctic fox became a prized commodity in Europe and America. Pelts sold for as much as $50, and rarer blue fox skins brought up to $100. To cash in on the rage for fox fur, the Hudson's Bay Company and other organizations set up dozens of trading posts across the Arctic. The companies grubstaked the Eskimos with traps, guns, and food, and then the Eskimos spent the winter trapping the foxes and preparing the sought-after pelts.

With the establishment of the trading posts and their growth as Eskimo population centers, representatives of the white man's church and state began to penetrate the Arctic. The Royal Canadian Mounted Police came to keep order in Canada's large expanse of Eskimo territory, putting an end to the kind of rough justice the Eskimos had dispensed by themselves. (Had Apitok lived in modern times, his execution of Ugak would probably have led to the assassin's own arrest and imprisonment.) The mounties also took censuses, handed out welfare benefits, and generally made the Eskimos aware of law, government, and other aspects of the white man's world.

Along with the mounties came the missionaries. Protestants and Roman Catholics set up schools and taught the Eskimos the rudiments of English. They also brought the Bible and Christianity. One by one the Eskimo groups abandoned their taboos and amulets. The shamans came into disrepute and gradually ceased to exist. As explained by Christian gospel, the universe seemed less harsh and threatening. Instead of chanting appeals to Sedna, Tatqeq, or the Mother of the Caribou, the Eskimos appeared at the white man's missions to learn of his God and sing his hymns to the Almighty.

By the 1920's the Eskimo traditional life that had survived about three millennia in the harshest environment on earth was all but extinct. The white man's culture reached into nearly every corner of the Arctic. Anthropologist Diamond Jenness described its impact: "We replaced their stone knives with knives of steel, their bows and arrows with rifles and shotguns, their garments of caribou fur with clothes of factory-woven cotton and wool, their homemade boats with motorboats, their log cabins and snow huts warmed by lamps burning animal fat with frame houses heated with wood-burning and oil-burning stoves; and for the ancient songs and dances which relieved the tedium of their long winter nights we substituted Christian hymns. They may speak the Eskimo language still; they may still roam the hunting grounds of their forefathers; but most of them are Eskimos no longer."

New Eskimo Sculpture, Drawings, and Prints

As a people frequently on the move, wresting a living in one of the world's most inhospitable regions, the Eskimos have had little time to build a strong artistic tradition. Though they have produced some works of great beauty through the centuries—small carvings, ivory amulets, basketry, and other items—it has only been in recent years, with the growth of an export market, that art has become a matter of considerable interest among the Eskimos. In large measure this birth of an esthetic consciousness was generated by Canadian artist and art collector James Houston, assigned by his government in the 1950's as an administrator in Eskimo territories. Under Houston's guidance numerous Eskimo artists have come to the fore, specializing in sculpture, drawing, and printmaking. Traditional materials, such as ivory, and new (to the Eskimos) substances, such as jade, have been integrated into several distinct regional styles.

An Eskimo drummer, beating time to a song, is the subject of this 1962 gray stone sculpture by Madeleine Issirkrut of Repulse Bay, Northwest Territories. In keeping with tradition, the drummer taps the rim of the instrument rather than the head of the drum.

"The Enchanted Owl," perhaps inspired by Eskimo mythology, was carved by printmaker Kenojuak, of Cape Dorset. The artist carved the design on a polished stone, then inked the stone and covered it with paper. By rubbing the paper with her fingers or a piece of sealskin, she transferred the design.

Sculpted in stone, its gray-green color reminiscent of the ocean depths, the goddess Sedna rides on the back of a seal. The statue, by Niviaksiak, of Cape Dorset, refers to a deity that lived at the bottom of the sea. She was vengeful and punished hunters who offended her by keeping sea mammals far from shore.

Ivory and stone are the two materials used in this statue portraying an everyday scene. The tattooed woman, her child tucked snugly in her parka, carries an ivory knife in one hand and dangles a fish from the other. This highly stylized 1955 work was fashioned by an unknown artist at Port Harrison, Quebec.

CONTEMPORARY INDIANS: Renaissance of an

During the late 19th and early 20th centuries many knowledgeable observers thought that the Indians of North America were doomed by the onslaught of white civilization. Their cultures, their traditional ways of living, perhaps even the Indians themselves would soon vanish completely. Like the erroneous report of Mark Twain's death, this obituary, too, was "an exaggeration." In fact, with a population of well over a million in the United States and Canada, and a birthrate nearly twice that of the general population, there seems little cause for concern about the disappearance of the first immigrants to North America.

Rebirth of Cultures

To many contemporary Indians this resurgence is much more than a matter of numbers. Indians also have a revitalized awareness of their tribal traditions and a renewed determination to carve out their own destiny within the larger society. The task is not simple. Indian leaders argue that their people have been harried and tricked out of tribal lands, herded onto reservations only to be done out of even those lands, romanticized as noble savages and denounced as shiftless incompetents, and subjected to numerous social experiments of government bureaucrats.

Yet centuries of such treatment have failed either to eradicate the Indians or to make them part of the prevailing white culture. The situation was summed up in the Final Report issued in 1977 by the American Indian Policy Review Commission, a congressionally created body made up of three senators, three members of the House, and five Indians. The report, which opposed forced assimilation and endorsed the idea of tribal self-government, stated in part: "From the earliest days of European settlement . . . and, more pertinently, since the founding of the Republic, the Indians have been subjected to ambivalent attitudes and policies by the advancing non-Indian society and, after 1789, by the United States Government itself. On the one hand, every method has been employed to force them to cease being Indians and to conform to the dominant society, while on the other hand they have been led to believe . . . that the government would support their right to survive as Indians. . . . Today we must ask the central question: Is the American nation—now two hundred years old, and one hundred full years beyond the era of the Little Bighorn—yet mature enough and secure enough to tolerate, even to encourage, within the larger culture, societies of Indian people who wish to maintain their own unique tribal governments, cultures and religions?"

To keep their cultural roots alive, to protect their remaining lands, to preserve the hundreds of diverse tribal identities and yet find ways to take part in a modern technological society is no mean task for the Indians. Like everyone else, they have been affected by social and economic change. Today nearly half the Indian population in the United States lives outside the 268 reservations officially recognized by the federal government. Big cities are the homes for many of them. Numerous others live in rural areas. Yet they have not disappeared into the American "melting pot" and do not wish to; increasingly, they demand the right to live in a society in which cultural diversity is accepted. Then, too, the Indians are understandably weary of being viewed as a "problem"—a people unable to adjust to the dominant culture and who are, therefore, regarded as a burden on it. And many feel that, in any case, assimilation would merely leave them homeless in both worlds. Past efforts at forced assimilation—notably the 1887 Dawes General Allotment Act, which broke up 86 million acres of tribal lands, and the federal "termination" policies of the 1950's, which sought to end all government services to Indian reservations—proved dismal failures.

There is little, if any, argument among Indians and their supporters about the need of government assistance for the foreseeable future. Indians simply want a much larger role in administering that assistance. They point out that such traditional Indian practices as placing the welfare of the community above that of the individual, holding lands in common, and sharing necessities during lean times require policies foreign to many non-Indians.

A Legacy of Conflicting Policies

After the 19th-century Indian wars had ended, the U.S. government, eager to relieve itself of the burden of caring for the recently subdued tribes, turned toward a policy of forced assimilation. This policy found its chief expression in the Dawes General Allotment Act of 1887, which sought to break up tribal lands and transform the Indians into a rough equivalent of white yeoman farmers on individually owned 160-acre plots; all "surplus" lands would be available for sale to whites. The results of this attempt at wholesale assimilation were disastrous for the Indians—86 million reservation acres lost, 90,000 Indians left landless. In part these developments occurred because many Indians were unprepared to adapt to farming, and in part because much of the land allotted to them was unsuited for agriculture. By the 1920's the Indian population of the United States had shrunk to approximately 245,000—a battered, demoralized remnant riddled with poverty and disease. Those who had been forced into missionary- or government-run boarding schools were fitted for neither the tribal nor the white world. Many found their only solace in alcohol.

In the early 1930's, spurred by the failure of the Dawes Act, the pendulum of white attitudes began to swing in the opposite direction, owing largely to the influence of Secretary of the Interior Harold L. Ickes

Ancient People

and to the tireless efforts of John Collier, who was commissioner of Indian Affairs from 1933 to 1946. Collier sought to expand tribal holdings, encourage traditional cultures, and create internal self-government on the reservations. Many of his ideas were incorporated into the Indian Reorganization Act of 1934 (Wheeler-Howard Act). It halted all land allotment to whites, provided for improved educational and health facilities, granted funds by which tribes could expand their holdings and attempt to become self-sustaining, returned to the Indians the freedom to practice their old religions, and gave tribes the rights to internal self-government and to form corporations for the management of their own resources. Further, each tribe was allowed to vote by secret ballot on whether it wished to accept the terms of the act. Of the 263 tribes eligible, 192 approved.

The Effects of War

Under the provisions of the Wheeler-Howard Act, Indian holdings were actually increased for the first time. The concept behind the act was a generation ahead of its time, and its implementation was hampered by such factors as Indian suspicion of all "reforms," white opposition, inadequate funds, and later, the onset of World War II. The war itself brought many changes. Indians by the thousands left their reservations to man defense plants in the cities, some never to return. About 25,000 served in the armed forces—among them Pima tribesman Ira Hayes, a marine who helped raise the flag at Iwo Jima, and Cherokee Jack Montgomery and Creek Ernest Childers, both of whom won the Medal of Honor for valor in the European theater. Indians were especially valuable in communications teams, using their tribal languages as codes to confuse enemy interceptors.

For many Indians the war was their first real experience of the outside world. Some, like Hayes, found only despair when they returned to their impoverished reservations. But others, gaining confidence from their war experiences, developed a new political consciousness and a determination to organize and protect their rights. In 1944 some 100 representatives of more than 40 tribes gathered in Denver to form the first nationwide organization composed solely of Indians, the National Congress of American Indians (NCAI).

The group's stated purpose was to promote legislation favorable to Indians, and the NCAI soon became active in the effort to establish an Indian Claims Commission. This body was created in 1946 to provide a means by which tribes might file claims directly against the U.S. government—largely in compensation for lands earlier ceded or expropriated. Before the creation of the commission the tribes had been forced to obtain a special Act of Congress each time they wished to sue the government. (A somewhat similar Canadian commission deals with Indian claims there but does

not have the power to adjudicate them. However, the commission has been an effective mediator between the Indians and the government.)

Despite such encouraging signs the postwar years marked the beginning of yet another swing of the pendulum—this time back to the old policy of "getting the government out of the Indian business" and ending expensive federal services to the tribes as quickly as possible. One sign of this new attitude was the adoption of a "relocation" policy by the Bureau of Indian Affairs. To any Indian seeking a way out of reservation life, this program offers transportation to a large city and help in finding work and housing. Many Indians have made the transition to the cities successfully, but others have found themselves stranded in an alien world. The Bureau of Indian Affairs estimates that more than a third of those who resettle eventually return to their reservations. Another far-reaching measure of the postwar period was a 1953 Act of Congress authorizing the states to assume jurisdiction over criminal and civil trials on the reservations without the consent of the tribes.

Changing National Policy

By far the most drastic change in policy, however, was embodied in the provisions of Concurrent Resolution 108, also adopted in 1953, that sought early termination of federal relationships with certain designated tribes (and eventually all the tribes). The intention of this termination policy was to cut off all financial and administrative assistance to the affected tribes, to release them from the restrictions of reservation life. The effect was to force the Indians to compete in the white world with little or no preparation. Among the tribes most seriously affected by the new policy was the Menominee of Wisconsin, who were pressured into termination in 1961, after being informed that they would be denied certain financial claims owing them unless they accepted their new status. The results were disastrous. The Menominees, who had formerly been relatively self-sufficient, had to automate their once-profitable sawmill to pay for such new burdens as sanitation and police and health services. Within a decade Menominee County, Wisconsin, was rife with unemployment and had become one of the 10 most depressed counties in the United States.

The Klamaths of Oregon had no better fortune. Having yielded to the temptation to liquidate their assets—which included timber valued at $120 million—and distribute the proceeds among themselves, they were soon left bankrupt and demoralized. Fortunately for the Indians, the drive toward termination began to lose momentum in the late 1950's. (The Menominees, for example, were finally restored to federal trust status, at their own request, in 1973.) But before the policy fell out of favor, some 19 tribes had been deprived of their federal support and more than 2.5 million acres of reservation land had been lost. Even after termination was abandoned, many Indians continued to fear its revival.

The New Activism

During the early and mid-1960's, under the Kennedy and Johnson Administrations, government policy shifted once more toward the principles embodied in the Wheeler-Howard Act of 1934: the encouragement of tribal self-government and the development of reservation resources. By this time many Indians had begun to speak out for self-determination and had rallied considerable public support. A clear sign of the new activist spirit was the historic conference of Indians convened at the University of Chicago in 1961. The meeting was attended by 500 Indians from 70 U.S. tribes as well as by Indian observers from Canada and Mexico. The participants signed a Declaration of Indian Purpose that rejected what they called "charity and paternalism" but asked for "assistance, technical and financial, for the time needed" in order to develop their own programs and policies in such fields as economic development, education, and health.

Another outgrowth of the conference was the formation soon afterward of the National Indian Youth Council (NIYC) by some of the younger, college-educated participants. Considerably more militant than the National Congress of American Indians, the NIYC in 1964 sponsored "fish-ins" along the rivers of Washington State in order to protest laws restricting age-old Indian fishing rights. The NIYC also urged the abolition of the Bureau of Indian Affairs and its replacement by agencies that would advise and help Indians without trying to control them.

The group's recommendation was well timed. In 1964 a conference on Indian poverty was held in Washington, D.C., to publicize the economic plight of Indians and urge their inclusion in the benefits of the Economic Opportunity Act, then being drawn up as the chief instrument of President Lyndon B. Johnson's "War on Poverty." America's Indians—with the nation's lowest life expectancy and annual income, and the highest rates of suicide, alcoholism, infant mortality, unemployment, and tuberculosis—rightly felt themselves to be experts on poverty, and they won their point. For the first time, under the Office of Economic Opportunity (OEO), they were given access to funds, agencies, and programs not under the control of the Bureau of Indian Affairs. For the first time Indians were able to design and run many programs themselves.

By the end of the 1960's there were some 60 community-action programs scattered through 17 states, and the results of some of the Indian-run projects were spectacular. The Lummis of coastal Washington, for example, developed an innovative and highly profitable sea-farming operation. The Navajos of the Southwest, given free rein to spend a yearly $11 million in OEO funds on their vast reservation, developed a demonstra-tion school at Rough Rock, Arizona. The policies were set by an all-Navajo school board, and English was taught only as a *second* language. Among other projects, the Navajos also established the first Indian-owned-and-operated community college (1968), which has a tribal center designed by Navajo medicine men, and established a network of fire, police, health, and legal services.

Other tribal enterprises in various areas include logging operations, housing projects, museums, and a number of highly successful tourist resorts. The OEO programs also provided opportunities for educated Indians by creating new jobs in federal agencies and on the reservations themselves. Then, too, programs such as Head Start (for preschool children) and Upward Bound (for those who wanted to attend college), as well as the new Indian-controlled and often bilingual schools springing up on many reservations, gave a much-needed boost to Indian education.

The Rise in School Enrollment

By the 1970's some 87 percent of Indian children were enrolled in school. The dropout rate was still alarmingly high—about 35 percent—but college enrollment jumped from a mere 2,000 in 1960 to approximately 35,000 in the mid-1970's. The average life expectancy of Indians in the United States rose from 60 to 65.1 years between 1950 and 1970 (as compared to 68.2 and 70.9 for all races). The infant mortality rate dropped from 62.5 per 1,000 births in 1955 to 18.2 in the mid-1970's (compared to 16.1 for all races). Unemployment, which stood as high as 40 percent in the 1960's, had dropped substantially by the mid-1970's. In part, this decrease in unemployment can be credited to improved educational opportunities and to Indian-owned-and-operated businesses (about 400 in the mid-1970's), as well as a trend toward preferential hiring policies by such government agencies as the Bureau of Indian Affairs.

Economic and health problems remain acute for both tribal and urban Indians, however. In 1975 per capita income of reservation Indians averaged about $1,500. Wealthy tribes, such as the Agua Caliente of Palm Springs, California, and the Yakima of Washington State, remained exceptions. The average income of Indians living off reservations was higher, but they benefited little from government-operated reservation programs in health, welfare, and education.

Like unemployment, health remains a chronic problem for today's Indians. Because many of them still live in substandard, overcrowded dwellings with minimal sanitation, tuberculosis, influenza, and pneumonia are rampant. Even more telling, the suicide rate among Indian adolescents is 100 times that of whites, and alcoholism—despite the banning of alcoholic beverages on many reservations—is commonplace. While the level of Indian health has improved, it is still "significantly below the level of the general United States population," according to a government report issued in the mid-1970's. The report went on to say: "This disparity is not only manifested in terms of incidence of . . . disease, but also in terms of severity of diseases."

An impressive number of contemporary Indians have taken strong measures to bring their plight to public attention. All U.S. Indians have been citizens since 1924, but widespread political assertiveness among them is a relatively recent phenomenon. In 1969 came the first in a series of dramatic, well-publicized confrontations between young Indian activists and the U.S. government. That year a group composed largely of students, who called themselves Indians of All Tribes, occupied the abandoned federal prison island of Alcatraz in San Francisco Bay. Pointedly offering the government $24-worth of beads and cloth in exchange for the facility, which they hoped to turn into a cultural center, they managed to occupy Alcatraz for 19 months before government agents cleared them out. More occupations followed—along beaches, on other islands, and on abandoned army posts—and new activist groups were quickly formed in both the United States and Canada.

Alarming the Elders

The new militants, many of whom lived in urban areas, alarmed the older, more traditional tribal leaders, some of whom felt that their younger rivals' activities would endanger much-needed federal support. The older leaders, in turn, were dismissed by many activists as "Uncle Tomahawks" who connived with whites to run the reservations as if they were domestic colonies of the U.S. government.

The most controversial of the activist groups, the American Indian Movement (AIM), was launched in 1966 by a group of young Chippewas in Minneapolis, initially in protest against police treatment of the city's Indian residents. An Indian Patrol was organized to monitor police activities, and the movement quickly spread to other cities. It was AIM that spearheaded the so-called Trail of Broken Treaties, a group of militants who moved on Washington, D.C., before the 1972 elections to demand improved programs for Indians. The group forcibly occupied the central offices of the Bureau of Indian Affairs, vandalized them, and departed with masses of BIA documents, many of which were later recovered.

But a far deadlier confrontation—and one that exacerbated the conflict between young militants and old tribal leaders—began in early 1973 at the village of Wounded Knee on South Dakota's Pine Ridge Reservation—the same village where, in 1890, some 150 to 300 Sioux (estimates vary) had been massacred by the U.S. Cavalry.

On February 27, 1973, a force of about 200 armed Indians, led by AIM organizers, took over Wounded Knee. This confrontation began as an Indian-versus-Indian dispute, the dissidents charging older Sioux leaders with corruption and dictatorial tactics. Roadblocks were set up by AIM, and the village was quickly surrounded by FBI agents, federal marshals, and droves of newspaper and television reporters. For 71 days the militants held out, determined to publicize their demands for self-determination, for hearings on U.S.-Indian treaties, and for a senatorial investigation of the government's treatment of the Indians. By the time a withdrawal was finally negotiated, two Indian militants were dead, one marshal had been wounded, and the issues themselves had been "drowned in hatred, rhetoric and media stunts," according to Sioux lawyer and author Vine Deloria, Jr. Two AIM leaders, Russell Means and Dennis Banks, were later arrested, but the charges against them were dismissed in 1974, largely because of evidence of perjury by government witnesses.

What, if anything, was actually accomplished at Wounded Knee is open to question, but according to one writer, Wilcomb Washburn, it was an important symbol of "the emergence of a new and raucous Indian voice, a voice which celebrated separatism instead of integration, political activism instead of dignified acquiescence, repudiation of white goals and values, and the rejection of existing tribal organizations."

The Search for Legal Remedies

Although the political results of violence have been minimal, there is little question about the effectiveness of court actions started by Indian tribes seeking redress of wrongs. In practice, if not in law, Indian land rights and treaties had always been subject to unilateral abrogation by whites. In recent years, however, tribal lawyers have had considerable success in challenging the legality of these old land cessions. The hundreds of claims filed against the U.S. government through the Indian Claims Commission since its establishment in 1946 have led to some important victories for the tribes. Created to make a final settlement of all Indian claims for lost lands—sometimes by financial compensation and sometimes by acreage grants—the commission has also yielded a measure of real sovereignty to certain tribes. For example, some have won the right to arrest and try non-Indian as well as Indian lawbreakers on reservations. Others have been awarded authority to collect taxes or to be exempt from outside taxes. Still other tribes have gained the right to hunt and fish on, and sometimes off, reservations without state permits. A number of tribes have been permitted to collect substantial royalties for mineral leases and to cancel certain contracts with mining companies.

One of the most important land victories in recent years was won by the Taos Pueblo of New Mexico. These Indians had been seeking the return of their mountain shrine at Blue Lake ever since the land was annexed to the Kit Carson National Forest in 1906. Rejecting a Claims Commission offer of financial compensation for the loss of Blue Lake, the Taoseños finally convinced Congress of the area's religious significance to them, and in 1971 the 48,000-acre tract was restored. The return of the land on purely religious grounds was precedent-breaking legislation.

That same year Alaska's 53,000 Indians, Eskimos, and Aleuts were awarded the largest settlement to date—40 million acres and nearly $1 billion in compensations for outstanding land claims. This enormous award was won through an alliance of strange bedfellows: the natives themselves and representatives of the oil industry, who discovered that they could not negotiate a corridor on which to build the Trans-Alaska Pipeline until clear ownership of the land was established.

Large areas have also been claimed by the tribes of the Northeast. The Oneidas of New York State, for example, want 300,000 acres restored to them, and Maine's Passamaquoddy and Penobscot tribes have asked for the return of as much as 5 million acres of the state's land. In all, by the late 1970's, the Indian Claims Commission had awarded $640 million to settle 275 land disputes, and some 200 cases were still pending.

There have also been legal actions in Canada. In 1975, 10,000 Canadian Eskimos and Cree Indians from the James Bay area won a $225 million award, a 5,345-square-mile reserve, and hunting and fishing rights on nearly 60,000 square miles. The award was in the form of royalties against future development of the James Bay hydroelectric project, a $12 billion facility planned by the Quebec government whose construction was blocked by the Indians and Eskimos until their land rights could be clearly established. And in western Canada other Eskimos and Indians organized to prevent the building of oil and gas pipelines through their areas until their land claims were settled.

Opposition to Indian Aspirations

The growing pressure for Indian self-determination and tribal sovereignty has not gone unopposed, however. In the United States whites have formed such opposition groups as the Interstate Congress for Equal Rights and Responsibilities. This organization, many of whose members are western farmers and ranchers, would like to see the entire reservation system ended and Indians integrated into the larger society. Resentment has also been aroused by Indian land-claims suits, which threaten established holdings, and by court decisions extending Indian fishing, hunting, and water rights and the internal sovereignty of the tribes.

Even today there are enormous differences in outlook between Indians and whites. Many Indians hold to a traditional view of land as something sacred, a gift to use, share, and preserve for future generations. The concept of owning land, of buying and selling it, remains foreign to them. Whites, on the other hand, have generally regarded land as private property to be possessed by individuals or companies, utilized for the benefit of the owner, and bought and sold like any other commodity. Whether these opposing viewpoints will be resolved, whether the old argument over assimilation versus self-determination for the Indians will ever be settled, remains open to question.

Cultural Renewals

Despite the inevitable acculturation that has taken place among U.S. Indians and despite the movement of nearly half of them to urban centers and rural areas in recent years, the Indians have never entirely abandoned or lost their tribal cultures. As Melvin Thom of the National Indian Youth Council put it: ". . . you might say we are the only people in this melting pot who have kept their culture. . . . It's the urban white American who is culturally deprived. It's the tourist who is culturally deprived. What culture has he got? The culture of the mass media that is fed to him."

Traditional Indian religions have survived, though sometimes in altered form, despite the fact that they were officially banned for 30 years. The ancient priesthoods and ceremonies of the Pueblo peoples, for instance, remain virtually unchanged, even though many Peublos also attend Roman Catholic services; they see nothing contradictory in practicing the two religions simultaneously. And many Iroquois in New York State and Canada still follow their old beliefs as codified and reformed in 1799 by the Seneca prophet Ganyodaiyo ("Handsome Lake"). This religion is influenced to some degree by Quaker beliefs, but it is essentially Indian. Ceremonies are conducted in Iroquois longhouses and are closely tied to farming and the seasons; only Iroquois languages are used, although virtually all Iroquois people are now English-speaking.

The Native American Church, which is the most widespread religion among U.S. Indians today, is also found in Canada. The church's tenets combine traditional Indian and fundamentalist Christian elements. Christianity's Trinity, Cross, and baptism are part of the religion, but the most important sacrament is the eating of the buttons of peyote, a hallucinogenic cactus, in order to induce contact with the supernatural. Ingestion of peyote, which grows wild in Mexico and the American Southwest, causes visions that often take the form of beautiful, kaleidoscopic designs.

The Native American Church is most influential among the Plains tribes, for whom the vision quest has long been an important ritual. But unlike the 19th-century Ghost Dance religion, which also swept the Plains, the Native American Church does not promise a future in which the white men and their works will be swept away. Many Indians have also joined more orthodox churches, but whatever their beliefs, religion usually touches all aspects of Indian life.

Contemporary Indians have also taken a renewed interest in their ancient healing arts, their languages, their arts and crafts, their songs, dances, and stories. The Navajo medicine men of the Southwest still practice healing by means of chants and elaborate rituals. The psychological benefits of these ceremonial cures are often impressive, and the National Institute of Mental Health has recently financed the training of Navajo healers. Tribal festivals and powwows—a word derived from the Algonquian term for "conjuror"—are held today on many U.S. and Canadian reservations. Like the amalgamation religions and the movement toward self-determination, these powwows encourage intertribal contact and the affirmation among Indians of their common interests and problems. Undeniably, the ceremonies also attract, and are affected by, the tourist trade, but basically they remain festivals held by Indians for themselves. One of the largest is the Crow Agency Powwow in Montana during August. Among other ceremonies are the Kachina Dances of the Hopis, the Sioux and Arapaho Sun Dances, and the Inter-Tribal Ceremonial in Gallup, New Mexico.

Artists and Craftsmen

Indian arts and crafts, both traditional and modern, are also enjoying a renaissance. In the 1930's the U.S. Department of the Interior created an Indian Arts and Crafts Board to train craftsmen, open new workshops, and set up cooperative marketing groups for Indian artists. The federally funded Institute of American Indian Arts in Santa Fe, which opened in 1962, offers courses each year to 300 Indians and native Alaskans. The students, who are from tribal, rural, and urban backgrounds, are trained not only in painting, sculpture, textiles, and ceramics, but also in commercial art, writing, drama, music, and dance. They are encouraged to experiment freely rather than work in the purely decorative "Indian" styles once demanded by collectors.

Indian jewelry, especially in silver and turquoise, has skyrocketed in both popularity and price in recent years. Navajo and Pueblo artists still produce the massive, much-imitated silver and turquoise jewelry for which the tribes have long been known, but some of the best new work is experimental and even futuristic in design. Hopi artist Charles Loloma, for example, freely combines gold, silver, turquoise, wood, and coral. Another Hopi, Lawrence Saufkie, is known for silver jewelry in the unique overlay style originated by his father, Paul Saufkie, and Fred Kabotie.

Indian writers, too, are finding a growing audience. In 1969 N. Scott Momaday, an established novelist and professor of comparative literature at the University of California, won the Pulitzer Prize in fiction for his novel *House Made of Dawn*, which dealt with the conflicts experienced by an Indian veteran of World War II. Vine Deloria, Jr., a Sioux lawyer and an outspoken advocate of Indian self-determination, is another Indian writer who enjoys critical and popular success. His

1969 book, *Custer Died for Your Sins*, lambasting government bureaucrats, missionaries, and anthropologists for their paternalistic attitudes, struck a responsive chord with both Indian and non-Indian readers.

In the early 1970's the Smithsonian Institution listed more than a hundred publications aimed at Indian, Eskimo, and Aleut audiences. Among the newspapers produced by native peoples are Los Angeles' *Talking Leaf*, the *Tundra Times* of Alaska, and *Akwesasne Notes*, published by the Mohawks of New York State.

Indians have also made their mark in the entertainment field—and not simply as the perpetual losers in Hollywood westerns. In dance, the Osage ballerinas Maria and Marjorie Tallchief were ballet stars in the United States and Europe. In music, there is the well-known Canadian Cree folksinger Buffy Sainte-Marie. Even the movies are finding nonstereotyped roles for Indians.

Silent No Longer

The assumptions long held by many whites—that the Indians would either die out, continue to endure their lot in stoic silence, or finally, be absorbed into the mainstream of society—have all proven untrue. The Indians are still there, still affirming their ancient cultures and speaking out in ever-increasing numbers for their rights as the original inhabitants of North America. The feelings, shared by many non-Indians, were well expressed in the Declaration of the Five County Cherokees of Oklahoma, who banded together in 1966 to protest abrogation of their treaty rights:

"Now, we shall not rest until we have regained our rightful place. We shall tell our young people what we know. We shall send them to the corners of the earth to learn more. They shall lead us. . . .

"In these days, intruders, named without our consent, speak for the Cherokees. When the Cherokee government is the Cherokee people, we shall rest.

"In these days, we are informed of the decisions other people have made about our destiny. When we control our destiny, we shall rest.

"In these days, the high courts of the United States listen to people who have been wronged. When our wrongs have been judged in these courts, and the illegalities of the past have been corrected, we shall rest.

"In these days, there are countless ways by which people make their grievances known to all Americans. When we have learned these new ways that bring strength and power, and we have used them, we shall rest.

"In these days, we are losing our homes and our children's homes. When our homeland is protected, for ourselves and for the generations to follow, we shall rest.

"In the vision of our creator, we declare ourselves ready to stand proudly among the nationalities of these United States of America."

Seeing Indian History

Museums, reconstructed villages, archeological sites, and other attractions open to the public

Key for listings ▥ *Museum* ⚱ *Archeological site (usually includes museum)* ⚑ *Reconstructed site* ⬥ *Historic site*

UNITED STATES

Alabama

▥ Birmingham Museum of Art, *Birmingham*
⚱ Indian Mound and Museum, *Florence*
⚱ Mound State Monument, *Moundville*
⚱ Russell Cave National Monument, *Northwest of Bridgeport*

Alaska

▥ Alaska State Museum, *Juneau*
▥ Anchorage Historical and Fine Arts Museum, *Anchorage*
▥ Sheldon Jackson Museum, *Sitka*
⬥ Sitka National Monument, *Sitka*
▥ Tongass Historical Society Museum, *Ketchikan*
▥ University Museum, *University of Alaska, Fairbanks*

Arizona

▥ Arizona State Museum, *Tucson*
⚱ Besh-Ba-Gowah, *South of Globe*
⚱ Canyon de Chelly National Monument, *Near Chinle*
⚱ Casa Grande Ruins National Monument, *Coolidge*
▥ Colorado River Tribes Indian Museum, *Parker*
▥ Gila River Indian Museum, *Sacaton*
⚱ Grand Canyon National Park, *South Rim, North Rim*
▥ The Heard Museum, *Phoenix*
⚱ Kinishba Pueblo, *West of Whiteriver*
⚱ Montezuma Castle National Monument, *South of Flagstaff*
▥ Museum of Northern Arizona, *Flagstaff*
⚱ Navajo National Monument, *Northwest of Tuba City*
▥ Navajo Tribal Museum, *South of Window Rock*
⬥ Oraibi Pueblo, *Southeast of Tuba City*
⚱ Pueblo Grande Museum, *Phoenix*
⚱ Tonto National Monument, *Northwest of Globe*
⚱ Tuzigoot National Monument, *Northwest of Cottonwood*
⚱ Walnut Canyon National Monument, *Southeast of Flagstaff*
⬥ Walpi Pueblo, *Southeast of Tuba City*
⚱ Wupatki National Monument, *Northeast of Flagstaff*

Arkansas

▥ Arkansas State University Museum, *Jonesboro*
⚱ Caddo Burial Mounds, *West of Murphreesboro*
▥ Hampson State Museum, *Wilson*
▥ Henderson State University Museum, *Arkadelphia*
▥ University of Arkansas Museum, *University of Arkansas, Fayetteville*

Special Events
For information about the times and places of Indian ceremonials, rites, and other events open to the public, write to
Bureau of Indian Affairs
U.S. Department of the Interior
Washington, D.C. 20245.

California

▥ Antelope Valley Indian Research Museum, *Near Lancaster*
⬥ Big and Little Petroglyph Canyons, *Near China Lake*
▥ The Bowers Memorial Museum, *Santa Ana*
⚱ Calico Mountains Archaeological Project, *Northeast of Barstow*
▥ California State Indian Museum, *Sacramento*
▥ Catalina Island Museum, *Santa Catalina Island*
▥ Clarke Memorial Museum, *Eureka*
⚑ Clear Lake State Park, *Northeast of Kelseyville*
⚱ Coyote Hills Regional Park, *South of Alvarado*
▥ Fine Arts Museums of San Francisco: M. H. de Young Memorial Museum, *San Francisco*
⬥ Indian Grinding Rock State Historical Monument, *Pine Grove*
⚱ Joshua Tree National Monument, *Twentynine Palms*
▥ Kern County Museum, *Bakersfield*
▥ Los Angeles County Museum of History and Science, *Los Angeles*
▥ Lowie Museum of Anthropology, *University of California, Berkeley*
▥ Malki Museum, *Banning*
▥ Oakland Museum, History Division, *Oakland*
▥ Pioneer Museum and Haggin Galleries, *Stockton*
▥ Riverside Municipal Museum, *Riverside*
▥ San Bernardino County Museum, *Badlands*
▥ San Diego Museum of Man, *San Diego*
▥ Santa Barbara Museum of Natural History, *Santa Barbara*
▥ Southwest Museum, *Los Angeles*
▥ Adan E. Treganza Anthropology Museum, *San Francisco State University, San Francisco*
▥ Tulare County Museum, *Visalia*

Colorado

▥ Colorado Springs Fine Art Center, Taylor Museum, *Colorado Springs*
▥ Colorado State Museum, *Denver*
▥ Denver Art Museum, *Denver*
▥ Denver Museum of Natural History, *Denver*
▥ Gem Village Museum, *Bayfield*

▥ Koshare Indian Kiva Museum, *La Junta*
⚱ Lowry Pueblo Ruins National Historic Landmark, *Northwest of Cortez*
⚱ Mesa Verde National Park, *East of Cortez*
▥ Pioneers Museum, *Colorado Springs*
▥ University of Colorado Museum, *Boulder*
▥ Ute Indian Museum, *South of Montrose*

Connecticut

▥ Peabody Museum of Natural History, *Yale University, New Haven*
▥ Slater Memorial Museum, *Norwich*
▥ Tantaquidgeon Indian Museum, *Uncasville*

Delaware

▥ Island Field Archeological Museum and Research Center, *South Bowers*

District of Columbia

▥ Museum of Natural History, U.S. National Museum, *Smithsonian Institution*

Florida

⚱ Crystal River State Archeological Site, *Northwest of Crystal River*
▥ Florida State Museum, *University of Florida, Gainesville*
▥ Museum of Florida History, *Tallahassee*
▥ Seminole Museum, *West Hollywood*
▥ Southeast Museum of the North American Indian, *Marathon*
⚑ Temple Mound Museum and Park, *Fort Walton Beach*

Georgia

▥ Creek Museum, *Indian Springs*
⚱ Etowah Mounds Archeological Area, *Cartersville*
⚱ Kolomoki Mounds State Park, *North of Blakely*
⬥ New Echota Historic Site, *Calhoun*

Idaho

⚱ Nez Perce National Historical Park, *Spalding*

Illinois

⚱ Cahokia Mounds State Park, *East St. Louis*
⚱ Dickson Mounds Museum of the Illinois Indian, *Outside Lewistown*
▥ Field Museum of Natural History, *Chicago*
▥ Illinois State Museum, *Springfield*
▥ University of Illinois Museum of Natural History, *Urbana*

398

Indiana

- Angel Mounds State Memorial, *Near Evansville*
- Children's Museum, *Indianapolis*
- Indiana University Museum, *Bloomington*
- Mounds State Park, *East of Anderson*
- Museum of Indian Heritage, *Indianapolis*

Iowa

- Davenport Museum, *Davenport*
- Effigy Mounds National Monument, *North of McGregor*

Kansas

- El Quartelejo Indian Kiva Museum, *Scott City*
- Fort Larned National Historic Site, *Larned*
- Indian Burial Pit, *Near Salina*
- Inscription Rock, *Lake Kanpolis State Park, Southeast of Ellsworth*
- Kansas Sac and Fox Museum, *Highland*
- Kansas State Historical Society, *Topeka*
- Pawnee Indian Village Museum, *Northwest of Belleville*

Kentucky

- Adena Park, *North of Lexington*
- Ancient Buried City, *Southeast of Cairo*
- Museum of Anthropology, *University of Kentucky, Lexington*
- J. B. Speed Art Museum, *Louisville*

Louisiana

- Louisiana State Exhibit Museum, *Shreveport*
- Marksville Prehistoric Indian Park State Monument, *Marksville*

Maine

- Robert Abbe Museum of Stone Age Antiquities, *Bar Harbor*
- Wilson Museum, *Castine*

Maryland

- Baltimore Museum of Art, *Baltimore*

Massachusetts

- Bronson Museum, *Attleboro*
- Fruitlands Museum, *Harvard University, Cambridge*
- Longhouse Museum, *Grafton*
- Memorial Hall, *Deerfield*
- Robert S. Peabody Foundation for Archeology, *Phillips Academy, Andover*
- Peabody Museum, *Salem*
- Peabody Museum of Archeology and Ethnology, *Harvard University, Cambridge*
- Plimoth Plantation, Inc., *Plymouth*
- Springfield Science Museum, *Springfield*

Michigan

- Jesse Besser Museum, *Alpena*
- Chief Blackbird Home Museum, *Harbor Springs*
- Cranbrook Institute of Science, *Bloomfield Hills*
- Fort Wayne Military Museum, *Detroit*
- Grand Rapids Public Museum, *Grand Rapids*
- Great Lakes Indian Museum, *Cross Village*
- Kingman Museum of Natural History, *Battle Creek*
- Norton Mounds, *South of Grand Rapids*
- University of Michigan Exhibit Museum, *Ann Arbor*
- Wayne State University Museum of Anthropology, *Detroit*

Minnesota

- Crow Wing County Historical Society, *Brainerd*
- Mille Lacs State Indian Museum, *Mille Lacs*
- Pipestone National Monument, *South of Pipestone*
- St. Louis County Historical Society, *Duluth*
- The Science Museum of Minnesota, *St. Paul*

Mississippi

- Emerald Mound, *Northeast of Natchez*
- Natchez Trace Visitor Center *North of Tupelo*

Missouri

- Cherokee Museum, *St. Louis*
- Ralph Foster Museum, *School of the Ozarks, Point Lookout*
- Graham Cave, *Graham Cave State Park, Interstate 70 near Danville*
- Kansas City Museum of History and Science, *Kansas City*
- Lyman Archeological Research Center and Hamilton Field School (Utz Site), *Northwest of Marshall*
- Missouri State Museum, *Jefferson City*
- Museum of Anthropology, *University of Missouri, Columbia*
- Museum of Science and Natural History, *St. Louis*
- William Rockhill Nelson Gallery and Atkins Museum of Fine Arts, *Kansas City*
- St. Joseph Museum, *St. Joseph*

Montana

- Chief Plenty Coups Museum, *Pryor*
- H. Earl Clack Memorial Museum, *Havre*
- Custer-Sitting Bull Battlefield Museum, *Crow Agency*
- Museum of the Plains Indians, *Browning*
- Poplar Indian Arts and Crafts Museum, *Poplar*

Nebraska

- Fort Robinson Museum, *Nebraska State Historical Society, Fort Robinson*
- Fur Trade Museum, *Chadron*
- Nebraska State Historical Society, *Lincoln*
- University of Nebraska State Museum, *Lincoln*

Nevada

- Lost City Museum of Archeology, *Near Lake Mead*

New Hampshire

- Dartmouth College Museum, *Hanover*

New Jersey

- Hopewell Museum, *Hopewell*
- Newark Museum, *Newark*
- New Jersey State Museum, *Trenton*

New Mexico

- Abo State Monument, *Southeast of Albuquerque*
- Acoma Pueblo, *South of Casa Blanca*
- American Indian Arts Museum, *Santa Fe*
- Anthropology Museum, *Eastern New Mexico University, Portales*
- Aztec Ruins National Monument, *Aztec*
- Bandelier National Monument, *Los Alamos*
- Blackwater Draw Museum, *Highway 70 north of Portales*
- Chaco Canyon National Monument, *Bloomfield*
- Coronado State Monument, *Bernalillo*
- El Morro National Monument, *West of El Morro*
- Gallup Museum of Indian Arts, *Gallup*
- Gila Cliff Dwellings National Monument, *Gila Hot Springs*

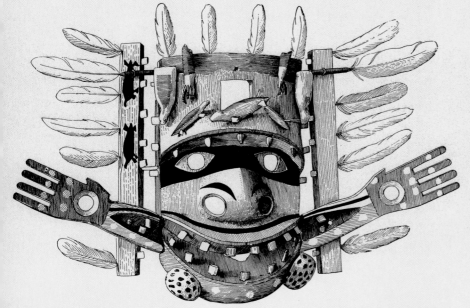

New Mexico (cont.)

- Gran Quivira National Monument, *South of Mountainair*
- Jemez State Monument, *Southwest of Los Alamos*
- Jicarilla Apache Tribal Museum, *Dulce*
- Kwilleylekia Ruins Monument, *Cliff*
- Laguna Pueblo, *West of Albuquerque*
- Maxwell Museum of Anthropology, *The University of New Mexico, Albuquerque*
- Miles Museum, *Eastern New Mexico University, Portales*
- New Mexico State University Museum, *New Mexico State University, Las Cruces*
- Palace of the Governors, *Santa Fe*
- Pecos National Monument, *Pecos*
- Picuris Pueblo, *Southwest of Taos*
- Puyé Cliff Ruins, *Santa Clara Indian Reservation, Southwest of Española*
- Millicent Rogers Museum, *Taos*
- Salmon Ruins Museum, *3 miles west of Bloomfield*
- Sandia Man Cave, *Northeast of Albuquerque*
- San Juan Pueblo, *North of Española*
- Santa Clara Pueblo, *Northwest of Santa Fe*
- Taos Pueblo, *Taos*
- The Wheelright Museum, *Sante Fe*
- Zia Pueblo, *North of Santa Ana*
- Zuni Pueblo, *Southwest of Gallup*

New York

- American Museum of Natural History, *New York*
- Brooklyn Museum, *Brooklyn*
- Buffalo and Erie County Historical Society, *Buffalo*
- Buffalo Museum of Science, *Buffalo*
- Canandaigua Historical Society Museum, *Canandaigua*
- Castile Historical Society Museum, *Castile*
- Cayuga Museum of History and Art, *Auburn*
- Chemung County Historical Museum, *Elmira*
- Cooperstown Indian Museum, *Cooperstown*
- Fort Plain Museum, *Fort Plain*
- Fort William Henry Restoration and Museum, *Lake George*
- Mohawk-Caughnawaga Museum, *Fonda*

- Museum of the American Indian, *Heye Foundation, New York*
- New York State Museum and Science Service, *Albany*
- Owasco Indian Village, *Owasco*
- Oysterponds Historical Society, *Orient*
- Rochester Museum and Science Center, *Rochester*
- Six Nations Indian Museum, *Onchiota*
- Yager Museum and Library, *Oneonta*

North Carolina

- Museum of the American Indian, *Boone*
- Museum of the Cherokee Indian, *Cherokee*
- Oconaluftee Indian Village, *Cherokee*
- Town Creek Indian Mound, *State Historic Site, Northeast of Mount Gilead*

North Dakota

- Affiliated Tribes Museum, *Newtown*
- Lewis and Clark Trail Museum, *Alexander*
- Slant Indian Village, *Fort Lincoln State Park, South of Mandan*
- State Historical Society Museum, *Bismarck*

Ohio

- Allen County Museum, *Lima*
- Butler Institute of American Art, *Youngstown*
- Cleveland Museum of Art, *Cleveland*
- Cleveland Museum of Natural History, *Cleveland*
- Fort Ancient State Memorial, *Southeast of Lebanon*
- Indian Museum, *Piqua*
- Johnson-Humrickhouse Memorial Museum, *Coshocton*
- Miamisburg Mound State Memorial, *Miamisburg*
- Mound City Group National Monument, *Chillicothe*
- Ohio Historical Society, *Columbus*
- Ohio State Museum, *Columbus*
- Seip Mound, *East of Bainbridge*
- Serpent Mound State Memorial, *Northeast of Peebles*
- Story Mound, *Chillicothe*
- Western Reserve Historical Society, *Cleveland*

Oklahoma

- Andarko Museum, *Andarko*
- Bacone College, Ataloa Lodge Museum, *Muskogee*
- Cherokee Center, *Tahlequah*
- Cherokee History Museum, *Tahlequah*
- Creek Indian Museum, *Okmulgee*
- Five Civilized Tribes Museum, *Muskogee*
- The Thomas Gilcrease Institute of American History and Art, *Tulsa*
- Indian City, U.S.A., *Andarko*
- Kerr Museum, *Poteau*
- Museum of the Great Plains, *Lawton*
- Oklahoma Historical Society, *Oklahoma City*
- Osage Tribal Museum, *Pawhuska*
- Ottawa County Historical Society, *Miami*
- Pawnee Bill Museum, *Pawnee*
- Philbrook Art Center, *Tulsa*

- Ponca City Indian Museum, *Ponca City*
- Sequoyah's Home, *Sallisaw*
- Southeastern Plains Indian Museum, *Andarko*
- J. Willis Stovall Museum, *University of Oklahoma, Norman*
- Tsa-La-Gi Indian Village, *Tahlequah*
- Woolaroc Museum, *Southwest of Bartlesville*

Oregon

- Collier State Park, *North of Klamath Falls*
- Coos-Curry Museum, *North Bend*
- Horner Museum, *Corvallis*
- Klamath County Museum, *Klamath Falls*
- Museum of Natural History, *University of Oregon, Eugene*
- Portland Art Museum, *Portland*

Pennsylvania

- American Indian Museum, *Harmony*
- American Indian Museum, *Pittsburgh*
- Carnegie Museum of Natural History, *Anthropology Center, Butler*
- Everhard Museum, *Scranton*
- Hershey Museum, *Hershey*
- Indian Steps Museum, *East of York*
- E. M. Parker Indian Museum, *Brookville*

Rhode Island

- Haffenreffer Museum, *Brown University, Bristol*
- The Museum of Natural History, *Roger Williams Park, Providence*
- Tomaquag Indian Museum, *Exeter*

South Dakota

- Badlands National Monument, *Southeast of Rapid City*
- Buechel Memorial Sioux Indian Museum, *St. Francis*
- Indian Arts Museum, *Martin*
- Land of the Sioux Museum, *Mobridge*
- Museum of the University of South Dakota, *Vermillion*
- Red Cloud Indian Museum, *Kadoka*
- Robinson Museum, *Pierre*
- Mari Sandoz Museum, *Pine Ridge Reservation*
- Sioux Indian Museum, *Rapid City*
- Sioux Land Heritage Museum, *Pettigrew Museum, Sioux Falls*

Tennessee

- Chucalissa Indian Town and Museum, *Southwest of Memphis*
- Frank H. McClung Museum, *University of Tennessee, Knoxville*
- Shiloh Mounds, *Shiloh National Military Park, Southwest of Savannah*

Texas

- Alabama-Coushatta Indian Museum, *Livingston*
- Alibates Flint Quarries National Monument, *Sanford*
- Dallas Museum of Fine Arts, *Dallas*
- El Paso Centennial Museum, *University of Texas, El Paso*
- Fort Concho Preservation and Museum, *San Angelo*

- Fort Worth Museum of Science and History, *Fort Worth*
- Indian Museum, *Harwood*
- Museum of Texas Tech University, *Lubbock*
- Museum of the Big Bend, *Alpine*
- Museum of the Department of Anthropology, *University of Texas, Austin*
- Panhandle-Plains Historical Museum, *Canyon*
- Texas Memorial Museum, *University of Texas, Austin*
- The Wilderness Park Museum, *El Paso*

Utah

- Anasazi Indian Village State Historical Site, *East of Escalante*
- Anthropology Museum, *Brigham Young University, Provo*
- Canyonlands National Park, *Southwest of Moab*
- Hovenweep National Monument, *At Utah-Colorado border northwest of Cortez, Colorado*
- Information Center and Museum, *Salt Lake City*
- Natural History State Museum, *Vernal*
- Newspaper Rock, *Indian Creek State Park, Northwest of Monticello*
- Dr. & Mrs. William R. Palmer Memorial Museum, *Cedar City*
- Utah Museum of Natural History, *University of Utah, Salt Lake City*

Virginia

- Hampton Institute Museum, *Hampton*
- Valentine Museum, *Richmond*

Washington

- Anthropology Museum, *Washington State University, Seattle*
- Eastern Washington State Historical Society, *Spokane*
- Lelooska's, *Ariel*
- Museum of Anthropology, *Pullman*
- North Central Indian Museum, *Wenatchee*
- Pacific Northwest Indian Center, *Spokane*
- Roosevelt Petroglyphs, *East of Roosevelt*
- Seattle Art Museum, *Seattle*
- State Capitol Museum, *Olympia*
- Wanapum Tour Center, *Wanapum Dam*
- Washington State Historical Museum, *Tacoma*
- Washington State Museum, *University of Washington, Seattle*
- Yakima Valley Museum, *Yakima*

West Virginia

- Archeology Museum, *West Virginia University, Morgantown*
- Grave Creek Mound State Park (Mammoth Mound), *Moundsville*

Wisconsin

- Aztalan State Park, *Aztalan*
- Kenosha Public Museum, *Kenosha*
- Lizard Mound State Park, *Northeast of West Bend*
- Logan Museum of Anthropology, *Beloit College, Beloit*
- Milwaukee Public Museum, *Milwaukee*

- Museum of Anthropology, *Wisconsin State University, Oshkosh*
- Neville Public Museum, *Green Bay*
- Ojibwa Nation Museum, *Hayward*
- Sheboygan Mound Park, *South of Sheboygan*
- State Historical Society of Wisconsin, *Madison*
- Venne Art Center, *Wausau*
- Winnebago Indian Museum, *Wisconsin Dells*

Wyoming

- Arapahoe Cultural Museum, *Ethete*
- Buffalo Bill Museum and Plains Indian Museum, *Cody*
- Colter Bay Indian Arts Museum, *Colter*
- Fort Bridger Museum, *Fort Bridger*
- Fort Casper Museum and Historic Site, *Casper*
- Fort Laramie National Historic Site, *Fort Laramie*
- Wyoming State Museum, *Cheyenne*

CANADA

Alberta

- Glenbow-Alberta Centre, *Calgary*
- Provincial Museum of Alberta, *Edmonton*
- Writing-on-Stone Provincial Park, *Milk River*

British Columbia

- British Columbia Provincial Museum, *Victoria*
- Campbell River Centennial Museum, *Campbell River*

- Kelowna Centennial Museum and National Exhibit Centre, *Kelowna*
- Ksan Indian Village, *Hazelton*
- Museum of Anthropology, *University of British Columbia, Vancouver*
- Museum of Northern British Columbia, *Prince Rupert*
- Queen Charlotte Islands Museum, *Skidegate, Queen Charlotte Island*
- Thunderbird Park, *Victoria*
- Vancouver Centennial Museum, *Vancouver*

Manitoba

- Manitoba Museum of Man and Nature, *Winnipeg*

New Brunswick

- Red Bank Indian Reserve, *Red Bank*

Newfoundland

- L'Anse-Amour, *Southwest of Red Bay, Labrador*
- Newfoundland Museum, *St. John's*
- Port Au Choix National Historic Park, *Port Au Choix*

Nova Scotia

- The Micmac Museum, *Pictou*

Ontario

- Agawa Indian Rock, *Lake Superior Provincial Park, South of Agawa*
- Bon Echo Provincial Park, *Highway 41*
- Brant Museum, *Burlington*
- Chiefswood, Six Nations Indian Reserve, *Ohsweken*
- Huron Indian Village, *Midland*
- Huronia Museum, *Midland*
- Kanawa International Museum of Canoes and Kayaks at Kandalore, *Dorset*
- Museum of Indian Archaeology and Pioneer Life, *University of Western Ontario, London*
- National Museum of Man, *Ottawa*
- Nodwell Indian Village, *Port Elgin*
- Petroglyphs Provincial Park, *Highway 28 East*
- Royal Ontario Museum, *Toronto*
- Serpent Mounds Provincial Park, *Keene*
- Ska Nah Doht Indian Village, *Delaware*

Prince Edward Island

- Fort Amherst National Historical Park, *Rocky Point*

Quebec

- McCord Museum, *McGill University, Montreal*
- Musée des Abenakis d'Odanak, *Odanak*
- Musée de Quebec, *Quebec*

Saskatchewan

- Saskatchewan Museum of Natural History, *Regina*
- Willow Bunch Museum, *Willow Bunch*

Yukon Territory

- MacBride Centennial Museum, *Whitehorse*

Index

*Page numbers in **bold** type refer to illustrations, maps, and captions.*

*Page numbers in **bold** type refer to illustrations, maps, and captions.*

*Page numbers in **bold** type refer to illustrations, maps, and captions.*

*Page numbers in **bold** type refer to illustrations, maps, and captions.*

*Page numbers in **bold** type refer to illustrations, maps, and captions.*

Credits

Art

Neil Boyle   **Cover Stamping**

George Buctel   **All maps** (*except page 12*)
Eva Cellini   **61, 258, 335, 371**
Joseph Cellini   **368**
Michael Hampshire   **18, 20, 21, 26–27, 65, 72–73, 119, 124–125,
131, 137, 174–175, 176, 179, 194, 267,
274–275, 297, 299, 300–301, 311, 316,
336–337, 338, 345, 367, 375**
Michael Herring   **134–135, 228–229, 322–323**
Vic Kalin   **8–9** (*illustrations*), **23, 33, 36–37, 57, 90–91, 122–123,
141, 148, 170, 223, 256–257, 302–303, 314** (*illustrations*),
358–359, 360, 363, 378, 384–385
Gabor Kiss   **12, 15, 95, 168, 243, 268–269, 285, 317–319**
Mara McAfee   **102–103**
William Smith   **190–191**
Darrell Sweet   **17**

For assistance in editorial research, the editors are especial-
ly grateful to the following individuals: Richard Conn, Curator of
Native Arts, Denver Art Museum; Dr. Lawrence E. Dawson, Senior
Curatorial Anthropologist, Lowie Museum of Anthropology, Univer-
sity of California, Berkeley; Francis A. Riddell, California Depart-
ment of Parks and Recreation; Dr. Stuart Struever, Director of the
Northwestern University Archaeological Institute, Northwestern
University; Dr. William C. Sturtevant, Curator of North American
Ethnology, Department of Anthropology, Smithsonian Institution;
Philip H. Tarbell, Specialist in Indian Culture, New York State
Museum; Dr. James W. VanStone, Curator of North American
Archaeology and Ethnology, Department of Anthropology, Field Mu-
seum of Natural History.

Photographs

For invaluable help in picture research, the editors are
especially grateful to the following organizations and their staffs:
The American Museum of Natural History; The Brooklyn Museum;
Amon Carter Museum; Cranbrook Institute of Science; Denver Art
Museum; Field Museum of Natural History; The Thomas Gilcrease
Institute of American History and Art; Glenbow-Alberta Institute;
The Heard Museum; The Museum of the American Indian, Heye
Foundation; Museum of the Cherokee Indian; National Museum of
Man, National Museums of Canada; The New York Public Library,
Rare Book Division; Ohio Historical Society; Peabody Museum,
Harvard University; Peabody Museum of Salem; Royal Ontario Mu-
seum; Smithsonian Institution, National Anthropological Archives,
National Collection of Fine Arts, Photographic Services; University
Museum, University of Pennsylvania.

Special appreciation is also extended to the following
individuals: Denis Alsford, Curator of Collections, National Museum of Man, National Museums of Canada; Delbert R. Baston, Foundation of Illinois Archaeology; Lee and Carol Boltin; Robert N.
Bowen, Director, Cranbrook Institute of Science; Maud Cole, Librar-
ian, Rare Book Division, The New York Public Library; Alison Dodd;
Paula Fleming, Museum Specialist, National Anthropological Archives, Smithsonian Institution; Dorothy Fulton, Associate Manager,
Picture Library, The American Museum of Natural History; Campbell Grant; Carmelo Guadagno and S. Alexandride, The Museum of
the American Indian, Heye Foundation; Joan Heim; Jerry Jacka; Paul
Jensen; Dan Jones, Photographic Archivist, Peabody Museum, Harvard University; Debbie King, Ohio Historical Society; Dr. Duane H.
King, Curator, Museum of the Cherokee Indian; Linda Licklighter,
Processing Lab, Smithsonian Institution; Arthur L. Olivas, Photographic Archivist, Museum of New Mexico; Richard A. Pohrt, Curator, Chandler-Pohrt Collection; Dylis Poole; Beverly Rosenberg, Public
Information Officer, William Rockhill Nelson Gallery of Art; Mark
Sexton, Peabody Museum of Salem; William Sonntag; Sam Spangen-
berg, Long-Spangenberg Associates; Ron Testa, Field Museum of Natural History; Dr. Joe Ben Wheat, University of Colorado Museum.